Joe Cousins

The World's Students in the United States

Seth Spaulding
Michael J. Flack
with
Sean Tate
Penelope Mahon
Catherine Marshall

The Praeger Special Studies program—utilizing the most modern and efficient book production techniques and a selective worldwide distribution network—makes available to the academic, government, and business communities significant, timely research in U.S. and international economic, social, and political development.

The World's Students in the United States

A Review and Evaluation of Research on Foreign Students

PRAEGER SPECIAL STUDIES IN U.S. ECONOMIC, SOCIAL, AND POLITICAL ISSUES

Praeger Publishers   New York   Washington   London

Library of Congress Cataloging in Publication Data
Main entry under title:

The World's students in the United States.

(Praeger special studies in U.S. economic, social, and political issues)
    Bibliography: p.
    Includes indexes.
    1. Students, Foreign--United States. 2. Students, Foreign--United States--Bibliography.
I. Spaulding, Seth.
LA203.W67   378.1'98   75-23992
ISBN 0-275-56130-5

PRAEGER PUBLISHERS
111 Fourth Avenue, New York, N.Y. 10003, U.S.A.

Published in the United States of America in 1976
by Praeger Publishers, Inc.

Printed in the United States of America

Each year, U. S. educational institutions enroll large numbers of foreign students in both graduate and undergraduate programs, and many other persons from abroad participate in training programs arranged by the U. S. Government, international agencies, or by private organizations. This report examines research pertaining to these students and trainees conducted primarily since 1967. Over 450 items of literature were collected (books, pamphlets, journal articles, conference reports, policy statements, sponsored studies, dissertations, etc.), abstracted, and analyzed. These items, which are listed in an annotated bibliography, are discussed within five principal categories: what happens to foreign students while in the United States (Chapter 2); the structure, administration, and finance of foreign student programs (Chapter 3); new approaches to technical cooperation in the preparation of human resources for development (Chapter 4); the migration of talent (Chapter 5); and foreign and international organization research (Chapter 6).

Three similar evaluative studies sponsored by the U. S. Government appeared during the 1960s, those by Margaret L. Cormack (1962), Margaret T. Cussler (1962), and Barbara J. Walton (1967). These, and several other macro-reviews, assess the quantity and quality of research on international educational exchange, identify major research areas and gaps, and address recommendations to researchers and to the U. S. Government. Their recommendations focus on improving communications between the research community and U. S. agencies which sponsor foreign students, on developing more accurate and extensive information abroad about study in the United States, on articulating exchange objectives on the basis on worldwide needs, and on improving the conceptual and methodological quality of foreign student research.

What Happens to Foreign Students While in the United States

The largest number of items from the bibliography (160 empirical and 44 non-empirical studies) concern what happens to foreign students while in the United States. Forty-two empirical items focus on foreign student attitudes and problems of social adjustment, 17 of them using sophisticated methods of data analysis. Those which examined basic cultural and religious attitudes found that the sojourn, particularly if shorter than two years, affected them only marginally; attitudes toward the United States are more subject to change and are apparently substantially influenced by the mass media. Studies of social adjustment indicate that foreign students are frequently isolated from social life on U. S. campuses and tend to form co-national groups which provide a surrogate for the home culture, protect members from psychological conflicts in adjusting to American society, and ease the transition upon return home. Degrees of social isolation may be related, either as cause or effect, to the finding that there is frequently little interaction between foreign and American students on campus. Few of the adjustment studies, however, make any attempt to develop interdisciplinary theory: the U-curve hypothesis has been tested and expanded with inconclusive results.

A second group of 25 empirical studies considers academic achievement, focusing primarily on the validity of certain tests in predicting academic success. An extensive AACRAO study of AID participants found the SAT-Math test to be a good predictor of undergraduate performance. Numerous other studies report that proficiency in English language correlates most often with academic success as measured by grade point average. Recommendations suggest: (1) that more emphasis be placed on the quality and made of teaching than on the selection of successful students, (2) that standard measures of academic success, for example, GPA, be re-evaluated in relation to foreign students' goals; (3) that departmental admissions criteria be more adequately studied and articulated, and (4) that more attention be given to techniques for coping with language problems.

A group of 27 studies examines both social adjustment and academic achievement (and often the relationship between the two), the most extensive being the series of exit interviews conducted in Washington, D. C., by DETRI for AID. Based on an earlier finding that utilization of training was strongly related to satisfaction with the total training experience, this project used self-reported participant satisfaction as a measure of program effectiveness. Other researchers have used a variety of problem checklists, questionnaires, and interviews to generate data which suggest a complex relationship between personal and social adjustment and academic achievement although none establish a firm cause and effect relationship between the two. It is frequently recommended, by researchers and by foreign students, that orientation, advising, and counseling procedures be improved.

A number of studies use a multidimensional approach, collating the information derived from the foreign students with that elicited from other groups involved in the exchange process. One of the most extensive, by Deutsch, is a two-year community study of foreign students and the international milieu at five colleges and universities in the Cleveland area; he found considerable community support for international education and for internationalizing the academic curriculum. Most studies, however, indicate a wide gap between: (1) the foreign students and those who determine campus policy, and (2) between the agencies which program foreign students and institutional administrators. More study is needed of the impact which foreign students and international programs have on both institution and community.

Studies of foreign students after return home form a final group of 26 empirical items. Research on returned AID participants, conducted in the early sixties, reported the desire by participants for longer sojourns and more extensive on-the-job training; utilization of training in various professional fields differed by country and world region. Other studies showed that technical knowledge was more valuable upon return than were more abstract research skills. Departmental offerings for foreign students might be improved, particularly in terms of increasing their relevance to professional needs, by departmental studies of alumni.

Structure, Administration, and Finance

Items relating to structure, administration, and finance form the second largest category in the bibliography: 35 empirical and 126 non-empirical studies. The topics addressed range widely:

Admissions procedures. The problem of correctly evaluating foreign credentials has been the subject of a series of NAFSA conferences and publications, of a UNESCO analysis, and of several other studies. Despite expanded information on foreign educational systems, credential evaluation remains difficult; two studies recommend the establishment of a central non-governmental evaluation service, and another the creation of a worldwide network of Counseling, Evaluating, and Testing Centers. Other factors in the admissions decision include test scores, English proficiency, financial resources, etc. A 1972 NAFSA study found that most U. S. universities do not have generally defined institutional policies regarding admission but that such decisions were made almost exclusively by individual departments.

Some writers argue that institutions must articulate admissions policies that would select students not only on the basis of probable academic success, but also on the basis of such social factors as the manpower requirements of developing countries, the provision of advanced education to potential leaders or social dissidents regardless of their prior academic training or English proficiency, and the encouragement of less privileged minority groups.

English language training. Studies of adjustment and academic achievement stress the importance of adequate ability in the English language. Several authors recommend that good command of English not be a college entrance requirement, but that institutions offer language training to students who need it. Several innovative language programs are described, and universities are encouraged to support them and/or develop local or regional language center.

Advising and counseling. From the moment he or she considers enrollment in an American college, university, or training program, the foreign student is in need of expert advice and counsel. Pre-departure orientation, particularly for the non-sponsored student, is generally weak; responsibility for orientation falls primarily on the academic institution. In attitude and adjustment studies, foreign students frequently criticized the usefulness of the programs they had attended. Other studies found that many institutions do not offer adequate orientation. On campus, it is the office of the foreign student adviser that must supply the needed personnel and practical counseling. A number of studies find that, especially in smaller or two-year institutions, the foreign student adviser's office is under-funded and under-staffed, its personnel do not have professional qualifications, and cooperation with academic advisers is minimal. A series of NAFSA publications in recent years has sought to familiarize institutional administrators with the functions of the foreign student adviser and to define professional standards for persons holding that position. It is recommended that orientation and counseling be available throughout the sojourn, including terminal or re-entry orientation prior to departure for the home country.

Programs. A variety of programs and services for foreign students are described and evaluated in the literature reviewed. Government programs include the Participant Training Program of AID, the Fulbright-Hays Program, exchanges with the Soviet Union and Eastern Europe, etc. The reports show an increasing concern for achieving the optimum impact with such funds as are available through improved communication with participants and educational institutions, cooperative ventures with other agencies and organizations, and the encouragement of exchange relationships among other countries. Private organizations administer such programs as the African Scholarship Program of American Universities, the African Graduate Fellowship Program, the Latin American Scholarship Program of American Universities, and exchange programs with many regions of the world. A common problem cited in the functioning of these programs is the conflict in training goals as stated or perceived by participant, agency, and institution. One attempt to improve programs through better communication was the holding of joint NAFSA-AID workshops and the establishment of a standing liaison committee for the two agencies.

International relations. A small but significant group of authors consider educational exchange and international relations. Those reviewed argue that educational and cultural activities must be accorded greater recognition as an important dimension of foreign policy, that they can play a role in the reduction of international tension and the creation of closer intercultural links, understandings, and stabilities.

Broad overviews. The studies which take a broad perspective on educational exchange stress the need for articulated rationales, at the institutional as well as the national level, for the presence of foreign students in the United States. Clear goal statements could then form a basis for policy decisions in such areas as admissions criteria, optimum numbers of students on campus, curriculum design, personal and community services, financial support, etc.

New Approaches

In addition to the enrollment of foreign students in traditional or special university programs, several other approaches have been devised for the dissemination of human knowledge. One of them involves technical training programs conducted under the auspices of various international organizations; major problems appear to be lack of central coordination (for example, of institutions within the UN family), lack of any emphasis on developing group rather than individual capability, failure to train participants at technological levels suitable to home country conditions, and the absence of programs to facilitate adaptation upon return home. Another approach involves linkages between U. S. universities and universities abroad, individually or as consortia, which provide for exchanges of faculty and students, longer-term and more coordinated international programs, and participation in government-funded technical assistance projects. The evidence suggests, however, that such international involvement has only seldom had an effect on the participating U. S. university.

Migration of Talent

The phenomenon of talent migration, or brain drain, is the subject of 66 studies (40 empirical and 26 non-empirical) which range from doctoral dissertations based on small sample populations to the larger studies of Glaser, Myers, UNITAR, and the Committee on the International Migration of Talent. They assess the saliency of a variety of factors affecting the decision to migrate, although many decry the absence of consistent definitions of significant terms (non-return, migration, re-migration) and of reliable statistics. Generally, the studies consider migration from developing to developed countries, or regional flows between developed countries. No truly global study of migration has yet been undertaken.

Structural conditions in donor countries found to be generally associated with talent migration are underdevelopment, imbalances in the system of higher education, and dislocation in the job market. Secondary factors include working conditions in the home country (for example, lack of advanced research facilities or stimulating colleagues), lack of social support from government or prospective employers, and the system of sponsorship.

Recipient countries attract international talent through their continuing demand for certain skills, their ability to satisfy the professional needs of employees, and the character of their migration and visa policies.

A third group of variables in the migration decision is circumstantial, that is, they vary according to the unique situation of each foreign student or professional. Home-country ties, patriotism, field and level of study, age, socio-economic status, length of sojourn, etc., all influence the individual's decision to return home or to remain abroad.

Although there is no unanimity in the findings of diverse studies, the following seem to command general support. Older students, those with strong family and cultural ties to their home countries, those sponsored by their home governments, and those from higher socioeconomic strata are less likely to remain abroad. On the other hand, those who begin to study abroad at a young age, those who pursue doctoral degrees, those who specialize in professions for which there is continuing demand in developed countries (that is, science, medicine, engineering), and those who are cultural or political dissidents are more likely to remain abroad. The migration decision is strongly influenced by opportunities for employment, including the degree of contact between students and potential employers in the home country, and by working conditions, which include the nature of the working environment as well as salary level.

The effect of talent migration on donor and recipient country has not yet been extensively researched. Some argue that manpower losses retard development efforts and have an adverse welfare effect on the remaining population; others challenge these findings. This area requires further study to develop more precise conceptualizations, measurement techniques, and reliable data.

Foreign and International Organization Research

The volume of literature reviewed which had its origin outside the United States is small, in part due to lack of response from researchers and institutions abroad. Several studies obtained from UNESCO, FAO, and the United Kingdom offer evaluations of training programs, revealing many of the same problems as in U. S. programs—difficulties in language and social adjustment, the desire for longer sojourns, variability in utilization. It would be helpful if further research compiled and assessed literature on foreign students published abroad in both English and other major languages.

Overview, Findings, and Recommendations

The final chapter of the report contains an overview that summarizes the quantity and types of publications reviewed, the analytical methods employed, the development of concepts and theory, and the topics addressed. The second section presents a profile of the major findings discussed in each chapter. In the final section are 19 recommendations for further research, for specific action, and for overall policy. The 11 action recommendations stress the need for implementation of suggestions that have been made repeatedly in foreign student literature and are largely based on the findings of empirical research. The four policy recommendations suggest new directions for research on educational exchange which would lead to a more standardized, coherent, accessible body of knowledge while encouraging innovation and creativity.

This study is one of a number done by academic and other research institutions for the Department of State as part of its external research program. These studies are designed to supplement the Department's own research capabilities and provide independent views to policy officers and analysts on key questions with important policy implications.

The external research program is planned and managed by the Bureau of Intelligence and Research. Comments on this study or queries about the program may be addressed to: The Director, Office of External Research, Bureau of Intelligence and Research, Department of State, Washington, D. C. 20520.

This research is supported by the Department of State under Contract 1724-32009. Views or conclusions contained in this study should not be interpreted as representing the official opinion or policy of the Department of State.

ACKNOWLEDGMENTS

Many persons have contributed time and counsel to this project. Among them, the following have offered written comment and suggestions: George V. Coelho, Philip H. Coombs, Johan Galtung, Richard H. Humphrey, A. K. Kinany, Ivan Putman, Jr., E. B. J. Postma, N. Pattabhi Raman, Boem van Ravenswaaij, and Philip I. Sperling. In addition, Margaret L. Cormack and Barbara J. Walton served as consultants, assisting particularly in the formulation of our working hypotheses.

The following discussed the project with the authors and offered information and advise: in Washington, D. C., Claudia Anyaso, Richard Arndt, Stephen K. Bailey, Katherine Bangs, Samuel Belk, III, Leo R. Crespi, Wilson Dizard, James Donovan, David Heft, Hugh Jenkins, George Jespersen, Frederick Lawton, Ernest Lefever, Alan Reich, Marshall Swan, Marion Terell, and Francis A. Young; in New York, Eleanor Barber, Howard Cutler, William Edgerton, Melvin J. Fox, William Glaser, John Matthews, Ward Morehouse, Delores di Paola, Pearl Purcell, Orlando Rodriguez, Oscar Schacter, M. J. Shoukletovich, Ronald Springwater, Steven Stackpole, James Tierney, Champion Ward, and William Warnock; in Pittsburgh, Marcha Ciesielski, Eleanor Dym, Otto Klineberg, Paul Peters; and, also in Pittsburgh, a group of foreign student advisers, Shiv Gupta, William Lenaghen, Jack Lozier, Virginia Mulligan, Norman O'Dell, and Betty Tillman. We are beholden to each and all of them.

While we do not list, after each name, their institutional affiliations, in part because their views and counsel were often given as individuals and not as representatives of their organizations, it may be noted that the organizations in which they work include the Department of State, the Agency for International Development, the United States Information Agency, the National Institute of Mental Health, the International Research and Exchanges Board, the United Nations Development Programme, the United Nations Institute for Training and Research, the United Nations Educational, Scientific and Cultural Organization, the Food and Agriculture Organization, the Organization of American States, the Institute for International Education, the National Association for Foreign Student Affairs, the American Council on Education, the Carnegie Corporation, the Ford Foundation, the African-American Institute, the International Council for Educational Development, the Brookings Institution, a number of U. S. universities, and the Ecole Pratique des Hautes Etudes, the Netherlands School of Business, and the University of Oslo.

Special thanks go to Pio D. Uliassi, Senior Program Officer, Office of External Research, Department of State, who, by arranging two most helpful inter-departmental progress consultations, has facilitated the articulation and completion of this study. Although we do not mention all of the members present at these meetings, we greatly appreciate their advice and counsel.

Our thanks go also to Sean Tate, who was instrumental in organizing and supervising the initial phases of the project; to Catherine Marshall, who undertook the final editing of the manuscript and preparation of the annotated bibliography; and to Carol Jones who provided invaluable editorial and administrative support and typed the entire manuscript.

While the entire project was essentially a team effort, major responsibilities were as follows: Chapters 1 and 7 by Michael J. Flack; Chapters 2 and 4 by Seth Spaulding; Chapters 3 and 6 by Sean Tate; and Chapter 5 by Penelope Mahon.

CONTENTS

LIST OF TABLES AND CHARTS

LIST OF ABBREVIATIONS USED IN CHARTS

Sponsorship

Inter-Gov.	Inter-governmental agency, e.g., UN, UNESCO, OAU, etc.
Gov. Ag.	Governmental agency
Priv./Non-Gov. Ag.	Private and non-governmental agency
Found.	Foundation
Univ.	University
Diss.	Dissertation

Population Studied

For. Stud.	Foreign Students
	Before—Before coming to United States
	In U. S.—While in United States
	In other hosts—While in other countries
U. S. Fac.	U. S. Faculty members
U. S. Stud.	U. S. Students
U. S. Comm.	U. S. host community
F. S. Admin.	U. S. administrators of foreign student programs
For. Emp.	Foreign employers
For. Comm.	Foreign community
U. S. Emb.	U. S. embassy

Geographic Emphasis (when not a specified country)

Multi-Nat.	Multi-national
N. Af.	North Africa
S.S. Af.	Sub-Saharan Africa
W. Eur.	Western Europe
E.E. & USSR	Eastern Europe and the USSR
M. East	Middle East
E. Asia	East Asia
S.E. Asia	Southeast Asia
M.S. Asia	Middle South Asia
Amer.	the Americas
L. Amer.	Latin America

Student Specialization

Multi-Disc.	Multi-Disciplinary or profession
Phys. Sci.	Physical Science
Soc. Sci.	Social Science
Soc. Prof.	Social Professions
Med.	Medical science and professions

Agric.	Agricultural Sciences
Lib. Arts	Liberal Arts
Arch.	Architecture
Educ.	Education
Engr.	Engineering
Pub. Adm.	Public Administration

Data Collection Methodology

Quest.	Questionnaires
Struct. Anal.	Structured Interviews
Inf. Inter./Ob.	Informal Interviews and/or observation
Ach.	Scholastic aptitude and/or achievement tests
Eng.	English language tests
Anal. Case	Analytic case study materials
Cas. Samp.	Casual sampling
Sci. Samp.	Scientific sampling including stratified, random
Hist.	Historical
Res. Rev.	Review of other research studies

Data Analysis Methodology

Simp. Anal.	Simple reporting of total responses and percentages
Soph. Anal.	More sophisticated techniques involving analyses of reliability, validity, and variance
MRA	Multiple regression analysis
Case Anal.	Case study analyses
Res. Rev.	Review of other research results

Disciplinary Emphases

Multi.	Multi-disciplinary
Psych.	Psychology
Soc.	Sociology
Anthro.	Anthropology
Econ.	Economics
Ad. Sci.	Administrative science
Ed. Sci.	Educational science

LIST OF ACRONYMS

AACRAO	American Association of Collegiate Registrars and Admissions Officers
AAI	African-American Institute
AFGRAD	African Graduate Fellowship Program
AGSA	African Graduate Study Awards
ATSA	African Transfer Student Awards
AID	United States Agency for International Development
ASPAU	African Scholarship Program of American Universities
CEEB	College Entrance Examination Board
DETRI	Development Education and Training Research Institute, American University, Washington, D. C.
EWA	Education and World Affairs
FAO	Food and Agriculture Organization
HEW	U. S. Department of Health, Education, and Welfare
ICA	International Cooperation Administration
IIE	Institute of International Education
JUSPAO	Joint United States Public Affairs Office
NACDRAO	National Association of College Deans, Registrars, and Admissions Officers
NAFSA	National Association for Foreign Student Affairs
OIT	Office of International Training, AID
PSAT	Preliminary Scholastic Aptitude Test
SASP	South African Scholarship Program
SAT	Scholastic Aptitude Test
TESOL	Teachers of English to Speakers of Other Languages
TOEFL	Test of English as a Foreign Language
UNESCO	United Nations Educational, Scientific, and Cultural Organization
UNITAR	United Nations Institute for Training and Research, 801 UN Plaza, New York, New York 10017
USIA	United States Information Agency
USIS	United States Information Service

It might be best to begin with the broader picture. In the last 25 years, several million young men and women and hundreds of thousands of trained technicians and specialists from around the world received their advanced academic education or training in institutions of higher learning located in countries other than their own. In a very real sense, they represent a significant segment of today's leadership and management in the world—in some countries the decisive segment.

A considerable percentage of these persons chose to study in the United States. In 1974-75 alone, the most recent year for which statistics are available, some 216,000 students from around the world enrolled in U. S. universities and colleges as regular undergraduate or graduate students. Upon completion of their studies and return, many of them, together with other colleagues, will put their imprint on the contours of tomorrow in their own societies, some on those of whole regions, and a few on developments or arrangements that may affect the world as a whole.

Each of them represents a multiply selected and thus promising individual. In the host country, these students pursue, as appropriate, specialized courses intended to equip them for a professional, social, and personal competence of their own choice, or that of their organization or society. But at the same time, the individuals are involved in the daily life and events of their temporary host society and thus, unavoidably, are exposed to varyingly consonant and divergent conceptions of societal values, of individual roles, rights, and responsibilities; of institutions and their functioning; of equality and authority; of opportunity and standards; and of differing modes of interpersonal action. This raises the continuous question of how these cultural factors compare, and how pertinently, to those at home, and how they relate to the goals that the foreign student and others envisage for the period after return. As all deep involvements, and particularly those

1

of an intercultural nature, both the multi-pronged learning and the bio-social maturation experienced during the sojourn abroad require energy and can be taxing. Depending on the person, the length of stay, and the cultural "distances" involved, the sojourn abroad can be exhilarating and liberating, disturbing and exhausting, and/or, in complex combinations and varieties, both.

Every admission and/or assignment of a student to a course of higher education in a foreign country, and thus to an extended sojourn and exposure abroad, represents a major assumption of responsibility, a considerable investment in funds, and a significant opportunity to contribute both to the individual concerned and to articulated or implied broader common goals, national and international. Educators, administrators, governments, and international organizations have on occasion sought to secure salient knowledge about how, and how well, the process of education abroad functions, what problems it generates, how useful what is acquired is perceived to be by the students, by their sponsors, and by those who hope to benefit from their future work. Also, there has been a continuing interest in learning what broader effects study abroad may exert on specific binational and overall international relationships between individuals, professions, institutions, nations, and regions.

The major instrument for acquiring such monitoring knowledge, and suggestions on how the content and process of educational exchange can be improved, is continuous, multi-faceted, and purposeful social science research. Ideally, such research ought to be undertaken by analysts in both the sending and receiving countries. Even more ideally, it ought to be undertaken periodically by joint teams. At present, however, the resources needed, the personnel available, and the techniques used make it most likely that research on foreign students will be conducted primarily in those countries which possess developed social science establishments. These, not surprisingly, tend to be the countries to which high proportions of students from abroad come to study, and where universities and colleges accompany education with research in search of better education.[1] The United States, with more than half of the universities and colleges in the world, and with the largest single presence of foreign students in any nation, is one of these countries.

Procedure and Method

In response to RFP-ST-73-58 of the United States Department of State, requesting a Research Study on "Foreign Students in the U. S.," and its submittal of a proposal, the University Center for

International Studies at the University of Pittsburgh was awarded, on June 29, 1973, Contract No. 1724-320097.

The Department of State's Work Statement on the Project speci- fies that the purpose of the study is:

> . . . to produce a critical review of existing research on foreign students in the United States as a basis for determining: (a) what is already well-established re- garding the personal, professional, and social impact of the study in the U. S., (b) deficiencies or gaps in the literature, and (c) areas in which government-sponsored or other research might be especially suitable or de- sirable.

The Work Statement refers to the:

> . . . uncertainty about the current state of social re- search on educational exchange—its extent, its current timeliness and validity (especially in the size and com- position of the foreign student population), and its ade- quacy for the purposes of policy consideration and program planning.

Referring to one past governmentally sponsored bibliographic compila- tion and two "state of the art" reviews,[2] the Work Statement expresses the expectation that: ". . . a new survey would build on these earlier studies and cover, moreover, the considerable but scattered empirical literature that has accumulated in the last few years."

Specifically, the contractor for the project would prepare:

1. A comprehensive annotated bibliography of published and unpublished research on foreign students in the United States, focusing especially on the more recent literature available in English, and drawing for it on all sources of studies, including those sponsored by international organizations, U. S. Govern- ment agencies, and those carried out under private auspicies.

2. A critical analysis of the literature, dealing, among others, with (a) the personal adjustments of foreign students in the United States, (b) their professional goals and expectations, (c) the effects that living and studying in the United States have on their social and political orientations, and (d) the impact, if any, they have on American society, especially on colleges and universities.

In doing so, the contractor was expected to evaluate existing re- search in terms of the quality of the data, the conceptual schemes, and the analytic methods employed by the authors, and identify seeming duplications, over-concentration in some areas, and significant gaps in the research literature.

Finally, the contractor was to identify in the concluding sections of the project: ". . . areas or problems in which government-sponsored research would be especially suitable and desirable, giving reasoned justifications for such suggestions." The project was to be "carried out on an unclassified basis" and the final report was to be "available for public distribution." In undertaking the study, the research team adopted the following procedures.

Scope and Types of Materials

Since three prior evaluative studies by Cormack (398/ 1962), Cussler (96/ 1962) and Walton (407/ 1967) have rather comprehensively covered pertinent research published before 1967, and since it was evident that the period thereafter, covering seven years, not only would include a very large number of research items, but also is of priority interest to the Department of State and others interested in this study, it was proposed that this review should focus primarily on post-1967 publications. In a number of instances, however, earlier items, especially dissertations not included in other studies, were also reviewed. It should be noted that post-1967 publications do not necessarily include only post-1967 data. In fact, several studies published within the period under review present and analyze data assembled before the cut-off date. Most studies, however, deal with the record of the last seven years—whether in terms of data, or of interests, categories, or concepts used.

The types of materials sought by the research team include pertinent books, articles in scholarly journals, research reports (whether printed or issued for more limited use by contractors), policy statements by governmental, professional, or university of college leaders or associations, dissertations and other unpublished studies as might be made available to it, or as could be secured. The search would include empirical studies, using some type of originally generated data, and non-empirical studies, reflecting the experience, views, or recommendations of the authors, reviews or critiques of secondary sources, etc.

To identify these materials, we surveyed a number of bibliographic compendia and addressed written queries to many persons and institutions in the United States and abroad. The personal libraries of team members yielded many research papers and reports presented at professional conferences. These were supplemented by references or publications received at, or duplicated from, the holdings of the Institute of International Education, the National Association of Foreign Student Advisers, the Agency for International Development, the

Historical Project of the Bureau of Educational and Cultural Affairs, Department of State, and other organizations.

In addition, the team solicited comments and suggestions from a select number of persons who had, over the years, exhibited professional concern for the topic. Where responses were received, they too were taken into account in this study.

Finally, we had the benefit of two meetings with an interdepartmental advisory group in Washington, D. C., to which we gave reports on the progress of the study and from which we received encouragement; and of a meeting with six foreign student advisers from institutions in the Western Pennsylvania-Eastern Ohio region, who made valuable suggestions and drew the team's attention to concrete problems to which foreign students are exposed.

Abstracting and Coding Procedures

In order to cope with the expected massive and diverse research product, a procedure was devised whereby each item was abstracted and coded according to a list of hypotheses which stated in concise terms various commonly held assumptions about foreign students in the United States. While many of these hypotheses were known to be open to question, it seemed to us that their articulation permitted the abstract to be so written that pertinent data could be related to the categories to be examined for the final report. Needless to say, the hypotheses were not meant to be proven right. In fact, the research perused was meant to test them, amend them, and add to them wherever relevant.

The abstracts were placed on specially designed McBee Cards, which, when appropriately punched, made it possible to select cuts of cards that combined pertinent items of information on each of the aspects studied.

Organization of the Report

The Report is organized in chapters which offer quantitative information on the number of studies perused in the category under review, identify the major thrusts, findings, and recommendations of specific studies, and comment on concordant or divergent features characterizing certain groups of studies in each area. Understandably, there is a certain amount of overlap in the studies themselves, and some will be discussed in more than one context. To provide the reader with additional information about each study, charts have been included at the end of each chapter which list the publication data and sponsor or publisher and, for empirical studies, the data collection method, sample population, geographic emphasis, and professional orientation of studies discussed in that chapter.

The remainder of this chapter will be devoted to a review of earlier evaluative studies. Chapter 2 will consider what happens to foreign students while in the United States, particularly in terms of social adjustment and academic achievement. Chapter 3 reviews those studies which address problems of structure, administration, and finance of foreign student programs in the United States.

During the process of organizing the materials collected, we found several studies which dealt with new approaches to technical cooperation in the preparation of human resources for development. Although these studies are not directly concerned with foreign students in the United States, they refer to alternate ways of achieving the same goal, namely educating and training people for productive professional employment and for extending their intellectual horizons. Collection of such materials was not a primary purpose of this review, but we include, as Chapter 4, a brief evaluation of those we received.

Chapter 5 considers the international migration of talent, enumerating the structural and circumstantial conditions which affect the individual's decision to migrate, particularly from the developing to the developed countries. In Chapter 6 we have collected a number of studies published abroad or by international organizations which discuss foreign students in other countries. The acquisition of foreign research was not a major goal of the study, but we include the items received for purposes of comparison and contrast.

In the final chapter we present a summary of the research findings and major recommendations for both research and action.

The Appendix contains the list of our working hypotheses together with an indication of whether they were supported or rejected by the literature. Next are a subject index to the studies reviewed, and two bibliographies. References in the text are accompanied by the bibliographic number and date of the study; those preceded by the letter R will be found in the non-annotated bibliography.

Throughout the Report we have attempted to limit the use of acronyms as much as possible. In the interests of space, and to avoid tiresome repetition, some of the more common ones do appear, and a listing of them is included in the front of the book. A further editorial decision was to use world geographic divisions based on the United Nations Statistical Handbook.

Review of Prior Evaluative Studies

The Work Statement suggested that the present study "build on similar earlier studies." Three such studies will be briefly characterized, indicating first their major themes or conclusions, and then enumeratively listing the Policy Action and Research Recommendations that are offered in all of them. The three studies are:

Margaret L. Cormack. An Evaluation of Research on Educational Exchange, Prepared for the Bureau of Educational and Cultural Affairs, August 1962. 137 pages.

Margaret T. Cussler. Review of Selected Studies Affecting International and Cultural Affairs, Prepared for the United States Advisory Commission on International and Cultural Affairs, November 1962. 94 pages.

Barbara J. Walton. Foreign Student Exchange in Perspective: Research on Foreign Students in the United States, Prepared for the Office of External Research, U. S. Department of State, September 1967. 59 pages.

Cormack's 1962 review (398), in many respects an analytical inquiry in its own right, notes that the research surveyed seems to be only partially adequate since it insufficiently focused on "what really happens to people" during the exchange process, that is, what internal processes of culture conflict, change, accommodation, and learning occur, and what effects these exert on the foreign student's personality and behavior. She notes a concentration of studies on foreign students' attitudes toward the United States—whether involving changes occurring during the sojourn, or the dissemination of acquired information and attitudes after return home. The other major concentration in research on foreign students centered on possible improvements in the content, milieu, and administration of exchange programs. Only few studies were found to deal in some depth with divergent cultural values and the impact of the surrounding American society on these values.

The methods used in government-sponsored studies during the period surveyed were found to be largely of the public-opinion survey type, asking direct questions on attitudes or changes in attitudes. Such approaches are viewed by Cormack as "superficial" and even "harmful" since they tend to offer "the illusion of knowledge based on empirical evidence," rely on "verbal responses," give no consideration to social conditions, and ignore the "deeper aspects of psychological affect." As Cormack notes: "Opinion is not an accurate measurement of 'belief and action'" (p. 36).

To move toward a theory of cross-cultural learning, many more studies in non-U. S. settings are needed; the examination and discussion only of foreign students in the United States appears to be "increasingly unrealistic" (ibid.). Cormack notes that doctoral dissertations, and other non-sponsored research, range more widely in topic and method, but that even they concentrate in large measure on "adjustment during sojourn." Cormack concludes that the sojourn period has been over-emphasized and that pre- and post-sojourn factors have been largely neglected. Data on expatriation are found to be meager (p. 54).

Regarding the nationalities studied, much research focused on students from India and Europe. Cormack emphasizes particularly the need to study students from Africa and some of the problems that can be envisaged as the volume of students from that continent shall increase.

Four subject areas are identified on which attention should concentrate: (1) evolvement of clear aims and value positions on exchanges, (2) development of functional (and at least partially standardized) methodologies and terms, (3) conduct of more definite studies of culture and personality in a universal frame of reference, and (4) contributions of, and to, sound theories of learning (p. 103).

Margaret T. Cussler's 1962 Review of Selected Studies Affecting International Educational and Cultural Affairs (96) critically reviews some early assumptions in exchange programs, namely, that understanding would lead to liking, that pre-departure attitudes toward the United States would resemble later attitudes, and that adjustment to American culture is extremely desirable. Later studies reflect some change in these assumptions, especially a growing realization that grantees' subsequent behavior is more important than favorable attitudes, that knowledge and experience acquired are more pertinent gains than the liking of the host, and that a desirable acculturation is one that is optimal, rather than maximal.

Cussler's survey of the research literature perused indicates that:

1. Foreign grantees have tended to come from the top or upper-middle classes, have been predominantly urban and male, and have not represented the political opposition, unions, or small business strata (p. 25).
2. Not all students, or student groups needed initial "orientation programs," and different groups indeed might need differing types of "orientation" (p. 27).
3. Length of stay and language competence tended to be major variables in adjustment, over-adjustment, academic success, and relationship to the home country (p. 28).
4. Interaction usually engendered positive feelings and lessened hostile stereotypes if the roles accorded the foreign student implied high status or equality focused on a common task (p. 24).
5. The student's perception of what status the U. S. environment accorded his or her own country affected both self-esteem and attitudes (p. 29).

TABLE 1.1

Characteristics of the Three Studies

	Cormack (1962)	Cussler (1962)	Walton (1967)
Sponsorship	Bureau of Educational and Cultural Affairs, Department of State	U. S. Advisory Commission on Educational and Cultural Affairs	Foreign Area Research Coordination Group (FAR), Office of External Research, Department of State
Period Reviewed	1948–1962	1954–1962	1946–1967
Number of Studies Perused	48	77	200 (approx.)
Subjects of Research	Educational Exchange; Foreign Students in the United States	Foreign Students and Leaders in the United States; American Students Abroad	Foreign Students in the United States
Types of Research Evaluated	Predominantly empirical	Empirical, analytical, and policy	Empirical, analytical, and policy
Recommendations Addressed to:	Sponsor, Researchers	Sponsor, Researchers	Researchers
Appendices and Bibliographies	Annotated bibliography of evaluated studies. List of studies sponsored by Department of State, 1951–63. Illustrative list of theses and dissertations on cross-cultural learning.	Statistical survey of Ph.D. dissertations, 1953–61. Bibliography of central studies reviewed. Annotated reading list.	List of perused research references.

9

6. "Cultural distance" and "cross-cultural contradictory expectations" were factors predictive of difficulties in adjustment (p. 27).
7. Those who arrived with strong anti-U. S. prejudices were likely to keep them and be rejectors (p. 26).
8. Over-adjustment led to alienation from the home culture and the desire to stay in the United States permanently (p. 29).

Cussler expresses skepticism about the reliability and pertinence of data or findings presented in some quantitative research studies. What is needed are more adequate and meaningfully arranged data, and evaluations of programs and processes by stated objectives. But many objectives are found to be vague, contradictory, and some may have become operationally obsolete. Due to administrative-political factors, and the desire to present precise results, a considerable part of the research employs samples, questionnaires, interviews, tabulations, polls, etc. Cussler cites cultural and political factors, biases in sampling and selection, and frequent "no answer" items as raising questions about the reliability and occasionally even the suitability of these methods. Most yield "verbal" data. She commends a greater use of control groups, of open-ended interviews, and of recommendations by foreign students themselves.

Walton's 1967 review (407) summarizes two decades of research on foreign students by indicating that the basic values in exchange should be sought in (1) what it does, personally and professionally, for the individual student, (2) its impact and contribution to cross-cultural understanding in a politically fragmented world, (3) the basically psychological and educational character of the experience, and the essentialness that administrative arrangements serve and relate to the latter. As she puts it: "Where goals are misconceived or unrealistic, no amount of change in administrative structure can bring about the desired results" (p. 41).

Walton's overview draws the following generalized conclusions from the research surveyed.

1. Foreign students tend to like the sojourn experience in the United States. They find it especially satisfying to meet Americans as persons, tend to evaluate positively some, though not all U. S. social behaviors and practices, and approve least of all U. S. foreign policies. The images and attitudes in each case are not simple and differentiate into positive and negative evaluations of almost every American characteristic. The question arises to what extent the findings of favorable attitudes reflect opinions present at the time of entry, thus challenging the breadth of the criteria used in selection, admission, and sponsorship of foreign students.

2. Too much attention has been accorded to the study of foreign students' attitudes toward the United States. There is need for a moratorium on such research, for a broadening of the "narrow band of attitudes" studied, and for more research on attitudes toward the students' own countries, their roles in society, and their conceptions of life and work.

3. Research on the leadership achievements of foreign students should be seen in perspective, since the largely selective, success-oriented, biographical case histories used leave influences exercised by the specific educational experience in the United States inconclusively demonstrated. Walton urges that research on ex-students' leadership roles in domestic social reform movements be conducted by researchers in the home society (p. 42).

4. Regarding utilization of the acquired knowledge at home, research tends to indicate that the returnees' degree, competence, and skill form only one cluster among many other factors; the prospect for utilization in positions of influence is higher where the training abroad was preceded by careful planning, institutional participation throughout the assignment abroad, and the commitment of home institutions to receive and employ the returnee. Short of this, there is no guarantee that successful study abroad will necessarily lead to its utilization at home, or that it may not result, due to factors inherent in the home situation, in alienation, frustration, and possible remigration. The question is raised whether short-term programs in specially designed training institutes might not, in skills training terms, be more useful and effective. U. S. institutions would need to decide in each case whether providing such training is an appropriate function for their university and for exchange programs as such (p. 43).

5. Regarding the non-returning foreign student and research on the "brain drain," Walton notes a lack of reliable student data and the use of non-consistent criteria for defining non-returnees. Research deals with the "push-pull" factors and has tended to see the root of the problem of migrating talent in the home countries (p. 44). Referring to research findings on alienation and acculturation, Walton remarks that a degree of detachment from one's home society is, in fact, a positive desideratum. An acculturation to the broader world society is and should be, after all, a part of the content and purpose of educational exchange. Reference is made to the Useems' concept of the "third culture."

6. Regarding the cross-cultural adjustment of foreign students, Walton notes the plenitude of studies on foreign students' problems—culture shock, U-curve, etc. Few studies seem to have explored empirically the conditions under which such problems occur, the role of differing environments, and the impact that advance preparation might have in preventing or mitigating effects. Attention is also drawn to

some studies that question the over-generalized "traumatic" interpretation of adjustment problems which in many instances represent temporary functional disorientations and preliminaries to new learning. Walton strongly urges that foreign students be viewed, and studied, more as "students" than as "foreign," and that it be borne in mind that their primary concerns while here are doing well in their studies and getting along with their professors (p. 47).

7. Regarding orientation and academic performance, research seems to indicate that certain types of orientation have tended to affect some, though not other, aspects of foreign students' perceptions, social relations, and performances in educational programs. In this connection, Walton poses the question whether orientation should be concerned only with facilitating the entry into the new environment and the foreign students' functioning in it, or whether it should relate to the entire course of the exchange, that is, include also the motivation and work roles after the student's return home (p. 48).

8. In reviewing research on foreign students' academic performance, Walton notes its limited character, reports a questioning of the comparability and reliability of grades as indicators of performance, and concludes that there is adequate evidence that, on the average, foreign students perform as well as American students. The literature overwhelmingly opposes a "dual standard," although the actual practices in institutions and departments have not been adequately studied and compared. Major factors accounting for poor performances include combinations of such variables as language deficiency, adjustment problems, personality, motivation, adequacy of prior preparation, and stage in the sojourn and career of the individual. Efforts to correlate some of these factors with performance have yielded diverse and inconclusive results.

9. Finally, regarding research literature evaluating foreign students' roles in, and impact on, the United States, Walton comments that "It may well be that the "foreign student problem" should be conceived primarily as a problem facing American educational institutions, rather than as a series of problems experienced by the [foreign] students themselves." (p. 48)

The issue is what role the education of foreign students can play, and what assistance they can offer, in the expanding international responsibilities of U. S. universities and colleges. Although some studies have traced specific or local types of impact, Walton points to the need for studies on the impact of worldwide education and training programs on U. S. universities. She notes the potentially internationalizing influence that foreign student advisers might play in their institutions and the effects of new ways of teaching English as a second language. She also notes that research has concerned itself much more with the impact of American on foreign students than vice versa. Some studies have focused on the conditions, organized actions, and factors that might optimize "international potentials" among them. However, many more studies are needed in this area.

Walton concludes with a call for research on the overall impact of exchange programs on American society. Has that impact been substantial, necessary, beneficial? Has U. S. society gained as much as it has given? Should future programs and policies place greater emphasis on "mutuality?" The implied answer is "yes" (p. 49).

Recommendations

A bringing together of the major themes, general and specific, identified as recommendations in one or more of the three reports, yields the following profile of needs as of 1962 and 1967:

Action-Policy

1. The Bureau of Educational and Cultural Affairs should act as a liaison in the coordination and sponsorship of research on international educational exchanges, organize regular meetings and conferences, and assist in the publication of periodical information and research, thus facilitating communication with the research community. (Cormack)

2. The Bureau should improve information available abroad about U. S. higher education, its resources, and the procedures related to foreign study in the United States. It should also establish closer liaison with counterpart government agencies abroad. (Cormack)

3. The Bureau should identify, sponsor, and periodically convoke a small group of appropriate social scientists specializing in the field to act as permanent consultants on international educational exchange research. (Cormack)

4. The U. S. Advisory Commission on Educational and Cultural Affairs should articulate exchange objectives on the basis of worldwide needs and trends and develop appropriate exchange programs. (Cussler) Government and others should provide funds that would assist universities and colleges in coping with their international responsibilities. (Walton)

5. Specific recommendations:
- Develop effective methods for maintaining contact with former grantees and alumni. (Cussler)
- Facilitate work-experience programs for foreign students while in the United States, especially for students from developing regions. (Cussler)
- Increase the percentage of women among foreign students. (Cussler)

- Review selection criteria to increase component of students who, while deficient in language competence or some other respect, have leadership qualities relevant to socio-economic change. (Walton)

Research

1. Formulate several master research plans that would permit the use of at least partially standardized methods and terms, thus yielding coordinated, comparable, and cumulative results, and contributing to a development of theory. At least one such plan should be worldwide in scope and research personnel. (Cormack)

2. Broaden research methods used beyond the general survey techniques (questionnaires, interviews, etc.) to include case histories of persons and projects, culture-free projective or sociometric tests, small group experiments, participant observations, documentary analyses, etc. (Cussler)

3. More longitudinal studies to yield findings about long-term effects of educational exchanges and role of returnees in their home countries. (Cussler, Walton)

4. Comprehensive studies of the "brain drain" and U. S. and home country factors accounting for non-return. (Cormack, Walton) Also, attention to the emancipatory, internationalizing, and "third culture" effects of study abroad. (Walton)

5. Study foreign students in the context of the wider university group of which they are a part since only in this manner can significant conclusions be drawn concerning the relationship between their performance and other factors. Study of foreign students in a vacuum makes it impossible to say whether the conclusions reached apply equally to all students or are a function of their special roles as foreigners. (Walton)

6. Study overall impact of international educational exchanges and of worldwide educational and training programs on U. S. society. So far only specific or local impacts have been traced. (Walton)

7. Comprehensive review of studies on foreign students in other host societies, and comparison of differential factors and findings, and their purport. (Cormack, Cussler)

8. Specific Research Topics Needing Attention

- Comparative educational advantages in "third country" training of students from developing regions. (Cussler)
- U. S. training programs for foreign military personnel. (Cussler)
- Special problems of women students and of their role as future leaders in their societies. (Cormack, Cussler)

- Interaction patterns, contacts, and problems between foreign and American students and their mutual impact on the attitudes of each. (Cormack, Cussler, Walton)
- Foreign students' involvement in significant community experiences. (Cussler)
- Case studies of successful grantees. (Cussler)
- Less research on attitudes toward the United States and more on the total experience and the acquisition of academic and social knowledge. (Cormack, Cussler, Walton)
- Optimum length of sojourn. (Cormack, Walton)
- Comparative effectiveness of varying types of orientation, guidance, and learning programs for persons from differing cultures studying differing fields. (Cormack)
- Motivations for study in the United States and of exchange programs. (Cormack)
- Relation of background and motivational factors to success or failure in academic study. (Cormack)
- Comparative grading practices in U. S. institutions, relating both to U. S. and foreign students. (Walton)
- Function and substance of "culture shock" and its effect and relation to achievement and study goals. Role of "adolesence" and "maturing" as explanatory factors in problems and sojourn experience. (Walton)

Other Macro-Reviews

In addition to the preceding three government-contracted review studies, the literature of the 1960's, and one study published in 1971, include a number of broad reviews of policy and research aspects relating to foreign students, and/or on problems, issues, and trends in the United States or in worldwide educational exchange. Juxtaposed, these studies help to round out the "state of the field"—its knowledge, problems, needs—and the recommendations proposed to meet these needs. These studies will now be briefly reviewed.

Klineberg's International Exchanges in Education, Science and Culture: Suggestions for Research (219/1966) notes the increasing volume of international educational exchanges, the requirement to enhance their effectiveness, and suggests that the task of research—beyond generating new knowledge—is to bring together and collate what has been found, as well as testing and probing for more universal validity the hypotheses, findings, goals, and theories that have been, or as yet are to be, articulated. Research should systematically compare the findings of U. S. studies with research findings and experiences in other societies. It should also compare the roles and effects of other types of "personal contact," for example, technical cooperation

missions, binational aid or research projects, tourism, sport, immigration, etc., and "non-personal contacts," for example, media, textbooks, the arts, literature, etc., in order to provide a more comprehensive understanding of intercultural transactions and their possible
effect on the growth of positive international activities and attitudes.
Three unconventional research recommendations are advanced: (1) to
study the rationales, operation, and effects of special Soviet university
programs for foreign students and to compare them, in terms of academic achievement and of international understanding with those in
Western societies; (2) to explore the Useems' finding of a high diver-
gence between the specialized field studied abroad and the actual field
of employment entered upon after return; and (3) to inquire into the
overall benefits to science and international understanding accruing
from aspects of the "brain drain."

Major's Review of Research on International Exchange (231/
1965) considers an array of studies on foreign students as (1) individual and cultural personalities, (2) participants in multi-faceted sojourn experiences, and (3) travelers and absorbers of new attitudes
and information. He notes the need for stronger conceptual and theoretical emphases. Particular research needs include the impact on
the foreign student on the host culture and on families and friends at
home, and on the student of protracted isolation during the sojourn
abroad. Additionally, he identifies a need for further research into the
general validity of the U-curve hypothesis, the ramifications of ethnocentrism and xenophilia, the liberalizing versus nationalizing impacts
of foreign travel, factors favoring the development of multi-cultural
personalities and orientations, and the modes and processes that facilitate the acquisition of "third culture" understandings and competencies.

Contacts, friendship, interaction, and participation are identified as the most influential factors in attitude change, and attention is
drawn to Selltiz's finding that the latter tend to be most intensive in
small colleges located in small towns.

Cormack's "International Development through Educational Exchange" (88/1968), essentially reviewing literature similar to that in
her prior study, also calls for greater emphasis on comparative
studies. The need, she says, is to compare: different foreign cultures
represented in one institution; members of one culture studying at different institutions; members of different social strata or sub-cultures
in one, and in several institutions; members of one culture at one institution under different conditions; members of one culture studying
in different countries; and foreign and American students on the same
campus. Such studies could be general or more specialized, that is,
focusing on particular fields or problem areas, such as adjustment
processes and outcomes, the "brain drain," propensities to adopt

foreign traits, roles accorded to national status, etc. Especially important are studies of institution building, and those that would consider institutional rationales, means, and goals together with individual motivations, adaptations, and success. What is also needed are more extensive longitudinal studies employing extensive background and follow-up data, more frequent uses of control groups, and the broadening of research approaches beyond the opinion survey generally encountered. A frequently overlooked factor is identified: the effect of the particular politico-social time period when the student happened to be abroad and/or returned home. The implication, while not developed, is significant: there is need not only for cross-cultural, but also for cross-temporal comparisons.

Walton's "Research on Foreign Graduate Students" (420/1971), representing an update of her 1967 survey, but concentrating on graduate students, reviews more recent studies on the usual range of foreign student topics, on special problems in several professional fields, on foreign students as professionals, and refers to research (then) in progress.

As in her 1967 review, Walton emphasizes the need to study foreign students within the context of the total student and university environment and to examine their relationships and roles in social and technological change. She notes that, until recently, there had been little systematic differentiation of undergraduate and graduate students in research; some studies on the latter seem to suggest fewer of the usual adjustment problems and a greater satisfaction with academic programs, particularly where such pursue concrete educational goals; varied but inconclusive evidence about differentials in academic performance; greater homesickness and feelings of discrimination; a greater need to participate in rather than merely to observe American life; and a feeling of greater pressure to succeed academically—one that often impedes the development of personal relationships with American fellow students.

Additional topics dealt with in more recent studies include the usefulness and relevancy of curricula for home country needs; benefits deriving from special courses or institutes; special "cultural" styles of American institutions and professional agencies; the problems of affecting changes upon return in their organizations and home countries; differing perceptions of the utility of advanced degrees for certain fields; and the value of specialized versus more general competence training. Studies relating to the "brain drain" noted the role of high specialization in non-return, the considerable incidence of non-return in the culturally non-circumscribed fields of science, engineering, and medicine; and the greater propensity to return by self-sponsored, graduate, and lower-class students. (Some of these findings, however, are contradicted in other studies.)

Apart from the already referred to recommendation that foreign students be studied primarily as students, and only secondarily as foreign, Walton recommends that future studies consider a number of broader areas, such as the general learning process, perceptions of self and culture, research on curriculum, conflict and peace theory, and the potential and actual roles and responsibilities of foreign students in innovation and social and technological change.

Angell, in his book Peace on the March (25/ 1969), devotes one chapter to an examination of the effects of study abroad on attitudes favoring transnational accommodation. He finds that the research does not offer consistent evidence, but that, systemically, transnational participation and exchanges between members of equally developed societies are more likely to result in positive accommodative attitudes than those involving members of developed and less-developed societies. Even here, however, there are positive results: the evolvement of friendships and of counterpart roles and functions between the respective professional elites; the transmission of status and experience roles to their own lands; and the effect that the new professionals may have on the climate in which decisions and policies are formulated and carried out.

The above propositions by Angell are based on an examination of literature as well as on original linkage research by the author. The research represents one of the few studies that focus on: (1) the nature and role of lateral functional relationships that, among others, link college and university personnel across national borders; and (2) on the question whether study abroad tends to produce internationalist frames of mind and thus may act as a factor in international accommodation and peace.

Eide's "Students as Bridges between Cultures" (124/ 1972), an article published in a Yugoslav periodical, draws on statistical and other data contained in her UNESCO project (125/ 1970). The essay takes a world view of foreign student flows and conceives of international study as: (1) a "bridging" from "the culture of yesterday to the culture of today," and thus from the present to the future; (2) the absorption of past and present achievements in knowledge created in many parts of the world; and (3) the incorporation into "knowledge" of new social strata and peoples that, traditionally, had not been part of the international university community. Knowledge is presented as a "bridge between cultures," in many instances facilitating a basically global perspective. Students are held to have always been exposed to foreign influences and their current task is to "bridge" their own "ideological commitments, political insights, and professional skills to the conditions of the society around them."

The study cites significant UNESCO statistics:

- As of 1968, 20 percent of all Arab and 15 percent of all African university students studied abroad;

- Two-thirds of the world's foreign students come from developing countries; but also,
- One-quarter of the world's total foreign students studied at institutions in other developing countries.

Eide regards the final statistic as particularly significant since it indicates the building of bridges within regions, and of lines of communication among former fellow students, many of whom will become local or national decision makers.

Spencer's "The Academic Performance of Foreign Students in American Colleges and Universities: Comments on the Literature 1960-1967" (362/ 1967), beyond the focus suggested by the title, includes an incisively critical review of the major features which characterize the literature on foreign students in the United States. He stresses the heterogeneity of the "foreign student" category; the facile way in which it has been employed; the procedural and substantive diversity of the criteria used to identify and evaluate academic success; and the dubious cross-cultural validity, utility, and relevance of such criteria. He recommends that future research include: (1) cross-cultural re-examinations and definitions of objectives in foreign study, anchoring such objectives in the student's home culture, not in that of the host; (2) greater attention to psychological as compared to sociological research approaches; (3) more frequent follow-up studies to individual research projects in order to counteract the tendency to constantly unrelated new starts; (4) greater refinement of statistical, methodological, terminological, conceptual, and substantive approaches used in research, many of which have yielded superficial and non-generalizable results; and (5) an effort to construct and standardize measuring instruments relevant to the cultural motivations, attitudes, and objectives of students from divergent cultural environments.

Finally, Allaway's International Educational Exchange in the United States: A National Profile (16/ 1971) deals with a broad range of problems and issues characterizing the international exchange situation in the United States: the decrease in available funds accompanied by a steep rise in costs; the lack of internal and external coordination in admission and selection procedures; the apparently less than satisfactory extent of contacts between foreign and American students on campuses; the overall paucity of curricular revisions that might meet the specific needs of students from the third world; the confrontation of linguistic prerequisites with those favoring the admission of promising potential leaders; the lack of cooperation and coordination between academic and foreign student advisers; the desirability of more differentiated orientation seminars; and the benefits that could accrue from a greater utilization of foreign students in classroom teaching and community work.

Using data from Bridges to Understanding (335/ 1970), The University of California Self-Study (410/ 1970), and Open Doors (185/ 1973),

Allaway devotes substantial attention to the organization of universities for the conduct of international, area study, and overseas cooperation programs, and the attendant problems of staffing, funding, teaching, research, and service by faculty. He draws attention to new forms of inter-institutional cooperation that have helped in recent years, conjoining a number of institutions around a mutual international interest. He makes particular reference to "inter-university consortia" and notes that, in 1967-68, 110 such consortia in the United States were involved in no less than 211 programs.

The Basic Questions

Cormack and Walton, in addition to drawing certain conclusions about the research surveyed in each of their studies, and making general or specific recommendations, raise a number of basic questions relating to international educational exchange which deserve recapitulation as a conclusion to this introductory chapter.

Are favorable attitudes toward the United States really what should be wanted from educational exchange?

Has U. S. society gained as much, or more, as it has contributed; has its life been affected, and how; and can it change others without being changed in the process?

Have we relied too much on a single formula in educational exchange?

Is it always a "good thing" to bring students to the United States?

Is it better to bring students to participate in our education— or render aid in their institutions?

Should priority be given to aiding professional growth and competence, or to personal growth and development?

To what extent should U. S. institutions change their degree requirements and procedures to accommodate individuals returning to societies with different conditions and aims?

Is the United States unwittingly aiding elite systems and individuals in the preservation of their status quo?

Is the United States unwittingly draining nations of much of their best professional potential, many students electing expatriation?

Should it matter where individuals elect to spend their lives? Doesn't education liberate minds toward freedom of choice?

These basic questions, asked in one case 12, and in the other seven years ago, continue—if we be permitted to comment from the perspective of the research published since then—to be alive and have as yet not received coherent, consistent, conclusive, and, in a number of respects, even adequate research attention.

International educational exchanges represent a complex area of mutual human impacts, learnings, broadenings, and reciprocal examinations—and beyond them, an intricate mechanism and social process in the course of which diverse human wisdom and experience become more widely diffused, and the competence to deal with national and common worldwide problems is advanced. In this perspective, the empirical sociologist, anthropologist, economist, etc., find themselves side by side with the historian of ideas, the macro-sociologist, the student of modernization and integration processes, and even the philosopher. While the research to be reviewed in the subsequent pages focuses on "The World's Students in the United States," it is essential to remember that this legitimate geographically specialized attention represents a cut-out from a much larger global process in the course of which, along with other factors, the newly emerging values, institutions, and procedures of all human survival and existence are being defined and, in increasing measure, readied for implementation.

NOTES

1. For 1968 alone, UNESCO reports the world total of "foreign students" as 428,883, of which "Europe and the USSR" had a total of 164,655, the United States 121,362. "Europe and USSR" and the United States and Canada together had a total of 71.9 percent of the 1968 world total of foreign residents studying at their institutions. See UNESCO, Statistics of Students Abroad, 1962-68, Paris, 1971, p. 19.

2. Cross-Cultural Education: A Bibliography of Government-Sponsored and Private Research on Foreign Students and Trainees in the United States and Other Countries: 1946-64, issued in 1965 by the Office of External Research, Department of State; and the reviews by Margaret Cormack (398/1962) and Barbara Walton (407/1967).

2

WHAT HAPPENS TO
FOREIGN STUDENTS
WHILE IN THE
UNITED STATES

Americans exhibit a continuing interest in finding out what happens to foreign students while they are studying in this country. The largest number of items from our bibliography fell into this category: 160 empirical and 44 non-empirical studies, most of which were published after 1967. These studies vary enormously in intent, content, and methodology. The focus may be on a group of students at a particular campus, or on students of certain nationalities at several campuses; other studies will look at short-term visitors, or immigrant students. Methodology ranges from interviews, to examination of scholastic records, to special testing; a variety of statistical devices are used to analyze the resulting data. The great majority of studies take a psychological or sociological approach, although the researchers themselves may be university administrators, foreign student advisers, faculty members, or Ph.D. candidates.

This wide variation is in itself part of the problem. There has been little effort to achieve a standardized or replicable methodology (with some notable exceptions such as the Michigan International Student Problem Inventory). Hence a questionnaire designed for one study is never used again, and findings based on it cannot be compared to results achieved in another study. A second major problem is definitional. Who exactly are foreign students? What, in fact, is "foreign?" If we want to use academic success as a criterion of a successful sojourn, how are we to measure success? Several studies, discussed below, suggest that conventional measures of academic success are inappropriate when applied to foreign students. A third problem to bear in mind is that most of the empirical research was conducted at a given point in time and few investigators have been able to follow students through their sojourns to see how their attitudes, life styles, English ability, grade point average, etc., change over time as a result of the foreign study experience.

In this chapter, we will identify and discuss research which focuses on the attitudes and achievements of foreign students while in the
United States, and on what happens after the students return home. A
significant preliminary question is: Why do foreign students come to
the United States to study?

A frequently reiterated complaint in the literature is that goals
of different persons and organizations involved in educational exchange
are often widely divergent. In particular, the student, the sponsoring
agency, if any, and the college or university may have goals that di-
verge or even conflict. The institution may aim at developing the full
intellectual potential of the individual; the agency may want a person
with very specific, technical skills to fill a position in the home country. Before we proceed to the studies of what happens to students during the sojourn in the United States, let us consider what they preceive
their goals to be.

We have identified only three studies devoted exclusively to an
analysis of reasons for study abroad, although others also provide
some information. Byers (57/1971), using IIE statistics, informal
interviews, and seven years' experience in dealing with foreign students, concludes that the influx of Asian students will continue as long
as the United States remains a business and industrial leader, English
remains the lingua franca of the world, the quality and availability of
U. S. higher education remains as it is, our economy can absorb all of
the professional people produced by higher education, and the political
situation in Asia remains unsettled. He implies that lack of higher-
education facilities and/or unsettled political or economic conditions
are factors motivating many students.

Meredith (241/1968) compares the reasons given by Asian and
U. S. students for attending the East-West Center in Hawaii. He finds
that there are differences between the two groups in reasons for coming, values, interests, influences, and needs as they relate to educational-vocational choice. Meredith used Dole's Reasons for Going
to College Inventory, an instrument not noted or used in any other
study which we have reviewed.

Finally, Cowan (94/1968) found no positive correlation between
the English ability of Japanese students and their reasons for coming
to the United States. She did, however, find that Japanese students
with better English tended to integrate more into American culture.

From these studies, and from data presented in broader studies
discussed later in this chapter, we may conclude that the major reasons for coming to the United States are to get advanced education or
training that is not available at home, to acquire prestige through a
degree from a U. S. institution, to take advantage of available scholarship funds, to escape unsettled political or economic conditions, and,
simply, to learn more about the United States.

The studies discussed below relate primarily to the central issue of how well American society and, in particular, American educational institutions are responding to the needs and desires of foreign students as revealed in the students' attitudes and academic achievement.

To structure the presentation and show research trends, we shall categorize and discuss the studies in six sections. The first five deal with empirical studies, namely: (1) those which examine students' attitudes and social adjustment; (2) those which examine academic achievement and/ or the relevance of academic programs to students' goals; (3) those which relate adjustment and academic achievement; (4) multidimensional studies, comparing perceptions of foreign students to those of American students, faculty, university administrators, or persons in the community; and (5) follow-up studies of foreign students after they have returned home. The sixth section reviews non-empirical reports on attitudes and/ or achievement, including studies which refer to empirical research but do not use original data in formulating conclusions. In the final section we present conclusions and a summary of the recommendations contained in the studies. The charts at the end of the chapter present pertinent information on the studies reviewed.

Attitudes and Social Adjustment

During the course of this review, we have analyzed 42 studies which, in one form or another, sought to obtain information directly from students while abroad and which focus on foreign student attitudes and problems of social adjustment. In two of these studies, Klein, et al. (218/ 1971) and a USIA report (409/ 1971), students were interviewed before they arrived in the United States as well as while they were here. The following table briefly summarizes the populations studied. See also Chart 2.1, p. 79.

It will be noted that there were no studies in this group pertaining to Latin American students, although several such studies will be referred to in later sections. Forty of the studies deal with students enrolled in a variety of disciplines and professional schools, while one deals exclusively with engineering students and one with with medical residents. Seventeen use sophisticated methodology and analysis involving scientific sampling, standardized instruments, multiple-regression equations, tests of reliability and significance, etc. Another 25 present only tabulations of averages and gross comparisons of data from different groups in the sample. A psychological or sociological approach predominates, although philosophy, political science, and psychiatry form the basis for one study each, and two have a journalism-mass communications orientation.

TABLE 2.1

Attitudes and Social Adjustment: Nationalities Studied

Multinational	21
Regional	
Sub-Saharan Africa	4
Middle East	2
Asia	1
Comparative	
Sub-Saharan Africa	
and Asia	1
India, Europe, Asia	1
Great Britain and United	
Arab Republic	1
Philippines and India	1
Countries	
Taiwan	3
India	3
Kenya	1
Nigeria	1
Saudi Arabia	1
Thailand	1

Foreign Student Attitudes toward Self, Career, and Home Country

These topics attracted the attention of relatively few researchers in the post-1967 period. Victor Coelho (74/ 1972), studying a small group of students in the Chicago area, found that Indians of Catholic, Protestant, and non-Christian backgrounds had different ethical belief systems and that their religious practices changed during their sojourn in the United States. Indian Catholics believed in the necessity of religious or ethical belief systems based on absolute and traditional values; non-Christians stressed ethical and social content; the Protestants' beliefs were between the two extremes. Coelho found that the longer the students were in this country, the less regular and consistent their religious observance became. He suggests the need for a general education curriculum for foreign students who come from religious societies, a curriculum adjusted to their belief systems.

Gandhi (146/ 1972) found that Indian students staying in the United States for less than two years tend to maintain traditional life styles. After four years in this country, however, they exhibit more modern life styles. If strict religious observance is considered an aspect of the "traditional," then Gandhi's study would confirm Coelho's findings. Similarly, among the Thai students studied by Antler (26/ 1970), religious beliefs and values were least subject to change over time. Areas in which change was noted were openmindedness, the value placed on knowledge, and greater freedom in the relationship between the sexes, a change also found by Coelho. Antler's analysis shows that most non-religious attitudes were affected according to length of stay, sex, age, and source of financial support.

Becker (39/ 1971) confirms these trends and suggests that the preservation of basic religious and cultural values safeguards the likelihood of successful re-adjustment upon return. Longer-term students (over two years) showed less patriotism and increased favorableness toward the United States, but often showed hostility to both. She suggests that such students may become "marginal," rejecting both home and host cultures. Markham (233/ 1967) reports that foreign students' images of peoples and political leaders in their homelands changed only slightly during their stay and, if anything, students became more positive toward their home country. Heise (169/ 1971) found that educational and vocational values held by foreign students were little changed by the environment of the U. S. institution attended. Heise, as others before him found, however, that there are background variables which do influence student values: the geographic area from which they come, their choice of a major, religious background, academic level, and employment prospects upon return home. Heise suggests that institutions should examine the values which they wish to inculcate and compare them with those which students actually hold. If values are a goal of institutional curricula, it may be that institutions are not communicating these values successfully.

In a study of Arab intellectuals' attitudes toward democracy, socialism, nationalism, and/ or global alignment, Ibrahim (180/ 1968) found that such values were significantly related to social background and the variety of experiences to which students were exposed in the United States and elsewhere. The more traditional their background and the more limited the variety of their experiences, the more traditional the attitudes. Egyptians studied by Hegazy (167/ 1968) revealed greater changes in dress and food habits than in religious and sexual mores.

If one can generalize about the above studies, it would appear that foreign students in the United States for up to two or three years change their basic cultural and religious attitudes very little. They appear to move toward greater "openmindedness" and toward greater value placed on knowledge, and those from countries with constraints in relationships between women and men increase in desiring greater freedom. Career goals and attitudes toward the home country are, however, fairly resistant to change.

Methodologically, this group of studies exhibits little consistency. Despite the diversity of research instruments used, however, the results recorded tended to be reasonably consistent.

Attitudes Toward the United States, Other Countries, and Students of Other Nationalities

A considerable number of researchers are interested in foreign student attitudes toward the United States, toward other countries, and toward other U. S. and foreign students. Clements (8/1967) found marked changes in attitudes toward the U. S. immediately after students arrived; and less change later. The study conducted by the Development Education and Training Research Institute (DETRI) for AID (10/1969), however, found little change in beliefs about the United States as a result of short-term orientation sessions immediately after arrival.

According to Markham (233/1967), most foreign students arrive with positive images and attitudes toward the United States. Affected by the mass media, these images tend to become more negative, especially regarding social discrimination.

Mowlana and McLaughlin (258/1969) also found that foreign students develop attitudes about the United States primarily from aural media such as radio and television, then from U. S. publications, foreign publications, and only lastly from personal communication. Background variables such as home country, field of study, tenure in the United States, or place of residence did not yield any consistent pattern.

Maslog (236/1967) found that Filipinos and Indians bring with them images of the United States which they had obtained from the local media in their own countries. Filipinos upon arrival think Americans are hard-working and possessed of a superiority complex; that they are practical, materialistic, affluent, and good. Indians, upon arrival, also think that Americans are hard-working, materialistic, and practical. The Filipino image of Indians upon arrival is that Indians come from a poor, underdeveloped, and overpopulated country and that they are dark, ugly, and materialistic. The reverse Indian view of Filipinos is much more positive—they come from a poor and underdeveloped country, but they are "happy islanders." In a similar study, Heath (166/1970) found a favorable pre-disposition toward Americans. The students he interviewed characterized Americans as friendly, democratic, egalitarian, optimistic, ambitious, and informal, but also immature, materialistic, and ephemeral in their social relations. Favorable attitudes, he believes, are a function of foreign student satisfaction with sojourn, academic program, and frequency of travel.

Chang (65/ 1972) found that attitudes of Chinese students toward the United States were positively related to the extent of association with Americans and to the foreign student's perception of America's relationship to his or her own country. On the other hand, the student's degree of frustration, sex difference, field of study, or religious affiliation showed no relationship to positive or negative attitudes to the United States.

Middle Eastern students studied by Davis (100/ 1960) were impressed with the quality of U. S. graduate education but critical of the emphasis on an intense and varied social life. They felt that ethnic groups are treated fairly but that racially distinct sub-groups are not. They further criticized aspects of egalitarianism as reflected in U. S. marriage and family life and reported contradictory impressions of U. S. patterns of friendship and hospitality. Klein, et al. (218/ 1971), found that attitudes and problems varied according to length of stay in this country: early attitudes and problems related to getting settled; mid-sojourn attitudes to academic problems; and end-of-stay attitudes to conflicts over the return home, and to the resolution of relationships with Americans.

Two studies compared attitudes of students from different geographical areas. Both agreed that Europeans tend to be most negative in their opinions about the United States, or "less favorable" in Heath's terminology. Markham (233/ 1967) reports that Asians viewed the United States in the most favorable light; Africans and Latin Americans only slightly less so. In a study of attitudes toward U. S. advertising, Pierce (312/ 1969) found that students from underdeveloped countries regard U. S. advertising more favorably than do students from European countries.

In a study which mixes sociological research with social philosophy, Restivo (324/ 1971) investigated the attitudes of visiting foreign scientists in the United States. He found that they tend to isolate themselves from social and political activity and stress efficiency and skills rather than innovation. Since science as an ideology tends toward "disinterestedness" as regards present and future social consequences of scientific research, foreign scientists in the United States tend to see science as a social process with no commitment to post-modern notions of a world community. However, scientists have a professional commitment that transcends commitments to neighborhood, community, and society, and this perhaps creates the pre-conditions for the growth of post-modern societies. Restivo, however, also finds that scientists tend toward bureaucratization, standardization, and simplification, and this may decrease the evolutionary potential of human culture. In essence, the developing international community of scientists may exhibit a loyalty to one another, but have no particular depth of feeling or sophistication about the community and society that science is affecting.

African Attitudes Toward the United States and Toward American Blacks

Four recent studies of black Africans' attitudes toward the United States and toward U. S. blacks carry particular interest. Becker (40/ 1973) found that black Africans could communicate better with U. S. whites than with U. S. blacks, and that they preferred dating whites. The Africans' tendency to emphasize their separate identity and to restrict contact with black Americans was strengthened by socio-cultural differences, the tangible benefits accorded Africans, and a perceived rejection of the Africans by U. S. blacks.

Miller (246/ 1967) found that a majority of Africans came to the United States with unfavorable anticipations regarding race relations in the United States, and that their attitudes became more unfavorable during their stay. They were unhappy with U. S. policy toward South Africa and disillusioned with race relations, especially in the North. Those interviewed in the Miller study tended to find hypocrisy in the United States and noted that they were treated better when they were known not to be Americans. On the other hand, they reported a very positive attitude toward the U. S. educational system and U. S. industrialization.

Among Nigerians, Sofola (358/ 1967) discovered positive attitudes toward this society's social, political, economic, and spiritual ideals upon arrival, but increasing bitterness and ambivalence during the sojourn. While here, they developed an enhanced appreciation of their home country.

A study undertaken by the United States Information Agency (409/ 1971) questioned African participants before and after a short-term study visit to the United States. Most arrived with a favorable opinion of the United States; about half left with more favorable, and half with less favorable attitudes. The visitors identified race relations as a concern, but found Americans more sympathetic to the problem than they had anticipated. Although they found the situation of black Americans better than they had expected, they found the American Indian situation much worse. They also felt that Americans tended to show little interest in international affairs, did not participate in domestic politics, had weak family ties, but were concerned with urban and industrial pollution.

As a whole, these studies support the notion that black Africans do not strongly identify with black Americans, but are inconclusive as to whether the general direction of attitude change during the sojourn is positive or negative.

Social Behavior and Adjustment to Life in the United States

A considerable number of recent studies focus on the social behavior of foreign students and their relationships with Americans and

American students. Most of these studies show that foreign students
from Western industrialized countries tend to socialize more with
Americans than do students from non-Western and less-industrialized
countries (see particularly Tanner [373/ 1968]). Supporting this general conclusion are studies by Antler (26/ 1970), who finds that foreign
medical residents have more intense social contacts with fellow countrymen than with host-country nationals, and Becker (39/1971), who
shows that students who have been in the United States for two years
or longer tend to withdraw into congenial social niches and live with
compatriots rather than with foreigners.

This phenomenon, which we may term social isolation, has been
investigated in several studies, particularly as it is exhibited by students from certain geographic regions. Klein, et al. (218/ 1971),
found that more than half of the Asian students studied had not established significant social relationships with Americans during their
stay; yet those who did not do so considered Americans insincere,
superficial, and incapable of real friendships. This is the only study
we have identified which uses a psychiatric approach to the study of
social adaptation. It suggests that among Asians, role conflict and
self-esteem are essential elements in determining social adaptation
and that situational factors over time determine its patterns. These
patterns are different in the early (getting settled) stages, the middle
(academic) stages, and the late (preparation for return home) stages.
It also suggests that the wholistic concept of "adaptation" must be dis-
aggregated and foreign students studied in terms of whether or not
they realize their professional goals, develop positive contacts with
Americans, increase their tolerance and flexibility, and strengthen
their identification with the home country.

Wakita (419/ 1971) studies the attitudes and social adjustments
of various categories of Asian students in California. He finds that
foreign-born Asians feel superior to American-born Asians who do
not speak Asian languages. The American-born react more strongly
on questions of discrimination than those born abroad, and Hawaii-
born Asians studying in Los Angeles believed that both foreign-born
and American-born Asians were prejudiced against them. Hawaii-born
Asians tended to congregate together, finding foreign-born Asians shy
and American-born Asians unfriendly.

In a study at the University of Minnesota, Kang (205/ 1971) found
that 80 percent of the Chinese students create their own small community which contributes to the maintenance of traditional values and belief systems. They live together, support their own church, belong to
only Chinese organizations, maintain close ties with the homeland, and
do not read many magazines generally familiar to U. S. students.
Kang, in another study (204/ 1971), found that Chinese students who
anglicize their names are more fully socialized, flexible, and varied

in economic adjustment, and have greater access to lines of influence and power in the host community than Chinese students who do not do so.

Indian students reveal the same tendency to congregate together. Ninety percent of those studied by Gandhi (145/1970), also at the University of Minnesota, lived with or close to other Indians. Regional differences among Indians created occasional conflict, but this was suppressed, producing what Gandhi calls "unity in diversity, cohesion in conflict." Regional and linguistic sub-groupings among Indians overrode caste differences as Hinduism, in turn, overrode regional differences. In a later report on data from the same study (146/1970), Gandhi shows that Indian students were more or less equally divided between those practicing traditional and modern life styles. Many Indians became "more Indian" after arrival and many developed a Western life style only after four or more years in this country. Those who adopted a new life style held more graduate assistantships on campus, exercised more power and influence, and had more social and cultural contacts with Americans. Gandhi further found that life styles could be predicted through attitude tests, suggesting that American universities could identify foreign students with traditional life styles and make special efforts to expand their opportunities for social contacts.

The pattern continues in studies of African students. Cohen (76/1971) found that Kenyan students preferred living with compatriots, forming the closest friendships with members of the same tribal groups. He suggests that the co-national group functioned as a temporary surrogate for the home culture. Among the Nigerians studied by Sofola (358/1967), those that did not have sufficient social contact with their countrymen and who had problems with their studies were particularly unhappy with their stay in the United States. Nigerians, he found, had problems adjusting to the individualistic approach to life in the United States and missed the extended-family tradition of their home country.

Egyptians too tend to form temporary communities while studying in the United States. Those studied by Hegazy (167/1968) had less contact with American society than did British students in the United States, and more frequently developed a temporary community within the larger social setting.

As this series of studies shows, the phenomenon of social isolation is a well-documented facet of the foreign student's adjustment to life in the United States. A few authors have tried to assess its causes and effects. One such study is that by Guglielmo (157/1967), who finds that students living longer in the United States had a better knowledge of U. S. civil regulations relating to immigration, automobile-licensing requirements, the income-tax and social-security systems, and housing and employment. Students living with other foreign students from the same country scored lowest, while students who had lived in several countries, who had jobs, and who had fathers in teaching or business scored highest. Orientation programs and contacts with U. S. families made no significant difference in knowledge of civil regulations.

Size of college and field of study may be related to degree of isolation. Selltiz, et al. (341/1956) found that foreign students in small colleges and towns had greater opportunities for contact and interaction with Americans than students in large towns and universities. Jammaz (194/1972) found that Saudi Arabian students adjusted better at small than at large colleges and that science and engineering students tended to adjust better than students in the humanities or the social sciences. He found academic difficulties associated with inadequate adjustment. These two studies imply the need for a closer examination of the way in which large colleges and universities facilitate social interchanges and deal with adjustment problems of foreign students.

Rising and Copp (326/1968), in a more general study of foreign students, confirm what many of the studies of students from geographic regions have found, namely, that those from non-Western and less-developed countries have greater difficulties in adjusting to academic work, to new personal relationships with persons from countries other than their own, and to U. S. culture. They suggest the need for special attention to orient and help students from such countries.

The psychological implications of adjustment problems are discussed by Pratt (316/1956), who suggests that emotional problems of foreign students stem from an inability to adjust to his or her own cultural tradition and have little to do with educational travel or with the impact of an alien culture. Inability to adjust to American values and the "American way of life" is more likely to be the neurosis of an American student than that of a Japanese student. If a Japanese student is neurotic, he or she is probably having trouble with Japanese values—not American. This thesis is partially supported by some of the above studies which show that foreign students who congregate together and preserve traditional values have fewer coping problems than those who do not and who cannot find a surrogate foreign student community in this country to temporarily replace traditional social relationships.

In order to identify the problems experienced by foreign students, several researchers have used the "Michigan International Student Problem Inventory," an instrument developed in 1962 by Porter (315/1962) and used by foreign student offices at a number of colleges and universities. For example, Breuder (52/1972) found that foreign students in Florida colleges cited problems in connection with financial aid, English-language placement, and admissions. Males and females, junior-college and four-year college students, and short- and long-term students identified about the same range of problems. Day (105/1968) reports that problems experienced by foreign students change according to how many months the students had been in the United States. Graduates and undergraduates, when divided into groups according to length of time spent in the U. S., reveal distinct categories of problems that are characteristic of that group but not necessarily found at any other time during the sojourn. Moran, et al. (255/1974), found that role-playing and simulation in orientation programs had helped students and that they felt that they had fewer problems after orientation than before. Ursua (412/1969) believes that English-language proficiency is not strongly related to the intensity or scope of problems. Major problems cited by students in this study included difficulty in securing good academic advice, financial difficulties, insufficient orientation, and the lack of social/personal guidance.

The Michigan International Student Problem Inventory is a quick and reliable way of identifying problems perceived by students on an individual campus, but can offer no solution to these problems. Unless the results of other research are taken into account in formulating foreign student policy, approaches to dealing with the problems might well be unproductive. (For further discussion of problem checklists, see below, pp. 47-48.

Theoretical Proposals

The studies discussed above throw considerable light on the life style and life space of diverse groups of foreign students while in this country. The problem which they present is how to interrelate the various disciplinary perspectives in order to design better academic programs and host relationships with the students.

Very few studies attempt such interdisciplinary theory or model building. Most examine specific aspects of life styles and social relationships or problems of foreign students and, by implication or expressly, tend to overstress the significance of the results by not taking into account other socio-psychological factors important to an individual and his or her nationality group in the present and in the future.

Few studies proceed to higher levels of suggested explanation. Of those reviewed above, only Ibrahim and Klein show any inclination toward theory building. Ibrahim posits a theory of attitude organization and deals with congruency patterns, particularly in terms of political attitude and student background. Klein reports on a long-term study taking a psychiatric approach to attitude building and adjustment.

Several studies critique and expand the U-curve hypothesis first described by Lysgaard ("Adjustment in a Foreign Society: Norwegian Fulbright Grantees Visiting the United States," International Social Science Bulletin, 1955, pp. 45-51). In its original version, this hypothesis proposed a sequence of periods and types of experiences common to many foreign students. The first period, immediately upon arrival, is marked by high expectations, a friendly reception, and the pleasures of discovery, but is soon followed by a period of increasing difficulties during which the student has to cope with a multitude of emerging problems. This low point in the curve ultimately yields to a third period, as departure for home approaches, in which the student has learned how to function in the host country and thus exhibits a more positive attitude toward the society and environment. Often this more positive stage is reached only during the second year of the sojourn so that many students on shorter courses of study leave at periods of considerable adaptational distress.

Among more recent studies are those by Heath (166/ 1970), who found that the U-curve proposition generally applied to students residing in the Berkeley International House, and by Selby and Woods (340/ 1966), who report an angular V-curve whereby non-Europeans showed a sharply dropping morale during the early months and a more gradually rising morale in later months of a one-year stay. They suggest the need to study not only cultural, but also institutional impacts upon their students, but do not elaborate further. Tanner (373/ 1968) found a U-curve progression operating in friendship patterns. At first foreign students would make friends with other nationalities, then contact and associate with compatriots, and toward the end of their stay begin to have friends of other nationalities again.

In a comparative study of Indians, Israelis, and Europeans at UCLA, Becker (38/ 1968) found that the U-curve operated in reverse for students from semi- or underdeveloped countries. Students from these countries arrived with greater anxieties and exhibited hostile attitudes early and late in their visits, but developed more favorable attitudes toward the middle periods of their sojourn. Moreover, "psychological time," the overall percentage of sojourn elapsed, was more important than actual time, number of months or years, in examining the U-curve phenomenon. She proposes a theory of "anticipatory adjustment," the selective adoption of attitudes on the basis of their utility in easing the individual's adjustment to anticipated imminent and drastic changes in environment.

Since U-curve-oriented studies tend to indicate the significance of adjustment problems and the related growth of negative attitudes after arrival in the United States, one might assume that orientation programs for foreign students would be ameliorative and important. Three evaluations of such programs which we have reviewed do not indicate that traditional orientation is particularly helpful. DETRI (10/ 1969)evaluated orientation sessions for AID participants coming to this country, and, although they found that participants averaged a ten-percent gain in information in before-and-after tests, there was little change in beliefs about the United States. Clements (8/1967), in a very limited study of nine students in a summer enrichment and leadership-training program, also found no significant changes in attitude, although participants liked the seminar. Marked changes in attitudes toward the United States and toward Americans took place shortly after arrival, but much less change occurred subsequently. Moran (255/1974) found that the role-playing and simulation exercises in orientation sessions apparently make a difference and need further examination to determine which techniques are most appropriate to the group involved.

Summary

It will be seen from the above discussion that, of the attitudes which students bring with them upon arrival in the United States, those pertaining to basic cultural and religious values are most resistant to change. This is especially true of students whose sojourn is less than two years. In their attitudes toward the United States, students from Europe tend to arrive with the most unfavorable attitudes, although black Africans who are apprehensive about race relations may also be said to display unfavorable attitudes. The studies show no consistent direction of attitude change during the sojourn and several suggest that attitudes to the United States can be understood only as a function of the student's experience, social and academic, while in this country.

In several studies, foreign students are reported to be critical of Americans' ability to form friendships; Americans are immature, superficial, etc. This may be related to the frequency with which foreign students form co-national groups. The research shows that such groups offer many positive benefits in helping the foreign student to cope with the new environment and in keeping alive traditional values which later on may assist in re-entry into the home culture. It would be interesting to know whether foreign students are encouraged to rely on co-nationals because their American peers cannot offer friendship of sufficient depth, or whether, having invested their emotional energy in a co-national group, foreign students have little left over for American friendships. In either case, the findings on social isolation raise the question of how much U. S. academic institutions and communities should attempt to change traditional values among foreign students if they wish to prepare students for an effective role when returning home and avoid creating psychological conflicts among foreign students while they are in this country. Perhaps the most appropriate goal is to attempt to develop positive attitudes toward the value of knowledge and technology which will be helpful to the development of the home country, with less concern for attempting to integrate foreign students into the "American way of life" in such a way as to create conflicts with traditional values.

With regard to the U-curve hypothesis, recent studies are inconclusive. It has been found to operate in some situations and not in others, suggesting that it is by no means universally applicable and needs to be further tested with a variety of carefully defined independent variables.

Academic Achievement and the Relevance of Academic Programs

We now move from studies which examine social and psychological adjustment to those which look exclusively at academic achievement and the relevance of academic programs to the needs of foreign students. There are 25 items in this group, three of which discuss the same research study. Eleven are doctoral dissertations and one is a master's thesis. All present data gathered from foreign students while in the United States except Moravcsik (256/1972) which examines data collected from students both before and after their arrival. The following tables summarize the nationality and disciplines of the populations studied. A further description of these studies is given in Chart 2.2, p. 84.

TABLE 2.2

Academic Achievement and Relevance:
Nationalities Studied

Multinational	17	Comparisons	
Latin America	1	Indonesia, Korea,	
Asia	1	Pakistan, Thailand	1
South Asia	1	Speakers of Spanish, Dutch, Japanese,	
India	1	Turkish	1

TABLE 2.3

Academic Achievement and Relevance:
Disciplines Studied

Multidisciplinary	20
Education	1
Military Science	1
Physical and Biological Science	1

Eleven of the 23 studies use a relatively sophisticated analysis of data involving tests of significance, multiple regression analysis, and/or tests of validity and reliability. As might be expected, since these studies examine the learning behavior of students, most of the researchers have a background in psychology.

Academic Programs

We will first look at studies which examine the perceptions of foreign students concerning their academic programs in general and which describe how foreign students are handled academically. Three items refer to an extensive project undertaken in 1967-68 by the American Association of Collegiate Registrars and Admissions Officers (AACRAO) under contract to AID (20/n.d.; 417/1970; 418/1971). The purpose of the project was to assess the effectiveness of the selection and placement of AID-sponsored academic participants in the U. S. colleges and universities and to suggest how the total process might be improved.

Upon arrival in the United States, 1,004 participants completed a questionnaire, two English-language tests, and a scholastic aptitude test. These data were supplemented with biographical details, a review of the relevant training documents from the field, and academic credentials. Additional data were collected on campus as the participants proceeded through their academic programs.

The study found that AID-supported participants differed significantly from the total foreign student population both in terms of geographic balance and the fields of study pursued. They tended to be more mature, more established professionally, and more likely to return to work in the public sector. About 80 percent were regarded as capable of doing satisfactory work in an American college or university of average academic competition and, although between one-third and one-half lacked sufficient English to begin a full academic program upon arrival, more than 85 percent ultimately met their training objectives. The field of study expected by participants agreed with their prescribed majors only 65 percent of the time, however, and some 35 percent felt that they should have been placed in degree programs other than those prescribed. In the opinion of the credential analysts and campus representatives, over 70 percent of the students were properly placed.

Contrary to findings in other studies discussed below, the SAT-Math test proved to be a good predictor of undergraduate performance; on the other hand, verbal scores on U. S. aptitude tests (SAT or Graduate Record Examination) proved of little value. Surprisingly, and despite strong evidence in other studies, English-proficiency tests had only marginal value in predicting performance as measured by grade point averages (GPA).

This study implies that there is considerable "slippage" in the process of providing training for AID participants appropriate to the positions that they expect to assume upon return home. Recommendations in the study suggest various ways of improving the selection, placement, and training process.

The study by Mozden (259/1973) describes and assesses the military-assistance training programs conducted by the United States Government. Although much more limited in its methodology than the AACRAO-AID study, it is of special interest since these programs include trainees from more than one-half of the world's nations and have produced more graduates than all other training programs sponsored by the U. S. Government. Working from a combination of primary and secondary sources, the author concludes that most trainees return home having acquired both specialized military skills and a variety of more general technical skills. He finds that the goals of these programs are rather general and ill-defined, and recommends that, considering the large funds invested in such programs, a study of their long-term effect would be appropriate.

Several other studies look at the academic side of the foreign student experience in general. Paraskevopoulos and Dremuk (303/1968) calculate the reduction ratio of foreign students at the University of Illinois. Of 5,800 foreign student applicants in one year, less than one-fifth actually became registered students at the University. The authors suggest that the freshmen yield is very low and that foreign students transferring from other American universities provide a higher yield. They criticize the time and money expended in application and admission procedures and believe that foreign students could be better screened at home. They also recommend a procedure whereby foreign applications could be pooled among various colleges and universities.

Halsz (159/ 1969) reports on an extensive analysis of academic performance data of graduate students from Indonesia, Korea, Pakistan, and Thailand registered at the University of California (Los Angeles) from the fall of 1959 through the spring of 1967. Relevant findings indicate that academic performance prior to arrival in the United States was reasonably predictive of grade point averages achieved in the United States, that English proficiency correlated highly with scholastic achievement, that family-supported students were less successful than sponsored students, and that the Thai and Pakistani students tended to pace themselves better and stay longer than the Indonesian and Korean students. The study also discusses in some detail the higher education credentials of these countries and the interpretation given them by the University of California.

A final study in this group is that of Pavri (306/ 1963), who undertook a study of foreign student records at the University of Virginia, supplementing their data by a questionnaire administered to foreign students. Among the significant findings of this study are the following: younger students were less successful than older students; married students living with their families achieved at a higher level and experienced fewer difficulties than those who lived alone, a result which conflicts with some attitudinal studies discussed above which indicated that married foreign students tended to have more problems than single foreign students; students with scholarships were more successful than those who were self-supporting; foreign students had difficulty with English; most were satisfied with their programs, though some felt there was not enough flexibility; nearly half were unsuccessful in their U. S. university careers; and most experienced various personal and social problems while in the United States.

Predictive Value of Academic Aptitude Tests, English-Language Tests, and Background Information Data

Of all the variables that might affect the scholastic aspect of a foreign student's sojourn, proficiency in English correlates most often with academic success. Heil and Aleamoni (168/ 1974) present a comprehensive review of literature on the prediction of academic success of foreign students, including their own data on foreign students at the University of Illinois. They find that the Test of English as a Foreign Language (TOEFL) "appears to be no better or worse than those admission tests used to predict success of native American students."

Other studies would seem to support this conclusion. Allen (18/ 1965) found a positive correlation between English test scores upon admission and academic success in the first semester; graduate students scored higher on the English test and made higher grade point averages.

Martin (235/ 1971) found that students with high TOEFL scores prior to admission achieved higher grade point averages in the year of graduate study than their non-tested counterparts, although sub-tests of TOEFL were in themselves not significantly predictive of academic success.

Melendez-Craig (240/ 1970) found that English proficiency correlated highly with academic achievement, that graduate and upper-level undergraduate students performed better than lower-level students, and that marital status or sex was not related to academic achievement. Uehara (379/ 1969) found English proficiency closely related to academic success, although in this study TOEFL was not used. English-language proficiency was determined either by an interview, by taking the School and College Aptitude Tests (SCAT), or by submitting a report of proficiency in English. Sharon (344/ 1971) hypothesized that the Graduate Record Examination (GRE) results for foreign students who scored high on TOEFL would be more predictive of academic success than results of students who scored low on TOEFL. This hypothesis was only moderately supported and Sharon believes that foreign students with low English verbal aptitudes can succeed at American graduate schools. Sharon also discusses the limitations of using grade point averages as a criterion of graduate school success by foreign students.

Burke (56/ 1968) studied the predictive validity of a battery of six ability and achievement tests administered to foreign students at the University of Southern California and found that the three most valid measures of predicting academic achievement were the California Reading Test, a speech interview, and the Larry Ward English Examination for Foreign Students. Elting (131/ 1970), in a study at the University of Miami, found that of eight pre-admission variables, two, namely, class-rank score and Cooperative English Tests—Level of Comprehension score, in combination effectively predicted expected grade point averages of foreign students in their freshman year. In addition, other background variables (age, geographic area, native language, and educational system) showed some relationship to academic success.

Burgess and Marks (55/ 1968) found that the Lado Test of Aural Comprehension did not predict in any significant way the academic success of students, although there was some correlation with grades in English classes. Although not directly related to academic success, Van de Guchte (414/ 1969) studied the foreign accents of students, found that the Lado Test of Oral Comprehension was a good predictor of accent, and that other aural and visual cues also affected the judgment of native speakers as to the extent of foreign accent demonstrated by foreign students. This study raises the question as to whether or not severe foreign accents lead to lack of communication between foreign students and professors and affect the judgment of faculty as to the academic ability of students.

The above and similar studies show that the level of English ability, as measured by TOEFL or other standardized English-as-a-Foreign-Language tests, is a valid predictor of academic success for undergraduate and graduate foreign students. Unfortunately, few studies go beyond this straightforward information. Questions abound. What kinds of remedial programs to assist foreign students in English ability have been successful at various universities? In what ways do foreign students who rapidly acquire English facility and academic success differ from those who are unable to do so? Do foreign students from certain language groups have more difficulty with English than do others? Should foreign students with low TOEFL scores be permitted to enter only colleges and universities with remedial English facilities?

A number of studies do, of course, look at other background variables to see which correlate with academic success. Ellakany (126/ 1970), for example, found moderate correlation between academic success and sex, age, and source of support variables at the undergraduate level. Native language and marital status were found to have some significance at the undergraduate and graduate levels. Sugimoto (369/ 1966) found that the most significant pre-admission predictors of the academic success of foreign students were graduate standing, age, and type of visa held. Academic success as defined by Sugimoto was not based on a grade point average, but rather on whether or not the student had obtained a degree, a certificate, a credential, or permission to continue university studies at a higher level. Using these criteria of success, he found that little predictive value could be attached to such standard pre-admission items as scores on the English examination, admissions status, and the date of entry into the United States. First-semester grade point averages were the best index of the student's eventual success in obtaining some kind of certification. These results are surprising since most other studies show a correlation between first- and second-term grade point averages and results on TOEFL tests when entering.

Telleen (374/ 1970) summarizes the findings of 41 authors on the subject of academic achievement for the period 1924 to 1969. She then describes the characteristics of Indian graduate students attending the University of Michigan from 1947 to 1968 and formulates a model which can be used to predict the academic achievement of Indian applicants to the graduate program. Of the 15 variables found to be significantly related to academic achievement, eight were selected for use in the predictive model. This model was also found to predict accurately the cumulative letter grade of Indian students who were not part of the original 300 students in the study. Variables included background information on the applicant's academic career in India; this is one of the few studies showing a reasonably high correlation between academic background in the home country and a grade point average in the

United States. Marital status and sex were not among the variables significantly related to academic achievement.

Farrar (134/ 1968), studying the population of a junior college in Los Angeles, points out that immigrant foreign students outnumber foreign students temporarily in the United States and that much more study is needed of factors related to their academic success. He found that the School and College Aptitude Tests (SCAT) had negligible value for predicting academic aptitude of immigrant foreign students; that the foreign students were superior to native students in grade point average and in all other parameters which were used to measure academic achievement; and that they differed considerably from the foreign student temporarily in this country in many significant ways.

Moravcsik (256/ 1972) reports on a project of the Committee on International Education in Physics designed to improve the selection of graduate students in physics from abroad. This study suggests that Graduate Record Examination results and letters of recommendation do not effectively predict the potential for success of foreign students in physics. Interviews conducted with applicants in their home countries by a team of U. S. faculty produced successful students and also acquainted the faculty with foreign educational systems, thus enabling them to prepare a better program for the foreign students.

A number of other studies of admissions requirements as they correlate with academic success were undertaken by university admissions offices (for example, University of South Carolina [411/ 1967]). We have found, however, no studies by faculty in academic departments designed to help them improve their selection of foreign students, other than that by Moravcsik, above.

Perceived Relevance and Quality of the Academic Program

A number of studies already discussed, including the AACRAO-AID study (418/ 1971), touch on foreign students' perceptions of the relevance and quality of their academic programs. In addition to the two studies reviewed here, the topic appears below in the discussion of research on students who have returned home.

The American Association of Colleges for Teacher Education (19/ 1973), in a pilot study of educators from abroad who participated in an AID-financed internship program in this country, report that 90 percent rated the benefits of this internship program as above average but that they would have preferred a longer sojourn. A follow-up study of all 131 participants was recommended.

Ford (140/ 1969) conducted a more comprehensive study of students from the Middle East, South Asia, and Southeast Asia focusing on the reaction of foreign students to their academic environments in the United States. Using in-depth interviews with a relatively small sample (15 students), Ford found that 11 had strong reservations about the relevance of what they were learning to their own career objectives. Many of these students had jobs waiting for them upon return but the academic advisers on campus did little to develop individual study programs which matched the job requirements. Ford found that students who did not have a job waiting were more apt to view as moderate or high the relevance of what was being learned. If one can over-generalize from this study, it would appear that foreign students who have vague career expectations are much more satisfied with their college careers than those who have clearly defined career expectations. This issue clearly should be the subject of further research. Ford suggests the need for much more intense and meaningful interaction with faculty and other graduate students on the part of foreign students.

Summary

It is apparent from the above discussion that the large majority of studies concerning the academic success of the foreign student consider only formal, university-wide admissions processes. Few studies related to or involved academic departments in such a way as to acquaint academic staff with the learning needs of foreign students or to suggest solutions to difficulties stemming either from personal or academic background differences or from language difficulties. In essence, most studies thus assume that we must find ways of selecting students who can do well what American students do, while few consider how we can teach foreign students so as to increase their chances for academic success.

Several studies make the valuable suggestion that the standard measures of academic success need to be re-evaluated when dealing with foreign students. The grade point average has limitations as a criterion and a measure. Success in obtaining a degree or certification similarly has limited value, although it probably is more significant in terms of the practical needs of foreign students than the grade point average as a sole measure. The role of varying standards between institutions and departments granting the degree or certificate is another question. No research has addressed the problem.

Although English ability as measured by various tests seems to correlate highly with early academic success, at least as measured by the grade point average, it would appear that there is much we do not know about the relationship between language problems and academic success. Further study is needed, for example, of the effectiveness of various approaches to eliminating language problems in the early stages of the sojourn. Some of these matters are discussed in Chapter 3.

The paucity of research on foreign students' perception of quality and relevance of academic programs would appear to reflect the somewhat limited approach to dealing with foreign students in the academic departments of most colleges and universities. Again, the goal of most institutions in the United States appears to be the training of foreign students to know and do the same things that American students know and do. There appears to be little research concern for finding out what the academic needs of foreign students indeed are, in terms of the positions waiting for them at home, the careers desired at home, or the foreign student's own perceptions of what may be meaningful for his or her life.

Studies of Both Adjustment and Academic Achievement

This section will discuss 27 studies which differ from those discussed in earlier sections in that they examine both attitudinal and adjustment elements of the foreign student experience and factors relating to the foreign student's academic success. Nineteen of the studies use some form of sophisticated sampling, questionnaire design, and/or data analysis, while the rest use relatively unsophisticated approaches to data collection and analysis. The nationalities and disciplines studied are shown in the following tables. Further details are supplied in Chart 2.3, p. 88.

Studies of AID Participants

For studies attempt to examine the total experience of being a foreign student in such a way that the relationships among background, attitudinal, adjustment, and academic achievement factors are clearly revealed. Such studies would necessitate an inter-disciplinary approach and, to be comprehensive, they would need to include case studies of students over time.

Most of the studies which do attempt comprehensive analysis are point-in-time examinations of students' perceptions of adjustment or academic problems. Probably the most careful and extensive such study recently undertaken is the International Training Assessment Program contracted for by the Agency for International Development with the Development Education and Training Research Institute (DETRI) of the American University in Washington, D. C. (11, 12, 113/1972). This project was an attempt to yield standardized objective results amenable to the aggregation necessary for an overall evaluation of the entire international training program. Only one similar prior effort had been undertaken, namely the worldwide evaluation

TABLE 2.4

Studies of Adjustment and Achievement:
Nationalities Studied

Multinational	19	Comparisons	
India	2	China, Pakistan, India,	
Middle East	2	Middle East	1
Latin America	1	Thailand, India, Pakistan	1
		India, Japan	1

TABLE 2.5

Studies of Adjustment and Achievement:
Disciplines Studied

Multidisciplinary	16
Agriculture	3
Health and Agriculture	1
Aviation	1
Education	1
Public Administration and Education	1
Internal Revenue	1
Labor	1
Public Health	1
Social Science	1

survey, 1960 to 1964, conducted by the International Cooperation Administration, predecessor of AID, in which participants were interviewed six months or more after return home. (This study is reviewed below, p. 66.) A major finding of this earlier survey was that the satisfaction with which a participant viewed the total training experience was strongly related to post-return utilization of training. Hence, the DETRI project used self-reported participant satisfaction as a measure of program effectiveness.

During the course of the project, November 1966 through March 1972, interviews were conducted with 10,825 AID participants from 75 countries as they passed through Washington, D. C., on their way home. The instruments developed for these "exit interviews" consisted of a standardized, structured questionnaire, an unstructured but focused oral interview for individual trainees, and, for observation-training team participants, a standardized, structured oral interview in a group session. A time-sharing information retrieval system was developed for the exit-interview data. In addition to a computer tape containing all the information in the data bank, DETRI prepared a number of reports for AID.

Most of the AID training programs were administered through individual government agencies; the DETRI reports summarized reactions of trainees programmed by each agency or department. Generally, between 50 and 70 percent of the participants rated both their feelings of welcome and acceptance in the United States, and their satisfaction with their total experience as AID participants at one of the top two scale positions. There was a marked trend for participants in the later years of the 1966-72 time period to have a less favorable attitude toward the United States as a society. The reports offer no explanation for this change.

Conclusions presented in the annual reports (11a/ 1969; 11b/ 1970; 11c/ 1971; 11d/ 1972) are partly supportive of other research findings, and partly in conflict. Generally compatible with other studies are conclusions such as the following: (1) participants who reported irrelevance or duplication of content were less satisfied with their technical training programs; (2) participants who felt more involved in planning their programs, and who believed that their supervisors were also involved, were more satisfied with their technical training program; (3) participants who felt that they were in some way discriminated against by Americans were less satisfied with the social-personal aspects of their sojourn; (4) participants who reported difficulties with living arrangements were less satisfied with the social-personal aspects of their sojourns. Both the First and Second Annual Reports indicate, however, that participants who met American friends, lived with Americans, participated in social, cultural, and recreational activities, and utilized support services made available by AID were more satisfied with both the technical and social-personal aspects of their sojourns. This finding seems to be in partial conflict with other findings of adjustment studies analyzed above which indicated that for regular academic students, a major factor in adjustment and satisfaction was the ability of the foreign student to form a small community with co-nationals while in the United States; students in such groups did not find lack of contact with Americans particularly disturbing. A further conflict with other research is the finding that difficulty with the English language, participation in pre-university workshops, and difficulties with money allowances were not related to participants' satisfactions or dissatisfactions.

Considerable and important data collected during this project exist on computer tape for further study and analysis. It is our understanding that AID would be happy to make such data available to interested researchers.

One other study of AID participants is that conducted by Frank (141/ 1965) among persons attending communications seminars at Michigan State University. The study focused on the participants' attitudes toward their personal ability to introduce change. Independent variables in five areas were considered: attitude toward change; perceptions of supervisory behavior; influence of physical factors; training program relevancy; and background or demographic factors. Frank found that participants who professed high expectations of success in introducing change tended to be those who felt that their training programs were relevant, who did not perceive physical factors as obstacles, and who held favorable views concerning the record of past change.

Studies of Students in General

The other studies which we have identified as relating attitudinal and adjustment problems to academic achievement and program relevance do not limit their attention to sponsored students; in fact, it is often difficult to disaggregate the sponsored from the non-sponsored or self-sponsored students in these studies. The first five refer specifically to the use of some form of foreign student problem inventory.

A 1970 study by Erickson (132) relied on the Mooney Problem Checklist, developed for use by U. S. students, in conjunction with a standardized attitudinal questionnaire on values and a specially constructed overseas student questionnaire. Probing for differences among male graduate students of Chinese, Indian-Pakistani, and Middle Eastern origin (and a fourth group identified only as "other"), he found that there was no significant difference on the Test of English as a Foreign Language scores, but that there were moderately significant differences in some of the other test results in problem and value areas. The Chinese students were academically superior to the other groups, and the Middle-Eastern students proved to be academically the weakest. In many problem areas there were no significant differences among the four groups, but the "other" group scored higher on social-psychological problems. Erickson concludes, however, that the similarities among the four groups outweigh the differences.

Sharma (343/ 1971) elected to construct a new foreign student problem inventory. In this study, foreign students attending universities in North Carolina considered the following academic problems as most difficult: giving oral reports, participating in class discussions, taking notes in class, understanding lectures and preparing written reports. The most serious personal problems involved homesickness, housing, sufficient funds, and appropriate companionship with the opposite sex. Students from South Asia seemed to make better academic adjustments than students from the Far East or Latin America. Length of residence in the United States and age upon entering the United States seemed to have little effect on the problems of the students.

Hill (176/ 1966) administered a problem checklist and a personal-data questionnaire at Indiana University to 78 students from Indonesia, Thailand, Pakistan, and India. He found that students of all four nationalities experienced substantial difficulties with academic, personal, and financial problems. Thai students experienced more academic problems than the other groups, specifically in areas requiring English proficiency. Thai and Indian students had much more difficulty getting acquainted with American students than did other nationality groups.

U Kyaw Win (424/ 1971) used a checklist to identify the problems of Indian and Japanese students at the University of Southern California, finding that Japanese students encountered many more difficulties than did Indian students in registration, understanding lectures and textbooks, reciting in class, and preparing oral and appropriate courses. He attributes the above to the Indian students' better peer group rapport, better historial understanding of administrative policies and procedures, and better English. The Indian students were more aggressive in seeking the help of the foreign student adviser than were the Japanese students.

Jarrahi-Sadeh and Eichman (195/ 1970) found that although Middle Eastern and Indian students at the University of North Carolina identified academic problems as a major source of discontent in the United States, many more of the foreign students had social adaptation problems on the college campus than did American students completing the same questionnaire. The foreign students were confused by the schizoid nature of America's attitude to them: on the one hand, the government and foundations encouraged them to study here; on the other, many U. S. university officials, faculty, and students showed little interest in them.

The remaining studies in this group used questionnaires, occasionally supplemented by personal interviews, to assess adjustment and academic achievement.

Lozada (230/ 1970) administered a questionnaire to foreign students at Purdue University in 1969, and found that foreign students were achieving grades equivalent to those of the average American student and were generally satisfied with study in the United States. A majority were academically well-equipped for their study, and language problems encountered upon arrival were largely overcome after the first year. Many students, however, did express dissatisfaction with informal aspects of college life. About one-fourth felt

dissociated from the mainstream of American life, and general dissatisfaction was expressed with the strength and nature of friendships
formed with Americans. The author recommends better orientation
and greater emphasis on work-study programs.

Shepard (347/1970) reports on a sample of 247 foreign students
in 38 universities and colleges in the southern United States. Many of
these colleges had no orientation programs, no English-as-a-Foreign
Language classes, and no scholarships or loans, international clubs,
or community services. A majority of the foreign students were self-
supporting, and most were pleased with their academic and social experience. Some 40 percent, however, said that they felt unwelcome,
lonely, and isolated. They complained of inadequate pre-departure
information, inadequate orientation on campus, and most felt that
their presence made little or no difference to the inter-cultural attitude of the campus as a whole, despite successful individual relationships with other students and faculty. Since the study was limited to
southern campuses, one cannot compare the results of this study with
what might have been found in northern campuses. This, of course,
applies also vice-versa. It seems, however, that fewer sponsored
students tended to attend southern campuses.

Among the 314 Indian graduate students in agriculture at 17 selected land-grant institutions who were studied by Basu (36/1966),
homesickness and living arrangements caused problems for many and
about 25 percent had financial problems. Fewer than 25 percent of the
students felt that they had experienced any discrimination and, although
some criticized Americans for lack of personal warmth, unfamiliarity
with other nations, and the superiority complex exhibited by some individuals, most held favorable views of Americans. About 90 percent
were satisfied with their studies, those pursuing doctoral degrees ex-
hibiting greater satisfaction than those enrolled for the Master's degree. Those who were successful in meeting course and degree requirements were more satisfied with the offerings than those who were
unsuccessful. Over 80 percent thought that their academic work was
relevant to their work at home, although many were apprehensive about
returning and expected difficulties in personal and professional life
upon return. Basu suggests the need for more basic sciences in the
college-level curriculum at Indian agricultural institutions and that
U. S. land-grant institutions should consider offering special courses
geared to the needs of students from developing countries.

A more general study by Keshav Dev Sharma (214/1969) of 1,416
Indian students enrolled during 1965-66 at 322 major institutions in the
United States attempts to identify the socio-economic and cultural backgrounds of such students and their academic and non-academic experiences and interactions. The students were most satisfied with general
academic standards in the United States and least satisfied with the

advisory system. Less than one-third attended any orientation program and half of these felt it helpful only in a very limited sense. The study concludes that the students experienced attitudinal changes on three levels: social-institutional; economic-technological; and political-ideological. Orientation and foreign student service programs are areas needing improvement.

Hagey (158/1968) found that Middle Eastern students attending colleges and universities in Oregon experienced academic and social adjustment problems which were related to such background factors as English ability, number of years spent in the United States, size of school attended, age, marital status, and financial support. Differences in academic and social adjustment were related to nationality and to different college environments, for instance, large vs. small.

Ruscoe (270/1968) studied about 1,000 Latin American students in U. S. colleges and universities by means of questionnaires seeking information about their backgrounds, current attitudes, and future aspirations. Most were found to be fairly well-satisfied with studies and life in the United States, reasonably well-informed about university academic life, relatively unencumbered by difficulties in pursuing academic studies, and moderately confident about their future educational and occupational success. Orientation in the United States was criticized and the study recommends that greater stress be placed on in-country orientation programs and on preparing Latin American students for the informal aspects of university and college life in the United States.

Longest (229/1969) evaluates an orientation program for foreign students conducted by Cornell University's College of Agriculture. He found that those who participated in the orientation program exhibited: (1) lower trans-cultural anxiety scores; (2) significantly higher knowledge of the United States and its universities' requirements; (3) significantly higher English-language test scores; and (4) higher grades. This study would appear to be in conflict with several other studies which seem to show that many orientation programs did not appreciably assist the students.

Summary

The studies reviewed in this section, which examined aspects of the foreign student's academic career and problems of adjustment, add another dimension to the studies reviewed earlier which looked at only academic adjustment or social adjustment. They suggest that there is a complex relationship between personal and social adjustment and academic-achievement problems, although none firmly establish cause-and-effect relationships between the two.

The evidence does suggest the rather self-evident conclusions that students who succeed academically are most satisfied with their academic experience and that students who have difficulties with oral and written English tend to have both academic and social adjustment problems. The evidence also supports the notion that, although certain difficulties are common to all foreign students, students from substantially different cultural backgrounds tend to have special types and intensities of academic problems.

Some studies which examined both social and academic problems argue that foreign students should be encouraged to mingle more with Americans, to become an integral part of the surrounding social and cultural milieu. (This point is also raised in Chapter 3, in discussing the role of the foreign student adviser. See p. 124.) Other studies however, show that the foreign student benefits both socially and academically from the existence on campus of foreign student communities which can provide a kind of surrogate home culture and assist members who may have social and academic problems. These findings suggest that one should not push U. S.-foreign student interrelationships beyond the point where they are naturally acceptable to the foreign student. Universities might do well in recognizing the value of the various nationality groups on campus and assist them in identifying and further developing the various roles and functions which they can serve.

At the same time, many studies indicate that foreign students receive little or inadequate pre-departure and/or on-arrival orientation, that on many campuses there exist inadequate foreign student services, and that inadequate attention is paid by academic advisers to these students' special needs.

In the more complex studies of both social and academic problems, there is little evidence of a clear-cut U-curve, due in part to the time limits of most studies. Those which disaggregate students by age, sex, educational background, nationality, competence in English, level of study, traditional and modern life styles, etc., find that social and academic adjustment processes do not present a clear-cut single pattern and that few generalizations can be made that would hold for all foreign students.

Almost totally unexplored during the 1967-74 period is the possible role of the major field of study while in the United States and its relation to attitude formation. The great preponderance of students—especially but not only on the graduate level—enrolled in engineering, the physical life sciences, business administration, education, and medicine would lead one to expect research concerning foreign students by fields. Although one study (324/1971) speculates on the possibility that scientists develop an ideology which disassociates itself from social problems, few others examine the possible impact of study in the natural and physical sciences on social, economic, or political attitudes of the foreign students. Some studies find that foreign students in science and engineering fields feel more confident about their ability to do something useful with their training when they return, while those who major in the social sciences are more change-oriented but less certain that they can implement their ideas. Most of these studies are inconclusive with respect to what the policy implications might be for institutions that offer higher education to substantial numbers of foreign students.

On the whole, the studies are only modestly sophisticated and tend to be dominated by the question of whether or not foreign students like their academic programs, the universities in which they are studying, and the American community—local or national-cultural. A few studies concern themselves with the relevance of U. S. training to the social, economic, and cultural conditions in the foreign students' home countries and these generally point out that few attempts are made to adjust academic programs to the home needs of students.

In general, the research surveyed offers an increasingly clear picture of attitudes, opinions, and academic achievement problems of foreign students in the United States, but also implies that few governmental, non-governmental, or higher-education institutions are making any major effort to take this information into account in devising programs for foreign students. This issue will be discussed more fully in Chapter 3.

Multidimensional Studies

Adding an important dimension to the studies reviewed above are those which interview not only the foreign student about attitudes, adjustment, and academic progress, but which also seek information from faculty, other students, members of the host community, home-country employers, government administrators, and so on. Although many of these studies confirm what was found by the uni-dimensional studies, in some cases significant additional information is produced. See Chart 2.4, p. 92.

This group includes 25 bibliographic items, representing 24 separate studies, which in varying ways examine attitudes and opinions of one or more groups other than the foreign students themselves, and which in some manner relate these attitudes or opinions to those obtained from foreign students. Nine of these studies are dissertations. The geographic areas of concern in these studies are as follows:

TABLE 2.6

Opinion Studies: Nationalities

Multinational	14	Canada	1
Asia	2	Ghana	1
Sub-Saharan Africa	1	Kenya and India	1
		Nigeria	1
		Korea	1
		Philippines	1
		Taiwan	1

Twenty-one deal with foreign students in general, two examine foreign students in medical studies, and one is concerned with foreign students studying agriculture and home economics. Ten studies use a relatively sophisticated data-analysis approach while 14 generally limit the reporting of data to tabular listings, percentages, and averages. We will examine first those studies which deal primarily with attitudes, then those dealing with academic achievement, and finally those which deal with both attitude and academic achievement.

Attitude Studies

Allen and Arafat (17/ 1971) studied American and foreign students to test two hypotheses: (1) that differing motivation can be explained by differing cultural backgrounds, and (2) that common educational experiences tend to eliminate differences in attitudes. Questioning the two groups of students as to their attitudes toward the procreative family, the authors found that attitudes were similar by social class and religion but did differ significantly by nationality. Similar education, in this case attendance at Oklahoma State University, had very limited consensual effect on the attitudes of foreign students, and the second hypothesis was not supported.

Bae (32/ n.d.) studied Korean students at the University of Wisconsin and a matched comparison group in Seoul. Results showed that Korean traditionalism is essentially stable; students in the United States returned to Korea as traditional as when they left. Traditionalsim, although a crucial barrier to satisfactory adjustment of Korean students to American society, did not decisively influence a student's decision to remain in the United States or return to Korea.

Chu et al. (68/ 1971) studied 67 Chinese students and faculty members at the University of Hawaii and correlated the results with the findings of a similar study by Yeh, et al., which had compared students in Taiwan who were ready to leave for study in the United States with a group of students who were remaining in Taiwan to complete their graduate study. As revealed by an adjective checklist, there was considerable consistency in the definition of American and Chinese character traits identified by Chinese students in Taiwan and Chinese students who have studied in the United States. There was a striking similarity between what the students expected before going to the United States and what they had experienced in the United States. Also, a relationship was found to exist between the personality patterns identified in the study and the adjustment of the Chinese students in the United States. On the attitude scales, the most mentally healthy group—as defined by apparent adjustment to U. S. life and responses to a "Mental Health Questionnaire"—was the one with a low "Chinese attitude" and high "American attitude," while those who had a high "Chinese attitude " and a high "American attitude" turned out to be less "mentally healthy."

Miller, et al. (247/1971) report on another aspect of the five-year study by Yeh, et al., mentioned above. The authors compared East Asian students at the University of Wisconsin with American students in East Asia and found that: (1) both groups tended to limit their warm and intimate contacts almost exclusively to co-nationals; (2) their relations with host-country nationals rarely went beyond superficial pleasantries; and (3) they were rather discouraged about prospects for deep inter-cultural friendships. Interviews with ten Ethiopian students gave further support to these observations. The authors speculate that the inability of foreign students to develop close friendships characterizes almost all inter-cultural university situations, but since important background variables (age and educational level) were not included, the hypothesis, for instance, that meaningful friendships between older graduate students in different cultures may develop more often than on the undergraduate level could not be tested.

Colacicco (77/ 1970) administered a personal information form and the Minnesota Multi-Phasic Personality Inventory to 53 male Indian, 58 male Latin American and an equal number of male American students. The data showed both foreign groups to be more prone to illness and depression than the American group, and more apt to behave in "unusual" or socially inappropriate ways. The differences between the Americans and either of the two foreign groups were larger than those between the foreign groups themselves.

Johnson (197/ 1971) administered a long questionnaire to both American and foreign students at the University of Tennessee and

discovered that the Americans expected the foreign students to have
many more problems than the foreign students themselves reported.
Certain areas, such as English proficiency or finances, were of less
concern to the foreign students than was expected. Surprisingly, Americans reported more problems with food than did the foreigners. These
findings, Johnson believes, corroborate Walton's contention that foreign students need to be studied more as students than as foreigners.
They display greater similarities to their American counterparts than
differences.

Two recent studies examine the attitudes toward one another of
black African students and U. S. students. Odenyo (291/1970) describes the ambiguity which has characterized the relationship of black
Americans to black Africans since the first black African student
came to the United States in the 1890s. He explains the ambiguity in
a number of hypotheses which were supported by questionnaire data
from students in Minnesota: (1) the ambivalence of the Africans rests
in part on the fear of being identified with an underprivileged American
minority; (2) and in part on what they perceive to be an exaggeration
or distortion of African culture by the Afro-American; (3) the ambivalence of Afro-Americans toward the African students rests in part on
their perception of them as free, high-status black foreigners who do
not wear the stigma of former slavery; and (4) the ambivalence of the
African and Afro-American students is partly the result of the fact that
the two view each other as foreign despite the commonality of the ancestral homeland. Other hypotheses which appear to be partially or
wholly supported by the generated data relate to the technological differences between African and American cultures and the apparent
perception of many black Americans that black Africans do not fully
support the worldwide black struggle for liberation.

In the second study, the National Association of College Deans,
Registrars, and Admissions Officers and the National Association for
Foreign Student Affairs (286/1973) examined U. S. and foreign student
relations at 42 predominantly black colleges in the United States, using
a questionnaire completed by 301 foreign students and 188 American
students. The study found that the foreign students often came from
more sophisticated backgrounds than their U. S. counterparts; that a
slight majority of the foreigners would have preferred to attend white
schools believing them to have better academic standards and facilities,
whereas the vast majority of U. S. students preferred a predominantly
black institution; the majority of foreign students believed that they
should not become involved in American socio-political activities
whereas U. S. students believed that such involvement would contribute
to the foreign students' understanding of the American system; both
U. S. and foreign students felt that hostility and lack of in-depth communication existing between the two groups were caused by prejudice,

misconceptions, lack of understanding, and attitude superiorities on both sides. The study recommends a variety of activities to encourage U. S. and foreign students to interact more fully.

Three studies considered the problems of communication and counseling. Snipes (357/ 1969) compared communication behavior of foreign and American students but found no correlation between communication behavior and personality characteristics nor was there an apparent relationship between communication behavior and personal adjustment. From an experimental study examining culture-conditioned communication variables that might affect the process of counseling, Coelho-Oudegeest (75/ 1971) suggests that, since the results were somewhat inconclusive, further research is needed on personality and background variables which may affect the counseling relationship. Finally, Arkoff, et al. (28/ 1966), explored the mental health and counseling ideas of Asian and American students and concluded that Asian students are less ready to avail themselves of counseling facilities than are American students. If they were involved in such processes, they would be more likely to expect the counselor to be a strong and authoritarian figure who could provide them with advice for a specific course of action.

Two techniques which encourage interaction between Americans and foreign students are the Inter-Cultural Small Group Experience (ISGE) and the Ogontz Plan. The ISGE, used extensively on college campuses since 1966, was evaluated by a NAFSA Task Force (281/ 1973) which concluded that the sessions, when designed and conducted responsibly, promote inter-cultural communication, the realization of assistance goals, and a more effective functioning of persons working with foreign students. The ISGE can also be useful in providing a forum for group discussion of adjustment problems and in training host families and expanding contact between host culture and foreign guests. (See also, p. 72.)

Under the Ogontz Plan, which originated in Philadelphia, selected foreign students in U. S. universities visit local elementary and secondary schools to talk about their home cultures and become acquainted with American educational milieus and techniques. Through a variety of interviews and questionnaire techniques, Brickman (53/ 1967) found that both foreign and U. S. students enjoyed and profited by the experience and believed that it was making a contribution to international understanding. He reports considerable interest in expanding the activity of the Ogontz Plan.

Perception of Academic Achievement

Methodologically, relatively few studies use comparisons of different groups to assess academic achievement or relevance of training to home-country needs. An exception is a study by Swan (372/1969), who compares perceptions of Filipino agricultural and home economics students, their major professors, and home-country officials regarding American graduate education. He found that students' satisfaction and performance levels were higher when their major professor and home-country authorities agreed with their own perceptions of objectives, policy, and procedures. Professors, however, were less concerned than home-country authorities with the need to develop special courses and non-credit experiences for the Filipino students. The study suggests the need for a greater degree of direct communication between academic advisers, teaching faculty, and home-country authorities.

Clark (69/1963) studied Ghanaian students in the United States, comparing their satisfaction with their academic achievement to the U. S. university's judgment of their success or failure. She found that students who held government grants were performing significantly better than those who did not; that those in the last two phases of cultural adjustment were more successful than those in the first two phases; and that those who attended accredited universities did more satisfactory work than those who did not. Significantly more students expressed satisfaction if they were 30 years of age or older, were married, held U. S. Government grants, or were self-supporting, as opposed to students who held Ghana Government grants.

Ohuche (292/1967) questioned undergraduate Nigerian students and their faculty advisers and found that previous educational experience as measured by the grade in the school-certificate examination did not satisfactorily predict academic achievement as measured by the students' cumulative grade point average in the United States. Undergraduates who had completed the equivalent of the Higher School Certificate Examination performed better academically than those who had not, and there was no difference in academic achievement between scholarship and non-scholarship Nigerians at the undergraduate level. Nor was there any significant difference in academic achievement between Nigerian graduate students who received Bachelor's degrees in the United States and those who received such degrees elsewhere. This comparative study challenges the findings cited above by questioning the reliability of using academic credentials of foreign students as bases for predicting academic success in U. S. institutions. (cf. pp. 40, 42.)

Comparative Studies of Both Attitudinal and Academic Issues

A number of studies were identified which examine both attitudinal and academic achievement issues relating to foreign students and which utilize a multi-dimensional methodology. Perhaps the most extensive is that of Deutsch (109/ 1965; 111/ 1970) who conducted a two-year community study of foreign students and the international milieu at five colleges and universities in the Cleveland area. Historical analysis, informant techniques, personal interviews, and observations were used, including questionnaire studies of 286 foreign students, 376 American students, 213 American faculty members, and 143 host families.

The foreign students, mostly male graduate students from the less-developed nations, were generally satisfied with the opportunities for meeting Americans and with their academic experience although many felt that much of the theoretical knowledge with which they were presented was inapplicable to the practical problems they would face in their home countries. Language was identified as a problem, though not a serious one. American students and faculty members appeared to be interested in and supportive of international education, but the latter were not very knowledgeable about the programs or services provided for foreign students. Community hosts to foreign students were found to be active, well-educated persons who viewed international education programs as service-oriented and were less cognizant of their own personal rewards than they were of the benefits to their foreign student guests.

Questioning of college and university administrators showed that the educational institutions generally lacked an articulated policy for international education. The distance between top academic administrators and persons directly concerned with foreign students was judged so great as to make the latter largely autonomous. The administrators were aware of developments in international education in other colleges and universities, but they seldom read advisory reports on aspects of international education which might have affected program development and implementation.

Deutsch concluded that there was considerable community concern for international education but apparently more interest in student than in faculty exchanges, and more interest in internationalizing the curriculum than in implementing technical assistance programs. Large-scale research is recommended by the author to assess the effect of external agents of change upon American institutions of higher education and to elucidate the role of the various organizations, agencies, and foundations in influencing the international commitment of colleges and universities.

The Deutsch study appears to be unique in its comprehensive approach to the study of foreign student programs in one community. The other studies which we have identified are much more limited in objective and scope. Few others examine in any depth the impact of foreign students on U. S. individuals or institutions.

A dissertation by Bohn (48/ 1957) administered a variety of aptitude, attitude, and achievement tests to foreign students and questionnaires to faculty advisers of students who were sponsored under the Technical Training Section of the U. S. Office of Education. Although conducted in 1957, this study is worth noting in that its results do not differ markedly from those of later studies. The students consistently rated below college freshmen in all types of language ability. Because of the effects of this language deficiency, the California Test of Mental Maturity provided little or no information relating to the native ability or intelligence of the students. The grades received by foreign students were equal to or better than the grades of American students, but a number of faculty indicated that they graded foreign students on a special scale and did not expect the foreign students to compete with American students. The major problems encountered by these students were inability to use the English language, inability to adjust to American food, inadequate housing during the summer months, and inability to adjust to different climatic conditions. One-third indicated that the educational program had failed to fulfill either their own personal objectives or the original objectives established for study in the United States. The major causes of this failure were misunderstandings between the sending country, the Office of Education, and the student; misinterpretation of curriculum offerings; and lack of adequate facilities for learning highly specialized activities.

Daniel Yankelovich, Inc. (401/ 1971) conducted a short exploratory study of the impact of campus unrest on foreign students. Both non-European foreign students and U. S. faculty members were interviewed on ten university campuses. It was found that foreign students were largely unaffected by student demonstrations, counter-culture life styles, or the rhetoric of the student left, and that about 40 percent preferred to associate with other foreign students. They were satisfied with the education they were receiving although they realized that overtraining and Americanization might make readjustment to their home countries difficult. Many foreign students disapproved of American foreign policy, especially toward underdeveloped countries, and were dissatisfied with U. S. domestic regulations which hindered their finding employment needed to supplement their meager funds.

Clarke and Ozawa (70/ 1970) report the opinions of foreign students and faculty members at the University of Wisconsin. Major adjustment problems cited by the foreign students were loneliness, homesickness, and lack of time for study. Academic problems included curricula inadequate for the needs of foreign students, the qualifications and quality of staff, inadequate funds to finance expanded programs in international education, and the lack of coordination mechanisms to insure communication between educational institutions, the government, foundations, and foreign countries.

A unique section of this study is the portion devoted to the story of Martha Ozawa's personal experience as a graduate student at the

University of Wisconsin. Her observations on her relationships with
students, her academic interests, and her comparisons of the United
States and Japan provide an instructive in-depth view of the thoughts
of foreign students. Ms. Ozawa's autobiographical case study is an
example of a useful form of commentary on the foreign student experience which perhaps should appear more often in print to supplement
other kinds of more quantified data.

Halberstam and Dasco (160/ 1965) examine the training experience of foreign medical residents in the United States as it compares
with the training of U. S. medical residents. Results show that foreign medical residents have an average of 17 years of schooling by the
time they receive their medical degree while U. S. physicians have an
average of 20 years. Supervisors felt that about four times as many
U. S. students as foreign students could work with no supervision.
Ninety percent of the U. S. residents considered U. S. physicians
better, or much better than foreign physicians insofar as their basic
scientific knowledge is concerned. A vast majority of both foreign and
U. S. residents expressed basic satisfaction with their academic experiences, although supervisors believed that there were a larger
number of dissatisfied residents among the foreign students. Supervisors also felt that a greater proportion of poorly performing residents occurred in the foreign as compared with the U. S. group, and
that there was urgent need for the establishment of criteria for the
selection of foreign physicians applying for U. S. hospital staff positions. The need to develop special programs to assist foreign students
was recognized, as was the need for follow-up training upon return to
their home countries.

Halberstam and others (161/ 1970) also studied foreign surgical
residents in university-affiliated hospitals to compare their own perceptions and evaluations of their training programs with their supervisors' evaluations of their performance. This study showed that
perceptions of foreign surgical residents were remarkably similar to
those of their U. S. counterparts, both in evaluation of the training
programs and the evaluation of their performance. A number of personal and social variables also were remarkably similar between the
two groups. Foreign surgical residents were considered to be competent physicians who found it easier to adjust to life and medical practice in this country than did foreign residents in other medical specialties. Even though about 40 percent of the foreign residents expressed
their intention to become U. S. citizens, both supervisors and residents expressed opposition to any limit on the time of training as a
means of solving the brain drain problem.

Kwochka (222/ 1970) studied the effects on American students
of residence in the International House of New York. She found that
the longer they resided in the House, the closer the friendships they

established with non-Westerners and non-Americans. A large minority, however, reported that residence had no effect on their educational progress. The author recommends programs that would establish a better balance between American and foreign students in the International House.

Grady (152/ 1969) studied American and Canadian students to find variables which related to academic achievement of the two groups. He concluded that the American College Test and high school grade point average provided the best prediction of college achievement for the American freshman, but these variables were not useful in the prediction of college achievement for the Canadians. Personality variables related to college achievement differed somewhat for the two samples of students as well. Selected biographical data were not significantly related to the college achievement of either the American or Canadian freshmen.

Summary

Studies reviewed in this section add a significant dimension to our understanding of the total context in which foreign students find themselves. Attitudes of U. S. students, the U. S. community, and U. S. faculty advisers toward the foreign students, their achievement, and their impact on the U. S. help to place foreign student perceptions into context.

The most extensive study of this group, that of Deutsch, clearly indicates the depth of interrelationships that may form within a community around the foreign student involvement in academic and community activities, although few of these studies, including that by Deutsch, show any major impact on U. S. academic institutions and their constituents that could be attributed to the presence of foreign students on campus.

Most of the studies indicate a considerable distance between those who deal directly with foreign students and those who determine policy on the campuses of colleges and universities. They also suggest considerable slippage in communication between the agencies which program foreign students and institutional administrators.

Studies comparing American and foreign students reveal similarities between the two, as well as many differences. Although certain nationality groups tend to cluster together for mutual support, there are many individuals who do not fit this pattern. Thus, although certain patterns and tendencies can be noted, each foreign student should be viewed as an individual and as a student, and not automatically presumed to be a sample unit of an expected pattern.

Finally, interrelationships entered into by foreign students with others while in the United States are extremely complex and, although questionnaire and interview studies have identified some apparent patterns, most of these studies are somewhat simplistic and often depend on rather primitive measures of attitude and behavior.

Foreign Students after Return Home

All of the studies discussed so far have presented data gathered from foreign students while they are in the United States or, in some instances, prior to arrival. In this section we will review studies which focus on students after they have returned to their home country. Twenty-six items in the bibliography relate to such research, representing 21 separate studies. There are only four doctoral dissertations in this group, reflecting the fact that few graduate students have the resources to question or interview foreign students after they have returned home. See Chart 2.5, p. 96.

The geographic focus of these studies is as follows:

TABLE 2.7

Post-Sojourn Studies: Nationalities Studied

Multinational	4	Iran, India, UAR	2
Asia	3	Turkey	2
East Asia	1	China	1
South Asia	1	England, Ireland	1
North Africa	1	Ghana	1
Latin America	1	India	1
		Thailand	1
		Vietnam	1

Seventeen of the studies deal with students in a variety of disciplines are professions and four with students in specific professional areas: one each in broadcasting, education, engineering, and library science. The great majority of these studies are surveys using relatively unsophisticated data analysis. Most report data in tabular form and give, at most, averages and percentages of response. Two are more sophisticated, offering correlations, regression analysis, or the development of standardized instruments.

In addition to the studies discussed here, there are several post-return surveys conducted by multi-lateral organizations. These items, including UNESCO studies in the Cameroons and Iran and an FAO study of participants in its fisheries program, are reviewed in Chapter 6.

Most of the studies below question students concerning their social and political attitudes as well as their satisfaction with the education which they have received. Three studies, however, deal solely with attitudes and nine primarily with the students' perceptions of the value and relevance of the training they have received in the United States. Most of the latter have to do with the relative strengths and weaknesses of training sponsored by AID.

Attitude Studies

Two researchers focused on opinions about the United States. Davis (101/ 1970) found that Middle Easterners showed favorable attitudes depending on the length of time they had lived in the United States. A sojourn of two to three years produced the least favorable attitudes, four to five years the most favorable, while a sojourn of more than five years resulted again in less favorable attitudes. Two-thirds of the students thought that American study had enhanced their career opportunities and nearly three-fifths agreed that the cross-cultural experience may have been more valuable than the formal education they received. Davis' data indicate that the smaller the discrepancy between the foreign student's aspirations and his or her self-perceived progress in achieving them, the more satisfied he or she will feel and the more favorable will be the attitudes toward the host country. His data also supports the two-way mirror concept that favorableness to America will vary with the student's perception of American favorableness to the home country.

Mastroiani (237/ 1971) studied short-term exchange participants in a United States Educational Exchange Project in radio and television. He compared the attitudes of this group with a group of broadcasters who had not visited the United States. No significant differences between the grantees and the comparison group in their average attitude-scale ratings were noted, although there were significant differences on certain items. For example, there was a significantly higher favorable response by the grantee group toward questions relating to the United States Government and politics. The non-grantee group was significantly more neutral. The major conclusion was that, as a result of their sojourn, the grantees were able to offer more discriminating and more definite responses to attitude statements regarding the United States.

In the third study in this group, Galtung (144/ 1965), using data from a UNESCO study (see No. 125), reports that students from the UAR, Iran, and India who had returned home after two or more years of study in Germany, the United Kingdom and the United States had achieved varying degrees of adjustment to the culture of their host countries. Factors which related to adjustment and the degrees of acceptance of the host culture included the degree to which the foreign student had received training in cultural pluralism, the cultural distance between the home country and the host country, the image (as perceived by the student) held by the host country of the home country (the two-way mirror concept), and the home country's perceived rank in the international system.

Academic Satisfaction and Relevance

Nine studies inquired primarily into the satisfaction expressed by returned students with their academic program and/or the perceived relevance of the program to their work at home. Seven of the nine studies sought data on returned AID grantees; six of them summarize evaluation of participants who had returned home prior to 1961; and one of participants who returned prior to 1967. These surveys were undertaken in some 40 countries and the AID Reports summarize the results, usually by region, though several country reports were issued separately.

The India study (14a/1966) found that less than half of the participants made considerable use of their training, either directly or indirectly, although many had better jobs than before their training. Participants agreed that the lack of material resources in India, the attitudes of colleagues and superiors, and a slow rate of progress and organization in India had precluded use of the training. Participants and their superiors voiced considerable satisfaction with the training program, however, and recommended that training should be longer, participants should have more advance information and opportunity to consult in program planning, and program content should be more practical, specialized, and relevant to the needs of India. About 75 percent of the participants were satisfied with their orientation program in the United States and enjoyed community hospitality and activities. Only one-half, however, were satisfied with their program upon departure from the United States, and only one-half had been in contact with AID technicians since their return.

The Ghana study (14f/1968) also recommended longer training periods although most of the participants and supervisors judged the program as satisfactory. Far greater numbers of Ghanaian participants (88 percent) reported using their training in their current work than did the Indian participants. Ninety-four percent stated that they had in some measure transmitted their knowledge or skill to others. The aspect of the training experience most frequently mentioned as most useful was on-the-job training.

In the studies summarizing results of evaluations by region, it is reported that the Far Eastern participants (14b/1966) were older and more educated than those from other regions, but were somewhat less satisfied with their training, particularly with the length of the programs and the excess of things they were required to do and see. Utilization of their training varied according to the professional specialization of the trainee.

Latin American and Caribbean-area participants (14c/ 1966) expressed greater satisfaction with their training programs than did those from other regions. Trainees who studied at universities were the highest utilizers of training and longer programs apparently enhanced utilization. Again, longer programs were judged as more important.

The participants from the Near East and South Asia (14e/ 1966) differed from those in other regions in having had less prior contact with American technicians in their home country before leaving for the United States, and they were more often selected for training by ministries than by their supervisors. Two-thirds were satisfied with their pre-departure information, but they were least satisfied with the content of their program before they departed. They experienced fewer language difficulties than did participants from other regions and about half of them were very satisfied with their program. They were most satisfied with the level of training and least satisfied with the program's length. Trainees in community development and in health and sanitation were the highest utilizers of their training, followed by those in transport and communications, agriculture and natural resources, and education.

Participants from North Africa (14d/ 1966) had fewer years of education and job experience than trainees from other regions. Almost half of the programs were conducted outside the United States, in Lebanon and in other countries; these third-country programs were rated as much less effective than those conducted in the United States. As with the other regions, the participants were least satisfied with the length of their programs and the variety of training activities. Participants trained in transportation and communications, and in industry and mining, utilized their training more than others, while those trained in health and education used their training least upon return. Those who participated in on-the-job training assignments tended to use more of what they had learned upon return.

Rather consistently, these reports cite recommendations from both participants and supervisors that longer training would increase participant satisfaction and positively affect utilization of training. It is also significant that participants who received on-the-job training were more satisfied with their programs than those who pursued academic studies exclusively. A third consistent finding is that in many countries there was little follow-up contact between AID and return participants. It should also be noted that there were differences by region in the degree of utilization of training in certain professional specialties.

A doctoral dissertation (151/ 1967) and a report by Gollin (149/ 1966) further summarize the results of the various AID studies described above. Gollin's conclusions are that non-technical aspects of the training program, while contributing to a pleasant stay in the United States, have little significance in determining the usefulness of the training when the students return home; that third-country sites are associated with lower approval of technical training but greater satisfaction with non-technical aspects; and, finally, that the least effective type of program, in terms of later utilization of training, was the observation tour or the special group program, when it was the sole form of training experience.

Except for the Ghana study, all of these studies involved participants in training prior to 1961. It would seem essential to undertake more up-to-date re-studies and studies of more recent participants to see if the trends noted in these studies have continued or varied in subsequent years.

One somewhat more recent study is a 1967 dissertation by Vorapipatana (416). Thais in the field of education who had returned home after a graduate-level academic program in the United States under AID auspices were surveyed, as were a number of their immediate superiors. The author found that the graduates were able to put into practice much of what they had learned in the United States, a high utilization rate based in part on the practice within the Ministry of Education whereby each department gives foreign trainees priority consideration for vacant positions. As in the earlier studies, participants criticized the program for not providing enough practical experience and for being too short.

In the first of two studies not related to AID participants, Carnovsky (61/ 1971) found that most library-school graduates who had returned to their home countries experienced satisfaction with their library-school education, but many had suggestions for improving the library-school curricula, in particular to make it more appropriate to foreign library situations.

Susskind and Schell (182/ 1968) made an extensive quesionnaire survey of engineering graduates from the University of California who had returned to their home countries. High use of the technical knowledge acquired was reported by over half of the master's graduates and by most of those who had completed doctorates, and high use of the acquired research skills by about one-third of the M.A.s and over two-thirds of the Ph.D.s. More than 90 percent of the Ph.D.s and 67 percent of the M.A.s from developing countries thought that their training had been "about right," compared to 83 percent of the M.A.s from developed countries who gave it this rating. About a third of the M.A.s from developing countries found the program too theoretical. The returned students made a variety of suggestions for improving the handling of foreign students in the United States and a number of them thought that graduate engineering education in the United States was more suitable for people working in a highly specialized position in a technologically advanced setting than for people who were returning to work in a developing country. High utilization of U. S. engineering education was positively affected by the presence of colleagues and supervisors who had also been trained in the United States, and many found that they had few such colleagues nearby.

Studies of Political and/or Social Attitudes and of Academic Adjustment upon Return Home

By far the largest number of studies of students who have returned home investigate both the socio-political attitudes of students and matters related to the relevance and usefulness of the training which the participants had received.

One of the earlier comprehensive studies is the so-called Gardner Report, issued in 1963 in two forms, one as a report to Congress (390a/1963) and the other as a publication for general distribution, A Beacon of Hope (390b/1963). This study was undertaken under the auspices of the U. S. Advisory Commission on Education and Cultural Affairs. Some 2,969 former grantees from 20 countries who had visited the United States between 1949 and 1960 completed questionnaires, and their opinions were compared to those of 1,116 nongrantee leaders in the same countries. A number of U. S. embassy officials, high-level Washington officials, private individuals involved in educational and cultural exchange, foreign student advisers on U. S. campuses, and others were also interviewed. Although the returned grantees were exclusively those who had studied in the United States under State Department-sponsored programs, the results of this early study bear remarkable similarity to those of many other studies of foreign students in general and of students sponsored by various other technical assistance and exchange groups.

On the basis of the massive data assembled, the report concludes that exchange has proven to be an essential part of America's total international effort. There has been an increased understanding of Americans as well as an increased understanding by Americans of different countries. Exchange helped dispel stereotyped misconceptions of Americans held by grantees and many grantees spoke appreciatively of the American character. The most common single criticism—less than 20 percent—was that Americans had no knowledge or interest in foreign countries. Race relations received the lowest ratings of all aspects of U. S. life. These findings parallel those of many later studies.

Grantees named increased knowledge in their field as the most valuable personal result of exchange. Seventy-five percent reported that the exchange experience had influenced their career and only eight percent reported that their experience had created professional difficulties upon return. A high percentage reported that they had continued to maintain professional contact with U. S. colleagues over the years.

In 1970, UNESCO sponsored a significant book, edited by Eide, which summarizes the views of a number of social scientists concerning the effect of student exchange (125). The first portion of the book represents one of the rare efforts to develop theory; it includes articles on exchange strategy, psychological aspects of student exchange, research critiques, and an article on exchange evaluation. The second section of the book analyzes data collected by UNESCO on students from the United Arab Republic, Iran, and India who had studied in Western countries in order to isolate factors that may be of importance in understanding whether, and how, different cultures are moving toward homogeneity. The factors included age, degree of homogeneity of home-country culture, nationality, differences in idiom, cultural distance, the importance of being accepted as culturally different, degree of prestige of the home country in the international system, the importance of being in larger groups of fellow nationals, and alternative adjustments in human relations. The study concluded that regardless of the host country, differences between the three groups of students (Egyptians, Iranians, and Indians) were maintained. Neither background variables nor social factors such as frequency of association with fellow nationals could explain away the characteristic differences between the three groups.

Two studies, one by the East-West Center (423/n.d.) and the other by Johnson (196/1970), report on what happened to Asian students after they had returned home from the University of Oregon. These respondents generally felt that their American education had been useful but that, although Americans were friendly, they had not made as many American friends as they might have.

Another study of Asian students, by the Joint United States Public Affairs Office in Saigon (201a/1967; 201b/1967), found that Vietnamese who had studied in the United States and returned home viewed their U. S. educational experience as useful and important in the advancement of their careers and of their social status. They thought that their attitudes had been affected by the U. S. sojourn in two basic ways: they now believed that people should be more active in a democracy and that the military were excessively influential in South Vietnam.

The problems of development in Turkey as seen by Turks who had returned home from study in American universities is the subject of a study by Davis (102/1973). He found that graduate students in the sample who had been in the United States longer were more prone to answer affirmatively the question of whether they would be able to contribute to development or influence social change in Turkey. Almost all who so responded said that their study in the United States had increased their ability to contribute to their nation's development. All those who had studied business had this confidence while many of those who had studied in the social sciences felt that they were less able to personally influence change. Queried as to the nation most highly regarded as a development model, the respondents cited West Germany first and the United States second. Other countries mentioned were Japan, Israel, France, Sweden, and Yugoslavia. The main reasons for selecting the United States were its efficient organization of effort, advanced science and technology, democracy, and high level of economic development.

A rather different type of study is that by Dow (119/n.d.) who used data from U. S. and Hong Kong publications, unpublished dissertations, U. S. government documents, and personal recollections to assess the impact on China of Chinese students who were educated in the United States and then returned home, focusing on 1911-49. He concludes that, although American-trained students did not transform China into an image of America, American-trained students did achieve significant objectives: Western science and technology were transferred to China; the American educational system supplanted the ancient Chinese examination system; and American-trained scientists and engineers continue to form the nucleus of China's technological life.

Two researchers focused on persons who did not participate in formal academic programs. Norton (403/1972) studied the effects of short-term study tours in the United States as perceived by participants in the Asian and Pacific Student Leader Project. Davis (103/1973) evaluated summer work experience in the United States through interviews with participants during and after their stay. The first few weeks of a work experience were deemed to be crucial. By midsummer those who showed personal growth and evidence of positive change tended to become substantially involved in at least one aspect of American life. They developed more positive attitudes toward America, while uninvolved students were likely to reinforce or create their own critical attitudes. Both positive and negative attitudes persisted at least six months after return home.

Finally, there are two studies which offer reviews of the literature on what happens to students after return home. One is the report on engineering students by Susskind and Schell (182/1968) described above, p. 66-67, which includes a survey of related research from 1957 to 1965. The other, a doctoral dissertation by Orr (296/1971), confirms most of the trends noted above and cites a further finding, that many exchangees experience readjustment problems upon return home. The studies which he reviewed showed, however, that 80 percent of the returnees were able to secure employment easily, and that those who were not—about 20 percent—usually resided in rigidly structured and/or developing countries, or lacked influential friends or relatives. At least three-fourths of the returnees were able to use their American training at least partially and about the same number claimed to have conveyed their knowledge and skills to others through their jobs. Orr suggests the need to improve the planning process and the extent of communication between the various players in the international-exchange game.

Summary

The post-return studies of utilization generally show a majority of students reporting considerable use of training received, but indicate wide regional differences which further research might show to be based on such factors as age, amount of education and job experience, etc. Almost universal are the preferences for longer training and for practical experience as part of the program. Other studies also show that technical knowledge is more valuable upon return than are more abstract research skills.

The attitude studies point to possible relationships between favorable views of the United States and length of sojourn, perception of academic success, etc., factors relating to the U. S. experience. Attitude toward the United States also seems to relate to what one author calls the "cultural distance" between the host country and the home country; the image held by the host country of the student's home country (as perceived by the student); and the student's perception of the rank of the home country in the international system. Clearly, both subjective and objective elements are at work and merit further study.

Non-Empirical Reports and Articles on Foreign Student
Attitudes and Achievements While in the United States

During the years under review, a number of governmental or private agencies commissioned study groups, held working conferences, and in many ways encouraged explorations of what happens to foreign students while in the United States. The non-empirical reports which are briefly summarized in this section represent much cumulative wisdom and experience, and make many valuable suggestions for improving the quality of the foreign student's sojourn in the United States. Chart 2.6 lists these articles and reports, gives a tabular analysis of some features of these reports and articles, and notes one or two key ideas in each item. (See p. 100.)

The Need to Adjust University Curricula to the Needs of Foreign Students

The largest number of these non-empirical studies deal with what the authors perceive as a need to adjust U. S. curricula to the needs of the student and of his home country. This issue is discussed in general by Canter (59/ 1967), the Committee on International Educational Policy (187/ 1966), Harari (162/ 1970; 163/ 1972), Jacqz (3/ 1967), Kaplan (267/ n. d.), NAFSA (404/ 1973), and Rogers (278/ 1971). Most of these deal with academic-relevance problems of foreign students in general, although the Rogers study deals primarily with the needs of students from Latin America.

A number of items go into some detail in a specific academic area. Kelly (211/ 1966) points out that much of the horticultural training in the United States is irrelevant to the agricultural situation in foreign students' home countries. Lewis (227/ 1967) discusses the special needs of foreign students from a variety of countries in the area of agricultural economics. Moravcsik (257/ 1973) suggests that much of the U. S. academic program in the natural sciences needs to be adapted to the needs of foreign students and their home countries. Ronkin (332/ 1969) suggests that pre-doctoral science students have had great difficulty in applying their knowledge once they return home and Stone (368/ 1969) indicates that supplemental training is needed for science students from foreign countries to help them identify researchable problems, maintain their skills, and develop basic administrative techniques that they will need to use after they return home. A NAFSA study committee (277/ 1971) found that there was a need to adjust U. S. business administration curricula to the needs of foreign students. Finally, Shearer (345/ 1970) proposed a technical and structural index to gauge how patterns and trends of training in the United States relate to the development needs of other countries. Schuler (337/ 1969) suggests that one answer might be to set up graduate training centers in other countries, thereby helping U. S. faculty members to understand the needs of those countries and at the same time assuring that foreign students not be excessively isolated from their own culture during training.

Two authors, Holland (178/ 1956) and Putnam (268/ 1965), point out that the goals of the various players in the international exchange process often are not the same and indeed often are in conflict. Until there is better communication and understanding of goals among students, their home-country authorities and employers, the U. S. government, and the U. S. institutions training them, these problems will continue to exist.

Cultural Adaptation, Adjustment, Communication, and Change

A number of authors examine methods for encouraging intercultural communication, or for the study of the process: Althen (274/ 1970) discusses two methods, sensitivity training and the intercultural communications workshop, concluding that the latter is more useful in promoting understanding between foreign and American students; Heath (165/ 1969) describes the one-week summer sessions offered by the Lodestar International Student Center in California. (See p. 56 for an empirical study of this subject.)

The articles by Bochner (47/ 1972), Mishler (250/ 1965), and Smith (356/ 1956) explore various aspects of cultural difference which affect mutual understanding. Niyekewa-Howard (290/ 1970) discusses the implications of "biculturality," the ability to identify with and appreciate the good aspects of two cultures. Observing that bicultural individuals have the potential to function with cognitive flexibility and to be creative in their thinking, she suggests that further research might focus on how such persons could make the best use of their biculturality. Finally, Stewart (367/ 1973) explores the differing effects of empathy and sympathy on cross-cultural communication.

The foreign student's images and perceptions of self, host country and home country, and the host's images of the traveler and the foreign country are explored in a variety of studies. Pool (314/ 1965) attempts to establish a theoretical framework for the examination of such images; Riesman (325/ 1968) discusses Brazilian students' perceptions of the United States; and Singer (350/ 1972) points out that foreign travelers establish cultural-identity ties with the host nation and thus, potentially, between elites in their home countries and the host country. Prince (317/ 1973) notes that in the fields of mental health and psychiatry, differences in world views and images pose problems of such magnitude that training in these fields is best done at home.

The mental health of foreign students is discussed by Coelho (393/ 1973) in an article describing a research program presently underway but not yet published as of mid-1974. He suggests the need for long-term longitudinal studies and is particularly interested in "coping behavior," that is, the behavior utilized by foreigners to establish emotional security within a culture distinct from their own. He further suggests the need to distinguish between students who do or do not follow the "U-curve" experience pattern, and to examine self-selection among foreign students. Cormack (89/ 1969) suggests the need to research growth, identity, and alienation factors as they affect the adjustment of foreign students.

Finally, there is a group of studies which review the effect on foreign students of the educational exchange experience. King (216/

1970) presents a history of African students at Tuskegee Institute in the 1920s; Melby (239/1966) and Pfnister (311/1972) both review academic and social problems of foreign students in the United States. Sanders and Ward (335/1970) discuss the effect of short-term training programs on foreign students and Spencer (363/1967) reviews factors which he feels have a bearing on the effectiveness of foreign student exchange programs.

Conclusion

During the course of this review of what happens to foreign students while in the United States, certain themes keep recurring, despite the great variety in focus and methodology. Although it is difficult to compare specific studies, it is possible to summarize them in terms of problem areas investigated.

In the studies which examined the effect of study in the United States on foreign students' basic values, it is generally agreed that, while external characteristics may change, the more deep-seated cultural and religious attitudes and educational goals are fairly resistant to change. Most students arrive with favorable attitudes toward the United States, although it is interesting to note that students from countries most like ours, namely European countries, are most apt to be critical on arrival. Black Africans form a unique subgroup; they arrive with apprehensions about racial discrimination and strive to maintain distinctions between themselves and black Americans. With this group, as with the others, there is little consensus on the direction of attitude change as a result of the sojourn. Several studies note, however, that foreign students' attitudes about the United States seem to be more influenced by the mass media, particularly radio and TV, than by personal contact. Attitudes toward the United States are also, to varying degrees, a function of the social and educational experiences of the student. We find little attempt in the research, however, to disaggregate the attitudes of students and to relate specific attitudes to specific educational and social experiences.

An issue that had attracted a good deal of research attention concerns for foreign student's success or failure in adjusting to America's social environment. Social adaptation has been examined in surveys using problem checklists, through case studies of particular national groups, and, in one instance, an in-depth biographical study of one student. The problems most frequently cited cluster around financial difficulties, the inadequacy of academic advice and personal counseling, and insufficient orientation. The specific problems encountered by students appear to vary, depending in part on the length of time spent in this country and on country or region of origin. Overall, however, similarities between groups of foreign students tend to outweigh the differences and, in some studies, foreign students display more similarities to their American counterparts than differences, suggesting that many problems arise because they are students rather than because they are foreign.

One technique much used by foreign students in coping with adjustment to a strange social milieu is the co-national group. Research has found that these cultural sub-communities help to maintain ties with the home country and provide emotional support to their members. On the other hand, they may be contributing to the frequently mentioned lack of contact between foreign students and the American community and, in some cases, to the isolation of foreign students from the campus power structure.

The adjustment studies make two points which should be of particular interest to university policy makers. First, foreign students appear to find counseling and orientation procedures inadequate, particularly the lack of coordination between academic advisers and foreign student advisers. (This issue is discussed further in Chapter 3.) Secondly, the phenomenon of social isolation, which is so deplored by those who wish to integrate foreign students more fully into campus or community, may in fact be fulfilling a very important psychological function if, indeed, students are able to find a co-national group within which they are comfortable.

Turning to studies of foreign students' academic achievement, we find that a major concern has been to develop methods of selecting those foreign applicants who are most likely to succeed in American academic institutions. The studies find rather consistently that scores on English language tests such as TOEFL are good predictors of academic success. Other aptitude and achievement tests, SAT, SCAT, GRE, etc., were less useful. Investigation of the applicant's academic record in the home country proved useful in some cases but not in others. The universal value of careful credential evaluation, discussed further in Chapter 3, is therefore open to question.

Several studies challenge the basic assumption that foreign students' academic success should be measured by the same criteria as the success of U. S. students. Essentially, American universities are trying to select foreign students who will do well the things that American students are expected to do well. No research has addressed the question of whether grade point average or the awarding of a degree are, in terms of the needs of the various kinds of foreign students, appropriate criteria of success. Similarly, as shown by the findings of several studies that around a third of the AID participants felt they had not been placed in appropriate degree programs, the universities have not been quick to adapt the educational environment to meet the personal or professional needs of the student from abroad.

The studies which were able to question students after return home were principally of sponsored students (often AID) in an effort to assess satisfaction and degree of utilization of training. Given the size of the self-sponsored foreign student population in U. S. academic institutions, it would seem essential that such research also be conducted by these institutions and, in particular, by individual academic departments to see how their alumni fare upon return home.

With a few exceptions, there has been little attempt in the literature to develop new theoretical positions. The U-curve theory has been tested and expanded, and found to be not as universally applicable as sometimes suggested. In particular, it appears to operate in reverse for students from less-developed countries. The "two-way mirror" concept, that the foreign student's image of the United States reflects the image of his or her home country commonly held by Americans, has been verified in some studies. Notably absent has been any concerted effort to relate socio-psychological factors to the attitudes, social adjustment, or academic success of either foreign students in general or in particular sub-groups. Only Klein and her colleagues, among the studies collected, have addressed this problem.

Although a number of studies question members of the academic or non-academic community concerning the experience of foreign students with whom they have been in contact, there is little research on how the foreign students affect American students, universities, or communities. Those studies which do examine this question seem to show that those Americans already interested in international affairs, either on campus or off, probably reinforce their interests through interaction with foreign students. There appears to be little major impact on the academic structure and program of universities as a result of the existence on campus of large numbers of foreign students, nor any major impact on the community as a whole. This conclusion is partly intuitive, it must be stated, and stems as much from what the many studies do not say as from what they do say.

The social adjustment and attitude studies are heavily dominated by opinion-poll methodology. Few make any effort to deal in depth with individual students or to develop a sophisticated methodology for validating responses to the polls, although in some cases questionnaires are supplemented by interviews.

The studies of academic achievement tend to compare background variables, including English-language ability, to grade point average or success in obtaining a degree. None look in depth at the kinds of specific academic problems students have in different disciplines and professions. Studies of the relevance of the academic program, of course, do query students as to how useful they think their program is (or was), but such opinion polling offers little detail to help improve the situation.

The studies which compare students' opinions with those of their advisers, other students, people in the community, and/or authorities in their own countries are equally general, on the whole. We suggest the need for more intensive case studies of small numbers of students and the academic and social community surrounding them, perhaps along the lines of the Deutsch study (111/1970), but including psychologists, political scientists, and perhaps anthropologists, as well as sociologists.

In general, the studies do not demonstrate a strong interest on the part of social scientists per se in the problems of foreign students. Although a number of sponsored, large-scale survey studies display a strong disciplinary competence in theory and statistical method, most of the other studies reviewed do not, indicating the need for greater sophistication in studies of these topics.

Recommendations

The majority of items considered in this chapter were empirical studies which presented findings rather than general policy recommendations. In this section, therefore, we shall summarize the suggestions made, specifically or by implication, in several problem areas.

Orientation

Improved orientation procedures are suggested in many studies. Orientation should be an ongoing program, beginning prior to departure from the home country, in the case of sponsored students or AID participants, and extending throughout the sojourn. It should consider both cultural aspects, practical advice on how to live in the United States and get along with Americans, and academic aspects, how to use the library, how to take objective tests, or write term papers. It should build on the knowledge and experience of the foreign student, but might be conducted in conjunction with campus orientation sessions for American students.

Counseling

In addition to better orientation, foreign students on campus need counseling facilities to help them with specific adjustment problems. This should be a high-level institutional service, and foreign students should be encouraged to use it. The foreign student adviser, at least, should be an expert in counseling techniques. A student advisory group might also be helpful.

Contact with Americans

Many authors express concern that foreign student contacts with Americans should be more frequent and more meaningful. Among the suggestions are that participants in training programs should have more time for social activities and, if the sojourn is for two years or more, should live part of the time with an American family. On campus, foreign students should live in dorms with their American counterparts, and other ways should be found to increase communication between the two groups.

Overexposure to American culture, however, poses some psychological coping problems for the foreign student, and it is also recommended that the foreign student adviser utilize the co-national group as a resource for helping foreign students both adjust to the new environment and preserve identity with home-country customs and culture.

Program Procedures and Design

It is suggested that improvements in procedures and program design could positively affect the attitudes and achievement of foreign students. Among the recommendations for more rigorous selection of foreign applicants were that in-country selection (for graduate programs) be conducted by traveling teams of academics, that special screening procedures be adopted for very young, single undergraduates on F or J visas, and that applications be pooled among a number of colleges and universities. Given the relationship between English-language ability and academic success, it is strongly recommended that universities either be more selective in admitting students lacking adequate English or be prepared to offer English-language training. Programs for AID participants should also include language training when necessary.

With regard to program design, it is suggested first, that sponsored students could be more accurately placed in appropriate programs if there were better communication among agency, student, and institution. Greater involvement of the participant in pre-departure planning is an important element. Secondly, universities are urged to devise special courses geared to the needs of students from developing countries and, in general, to be more flexible in program design. Programs which incorporate practical experience, or work-study programs, are strongly recommended.

Students Who Have Returned Home

Post-return studies indicate the need for more sponsor and home-government support of returned students and for better alumni contacts on the part of American institutions.

Future Research

The following are some of the topics suggested for further research:

Methods of developing a university climate favorable to international educational exchange.

Effect of sponsoring agencies on the international commitment of universities.

Effect on American students of contact with foreign students.

Impact of exchange programs on other countries (home countries).

Development of counseling techniques appropriate to the cross-cultural situation.

Design and testing of experimental approaches to the education of students whose personality and upbringing restrict their openness and sensitivity to a foreign culture.

Relationship of foreign student attitudes and habits to university policies regarding housing, social activities, curricula.

Reasons for Americans' preferential treatment of black Africans, and the mutual relationship between them and black Americans.

Number and distribution of immigrant students and comparison of this group with non-immigrant students.

Discipline and theory-based research on coping behavior of students from different cultures.

Longitudinal follow-up studies of students returned home in order to disaggregate the relevance or lack of relevance of U. S. university training in various professions to home-country needs.

CHART 2.1 - ATTITUDE AND ADJUSTMENT STUDIES: FOREIGN STUDENTS WHILE ABROAD

Item No./ Author(s)/ Date	Sponsor- ship	Population Studied/ Geographical Emphasis	Student Specialization/ Long- or Short- Term Stay	Data Collection Methodology/ No. of Respondents	Data Analysis Methodology/ Apparent Disciplinary Emphasis	Key Ideas
10/AID (DETRI)/ 1969	AID	For. Stud., In US/Multi-Nat.	Multi-Disc./ ST (Early Orientation)	Quest., Ob./ varied groups to 412	Soph. Anal./ Soc., Psych.	Shows little effect of one-week orientation on attitude, although there is information gain
26/Antler/ 1970	HEW	For. Medical Residents in US/Multi-Nat.	Med./LT	Quest., Att., Sci. Samp./ 170	Soph. Anal./ Soc., Psych.	
35/Barry/ 1966	Diss., Columbia Univ.	For. Stud. in US/Thai	Multi-Disc.	Quest./ 85% Response of 1,214	Soph.Anal./ Soc., Psych.	Religion, occupation, education, family
38/Becker/ 1968		For. Stud. at UCLA/Indian, Israeli, European	Multi-Disc./ LT	Struct. Int., Att. (Semantic Differential)/ 77	Simp. Anal./ Soc. Psych.	U-Curve adjustment hypothesis
39/Becker/ 1971	Univ. of Calif. (Los Angeles)	For. Stud. at UCLA/Multi-Nat.	Multi-Disc./ LT	Struct. Int., Sci. Sample/ 187	Simp. Anal./ Soc.	Cultural and ideological
40/Becker/ 1973	Univ. of Calif. (Los Angeles)	For. Stud. at UCLA/SS Africa	Multi-Disc./ LT	Struct. Int., Sci. Sample/ 57 (sub-group of study, above)	Simp. Anal./ Soc.	Relationships of SS Africans with Black and White US
52/Breuder/ 1972	Center for State & Reg'l Leader- ship, Florida	For. Stud. in Florida/Multi- Nat.	Multi-Disc./ LT	Quest. (Michi- gan Int. Stud. Problem Soc. Inventory)	Simp. Anal.	

Item No./ Author(s)/ Date	Sponsor- ship	Population Studied/ Geographical Emphasis	Student Specialization/ Long- or Short- Term Stay	Data Collection Methodology/ No. of Respondents	Data Analysis Methodology/ Apparent Disciplinary Emphasis	Key Ideas
65/Chang/ 1972	Diss., Univ. of Texas (Austin)	For. Stud. in US/China	Multi-Disc./ LT	Quest.	Soph. Anal./ Soc.	
8/Clements/ 1967	AID	For. Stud. in US/Multi- Nat.	Multi-Disc./ ST (six weeks)	Before and after Quest./ 9	Simp. Anal./ Psych.	Evaluation of effect of enrichment-internship program
74/Coelho/ 1972	Diss., Loyola Univ.	For. Stud. in US/India	Multi-Disc./ LT	Semi-Struct. Interviews, Anal. Case/ 56	Simp. Anal./ Soc.	Religious and cultural
76/Cohen/ 1971	Diss., Columbia Univ.	For. Stud. in US/Kenya	Multi-Disc./ LT	Struct. Int./ 35	Simp. Anal./ Soc.	Effect of co-national groupings of students
100/Davis/ 1960	Univ. of Minn. & Univ. of Michigan	For. Stud. in US/M. East	Primarily Grad. Engineer/LT	Quest./93 of 196 responded	Simp. Anal./ Soc.	Compares background of students and their opinions concerning US life
105/Day/ 1968	Diss., Univ. of Oklahoma	For. Stud in US/Multi-Nat.	Multi-Disc./ LT grad. and undergrad.	Michigan Int'l. Student Problem Inventory/199	Soph. Anal./ Psych.	Kinds of problems; change over time
145/Gandhi/ 1970	Author at Univ. of Calgary	For. Stud. in US/India	Multi-Disc./ LT	Quest., Int., Observ./134 (at Univ. of Minnesota)	Simp. Anal./ Soc.	Examines inter-action among Indian students
146/Gandhi/ 1972	Author at Univ. of Calgary	For. Stud. in US/India	Multi-Disc./ LT	Quest./138	Soph. Anal./ Soc.	Explores old and new life styles of Indian students
157/ Guglielmo/ 1967	Diss., Univ. of Arizona	For. Stud. in US/Multi-Nat. LT	Multi-Disc./ LT	Quest./146	Simp. Anal./ Soc.	Student background compared with knowledge of civil regulations

Item No./ Author(s)/ Date	Sponsorship	Population Studied/ Geographical Emphasis	Student Specialization/ Long- or Short-Term Stay	Data Collection Methodology/ No. of Respondents	Data Analysis Methodology/ Apparent Disciplinary Emphasis	Key Ideas
166/Heath/ 1970		For. Stud. in US/Multi-Nat.	Multi-Disc./ LT grad. and undergrad.	Inter./110	Soph. Anal./ Soc., Psych.	U-curve adjustment pattern found
167/ Hegazy/ 1968	Diss., Univ. of Minnesota	For. Stud. in US/England, UAR	Multi-Disc./ LT	Quest./148	Soph. Anal./ Soc.	Compares feelings of British and Egyptian students
169/ Heise/ 1961	Diss., Stanford Univ.	For. Stud. in US/Multi-Nat.	Multi-Disc./ LT	Quest./51% of 3,000 male grad. stud. responded	Soph. Anal./ Soc.	Educational and vocational values related to stud. background and not to institutional environment
180/ Ibrahim/ 1968	Diss., Univ. of Washington	For. Stud. in US/Arab (M. East)	Multi-Disc./ LT	Quest./400 (64% return on nat. survey)	Soph. Anal./ Soc., Pol. Sci.	Examines primarily political attitudes and student background
238/ ICSEE/ 1974	Int'l. Comm. for the Study of Educ'l. Exchange	A progress report on a seven-country survey of student and faculty exchange programs. Topics of the study include: the nature and extent of exchanges, changes in individuals over a period of time, relevant administrative arrangements, and problems encountered. Various research approaches are used, including questionnaires, interviews, records.				
194/Jammaz/ 1972	Diss., Michigan State Univ.	For. Stud. in US/Saudi Arabia	Multi-Disc./ LT	Quest./345 of 400 surveyed	Soph. Anal./ Soc.	Compares background variables with problems encountered
204/Kang/ 1971	Univ. of Minnesota	For. Stud. in US/China	Multi-Disc./ LT	Quest./170	Simp. Anal./ Soc., Psych.	Chinese who anglicized their names compared with non-name changers
205/Kang/ 1972	State Univ. of NY, Buffalo	For. Stud. in US/China	Multi-Disc./ LT	Quest./118	Simp. Anal./ Soc.	Analyzes functions of Chinese for. stud. ethnic community on one campus
218/Klein, et al./1971	Ford Fdn., Univ. of Wisconsin	For. Stud. before & in US/Asia	Multi-Disc./ LT	Quest., Int./ all foreign stud. entering Univ. of Wisc. since 1967	Simp. Anal./ Soc., Psych.	Part of a complex study of social experiences of foreign students and adaptation patterns

Item No./Author(s)/Date	Sponsorship	Population Studied/Geographical Emphasis	Student Specialization/Long- or Short-Term Stay	Data Collection Methodology/No. of Respondents	Data Analysis Methodology/Apparent Disciplinary Emphasis	Key Ideas
233/Markham/1967	Univ. of Iowa	For. Stud. in US/Multi-Nat.	Multi-Disc./LT	Quest., Int. over five-year period/340	Soph. Anal./Psych.	Examines attitude change as related to mass-media exposure
236/Maslog/1967	Diss., Univ. of Minnesota	For. Stud. in US/Philippines and India	Mult-Disc./LT	Quest./99 newly arrived students	Simp. Anal./Pol. Sci., Journalism	Examines political stereotypes and possible mass-media influence
246/Miller/1967	Diss., Univ. of N. Carolina (Chapel Hill)	For. Stud. in US/SS Africa	Multi-Dtsc./LT	Quest./130 at 7 universities	Simp. Anal./Soc.	African students come with unfavorable attitudes toward US race relations and have these attitudes strengthened while in US
255/Moran, et al./1974	Univ. of Minnesota	For. Stud. in US/Multi-Nat.	Multi-Disc./LT	Quest., Mich. For. Stud. Prob. Inventory/43	Simp. Anal./Psych.	Evaluation of role-playing orientation session showed positive results
258/Mowlana & McLaughlin/1969		For. Stud. in US/Multi-Nat.	Multi-Disc./LT	Quest.	Soph. Anal./Soc.	Explores media usage and relationship to attitudes
312/Pierce/1969	Diss., Univ. of Illinois	For. Stud. in US/Multi-Nat.	Multi-Disc./LT	Quest. (Semantic differential)/600+ at 36 uni.	Soph. Anal./Psych.	Students from developing countries had more favorable attitude toward advertising than those from rich countries
315/Porter/1962	Diss., Michigan State Univ.	For. Stud. in US/Multi-Nat.	Multi-Disc./LT	Mich. Int'l. Stud. Problem Inventory/108	Soph. Anal./Psych.	Establishes MISPI as a valid instrument for identifying for. stud. problems
316/Pratt/1956		For. Stud. in other countries/Multi-Nat.				Case analyses of culture goals which cause mental health problems within various nationality groups. Suggests that these culture goals are what cause mal-adjustment of individuals when abroad, rather han the culture of the host country. (Soc., Psych.)

Item No./Author(s)/Date	Sponsorship	Population Studied/Geographical Emphasis	Student Specialization/Long- or Short-Term Stay	Data Collection Methodology/No. of Respondents	Data Analysis Methodology/Apparent Disciplinary Emphasis	Key Ideas
324/Restivo/1971	Diss., Michigan State Univ.	Visiting For. Scientists in US univ./Multi-Nat.	Phy. and Bio. Science/LT	Quest., Int./144 resp. of 222 plus 82 interviews	Simp. Anal./Soc., Philo.	Explores conditions of work, science as an ideology, and modern/traditional orientation of foreign scientists in US
326/Rising and Copp/1968	Univ. of Rochester	For. Stud. in US/Multi-Nat.	Multi-Disc./LT	Quest., Int./20 returned of 45; 22 Int.	Simp. Anal./Soc.	Adjustment examined to aid in developing orientation program
340/Selby and Woods/1966		For. Stud. in US/Non-European (Multi-Nat.)	Multi-Disc./LT	St. Int. (3 over time)/18	Simp. Anal./Soc., Psych.	Adjustment declines sharply and improves gradually
341/Selltiz, et. al./1956		For. Stud. in US/Multi-Nat.	Multi-Disc./LT	St. Int. (early & late in sojourn)/348 attending 35 inst.	Simp. Anal./Soc.	Background of student as important as opportunity in determining intimate inter-action with hosts
358/Sofola/1967	Diss., The American Univ.	For. Stud. in US/Nigeria	Multi-Disc./LT	Quest., Int./265 respondents of 500	Soph. Anal./Psych., Soc.	Analysis of adjustment and attitudes of Nigerian students
373/Tanner/1968	Univ. of Michigan	For. Stud. in US/Multi-Nat.	Multi-Disc./LT graduate students	Quest./63	Simp. Anal./Soc.	Shows U-curve in friendship patterns with other US stud. and others of own nationality
412/Ursua/1969	Diss., Catholic Univ. of America	For. Stud. in US/Multi-Nat.	Multi-Disc./LT graduate	Mich. Int. Stud. Problem Inventory, Eng./201 grad. stud.	Soph. Anal./Psych.	Finds only limited correlation between English lang. problems and adjustment problems
409/USIA/1971	USIA	For. Stud. before and in US/Africa	Multi-Disc./ST	Quest. before (154) and after (119) short-term tours; Group discussion (60)	Simp. Anal./Soc., Psych.	ST Grantees left US with favorable impression, but major changes in attitude were few
419/Wakita/1971	Los Angeles City Coll.	For. Stud. in US/Asia (both native and for. born)	Multi-Disc./LT undergrad.	Quest./659 (39% response of 1,700)	Simp. Anal./Soc.	Finds various kinds of prejudice between foreign, native-born, and Hawaii-born Asians which affect inter-action between them

CHART 2.2 – ACHIEVEMENT AND ACADEMIC RELEVANCE STUDIES: FOREIGN STUDENTS WHILE ABROAD

Item No./ Author(s)/ Date	Sponsor- ship	Population Studied/ Geographical Emphasis	Student Specialization/ Long- or Short- Term Stay	Data Collection Methodology/ No. of Respondents	Data Analysis Methodology/ Apparent Disciplinary Emphasis	Key Ideas
20/AACRAO/ n.d.	AID	For. Stud. in US/Multi-Nat.	Multi-Disc./ LT grad. & undergrad.	Quest./Ach./ Eng./Att./Anal. Case/1,004	Soph. Anal./ Psych.	AID participant problems, with recommendations on selection & placement procedures
417/ AACRAO (Vroman)/ 1970	AID	For. Stud. in US/Multi-Nat.	Multi-Disc./ LT grad. & undergrad	Quest./Ach./ Eng./Att./Anal. Case/1,004	Soph. Anal./ Psych.	Journal article on above study
418/ AACRAO (Vroman)/ 1971	AID	For. Stud. in US/Multi-Nat.	Multi-Disc./ LT grad. & undergrad.	Quest./Ach./ Eng./Att./Anal. Case/1,004	Soph.Anal./ Psych.	Final report on study above
19/AACTE/ 1973	AACTE	For. Stud. in US/Multi-Nat.	Educ./ST Internships	Quest.; Anal. Case/14	Simp. Anal./ Psych.	Some interns felt that average of 4.2 months was too short
18/Allen/ 1965	Univ. of Houston	For. Stud in US/Multi-Nat.	Multi-Disc./ LT	Eng. Lang. test/ 90 for. stud.	Simp. Anal./ Psych.	Predictive validity of aural comprehension test challenged
55/ Burgess & Marks/ 1968	Portland State College	For. Stud. in US/Multi-Nat.	Multi-Disc./ LT	Eng. test scores compared with achievement/89	Soph. Anal./ Psych.	
56/Burke/ 1968	Diss., Univ. of S. Calif.	For. Stud. in US/Multi-Nat.	Multi-Disc./ LT (60% grad.)	Six English ability & achievement tests/178	Soph. Anal./ Psych.	Three tests validly predict: three do not

Item No./ Author(s)/ Date	Sponsor-ship	Population Studied/ Geographical Emphasis	Student Specialization/ Long- or Short-Term Stay	Data Collection Methodology/ No. of Respondents	Data Analysis Methodology/ Apparent Disciplinary Emphasis	Key Ideas
126/ Ellakany/ 1970	Diss., Iowa State Univ.	For. Stud. in US/Multi-Nat.	Multi-Disc./ LT	Quest., Case Anal./ 454	Soph. Anal./ Psych.	Correlates academic achievement with personal characteristics
131/Elting/ 1970	Diss., New York Univ.	For. Stud. in US/Multi-Nat.	Multi-Disc./ LT	Case Anal./695 undergrad. & grad.	Soph. Anal./ Psych.	Correlates pre-admission data with freshman grade point average
134/Farrar/ 1968	Diss., Univ. of Calif. (UCLA)	For. migrant stud. in US/ Multi-Nat.	Multi-Disc./ LT	Apt., Ach./268	Simp. Anal./ Psych.	Compares academic success of migrant students with that of native-born
140/Ford/ 1969	Diss., Michigan State Univ.	For. Stud. in US/Asia	Multi-Disc./ LT	Inter./15 grad. (over 3-mo. period)	Simp. Anal./ Soc.	Examines how students react to academic programs
414/Van de/ Guchte/ 1969	Diss., Michigan State Univ.	For. Stud. in US/Dutch, Spanish, Japanese, & Turkish speaking	Multi-Disc./ LT	Student judges of degree of foreign accent/32	Simp. Anal./ English as a Foreign Lang.	Explores visual and aural cues to foreign accent
159/Halasz/ 1969	UCLA	For. Stud. in US/Indonesia, Korea, Pakistan, Thailand	Multi-Disc./ LT	Graduate stud. admissions data/ 34 Indonesian, 100 Korean, 21 Pakistani, 22 Thai	Simp. Anal./ Psych.	Background characteristics compared to academic achievement
168/Heil & Aleamoni/ 1974	Univ. of Ill.	For. Stud. in US/Multi-Nat.	Multi-Disc./ LT	Eng. (TOEFL) compared with later GPA/148	Simp. Anal./ Psych. (good review of res.)	Finds TOEFL good predictor of academic standing

Item No./Author(s)/Date	Sponsorship	Population Studied/Geographical Emphasis	Student Specialization/Long- or Short-Term Stay	Data Collection Methodology/No. of Respondents	Data Analysis Methodology/Apparent Disciplinary Emphasis	Key Ideas
235/Martin/1971	Diss., Univ. of N. Carolina (Chapel Hill)	For. Stud. in US/Multi-Nat.	Multi-Disc./LT	Eng., academic records/72	Soph. Anal./Psych.	TOEFL was a good predictor of academic success
240/Melendez-Craig/1970	Diss., Brigham Young Univ.	For. Stud. in US/L. America	Multi-Disc./LT	Eng., Academic Records, Quest. (Mich. Int'l. Stud. Problem Inv.)	Soph. Anal./Psych.	Examines background variables and achievement; English Lang. ability good predictor of academic success
256/Moravcsik/1972	UCLA, Univ. of Oregon, Michigan, & Pittsburgh	For. Stud. before and in US/S. Asia	Physics/LT	Int. before coming, acad. achievement in US/145	Simp. Anal./Psych.	Showed high correlation between interview judgment and subsequent academic success or failure
259/Mozden/1973	Master's Thesis, Univ. of Pittsburgh	Using field visits, documents, interviews, and previous studies as a data base, author describes history of the Military Assistance Training Program, evaluates its work, and suggests that MATP's effect may be underestimated. Program consists of variety of activities, including university training in US, Mobile Training Teams, etc.				
303/Paraskevopoulous & Dremuk/1968	Univ. of Illinois	For. Stud. in US/Multi-Nat.	Multi-Disc./LT	Examines "reduction ratio" of 5,800 for. stud. applications at Univ. of Ill.		Only 11 of 58 applicants actually enter: reduction relates to various background factors
306/Pavri/1963	Diss., Univ. of Virginia	For. Stud. in US/Multi-Nat.	Multi-Disc./LT graduate students	Quest., Acad. Records/319	Soph. Anal./Psych.	Compares background factors with success rates of students
344/Sharon/1971	Educ. Testing Service	For. Stud. in US/Multi-Nat.	Multi-Disc./LT	Grad. Rec. Exam & TOEFL results compared with grade point avg.	Soph. Anal./Psych.	Students with low English verbal aptitude can succeed in graduate work; GRE not good predictor
369/Sugimoto/1966	Diss., Univ. of S. Calif.	For. Stud. in US/Multi-Nat.	Multi-Disc./LT	Examination of stud. records, admission tests, background, & first-term acad. records/2,075	Soph. Anal./Psych.	Pre-admission predictors of academic success are graduate standing, age, & type of visa held; standard pre-admission data such as TOEFL poor predictors

Item No./ Author(s)/ Date	Sponsor- ship	Population Studied/ Geographical Emphasis	Student Specialization/ Long- or Short- Term Stay	Data Collection Methodology/ No. of Respondents	Data Analysis Methodology/ Apparent Disciplinary Emphasis	Key Ideas
374/Telleen/ 1970	Diss., Univ. of Michigan	For. Stud. in US/India	Multi-Disc./ LT grad. stud.	Compares grad. stud. background variables with acad. achieve- ment/300	Soph. Anal./ Psych. (includes Res. Rev., 1947- 1969)	Develops model which can predict academic achievement based on background variables
379/Uehara/ 1969	Kapiolani Comm. College (Hawaii)	For. Stud. in US/Multi-Nat.	Multi-Disc./ LT undergrad.	Compares acad. achievement with original visa status and entrance test data	Simp. Anal./ Psych.	Shows high predictive value of English ability, no matter how tested
411/Univ. of South Carolina/ 1967	Univ. of S. Carolina	For. Stud in US/Multi-Nat.	Multi-Disc./ LT undergrad.	Compares grade point average & nationality	Simp. Anal./ Psych.	Students with good English and from countries with good relationship with US do well

CHART 2.3 – STUDIES OF BOTH ATTITUDE AND ACHIEVEMENT (OFTEN RELATING THE TWO): FOREIGN STUDENTS WHILE ABROAD

Item No./Author(s)/Date	Sponsorship	Population Studied/Geographical Emphasis	Student Specialization/Long- or Short-Term Stay	Data Collection Methodology/No. of Respondents	Data Analysis Methodology/Apparent Disciplinary Emphasis	Key Ideas	
						Student Attitudes or Adjustment	Academic Achievement or Relevance
12a/AID (DETRI)/1971	AID	For. Stud. in US/Multi-Nat.	Soc. Sci. (Demography)/largely ST	Quest./Inf. Int. (on leaving US)	Soph. Anal./Soc., Psych.	x	x This and next eight studies examine opinions of AID participants toward their specialized training as programmed by various government agencies
12b/AID (DETRI)/1971	AID	For. Stud. in US/Multi-Nat.	Agric./LT, ST	Quest., Inf. Int./916 LT; 228 ST	Soph. Anal./Soc., Psych.	x	x
12c/AID (DETRI)/1971	AID	For. Stud. in US/Multi-Nat.	Labor/ST	Quest., Inf. Int./293	Soph. Anal./Soc., Psych.	x	x
12d/AID (DETRI)/1971	AID	For. Stud. in US/Multi-Nat.	Aviation/ST	Quest., Inf. Int./213	Soph. Anal./Soc., Psych.	x	x
12e/AID (DETRI)/1971	AID	For. Stud. in US/Multi-Nat.	Internal Revenue/ST	Quest., Inf. Int./183	Soph. Anal./Soc., Psych.	x	x
12f/AID (DETRI)/1971	AID	For. Stud. in US/Multi-Nat.	Education/ST	Quest., Inf. Int./161	Soph. Anal./Soc., Psych.	x	x

Item No./Author(s)/Date	Sponsorship	Population Studied/Geographical Emphasis	Student Specialization/Long- or Short-Term Stay	Data Collection Methodology/No. of Respondents	Data Analysis Methodology/Apparent Disciplinary Emphasis	Key Ideas	
						Student Attitudes or Adjustment	Academic Achievement or Relevance
12g/AID (DETRI)/ 1971	AID	For. Stud. in US/Multi-Nat	Education, Public. Acmin./ LT, ST	Quest., Inf. Int./2,439 LT, plus 72 ST	Soph. Anal./ Soc., Psych.	x	x
12h/AID (DETRI)/ 1971	AID	For. Stud. in US/Multi-Nat.	Pub. Health/ LT, ST	Quest., Inf. Int./358	Soph. Anal./ Soc., Psych.	x	x
112/AID (DETRI)/ 1972	AID	For. Stud. in US/Multi-Nat. (at Univ. Mo.)	Agric., Health, Education/ST	Quest., Inf. Int. 37	Soph. Anal./ Soc., Psych.	x	x
11a/AID (DETRI)/ 1969 (First Annual Report)	AID	For. Stud. in US/Multi-Nat.	Multi-Disc./ LT, ST	Quest., Inf. Int./2,420	Soph. Anal./ Soc., Psych.	x This and next four reports describe results of exit interviews of AID participants as they leave the US	x
11b/AID (DETRI)/ 1970 (Second Annual Report)	AID	For. Stud. in US/Multi-Nat.	Multi-Disc./ LT, ST	Quest., Inf. Int./1,887	Soph. Anal./ Soc., Psych.	x	x
11c/AID (DETRI)/ 1971 (Status Report 3)	AID	For. Stud. in US/Multi-Nat.	Multi-Disc./ LT, ST	Quest., Inf. Int./2,853 ST, LT plus 129 ST "Observation Training Teams"	Soph. Anal./ Soc., Psych.	x	x
11d/AID (DETRI)/ 1972 (Status Report 5)	AID	For. Stud. in US/Multi-Nat.	Multi-Disc./ LT, ST	Quest., Inf. Int./5,501	Soph. Anal./ Soc., Psych.	x	x

Item No./Author(s)/Date	Sponsorship	Population Studied/Geographical Emphasis	Student Specialization/Long- or Short-Term Stay	Data Collection Methodology/No. of Respondents	Data Analysis Methodology/Apparent Disciplinary Emphasis	Key Ideas — Student Attitudes or Adjustment	Key Ideas — Academic Achievement or Relevance
113/AID (DETRI) 1972 (Final Report); see also Sperling [365], Clements [8], Lockett [228], Gollin [149], and AID country studies of participants after return home	AID	For. Stud. in US/Multi-Nat.	Multi-Disc./ LT, ST	Quest., Inf. Int./10,825 (includes all in indiv. reports, above)	Soph. Anal./ Soc., Psych	x	x
36/Basu 1966	Diss., Univ. of Missouri	For. Stud. in US/India	Agric./LT graduate	Quest., Struc. Int./314 in 17 univ. (85.1% response)	Simp. Anal./ Soc.	x	x
132/Erickson/ 1970	Diss., Univ. of N. Dakota	For. Stud. in US/China, Pakistan, India, M. East	Multi-Disc./ LT	Eng., Att., Ach./43 grad.	Soph. Anal./ Psych.	Compares personality, academic, & biographical characteristics of nationality groups	
141/Frank 1965	Diss., Michigan State Univ.	For. Stud. in US/Multi-Nat.	Multi-Disc./ LT	Quest./317	Soph. Anal./ Psych.	Examines AID participants' attitudes toward introducing change at home	
158/Hagey/ 1968	Diss., Univ. of Oregon	For. Stud. in US/M. East	Multi-Disc./ LT	Quest./272	Soph. Anal./ Soc., Psych.	Academic & social adj. compared to background & environment	
176/Hill/ 1966	Diss., Indiana Univ.	For. Stud. in US/Thailand, India, Pakistan	Multi-Disc./ LT	Quest./78 respondents of 150	Simp. Anal./ Soc.	Analyzes adjustment problems, academic and personal	
195/ Jarrahi-Zadeh & Eichman/ 1970	Univ. of N. Carolina	For. Stud. in US/M. East.	Multi-Disc./ LT	Quest./50 rep. 82% response	Simp. Anal./ Soc.	Compares academic & adjustment problems with earlier US student study	

Item No./ Author(s)/ Date	Sponsor- ship	Population Studied/ Geographical Emphasis	Student Specialization/ Long- or Short- Term Stay	Data Collection Methodology/ No. of Respondents	Data Analysis Methodology/ Apparent Disciplinary Emphasis	Key Ideas Student Attitudes or Adjustment	Academic Achievement or Relevance
229/Longest/ 1969	Cornell Univ. & Ford Fdn.	For. Stud. in US/Multi-Nat.	Agriculture/LT	Quest. given in 2 consecutive semesters/85 grad.	Simp. Anal./ Soc.	Pre- and post-quest. to evaluate effect of orientation program, as related to differential stud. background	
230/Lozada/ 1970	Diss., Purdue Univ.	For. Stud. in US/Multi-Nat.	Multi-Disc./ LT	Quest./476 respondents of 809 surveyed	Simp. Anal./ Soc.	Examines personal characteristics & problems	
270/Ruscoe/ 1968	NAFSA & Standard Oil (NJ)	For. Stud. in US/Latin America	Multi-Disc./ LT	Quest. 927 of 2,000 surveyed	Simp. Anal./ Psych., Soc.	Explores opinions of for. stud. concerning US sojourn; recommends better orientation & assistance only to those needing it	
214/Sharma/ 1969	Univ. of Chicago & Univ. of Wisconsin	For. Stud. in US/India	Multi-Disc./ LT	Quest./1,416 respondents of 3,862 in 322 inst.	Simp. Anal./ Soc.	Attitudes of students toward acad. program & to non-acad. experiences	
343/Sharma/ 1971	Diss., Univ. of N. Carolina (Greensboro)	For. Stud. in US/Non- European	Multi-Disc./ LT	Quest./195 grad. (all N.C.) (some interviews)	Soph. Anal./ Psych.	Basically, an inventory of acad. & personal adjustment problems	
347/ Shepard/ 1970	Diss., Univ. of Mississippi	For. Stud. in Southern US/ Multi-Nat.	Multi-Disc./ LT	Quest./247 (67% response) in 38 inst.	Simp. Anal./ Soc.	Finds many foreign students poorly adjusted & needy of more pre- departure orientation and on-campus help	
242/Win/ 1971	Diss., Univ. of S. Calif.	For. Stud. in US/India & Japan	Multi-Disc./ LT	Mich. For. Stud. Prob. Inventory/ 98 Indian, 47 Japanese	Soph. Anal./ Psych.	Two nationality groups showed sharp differences in problems encountered: also differences between grad. & undergrad.	

CHART 2.4 – COMPARATIVE STUDIES OF ATTITUDE AND/OR ACHIEVEMENT: DATA FROM FOREIGN STUDENTS COMPARED WITH DATA AND/OR OPINIONS OF HOST-COUNTRY STUDENTS, FACULTY, COMMUNITY, OR OTHERS

Item No./ Author(s)/ Date	Sponsor- ship	Population Studied/ Geographical Emphasis	Student Specialization/ Long- or Short- Term Stay	Data Collection Methodology/ No. of Respondents	Data Analysis Methodology/ Apparent Disciplinary Emphasis	Key Ideas
17/Allen & Arafat/ 1971		For. Stud. in US; US Stud./ Multi-Nat.	Multi-disc./ LT	Quest. Sci. Samp./ 100 US; 99 For.	Simp. Anal./ Soc.	Procreative family
28/Arkoff, et al./1966	Univ. of Hawaii	For. Stud. in US; US Fac.; US Stud./Asian US	Multi-disc./ LT graduate	Quest./118	Soph. Anal./ Psych.	Mental Health
32/Bae/ n. d.	Univ. of Wisconsin	For. Stud. in US; Stud. in Korea	Multi-disc.	Quest., Struc. Int./53 in US, 210 in Korea	Soph. Anal./ Soc.	Traditionalism
48/Bohn/ 1957	Diss., Wayne St. Univ.	For. Stud. in US; US Fac./ Multi-Nat.	Multi-Disc./ LT	Quest., Int., Att., Ach., Eng., plus Fac. Int./ 36 stud.	Simp. Anal./ Psych.	
53/ Brickman/ 1967	Ogontz Plan, Phila.	For. Stud. in US, Univ. & School Fac./ Multi-Nat.	Multi-disc./ LT	Quest., Inf. Int./63 For. Stud. plus US Fac. & Commun.	Simp. Anal., Case Anal./ Multi	Effect of for. stud. visits to US elementary & secondary schools
68/Chu, et al./1971		For. Stud. & Fac. in Hawaii, For. Stud. before Stud. in Taiwan	Multi-disc./ LT	Quest./67 in Hawaii, 132 in Taiwan before, 108 staying in Taiwan	Simp. Anal./ Soc.	Compares those in Hawaii with those about to come and those staying home

Item No./ Author(s)/ Date	Sponsor- ship	Population Studied/ Geographical Emphasis	Student Specialization/ Long- or Short- Term Stay	Data Collection Methodology/ No. of Respondents	Data Analysis Methodology/ Apparent Disciplinary Emphasis	Key Ideas
69/Clark/ 1963	Diss., Univ. of Michigan	For. Stud. in US, US Fac./ Ghana	Multi-Disc./ LT	Quest./100 stud. plus fac.	Soph. Anal./ Soc.	Attitudes toward academic achievement
70/Clark & Ozawa/1970	Univ. of Wisconsin	For. Stud. in US, US Fac./ Multi-Nat.	Multi-Disc./ LT	Quest., Anal. Case/861 For. Stud., 289 Fac., 1 for. stud. case in depth	Simp. Anal./ Soc., Anthro.	Includes fascinating auto-biographical case history of one Japanese student
75/Coelho-Oudegeest/ 1971	Diss., Univ. of Wisconsin	For. Stud. in US, F. S. Counselors/ Multi-Nat.	Multi-Disc./ LT	Struct. Int., Att., Anal. Case/24 for. stud.,11 counselors	Soph. Anal./ Psych.	Complex study of variables affecting counseling relationship
77/ Colacicco/ 1970	Diss., Purdue Univ.	For. Stud. in US, US Stud./ Kenya, India	Multi-Disc./ LT	Personality Inventory/ 111 For. Stud., 111 US Stud.	Soph. Anal./ Psych.	Compares personality characteristics
109/ Deutsch/ 1965	Funded by several	For. Stud. in US, US Fac., US Stud., US Commun., etc./ Multi-Nat.	Multi-Disc./ LT, ST	Hist., Quest., Int., Case Anal./1,018	Soph. Anal./ Soc.	A comprehensive sociol. study of for. stud., universities & community
111/ Deutsch/ 1970	Data from above study in book form					
152/Grady/ 1969	Diss., Univ., of N. Dakota	For. Stud. in US, US Stud./ Canada	Multi-Disc./ LT	Att., Ach./ 31 US & 31 Canadian freshmen	Soph. Anal./ Psych.	Academic, personality & biolcgical factors compared with achievement

Item No./ Author(s)/ Date	Sponsorship	Population Studied/ Geographical Emphasis	Student Specialization/ Long- or Short-Term Stay	Data Collection Methodology/ No. of Respondents	Data Analysis Methodology/ Apparent Disciplinary Emphasis	Key Ideas
160/Halberstam & Dasco/ 1965	HEW	For. Stud. in US, US Stud./ Multi-Nat.	Medical Residents/ LT	21 Questionnaires & Instruments/170 for., 150 US	Soph. Anal./ Psych.	Compares training experience and attitudes of US & foreign medical residents
161/Halberstam, et al./ 1970	HEW, IIE	For. Stud. in US, US Stud., US Supervisors/ Multi-Nat	Surgical Residents/LT	21 Quest. & Int. (similar to above)/50 for., 50 US	Soph. Anal./ Psych.	Compares US & foreign perceptions of training & supervisors' evaluations
197/ Johnson/ 1971	Univ. of Tennessee	For. Stud. in US, US Stud. Multi-Nat.	Multi-Disc./ LT	Quest./214 (representing 84% of sample)	Simp. Anal./ Soc.	FS problems not necessarily those thought to be problems by US students
222/ Kwochka/ 1970	Diss., Columbia Univ.	US stud. in Int'l. House, For. Stud./ Multi-Nat.	Multi-Disc./ LT	Quest./650 US Stud. of 1,200 former residents; info. from earlier FS study used	Simp. Anal./ Soc.	Degree to which Int'l. House helped US & foreign students meet their professional goals & understand others
247/Miller, et al./ 1971	Ford Fdn. & Univ. of Wisc.	For. Stud. in US, US Stud. in Asia/E. Asia	Multi-Disc./ LT	Quest., Int./ 59 for. stud., 35 US stud. in Taiwan	Simp. Anal./ Soc., Psych.	Concludes that both Asian & US students abroad fail to achieve warm friendships with host nationals
286/NACDRAO & NAFSA/ 1973	NACDRAO & NAFSA	For. Stud. in US Black Colleges, US students/ Multi-Nat. (largely SS Africa)	Multi-Disc./ LT	Quest./301 of 1,495 for. stud. surveyed; 188 of 930 US stud.	Simp. Anal. Soc.	Explores US & for. stud. attitudes toward each other; some superiority felt by each group
285/NAFSA/ n. d.	State Dept.	For. Stud. in US, US Fac. & Commun. Multi-Nat.	Multi-Disc./ ST Intercultural workshops	Quest./400	Simp. Anal.	An evaluation by participants in 3-day Intercultural Small Group Experience sessions

Item No./Author(s)/Date	Sponsorship	Population Studied/Geographical Emphasis	Student Specialization/Long- or Short-Term Stay	Data Collection Methodology/No. of Respondents	Data Analysis Methodology/Apparent Disciplinary Emphasis	Key Ideas
291/Odenyo/1970	Diss., Univ. of Minnesota	For. Stud. in US, US Black Stud./SS Africa	Multi-Disc./LT	Hist., Quest., Obs./Samples of US & For. Stud. in Minnesota	Simp. Anal./Soc.	Explores ambivalence of US & for. black students toward each other
292/Ohuche/1967	Diss., Iowa State Univ.	For. Stud. Admin, For. Stud. in US/SS Africa (Nigeria)	Multi-Disc./LT	Quest. & acad. record/Sample of 456 grad. & 1,426 under-grad. plus for. stud. admin.	Simp. Anal./Psych.	Found little predictive value in grades on school cert. exam in Nigeria; high-school cert. holders did better than non-holders, etc.
357/Snipes/1969	Indiana Univ.	For. Stud. in US, US Stud./Multi-Nat.	Multi-Disc./LT	Quest. & Personality Factor Test/112	Soph. Anal./Psych., Soc.	Personality factors not correlated with communication behavior: grad. students spent more time with mass media, undergrads most time in social communication activities
372/Swan/1969	Diss., Univ. of Wisconsin	For. Stud. in US, US Fac., For. employers/Philippines	Agriculture & Home Economics/grad. stud./LT	Int./113 stud., 68 prof., 76 home-country authorities	Simp. Anal./Psych., Soc.	Explores perceptions of respondents of US graduate education objectives, policies, & procedures
401/Yankelovich/State 1971	Dept. of State	For. Stud. in US, US Fac./Multi-Nat. (non-Europ.)	Multi-Disc./LT	Int./35 Stud., 15 US Fac. in 10 univ.	Simp. Anal./Soc.	Finds for. stud. little affected by campus unrest: some disapproval of US policies & with training in US

CHART 2.5 - STUDIES OF ATTITUDE AND/OR ACHIEVEMENT: FOREIGN STUDENTS AFTER RETURN HOME

Item No./ Author(s)/ Date	Sponsor-ship	Population Studied/ Geographical Emphasis	Student Specialization/ Long- or Short-Term Stay	Data Collection Methodology/ No. of Respondents	Data Analysis Methodology/ Apparent Disciplinary Emphasis	Key Ideas
14a/AID/ 1966	AID	For. Stud., Ret. Home/ India	Multi-Disc./ LT, ST	Quest./1,449	Simp. Anal./ Soc.	One of 40 country studies done by AID missions during early 1960's of returned AID training participants
14b/AID/ 1966	AID	For. Stud., Ret. Home/ E. Asia	Multi-Disc./ LT, ST	Struc. Int./ 2,567	Simp. Anal./ Soc.	Summary of five country studies
14c/AID/ 1966	AID	For. Stud., Ret. Home/ L. Amer.	Multi-Disc./ LT, ST (avg. 5.4 months)	Struc. Int./ 3,480	Simp. Anal./ Soc.	Summary of 11 country studies
14d/AID/ 1966	AID	For. Stud., Ret. Home/ N. Af.	Multi-Disc./ LT, ST	Struc. Int./ 1,122	Simp. Anal./ Soc.	Summary of five country studies
14e/AID/ 1966	AID	For. Stud., Ret. Home/ M. East, S. Asia	Multi-Disc./ LT, ST	Struc. Int./ 5,019	Simp. Anal./ Soc.	Summary of eight country studies
14f/AID/ 1967	AID	For. Stud., Ret. Home/ Ghana	Multi-Disc./ LT, ST	Struc. Int./ 143	Simp. Anal./ Soc.	
61/ Carnovsky/ 1971	HEW	For. Stud., Ret. Home/ Multi-Nat.	Library/LT	Quest./All Library School Grads., 1965-69	Simp. Anal./ Multi-Disc.	

Item No./Author(s)/Date	Sponsorship	Population Studied/Geographical Emphasis	Student Specialization/Long- or Short-Term Stay	Data Collection Methodology/No. of Respondents	Data Analysis Methodology/Apparent Disciplinary Emphasis	Key Ideas
101/Davis/1971	Illinois State Univ.	For. Stud., Ret. Home/Turkey	Multi-Disc./LT	Quest., Int./222 (of 600 returnees), one-half int.	Simp. Anal. of data/Soc.	Favorability to US varies according to time spent in US & perceived US attitude toward Turkey
102/Davis/1973	Fulbright Grant	For. Stud., Ret. Home/Turkey	Multi-Disc./LT graduate	Quest., Int./222 (selected from Fulbright lists)	Simp. Anal./Soc.	Attitudes toward Turkish & US development examined
103/Davis/1973	Council on Int'l. Educ. Exchange	For. Stud., in US & after Ret. Home/England, Ireland	Multi-Disc./LT	Quest., Int./8 randomly selected & studies over period of time	Simp. Anal./Soc.	Examines nature of & satisfaction toward summer-work experience
119/Dow/n.d.	Florida Atlantic Univ.	For. Stud., Ret. Home/China	Multi-Disc./LT	Secondary data from available publications	Historical	
423/East-West Center/West Center	East-West Center	For. Stud., Ret. Home/Asia	Multi-Disc./LT	Int./36		
125/Eide/1970	UNESCO	Variety of theoretical, data-based, and speculative articles on the effects of foreign student exchange on students, hosts, and home country. Portion is based on UNESCO questionnaire surveys of Iranian, Indian, and UAR students who had returned home after two or more years of study. Data basically same as used by Galtung, below.				
144/Galtung/UNESCO 1965 (see also Eide [125])		For. Stud., Ret. Home from US, UK, & France or Germany/UAR, India, Iran	Multi-Disc./LT	Inter.	Simp. Anal./Soc.	Examines adjustment & attitudes of for. stud. toward their host countries

Item No./ Author(s)/ Date	Sponsor- ship	Population Studied/ Geographical Emphasis	Student Specialization/ Long- or Short- Term Stay	Data Collection Methodology/ No. of Respondents	Data Analysis Methodology/ Apparent Disciplinary Emphasis	Key Ideas
390a/ Gardner/ 1963	Dept. of State	For. Stud., Ret. Home, For. Emp., For. Com., US Emb., FS Admin., US Com./ 20 countries	Multi-Disc./ LT, ST	Quest., Res. Rev./2,696 former Dept. of State grantees plus other US & for. informants	Simp. Anal./ Multi-Disc.	US Advisory Commission's report to Congress on the effectiveness of the US Dept. of State's exchange program, 1949–63
390b/ Gardner/ 1963	Dept. of State	The above Congressional Report issued for public distribution				
149/ Gollin/ 1966 (see also AID country studies, above)	AID	For. Stud., Ret. Home; For. Emp.; US colleagues/ multi-nat.	Multi-Disc./ ST, LT	Struc. Int. (stud.), Quest. (For. Emp. & US colleagues)/ 9,668 For. Stud.	Soph. Anal./ Psych., Soc.	An evaluation of AID training programs; data collected from 1959 to 1963
151/ Gollin/ 1967 (see also AID country studies, above)	Diss., Columbia Univ.	A further treatment of the data collected in the above study				
196/ Johnson/ 1970	Univ. of Oregon	For. Stud., Ret. Home/ Asia	Multi-Disc./ LT	Inter./38	Simp. Anal./ Soc.	Reasons for return home & opinion on relevance of US education
201a & b/ JUSPAO/ 1967	JUSPAO	For. Stud., Ret. Home/ Vietnam	Multi-Disc./ LT, ST	Quest., Int./ 446	Simp. Anal./ Soc.	Most found US training useful & are favorable to US

Item No./ Author(s)/ Date	Sponsorship	Population Studied/ Geographical Emphasis	Student Specialization/ Long- or Short-Term Stay	Data Collection Methodology/ No. of Respondents	Data Analysis Methodology/ Apparent Disciplinary Emphasis	Key Ideas
237/ Mastroianni/ 1971	Diss., Syracuse Univ.	Foreign Broadcasters Ret. Home/Multi-Nat.	Broadcasters/ ST	Att., Quest./ 78 who attended US Seminar, 76 who did not	Soph. Anal./ Psych.	Both those who attended & those who did not had favorable attitudes toward US, but attendees had more definite opinions
403/Norton 1972	Dept. of State	For. Stud., Ret. Home, Univ. Admin., Govt. Officials/Asia	Multi-Disc./ ST (70-day Asian student leader tours)	Quest., Int. in Asia/122	Simp. Anal./ Soc.	Evaluation of Asian & Pacific Student Leader Project showed favorable results
296/Orr, Jr. 1971	Diss., Columbia Univ.	For. Stud., Ret. Home/ Multi-Nat.	Multi-Disc./ LT	Critical review of existing research – 85% sponsored by US Govt., mostly of sponsored students		Examines adjustment, attitudes, & use of training
182/ Susskind & Schell/ 1968	Univ. of California (Berkeley); Ford Fdn.	For. Engineers after Degree (some returned home, some stayed)/Multi-Nat.	Engineering/ LT	Quest./345 of 676 surveyed	Simp. Anal., Res. Rev./ Soc., Psych.	Most satisfied with training; 31% from poor countries found training too theoretical; many stayed in US
416/ Vorapipatana/ 1967	Diss., Univ. of Utah	For. Stud., Ret. Home, For. Emp./ Thailand	Education/ LT (AID-sponsored)	Quest. (170 Ret. Stud., 75% response; 51 immediate supervisors, 82% response); Int. (25 grads., 15 superv.); Res. Rev. & Int. with AID officers in Thailand	Simp. Anal./ Soc., Psych.	Analysis of strengths and weaknesses of AID-sponsored training in education in US and uses of training by returned fellows

CHART 2.6 – NON-EMPIRICAL STUDIES: EFFECT ON FOREIGN STUDENTS OF STUDY ABROAD

Item No./ author(s)/ Date	Sponsor- ship	Represents Thinking of	Apparent Background of Author(s)	Geographic Emphasis	Student specialization (if specified)	Includes Reference to Empirical Research	Student attitudes or adjustment (general)	Academic Achievement or Relevance
								Key Ideas
274/Althen/ 1970	Priv./ Non-Gov.	Ind.	Psych.	Multi.	Multi-Disc.	Some	X Intercultural workshops advocated	
47/ Bochner/ 1972	Not Stated	Ind.	Chiefly Anthro.	Oceania	Multi-Disc.	Much	X Cultural Adaptation context used to describe for. stud. problems	
59/Canter/ 1967	Univ.	Ind.	Univ. Acad.	Multi.	Multi-Disc.	None		X The internationalization of U. S. education is advocated as a means of making that education more relevant for foreign students
393/Coelho/ 1973	Priv. Non-Gov.	Ind.	Psych.	W. Eur., E. Eur., Amer., M. S. Asia., E. Asia	Multi-Disc.	Some	X Describes two research proposals on mental health of foreign students and long-term consequences of exchange	
187/ Committee on Int'l. Exch. Policy/1966	Gov. Agy.	Group	Unclear	Multi.	Multi-Disc.	None		X Three problems faced by U. S. institutions admitting foreign students concern the extent curricula should be adjusted for them, the academic per- formance of foreign students vis-a-vis American students, and the degree of assistance to be given to foreign students on social and personal adjust- ment by the universities

Item No./ author(s)/ Date	Sponsor- ship	Represents Thinking of	Apparent Background of Author(s)	Geographic Emphasis	Student specialization (if specified)	Includes Reference to Empirical Research	Key Ideas: Student attitudes or adjustment (general)	Academic Achievement or Relevance
89/Cormack/ 1969	None	Ind.	Univ. Acad.	Multi.	Multi-Disc.	Much	X Research on adjustment should shift to inquiries on growth, identity, and alienation	
314/ de Sola Pool/ 1965	Priv., Non-Gov.	Ind.	Univ. Acad.	Multi.	Not specified	Much	X Reviews research on travellers' images of self and host country and host-countries' images of traveller	
162/ Harari/ 1970	None	Ind.	Unclear	Multi.	Multi-Disc.	Some		X More consultation recommended on development priorities of LDCs and on curriculum reform for foreign students
163/ Harari/ 1972	Priv., Non-Gov.	Ind.	NGO	Multi.	Multi-Disc.	Some		X There is a need for university departments to survey curriculum adequacy for foreign students
165/ Heath/ 1969	None	Ind.	Unclear	Multi.	Multi-Disc.	None	X Describes foreign student reactions to intercultural seminars run by the Lodestar International Student Center in Northern California	
178/ Holland/ 1956	Priv., Non-Gov.	Ind.	NGO	Multi.	Multi-Disc.	Much	X Students' goals do not match the goals of their sponsors	
3/Jacqz/ 1967	Priv. Non-Gov.	Group	NGO	S.S.Af.	Multi-Disc.	Some		X A major recommendation is that training for S. African foreign students should be in fields most needed in Africa
267/ Kaplan/ no date	Priv., Non-Gov.	Ind.	TOEFL, Univ.Acad.	Multi.	Multi-Disc.	Some		X A series of recommendations is made for improvement of international exchange, particularly in the adjustment and maximization of academic potential of foreign students

Item No./ author(s)/ Date	Sponsorship	Represents Thinking of	Apparent Background of Author(s)	Geographic Emphasis	Student specialization (if specified)	Includes Reference to Empirical Research	Student attitudes or adjustment (general)	Academic Achievement or Relevance	Key Ideas
211/Kelly/ 1966	Priv., Non-Gov.	Ind.	Horticulture	Multi.	Ag. Sci.	None		X	Horticulture training for foreign students is criticized as irrelevant for home-country use
216/King/ 1970	None	Ind.	Unclear	S. S. Af.	...	None	X	X	Examines the history of African students at US colleges; particular emphasis on Tuskegee Institute
227/Lewis/ 1967	None	Ind.	Ag. Econ.	Multi.	Ag. Econ.	None	X	X	The relevance of agricultural economics curricula is examined
239/Melby/ 1966	Gov. Agy.	Ind.	Unclear	Multi.	Multi-Disc.	None	X	X	Examines reasons why foreign students come to the US and their problems once here including relevance of education, discrimination, social problems
250/Mishler/ 1965	None	Ind.	Unclear	Multi.	Multi-Disc.	Some	X	X	Cultural differences, the foreign students' relationships to their home country and conflicting goals of sojourn (between student and sponsor) are examined
257/ Moravcsik/ 1973	None	Ind.	Univ. Acad.	Multi.	Phys. Sci., Bio. Sci.	None	X	X	Better pre-sojourn information, cooperation of the foreign student adviser with science faculty with experience in developing countries in planning curricula and other suggestions are made to improve the lot of foreign students in the natural sciences

Key Ideas

Item No./ author(s)/ Date	Sponsor- ship	Represents Thinking of	Apparent Background of Author(s)	Geographic Emphasis	Student specialization (if specified)	Includes Reference to Empirical Research	Student attitudes or adjustment (general)	Academic Achievement or Relevance	Key Ideas
277/NAFSA/ 1961	Priv., Non-Gov.	Group	NGO Univ. Acad., Univ. Ad.	Amer.	Business	Some	X		A report which examines ways of improving the Latin American business students' experience in US universities, using existing US university structures and resource limitations
290/ Niyekawa- Howard/ 1970	Univ.	Ind.	Anthro.	Multi.	Multi-Disc.	Much	X		Reviews literature on biculturality and suggests research on how bi-cultural individuals can make the best of their biculturality
311/ Pfnister/ 1972	Priv., Non-Gov.	Ind.	Univ. Acad.	Multi.	Multi-Disc.	Some		X	Finds that there is little research being conducted on foreign students abroad and that such research is needed
317/Prince/ 1973	Priv., Non-Gov.	Ind.	Psych.	Multi.	Mental Health	None	X		Differences in world views pose many problems for foreign students (particularly mental health workers)
268/ Putman/ 1965	Priv., Non-Gov.	Ind.	Univ. Ad. NGO	Multi.	Multi-Disc.	Some	X		Exchange participants (the student), home country, US government and US Institution are seen to have conflicting goals. The role and problems of the foreign student adv.ser are described

Key Ideas

Item No./ author(s)/ Date	Sponsorship	Represents Thinking of	Apparent Background of Author(s)	Geographic Emphasis	Student specialization (if specified)	Includes Reference to Empirical Research	Student attitudes or adjustment (general)	Academic Achievement or Relevance
281/Report of NAFSA Task Force on Intercultural Communications Workshop/1973	Priv., Non-Gov.	Group	Univ. Ad. Multi-Disc.	Multi.	Not specified	None	X	Intercultural workshops are found to be conducive to effective intercultural communication, realization of participants' goals and to the effective functioning of persons working with foreign students
404/Report on Meeting re Crucial Issues/1973	Gov. Agy.	Group	Univ. Ad., Univ. Acad., Govt. Ad., NGO	Multi.	Multi-Disc.	None		X — An important summary of the state of foreign student education. Includes proposals to make curricula and programs more relevant and to improve quality of orientation
325/ Riesman/ 1968	None	Ind.	Soc.	Amer.	Multi-Disc.	None	X	X — The theme of this group discussion of Brazilian students at Harvard was the social and economic changes in the US. Topics discussed included racial discrimination, anti-communism of North Americans, and the generation gap
278/ Rogers/ 1971	Priv., Non-Gov.	Group	NGO	Amer.	Engineering	None		X — The Latin American engineering student often finds his US training irrelevant to his needs
332/ Ronkin/ 1969	None	Ind.	Univ. Acad.	Multi.	Phys. & Bio. Sci.	None		X — Concerns problems of foreign predoctoral students in science in applying their education at home
335/ Sanders and Ward/ 1970	None	Ind.	Univ. Acad.	Multi.	Multi-Disc.	Some	X	Analysis offered on trainee reactions to short-term training programs

Key Ideas

Item No./ author(s)/ Date	Sponsorship	Represents Thinking of	Apparent Background of Author(s)	Geographic Emphasis	Student specialization (if specified)	Includes Reference to Empirical Research	Student attitudes or adjustment (general)	Academic Achievement or Relevance
337/ Schuler/ 1969	None	Ind.	Soc.	Multi.	Soc., Multi.	Some	X	X — Describes a research project on how well foreign students were being prepared for their work at home. Affirms a proposal to set up graduate training centers in various other cultures
345/ Shearer/ 1970	None	Ind.	Unclear	Amer.	Multi-Disc.	Some		X — A technical index and a structural index were devised by the author to gauge how patterns and trends of training in the US relate to development needs of other countries
350/ Singer/ 1972	None	Ind.	Pol. Sci.	Multi.	Multi-Disc.	Some		It is contended that foreign education creates perceptual and identity ties between the foreign students and the host nation, and thereby between developing nations' potential elites and the host nation
356/ Smith/ 1956	None	Ind.	Not specified, Anthro.	Multi.	...	None	X — Examines the conditions and processes by which one culture affects another	
363/ Spencer/ 1967	Univ.	Ind.	Univ. Acad.	Multi.	Multi-Disc.	Some	X — Examines (and speculates on) those factors which have a bearing on the effectiveness of foreign students on international educational assignments	

105

Key Ideas

Item No./ author(s)/ Date	Sponsor- ship	Represents Thinking of	Apparent Background of Author(s)	Geographic Emphasis	Student specialization (if specified)	Includes Reference to Empirical Research	Student attitudes or adjustment (general)	Academic Achievement or Relevance
367/ Stewart/ 1973	Priv., Non-Gov.	Ind.	Psych./ Cross-Cultural Studies	Multi.	Multi-Disc.	Some	X Empathy rather than sympathy is recommended in intercultural communication	
368/Stone/ 1969	None	Ind.	Univ. Acad. Phys. Sci.	Multi.	Sciences	None		X Supplementary training for science students from foreign countries is seen as necessary in the identification of research problems, maintenance skills, and basic administrative techniques

3

STRUCTURE,
ADMINISTRATION,
AND FINANCE

Overview

Material presented in the previous chapter was concerned with the general situation of the foreign student in the United States: reasons for coming, adjustment to American culture and the academic policies of American universities, academic achievement, and the relationship between adjustment and achievement. The principal focus of this literature, both empirical and non-empirical, was on the de facto presence of the foreign student in the United States and the problems and benefits deriving, or accruing, from that presence.

The literature reviewed in this chapter will encompass the response of institutions, organizations, and individuals to the needs and problems of foreign students. Consideration is given to what has been done for the foreign student, how it should be done, and the directions which research should take in the future.

The response to foreign student problems and needs comes from and is directed to several major groups of "players" in the international educational exchange process. First, there are the governmental players, principally of the U. S. government, who are concerned with immigration policies, economic impact of foreign student programs on the United States and other countries, educational and foreign policy impact of the programs, and other aspects of the exchange process. Second, there are the sponsors of foreign students. These players are of several types. They may be organizations which fund and administer fellowships for foreign students, or which administer fellowship funds for other organizations. Sponsors may be international agencies (UNESCO, UNDP, OAS), private foundations, religious organizations, or government agencies which are involved in training programs, for example, AID. The interests of sponsoring players from these governmental agencies often overlap or may conflict with those of other purely governmental players. Third, there are players from non-governmental organizations concerned with foreign student affairs. The Institute of International Education (IIE) and the National Association for Foreign Student Affairs (NAFSA) are the principal organizations in this category. The fourth group is composed of institutional players. These are faculty members, foreign student advisers and other administrative officials, and researchers, principally M.A. and Ph.D. candidates. Players from the world of business—corporate players—constitute a fifth group; the sixth and final response group consists of those key players in the exchange process, the foreign students themselves.

In simple quantitative terms, the response of the players to problems concerning structure, administration, and finance of foreign student programs is quite large: 161 items. Of this number, 35 items were empirical studies and 126 non-empirical. This category therefore ranked second to the category discussed in Chapter 1 which contained 204 items. One other quantitative comparison between these two categories might be pointed out here: studies of what happens to foreign students in the United States were predominantly empirical whereas those pertaining to structure, administration, and finance are primarily non-empirical. This reversal in the empirical/non-empirical ratios may be a function of the content involved but it is also suggestive of empirical research gaps and needs. The charts at the end of this chapter describe the 152 studies which are reviewed in this chapter in some detail.

Empirical Studies

In the following tables, we present a brief statistical summary of the literature reviewed in this section. Although 29 studies are considered, totals in the tables may be greater due to the appearance of some in more than one category. Further information on the studies is presented in Chart 3.1, p. 167.

The largest group of studies comes from the academic community, as either administrative, faculty, or graduate student research. Among the private organizations, NAFSA was the principal contributor.

Among the populations studied, those which received greatest attention were foreign students and "program administrators," chiefly foreign student advisers. American communities and university faculty members received little attention. Only four studies concentrated on more than one population.

TABLE 3.1

Empirical Studies: Auspices

Private Organizations	9
Dissertations	8
Inter-governmental Agencies	1
Universities	4
U. S. Government Agencies	3
Foundations	1
Master's Theses	1
None	2
Unclear	2

TABLE 3.2

Empirical Studies: Populations Surveyed

Program Administrators	12
Foreign Students	7
U. S. Faculty	3
U. S. Community	1
Foreign Employers	1
Other	6

TABLE 3.3

Empirical Studies: Geographic Emphasis

Multinational	24
Western Europe	2
The Americas	2
Middle South Asia	1
East Asia	1
South East Asia	1
Eastern Europe and USSR	1

Geographically, most studies looked at students from many nations. Few focused on any one geographical area, and only two studies concentrated specifically on several particular areas. North Africa and Sub-Saharan Africa were not selected for emphasis in this group of studies.

TABLE 3.4

Empirical Studies: Data Collection Method

Questionnaires	15
Structured Interviews	6
Research Review	4
Analytical Case Studies	2
Informal Interviews/ Observation	2
Records Analysis	2
Analysis of Economic Statistics	2
Historical	2
Theoretical	1
Not Stated	2

The data collection method most frequently used was the questionnaire. The number of respondents varied from 795 down to 10; seven studies had over 400 respondents, and only three had less than 100 respondents. The second most popular method was the interview, particularly the structured interview. A theoretical approach appeared in only one study and a historical emphasis was found in two studies. The analysis of economic statistics was central to two brief studies on the economic benefits of the foreign student presence to the income of two American states.

TABLE 3.5

Empirical Studies: Data Analysis Method

Simple Analysis	20
Case Analysis	10
Research Review	4
Sophisticated Analysis	3
Economic Analysis of Statistics	2

Data analysis was largely of the "simple analysis" type in which various responses and percentages are reported. More sophisticated techniques involving analysis of reliability, validity, variance, and other factors were found in only three studies. Case study analysis was found to various degrees in eleven studies, making this the second most popular method.

The subject matter of these empirical studies falls into three broad categories: (1) the selection, admissions, and related academic policies of institutions and organizations, including the problems of evaluating foreign student credentials; (2) the role, behavior, and effectiveness of foreign student advisers at American educational institutions; and (3) the extent and effectiveness of the services offered foreign students by various types of organizations and educational institutions involved in the exchange process. The cast of players in this last category includes personnel from international organizations, agencies of the U. S. government, four-year and graduate educational institutions, two-year junior and community colleges, and American communities.

There are several empirical studies which do not fit into the format outlined above: two short studies which attempt to justify in monetary terms the presence of foreign students in two American states, and one study in which the international market for higher education is examined theoretically and empirically. In addition, there is one study which traces the history of foreign students in American higher education. It seems appropriate to begin the review and analysis of the structure, administration, and finance of foreign student programs and services with this historical survey.

In her dissertation on A History of Foreign Students in American Higher Education from its Colonial Beginnings to the Present, Schulken (338/1968) identifies three major forces which contributed successively to the growth of the foreign student movement. First was the 19th century missionary movement, which, as the principal force bringing or sending foreign students to the United States, forged a close and lasting bond between the foreign mission and higher education.

During the close of the 19th century and especially in the first three decades of the 20th, private philanthropy emerged to supplement the efforts of the missionary movement, greatly enlarging the scope and purpose of the foreign student movement in American higher education. Finally, during the years just prior to World War II and continuing into the present, the U. S. government has played an increasingly active role in exchange programs and in foreign student activities.

The present is also marked, however, by increasing financial restrictions on the foreign student, particularly in the area of employment while studying in the United States. Administrators and others interested in foreign student affairs are looking for research that would justify the presence of foreign students in monetary terms and in particular to justify—educationally and otherwise—employment possibilities for foreign students. We have identified three small empirical studies on this topic.

Farmer and Renforth, in their study of "Foreign Students in Indiana: Our Intangible Exports" (133/1971), find that it is possible to make rough estimates of how much is earned from the sale of educational services to foreign students. In 1971 the state of Indiana was estimated to have received $17.6 million a year from having foreign students, $2 million of which came from the federal government through AID scholarships and other sources. Further "brain gains" were believed to accrue from the foreign students (approximately 10 percent) attending Indiana institutions who stay in Indiana and are employed there, and from those foreign students who help to broaden American students' horizons by also serving as instructors at Indiana universities. Despite these positive estimates, the authors found it impossible to put a cash value on the actual gain.

In a similar study, stimulated by the work of Farmer and Renforth, James Kent looked at "Foreign Students: An Economic Approach" (213/1973). This study focused on New York State and estimated that the foreign student "industry" trade ranked 18th among the state's exporters. The presence of foreign students was estimated to result in 6,571 jobs in New York State.

A third study, by Rives (331/1971), also examines the economics of educational exchange but on a much more international scale. A theoretical market framework is developed to examine production and exchange in higher education. This framework is extended to the international setting where demand factors, supply factors, and constraints on the international market are examined. Relationships among trade in education, human capital migration, and economic development are explored in the light of a theoretical framework and of reliable data relating to countries importing United States education.

The exploratory nature of the three studies above exemplifies the breadth of the research gap which exists concerning the economic impact, including the possible economic benefits, of the foreign student presence.

Selection, Admission, and Academic Policies

The selection, admission, and academic policies of various organizations and institutions, as they affect foreign students, form the subject matter of a major group of empirical studies.

The evaluation of foreign students' academic credentials is a problem that has received considerable attention. Two reports, both apparently based on the same study, were devoted to the feasibility of

establishing a central foreign student credential evaluation service
(FCES) under nongovernmental auspices. Frey (395/ 1969) reports
on a study in which admissions officers at 223 educational institutions
and representatives of 38 agencies were surveyed on the need for and
feasibility of setting up such a service. Participants replied that there
was a need, principally because the evaluative reports provided by the
FCES of the U. S. Office of Education were very general in nature. It
was proposed that the new FCES should supply data on the number of
years of students' formal education, quality of academic work in terms
of the countries' rating systems and of the U. S. grading scale, number of credit hours in all subjects, U. S. equivalence for foreign cer-
tificates and degrees, and other items. Dremuk (287/ 1969) also
reports on a study favorable to a new FCES, and includes a number
of policy recommendations concerning fees and billing arrangements
to universities and government agencies. It is suggested that federal
agencies might want to negotiate an annual contract for the evaluation
services while academic institutions would prefer arrangements based
on the size of foreign student enrollment. Institutions with a large enrollment might want an annual membership, whereas those with a
small foreign student enrollment could be charged a set fee for evaluation of specific foreign educational credentials.

In an attempt to provide useful information on the background
and structure of educational systems from which foreign students come,
NAFSA has sponsored a series of publications containing pertinent data
(264a-e). The information is primarily for the use of admissions officers and others involved in the evaluation of foreign student credentials, but should also be useful to comparative educators. One of these
studies, on The Admission and Academic Placement of Students from
Nordic Countries (264e/ 1974), while of the same general descriptive
nature as other publications in the series, also uses material gathered
by 22 American and Canadian admissions officers who visited Scandi-
navia in 1973 pertaining particularly to the grading systems of Norway,
Sweden, Denmark, Finland, and Iceland. (This series is discussed
more fully below, p. 127.)

A much more comprehensive and international analysis has been
published by UNESCO in Methods of Establishing Equivalences between
Degrees and Diplomas (188/ 1970), which examines six countries:
Czechoslovakia, France, the Federal Republic of Germany, U.S.S.R.,
the United Kingdom, and the United States. In addition to the description of equivalency practices in these countries, three major approaches for establishing equivalences are noted. First, there is the
multilateral approach, which lends itself to groups of countries with
related university and general cultural equivalences. The major disadvantage of this arrangement is that it is often difficult to find a common measure of the qualifications agreeable to all concerned. A

bilateral approach has the advantage of making the process of evaluation much easier but usually involves prolonged negotiations and much preparatory work. The third arrangement—a unilateral approach—takes two forms. In the first, competent authorities (for example, the universities) decide each individual case on its merits; in the second, the recognition of equivalences is standardized to the extent that lists are drawn up of acceptable foreign qualifications. This second method has the advantage of facilitating the work of authorities responsible for granting recognition but has the drawback of making the authorities less willing to enter into generalized commitments. The first form has the drawback that applicants do not know in advance whether their qualifications will be recognized, but has the advantage of flexibility.

Several studies focus specifically on the selection and admission criteria for foreign students in American higher aducation institutions. A master's thesis by Feinberg (135/ 1967) studies students of journalism in American universities and colleges. The admissions decision was found to be based on a wide variety of factors: secondary school records, test scores, English proficiency, financial backing, letters of recommendations, samples of writing, etc., although evaluation of foreign credentials was a perennial problem. A number of approaches had been developed to accommodate the foreign student lacking knowledge of the American language and culture: the University of Wisconsin Department of Agricultural Journalism had bilingual faculty members, permitting foreign students to write in their native language; nondegree programs, split-degree programs permitting the student to complete the degree in the home country, and professional seminars were some of the other approaches.

In a considerably broader study, Deluga (107/ 1970) examined the selection procedures for foreign students at the undergraduate level in 631 institutions throughout the United States. From his data he draws several interesting conclusions. Admissions officers and foreign student advisers, for the most part, were found to have insufficient backgrounds in comparative education to effectively evaluate credentials. Very few institutions were providing English for foreign students as part of their curriculum. It was also noted that one of the basic difficulties underlying America's commitment to international educational exchange is the diversity of the institutions of higher learning, making it impossible to develop a clear-cut controllable series of programs across the country. Deluga's conclusions also supported the studies discussed above that showed admissions officers favoring a central clearinghouse for the evaluation of foreign student credentials.

An Inquiry into Departmental Policies and Practices in Relation to the Graduate Education of Foreign Students (284/ 1972), a NAFSA study, revealed that most American universities do not have specific institutional and departmental policies regarding foreign student admissions. Admissions decisions were found to be made almost exclusively by departments and, while quotas are rarely stated, some departments do impose upper limits. It was recommended that the establishment of departmental quotas as a part of reasoned policy was preferable to an informal restriction based on expediency.

Only one study focused exclusively on the subject of grading patterns. Paraskevopoulous and Dremuk (304/ 1969) questioned faculty at the University of Illinois regarding differences in grading procedures and course requirements for foreign and domestic students. Findings of the study showed that 96 percent of the faculty expected foreign students to meet the same course requirements as Americans and 90 percent said their grading standards were the same for foreign and American students. The NAFSA study discussed above also found that university departments expect the same level of performance from foreign and American students. In addition, it found that foreign students perform as well academically as American students and receive degrees in the same amount of time.

The selection, admissions, and grading policies examined in the studies above refer almost exclusively to four-year and graduate institutions. There are several studies, however, which take note of such policies at the community or junior college level. Matthewson, in a national survey of international students and programs in community junior colleges in the United States (272/ 1968), discovered that 67 percent of the 410 colleges surveyed had foreign students and few of these had limitations on admissions or quotas. Hickey (174/ 1967), in a survey of foreign student admissions procedures in Kansas and Nebraska junior colleges, found that there were no standardized admissions procedures among the surveyed colleges and only three of the institutions required tests of English as a foreign language. Overseas interview services were not well-utilized by these schools. A small study of foreign student admissions at California junior colleges by Elliott (130/ 1969) also revealed a wide variance in policies. There was no organized effort to establish common policies or to exchange admission information with other schools. Recommendations of this study included the admission of transfer students to the junior colleges on a controlled-quota basis, simplification of admissions procedures by limiting proof of financial responsibility to the declaration by the student on the Certificate of Eligibility, and by limiting foreign student enrollment to two percent of the full-time enrollment of each institution.

The Foreign Student Adviser

The functions, behavior, and effectiveness of foreign student advisers form a second major grouping among the empirical studies.

An important early study on the status of foreign student advising was
published by Higbee in 1961 (175). This research remains one of the
most thorough, both substantively and methodologically, of the studies
on this subject. Among its findings was that the greater the institutional
involvement in international education, the greater the clarity of the
foreign student adviser's role. But in a majority of the institutions surveyed, the foreign student adviser's function was not given high-level
academic or administrative authority. The general recommendations
of the study continue to be relevant today: (1) top institutional officials
should be continuously apprised of the demand for an international dimension in education; (2) U. S. institutions of higher education should
view acceptance of foreign students as a mutually beneficial exchange
of knowledge; (3) there is an urgent need for English-language centers
in the United States; (4) information about American education must be
made more readily available to prospective foreign students before
they leave their home countries; (5) more attention should be accorded
the need of foreign students for academic advice; (6) the foreign student adviser must be an integral part of an international activity team
at the institution.   ￼

Several more recent studies expand on the subject matter of
Higbee's research. Miller, in a 1968 dissertation (249), examines the
perceptions of foreign student advisers for those aspects of their on-
the-job behavior which they consider significant in facilitating the academic progress and/ or personal development of the foreign students at
their institutions. Sixteen critical areas were identified including,
among others, the administration of the foreign student adviser's office, planning and program development, academic and financial guidance programs, immigration, personal counseling, and referral
services. Of considerable interest was the secondary purpose of the
study: to determine which functions are performed most effectively
and which are performed least effectively by foreign student advisers.
The advisers surveyed perceived themselves as working more effectively with people, and in particular, with non-university people, than
in areas concerning ideas, programs, or organizational structures.
They saw themselves as working least effectively in the academic advising of foreign students.

Two other studies consider the effectiveness of foreign student
advising. A small study by Irvine (191/ 1968) among the foreign students at Sacramento State College determined that the students had
unrealistic expectations of what their advisers could do for them and
recommended that advisers improve communication with their students.

A considerably more ambitious study by Lockett (228/ 1970) is
one of the few that makes use of data collected by the American University Development Education and Training Research Institute (DETRI)
as a part of the Agency for International Development Office of Inter-

national Training Exit Interview Project. (See Ch. 2, p. 44.) She found that foreign student advisers were judged to be effective in their role by the large majority of the foreign students interviewed. A major aspect of the usefulness of the foreign student advisers was their availability to the foreign students. The geographic origins of the foreign students did not seem to determine whether or not they talked with the foreign student adviser.

Several studies consider the role and effectiveness of foreign student advisers at junior and community colleges. Matthewson (272/ 1968) and Grafton, who reports on the study by Matthewson (153/ 1970), observe that, in a survey of approximately 70 percent of the nation's junior and community colleges, few reported special procedures of advisement, orientation, and admission for foreign students. In a study of foreign student admissions procedures in Kansas and Nebraska junior colleges, Hickey (174/ 1967) found that there were no full-time foreign student advisers in the 18 institutions surveyed. The foreign student adviser was usually a combination of things: teacher/ adviser, registrar/ adviser, or administrator/ adviser.

The observations of Matthewson, Grafton, and Hickey were supported by Marsh (234/ 1972) in a dissertation on foreign student advisers in community colleges in the State of Washington, where the "typical" adviser is a counselor with a master's degree who works with foreign students one-quarter time or less. The adviser tended to spend less than five years in the position, for which he or she had little preparation. The community college foreign student adviser thus had a role different from that of an adviser in a four-year institution. More likely to be trained as a counselor, the community college adviser could bring more skill to the advisory aspect of the job, but since these advisers do not concentrate their professional time in the role, they are in need of assistance to develop required technical expertise.

The studies on the role and effectiveness of foreign student advisers are somewhat mixed in their conclusions. There is evidence that, on the whole, advisers are effective in their role. Advisers at two-year junior and community colleges, however, tended to receive considerable criticism. At all institutions, there are limitations on the role of the foreign student adviser, particularly of time, money, and personnel. At a mini-conference of foreign student advisers from educational institutions in Pittsburgh and the surrounding area, held in conjunction with this evaluative study, the feeling was expressed that the adviser deals too often in "crisis situations." The pressure of the foreign student adviser's position, often caused by lack of personnel, may have much to do with the blunt and startling recommendation in Irvine's study that "students need to have their expectations lowered and be taught to seek out more help in spite of themselves."

Programs and Services

The third major group of studies in the Structure, Administration, and Finance category concerns the extent and general effectiveness of programs and services for the foreign student and the future needs for such programs and services. Five studies in this group were conducted under the auspices of international organizations and are not specifically concerned with students in the United States. They are discussed in Chapters 4 and 6.

The effectiveness of the U. S. government and other organizations at the national level in the implementation of educational and cultural exchange programs is the focus of a report from the Bureau of Educational and Cultural Affairs of the Department of State (399/ 1967) which summarizes 40 evaluation studies dating from 1951 to 1965. Each summary includes the purpose, design, conclusions, and recommendations of the evaluation. In-depth interviews and questionnaire surveys were used to obtain information on a wide variety of topics but the principal concerns were the participants' attitude changes as a result of their exchange programs, professional and social consequences of the experience, and general assessments of the problems the participants encountered.

Predeparture orientation for foreign students is a concern of government and private agencies as well as universities and colleges. A survey of facilities and programs for predeparture orientation in three Latin American countries—Mexico, Chile, and Colombia—was conducted by Bridgers and Hall for the National Association for Foreign Student Affairs (266/n.d.). It was found that U. S. government-sponsored students generally received adequate predeparture orientation but students sponsored by foundations, private agencies, or foreign governments may or may not receive adequate predeparture orientation depending on the degree of concern for the grantees' needs and the resources available. Non-sponsored students were generally not included in any of the programs surveyed. The informational materials available, mostly USIS publications, were frequently inadequate and out-of-date. It was suggested that a Council on In-Country Orientation be created in NAFSA to plan, in cooperation with local organizations and individuals, pilot projects of predeparture orientation in the three countries.

At a purely institutional level, a NAFSA survey of facilities (280/ 1973), again for Latin American students, in 481 American colleges and universities, presented raw data on the enrollment of Latin American students as of June 1971, TOEFL requirements, presence or absence of special English programs, financial aid, social organizations, and the names of campus contact persons.

Two brief studies focus specially on the housing of foreign students. Both studies were done by Coan at the University of Kansas (71/

1966; 72/1969). Similar studies probably exist for other campuses.
The Kansas studies showed that while students were fairly satisfied
with their housing, more must be done to make appropriate housing
available to older, graduate-level students. Other findings were that
most foreign students lived off-campus, that much off-campus housing
was inferior in quality and that many students had problems with legal
commitments.

The Inquiry into Departmental Policies and Practices in Relation
to the Graduate Education of Foreign Students (284/1972) conducted by
NAFSA at 12 universities reaches a number of conclusions on the
effectiveness of foreign student programs and services. It was found,
first, that most of the universities and departments surveyed did not
have functional policies supporting involvement in international education and foreign student enrollment. Most institutions, however, believe that existing programs have demonstrated their commitment to
international education, and departments could cite the benefits of the
foreign student presence: the addition of different perspectives, enhancement of the department's and the school's international reputation, and intercultural interchange and experience. A review of the
services and programs offered at the institutions showed that effective
cooperation existed between foreign student advisers and department
administrators but in some cases it was questioned as to whether faculty in general were aware of the cooperation. Departments did not
provide special orientation and counseling services, did not tend to accommodate foreign students' special needs and problems (except to
adjust course loads in initial semesters when necessary), and did not
offer courses designed to help foreign students understand how training could be transferred to their home countries. Doctoral candidates
were not encouraged to write dissertations in absentia on topics relevant to their home countries though permission to do so was obtainable
from most departments. Nor did departments maintain contact with
foreign alumni to determine the usefulness of U. S. education. In light
of these conclusions, the NAFSA study recommended additional research on the kind and quality of education received by foreign students,
follow-up after return, and foreign student perceptions as to the relevance (economically, socially, politically, and personally) of U. S.
education.

Several studies focus specifically on programs and services for
foreign students at two-year junior and community colleges. The
Matthewson study cited above (272/1968) found that of 410 junior colleges, 67 percent had foreign students but few had special programs,
offices, or staff for them. Only 23 percent gave special English
courses, and 18 percent had special organizations for foreign students.

A dissertation by Elliott (129/1967) identified major areas of
concern in the foreign student programs of several California public

junior colleges: the need to establish philosophical bases for supporting foreign student programs, to provide an adequate instruction program for foreign students, and to maintain effective foreign student personnel services.

Similar concerns are echoed in a 1970 dissertation study by Bloom on <u>Students from Other Lands in the Two Year College</u> (43). It found few support services exist for foreign students after acceptance at two-year colleges. Again, it was recommended that each college must define its international goals and investigate what is now being done to achieve them. It was also seen as imperative that the college understand a student's long-range educational goal. Rarely has the associate of arts degree been the ultimate goal for the majority of students. Most often, these students intend to continue in a four-year college for a baccalaureate and not uncommonly expect to engage in graduate study. The problems of transfer, and the course requirements for such transfer, must therefore be understood at the very beginning of the foreign student's college career. A consortium concept of several two-year colleges was suggested as an excellent means of better serving foreign students.

As noted earlier, only one empirical study deals with community services for foreign students. This study, by Kirstein (217/1971) was based on a very small questionnaire response (10). It concluded that the structure of community services, at least in the large metropolitan areas emphasized in the study, was for the most part ineffective. Specifically, most community services suffer from lack of coordination, poor communication with students and/or sponsoring agencies, and inadequate financing.

Conclusion

It is difficult to summarize the conclusions of the studies on the extent and effectiveness of foreign student programs and services due to the great variation in the type and quality of the studies. However, the repeated emphasis on some concerns prompts several observations.

First, poor communication among all the players—the foreign students, their advisers, institutions, home governments, and sponsoring agencies—is a constantly recurring theme. As one means of improving communication and coordination, the research particularly emphasizes the need for educational institutions, departments, and other organizations to develop clear policies supporting international education.

A second observation deriving from these studies is that while many programs and services are effective, others exhibit strong negative aspects. Many institutions and organizations, nominally dedicated to international education, are over-extended when it comes to providing effective support for foreign students; two-year junior and community colleges apparently provide little in the way of such support. Predeparture orientation for all students needs much more attention, with particular emphasis on non-sponsored students.

Admission and the evaluation of credentials of foreign students continue to be problems. Many universities and departments simply do not have any policy regarding foreign student admissions. There apparently is a desire and a need for a non-governmental credential evaluation board composed of persons well-trained in such evaluation.

The future directions of research on the structure, administration, and finance of foreign student programs and services will be examined following an analysis of the non-empirical literature and its contributions in this area.

Non-Empirical Studies

In this section we shall consider 123 non-empirical articles, reports, studies, and guides which represent the response of various players in the international educational exchange process to foreign student needs and services. These items are primarily descriptive, or policy oriented, discussing the type and nature of foreign student services, their deficiencies, and ways in which they can be improved. In the tables below we offer brief statistical summaries of these studies; further details will be found in Chart 3.2, p. 174. Totals may be greater than 123 due to the inclusion of some studies in more than one category.

TABLE 3.6

Non-Empirical Studies: Auspices

Private Organizations	52
Government Agencies	31
Intergovernmental Agencies	4
Universities	5
Foundations	3
Dissertations	1
None	34
Unclear	2

TABLE 3.7

Non-Empirical Studies: Geographical Emphasis

Multinational	87
Americas	15
Sub-Saharan Africa	10
East Asia	6
North Africa	4
Eastern Europe and USSR	4
Middle South Asia	3
Southeast Asia	3
Oceania	1
Western Europe	1

As was the case with the empirical studies, most were conducted under the auspices of private organizations. Government agencies, however, which produced only three empirical studies, here account for 31. The amount of non-empirical literature from universities is small, and foundations produced only three items—a response similar to that seen among the empirical studies (one study).

The geographical emphasis of a very large proportion of the non-empirical literature was multinational, as was the case with the empirical studies. The specific geographical area receiving most attention in the non-empirical literature was the "Americas" (15 items), a category which includes Latin America, the Caribbean countries, and Canada. The Asian countries accounted for 12 items (Middle South Asia, East Asia, and Southeast Asia), and Africa 14 (North Africa and Sub-Saharan Africa). Only one non-empirical item was concerned with

TABLE 3.8

Non-Empirical Studies: Categories of Literature

Nature of Foreign Student Programs and Services	49
Broad Overviews	24
Guides	15
Selection and Admission	9
English Training and Proficiency	9
Foreign Student Advisers	8
International Relations and Foreign Students	5
Response of the Business World	4

Oceania (there were no empirical studies receiving this geographical emphasis) which, while perhaps regrettable, is consistent with the small number of foreign students studying in the United States from this area—only one percent of the total foreign student population as reported in Open Doors, 1973.

In 61 of the non-empirical items, no reference was made to any empirical research. Fifty-five items referred to some empirical research but it should be noted that the emphasis placed on those references varied in terms of quality and quantity. Only seven items could be classified as having "much" reference to empirical research.

There are four major classifications of non-empirical literature, and we shall discuss them in the following order. First there are "guides" addressed to specific audiences, principally foreign students and foreign student advisers. Second, there is a large body of literature concerning specific problems in the structure, administration, and finance of foreign student programs and services. These problems fall into the following categories: (1) selection, admission, and related academic policies and practices of institutions and organizations, (2) English-language proficiency, (3) foreign-student advisers and their work, (4) the nature of foreign student programs and services. The third major classification is literature focusing on the relationships between educational exchange and international relations; the fourth consists of reports, articles, and studies which examine the exchange process in broad overview form, covering most of the above topics and outlining policies and practices, strengths and weaknesses, future directions, and research needs.

Guides

Fifteen publications stand apart from the rest of the non-empirical literature by virtue of their "self-help" orientation. The guides are directed toward several audiences. Eight are for the use of foreign student advisers; two are specifically for foreign students. One is a counseling handbook for the Office of International Training of the Agency for International Development. The remainder are written for broader audiences. There are several other bibliographies and reports, principally about selection and admission of foreign students, that are somewhat similar to these guides. They are discussed below, p. 127.

Of the eight guides for foreign student advisers, seven are part of the Guidelines series published by NAFSA. These are concise booklets which recommend policy and practices for selection and admission, English proficiency, housing, and orientation for foreign students, and discuss the responsibilities and ethical standards of foreign student advisers in their daily work. As with other NAFSA publications, the Guidelines address the problems of larger educational institutions;

there is a need for better recognition in this literature of the problems of the smaller school or the school with a small foreign student enrollment.

Guidelines: Responsibilities and Standards in Work with Foreign Students (265e/n.d.) is concerned with the maintenance of the highest professional and ehtical standards by every person dealing with foreign students. Responsibilities and standards are listed for foreign student advisers, admissions officers, teachers of English as a foreign language, community program workers, and others. The statement of standards was prepared and approved by the NAFSA Committee on Professional Development and the NAFSA Board of Directors in October 1970.

Three others in this series, Academic and Personal Advising (265b/1966) (also discussed below, p. 133), Selection and Admission of Foreign Students (265a/1966), and Housing of Foreign Students (265d/1967), discuss in considerable detail these specialized aspects of the foreign student adviser's job. The second is also of interest to admissions officers as it presents a model of the procedure for admitting foreign students.

Two Guidelines focus on American/foreign student relationships. The first, published in 1967 (265c), states that since it is an underlying assumption of any institution in enrolling foreign students that contact between U. S. and foreign students is beneficial, institutional programming, initiated by the foreign student adviser, should create opportunities for such relationships. Recommendations include combining and overlapping orientation for American and foreign students, encouraging existing campus groups to develop an international dimension and providing for foreign student participation in housing, student union, cafeterias, and classrooms. Similar suggestions appear in a 1972 Guideline (265g). A campus team approach is emphasized in order to aid the foreign student and the foreign student adviser. Students, faculty and others should be enlisted in a campaign to help foreign students adjust to American community and campus life. It is repeatedly stated that the foreign student adviser cannot act alone but must be a catalyst for others.

English-language proficiency and training is the subject of one Guidelines publication from NAFSA and a catalog from the Institute of International Education. Guidelines: English Language Proficiency (265f/1971) notes that English proficiency as a criterion of admission is seldom used consistently and if it were, only students with very high levels of proficiency would be admitted from other countries. According to several surveys, between 60 and 70 percent of the foreign students admitted in any given year need additional training in English. Regional English-language training centers are proposed as a way to achieve efficiency and lower cost in the operation of such programs. The catalog of the Institute of International Education on English Language and Orientation Programs in the United States (186/ 1973) lists and briefly describes 121 English-language programs, orientation programs with English-language training, and special opportunity programs at 108 institutions. In addition, this booklet lists 313 English language courses offered at 312 institutions, and degree and certificate programs in Teaching English as a Foreign Language at 54 institutions.

Two guides are specifically for the use of the foreign students. The first, Financial Planning for Study in the United States: A Guide for Students from Other Countries, by Maria Sasnett (78/ 1967), provides students with information on the costs of study in the United States, what responsibilities they will be expected to assume in meeting these costs, what help may be available from other sources, and how they should plan for the financial aspect of their visit to the United States. The second is The Two Year College in the United States: A Guide for Foreign Students (181). Published in 1967, this booklet presents information about junior colleges—their general nature, instructional methods, teachers, calendars, costs, admission requirements, and visa requirements—and provides a list of accredited junior colleges. This guide was published by the Institute of International Education, which also publishes periodically a larger Handbook on U. S. Study for Foreign Nationals (R47/ 1973).

The Counseling Handbook (13/ 1973) of the Office of International Training of AID summarizes the philosophy, functions, and services of the counseling staff of that agency. The counseling function is performed by professionals and consultants who provide a chain of supporting guidance to AID trainees. The principal categories of problems encountered by the counseling staff are inter-cultural adjustment problems, basic personality problems, and problems growing out of the mechanisms of the training programs themselves.

Three handbooks are broader in scope than those discussed above. The most recent of these is the Guide for the Education of Foreign Students by Benson and Kovach (283/ 1974). It offers succinct data for the foreign student, universities, sponsoring agencies, foreign governments, and other players in the international exchange process in a checklist format with the international exchange process divided into ten stages: planning and selection, preadmission, admission, notification, postadmission and pre-arrival, arrival and pre-enrollment, enrollment and first term, sojourn, pre-departure and re-entry, and follow-up, evaluation, and continuing education. The actions, admittedly ideal, of each of the parties involved in the exchange experience are outlined for each stage.

The Fact Sheet on the International Educational Exchange Program: 1946-1966 (397) briefly describes the principal features of the Department of State's efforts in international educational exchange as seen in

1966. The description includes a summary of the legislation which initiated the Exchange Program, a statement of purpose, financial organization, history, and philosophy.

A large number of recent programs in foreign student education are described in a 1970 NAFSA publication on Innovations and New Programs of Special Interest in Foreign Student Education: A Catalogue (275). The editor notes a trend toward greater foreign student participation in campus decisions. Other new directions include a view of foreign students as a resource in high schools, in-country and pre-departure orientation programs, group counseling, intercultural communications and human-relations training, U.S. business/ foreign student programs, and community action and service.

A final guide could serve a multiple audience, but focuses on a specific group of players. The Manual for Programs for Foreign Wives (282/ 1973), a NAFSA publication, discusses the needs of foreign student wives and the kinds of programs which may give foreign wives the attention and help they need. The pamphlet recommends that programs for foreign wives are best organized by a core of American wives who find out about existing services, maintain contacts with foreign student advisers or their counterparts, and plan an effective program which meets regularly and tackles one problem at a time.

The guides surveyed represent a most useful, direct-action type of literature on foreign student education. More are needed, focusing on other problems or other stages of the exchange process. Because of their format, one does not expect these guides to provide in-depth information on the various topics, and they do not. Several of those reviewed, however, are now out-of-date, and could be revised to incorporate new material gleaned from the empirical research. Such revisions and new guides could be more substantial in content without detracting from the simplicity of the format. Larger bibliographies, where appropriate, could be a useful addition, providing a valuable tool for the reading audiences.

Studies of Specific Problems

The second major category consists of studies devoted to specific problems in foreign student programs and services: selection and admission, English-language training and proficiency, foreign student advisers and their work, the programs and services of various agencies and organizations, and the response of business to the needs and problems of international exchange.

Selection, Admission, and Related Academic Policies

Nine studies focus on selection, admission, the evaluation of academic credentials, and the academic performance of foreign students.

Additional related information comes from some of the broad overviews and other literature. Five of the nine studies are reports of workshops sponsored by NAFSA and the American Association of Collegiate Registrars and Admissions Officers (AACRAO) on the admission, placement, and educational credentials of students from different world areas. One publication is basically a bibliography of reference materials on evaluating foreign student credentials. Two studies on selection and admission were published by the no-longer-existing Education and World Affairs (EWA). Three of the nine items appeared in 1966 and the most recent in 1974.

The five workshop reports from NAFSA and AACRAO concern the admission and academic placement of students from the Federal Republic of Germany, Asia, Latin America, the Caribbean, and Pacific-Asia. Because they provide valuable material on the historical background and contemporary practices of educational systems in a number of countries, the reports are useful resources not only for admissions officers and others interested in international exchange, but for comparative educators as well.

The evaluation of education credentials of students from India, Japan, the Philippines, and Taiwan is the subject of The Evaluation of Asian Educational Credentials: A Workshop Report (264a/1966). The workshop was held in late 1965, making it the earliest of those reviewed here. The report contains overviews of the four educational systems and information concerning quality factors, the grading system, admission and placement practices, and makes recommendations regarding admission, placement, and credentials to U.S. colleges and universities. The material contained in this report is less comprehensive than that of the later reports.

The Admission and Placement of Students from the Pacific-Asia Area (264b/n.d.) was discussed at a 1969 workshop. Countries discussed include Hong Kong, Malaysia, Pakistan, Singapore, Australia, New Zealand, Ceylon, Okinawa, the "Pacific Islands," and India. Again, an overview of the historical and cultural background of each country is given as well as considerable information on each education system. Workshop participants recommended that complete files on each applicant be compiled before deciding on admission or placement, that TOEFL be used, and that eligibility for the home university system be used as a criterion for admission. Clues for evaluating the quality of applicants included years of formal schooling, type of degree completed, examination and test results, and quality of the references. Suggested indicators for the evaluation of an institution were its age, curricula, library facilities, quantity and quality of the faculty, admissions requirements, and the grading system.

The only NAFSA/AACRAO report reviewed which focuses on a single country is the result of The German-American Conference on

Educational Exchange (279) held in 1972. The report is almost totally
devoted to an extensive description of the history and structure of the
educational system of the Federal Republic of Germany. All levels of
German education are described and an outline is provided of the equivalences between degrees awarded in Germany and the United States.
A particularly useful glossary of German academic terms and numerous curriculum outlines for many educational areas and levels add to
the value of this report.

The educational systems of Argentina, Chile, Ecuador, and Peru
were examined in a 1970 workshop on The Admission and Academic
Placement of Students from Selected Countries of Latin America (264c/
n.d.). General recommendations of the workshop participants were that
TOEFL be given to all applicants and that eligibility for higher education in the student's own country might not be a useful criterion for
admission to a United States institution because of the high degree of
selectivity for the few places in the higher education systems in the four
countries. This recommendation is in direct conflict with that made by
the workshop on the Pacific-Asia countries, indicating a wide difference
in educational policies of the countries considered. It was also suggested in the Latin American report that advanced standing be granted only
after arrival, if at all, and that the "open-door admissions policies of
junior colleges, while entirely valid for native students, should not be
applied to non-immigrant foreign students." A brief annex to the report
discusses Spanish-language tests developed in Puerto Rico which are
more reliable and valid for testing academic aptitude and achievement
than the standard English-language tests. This report is carefully prepared and contains much valuable material.

The last and most recent of the NAFSA/AACRAO reports to be
surveyed here is on The Admission and Academic Placement of Students
from the Caribbean (264d/n.d.). The report is based on a workshop
held in late 1972 and contains historical and educational background
material for Cuba, the Dominican Republic, the French West Indies,
Haiti, Puerto Rico, the U.S. Virgin Islands, and the countries employing the British pattern of education in the Caribbean.

One other report in this series, on The Admission and Academic
Placement of Students from Nordic Countries (264e), based on a 1973
study, has been reviewed as empirical research because of the data-
gathering approach used by the participants (see p. 113). In other respects, this report resembles others in the series both in format and
content.

In addition to this NAFSA/AACRAO series, four other publications
examine problems of selection and academic placement. One is a bibliography (21/1971) edited by Robert Hefling and issued by AACRAO containing references used by the Academic Advisory Staff of AID's Office
of International Training in analyzing and interpreting academic creden-

tials of AID participants from various contries. The other three discuss the issues in greater detail.

Barrientos and Schufletowski, in their article on "The Questionable Foreign Student" (34/1968), argue that for academic and political reasons, American institutions should do all they can to help the best foreign students to gain entry into this country and to create favorable conditions for them once they are enrolled in schools. They recommend that academic permissiveness, which encourages a double standard, be eschewed, that more selective admissions policies be enforced, and that foreign student offices be created which are committed to and competent in high-level, cross-cultural theory and practice as well as guidance and counseling.

One suggestion intended to help U.S. colleges and universities in coping effectively with the expanding number of applications from foreign students is the creation of a world-wide network of Counseling, Evaluating, and Testing Centers (CETCs). This proposal, made in a publication of Education and World Affairs on The Overseas Selection of Foreign Students (300/1966), argues that such centers could both assist American institutions in the selection of qualified foreign students and enable foreign students, both sponsored and unsponsored, to obtain accurate information on U.S. universities, thus facilitating their choice of program.

The need for more reliable information on prospective students is again discussed in an Education and World Affairs Study Committee article on "The Foreign Student: Whom Shall We Welcome?" (123/1966). The Committee observed that foreign student policies followed by U.S. colleges and universities were ambiguous and conflicting. Selection and admissions policies, in particular, should be formulated in congruence with the purposes of the institution, which should also consider whether admissions policies should be tied to the manpower policies of the developing countries, and whether foreign students are in danger of becoming permanently alienated from their native culture. Graduate schools must consider whether the specialized training they offer is relevant to the professional needs of the student upon return home. Finally, the Committee finds it especially urgent that all concerned agencies and institutions accept greater responsibility for unsponsored students.

The need for carefully developed institutional policy on foreign student admissions has been expressed in a number of other publications which look at the international educational exchange process in broader perspective. Forest Moore, in an article on "International Education in the Seventies: Revolution or Turmoil on the Campus" (253/1970), suggests that normal admissions documents be replaced with a policy statement that students unable to meet academic requirements will be dropped. A 1971 colloquium on The Foreign Student: Priorities for

Research and Action (430) urgently recommends development of national and institutional rationales for the presence of foreign students. Edward Carpenter, examining the "Roles of the Foreign Student Adviser" (62/ 1969), noted that the adviser's effectiveness depends on institutional policy which is too often non-existent. The result is that policy is set by the foreign student adviser with little conscious, rational determination beforehand.

The broad overview literature contains several other observations on the selection and admissions process. Francis Colligan, writing in 1963 on The College, the University, and the Foreign Student (82), feels that admissions should be flexible enough to admit students from developing countries whose objectives can be served by the institution even when their academic backgrounds are not equal to those of students from more advanced nations. Colligan also believes that English-language competence should not be a decisive criterion for admission— an observation echoed in several of the publications on English-language proficiency and training. Participants in a 1967 colloquium on the University, Government, and the Foreign Graduate Student (79/ 1969) agreed that a double standard (between American and foreign students) on admissions and grading is an unacceptable and inequitable institutional practice. It was also suggested that institutions aim at a "critical mass" of five to ten percent foreign students. Forest Moore, cited above, also believes in minimum quotas of foreign students, specifically five percent of the undergraduates and 25 percent of the graduates. Finally, the idea of Counseling, Evaluation and Testing Centers, noted earlier, is discussed in several broader publications discussed below, Speakman (361/ 1966), Sanders and Ward (335/ 1970), and the U.S. Advisory Commission (390c/ 1964).

English Training and Proficiency

Nine publications focus on English-language training and proficiency. Two of these are guides discussed previously (see pp. 124-25) All were published between 1968 and 1973.

A dissertation by Darian, A History of the Teaching of English as a Foreign Language in American Colleges and Universities, 1880-1965 (97/ 1968), shows that while the development of aural-oral mastery has always been the goal of such teaching, the aural-oral method is used less often than writing in present-day methodologies, at least at the intermediate and advanced levels. Further analysis of grammar texts reveals a lack of contextual material, i.e., presentation of grammar patterns in material of larger-than-sentence length.

An article which also uses a generally historical approach is Jameson and Malcolm's "TOEFL—The Developing Years" (193/ 1972-73) The purpose of the test is to serve both the admissions process and

placement of foreign students in intensive English courses by measuring
the foreign applicant's ability in five areas of English proficiency: listening and reading comprehension, vocabulary, grammar, and writing
ability. The authors emphasize the the test is not to be considered
an aptitude test or a predictor of academic success.

Robert Kaplan, in an address on "The Foreign Student and His
English Language Proficiency" (208/1968), agrees with the argument
advanced above that English-language proficiency should not be made
a college entrance requirement for foreign students (see p. 130). He
also believes, however, that institutions should not admit foreign students with inadequate English-language comprehension unless they are
prepared to support a training program to raise the language ability
of such students to the point where they gain full benefit from their
studies. Since it would be difficult for every U.S. institution to provide such instruction, Kaplan suggests regional centers or consortia
similar to those proposed in Guidelines: English Language Proficiency
(see p. 124). Both Kaplan and the Guidelines publication recommend
TOEFL as an evaluative measure, finding it clearly superior to other
English-language tests, most of which are fragmentary and unvalidated.

Two publications explore the actual instruction given in courses
on English as a Second Language. The first, Plaister's Reading Instru-
tion for College Level Foreign Students (313/1968), offers a very brief
description of the English Language Institute reading courses at the
University of Hawaii. The courses stress elimination of poor reading
habits, training in reading by structures, timed reading exercises,
lectures on important cultural concepts, and vocabulary development
using programmed texts. The second publication, by Arapoff, examines
Discover and Transform: A Method of Teaching Writing to Foreign
Students (27/1969). The "discover and transform" method of learning
writing is predicated on the observation that reading is an important
prelude to writing and that the persons who have done the most reading
are the best writers. The students first read and compare two written
models similar in content but different in form. Aided by a set of questions, the students then analyze the two models in order to discover
the grammatical and semantic rules which operate to transform the
first into the second. In the "transform" phase the students apply their
competence in performance—by using the transformation rules on a
written model.

A final report on English training and proficiency concerns FILI:
A Pioneer with Potential (200/1969). FILI, the Florida Inter-American
Learning Institute in Tallahassee, Florida, was established in 1968 as
a "half-way house" where foreign students can increase their ability to
communicate in English. Students enroll for one or two 11-week periods
in which they study reading, writing, speaking, and understanding English. When the students reach an established level of proficiency, they

are permitted to attend regular courses as unofficial auditors, thereby gaining exposure to classroom requirements similar to those of institutions where they will pursue their academic careers.

The principal observations of the non-empirical literature on English-language training and proficiency, then, are that English proficiency is seldom used consistently as a criterion of admission, that such proficiency should not play a major role in admission provided that the institutions are prepared to support English-language training programs, and that TOEFL is the most valid and useful measure of proficiency presently available. Many different programs for English-language training are in operation and, as previously noted, a listing and description of a large number of such programs can be found in the booklet English Language and Orientation Programs in the United States (186/ 1973).

The Foreign Student Adviser

Seven publications focus primarily on foreign student advisers and their work. Two are "guides" discussed above (p. 124). Two items contain some references to empirical research; five contain none.

The increasing importance of the foreign student adviser's role appears as a major theme in the non-empirical literature. Klinger, in "The Foreign Student Adviser: A Necessary Profession" (220/ 1967), argues that the advisers are specialists necessary to institutions and to the foreign students, not only because their duties and responsibilities to both of these parties are increasing, but because the situation of the foreign student is distinct from that of American students in several ways. First, there are academic differences. The foreign student adviser can advise admissions officers regarding equivalencies and credentials and can help to orient the foreign student to the academic system. Second, the adviser can counsel foreign students on legal problems, problems of finance, and relations with sponsors. Third, with regard to social contacts, the adviser can assist foreign students in developing social relationships on campus and in the community. The adviser also aids the student in maintaining ties with the home country and counseling the student about problems connected to the return home. Finally, the foreign student adviser is often responsible for maintaining institutional contact with foreign alumni.

A 1963 dissertation by Skinner on The Foreign Student Adviser's Office: Practices, Problems, and Procedures in Selected Colleges and Universities (353) also emphasizes the increasing importance of the foreign student adviser but acknowledges that there is some confusion on the intent, purpose, role, and goals of the foreign student adviser's office.

Much of this confusion is attributed by Carpenter, in his "Roles of the Foreign Student Adviser" (62/ 1969), to the lack of articulated insti-

tutional policy regarding the presence of foreign students on campus.
This lack of institutional policy, which was discussed above in the context of selection and admissions, becomes a major impediment to the
foreign student adviser as he or she attempts to define a role vis-a-vis
foreign students and the community. Carpenter also believes that the
foreign student advisers have been least successful at developing "meaningful relationships" between foreign and American students.

The problems most frequently encountered by foreign student
advisers are examined in two publications. One is that of financing the
student's education. Eddy, in looking at "Factors and Guidelines in
Foreign Student Guidance" (122/1972), notes the the tight money situation (in 1972, but even more true in 1974-75) makes loans difficult to
obtain and that inflation decreases the true value of the loan. Some
state institutions restrict out-of-state-students because they are deemed
a burden on the taxpayers. A shortage of jobs exists for all persons as
well as for foreign students, states Eddy, a situation which worsened
dramatically with the 1974 restrictions on job-holding by foreign students.
Because of these and other financial problems, Eddy takes a pessimistic
view of the opportunities for foreign student study in the United States
in the 1970's.

Jobs are also the subject of an article by DeAntoni on "Foreign
Student Career Counseling: A Personal View" (106/1972). DeAntoni
finds that the students have many difficulties in "job-hunting," whether
attempting to get a job in the United States or the home country. Career
counseling can help the foreign student learn the techniques of seeking
employment, but its success depends on the counselor's knowlege of the
foreign student's culture patterns and lifestyle, and the counselor's
ability to predict effects of American education on these factors.
DeAntoni adds that attempts of Cornell Univerisity's Career Center
to act as liaison between foreign students and their home countries often
found the countries less than willing to cooperate in attracting nationals
back home.

Other foreign student difficulties as well as additional facets of
the foreign student adviser's role are described in NAFSA's Guidelines:
Academic and Personal Advising (265b/1966). The problems include
insufficient knowledge of English, poor academic preparation, inappropriate study methods, and goal conflict. The adviser, who must deal
with sources of support, lines of communication and assistance,
methods of informing new students about the institution and other services, also has the responsibility of seeing that institutional resources
are wisely used according to the special needs and problems of the
foreign students.

To discover just which problems were most prevalent, the Office
of the Dean of Foreign Students at the University of Kansas kept a log
of the number and types of contacts with foreign students during one

term. "A Dean's Profile" by Coan (73/1969) summarizes that log, revealing that most of the office's time was spent on immigration advising, personal counseling, social referrals, and foreign student activities. The least time was spent on community relations, group meetings, or emergency situations. This was a very casual survey which does not claim to be representative.

In "Factors and Guidelines in Foreign Student Guidance" (122/1972), Eddy provides a useful list of policy recommendations aimed at making the foreign student adviser's role more effective. These recommendations include the appointment of at least one foreign student adviser per campus, development of a unified set of application forms, arrangement of links between institutions and foreign governments, more careful audits of student funds and refusal to accept students with insufficient funds, the writing of more realistic letters to foreign students on the prospects of studying in the United States at a particular college, and realistically advising students on their college careers and majors.

Despite the increasing importance attributed to the foreign student adviser's role by this non-empirical literature, there appears to be a drop in support for that position. Eddy, writing in 1972, believes that foreign student advisers are neither being added or supported by budgets as they were in the past. This situation makes the more efficient use of institutional funds for foreign student services not only a recommendation but a necessity.

Programs and Services

The non-empirical literature covers a wide variety of specific foreign student programs and services. This literature is broadly categorized here according to the professional origin of the players—government agency, private organization, university, or business—involved in the structure, administration, and finance of those programs and services. There are also three pertinent reports from international agencies, UNESCO (386, 426) and FAO (138) which are reviewed in Chapter 6.

Government Agencies

The non-empirical literature from government agencies consists of 26 publications. The largest group (16) is from the Bureau of Educational and Cultural Affairs of the Department of State. Four are from the Board of Foreign Scholarships, and two are from the Soviet and Eastern European Exchanges Staff of the Department of State. One study is from AID, and two others concern workshops conducted jointly by AID and NAFSA. Only two of the reports were issued prior to 1967.

Of the 16 reports issued by the Bureau of Educational and Cultural Affairs, 15 are part of a series on the Educational and Cultural Exchange of Persons and Related Activities under the Auspices of the United States Government and Private Agencies (400a-o). Each report concerns a different country: Argentina, Bolivia, Brazil, Chile, Colombia, Costa Rica, the Dominican Republic, Ethiopia, Japan, Kenya, Liberia, Mexico, Peru, Tunisia, and Venezuela. The reports are similar in format and provide very basic information on the numbers of exchangees for a given year, their fields of study, general program emphases, and the nature of other American assistance. Statistics in the reports come from the State Department, the Peace Corps, the Department of Defense, IIE, and other agencies and organizations. The reports surveyed here were issued between 1967 and 1969.

Students coming to the United States from the countries discussed in the above reports were clustered in certain fields of study. Engineering was one of the major interests of students coming from five countries: the Dominican Republic, Colombia, Peru, Bolivia, and Tunisia. Business Administration particularly attracted students from Japan, Peru, the Dominican Republic, Colombia, and Bolivia. English language and literature was a primary field of interest for many students from Japan, Colombia, and Peru. A large number of students from Tunisia, the Dominican Republic, and Brazil came to the United States to study various aspects of agriculture.

The reports contain evidence of a growing trend toward cooperation and coordination among various agencies in implementing study-abroad programs and other activities. In Tunisia, the International Development Association, UNESCO, and the Peace Corps worked together to strengthen secondary education while AID and FAO promoted agricultural development. In Mexico, two significant results of the programs have been the affiliation between educational institutions in the United States and Mexico and the impact of grants from the Rockefeller Foundation to the International Maize and Wheat Improvement Center in training scientists and promoting food sufficiency. Cooperative efforts were also noted in reference to Japan, Colombia, Ethiopia, and other nations.

A more recent publication by the Bureau of Educational and Cultural Affairs provides a brief overview of International Educational and Cultural Affairs (405/1974). Exchanges between the United States and the U.S.S.R., Eastern Europe, and the People's Republic of China are outlined as are exchanges with the Middle Eastern nations. Recent thrusts in exchange are noted and include the funding of special U.S.- African exchange projects for black college faculty and secondary school teachers, the development of a number of exchange programs on an institutional basis, and the growing support of other nations for exchange—in particular, exchange programs between Japan and the Federal Republic of Germany.

Three publications concern the operations of AID in international exchange. Preston briefly describes the Operations of the Participant Training Program of the Agency for International Development (7/ 1966) The program is a special form of planned education designed to provide technical and professional training to meet practical and immediate needs—for specific rather than general purposes. The training is therefore linked to specific developmental goals and the participants are brought to the United States (or sometimes to regional centers in other countries) to learn appropriate skills. Coordination between AID's Office of International Training and universities in the implementation of Participant Training was the theme of two workshop reports sponsored by AID and NAFSA: Report of the AID-NAFSA Workshop for Foreign Student Advisers (9a/ 1970) and the Report of the Second AID-NAFSA Workshop (9b/n.d.). The workshops brought together foreign student advisers, NAFSA representatives, staff of the office of International Training, and members of other government agencies. Proglems discussed included the lack of communication among universities, communities, and AID when personal problems arose for the participant; the lack of information possessed by AID and NAFSA about each other's orientation programs, resulting in overlap between AID and university faculties over requests for changes in the students' study programs. These latter disagreements arise because of the stipulation in the Participant Training Program that its grantees receive training for specific objectives; education in its fullest sense is not the primary goal of the Program. One method of improving communication, recommended in the Second Workshop Report, was the establishment of a standing AID-NAFSA liaison committee. The Committee would attempt to improve communication, not only between the two agencies, but also between the agencies and universities, particularly in terms of information on campus orientation programs, more information on the participants' background and academic objectives (from AID) and feedback information from faculty on returned participants (through NAFSA).

Four publications concern the role of the Board of Foreign Scholarships in the international exchange process. In its seventh Annual Report, Reviewing the Commitment (44a/ 1969), academic exchanges between the United States and other countries are described for the year September 1, 1968, through August 30, 1969, and statistics are presented summarizing grants made under various exchange programs authorized since 1949. In A Quarter Century: The American Adventure in Academic Exchange (46/ 1971), an informal history of the Fulbright-Hays Program is presented. Included in this review are the laws establishing that program, its binational aspects, the Board of Foreign Scholarships' responsibilities, and the program's achievements. Four recommendations were made for the future directions of the program: (1) binational commissions should concentrate on three or four broadly conceived programs and projects; (2) exchanges should be confined to persons in higher education or professions; (3) funds should be granted to "team activities" or the development of "institution-to-institution" programs; and (4) policy should be directed at increasing support from private sectors and cost-sharing by foreign governments. A statement entitled "Educational Exchange in the Seventies" (45/1971) by the Board offers essentially the same information and recommendations as A Quarter Century. The 1973 Report on Exchanges (44b) describes the reorganization of the Board and the introduction of a new system of sub-committees which will provide more effective liaison with co-operating agencies and increase contact with small and minority campuses. The report again noted the declining support for foreign students, although 22 countries now share the costs of the programs through regular annual contributions and a number of host universities make indirect contributions in the form of housing, maintenance, supplements, etc.

Annual reports from the Soviet and Eastern Europe Exchanges Staff of the Department of State examine Exchanges with the Soviet Union and Eastern Europe. The two reviewed here (408a/1969 and 408b/1970) describe officially negotiated exchanges such as exhibits, performing arts, scientists, scholars, and artists, as well as privately sponsored visits. The number of exchangees in scientific study programs remained approximately at the same level in the two years surveyed. Educational exchanges increased slightly—23 students and seven professors in 1968, 32 students, four newly accepted Soviet professors plus six scholars involved in long-term research in 1970. Long-term visits in 1970 with Eastern Europe fell below the 1969 level due to a sharp decline in the number of exchangees from Czechoslovakia. The emphasis placed on various fields of study by scholars from Eastern Europe varied by country, but science, medicine, technology, and agriculture received consistent priority interest. (See also IREX, pp. 142-43.)

The final government agency publication to be surveyed here is also the oldest and the only one focusing specifically on U. S. Government Exchange and Training Programs for Women (406). This 1964 study found that in Department of State programs, the proportion of women had remained almost constant at 23 percent since 1955. There was, however, a shift of geographic emphasis away from Western Europe to other areas. A similar geographic shift occurred in AID's programs where the proportion of women had doubled in three years, reaching 12 percent in 1963. Women in the Department of State programs were usually students or teachers while those associated with AID were in the fields of health, education, and community development. The age of this publication and the recent growing concern for the rights and opportunities of women indicate the need for a new, in-depth report specifically on women in government exchange and training programs.

The government agency reports, taken as a whole, cover a wide array of exchange activities. They show increasing concern among the agencies for achieving the optimum impact with such funds as are available. Methods of achieving that impact include attempts to improve communication among program staff, participants, and universities; cooperative ventures with other agencies and organizations (national and international); and the encouragement of exchange relationships among other countries.

Private organizations

Twenty non-empirical publications concern the exchange efforts of private organizations, excluding business corporations. Of these, four can be grouped together because of their focus on orientation programs. Five publications have no particular geographical emphasis; the final 11 publications concern programs and services for foreign students from specific geographic areas. Africa receives the most attention in this last group. Thirteen of the 20 publications contained no reference to empirical research. The remainder contained reference to such research.

The four articles on orientation cover several kinds of programs. (See above, p. 118, for an empirical study.) The Report on In-Country Orientation in the Dominican Republic and Venezuela (276/1970) by Bridgers (for NAFSA) presents a description and subjective evaluation of a highly recommended orientation program of the North American Association in Venezuela. The objective of Bridger's visit was to determine the desirability of using the program as a prototype for other countries where only a one-day program is feasible. He judged the program to be effective and recommended it as a model. A visit was also made to the Dominican Republic where efforts by the Fundacion de Credito Educativo to develop an orientation program were just beginning. It was recommended that better communication was needed between that organization and NAFSA, and that NAFSA take immediate steps to increase communication with other public and private agencies in Latin America that provide in-country and pre-departure orientation. There is a further need to explore the serious problems of returned students in securing recognition of credits and diplomas earned in the United States.

An entirely different kind of orientation is described by Owen and Colwell in "Orientation for Foreign Students: The Lesson of the Summer Economics Institute" (301/1968). The Institute was established in the late 1950's by the American Economic Association and the Ford Foundation as an orientation program for foreign graduate students, primarily from the less-developed countries, in economics. The program is based on the assumption that most problems stem from inadequate academic preparation. The Institute, therefore, offered, in 1968, intensive summer sessions on economic theory, mathematics, and/ or English, tailored to fit the students' special needs. It is noted that similar programs were developed in law (at Princeton) and engineering (at Purdue).

"Orientation of Foreign Medical Graduates" (371/ 1971) by Sutnick, Reichard, and Angelides, describes orientation programs organized by the Philadelphia County Medical Society and various community organizations for foreign doctors and nurses serving in Philadelphia hospitals. The programs include information about Philadelphia, insurance, vacation opportunities, hospitality programs, and English-language programs. A survey by the Association for Hospital Medical Education, quoted in the article, found that the major difficulties confronting foreign medical graduates were unfamiliarity with the English language, confusion with unfamiliar medical techniques and procedures, and unfamiliarity with American methods of practicing medicine and the structure of hospital organization. Recommendations to the Philadelphia Medical Society included the expansion of programs to include systematic orientation of foreign medical graduates to conditions in those cities in which they work.

Yet another type of orientation is discussed in The Tenth Mohonk Consultation with International Students: A Proposal for Pre-Departure Seminars (375/ 1973). Thirteen students from 12 countries at this small conference prepared a proposal for seminars to prepare foreign students for departure from the United States. The proposed seminars, which would take place outside or within school curricula, were seen as essential for several reasons. First, it was felt that U. S. education does not adequately prepare the foreign student to use the skills he or she has learned. Second, prolonged exposure to a new culture and adoption of many of its facets poses a problem to the student's ability to communicate upon return. Third, there is a decrease in the ability of students to keep up with the changes in their home societies during their absence. This type of re-orientation deserves serious consideration and greater emphasis in future research.

Five articles and reports deal with specific examples of programs and services, including orientation, offered foreign students in the United States. Rayner and Jones, in "Foreign Nurses: Dedicated Exchange Visitors" (321/ 1973), describe the Exchange-Visitor Program for Foreign Nurses at Columbia Presbyterian Medical Center in New York City. This is an example of a long-term (one-year) training program designed to familiarize visiting nurses with American health services through coordinated educational contact and supervised clinical practice. This program appears to cope with most of the

problems of foreign medical graduates outlined above in the survey of
the Association for Hospital Medical Education (see p. 139).

The Preconference Institute: Papers and Speeches (23/1970) of
the American Library Association contains a subjective discussion of
foreign-trained librarians in American libraries and foreign students
in North American library education programs. Policies and practices
are reviewed and library education programs in selected countries of
Latin America and the Caribbean, Europe, Asia, Africa, and Australia
and New Zealand are described.

The administration, structure, and financing of the Pittsburgh
Council for International Visitors (PCIV) is examined by Witman in
"COSERV's First Decade in One Community in Pittsburgh, Pennsylvania" (425/1972). The Pittsburgh Council is a community organization
designed to welcome international visitors to Pittsburgh but whose
commitment is seen to extend beyond hospitality programs to the development of intercultural communication skills between community
citizens and foreign visitors. Volunteers are recognized as having a
key role in the organization.

The promotion of intercultural understanding is the goal of the
Lodestar International Student Center, established in 1963 as a non-
profit, non-sectarian educational and recreational center in northern
California. The Center, as described by Heath (165/1969), operates
eight one-week sessions each summer, accommodating 16 students
and one discussion leader. American and foreign students are brought
together to provide an experience in cultural exchange apart from the
educational setting.

Kaplan worries about the role of one of the largest organizations
for and about foreign students in the United States—NAFSA—and at the
same time is concerned about the growing reaction against international
education. In "NAFSA in the Mod, Mod World" (210/1970), Kaplan
argues that NAFSA must encourage educational institutions and government to adjust to the presence of foreign students (rather than the reverse) by making every effort to ensure the relevance of U. S. education to global problems. He feels that we have not internationalized
American education; we have Americanized international education.

Of the reports which focus on programs and services for foreign
students from specific geographical areas, six concern programs of
the African-American Institute (AAI), an organization central to educational exchanges with African nations. Two reports concern the
African Scholarship Program of American Universities (ASPAU) which
is administered by AAI. A Report on the African Scholarship Program
of American Universities: 1960-1970 (95/n.d.) traces the history of
the program from 1960 to 1970 and discusses major administrative
problems: (1) conflict between training goals of AID and the educational goals of the participating institutions, a problem noted elsewhere;

and (2) rising costs of U. S. education and changes in funding priorities of both educational institutions and U. S. agencies. As a program to provide trained manpower, ASPAU was considered to be only moderately successful, since, by 1970, only 711 of the 1,338 graduates had returned to Africa. Some, however, were expected to return subsequently. It was concluded that new and more flexible responses are needed to meet the challenges of the seventies. An Annual Report (July 1, 1972, to June 30, 1973) of ASPAU (6/n.d.) notes that the rate of repatriation continued to increase and that a significant number of students graduating in 1973-74 were pursuing graduate education in the United States.

Another AAI program—the African Graduate Fellowship Program (AFGRAD)—is discussed in a 1972 Annual Report (5/1972). As of June 1972, AFGRAD had granted awards to 693 Africans from 31 countries, with an overall repatriation rate by 1972 of 88.6 percent. Several major changes occurred during the life of the program. First, a growing demand for doctorates has led to an increase in Ph.D. students. Second, a high rate of non-return among medical students forced AFGRAD to reduce its emphasis on medical studies. Third, there was the development since 1967 of the African Graduate Study Awards (AGSA) to aid employed applicants who did not meet AFGRAD standards. Finally, provision was made for financial aid to grantees wishing to conduct dissertation research in Africa. Two of these changes are directly concerned with the growth of Ph.D. study among African students resulting from the rapid expansion of African universities which has created a demand for Ph.D.-level teachers, and from an increasing emphasis in American universities on "straight" Ph.D. programs, that is, graduate study without pause to receive a master's degree.

The manpower needs of African nations, including the demand for university teachers noted above, and the responsiveness of American colleges and universities to those needs, was a major issue for debate at a Conference on the Admission and Guidance of African Students in 1967 at Howard University. As summarized by Jacqz in African Students at U. S. Universities (2/1967), the principal speakers at the Conference believed that U. S. institutions should be responsive to African needs and should also assume responsibility for encouraging students to return to Africa. Conference participants echoed criticisms heard in other quarters in noting that many difficulties of responding to manpower needs arise from the differing and frequently conflicting objectives of student, U. S. government, U. S. institution, and home government. The need for better communication among those parties was emphasized. Other suggestions to improve the response to African manpower needs included better manpower planning by African governments, stricter control over issuance of passports and expanded use of bonding, more effective academic counseling in U. S. institutions, and provision of information on African manpower plans and employment opportunities.

A different type of training was emphasized in a second report by Jacqz on the Refugee Students from Southern Africa (3/1967). This report, also of a 1967 conference, noted that there were 350,000 to 440,000 refugees from southern Africa, most of whom could not return home. The primary goal of training, according to conference partici- pants (members of international, American, and European govern- mental and private agencies, and African governments and liberation movements), was to prepare for participation in the struggle for free dom. Secondary objectives were to prepare students for service among refugee groups or in their country of asylum.

The sixth study in this group, "A Current Assessment of the Southern African Student Program," by Kletzien (4/1972), describes the program initiated in 1961 by the Department of State as an urgent effort to provide educational training for African students, especially from countries expecting independence and majority rule in the near future. By January 1972, 465 students had participated in the program. The study found that while most participants would have preferred to return to their home country, the continuation of white minority rule and the prospect of persecution made this in many cases inadvisable. The program's efforts are currently oriented toward helping such refu- gees in their efforts to adjust to life in the United States and to obtain employment.

An evaluation of several of these African programs was prepared by Practical Concepts, Inc., to develop a factual basis for further AID efforts in assisting African countries to meet their needs for trained manpower (431/1973). It found, as did the studies cited above, that AFGRAD had a higher repatriation rate than ASPAU although delays in return were frequently due to the desire for further study or for prac- tical work experience. The value of work-study programs or practical work experience is stressed, whether or not it is related to academic preparation; on-the-job success was not importantly related to the quality or type of degree or to initial academic preparation. Of those who returned, 20 percent held "high leverage" positions in "high lever- age" organizations. In many instances, however, the degree sought by the participant was in an area not relevant to African development priorities. Finally, the study found that the intermediary programming organizations played an important and critical role in the success of the programs.

The five remaining studies on programs of private organizations focus on Eastern Europe and the U.S.S.R. (two items), Asia (one item), and Latin America (two items).

Two Annual Reports from the International Research and Ex- changes Board (IREX) (189a/1972 and 189b/1973) describe the progress made in expanding the exchange of scholars with the Soviet Union and Eastern Europe despite such problems as Soviet rejection of Americans working in "sensitive areas." The 1973 report expresses the belief that the academic public should understand that detente has not solved any fundamental problems of scholarly contact with the Soviet Union.

A report on Educational and Cultural Exchange with the Asian Countries (269/ 1967) from the 18th Annual NAFSA Conference addresses basic issues of developing cooperative educational relations between nations. Workshops at this conference covered an extensive range of topics including Asian historical and cultural background, the structure of educational systems in specific Asian nations, and communication problems of and with foreign students. A number of policy recommendations for future research emerged from the Conference: (1) manpower studies and placement in positions after return (also suggested in the previous African reports); (2) studies of readjustment and attitudes toward America; (3) quantitative studies of correlations between language proficiency and academic achievement; (4) development of tests to determine capacity of students for improving ability in English; (5) a general study of criteria used by institutions in selecting foreign students; (6) development of a case-study manual for the in-service training of foreign student advisers; (7) a study of the expectations of the student concerning services of the foreign student adviser; (8) the relationship of personal counseling to academic achievement; and (9) studies of the dominant role of inter-personal relationships in different cultures.

Further recommendations, directed to Latin American students, appear in a report by Jenkins on "Various Proposals for the Improvement of Educational Programs Provided for Latin American Students in the USA" (271/ 1968). A greater emphasis on in-country orientation programs (also noted above, p. 138) is a major recommendation of the report. Other proposals include the examination of English proficiency standards and ways to meet the needs of Latin American students in that area, study of the relationship of curricula to the specific educational needs of Latin American students, and the organization of community workshops on Latin American exchange to establish more clearly who the students are and which are the countries from which they come.

One of the most important programs in the Latin American area is the Latin American Scholarship Program of American Universities (LASPAU), described by Henry (173/ 1972), a cooperative undertaking of more than 300 North American and Latin American institutions of higher education. This seeks to give well-qualified, well-motivated, but financially limited Latin American students an opportunity to obtain the academic training required for successful careers as university teachers in their home countries. The long-term, continuous

linkages between universities sponsoring this program would appear
to be promising, although no formal evaluations appear to have been
undertaken to date.

The 20 non-empirical publications from and about private organizations describe a large variety of activities and present numerous
recommendations for research and action, making a summary of content difficult. There are, however, several recurring themes.

One theme is the need for improved orientation procedures. In-
country orientation, regarded as an effective means of helping the foreign student adjust to American social patterns and the U. S. educational system, is recommended in two publications, both concerning
Latin American students. Orientation to fit the needs of students in
specific academic and professional fields is also considered beneficial
by several authors. The extension of such academic orientation into
longer-term training programs has apparently met with success in a
program for foreign nurses and could be considered for other fields.
Intercultural communication as an orientation technique is of particular
importance in two programs, the Lodestar Center and the Pittsburgh
Council for International Visitors. Terminal orientation programs
for students returning to their home countries is the subject of only
one publication, but the importance and difficulty of such orientation
would seem to call for much increased attention.

Three other interrelated themes appear in the non-empirical
literature from and about private organizations. One of these is the
conflict of training goals as enunciated by different agencies and institutions. A second theme, expressed in reports of African and Asian
programs, is the debate over the extent to which agencies and institutions should relate training goals and efforts to the manpower needs
of the countries from which the students come. Finally, there is the
closely related need to increase the amount of effective communication
among governments, private organizations, educational institutions,
and the foreign students themselves.

The Universities

University programs for foreign students are given particular
attention in 11 publications. Eight of the 11 make no reference to empirical research. Geographically, with the exception of one article
on African students, the items are of a general multi-national character. Only one of the publications was written before 1967.

The historical nature of "African Students in Negro American
Colleges: Notes on the Good African" by King (216/ 1970) sets it apart
from the other non-empirical literature on university programs. The
growth of African interest in higher education after World War I, the
heavy rural emphasis placed on education in the colonial universities
and the links forged between black Africans and black Americans during

this same period, are described as leading to an interest by the Africans in the black colleges and universities of the southern United States. The colonial powers were concerned that students from their African colonies would be exposed to radical and militant attitudes at these American institutions. King shows that this did indeed happen at Tuskeegee Institute, despite its reputation among whites as a "safe" school where Africans could study without becoming political radicals. He concludes that the school served as a stimulus for black separatism, an incentive to aggressive business enterprise, and an inspiration for independent, non-sectarian African schools.

Two articles deal with the quality of agricultural training for foreign students. Kelly, in a paper on "Horticultural Training of Graduate Students from Developing Countries" (211/1966), expresses three criticisms. First, the students are not prepared for the positions and tasks they will need to fill at home. Second, they are taught with equipment they will never use again. Third, standards are lowered for foreign students and they get second-class degrees. The need for "applied" horticulture is emphasized but the author also observes it would be a misfortune if horticultural courses were so provincial as to apply to a single country. One attempt to adapt agricultural training to the needs of foreign students is described in Peterson's article on "Some Reflections on Conducting a Foreign Student Training Course" (309/1968). The course, on the economics of agricultural production and resource use, was offered by the University of Nebraska from 1961 through 1966 as a response to the criticism that foreign training programs had been too specifically geared to knowledge of the U. S. economy and introduced technical skills inappropriate to developing countries. The special course for foreign students required that the students be removed from their immediate academic programs and placed in a practical workshop situation. Methods of instruction included lectures, field trips, individual projects and reports, and library study.

A short report by Brettell and Gildseth, Foreign Student Programming at Kansas State University: An Inventory (51/1969), very briefly presents an overview of International Student Programs at the Manhattan, Kansas, campus, including those of religious organizations, international organizations, and community volunteers.

Thompson, in "International Programs: Communication or Obfuscation" (377/1971) describes the results of an unsystematic survey of "key people" in ten large universities concerning the existence and vitality of international clubs and the extent of foreign student participation in programs planned for them. Only two of the universities had international clubs, suggesting that such clubs are perhaps becoming obsolete. Most of the universities reported a definite decline in foreign student program participation. Thompson explains this decline by the growth of campus-wide opportunities that encourage foreign student involvement and the fact that more foreign students are graduates and consequently less interested in group programs.

Two publications describe programs and services for foreign students at two-year junior and community colleges. The advantages for foreign students at such institutions are identified in Foreign Students in Community and Junior Colleges by Kerr (22/ 1973). They include specialized two-year training, low fees, and close association among students, faculty, and community. Advice is offered to college personnel on admissions procedures, counseling of foreign students, and academic and non-academic orientation programs. The advantages of junior and community colleges for foreign students are also described by Davis in "Foreign Students in the Two-Year Colleges" (104/ 1971), who claims that such colleges frequently offer better facilities and equipment, teaching, administration and counseling staffs, and smaller classes than larger institutions. One disadvantage of the two-year institutions, however, is the tendency towards provinciality. Recommendations for counteracting that tendency include field trips, special projects, programs to welcome foreign students, and study-abroad programs.

A university-sponsored study-abroad program for American students is the subject of an article by Cormack, "American Students in India: Ambassadors of Cultural Polluters?" (91/ 1973). It is included here because it offers some observations useful in the administration of foreign student programs in the United States. The program examined is the "Callison-in-Bangalore Program," through which sophomores at Callison College, University of the Pacific, attend Bangalore University in India. The general aim of the program is "broadening one's horizons" but Cormack believes that more specific aims must be formulated which will consider the negative experiences of some students and will avoid exploitation of the Indian hosts and "polluting" of Indian culture. She redefines the major purpose of the program as intercultural education based on a clear intercultural aim, with selection and orientation appropriate to this aim, a continuous intercultural seminar in the field, and an integration of the intercultural experience into the college cirriculum. The formulation of specific aims which consider the negative experiences of some students and the suggestions on intercultural education could be helpful in the context of foreign student education in the United States.

An article which looks specifically at the administration of international programs in U. S. educational institutions is "How to Run Programs" by Michie (243/ 1967). Two different administrative approaches are envisaged. The first is the institution-wide approach by which administration, preferably with faculty participation, works to an overall plan to extend the international dimension throughout the institution. The second approach is the slower, selective method of identifying and encouraging individuals, disciplines, schools, and colleges within the institution where the international dimension has already become rooted and providing the atmosphere in which they can interact. Between the two approaches are, of course, a number of other institutional mechanisms and techniques.

International programs in U. S. universities face many problems in the 1970's as both government and private foundations shift their support priorities toward urgent domestic issues. Perkins, in Inter-national Programs of U. S. Colleges and Universities: Priorities for the Seventies (308/1971), outlines some specific suggestions as to how universities and colleges may restructure the goals and content of their international programs in the light of a changing definition of national interest. He recommends that language and area-studies centers tie their goals more closely to new domestic and foreign policy directions; that study-abroad programs receive careful reevaluation; that foreign students in the United States be selected with greater care and regard to the needs of developing countries; that two-way exchanges of visiting scholars be upgraded and widened to include more institutions; that universities consider, as an approach to funding from international agencies, a procedure in which the contracting agent is an individual rather than the university itself; and that international programs become an integral part of the university's basic curriculum. The suggestions made in this significant paper summarize and in many cases extend recommendations made in the other literature on the nature of international education and exchange programs.

Business

The response of the business world to foreign student programs consists, in our bibliography, of four publications.

The proceedings of a 1969 conference on Closing the Worldwide Learning Gap: How Can Free Enterprise Help? (183/1969), sponsored by the Institute of International Education, indicated that conference participants believed four elements—specific goals, sound organization, operational flexibility, and assured funding—were essential to any program of cooperative assistance to education in developing nations by business and government. A pilot project was proposed, as was an educational foundation which would have the specific function of developing and administering cooperative efforts between government and business in the field of international educational exchange.

The Shape of Change in International Business and Higher Education's Response (322/n.d.) was the title of another conference, sponsored by the Regional Council for International Education in Cleveland, Ohio, in 1973. Among the recommendations of conference

participants were that corporations should provide their own language
training; that universities should develop new curricula and methods to
cope with third world demands for training in maintenance; and that
foreign and American students would be better prepared for careers in
international commerce if a more fully integrated curriculum were
available.

The role played by the corporate side of the private sector, particularly multinational corporations, in helping to support educational
and cultural exchange is examined in an article by Ackerman on "Private Support Activities in International Education" (1/ 1970). The principal form of overseas support by corporations is grants to graduate
foreign students for study in America. One recommendation of interest in this article, made by Charles Robinson, president of the
Marcona Corporation, is the creation of regional educational foundations supported by contributions from corporations proportional to
their total investments in that region.

Two basic types of cooperative relationships between business,
a university, and students are outlined in A Status Report and Development Plans for an International Program in Cooperative Education
(251/ 1967). The university in this case is Mississippi State University. The first type of relationship applies to international firms that
have facilities in the United States and business, industrial, or li-
censee arrangements in foreign nations. The U. S. operation is asked
to provide the university student with a tax-free scholarship or the
employer may pay the student for his or her work. On completion of
study the graduate returns home to work for the sponsoring organization. The second type of relationship is designed to apply to the student who either is not sponsored or is sponsored by a company with
only U. S. operations and affiliation. In this case temporary work experience is arranged with a U. S. firm that wishes to employ the student when not in school or that may be interested in the student as a
potential employee.

The business world, then, has some definite ideas on the role
it can play in international education and exchange. Cooperative relationships with universities, and students, joint programs with governments of developing nations, the formation of educational foundations
or corporate foundations to administer international programs and
activities, and a call for greater relevance of curricula for foreign
students at American universities are expressions of the business
response to international education and exchange needs.

International Relations and Foreign Students

This is a subject which occupies a small but distinct place in the
literature on educational exchange. Only five publications are reviewed, all published before 1968.

A paper by Heft on The Training of Foreign Students: Its Impact on Tensions Among Nations (295/ 1963) attempts to determine whether and how the training of foreign students in the United States may contribute to the reduction of tensions which threaten world peace. Training is examined in terms of its effect on the students, on the United States, on the economic and social development of the students' countries, and on the relations between the United States and other countries. In all of these aspects, it is concluded that foreign student training can be beneficial. Suggestions are offered to help make training more effective: (1) cooperation between American and foreign institutions; (2) training for youth leadership; (3) favoring the training of those who will train their countrymen; (4) emphasis on training related to economic opportunities and the general economic and social conditions in the students' home countries; and (5) greater use of multinational agencies.

The thesis of Coombs' Fourth Dimension of Foreign Policy (86/ 1964) is that educational and cultural activities constitute a fourth dimension of foreign policy that must supplement political, economic, and military elements and add badly needed flexibility, breadth, and depth. It is urged that this component be given equal status with the other three. In order to fulfill its proper role in the future, educational policy must be shaped by a clear set of objectives, better planning, and more vigorous and imaginative administration. Greater political and financial support and the strengthening of relationships between the government and private sectors are advocated. In addition, Coombs believes that the United States should strengthen international mechanisms of cooperation by expanding multilateral approaches through UNESCO and other such agencies.

A similar awareness of the relationship between foreign policy and international exchange is expressed by Frankel in The Neglected Aspect of Foreign Affairs (142/ 1966). Educational and cultural relations with other countries are viewed as a neglected facet of American foreign policy. He argues that the goals of educational and cultural exchange must be reinstated if American policy in this area is to be more effective and enlightened. Frankel suggests that goals be reformulated as (1) the lacing together of educational systems, (2) improvement of the context of communication, (3) disciplining and extending international intellectual discourse, (4) international educational development, and (5) the furthering of educational and cultural relations as ends in themselves. Among the basic reforms which he believes necessary to implement these principles are a further upgrading of educational/ cultural relations in the Department of State so that their significance is recognized; changes in policy-making structures so that exchange is not seen from distorted agency perspectives; and formation of new, more cooperative and binding relationships between government and private educational and cultural communities. The creation of a semi-autonomous foundation for educational/cultural affairs with responsibility for planning and implementing policy abroad is also recommended.

In the concluding chapter of his book on International Behavior, Kelman examines the "Social-Psychological Approaches to the Study of International Relations: The Question of Relevance" (212/1965). He asks whether international cooperation, and specifically educational exchange, has some bearing on conditions for peace, and whether research in this area has potential political relevance. In answering, he defines four ways in which international cooperation and exchange may affect relations between nations and hence create conditions for peace. International education may produce (1) increased openness among key individuals in attitudes towards other nations, (2) reduced levels of tension, (3) increased world-mindedness and commitment to internationalist theory among participants, and (4) development of networks of relations cutting across national boundaries. Kelman recommends research which would evaluate exchange programs to ascertain whether they have achieved their goals and offer insights into ways of enhancing effectiveness of future programs.

An interesting case study of the long-range consequences of academic exchanges is presented in "Pragmatism Goes West" by Ukai (380/1967). The tangible effects of American-Japanese exchanges include new thrusts in Japanese education—the development of American studies in Japanese universities and interdisciplinary and intradisciplinary communication across national boundaries. The intangible effects of exchange have to do with attitudes such as a sharpened awareness on the part of Japanese intellectuals of the significant differences between Japanese and American modes of thinking.

Publications on international relations and foreign students including those written 8 to 12 years ago contain a large number of suggestions and recommendations that deserve serious consideration. Common areas of agreement in this literature appear to be that educational and cultural activities should receive greater recognition in terms of their relevance to foreign policy, and may be beneficial in reducing international tensions, that inter-university cooperation is a useful method of cutting across national boundaries, that multilateral approaches to exchanges through international agencies should be strengthened, and that there should be precise objectives or goals set for international educational and cultural exchange.

The Broad Perspective

Alan A. J. Elliott, in "Foreign Students in Perspective" (128/1967), notes that the growing body of literature on foreign students includes a great variety of approaches to the subject: educational, political, humanitarian, statistical, and others. He advocates and encourages a broad approach in such literature. It is this broad approach which characterizes the 24 remaining publications.

The first five, published between 1956 and 1964, are grouped together for easier comparison of early recommendations with those of more recent literature.

"Statistics and Comments on Exchange with the United States" (178/ 1956) is an article by Holland which comments on several IIE publications. Taba, in discussing cultural attitudes and international understanding, concludes that foreign experiences do not automatically create international-mindedness, and that international travel does not necessarily contribute to world understanding. The conflict between the goals of sponsoring agencies and those of the participants, the subject of a number of later articles and reports, is also analyzed. She argues that the purposes of any international educational exchange program should be education first, and understanding and liking for the United States second.

Coombs, writing on the fifteenth anniversary of the signing of the Fulbright Act, assesses the accomplishments and failures of the international educational exchange program in "International Educational Exchange: A Work of Many Hands" (85/ 1961). Areas of particular concern and in need of improvement in the structure and administration of exchange programs at this time included: better predeparture and academic placement, tailoring of academic programs to the special needs of foreign students; increased community contacts; creation of an admissions and guidance office in each major contributing country; and increased follow-up on returnees.

The Professional Education of Students from Other Lands (334), edited by Sanders in 1963, offers recommendations in several different areas. For universities in general, it is recommended that selection should be based on the potential of an individual to use training upon return as well as personal criteria, and that counseling and orientation should begin before departure and continue through reorientation counseling before return. In addition, it is recommended that follow-up studies be conducted to evaluate U. S. programs.

Colligan, also writing in 1963, examines The College, the University, and the Foreign Student (82). He thinks it essential that colleges and universities provide leadership in assessing program objectives, and in cooperating with government and private agencies in achieving them. Suggested improvements in programs for foreign students include greater dissemination of information on U. S. institutions, more flexible admissions standards, English-language training centers, continuing orientation programs, professional academic advising and personal counseling, and greater budgetary support for foreign student services.

The U. S. Advisory Commission on International Education and Cultural Affairs issued its second annual report in 1964 entitled A Sequel to a Beacon of Hope (390c). The report discusses the various activities of the Commission and progress made since its first report, A Beacon of Hope. That progress included the creation of the Council on International Educational and Cultural Affairs in 1964, a survey of government English-language programs undertaken by the Inter-Agency Committee on English Language Teaching, and the formation of inter-agency groups on youth activities, international athletics, and research in international education.

This brief summary of early and important publications reveals that certain topics have long been of concern to those writing in this field. In the review of more recent literature which follows, it will be apparent that many of the same concerns are expressed, and similar recommendations made.

Of this literature, only two publications challenge underlying assumptions about the basic worthwhileness of bringing foreign students to the United States. In "Advanced Training for Foreign Students: The Regional Approach" (336/1971), Schmidt and Scott see the chief short-comings of educating foreign students from less-developed countries in industrialized nations as: (1) the inappropriateness of training for the needs of the developing countries; (2) long and costly training periods; (3) paternal attitudes of training institutions; (4) dissertation research topics often based on the host country's problems; and (5) the brain drain. The authors also note that although the developing countries are predominantly agricultural, the training of agricultural scientists, as compared to other fields of study, has received little emphasis. They argue that because of environmental and cultural factors, there is much to be said for regionally based research and training in developing countries. A regional approach would allow for more productive orientation of research and education programs than is now possible in fragmented, short-term programs being supported by foundations and AID, and would also provide a better prospect that students return to their own countries as productive citizens.

A similar point is made by Regueira in an article on "Cursos de Formacao em Desenvolvimento Economico: Alguns Aspectos Caracteristicos" (Educational Courses in Economic Development) (323/1966). He notes two methods by which developing countries can satisfy their need for professional personnel trained in various aspects of economic and social development. The first is to integrate their students into the regular programs of foreign universities. The second is to send them to specially created institutes which offer courses in economic and social development. Despite their many drawbacks, Regueira believes that the institutes offer a much more useful and comprehensive program of education for students from developing countries.

Thomas Cotner, in A Summary of the Exchange and Training Programs, Office of Education, U. S. Department of Health, Education, and Welfare, 1939-1967 (394/ n. d.) reviews the various programs administered and the number of grantees involved since 1939 when the Office of Education first became engaged in international exchange and training. Among the programs described are the International Teacher Development Program (begun in 1944), the Leader and Specialist Program (1949 to 1954), and the exchange activities of the International Cooperation Administration (since 1955) and the Agency for International Development (since 1961).

The need for each university and college to analyze what it is trying to do in participating in international exchange programs and to adjust its policies accordingly is the central theme of an AACRAO conference report, Rationale for International Students 1 (29/ 1970). Exchange programs are one way for American educational institutions, while pursuing their own primary goals—the advancement and transmission of knowledge—to contribute as well to a primary goal of U. S. foreign policy—the creation and maintenance of free nations around the world. The responsibilities of the institution include adequate preadmission information, high standards of classroom education, instruction in English as a Foreign Language, and competent advisory staff for foreign students.

Also emphasizing policy clarification, "The Goals and Definitions of International Education" (354/ 1971) by Smart begins with the premise that what international education is depends on its goals, and therefore an attempt is made to clarify possible goals and related definitions of international education. Eight basic goals are cited: (1) permeation of new ideas, (2) synthesis of value systems and world cultures, (3) national development, (4) the development of national political power, (5) mutual understanding and cooperation, (6) basic preparation for life in the global context, (7) developing a creative attitude towards diversity, and (8) the discovery of truth. It is concluded that the issue facing the United States regarding international education is the need to define goals, to face their implications by relating them to other goals, and finally to develop programs which will achieve the objectives.

The need for clear goal statements by planners and administrators is important in educational evaluation. The difficulties in evaluation of the foreign study experience have been the subject of an increasing quantity of literature in recent years but Elliott, in "The Evaluation of International Education: An Administrative Approach" (127/ 1965), believes that an insufficient place has been accorded to the role of "fellowship administrator" in evaluating the programs for which he or she is responsible. He recommends further examination and development of the role of evaluation in administrative procedures.

Sinauer, in The Role of Communication in International Training and Education: Overcoming Barriers to Understanding with the Developing Countries (349/1967), assesses international education in the United States and other countries, examining the role of oral, written, visual, and other modes of communication in meeting the educational needs of students from the developing nations. He considers such alternative proposals as presentation of programs in foreign languages, presentations in English through interpreters, the use of transition programs and personal contacts, and learning through field trips.

It has been observed elsewhere that America's "international era" may be giving way to a period of domestic introspection and isolationism. In "The Erosion of the American Commitment to International Educational Change" (223/1973), Landers sees this trend as posing acute problems for the future of international educational exchange. The declining support for and rising costs of education for foreign students is decried and recommendations for remedial action are suggested. (1) National goals should be reassessed and our national commitment (expressed in dollars) to the underlying rationale of international educational exchange renewed. (2) Foreign students must be provided equal opportunities for scholarships, fellowships, and employment. The burden of this assistance to be shifted from the financially troubled local institutions to the federal government. (3) Overseas counsellors should be supplied with more complete information about low-tuition colleges in low cost-of-living areas and attempt to direct foreign students to these schools.

Another series of recommendations on dealing with foreign students is contained in Kaplan's Towards a Model for International Educational Exchange (A Large University System) (267/n.d.). These recommendations are specifically addressed to the State University System of Florida but have more general application. Kaplan suggests the establishment of a contralized clearinghouse to process admissions; establishment of a system-wide institute for the teaching of English; creation of a uniformly defined position entitled Foreign Student Adviser; designation of one faculty member in each academic unit having foreign students to advise those students on a long-term rotational basis, and to report back to the administrator on curriculum and use of foreign students as an educational resource; that the system should make available substantial tuition waivers and a low-cost loan fund for foreign students; development of comparative courses in those units having foreign students in order to maximize the potential of those students to contribute their "informant knowledge"; development of courses for the first and last terms in residence of foreign students (for orientation and re-orientation respectively); and the encouragement of faculty individually and collectively to seek and develop inter-institution and institution-governmental relationships across national boundaries to develop joint curricula.

The diversity of activities and problems in international education is examined in two publications by Allan Michie. Diversity and Interdependence through International Education (245/1967) is a lengthy edited report which brings together the major statements and discussion of a symposium held at Columbia University in 1966 to mark the Twentieth Anniversary of the International Educational Exchange (Fulbright) Program. Questions noted in the symposium for future attention included: (1) How can the quality of the Fulbright Program be maintained? (2) How can we avoid playing numbers games by supplying live bodies or bringing live bodies who are not really wanted in other countries? and (3) Who from other countries could most profit by being in the United States? In Higher Education and World Affairs (244/1968), Michie addresses those institutions which are just beginning to move into the international field. He therefore includes a survey of present activities in international education, the strengths and problems to be considered, and the resources available to institutions.

The Student in the International Scene (273) also surveys international education through a collection of 65 abstracts of papers presented at the International Education Year Conference in 1970. Topics included admissions priorities, new directions for NAFSA, intercultural workshops, the brain drain, and others.

In The Foreign Graduate Student (366/n.d.), Springer recommends that foreign student programs would benefit from the introduction of a computerized two-way information system. Such a system would provide coordinated and efficient processing of information for both foreign student applicants and for institutions and agencies.

A 1967 colloquium, attended primarily by graduate deans, is summarized in The University, Government, and the Foreign Graduate Student (79/1969). The colloquium considered several broad questions concerning graduate programs. Noting that foreign graduate students sponsored as part of an institution-to-institution arrangement have the best possibility of being matched to an appropriate U. S. institution, and that growth in international programs (in 1967) poses questions regarding program design and the treatment of foreign students, the colloquium participants recommended that: (1) institutions aim at a critical mass of five to ten percent foreign students in graduate programs; (2) special efforts be made to orient prospective students to the U. S. educational system; (3) a double standard for admission and qualification for degrees has no justification in universities; and (4) additional scholarship funds be sought to maintain the recommended proportion of foreign students.

Speakman, writing on International Exchange Education (361/1966), examines a number of issues. Better selection procedures are advocated through creation of a system which will screen increasing

numbers of applicants, counsel them, and test them. For the system
to function effectively, future demand at graduate and undergraduate
levels must be estimated, advantages and disadvantages to U. S. education as a result of increasing foreign student enrollment must be
assessed, and goals must be established for numbers of foreign students. Speakman regards overseas Counseling, Evaluating, and Testing Centers as a useful device but one that would require the cooperation of colleges and universities to be successful. He feels that many
other foreign student problems could be alleviated if institutions would
ask questions regarding the timeliness of sojourn, ability to accept the
financial burden, and preparation for study abroad.

Moore, in "International Education in the Seventies: Revolution
or Turmoil on the Campus" (253/ 1970), offers a wide variety of recommendations for educational institutions and government. With regard
to immigration regulations and procedures, he advocates the granting
of blanket work permission contingent upon satisfactory academic performance, the abolition of reporting requirements except in cases of
unsatisfactory academic performance, and the creation of a new legal
status which would give enhanced privileges but require responsibility
in return. Recommendations for universities and colleges fall into
several categories. Concerning admissions, selection, and academic
performance, he regards the establishment of minimum quotas as desirable and recommends that normal admissions documents be replaced with a statement of the institution's policy which makes it explicit that students unable to meet academic requirements will be
dropped. An interesting and related suggestion is that institutions
require different levels of performance according to a student's year
of study. To encourage foreign student participation in university
government, it is recommended that a respresentative governing body
among foreign students be developed, that there be regular consultation
between the foreign student representatives and a foreign student adviser, and that U. S. governing bodies enunciate policy on exchange
and work for its implementation. To provide against social and cultural exclusion, he sees a need to update university and state regulations so that foreign students and their dependents will not be
excluded from work opportunities, social life, and community participation. A number of suggestions are also made to promote and
institute curriculum changes: (1) initiate co-curricular programs which
integrate and apply class learning to situations in foreign students'
home countries; (2) recommend to departments foreign students who
can be used as teachers or aides in courses related to international
education; (3) stimulate course evaluations; (4) encourage foreign students to lobby for the right to participate in curriculum committees,
and for inclusion in graduate curriculum or core courses that relate
to development—particularly to cultural, psychological, and socio-

logical barriers to change; and (5) encourage the development of internships that approximate human and environmental conditions in foreign students' home countries.

The problems and failures encountered in the sponsorship and administration of foreign student exchange programs, and recommended responses to them, are discussed extensively in a valuable book by Sanders and Ward entitled Bridges to Understanding: International Programs of American Colleges and Universities (335/1970). On selection and admission procedures for foreign students, a failure is seen in internal coordination among admissions offices, foreign student advisers, and departments. Coordination is again a problem in the work of the foreign student adviser who shares responsibility, but not information, with the academic adviser regarding the success or failure of the student. Regarding financial problems, so frequently mentioned by foreign students and their advisers, the authors find universities less able to help because private and international assistance is decreasing, U. S. aid is not increasing, and increased funding is needed for, and being allocated to, minority students.

Sanders and Ward also discuss the limitations placed on foreign students by the curriculum at American educational institutions: that training is based upon U. S. experience and within the U. S. setting; that American professors have little or no foreign experience (Asia is given geographical emphasis here) and are unfamiliar with the human and economic issues foremost in the minds of foreign students; and that degree requirements are narrowly prescribed and foreign students have little opportunity to mold programs of study to fit their needs. Reasons for the failure of colleges and universities to tailor curricula to fit foreign student needs may be lack of resources or of qualified personnel, fear of lowering standards, and reluctance to further compartmentalize the curriculum.

The authors make recommendations to university trustees, presidents, and other administrators, faculty, and students; to foundations, legislators, governmental officials, and communities. Trustees are advised to issue policy statements supporting the importance of international programs and indicating that leave and promotion policies will encourage those who choose to work with such programs. In addition, a trustee committee is recommended to work with univerwity representatives in providing a continuous appraisal of an institution's international efforts and to seek support for programs. University presidents and other administrators are asked to assure a high place for international programs among institutional priorities. Faculty are asked to ensure that participation in exchange programs meets the criteria of: (1) academic substantiveness of the programs, (2) treatment of scholars as scholars and not mere beneficiaries, and (3) return of some dividends to institutions through library acquisitions,

broadened contacts, and an increase in numbers of faculty exposed to
international issues in education. For foundations, the recommendations include the distribution of substantial grants that would lead to
development of an international intellectual network through support
of inter-institutional arrangements, and the maintenance of an overall pattern of grants to assure that the pendulum of interest does not
swing so far toward domestic issues that the previous heavy investment in international programs is dismantled for lack of support. The
legislators are requested to adopt and fund proposals which provide
effective exchange arrangements, and government officials are asked
to base planning and grant-making processes on continuous consultation with members of the academic community, other government
officials, and non-academic leaders in international affairs. It is also
recommended that government officials draw up guidelines for program evaluation. Finally, the suggestion is made that communities
cooperate with foreign student advisers in efforts to acquaint foreign
students with off-campus activities and in helping to make visiting
foreign scholars and their families feel welcome.

　　The last of the broad overviews on foreign students and foreign
student programs is The Foreign Graduate Student: Priorities for
Research and Action (430/1971). It, again, is the result of a
colloquium, held in 1970, and is a most useful discussion of the
future directions of exchange programs. The prospects for foreign
students are worsening as the demand for the opportunity to study in
the United States continues to rise. The era of affluence in American
graduate education has come abruptly to a halt and costs of graduate
education are soaring. In addition, other countries are facing an
educational glut of overtrained or wrongly trained people, and with
the prospect of no employment or unsuitable employment, many
foreign graduates fail to return home. This gloomy outlook has,
according to colloquium participants, several implications. In the
area of policy formation, they urgently recommended the development of national and institutional rationales for the presence of
foreign graduates. With regard to the administration of exchanges,
they recommended that policies be developed concerning the admission and training of foreign graduate students, and that sustained
efforts be made to consult with appropriate people overseas involved
in the formal educational system as well as others with legitimate
concerns in national manpower objectives. In other words, better
links should be established with foreign governments, universities,
and organizations as a basis for planning.

　　Perhaps the most valuable aspect of The Foreign Graduate
Student: Priorities for Research and Action, and one of the reasons
that it is considered last here, is its collection of recommendations
for research. These recommendations encompass what foreign

nationals are being trained, where, and at what levels; foreign manpower needs, educational opportunities, and governmental policies
regarding utilization of trained manpower, especially in developing
areas; policies of American universities and departments in respect
to admission of foreign graduate students; the rise in applications from
foreign student immigrants; the use of foreign students as laboratory or
teaching assistants; and "true costs" of American graduate education,
rates of production of American Ph.D.s, and probabilities of appropriate employment after completion of study. It is also suggested that a
more complete annual census of foreign students be instituted, going
beyond the data reported in Open Doors to include sources of financial
aid. Intermediate and longer-term research is recommended on a
wide range of issues: how to assess the foreign graduate student pool,
with special reference to the students' social and economic backgrounds;
effective selection and screening practices; determination of the
desirable "critical mass" of foreign students in U.S. institutions; the
cultural dimension of the learning process; education for social change
and how to effect social change; foreign students' performance in relation to data known at the time of their admissions; and the relevance
of U.S. curriculum for foreign graduate students. It is emphasized
that much information is already available on many of these issues,
and might be tapped profitably for research purposes.

It is evident that the broad non-empirical literature on the
structure, administration, and finance of foreign student programs and
services represents a highly valuable source of ideas, criticisms, and
recommendations for the future. The plethora of recommendations
found in these publications is the principal contribution of this literature. The extensive attention paid here to these recommendations,
often at the risk of repetition and overlap, is indicative of the importance attributed to them. Although this literature most often contains
little reference to empirical research, its value is high as an articulation of needs and a catalyst for future research and action.

Conclusion

In reviewing the non-empirical literature, observations were
made on the quality and quantity of publications in each category,
and on the central themes that appeared to receive the most emphasis.
The "guides" were found to be a useful type of direct-action literature
on a variety of topics: the need for updating some of these guides was
noted and somewhat greater depth in content, drawing upon recent
empirical studies, was advised as a means of enhancing their value.
In the literature on selection and admissions, repeated emphasis
appeared on the need for institutional and national rationales for the
presence of foreign students. The creation of a worldwide network of

Counseling, Evaluating, and Testing Centers (CETCs) also received attention in several publications. Analysis and interpretation of academic credentials of foreign students is aided by the publications which provide detailed background information on the educational systems of various countries. The principal conclusions of the non-empirical literature regarding English-language training and proficiency are that English proficiency is seldom used consistently as a criterion of admission to educational institutions, that such proficiency should not play a major role in admission provided that the institutions are prepared to support English-language training programs, and that TOEFL is the most valid and useful measure of proficiency presently available.

The literature on the foreign student adviser describes many of the difficulties of this position, due in part to the absence of institutional policy regarding the role of foreign student adviser or the presence of foreign students on campus. Despite increasing importance attributed to the foreign student adviser's job and an increase in duties and expectations, there appears to be a reduction in support for that position. A repeated emphasis on cooperation and communication is expressed in all quarters. Government agencies, in an era of tight money, show increasing concern with achieving the most impact with the funds available. Toward that end there have been, and will be, attempts to improve communication among program staff, participants, and universities, to initiate cooperative ventures with other agencies and organizations, and to encourage exchange relationships between other countries.

In the literature on the activities of private organizations, considerable attention is paid to orientation programs; in-country, academic orientation in specific disciplines and professions, and terminal orientation for students returning to their home countries. Other interrelated themes in the literature on private organizations include a concern for the conflict in training goals among different agencies, institutions, and organizations; the question of relating training goals to the manpower needs of developing countries; and, again, the need to increase the amount of communication among governments, private organizations, educational institutions, and the foreign students.

Universities and colleges were found to be taking a number of approaches to the training of foreign students. Their international programs were being threatened, however, as government and private foundations shift their support toward pressing domestic issues. Suggested solutions to this problem included language and area-studies centers that tie their goals more closely to domestic and foreign policy; better selection of foreign students; careful re-evaluation of study-abroad programs; better communication with other educational

institutions, organizations, and agencies; and, again, the formulation
of rationales for the presence of foreign students and of goals for international programs.

The business world appears to be investigating cooperative
relationships with universities and with governments of developing
nations, and formation of educational foundations by corporations to
administer international programs.

Finally, the publications which focus on international relations
and foreign students indicate that educational and cultural activities
should receive greater consideration in foreign policy thinking, that
such a broadened conception may be helpful in mitigating international
tensions, that inter-university cooperation is a useful method of
cutting across national boundaries, that multilateral approaches to
exchange through international agencies should be strengthened, and
that there should be precise objectives set for international educational and cultural exchange.

Recommendations

A principal feature of the literature on the structure, administration, and finance of foreign student programs and services is the large
number of recommendations made for both action and research.
Summarized below are the major recommendations contained in the
studies reviewed in this chapter.

Recommendations for Educational Institutions

The most frequently made recommendation is that institutions
must develop rationales for the foreign student presence. Once the
international education goals of the college or university are clarified,
the administration and faculty are urged to support and develop them.
It is suggested, for instance, that university trustees issue policy
statements supporting the importance of international programs and
indicating that leave and promotion policies will be adjusted to
encourage faculty who choose to work with such programs. A trustee
committee should work with university representatives in providing
continuous evaluation of an institution's international efforts to seek
support for its programs. Presidents and other high university officials
are also asked to ensure a high place for international programs
among institutional priorities.

Another area which concerns general university policy is the
need for more cooperative efforts between U. S. institutions and
both foreign institutions and foreign governments. Some universities

and university consortia which are developing linkages of this type are described in Chapter 4. More specifically, it is here recommended that two-way exchanges of visiting scholars should be upgraded and widened to include more institutions; that universities should consider, as an approach to funding from international agencies, a procedure in which the contracting agent is an individual rather than the university itself; and that universities encourage faculty individually and collectively to seek and develop inter-institutional links across national boundaries to devise joint curricula.

A number of recommendations concern the expansion of the international dimensions of the campus. In several reports it is suggested that a "critical mass" of foreign students is needed and that therefore there should be institutional and departmental quotas for foreign students. These students should then be encouraged to participate in university governance and to develop their own representative governing bodies. Existing campus groups should make a special effort to attract foreign students, and there should be a foreign student dimension in housing, student unions, and cafeterias, as well as in the classroom. As for the faculty, their involvement in exchange programs must meet the criteria of academic substantiveness, treatment of scholars as scholars and not as mere beneficiaries, and, most importantly, the return of dividends to the institution through library acquisitions, broadened contacts, and increased numbers of faculty exposed to international issues.

Finally, the institution must accept greater responsibility for the unsponsored student.

Selection and Admission

The problem of developing better admissions criteria is addressed in several studies which recommend that complete files on each applicant be compiled before deciding on admission and placement; that standardized application forms be adopted; and that institutions should query each applicant as to the timeliness of the sojourn, the ability to accept the financial burden of study abroad, and the degree of academic preparation. There is also general agreement that academic permissiveness, encouraging a double standard for foreign students, should be eschewed.

Less agreement is found regarding specific admissions criteria. Some studies suggest that eligibility for home university systems is a useful admissions guideline; others recommend the contrary. Similarly, some studies recommend more selective admissions standards and others the adoption of more flexible criteria. There is also disagreement on whether TOEFL should be used as an aptitude test or predictor of academic success, although most studies agree that American institutions should be prepared to offer programs which raise the English-language proficiency of foreign students or be willing to participate in regional language centers. Another problem area concerns the degree to which institutions should consider the manpower needs of developing countries. If such a policy is adopted, the institution should make sustained efforts to consult with appropriate persons in the home country, and query the applicant on his or her ability to utilize training upon return home.

Orientation

In general, it is recommended that orientation be a continuing process. Greater emphasis should be placed on orientation in the home country prior to departure, on academic orientation in specific disciplines upon arrival at the U.S. institution, and on terminal orientation immediately before return home. A related recommendation is for a worldwide network of Counseling, Evaluating, and Testing Centers for prospective foreign students.

Curriculum

In the area of curriculum development, it is recommended that international programs become an integral part of the university's basic curriculum, resulting in academic advantages to both foreign and American students. Within such programs, full use should be made of the special abilities and knowledge of foreign students, as teachers, aides, and "informants." One of the most frequently made recommendations is that curricula for foreign students should be more relevant to their professional needs and to the needs of the developing nations.

Advising and Counseling

Foreign students need both academic and personal advice; recommendations in this field focus on the role of the foreign student adviser. Each institution which enrolls foreign students should have a full-time, professionally qualified foreign student adviser who is competent to perform high-level, cross-cultural counseling. Closer cooperation between this person and the academic adviser is recommended, and some studies suggest that the foreign student adviser be part of a campus team which will provide a variety of services for the foreign students.

Recommendations for Government

As in the case of institutional policy, it is recommended that national goals regarding international education be reassessed.

Regarding funding, it is suggested that there be a renewal of the national commitment to international exchange, and that the burden of assistance be shifted from financially troubled local institutions to the federal government. Government officials are asked to base planning and grant-making decisions on continuous consultation with members of the academic community, other government officials, and non-academic leaders in international affairs. Educational and cultural activities should receive more attention in foreign policy, and better channels of communication opened among governments, sponsors, and academic institutions. This is particularly true of the government-sponsored training programs such as AID. Concerning the Fulbright-Hayes program, it is recommended that efforts be made to increase support from the private sectors and from foreign governments; that funds should be granted to "team activities," and that grantees should be primarily persons in higher education or other professional fields.

Consideration should also be given to the creation of regional training institutes which could offer less expensive and more appropriate courses of study for students from developing countries.

Recommendations for Foreign Governments

Recommendations in this area focus on the need for better man-power planning and coordination of such plans with training abroad programs. Each developing country should forecast its manpower needs, select candidates for study abroad, and finance and supervise that study in appropriate institutions. This idea is discussed further in Chapter 4.

Recommendations for Private Organizations

General recommendations concern, again, the need for better communication between the sponsoring organization and the government, and for the strengthening of relationships between the government and the private sector. It is suggested that private organizations should be responsible for a Foreign Credential Evaluation Service, a centralized clearinghouse to process admissions, and for improving in-country orientation programs. Foundations should be aware that students prefer longer sojourns, and should maintain an overall pattern of grants which assures that the pendulum of interest does not swing so far toward domestic issues that previous heavy investment in international programs is dismantled for lack of support.

Recommendations for Business

It is recommended that cooperative relationships be developed between corporations (particularly international corporations) and universities, on the one hand, and between corporations and governments on the other. Educational foundations should be established which would have the specific function of developing and administering such programs in developing countries. These foundations should be supported by contributions from corporations proportional to their total investment in the developing country.

Recommendations for Communities

Recommendations in this area concern primarily the need for better coordination of community services for foreign students; improved communication with academic institutions, sponsoring agencies, and government; and planned financing of such services. Communities should, for instance, cooperate with foreign student advisers in efforts to acquaint foreign students with off-campus activities and in making visiting scholars and their families feel welcome.

Future Research

The following is a listing of topics suggested for further research.

Curriculum

1. On the kind and quality of education received by foreign students.
2. On the relevance of U.S. curriculum for foreign graduate students.
3. On foreign students' perceptions about the relevance of U.S. education to their future needs (economic, political, and personal).
4. On the cultural dimension of the learning process.
5. On the utility of master's-degree programs for foreign students.

Admission and Selection

1. On effective selection and screening practices.
2. On policies of American universities and departments with respect to admission of foreign graduate students.
3. On the criteria used by institutions in selecting foreign students.
4. On the desirable "critical mass" of foreign students in U.S. institutions.

5. On the rise of applications from foreign student immigrants.
6. On how to assess the foreign graduate student pool, with emphasis on social and economic backgrounds.
7. On foreign student performance in relation to data known at time of admission.

Advising and Counseling

1. On the expectations of foreign students concerning services of foreign student advisers.
2. On the relationship of personal counseling to academic achievement.
3. On dominant influences on interpersonal relationships in different cultures.

Language

1. Quantitative studies on correlations between language proficiency and academic achievement.
2. Examination of English proficiency standards and ways to meet the needs of Latin American students.

Other

1. On readjustment to the home countries and attitudes toward America.
2. Applied research conducted in the form of evaluation of exchange programs.
3. Follow-up studies of foreign students after return to their home countries.
4. On what foreign nationals are being trained, where, and at what levels.
5. On foreign manpower needs, educational opportunities, and governmental policies regarding utilization of trained manpower, especially in developing areas.
6. On the use of foreign students as laboratory or teaching assistants.
7. On the "true costs" of American graduate education and rates of production of American Ph. D. s and probabilities of appropriate employment.
8. On education for social change and how to effect social change.

CHART 3.1 - EMPIRICAL STUDIES: STRUCTURE, ADMINISTRATION, AND FINANCE

Item No./ Author(s)/ Date	Sponsorship	Population Studied/ Geographical Emphasis	Data Collection Methodology/No. of Respondents	Data Analysis Methodology	Key Ideas
43/Bloom/ 1970	Diss.	U. S. Fac./Multi-Nat.	Unstated/ Unstated	Simp. Anal.	The study indicates the need to analyze and design the existing foreign student programs in two-year colleges to meet the real needs of this student group. The study indicates that foreign students are accepted by colleges with little prior planning. Lack of organization in foreign student programs and lack of communication between colleges' administration and the students are major problems. Each college must define international goals.
266/ Bridgers and Hall/ n.d.	Priv./Non-Gov./Amer.	For. Emp., Other	Struct. Inter., Res. Rev./ Not stated	Simp. Anal., Case Anal.	Survey revealed inadequacy of pre-departure orientation of non-sponsored students from México, Colombia, and Chile. Informational materials available to students coming to the US from these countries was also found to be inadequate.
399/Bureau of Educational and Cultural Affairs/1967	Gov. Ag.	For. Stud., Other/ Multi-Nat.	Res. Rev., Struct. Inter./Unstated	Simp. Anal., Res. Rev., Case Anal.	Summaries of 40 evaluation studies of programs in international and educational exchange. Describes attitude change as a result of exchange programs (mostly Fulbright and "Foreign Leader" Programs) and problems of exchangees.
71/Coan/ 1966	Univ.	For. Stud./Multi-Nat.	Quest./187	Simp. Anal.	Showed that foreign students on University of Kansas campus were fairly well-satisfied with their housing. However, more effort was needed to find more attractive housing for older graduate-level students. Many legal problems with housing.

Item No./ Author(s)/ Date	Sponsorship	Population Studied/ Geographical Emphasis	Data Collection Methodology/No. of Respondents	Data Analysis Methodology	Key Ideas
72/Coan/ 1969	Univ.	For. Stud./Multi-Nat.	Quest./302	Simp. Anal.	Study on housing for foreign students at University of Kansas. Preferences in housing as well as dislikes and disadvantages concerning on-campus and off-campus housing examined.
107/Deluga/ 1970	Diss.	Prog. Ad./Multi-Nat.	Quest./631	Simp. Anal.	Primary objectives of the study were analysis of selection procedures for foreign students at U. S. universities (undergraduate students only were considered) and evaluation of the effectiveness of the present system of selection. Admissions officers were found to have insufficient background and training to effectively evaluate credentials.
287/ Dremuk/ 1969	Priv./ Non-Gov.	Prog. Ad., Other/ Multi-Nat.	Not Stated/ Not Stated	Simp. Anal.	A report advocating the establishment of foreign credential evaluation services--under non-government auspices.
129/ Elliott/ 1967	Diss.	Prog. Ad./Multi-Nat.	Inf. Inter/Ob. Records/ Not Stated	Case Anal.	Examination of foreign student programs of selected California public junior colleges to identify administrative policies and salient problems. Twenty recommendations were made.

Item No./ Author(s)/ Date	Sponsorship	Population Studied/ Geographical Emphasis	Data Collection Methodology/No. of Respondents	Data Analysis Methodology	Key Ideas
130/ Elliott/ 1969	Univ., Priv., Non-Gov.	Not Stated/ Multi-Nat.	Records/Seven Colleges	Case Anal.	Admission policies and practices for foreign students at a sample of California junior colleges are examined.
133/Farmer and Renforth/ 1971	Not Stated	Other/Multi-Nat.	Economic statistics collected	Economic analysis of statistics	This study attempts to determine the effect in monetary terms of the presence of foreign students in the State of Indiana. It was found to be difficult to arrive at a cash value from the presence of foreign students.
135/ Feinberg/ 1967	M.A. thesis	Journalism Schools/ Multi-Nat.	Quest., Struct. Inter./22 schools. Total population not stated.	Simp. Anal.	Examines selection and admissions criteria of 22 western and mid-western journalism schools.
395/Frey/ 1969	Gov. Ag.	Prog. Ad., Other/ Multi-Nat.	Quest., Res. Rev.	Simp. Anal., Case Anal., Res. Rev.	The study was conducted to determine whether a non-governmental Foreign Credential Evaluation Service should be established. A survey revealed that such an agency could provide improved service over the present credential service of the U. S. Office of Education. No consensus on organizational structure. New service could be self-supporting after 5 years.
153/ Grafton/ 1970	Priv./Non-Gov.	Prog. Ad., Other/ Multi-Nat.	Quest./Not Stated	Simp. Anal.	Questionnaire survey revealed that community colleges enrolled few foreign students. More than one-half of foreign students in junior colleges were in 3 states: California, Michigan, and Illinois. Eight out of 10 foreign students in junior colleges were transfer students. Few special programs for foreign students in junior colleges.

169

Item No./ Author(s)/ Date	Sponsorship	Population Studied/ Geographical Emphasis	Data Collection Methodology/No. of Respondents	Data Analysis Methodology	Key Ideas
174/ Hickey/ 1967	Univ.	Prog. Ad./Multi-Nat.	Quest./19 public junior colleges in Kansas and Nebraska, 5 private Kansas junior colleges	Simp. Anal.	There were no standardized admissions procedures among the surveyed colleges. No full-time advisers. More variety among foreign students urged.
175/ Higbee/ 1961	Found. Priv./Non-Gov.	Prog. Ad., For. Stud., Other/ Multi-Nat.	Quest., Inf. Inter-Ob./1,365 institutions; 220 interviews with university officials	Soph. Anal., Case Anal.	Examines the status of foreign student advising in U. S. colleges and universities. Adviser's function was generally not given high administrative priority.
188/International Association of Universities/1970	Inter-Gov.	Other/W. Eur., E. Eur. & USSR, Amer.	Anal. Case/Six Countries	Case Anal.	Methods and practices of establishing equivalences between degrees and diplomas, and the nature of those equivalences, are examined for six countries: USSR, US, France, Czechoslovakia, Federal Republic of Germany, and the UK. Multilateral, bilateral, and unilateral approaches to establishing equivalences are discussed.
191/ Irvine/ 1968	Not Stated	For. Stud./Multi.: M.East, E. Asia, S.E. Asia, M.S. Asia	Quest./106	Simp. Anal.	The major finding of the study was that foreign students' expectations of what their advisers could do for them was much greater than what they actually experience. It was recommended that advisers need much improved techniques of communication.
213/Kent/ 1973	Gov. Ag.	Other/Multi-Nat.	Economic Statistics	Simp. Econ. Statistical Anal.	Attempts to determine the monetary benefits to the New York State economy of the presence of foreign students. Foreign student "industry" was found to rank 18th among state exporters.

Item No./ Author(s)/ Date	Sponsorship	Population Studied/ Geographical Emphasis	Data Collection Methodology/No. of Respondents	Data Analysis Methodology	Key Ideas
217/Kir- stein/ 1971	None	U. S. Commun., Prog. Ad./Multi-Nat.	Quest./10	Simp. Anal.	Examines community services for foreign students in some large metropolitan areas. For the most part the structure of these services was found to be ineffective, suffering from lack of coordination and inadequate communication with foreign students and sponsoring agencies.
228/ Lockett/ 1970	Diss.	For. Stud./Multi-Nat.	Quest./795	Soph. Anal.	Purpose of the study was to obtain an indication of the effectiveness of foreign student advisers as perceived by foreign students. Most advisers were seen as effective. The major determinant of usefulness of foreign student advisers as perceived by foreign students was their availability to the students.
234/ Marsh/ 1972	Diss.	Prog. Ad./Multi-Nat.	Quest., Struct. Inter./Not Stated	Simp. Anal., Case Anal., Res. Rev.	Describes the role of the foreign student adviser in the community college and his functions in that role. The community college adviser is seen to be more likely trained as a counselor than his counterpart in a four-year institution. Absence of institutional policy for foreign students may limit the foreign student adviser's role in the community college. Typical Advisers in community colleges serve in that role one-quarter time or less.
272/ Matthewson/ 1968	Priv./Non- Gov.	Prog. Ad./Multi-Nat.	Quest./410	Simp. Anal.	Provides data on topics concerning the housing, finances, English proficiency, and enrollment of foreign students at US junior colleges, as well as information on community services offered and institutional philosophy.

171

Item No./ Author(s)/ Date	Sponsorship	Population Studied/ Geographical Emphasis	Data Collection Methodology/No. of Respondents	Data Analysis Methodology	Key Ideas
249/ Miller/ 1968	Diss.	Prog. Ad./Multi-Nat.	Struct. Inter./48	Simp. Anal.	The critical incident technique was used to obtain information about those functions of the foreign student advisor which, if performed in an effective manner, have a significant effect on the adviser's successful performance; 200 common functions were identified.
284/ NAFSA/ 1972	Priv./Non-Gov.	For. Stud., U. S. Fac./Multi-Nat.	Struct. Inter., Anal. Case/ 2 depts. at 12 univ.	Simp. Anal., Case Anal.	This report is a synthesis of conclusions on institutional policy, departmental policy, admissions, financial aid, English competency, and foreign student services and programs. Findings show that most of the universities surveyed don't have policies supporting involvement in international education and foreign student enrollment, nor do most of the departments surveyed, Most of the surveyed universities had no specific institutional policies on foreign student admissions.
280/ NAFSA/ 1973	Priv./Non-Gov.	Prog. Ad./Amer.	Quest./481	Simp. Anal.	Provides data on the institutions enrolling Latin American students in the US. Information given includes enrollment, financial aid, TOEFL requirements, academic options, and names of campus contact persons.
264e/ NAFSA/ 1974	Priv./Non-Gov.	W. Eur.	Res. Rev., Hist.	Case Anal.	Report contains basic information on background and structure of 5 Nordic countries (Norway, Sweden, Denmark, Iceland, and Finland) including the grading systems of each country. Purpose of the report is to help admissions officers in evaluating academic credentials of students of these countries entering the US.

Item No./ Author(s)/ Date	Sponsorship	Population Studied/ Geographical Emphasis	Data Collection Methodology/No. of Respondents	Data Analysis Methodology	Key Ideas
304/ Paraske-vopoulous and Dremuk/ 1969	None	U. S. Fac./Multi-Nat.	Quest./565	Simp. Anal.	Contains information gathered from faculty of the University of Illinois concerning their differential course requirements and grading standards for foreign vs. American students. 96 percent of faculty said they did expect foreign students to meet same standards as Americans.
331/ Rives/ 1971	Diss.	...	Theoretical	Theoretical Soph. Anal.	The market framework established in the study provides a tool for relating factors of trade in higher education and related human capital migration.
338/ Schulken/ 1968	Diss.	.../Multi-Nat.	Hist., Res. Rev.	Res. Rev.	Examines several major forces which influenced the development of the foreign student movement in US higher education. The missionary movement, philanthropic foundations, and the US Government are seen to have each contributed significantly.

CHART 3.2 -- NON-EMPIRICAL STUDIES: STRUCTURE, ADMINISTRATION, AND FINANCE

Item No./ Author(s)/ Date	Sponsorship	Geographic Emphasis	Includes Reference to Empirical Research	Key Ideas
29/AACRAO Conference/ 1970	Priv./Non- Gov.	Multi-Nat.	None	Report of a discussion at an AACRAO conference. Makes a case for the continuation and expansion of international exchange programs. The need for each institution to analyze what it is trying to do is emphasized. Institutional obligations are discussed.
6/African- American Institute/ n. d.	Priv./Non- Gov.	Sub. Sah. Af.	None	Annual Report of African Scholarship Program (ASPAU). Nigeria accounted for 23.71 percent of ASPAU grantees. Was decrease (and later restitution) of AID maintenance support. There was repayment of travel obligations by several participating nations.
9a/AID and NAFSA/ 1970	Gov. Ag. Priv./Non- Gov.	Multi-Nat.	None	Report of a workshop to provide 32 foreign student advisers with information about the functions and services of the Office of International Training (AID) and to allow the foreign student advisers to describe their role and function. Recommendations were made to improve coordination between AID and the universities.
9b/AID- NAFSA/ 1971	Gov. Ag. Priv./Non- Gov.	Multi-Nat.	None	Describes the Second NAFSA-AID Workshop. Purposes were to broaden contacts between AID's Participant Training Program and NAFSA representatives on campus and in the community. Recommendations were made on orientation, counselling, community relations, and relations among campuses, AID, and participating agencies.
23/American Library Assn./ 1970	Priv./Non- Gov.	Multi-Nat.	Some	Four papers present a subjective look at foreign-trained librarians and North American Libraries and foreign students in North American library education programs. Analyzes policies and practices related to their employment.
1/Ackerson/ 1970	None	Multi-Nat.	Some	Examines role of corporations in educational change. Principal form of support is grants to foreign students for study in US.

174

Item No./ Author(s)/ Date	Sponsorship	Geographic Emphasis	Includes Reference to Empirical Research	Key Ideas
27/Arapoff 1969	Not stated	Multi-Nat.	Some	Describes the "discover and transform method" of learning written English.
34/Barrientos and Schufletowski/1968	None	Multi-Nat.	None	Elimination of permissive academic standards for foreign students, more selective admissions policies, and the creation of foreign student offices committed to and competent to perform high-level, cross-cultural theory and practice as well as guidance and counseling are suggested as the best ways to create favorable conditions for foreign students in US universities.
283/Benson and Kovach/ 1974	Gov. Ag. and Priv. Non-Gov.	Multi-Nat.	None	A guide for foreign students in the form of a checklist of actions in the ideal exchange experience. Ten stages of this experience are described, from planning and selection to follow-up, evaluation, and continuing education.
44a/Board of Foreign Scholarships/ 1969	Gov. Ag.	Multi-Nat.	None	Seventh annual report of the Board to the US Congress. Presents statistics summarizing grants made in exchange programs since 1959. Concern is expressed for cutback in private and federal funding for educational change.
44b/Board of Foreign Scholarships/1973	Gov. Ag.	Multi-Nat.	None	Annual report. A major feature of 1971-72 was the reorganization of the Board and the introduction of a system of sub-committees to provide more effective liaison with cooperating agencies. Statistics presented on various exchange programs in 1971-72.
45/Board of Foreign Scholarships/1970	Gov. Ag.	Multi-Nat.	None	A policy statement by the Board. Recommends that participants in exchanges be engaged in higher education activities. There should also be increasing numbers of persons from non-academic professions, too, however. The Board's programs should focus on a few subjects or problems at a time. There should also be an expansion of support to non-sponsored scholars and educational groups.

Item No./ Author(s)/ Date	Sponsorship	Geographic Emphasis	Includes Reference to Empirical Research	Key Ideas
46/Board of Foreign Scholarships/1971	Gov. Ag.	Multi-Nat.	None	Presents an informal history of 25 years of the Fulbright-Hayes Program. Future directions are discussed: (1) bi-national commissions to concentrate on 3 or 4 broadly conceived programs, (2) exchanges should be concentrated on persons in higher education or professions, (3) funds should be granted to team activities, (4) policy should be directed to increasing support from private sectors and foreign governments.
51/Brettell and Gildseth/ 1969	Univ.	Multi-Nat.	None	Overview of International student programs at Kansas State University.
276/ Bridgers/ 1970	Priv./ Non-Gov.	Amer.	None	Describes an orientation program conducted in Venezuela for Venezuelan students coming to the US. Recommends this program as a prototype for other nations. Also describes a less sophisticated orientation program in the Dominican Republic.
400a–o/ Bureau of Educational and Cultural Affairs/1968	Gov. Ag.		Some	These reports describe educational and cultural exchanges between the US and other countries: Argentina, Bolivia, Brazil, Chile, Colombia, Costa Rica, the Dominican Republic, Ethiopia, Japan, Kenya, Liberia, México, Perú, Tunisia, and Venezuela.
405/Bureau of Educational and Cultural Affairs/1974	Gov. Ag.	Multi-Nat.	Some	Describes a variety of exchanges between the US and other nations. Trends in exchange are noted, including funding of special US-African exchange projects for black college faculty and secondary school teachers, the development of a number of exchange programs on an institutional basis, and the growing support of other nations for exchange.
279/ Byers/ 1972	Priv. Non-Gov.	W. Eur.	Much	This report is aimed at American academicians concerned with admitting West German students to US universities. It is an extensive description of the history and structure of the German educational system. Also outlines equivalences between US and German degrees.

Item No./ Author(s)/ Date	Sponsorship	Geographic Emphasis	Includes Reference to Empirical Research	Key Ideas
62/ Carpenter/ 1969	None	Multi-Nat.	None	Describes the various roles of foreign student advisers in the US. Lack of institutional policy on foreign students at universities is seen as a major impediment to the advisers as they attempt to define their roles.
73/Coan/ 1969	Univ.	Multi-Nat.	Some	A descriptive profile of the number and type of foreign students at the University of Kansas.
79/College Entrance Examination Board/1969	Priv./Non-Gov.	Multi-Nat.	Some	Report on a colloquium focusing on broad questions relating to foreign student graduate programs: policies, prospects, assumptions and responsibilities from the standpoint of graduate schools; interplay in such programs between the university, government agencies, and sponsoring agencies; and how policies of universities can be defined and communicated.
430/College Entrance Examination Board/1971	Priv./Non-Gov.	Multi-Nat.	Some	Identifies pertinent questions related to the influx of foreign students and seeks to consensus on priorities for research and action. National and institutional rationales are seen as needed for the presence of foreign graduate students.
82/Colligan/ Priv./ 1963	Non-Gov.	Multi-Nat.	Some	The international commitments of US colleges and universities are seen as permanent and increasing. These institutions, it is recommended, must provide leadership in assessing program objectives and in cooperating with government and private agencies in achieving those objectives. Other recommendations include more flexible admission standards, continuing orientation programs, and greater budgetary support for foreign student services.
85/Coombs/ 1961	None	Multi-Nat.	Some	Briefly assesses the accomplishments and failures of international exchange programs, particularly by the US Government. Recommendations include more cooperation between private and federal agencies to provide for non-sponsored students, and the creation of admission/ guidance offices in countries sending large numbers of students to the US.

177

Item No./ Author(s)/ Date	Sponsorship	Geographic Emphasis	Includes Reference to Empirical Research	Key Ideas
86/Coombs/ 1964	Priv./ Non-Gov.	Multi-Nat.	Some	Educational and cultural activities are seen to comprise a fourth dimension of foreign policy that can bolster political, economic, and military elements. The contribution of educational and cultural exchange to foreign policy is traced and it is contended that in the future educational policies must be shaped by a clear set of objectives, better planning, and vigorous administration.
91/Cormack/ 1973	Univ.	M. S. Asia	Some	Examines the program of Callison College in sending American students to study in India. The cultural credits and debits to both countries are considered. The purpose of such a program is seen to be intercultural education, based on a clear intercultural aim, appropriate selection and orientation in relation to this aim, and integration of the intercultural experience into the college curriculum.
394/Cotner/ n.d.	Not stated	Multi-Nat.	Some	Reviews some of the various programs administered and the number of grantees involved since the US Office of Education became engaged in educational exchange.
95/Craig/ 1973	Priv./ Non-Gov.	Sub. Sah. Af.	None	Traces the history of the African Scholarship Program of American Universities (ASPAU) from 1960-70. Major administrative problems included: (1) conflict between the training goals of AID and the educative goals of the participating institutions, (2) rising costs of US education and changes in funding priorities of both educational institutions and US agencies.
97/Darian/ 1968	None	Multi-Nat.	Much	The purpose of the study is to determine the trends in the teaching of English as a Foreign Language in American colleges and universities from 1880 to 1965. Early materials were built around a semantic topic rather than a specific grammar pattern. An analysis of recent methodology reveals that the aural-oral technique is used less often than writing in the teaching of grammar.

Item No./ Author(s)/ Date	Sponsorship	Geographic Emphasis	Includes Reference to Empirical Research	Key Ideas
104/Davis/ 1971	None	Multi-Nat.	None	Examines those aspects of two-year community colleges that relate to foreign students and makes recommendations for their optimum success. Among recommendations for these colleges are: (1) clear information must be provided about these colleges to the students abroad, (2) selective admissions, (3) special orientation procedures, (4) professional advisers.
106/ DeAntoni/ 1972	None	Multi-Nat.	None	Examines the difficulties that foreign students have in job hunting. Many countries were found to be less than willing to cooperate in attracting nationals back home. Satisfactory career counseling was seen to be dependent on counselor's knowledge of foreign students' patterns of socialization and their lifestyle.
122/Eddy/ 1972	None	Multi-Nat.	Some	A shortage of jobs, tight money, restrictions in the acceptance of out-of-state students, and language difficulties are some of the principal problems facing foreign students. Support for foreign student offices appears to be declining. Policy recommendations, directed toward foreign student advisers, include: (1) arrangement of links between institutions and foreign governments, (2) refusal to admit students with insufficient funds.
127/ Elliott/ 1965	None	Multi-Nat.	None	An insufficient place is seen to have been accorded the role of the "fellowship administrator" in evaluating the programs for which he is responsible.
128/ Elliott/ 1967	None	Multi-Nat.	Some	Humanitarian, political, and educational approaches to the study of the foreign student are discussed. Statistics on foreign students are found to be limited in the kinds of information they can convey. Factors which should be considered in the present and future development of policies toward foreign students are discussed.
123/EWA Study Committee on Foreign Student Affairs/1966	Gov. Ag.	Multi-Nat.	Some	Foreign student policies of many US colleges and universities are seen to be ambiguous and conflicting. Further, admissions decisions are found to be hampered by the lack of reliable information of prospective students and of adequate means for evaluating foreign credentials. Much cooperative planning is needed among private and government agencies to reduce the confusion and conflict.

Item No./ Author(s)/ Date	Sponsorship	Geographic Emphasis	Includes Reference to Empirical Research	Key Ideas
300/Education and World Affairs/ 1966	Priv./Non-Gov.	Multi-Nat.	None	A world-wide network of Counseling, Evaluating, and Testing Centers is advocated to help US colleges and universities cope with the expanding number of foreign student applications.
397/Fact Sheet on the International Exchange Program:1946-66	Gov. Ag.	Multi-Nat.	Some	Describes the principal features of the US Department of State program including initiating legislation, a statement of purpose, history, and philosophy.
142/ Frankel/ 1966	Priv./Non-Gov.	Multi-Nat.	Some	Education and cultural relations with other countries constitute a neglected aspect of US foreign policy, according to the author. It is suggested that the goals of US educational and cultural exchange be restated to include: lacing together of educational systems, improvement of communications and furthering of educational and cultural relations as ends in themselves.
165/Heath/ 1969	None	Multi-Nat.	None	Describes the Lodestar International Student Center in northern California. The Center provides eight one-week sessions each summer for small groups of students from various cultures.
21/Hefling/ 1971	Priv./Non-Gov.	Multi-Nat.	Much	Lists reference materials which can be used in the analysis and interpretation of academic credentials of AID participants from various parts of the world.
295/Heft/ 1963	Inter-Gov.	Amer., Multi-Nat.	Some	The objective of the paper is to help determine whether and how the training of foreign students in the US can contribute to the reduction of world tensions. Suggestions for more effective training of foreign students include: (1) inter-university cooperation between foreign and US institutions, (2) training for youth leadership, (3) extension of the period of international fellowships beyond that devoted to sojourn abroad.

Item No./ Author(s)/ Date	Sponsorship	Geographic Emphasis	Includes Reference to Empirical Research	Key Ideas
173/Henry/ 1972	None	Amer.	None	Reports on activities of the Latin American Scholarship Program (LASPAU) 1969–71.
178/Holland/ 1956	None	Multi–Nat.	Much	Contains statistics on various aspects of the foreign-student experience in the US. An essay by Hilda Taba, entitled, <u>Cultural Attitudes and International Understanding</u> (1954) analyzes experiences of 45 American students on a European summer-study tour. It is concluded that foreign experiences do not automatically create international-mindedness. The aims and interests of orientation programs are considered in an essay on <u>Orientation of Foreign Students, Signposts for the Cultural Maze.</u>
181/Institute of International Education/1967	Priv./Non-Gov.	Multi–Nat.	None	For the foreign student who plans to enter a US junior college, this booklet presents information about the location, programs, instructional methods, costs, and requirements of such two-year schools.
183/Institute of International Education/1969	Priv., Non-Gov.	Multi–Nat.	Some	Proceedings of a conference on how business and government can jointly close the world-wide learning gap. Specific goals, sound organization, operational flexibility, and assured funding were seen to be essential to such cooperative assistance.
186/Institute of International Education/1973	Priv./Non-Gov.	Multi–Nat.	None	This booklet lists and briefly describes 121 offerings of English-language programs, separate orientation programs with English-language training and special opportunity programs at 108 institutions.
189a/International Research and Exchanges Board/1972	Priv./Non-Gov.	E. E. & USSR	None	Annual Report (1971–72) of IREX describing US exchanges with the USSR and Eastern Europe. Preparatory fellowships for US doctoral candidates have proven so successful that additional funds were obtained for 1973–74. Problems of exchanges with the USSR include continuing Soviet rejection of Americans working in "sensitive" areas.

Item No./Author(s)/Date	Sponsorship	Geographic Emphasis	Includes Reference to Empirical Research	Key Ideas
189b/International Research and Exchanges Board/1973	Priv./Non-Gov.	E. E. & USSR	None	Annual Report (1972-73) of IREX describing US exchanges with the USSR and Eastern Europe. Exchange successes were detailed, notably the visit of US Russian-language teachers to Moscow. The report stresses, however, that "detente has not solved any fundamental problems of scholarly contact with the Soviet Union."
2/Jacqz/1967	Priv./Non-Gov.	N. Af. Sub. Sah. Af.	Some	This is a report of a conference on the Admission and Guidance of African Students held at Howard University. A major issue at the conference was whether or not US colleges and universities should be responsive to African manpower needs in admitting and guiding African students. Suggestions were made to respond to African manpower needs: stricter passport control, emphasis on graduate programs, and provision of information on manpower plans.
3/Jacqz/1967	Priv./Non-Gov.	N. Af. Sub. Sah. Af.	None	Report of a workshop on refugee students from southern Africa. Estimated to be 350,000 to 440,000 such refugees. Discussion focused on factors affecting training and utilization of these students. The primary goal of training was seen to be preparation for participation in the struggle for freedom.
264b/Jameson/n.d.	Priv./Non-Gov.	Oceania, S. E. Asia, M. S. Asia, E. Asia	Some	Report of a workshop of admissions officers and resource persons from the Pacific-Asia area. Historical and cultural background and detailed information on educational systems of Hong Kong, Singapore, Malaysia, Australia, Pakistan, India, Ceylon, New Zealand, and the Pacific Islands is provided to help admissions officers evaluate degrees and credentials.
193/Jameson and Malcom/1972-73	None	Multi-Nat.	Some	Discusses history, development, and utility of TOEFL (Test of English as a Foreign Language).
271/Jenkins/1968	Priv./Non-Gov.	Amer.	None	A conference report which attempts to translate recommendations made in a study on Latin American students in US colleges and universities (Gordon Ruscoe, 1968) into specific program proposals. The proposals cover admissions and financial assistance, orientation, and English proficiency.

Item No./ Author(s)/ Date	Sponsorship	Geographic Emphasis	Includes Reference to Empirical Research	Key Ideas
200/Johnston/ 1969	Univ.	Amer.	Some	This report presents a review of the Florida Inter-American Learning Institute (FILI). Begun in 1968, FILI was designed as a "half-way house" where foreign students could increase their ability to communicate in English.
208/Kaplan/ 1968	Priv./Non-Gov.	Multi-Nat.	Some	The major assertion of this address is that English proficiency should not be a criterion for admission of foreign students to US universities, providing that the institution is willing to assume the obligation of English instruction.
209/Kaplan/ 1968	None	Multi-Nat.	Some	Educational institutions should not consider English-language proficiency as a criterion for admission of foreign students. Admissions policies should be related to the institutions' capability to provide English-language training.
210/Kaplan/ 1970	Priv./Non-Gov.	Multi-Nat.	None	It is argued that NAFSA must encourage educational institutions and government to adjust to the presence of foreign students by making every effort to insure the relevance of US education to global problems. NAFSA must also combat the growing reaction against international education.
267/Kaplan/ n.d.	Priv./Non-Gov.	Multi-Nat.	Some	Suggests a series of recommendations addressed to the State University System of Florida on dealing with foreign students. The recommendations are, however, seen as the basis for a more universal model to be applied elsewhere.
211/Kelly/ 1966	None	Multi-Nat.	None	Three criticisms of horticultural training for foreign students are identified: (1) students are not prepared for jobs to be done at home, (2) training is done on equipment they will never use again, and (3) standards are lowered and the students thus receive second-class degrees.

Item No./ Author(s)/ Date	Sponsorship	Geographic Emphasis	Includes Reference to Empirical Research	Key Ideas
212/Kelman/ 1965	None	Multi-Nat.	Some	Applied research in the form of evaluation of exchange programs is recommended to ascertain whether they have achieved their goals. The effects of international cooperation are discussed. Among the effects are increased openness of key individuals toward other nations, reduction in tensions, and increased world-mindedness.
22/Kerr/ 1973	Priv./Non-Gov., Found.	Multi-Nat.	None	Describes the advantages of enrollment of foreign students in two-year and junior colleges (low fees, close association among students, faculty, and community, and specialized two-year training). Detailed advice is offered on admissions procedures, housing, and advising and counseling of foreign students.
216/King/ 1970	None	Multi-Nat.	None	Historical background of the coming of African students to black American colleges and universities. In particular, the role of African students at Tuskeegee Institute is traced.
4/Kletzien/ 1972	Gov. Ag. and Priv., Non-Gov.	Sub. Sah. Af.	Some	Reports on the Southern African Student (SASP). Major problems encountered by students in the US related to their legal status.
220/Klinger/ 1967	None	Multi-Nat.	None	Foreign student advisers are seen as necessary to their institutions and foreign students, and the duties of the advisers are increasing.
223/Landers/ 1973	None	E. Asia Multi.	None	Declining support for and rising costs of education for foreign students is decried. Recommendations include: (1) renewal of US commitment to the underlying rationale of educational exchange, (2) foreign students should be provided equal opportunities for employment and fellowships, and (3) overseas counselors must be supplied with more complete data on low-tuition colleges in low-cost living areas.
244/Michie/ 1968	Priv./Non-Gov.	Multi-Nat.	Much	Surveys diverse activities which make up international education, institutional strengths and weaknesses, and resources available.

Item No./ Author(s)/ Date	Sponsorship	Geographic Emphasis	Includes Reference to Empirical Research	Key Ideas
245/Michie/ 1967	Priv./Non- Gov., Found.	Multi-Nat.	Some	Report of symposium marking the 20th anniversary of the Fulbright Program. Accomplishments of the Program and the problems and prospects of international education are reviewed. Maintenance of quality in international education, provision of education relevant to the needs of the countries from which students come, and determination of which students could most profit from a US education are problem areas discussed.
251/Mississ- ippi State Uni- versity/1967	Univ.	Multi-Nat.	None	Suggests cooperative programs between a university (Mississippi State), international employers, and students.
253/Moore/ 1970	None	Multi-Nat.	None	Reviews problem areas for students in general and foreign students in particular. Recommendations are made for changes in immigration policies, reforms in admissions and in selection and academic-performance standards, and in reform in the bureaucracy and functions of the foreign student adviser.
264a/ NAFSA/ 1966	Priv./Non- Gov.	M.S. Asia E. Asia S.E.-Asia	None	This report summarizes presentations made at a workshop on the evaluation of Asian educational credentials (specifically India, Japan, the Philippines, and Taiwan). The report contains an overview of the history and present structure of the educational systems of these four countries. Contains information on quality factors and grading systems.
264c/ NAFSA/ n.d.	Priv./Non- Gov.	Amer.	Some	Report on a workshop of the admission and academic placement of students from Argentina, Chile, Perú, and Ecuador. Presents historical and current information on the educational systems of those countries, particularly grading systems, and quality factors.
264d/NAFSA/ n.d.	Priv./Non- Gov.	Amer.	Some	This report contains historical and educational background material as well as descriptions of the educational systems of British-patterned education in the Caribbean, Cuba, the Dominican Republic, the French West Indies, Haiti, Puerto Rico, and the US Virgin Islands.

Item No./Author(s)/Date	Sponsorship	Geographic Emphasis	Includes Reference to Empirical Research	Key Ideas
265a/NAFSA/1966	Priv./Non-Gov.	Multi-Nat.	None	Suggests guidelines for the selection and admission of foreign students to US universities.
265b/NAFSA/1966	Priv./Non-Gov.	Multi-Nat.	None	Suggests guidelines for the day-to-day advising of foreign students by foreign student advisers.
265c/NAFSA/1967	Priv./Non-Gov.	Multi-Nat.	None	Suggests guidelines to assist the development of US/foreign student relationships.
265d/NAFSA/1967	Priv./Non-Gov.	Multi-Nat.	None	Suggests guidelines for the foreign student adviser on how to assist the foreign student with housing.
265e/NAFSA/n.d.	Priv./Non-Gov.	Multi-Nat.	None	Suggests guidelines for the responsibilities and standards of professional conduct of institutions and individuals working professionally with foreign students.
265f/NAFSA/1961	Priv./Non-Gov.	Multi-Nat.	Some	Discusses the foreign students' problems of English-language proficiency. Surveys show that English proficiency as a criterion for admission is seldom used consistently. "A relatively small group of the total mass of students (foreign)...have adequate proficiency. Describes tests of English proficiency.
265g/NAFSA/1971	Priv./Non-Gov.	Multi-Nat.	None	Suggests guidelines for the encouragement of US/foreign student relationships.
273/NAFSA/1970	Priv./Non-Gov.	Multi-Nat.	Much	Abstracts of papers presented at the International Education Year Conference. Topics covered include English Language Training, new directions for NAFSA, the brain drain, intercultural workshops and a number of others.
282/NAFSA/1973	Priv./Non-Gov.	Multi-Nat.	None	Discusses the needs of foreign student wives and the kinds of programs which may give foreign wives the attention and help they need.

Item No./ Author(s)/ Date	Sponsorship	Geographic Emphasis	Includes Reference to Empirical Research	Key Ideas
13/Office of International Training, AID/1973	Gov. Ag.	Multi-Nat.	None	Summarizes philosophy, functions, and services of the counseling staff of AID's Office of International Training.
275/ Ostrander/ 1970	Priv./Non-Gov.	Multi-Nat.	None	Describes programs in foreign student education that have been initiated at US colleges and universities. New directions include in-country and pre-departure orientation programs, group counseling, US business-foreign student programs and intercultural communications training.
301/Owen and Colwell/ 1968	None	Multi-Nat.	None	Discusses the goals, structure, administration and accomplishments of the Economics Institute, an orientation program for foreign graduate students in economics.
308/Perkins/ 1971	Priv./Non-Gov.	Multi-Nat.	None	US educational institutions are urged to restructure the goals and content of their international programs. Recommendations made include establishment of language and area studies centers, more careful selection of foreign students, funding from international agencies and greater two-way exchange of visiting scholars.
309/Peterson/1968	None	Multi-Nat.	None	Describes the objectives, organization, and problems of a course for foreign students in the economics of agricultural production and resource use held at the University of Nebraska. Practical workshop situations employed.
406/Pierson and O'Grady/ 1964	Gov. Ag.	Multi-Nat.	Some	Describes the activities of the US government agencies involved in training and exchange programs with special attention given to programs in which women have participated substantially.
313/Plaister/ 1968	None	Multi-Nat.	None	Describes the English Language Institute reading courses at the University of Hawaii.

Item No./ Author(s)/ Date	Sponsorship	Geographic Emphasis	Includes Reference to Empirical Research	Key Ideas
431/Practical Concepts, Inc./ 1973	Gov. Ag./	Af.	Much	Evaluates US programs for African students and trainees.
7/Preston/ 1966	Gov. Ag.	Multi-Nat.	None	Describes the Participant Training Program of AID and the specific standard procedures for each phase of the program. Phases discussed include pre-departure, selection, processing, training in the US, orientation in the US, and exit interviews. Difficulties in each phase are noted.
321/Rayner and Jones/ 1973	None	Multi-Nat.	None	Describes the functions and accomplishments of the Exchange-Visitor Program for Foreign Nurses at Columbia-Presbyterian Medical Center in New York City. Main objective of the program is to familiarize visitor nurses with American health services and nursing practices.
322/Regional Council for International Education/ n.d.	Priv./Non-Gov. Ag.	Multi-Nat.	None	Report of a conference. Objectives were to identify the circumstances and forces changing the atmosphere in which multinational corporations must function, and to recommend changes in curricula to enable graduates to better function in the international business community of the future.
323/Regueira/ 1966	None	Multi-Nat.	None	Examines alternatives in training individuals in educational courses in social and economic development. Integration of students into programs of foreign universities has two drawbacks: (1) knowledge taught may be irrelevant to home country's needs, and (2) foreign students may not return to their home countries. Special institutions for this training, despite other problems, offer a more useful education to the foreign students.
5/Rotach and Haas/ 1972	Priv./Non-Gov.	N. Af. Sub. Sah. Af.	Some	Describes the development and activities of the AFGRAD (African Graduate Fellowship) Program of the African-American Institute. Trends include: (1) increase in Ph.D. students, (2) a high rate of non-return among medical student forced a reduction in emphasis on medical studies, (3) provision for financial aid to grantees wishing to conduct doctoral dissertation research in Africa.

Item No. / Author(s) / Date	Sponsorship	Geographic Emphasis	Includes Reference to Empirical Research	Key Ideas
334/Sanders/ 1963	Priv./Non-Gov.	Multi-Nat.	Some	Based on conference materials and discussion, this book considers unsolved problems in the professional training of students from other countries. It reinforces the point that the selection and training cannot be considered apart from re-entry, nor orientation apart from academic practices.
335/Sanders and Ward/ 1970	Priv./Non-Gov.	Multi-Nat.	Some	Sponsorship and administration of foreign student exchange programs are examined. Presents summaries of findings of other studies. Major conclusions are that: (1) international studies are largely underdeveloped on most campuses, and (2) present levels of activity are in jeopardy due to financial, organizational, and other difficulties. Recommendations for policy and action are made.
78/Sasnett/ 1967	None	Multi-Nat.	None	A guidebook for students from other countries to the costs of study in the US, financial resources, and the planning of the financial aspects of foreign study.
336/Schmidt and Scott/ 1971	None	Multi-Nat.	None	It is argued that because of environmental factors (climate, diseases, culture of the people) there is much to be said for establishment of regionally based research and training in developing countries.
349/Sinauer/ 1967	None	Multi-Nat.	None	Assesses international training and education in the US and the role of various types of communication in meeting the needs of students from the developing nations.
353/Skinner/ 1963	Diss.	Multi-Nat.	Some	Describes the practices and procedures of the foreign student adviser in US higher education and the increasing importance of the foreign student adviser's role. The study also attempts to evaluate the effectiveness of the foreign student adviser.

189

Item No./ Author(s)/ Date	Sponsorship	Geographic Emphasis	Includes Reference to Empirical Research	Key Ideas
354/Smart/ 1971	None	Multi-Nat.	None	Attempts to clarify the goals and related definitions of international education. Among the stated goals are: permeation of new ideas, synthesis of value systems and world culture, national development, mutual understanding and cooperation and the development of creative attitudes towards diversity.
408a/Soviet and Eastern European Exchanges Staff/1968	Gov. Ag.	E. E. & USSR	None	This report discusses US exchanges with the USSR, Poland, Czechoslovakia, Hungary, Romania, and Bulgaria during 1968.
408b/Soviet and Eastern European Exchanges Staff/1970	Gov. Ag.	E. E. & USSR	None	This report discusses US exchanges with the USSR, Poland, Czechoslovakia, Hungary, Romania, and Bulgaria during 1970.
361/Speak-man/1966	Priv./Non-Gov.	Multi-Nat.	Some	Examines a number of facets of international exchange in education. Reviews the historic background of such exchanges and describes exchange programs (in 1966) of national and international institutions. Problems noted include the need for better selection and admissions, closer bilateral cooperation in the planning of exchange programs, and manpower shortages in staffing exchange programs.
366/ Springer/ n.d.	None	Multi-Nat.	Some	Reviews problems of foreign students, and the problems of administering and organizing foreign student programs. Recommends the introduction of a computerized two-way information system to benefit participating institutions and domestic as well as foreign applicants.
269/Steb-bins/1967	Priv./Non-Gov.	E. Asia S. E. Asia	Some	Report of a conference on educational and cultural exchange with Asian countries. Discusses the problems of developing countries and reviews the history and present structure of the educational systems of China, Malaysia, Indonesia, the Philippines, Taiwan, and Hong Kong.

190

Item No./ Author(s)/ Date	Sponsorship	Geographic Emphasis	Includes Reference to Empirical Research	Key Ideas
371/Sutnick, Reichard, and Angelides/ 1971	None	Multi-Nat.	Some	Describes orientation programs organized by the Philadelphia County Medical Society and various community organizations for foreign medical students.
375/The Tenth Mohonk Consultation with International Students/ 1973	Found.	Multi-Nat.	None	Terminal seminars (in US, before return to home countries) are proposed by a conference of 13 students from 12 countries. Objectives of the seminars: to help the students prepare to use the skills they have learned in the US, to reduce the threat that students will be unable to communicate with their home culture upon return, and to keep up with changes in the home culture.
377/Thompson/ 1971	None	Multi-Nat.	None	The existence and vitality of international clubs is discussed as well as foreign student participation in planned programs for international students.
380/Ukai/ 1967	None	E. Asia	None	Describes the growing number of exchanges between the US and Japan. Proposes that competent US scholars spend more than one year in Japan, that rigorously high standards be maintained and that funds for international educational exchange be entrusted to an international coordinating agency that can operate on a multilateral basis.
390c/US Advisory Commission on International and Cultural Affairs/1964	Gov. Ag.	Multi-Nat.	Some	Second annual report of US Advisory Commission on International Educational and Cultural Affairs. Activities of the Commission included creation of a Council on International Educational and Cultural Affairs, a survey of government English language programs being undertaken by the Interagency Committee on English Language Teaching, and the formation in the Department of State of an Overseas Schools Policy Committee.
425/Witman/ 1972	None	Multi-Nat.	None	Describes the administration, structure, and financing of the Pittsburgh Council for International Visitors (PCIV). The key role of volunteers in this organization, designed to welcome international visitors to Pittsburgh is stressed.

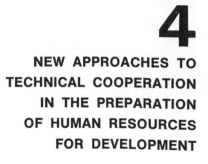

NEW APPROACHES TO
TECHNICAL COOPERATION
IN THE PREPARATION
OF HUMAN RESOURCES
FOR DEVELOPMENT

Many of the studies reviewed in earlier chapters suggest that U. S. universities should adjust their programs for foreign students to suit the requirements of developing countries. The largest number of foreign students in the United States are self-supporting and pursue studies which may or may not prepare them for available positions at home. The issue of the relevance of study programs becomes critical, however, when the students are sponsored by their governments, bilateral organizations, or multi-lateral organizations under technical cooperation projects which assume that they are preparing for well-defined leadership positions at home.

According to the Development Assistance Committee of the Organization for Economic Cooperation and Development, the wealthy countries spent some $922 million on technical assistance activities in 1964, of which $80 million were spent to train fellows from developing countries in skills appropriate to social and economic growth. In 1970, these same countries spent $1,526 million on technical assistance activities, of which $171 million were for the support of bilaterally sponsored technical training activities. These figures do not include multi-lateral (United Nations, Organization of American States, etc.) technical assistance activities, which grew from $200 million in 1964 to $367 million in 1970, with at least ten percent of this figure being spent on the support of fellowship training activities. Nor do these figures include substantial sums spent by many developing countries to finance their own fellows while training abroad for return to positions of leadership.

In addition to these fellowship programs under technical assistance schemes, probably four times as much money is spent on sending experts from highly developed countries to the poorer countries, primarily to train local personnel on the spot. These highly expensive experts ($749 million was spent on them under bilateral programs in 1970, according to the Development Assistance Committee) are presumably needed because of the lack of planning, programming, administrative, and technical skills in the poorer countries.

With this kind of public expenditure at stake, it is worth bringing together in one chapter a number of studies on the effect of technical assistance programs (which, in essence, are a form of training) and others which describe various new approaches to the preparation of human resources for development. Previous chapters have focused primarily, although not exclusively, on traditional forms of education; what happens to foreign students who enroll in American institutions of higher education and how these institutions respond to their needs. Education abroad is a phenomenon with long historical antecedents and will undoubtedly continue because it answers very basic human needs. In certain situations, however, traditional forms of education and training create more problems than they solve. Students may become over-specialized for the jobs waiting at home, alienated from their native culture, exposed to emotional and financial difficulties in the host country. The less-developed countries, which may have planned a very specific development project, see their young people spending their formative years in a different culture, acquiring skills which may or may not be appropriate to the project, and which may or may not be brought home to be utilized and transmitted to others. In this context, many persons, organizations, national governments have sought to devise alternate methods of sharing, on a global basis, the advanced technology which has become concentrated in the more developed countries. The selection of literature in this chapter is by no means comprehensive. Moreover, as will be noted, many of the studies are discussed more fully elsewhere in a different context. A brief description of the items is given in Chart 4.1, p. 203.

The Basic Issues

Within the past two years, the Society for International Development has included a supplement in its International Development Review entitled Focus: Technical Cooperation. A number of articles suggest a new look at technical cooperation strategies and at the fellowship components of technical cooperation projects. For instance, Spaulding (360/1974) suggests the need for large global research and development projects designed to answer some of the key questions being asked by educational policy makers and planners: What are the different ways of organizing for curriculum reform? What are the comparative costs of recent educational strategies such as television

and programmed instruction? What kinds of educational services should
be included in "life-long education"? Institutions anywhere which have
proven successful in answering such questions and in doing the kinds of
things that developing countries wish their institutions to do should
be encouraged to participate in the technical cooperation process through
institutional linkages with developing countries. Through such linkages,
tailor-made training programs can be planned both within the recipient
country and abroad. Such collaboration would lead to better definition
of skills needed in institution-building in developing countries and, in
turn, to better planned training programs. Built-in evaluation of training which should take place under technical cooperation projects would
help all players in the process to learn how to improve the system. This
and other suggestions would involve financial support for a more sophisticated infrastructure than the traditional fellowship support for students to take degrees at foreign universities.

In the same journal, Raman (319/1973) enumerates some frequently encountered problems in technical cooperation projects, in
particular the long delays in the appointment of counterpart project
personnel, in aligning national and international inputs of personnel,
and in the nomination of qualified candidates for training abroad. Evaluation studies reveal further problems arising from: the narrowness
of approaches to counterpart training; deficits in the scope and substance
of training; and shortcomings in the planning and execution of fellowships. He suggests the development of staff capability in the collective
sense rather than in the preparation of single individuals. This would
reduce the dependence of projects on individuals serving as single
counterparts to experts. The terminal objective of training should be
not simply an increase in the competence of the trainees in certain
subject matter fields, but also, and more importantly, the enhancement
of the knowledge and the formation of the skills and attitudes needed by
the staff to carry out institutional tasks in their home country. He proposes a seven-step process in identifying the skills needed under each
fellowship and the planning of the training program.

The brain drain and the extreme dispersion in planning and administration are the two major problems which have characterized study-
abroad programs for over 20 years, according to a UNESCO monograph
on Study Abroad and Educational Development (63/1973) by Carter.
Stressing the need for a more integrated approach to training, the author
discusses seven interrelated tasks which might serve as a framework
for new policies, as proposed by the United Nations Development Programme. These tasks are: (1) to promote greater recognition of the
centrality of training in development programs; (2) to improve knowledge of training activities which could improve coordination and suggest
new approaches in the field of training; (3) to improve awareness of
ways whereby needs and priorities could be identified more effectively;

(4) to improve the planning of training programs in general and the training component of specific projects; (5) to improve the capacity of outside experts and "trainers of trainers"; (6) to improve the training of local experts or counterparts on projects; and (7) to improve the quality of administration of international training at national, regional, and interregional levels. To implement these tasks, an administrative unit in each country is proposed which would correlate information and research, define the criteria needed in negotiating with foreign scholarship donors, define standards of candidate selection, and supervise orientation, placement, and follow-up of grantees.

In "International Training Policy in the Context of Economic Development," published by UNESCO ten years earlier (225/1963), Levy had presented a detailed proposal for such an agency. In order to foster the development of indigenous educational institutions, he suggests that each developing country establish a National Manpower Authority which would diagnose and forecast the country's manpower needs, select candidates for foreign study, finance and closely supervise their study in appropriate foreign institutions, and ensure their return through bonding arrangements, frequent home leaves, and contacts with potential employers.

From the international agencies which sponsor and coordinate technical training programs, there is a considerable amount of evaluative literature. Van Ravenswaaij (139/1973), for example, in discussing the Food and Agriculture Organization's training programs, suggests that "training for development" is the "aggregate of activities systematically geared towards developing the human resources potential of the third world into an effective instrument for the governments of the countries involved to reach their development target and objectives." Although training for development is a high-priority activity for FAO, he finds that no systematic attempt has been made so far to review and evaluate the effectiveness and efficiency of FAO's training activities as a whole. An occasional background sheet prepared by the External Training, Coordination, and Evaluation Unit of FAO in 1973 (137) showed that in only nine of the 27 group training activities surveyed in 1972 was there any attempt made to evaluate effectiveness. The objective, therefore, of the External Training Coordination and Evaluation Unit in charge of creating the FAO evaluation system was to design a standardized yet flexible system offering policy makers and practitioners responsible for development training a management tool to assist them in improving and changing their training-development approaches according to the changing needs of the societies served by it. This decision-making approach is an up-to-date design but its effectiveness in practice ("meta-evaluation") cannot be determined from the FAO report. Van Ravenswaaij believes that far-reaching changes in multi-laterally sponsored training activities are

necessary in order to find effective solutions to human resource
training problems.

From UN agencies come three reports which address the issue
of improving existing training programs. (For other studies, particularly those which evaluate the UNESCO Fellowship Programme, see
Chapter 6.)

The purpose of the report by UNESCO's International Committee
of Experts on Training Abroad Policies (386/1972) was to advise
UNESCO's Director-General on those policies. The report is largely
composed of recommendations for the improvement of UNESCO's efforts
in training abroad. The two recommended objectives of those efforts
are the training of key personnel from the less-developed countries and
the exchange of persons between member states. The implementation
of these objectives depends heavily on the coordination of policies and
personnel. It was recommended that UNESCO develop an overall training policy with a view towards democratizing education, innovating and
reforming curricula and teaching methods, and realizing life-long
education. Cooperative links between member states' universities, the
design of training programs that would train a coherent group of specialists from one country to aid in the development of a certain
sector of that country's economy, and the design of loan services to
facilitate study abroad were among the ways suggested to promote
training activities. The Committee emphasized the importance of local
and regional training and recommended the utilization, development,
and creation of local and regional institutions where necessary. A
final strategy involving coordination calls for the coherence of training
activity within each institution of the United Nations system and between
various United Nations institutions and bilateral programs.

An evaluation report (382/1968) of seminars, study tours, training
courses, and meetings of working groups of experts financed by the
United Nations Development Program (UNDP) identifies a number of
problems and makes recommendations for the implementation of
training-abroad programs. A major problem appeared to be the lack
of coordination between UNDP and the proper national government
coordinating agencies. Of particular interest is the concern paid to
teaching methods. It was suggested that significant improvements might
be obtained by strengthening the teaching, as distinct from substantive,
aspects of the projects. Greater reliance on participants for leadership
roles and the use of small discussion groups were included in the recommendations. Continuous evaluation and closer attention to problems of
innovation—the means by which participants learn how to apply back
home whatever was learned in the project—were advocated.

Finally, a UNITAR weekend seminar in 1972 was devoted to The
Search for New Methods of Technical Cooperation (432/1974). Acknowl-
edging that, in the 20 or so years since its inception, technical

assistance has undergone little in the way of innovation although its scope of activity has broadened considerably, the participants discussed a number of constraints inherent in assistance projects and possible solutions to them. The fact that technical cooperation is largely a government-to-government activity imposes constraints arising from the nature of the predicament facing developing countries' governments and the effectiveness of the machinery of government at their command. A second type of constraint arises from the nature of technical cooperation as ultimately a person-to-person activity; the "experts" recruited serve only two to three years and concentrate on transmission of conventional knowledge. Among the proposals resulting from the seminar were: (1) that assistance be extended to and through nongovernmental organizations, volunteers and voluntary agencies, and philanthropic institutions; (2) that new devices be utilized to augment the expert-counterpart relationship; and (3) that new machinery be developed to provide information and advice on technology which is appropriate, or can be adapted, to the needs of developing countries. In conclusion, the report states: "The scale of technological advance today offers the prospect of greatly enhanced development aid being made available. Its accessibility to the developing countries and its dissemination and adoption within them cannot be assured, however, unless the techniques employed in the process can keep pace with the growing volume and complexity involved."

University Programs

A number of items in our bibliography discuss the many ways in which U. S. colleges and universities have sought to develop and upgrade foreign institutions aside from the enrollment of students in traditional curricula. One section of the book by Sanders and Ward, Bridges to Understanding (335/1970), describes the technical assistance involvement of American colleges and universities during the 1970's. They find that there are contradictory assessments of university performance abroad and that the goals of the university and of the Agency for International Development often differ. Several innovative approaches used by American universities in attempting to improve their effectiveness as technical assistance change agents are listed. Among these are the Harvard Development Advisory Service, established in 1962, which sent two types of people overseas, operational change agents and researchers; the International Legal Center, founded in 1966, which attempts to strengthen legal institutions overseas through tailor-made training of foreign law students and instructors and by helping to build institutions; consortia of universities, including a project involving nine U. S. institutions which helped to establish an engineering school in Kanpur, India; the Midwest Universities Consortium for International Activities, set up, in part, to enable participating institutions to develop a greater capacity to render technical assistance; and the Associated Colleges of the Midwest, a consortium of liberal arts colleges which worked with Cuttington College in Liberia for a number of years. The authors feel that unless universities are encouraged to be more active partners in technical cooperation programs they are unlikely to retain a lively interest in development projects and in specialized training programs for international students.

Hayden (164/1973) describes in further detail the Midwest Universities Consortium for International Activities. The main objectives of this group of five universities are to build and sustain academic linkages with overseas universities and research institutions; to provide more effective technical cooperation; and to strengthen the international dimension of the members' campuses through faculty and student participation in international development work overseas. For its member institutions, MUCIA coordinates inter-university groups which focus on problem areas, awards small grants for special purposes, provides salary guarantees to facilitate participation of outstanding senior faculty in overseas projects, provides funds for exploratory travel, and conducts university seminars and symposia. Its major programs include a study of institutional development and technical assistance methodology under an AID grant and a distinguished visiting scholar program which provides campuses with research and teaching expertise from international agencies and overseas institutions in the field of international development. It also coordinates small top-level teams to provide on-site investigation of alternative strategies for projects, problem resolution, and so on. It is not clear to what extent the consortium is improving the training programs for fellows from abroad on member campuses, but the infrastructure would appear to offer potential in this direction. A recent study by Weintraub, "MUCIA Foreign Alumni" (433/1974), however, found that little has been done on an institutional level to maintain contact with alumni residing outside the U. S., a group numbering some 22,500. He believes that much could be done in building institutions which would formalize and strengthen international inter-institutional linkages. Several articles examine specific instances of technical cooperation between U. S. universities and foreign institutions.

Doty (118/1971) makes an attempt to evaluate the effectiveness of 15 years of technical assistance to higher education in West Pakistan provided through the Washington State University Pakistan Project under the auspices of the Agency for International Development. He finds that a number of programs and sub-projects continued in Pakistan after termination of technical assistance, suggesting that the project has been relatively successful, although qualitative measures are imprecise because of the lack of any built-in evaluation during the project. Furthermore, he suggests that there is little evidence of any impact on Washington State University as a result of the project. Case histories of a number of the participant trainees in the project are included.

Bjur (42/ 1967) uses an institution-building model to assess the success of a technical assistance project designed to create a school of public administration in Brazil. The University of Southern California maintained experts in Brazil and brought 53 Brazilian professors to the United States for graduate study programs in public administration. The project ultimately served five Brazilian public administration schools. The author suggests that participant training must be a part of a more broadly conceived institution-building model if the trainees are to be successful in maintaining a viable institution upon their return home.

Ojiaku (293/ 1968) suggests that the American land-grant tradition has been adopted by the higher education institutions in eastern Nigeria and in particular the University of Nigeria, Nsukka. He describes the various foreign influences on higher education in Nigeria and feels that the American influence, in part through the efforts of Michigan State University, have been the most beneficial. The role of American-trained Nigerians in higher education leadership is described in some detail.

Montgomery (252/ n.d.) studied five technical assistance projects sponsored by the Agency for International Development in Thailand under contract with the University of Texas, Indiana University, Wayne State University, Michigan State University, and the University of Kentucky. All five projects revolved around the central theme of the adaptation of American educational patterns to the Thai situation. It was assumed by the contract planners that a certain set of conditions was desirable and the process of assistance was one of influencing the recipient to adapt to these conditions. The author found the projects to be inflexible in adapting to local needs and conditions, and neither AID nor the universities were able to modify goals and activities sufficiently to meet the local problems encountered.

Seaquist (339/ 1968) discusses the relationship between the University of Alabama and binational elementary and secondary schools in Colombia. He suggests that American universities should work closely with the schools in preparing teachers for them and in helping them to collaborate with one another in resolving planning and programming problems.

In 1965 the University of California, with funding from the Ford Foundation, established the Convenio, a long-term involvement with the University of Chile. The Self-Study of International Educational Exchange (410/ 1970), a major evaluation of international programs on the

University of California's nine campuses, analyzes the value and problems of this approach. It finds that the association has been mutually beneficial, that 151 Chileans and 180 members of the University of California have been seriously engaged in the process of international educational exchange and research through the support and direction of the Convenio. Particularly valuable has been the work in the fields of veterinary medicine, entomology, and physical and earth sciences, leading to the growth of research facilities in both countries. This report stresses the importance of long-term involvement. The Convenio was originally funded for five years with the understanding that an additional five years of funding would be available after a mid-term review. Initial attempts to develop programs, particularly in the social sciences and arts, met with frustrations, miscalculations, and misunderstandings which were only gradually overcome. If the Convenio had been conceived as a two- or three-year project, no tangible benefits would have accrued to either institution in these fields.

The studies reviewed here merely skim the surface, typifying the many institution-to-institution linkages forged between U. S. and foreign universities. Many more exist, ranging from extensive programs of the Convenio type to more modest exchanges of scholars. Few evaluative studies have come to our attention, however. Further research would be necessary to identify them and judge whether this type of assistance is a viable alternative to traditional study abroad.

Government Programs

A further group of reports deals with government-sponsored technical assistance projects abroad. The major U. S. fellowship programs, either directly administered by the government or funded by the government and administered through non-governmental organizations such as the African-American Institute and Institute for International Education, are discussed elsewhere (see Chapters 2 and 3). One such technical assistance project had as its goal the establishment of a program budget and position classification scheme in Iran. In an evaluation by Osman (298/ 1970), it is suggested that program budgeting practices appear to be successful in Iran but that the use of program classification met resistence due to the Iranian cultural emphasis on status and rank. The conclusion of the study is that foreign institutions and agencies must take care to adapt foreign approaches to public administration to local cultures and environments.

The scope and variety of U. S. technical cooperation programs, whether initiated by government, private organization, or educational institution, is well-illustrated in the reports issued by the Bureau of

Educational and Cultural Affairs (400a-o). The extensive notes offer
information on such unconventional linkages as that of Tuskegee Institute and the Liberian Department of Instruction in an attempt to upgrade elementary school teaching (400k); and the advanced teacher
training course offered by the American Institute for Free Labor Development in Costa Rica (400f).

Finally, we have a report by Amir (24/1973) on the experience
of another country, Israel, in providing agricultural training. Between 1960 and 1972, some 4,500 trainees from 80 countries have participated in 160 courses, individual studies, or observation tours given
by Israel's Department of Foreign Training, Ministry of Agriculture.
In addition, some 1,700 trainees participated in 61 local courses held
by Israeli experts in 20 countries abroad. Amir makes the case that
there is advantage in having students from developing countries study
in another developing country such as Israel where they may find skills
and techniques which are more applicable to their home-country context. Alumni of Israeli training institutions are urged to form clubs
upon return home to foster exchange of information and follow-up activities. Amir suggests that the goals are specific: "The trainees must
leave the country convinced that changes can be achieved, as proved
by Israel's example, and that they possess the necessary techniques
to implement them."

Conclusion

Together with the steady increase in technical cooperation activities under the auspices of multilateral organizations, our research
reveals that a considerable number of American universities have embarked upon programs which involve them in technical training and institution building in developing countries. Relatively few of them,
however, are seeking to develop innovative, new approaches to the
preparation of human resources for development tasks in poorer countries. Nor is there any evidence presented to show that the university's
foreign involvement has much effect on the institution itself. The host
of problems encountered by foreign students, as described in Chapters
2 and 3 of this report, testify to the apparent difficulty or reluctance
of American institutions to adjust or modify their structure, content,
or teaching approaches to suit foreign students, or to otherwise profit
from participation in international training or technical cooperation
activities. Approaches such as MUCIA and the California Convenio
seem to hold promise, particularly in that they are long-term, institution-wide efforts. Consortia of universities, however, cannot substitute for direct international involvement on the part of individual
faculty, programs, and schools on one university campus.

Technical cooperation programs, whether bilateral or multi-lateral, tend to be a package of fellowships, equipment, and experts. Critics of these programs point out first that fellows are rarely trained in teams in an effort to develop group, as opposed to individual, skills, and secondly that experts are often inexperienced in adapting what they know to the cultures and contexts of the developing country. The policy implication is clear: technical assistance agencies must give more attention to the development of institutions in industrialized countries which will respond to the personal, human needs of the foreign student and which can accumulate the experience necessary for understanding how to adapt advanced technology to the needs of the developing country.

Since it was not the major purpose of this study to go into detail in this area, we have made an attempt only to sample the literature. We suggest a need for more extensive studies of the training component in technical cooperation and of new approaches to the preparation of human resources for development.

Recommendations

The studies reviewed in this chapter contain recommendations of two types. First are general recommendations relating to the structure and administration of technical cooperation programs and the training component thereof. All participants are urged to clarify their goals and working relationships in such programs—the employing agency, the placement agency, the country, the institution, the academic adviser, and the student. Related to this is the suggestion that better channels of communication are needed among the partners, as are better evaluation techniques at every level. Agencies are urged to develop funding for large global projects which will attempt to generate more relevant knowledge concerning the adaptation and transfer of technologies in all disciplines and professions. Other structural recommendations are that local and regional training centers be developed, and that each developing country create an agency to coordinate foreign training programs. Finally, it is recommended that universities recognize their role as international resources and develop more effective cooperation with counterpart institutions abroad.

The second category of recommendations concerns the implementation of specific projects. The major suggestions, directed to those who design technical cooperation programs, are that they consider the social and cultural setting of the recipient country; that they select technology appropriate to the needs of that country; that they provide flexibility in the use of funds; that they aim at developing collective staff capability as well as individual; and that they expand the role of non-governmental organizations and institutions in the project.

CHART 4.1 – STUDIES CITED: NEW APPROACHES TO HUMAN RESOURCE DEVELOPMENT

Item No./ Author/ Date	Sponsorship	Key Ideas
24/ Amir/ 1973	Min. of For. Aff., Israel	Description of training courses sponsored by Israeli Ministry of Agriculture.
42/ Bjur/ 1967	Diss.	U. S. technical assistance to Brazil in the field of public administration education.
400/ Bur. of Educ. and Cult. Aff./ 1967-69	Dept. of State	Statistical summaries of exchanges between US and other countries.
63/ Carter/ 1973		Reviews problems of study-abroad programs and proposes 7 inter-related tasks to serve as a framework for new policies.
118/ Doty/ 1971	Diss.	Assesses effectiveness of technical assistance to higher education in West Pakistan provided by Washington State University.
137/ FAO/ 1973	FAO	Describes a survey which revealed lack of evaluation in FAO group training.
139/ Van Ravenswaaij/ 1973		Proposes need for evaluation of FAO training activities.
164/ Hayden/ 1973		Describes objectives and programs of the Midwest Universities Consortium for International Activities (MUCIA).
225/ Levy/ 1967		Proposes a National Manpower Authority in each developing country.
252/ Montgomery/ n.d.	Diss.	Discusses problems encountered in educational assistance to Thailand provided by 5 US universities.
293/ Ojiaku/ 1968	Diss.	Compares the failure of English "Red Brick" model to the success of US "Land Grant" model for Nigerian universities.
298/ Osman/ 1970	Diss.	Analyzes US technical assistance program in public administration in Iran.
319/ Raman/ 1973-74		General discussion of problems encountered in technical assistance projects.
335/ Sanders and Ward/ 1970		Ch. 11 discusses university involvement in technical assistance.
339/ Seaquist/ 1968	Diss.	Discusses binational schools in Colombia and their association with the University of Alabama.
360/ Spaulding/ 1974		Suggests new modes and strategies for technical assistance.
386/ UNESCO/ 1972	UNESCO	Recommendations for UNESCO training abroad policies.
382/ UNDP/ 1968	UNDP	Evaluation of UNDP training programs.
433/ UNITAR/ 1974	UNITAR	Seminar devoted to discussion of new ideas for improvement of methods of technical assistance.
410/ Univ. of California/ 1970	University	Studies exchange programs at California's 9 campuses, including the joint program with the University of Chile, the Convenio.
434/ Weintraub/ 1974	University	Investigates contacts between MUCIA and its foreign alumni.

5

MIGRATION OF
TALENT AND SKILLS

The problem of talent migration, one aspect of which is commonly referred to as brain drain, has occupied a major place in international exchange research for the past several years. That there exists a vast amount of information available on this subject comes as no surprise to anyone familiar with the area. Due to the plethora of materials available and to the fact that the subject has been examined comprehensively in several works recently and in the past, we did not exhaustively review all existing literature but, rather, focused attention selectively. Our conclusions thus are based on the body of literature surveyed.

We collected 66 studies which deal almost exclusively with the migration of talent: 40 are empirical and 26 are non-empirical. The empirical research was undertaken by sponsored and unsponsored individuals and/or organizations, and by advanced students, both foreign and American. The majority of these studies take a sociological, economic, or politico-economic approach. Fifteen studies employ various types of sophisticated methodology and analysis involving scientific sampling, standardized instruments, multiple-regression equations, and tests of reliability and significance. Twenty use methods which involve no scientific sampling, standardized instruments, or sophisticated treatment of data. Only ten of the empirical studies focus in whole or in part on foreign students or professionals who have returned home; the rest examine migrants, primarily in the United States, although a few also analyze foreign students and professionals in other developed countries. None of these studies, however, examine the migration of talent from the perspective of students and professionals from developing countries who have migrated to other developing countries.

Brief statistical summaries of the empirical and non-empirical studies are presented in the following tables; totals may exceed those given above due to inclusion of some studies in more than one category. The empirical studies are further described in Chart 5.1, p. 252, and the non-empirical in Chart 5.2, p. 258.

TABLE 5.1

Empirical Studies: National Origin of Population Studied

Multinational	11	Taiwan and China	7
Asia	4	India	6
Africa	3	Korea	3
Middle East	2	Philippines	2
South America	2	Japan	2
Western Europe	1	Israel	2
Eastern Europe and USSR	1	Iran	1
		Palestine and	
		Jordan	1
		Peru	1
		Canada	1
		United Kingdom	1

TABLE 5.2

Empirical Studies: Discipline of Population Studied

General	29
Medical Sciences	4
Physical Sciences	3
Engineering	3
Social Sciences	1

Of 26 non-empirical studies, 20 were written by academics, professionals, or university administrators. Many of these studies are unsponsored and represent the thinking of the author. The remaining six represent institutional thinking and are authored by committees and governmental and inter-governmental agencies. A few studies appear to take an economic, political science, or sociological approach, although the perspective of the vast majority is general. Nine studies relied, to some lesser extent, on empirical research sources. The more comprehensive efforts are those by groups or agencies with a social science orientation, sponsored by inter-governmental organizations, foundations, or non-governmental agencies.

TABLE 5.3

Non-Empirical Studies: National Origin of Population Studied

Multinational	15	India	4
Asia	5	Iran	2
South America	2	Australia	1
East Africa	2	Cameroons	1
Africa	1	Colombia	1
Western Europe	1	Kenya	1
Middle East	1	Lebanon	1
		Nigeria	1
		Pakistan	1
		Philippines	1
		Thailand	1
		Trinidad and Tobago	1
		United Kingdom	1
		West Indies	1

TABLE 5.4

Non-Empirical Studies: Discipline of Population Studied

General	20
Medical Science	3
Physical Sciences and Engineering	2
Education	1

Conceptual Problems

In much of the research in this area, there is implicit agreement regarding the existence of a phenomenon of considerable magnitude called "brain drain." Several of the studies under review challenge this assumption and address themselves to the basic issues of definition and measurement. In so doing, they suggest that solutions to the problem of talent migration can be proposed legitimately only after it has been clearly defined and scientifically measured. In this section, therefore, we shall discuss various approaches to the problems of conceptualization and statistical measurement.

Definitional Problems

Four authors in particular are concerned with how the phenomenon of talent migration can be most appropriately and usefully concep-

tualized. Myers (261/ 1967; 263/ 1972) attempts to improve basic concepts and theory regarding foreign student non-return upon completion
of studies in the United States. In Education and Emigration, he discusses the ambiguity which prevails in the designation of national
affiliation, in deciding who is "foreign," and in distinguishing between
the "immigrant" and the "non-returnee." In the same work, he presents a paradigm by which to view the migration of talent. This paradigm incorporates and emphasizes the notion of remigration, or the
return home of college students, prodigal sons, disappointed job
seekers, retrained workers, retiring elders, or former political
exiles educated outside of their home countries. Remigration is a
concept which Myers believes will help to clarify the gains and losses
attributable to migration. Any viable overall definition and measurement of talent migration must somehow allow for it.

Glaser's conclusions (148/ 1974) are similar. Although he is not
directly concerned with problems of definition, his findings that most
students from developing countries do plan to return home eventually,
and that many non-returnees engage in temporary work to gain experience but plan to return later, suggest that emigration should not be
viewed as a permanent condition. What may appear as permanent migration is, in many cases, only temporary and remigration will follow.
The empirical works of both Glaser and Myers point not only to what
factors must be considered in defining brain drain, but also what concepts must be more precisely formulated.

Baldwin (33/ 1970) and Das (99/ 1971) examine this problem non-
empirically. Baldwin's thesis is that talent migration from developing
to developed regions is caused primarily by the inability of developing
countries to absorb high-level manpower. To the extent that brain
drain represents an overflow of talent, Baldwin argues first that the
ambiguity as to who is a "brain" and what is a "drain" serves only to
exacerbate the problems of definition and measurement and, second,
that migration is more usefully and realistically viewed from the perspective of a society's effective demand. Hence, for Baldwin, the definition of the brain-drain phenomenon must include notions of effective
demand and overflow.

Das' analysis is similar. He argues that "brain drain" is an
ambiguous term which needs further clarification, for in some cases,
talent migration is beneficial to both the donor and recipient countries,
as well as to individuals. This positive facet, more appropriately
termed "brain gain" or "brain exchange," appears where an individual
is trained in a specialized field that is not in great demand or where a
country cannot absorb all available manpower. Brain drain, on the
other hand, occurs only when migration retards the development of the
home country, and is thus dysfunctional. Like Baldwin, therefore, Das
urges an objective reconceptualization and redefinition of talent

migration to include both its eufunctional aspects and the notion of a society's and economy's absorptive capacity.

Problems of Measurement

Twelve studies comment specifically upon the inadequacy of statistics and the consequent difficulty of measuring the magnitude of talent migration accurately. The empirical studies in this group are Myers (260/ 1967; 263/ 1972), Niland (289/ 1970), UNITAR (389/ 1971), and Van der Kroef (415/ 1970); the non-empirical studies are Baldwin (33/ 1970), the Committee on the International Migration of Talent (84/ 1970), Grubel (156/ 1968), Kannappan (206/ 1968), Niland (288/ 1970), Parthasarathi (305/ 1967), and Watanabe (421/ 1969).

One group of these studies discusses the weaknesses of published statistical data in general. The Committee on the International Migration of Talent states that its study was impaired because reliable statistical data are scarce. It augmented its migration statistics with information from university alumni associations and from informed professionals in the field. According to Van der Kroef, statistics supplied by the U. S. Immigration and Naturalization Service do not agree with those of the Organization of Economic Cooperation.

Niland proposes that inaccuracies in estimates of student non-return based on immigrant visa statistics could be corrected by improvements in data on foreign student entry into the United States labor market and by publication of figures on immigrant visa applications. Immigration statistics should also specify the numbers of re-entering foreign students. Niland also argues that statistics must distinguish between de jure drain which occurs when the visa is issued and de facto drain which occurs much earlier when visa application is made: an annual tabulation of the number of applications that do not lead to issuance of an immigrant visa would provide a useful measurement tool. Yet, Niland argues, even with these adjustments, measurement of talent migration would still suffer the weakness of measuring a market phenomenon in terms of administrative technicalities. It would be more useful and accurate to measure international relocation at the time when the foreign student accepts first employment upon completion of study.

In his study, Kannappan considers statistics on migration published by the Institute of International Education (IIE), the Department of State, OECD, and UNESCO, and concludes that they are both limited and non-comparable in nature. Therefore, the most useful statistics for him are the numbers of students receiving foreign aducation. Myers also refers specifically to the problem of relying solely on IIE statistics. In an article entitled, "'Brain Drains' and 'Brain Gains,'" he states that migration statistics suffer from in appropriate sampling, misleading occupational titles, and questionable accuracy of reporting. In an analysis of foreign student non-return based on IIE's census for 1964-65, he finds several problems of measurement. Some institutions' foreign students are not included, since counts of students in September and October (when the census is taken) include only the students enrolled for the full year. The IIE census may thus underestimate the total yearly foreign student population by as much as 10 to 20 percent. Moreover, the IIE survey excludes many individuals who, by another definition, would be considered students. These include foreign medical residents or interns, industrial trainees, foreign nationals whose primary purpose is teaching or advanced research but who may also be students, and the like.

Three studies discuss the quality of developing countries' statistics. The UNITAR report notes the difficulties encountered in attempting to compile statistical data from these sources and cites specific unresolved inconsistencies. In discussing his use of published statistics from such countries, Baldwin notes that the data do not consider either the "quality" of migration (that is, the proportion of migration to total output of skilled manpower) and whether individuals would have found employment at home, or the rate of foreign student return. Parthasarathi, focusing his discussion on Indians, observes not only that available data on total manpower levels in science and technology outside of India are fragmentary and diffuse, but that data regarding this manpower's distribution among recipient countries is even more uncertain. His conclusions are based on data from UNESCO and the National Register of the Indian Council of Scientific and Industrial Research.

The incomplete, inaccurate, and non-comparable nature of migration statistics seems to have produced three important results. The first is that research has not generated reliable estimates of the number of persons involved in talent migration or meaningful empirical measures of the welfare losses to the population of "losing" countries. Secondly, attempts to measure the quality and rate of talent migration focus predominantly on gross figures of in-migration and out-migration, and thereby ignore the quantity and quality of its flows as would be characterized, for example, by remigration (Myers). Thirdly, and most significantly, inadequate country studies have hampered efforts such as Myers' to compare relative losses through student non-return on a cross-national basis.

In the next section of the report, we review a number of studies which attempt to describe the general pattern of talent migration. The conceptual problems discussed here, however, should be borne in mind, particularly as they relate to two major issues. The first concerns the need for standardization of statistical methodology and more precise definition of talent migration. Despite considerable scholarly effort, research has not and will not yield comparable, or, more importantly, accurate statistics, given the present state of conceptual and definitional development. At present, any researcher, analyst, or policy maker will be severely hampered in his or her attempts to measure, understand, or assess the phenomenon of talent migration.

The second issue concerns the uni-directional nature of the research: in no instance does one find figures on remigration, nor any indication of the extent to which talent migration occurs intra-regionally as, for example, within Africa, Latin America, or sections of Asia.

General Patterns and Trends in Talent Migration

While the remainder of this chapter will review the causes and effects of talent migration as revealed in this sample of the literature, it is perhaps useful to consider migration first from the larger perspective of who the non-returning students and professionals are and where they do or do not come from. It is curious to note that with perhaps the exception of Truscott's dissertation (378/ 1971) which takes a systemic view of the problem, we found no study which examines the international flow of talent and skills from a truly global perspective. Even the impressive works of Glaser (148/ 1974), the Committee of the International Migration of Talent (84/ 1970), Adams (429/ 1968), Myers (263/ 1972), and Henderson (388/ 1970) focus primarily on the flows of talent into the developed countries from developing countries. Glaser also reports on professionals who, having studied in developed countries, returned to India, Sri Lanka, Greece, Ghana, Brazil, Colombia, and Argentina. The flows from developed countries to other developed countries, or to those less developed is, on the whole, ignored in this body of research in spite of Van der Kroef's assertion that it is the global character of talent migration that endows it with such immediate and pressing significance. In this section we will, however, summarize what the literature has to say about regional flows of talent, its principal destinations, and the fields of specialization particularly affected.

Regional Flows

The Annual Indicator of the U. S. Immigration and Naturalization Service (396/ 1970) provides a statistical compilation of trends in immigration to the United States of persons in professional and related occupations. Important findings for 1969 were: (1) immigration totaled 358,579 persons of which 11.3 percent (40,427) reported their occupations in the professional, technical, and kindred work category, figures which represent a 21 percent decrease in overall immigration and a 17.1 percent decrease in professional and related fields compared with the previous year; (2) the number of immigrants from Asia in professional and related fields increased to 41 percent of the total over the previous year, while those from North America and Europe decreased to 24 percent, the latter representing a continuing downward trend from these two areas; (3) as in the previous two years of publication, engineers, teachers, nurses, accountants and auditors, and physicians and surgeons were the dominant occupations of aliens in the professional and kindred worker class.

The Committee on the International Migration of Talent provides estimates from national and international sources regarding worldwide migration from less- to more-developed countries and calculates that during the sixties, migration averaged about 300,000 persons per year, some 15 percent of whom had professional or technical training. Approximately 3,000 to 5,000 were persons of the highest ability whose loss can be particularly detrimental to the home country. The major donor countries have been India, Iran, Turkey, Pakistan, the Philippines, Taiwan, Korea, Greece, Colombia, and Argentina.

This study, and another by Baldwin (33/1970), analyze talent flows on a regional basis from East and Southeast Asia, South Asia, Middle East, East Africa, and Latin America. They find that in East and Southeast Asia all countries are experiencing problems caused by internal migration, which concentrates skilled manpower in the large urban centers, but South Korea, Taiwan, and the Philippines also have considerable out-migration, stimulated primarily by economic factors. In Thailand, Malaysia, and Singapore, however, employment opportunities for university graduates are relatively plentiful. Regarding Japan, Baldwin finds no problem of talent migration or immigration, but the Committee notes potential problems arising from the loss of a few highly qualified persons or mature scholars from the staff of universities and research institutes. Van der Kroef tends to concur with this latter view.

Both studies agree that migration from India is large, representing a substantial percentage of university graduates each year, and that this is due to economic and social conditions of the sub-continent which prevent full utilization of manpower. According to the Committee report, the key problem for the Middle Eastern countries of Lebanon, Turkey, and Iran is the occasional loss of exceptional indivuals rather than mass emigration. Baldwin adds that the latter two nations suffer from serious internal migration.

The studies agree that East Africa (Tanzania, Kenya, and Uganda) as of 1970 has not suffered due to migration of high-level nationals. The Committee suggests that migration may increase because African universities soon will produce too many graduates in fields not related to development requirements. As for Latin America, the authors' opinions differ only slightly. Baldwin states that Colombia, Ecuador, Peru, Haiti, and the Dominican Republic have lost heavily; the Committee sees regional losses (primarily to the United States) as significant, but not catastrophic.

Two other studies consider migration from Latin America. According to a 1966 World Health Organization report cited by Van der Kroef (415/1970), approximately 4,000 university-educated persons entered the United States from Latin America with immigrant visas in the early 1960's. About three-quarters were permanent immigrants. Oteiza's research (299/1965) analyzes data published by Argentina's Census Bureau. He observes that the percentage of the total of Argentine immigrants to the United States falling within the professional, technical, and kindred workers categories is an extremely high 35 percent. Among the graduate professions in Argentina, physicians and engineers are most numerous and members of both professions emigrate in considerable numbers to the United States. Hence, his analysis suggests that this immigration may in fact be an example of the overflow discussed earlier.

Sitler (352/1971) and Wei (422/1970) discuss out-migration from Asian nations and both characterize the outflow as severe. According to Sitler, Asian nations estimate that over 90 percent of their students in the United States fail to return. Wei states that less than five percent of the 8,163 Taiwanese graduate students who studied abroad during 1965-69 have returned home.

Related to the discussion of the magnitude of regional flows are those studies which consider the role played by the country of origin in migration. Glaser (148/1974) suggests that countries differ in the ability of their citizens to adjust to foreign societies. Ties with home, educational and language barriers, and discrimination all influence the rate of return. He finds this to be especially true among nationals from heterogeneous countries where emigration is high among linguistic, religious, and racial minorities.

In his survey of 1,400 students from 31 developed or developing countries in Asia, Africa, and Latin America, Das (99/1971) draws the general conclusion that students from developing countries are more likely to return home than those from developed regions. Specifically, he finds that Asian students, particularly those from developed countries, decide to settle in the United States more often than others. Finally, the Committee on Educational Exchange Policy (81/1958) hypothesizes that area of origin may be a factor in immigration as shown by data from the Rockefeller Foundation and IIE; a higher proportion of Europeans immigrated to the United States than Far Easterners during the 30-year period analyzed in this report. Clearly

one cannot draw conclusions from these studies regarding those countries which are more likely to exhibit high rates of out-migration. The
most one can say is that country of origin, for whatever reasons, is
a variable facilitating migration.

Destinations

As noted above, most studies examine the flow of talent from developing to developed countries and, in particular, to the United States
and Canada. In dissertations written in 1971, for example, Sours (359)
and Truscott (378) both focus on the United States as a major recipient
country. Truscott, however, examining factors which attract talent to
the United States, speculates on the possibility of reverse brain drain
out of the United States in the near future. There is some empirical
evidence to support this view: Watanabe (421/ 1969) notes that profes-
fesional immigration into Canada during the sixties increased at a
faster rate and was more labor-intensive than immigration into the
United States, and Glaser's (148/ 1974) survey results show that foreign students and professionals perceived Canada to be more receptive
to immigrants than France or the United States and thus attracting
more foreign students from minority groups and more permanent immigrants.

Fields of Specialization

From its empirical study of five developing countries (the Cameroons, Colombia, Lebanon, the Philippines, and Trinidad and Tobago),
UNITAR (389/ 1971) concludes that "emigration of high- and middle-
level manpower has gained momentum over the last decade." The report stresses, however, that while all manpower categories are
affected by emigration, certain professions have a particularly high
rate: scientists, physicians, engineers, and technicians. This conclusion, that migration is most serious in certain fields of specialization, is supported by numerous studies and will be discussed in
greater detail below. (See p. 230.)

Structural Conditions Related to Talent Migration

Discussion of the causes of talent migration commonly refer to
"push" and "pull" factors, meaning those conditions in the donor and
recipient countries which influence the decision to migrate. Recogniz-
ing the need for such categorization and at the same time its artifici-
ality, we shall discuss motivation in terms of "structural" and

"circumstantial" conditions. As used here, structural conditions include the social, economic, or political characteristics of both societies, while the circumstantial conditions refer to the personal situation of the individual involved. It should be noted that in almost all cases, research has focused on donor countries which are developing countries. It must also be emphasized that this analysis examines factors which are in fact independent variables in the process, any combination of which may result in a decision to migrate, to stay on, or to return. In the concluding section we shall attempt to weigh the variables and indicate which are most strongly related to migration.

Structural Conditions in Donor Countries

The literature identifies seven structural conditions in developing countries which are thought to influence the migration decision. They are: underdevelopment, higher education systems, employment opportunities, working conditions, system of sponsorship for study abroad, and the degree of social support.

Underdevelopment

In most of the studies under review, talent migration is linked to the level of economic development of the donor country, either implicitly or explicitly. The general view is stated in UNITAR's report (389/ 1971) on migration from five developing countries:

> In all recent studies on the problem of the outflow of trained personnel from developing countries, including those carried out for the preparation of this report, one basic cause stands out above others—the problem of underdevelopment. It has become clearer from these studies that the outflow is a consequence of, and in some cases, a causal factor contributing to underdevelopment.

This view is supported by Adams (429/ 1968), Sitler (352/ 1971), Watanabe (421/ 1969), and the Committee on the International Migration of Talent (84/ 1970) which describes migration as an "anomaly" of development, the result of a disequilibrium generally endemic to the development process. Calder (58/ 1967) agrees that migration is related to development and suggests that talent outflows would decrease if developed countries were more interested in scientific problems facing developing countries because foreign students and professionals would then have the opportunity to utilize their talents in areas suitable to their home country's needs.

Only Glaser (148/ 1974) does not find evidence to support what seems to be conventional wisdom. He tested several hypotheses based

on emigration and return data from different countries and found that
the level of economic development of the home country had only a
limited relationship to talent migration; some poor or stagnating countries had high return, whereas some rich or growing countries had low
return. Structural imbalances in the market for professionals had a
stronger relationship to emigration. Thus, if a developing country is
producing many educated persons, return by its foreign-trained nationals is discouraged, whereas in a developing country which educates
few people, there is a greater likelihood of return because there is a
greater certainty of employment.

Higher Education Systems

Eight studies, three empirical and five non-empirical, discuss
the relationships between migration and the system of higher education
in the developing countries. Henderson's study for UNITAR (388/1970)
offers the most comprehensive view. His findings, which are supported by many other authors, show that foreign and indigenous educational systems contribute to migration in the following ways: First,
they educate more people than the local economy can absorb. This
view is supported by empirical data given in Baldwin's study (33/1970)
of South Korea, Taiwan, and the Philippines, and in Valipour's study
(413/1967) of Iranian students. Second, they educate too many people
in fields inappropriate to manpower needs. Van der Kroef (415/1970)
cites as one cause of migration the persisting dysfunction of educational
and professional training in relation to national and developmental
needs in developing countries. The same point is made by the Committee on the International Migration of Talent (84/1970), Watanabe
(421/1969) and Myint (in Adams [429/1968]). Third, they educate too
many people in specialities which accord better with the professional
demands of the developed countries. Lefevre (224/1969), for example,
examines the inadaptive nature of education and science programs in
developing countries. The Committee on the International Migration
of Talent discusses the crucial role of rural improvement in developing
countries, using it as a prime example of the asymmetry between university output and needed expertise.

Henderson also examines five internal educational factors which
stimulate migration from developing countries. They are enumerated
in full below because Henderson specified what many authors only assume or make passing reference to:

1. Many students are majoring in fields irrelevant to developmental needs.

2. Many students enter science and engineering fields with the
intent to find jobs in developed countries. Moreover, the problems
they work on are unrelated to their home country's needs.

3. Low enrollment and high drop-out rates are characteristic of universities in Africa and Latin America.

4. Popular attitudes which view education as a good valued for prestige and satisfaction are not rational with respect to employment and productivity at home.

Henderson also makes the point that the educational system of a developing country, often modeled after that of a more developed country, may be inappropriate to the student's or country's needs. Parthasarathi (305/1967) supports this view in a provocative article which, in examining India's talent migration vis-a-vis international norms, also takes a systemic view of the whole problem. The magnitude of this migration suggests that India's system of higher education is alienating young Indians from their social and physical environment and cultural milieu. To attack the problem of talent outflow, there must first be a restructuring and reorientation in the methodology and philosophy of her system of higher education and its research emphases.

Sitler (352/1971) and Ritterband (328/1968) add that, for some countries, the lack of graduate facilities is a major, internal factor motivating talent migration.

Only one study in this group suggests that educational systems of developing countries are not strongly related to migration. Myers (263/1972), in attempting cross-national comparisons of relative losses through non-return, finds no consistent relationship between non-return and country statistics on educational development. Even though Myers warns his readers not to overrate the significance of cross-national comparisons, the results of his efforts are noteworthy.

Employment Opportunities

Closely related to, but somewhat distinct from the problems posed by the higher educational systems is the question of employment opportunities available in the home countries to highly trained and skilled individuals. Eighteen studies examine these opportunities from the perspectives of availability of employment, perception of opportunity, and manpower policies.

The empirical works of Comay (80/1969), Das (98/1969; 99/1971), Glaser (148/1974) Rodriguez (392/1974), Sheffield and McGrail (346/n.d.), Valipour (413/1967), and Van der Kroef (415/1970) and the non-empirical works of Baldwin (33/1970), Cervantes (64/1972), Jones (203/1966), and Henderson (388/1970) discuss job availability. In both of his studies, Das analyzes the same data. His sample consists of 1,400 male students from 31 developing countries in Asia, Africa, and Latin America enrolled in 20 American institutions during 1968-69 or working full-time as part of their practical training. He found that students whose home countries provide greater employment opportunities were more likely to return home. Similar findings are reported for Canadian and Iranian students.

The empirical findings agree with the non-empirical conclusions of Cervantes, Jones, and Henderson, all of whom assert that the condition of the job market in the home country is an important consideration in the decision to migrate. Baldwin's argument is more complex in that he relates talent migration to a society's "effective demand," understood in part as the availability of employment. Due to their inability to employ all of their university graduates, some countries suffer "external" migration or brain drain, while others suffer greater "internal" migration.

Four empirical works look at employment opportunities as perceived by the potential migrant. In his interviews with 100 Iranian students attending institutions in Southern California, Borhanmanesh (49/ 1965) finds that those who perceived better employment opportunities in Iran returned and vice versa. Rodriguez (392/ 1974) finds that such perceptions of opportunity are based on students' rational assessment of objective situations, such as where opportunities are or have been opened up. Similarly, for her sampling of Philippine students who had studied in the United States, Cortes (93/ 1970) reports that the propensity to migrate is higher among those who perceive little opportunity for themselves at home. Shin (348/ 1972), however, disagrees with these conclusions. In his survey of 103 Korean students, he finds that their return plans are not related to attitudes towards employment conditions back home. This conclusion is supported by the findings of several others and will be examined in greater depth below (see p. 219).

Three non-empirical studies discuss the effect on talent migration of manpower policies in the home country. Parthasarathi (305/ 1967) states that India's talent outflow will not be alleviated until she develops a sensible manpower policy which will allow for both the advanced training of individuals and their subsequent absorption by the economy. This view is supported by Sitler's article (352/ 1971) on Asian migration and Watanabe's study (421/ 1969) of migration from developing to developed countries in general.

Working Conditions

The studies of Baldwin (33/ 1970), Cervantes (64/ 1972), the Committee on the International Migration of Talent (84/ 1970), Glaser (148/ 1974), Henderson (388/ 1970), Jones (203/ 1966), Lefevre (224/ 1969), and Watanabe (421/ 1969) all agree that migration is related to working conditions in the donor country. Criticisms most frequently mentioned are the lack of adequate research facilities, the difficulty of

communicating with colleagues abroad, the unavailability of professional publications, and the dearth of opportunities for advancement
due to traditional bureaucracies, existing power structures, or the
attitudes of colleagues and superiors towards those trained abroad.
Glaser, in particular, finds that such variables are associated with
migration plans at all stages. It should be noted, however, that low
salary levels are not among the most frequently cited reasons for
enigrating. These authors agree with Baldwin's statement that the
strength of non-economic motives is one of the major findings of recent research (see below, p. 221). Furthermore, as Cervantes points
out, many countries, particularly in Asia, are acquiring modern scientific and engineering technology, which is lessening the amount of
migration prompted by poor working conditions.

Sponsorship

A fifth structural condition linked to talent migration is the system of financing or sponsoring of foreign education. The literature
makes specific reference to two kinds of sponsorship: public (or governmental) and private. The empirical studies of Palmer (302/ 1968),
Myers (260/ 1967; 263/ 1972), Chu (67/ 1968), and Das (99/ 1971) support Glaser's (148/ 1974) findings that students sponsored by their
home governments are more likely to return, or more often intend to
return, than self-sponsored students or students supported by non-
national sources.

In his study of student expatriation as a function of social support,
Chu questioned 106 male graduate students from Asia, Africa, Latin
America, and the Middle East. His hypothesis that student expatriation
will be negatively related to the amount of social support perceived
from the home culture is strongly supported by the findings that all
students sponsored by the home government or organization intended
to return, while self-sponsored or university-sponsored students did
not. Das found that those self-sponsored students who did plan to return had dependents at home, an instance of the powerful nature of
home-country ties discussed in a later section. Only Shin (348/ 1972)
in his study of Korean students, did not find a statistical difference
between return plans of sponsored and non-sponsored Korean students.

Social Support from the Home Country

The sixth and final structural condition which can be related to
migration is the degree of social support the student or professional
receives from the home country. Sixteen studies consider this issue.
The concept of Social support may be variously defined; some
authors, such as Chu (67/ 1968), include financial support which we

have treated separately above. We have also treated employment
opportunity as a separate category but review here those studies which
consider the degree to which national governments or prospective
employers display an interest in contacting students and professionals
abroad concerning employment in the home country. This contact from
home, whether or not it leads to a job, is a form of social support and
may influence the migration decision.

Seven non-empirical studies discuss this problem from the
perspective of what governments have done or should do. Lefevre
(224/1969) notes that a major cause of migration is simply that when
students return home, they are out of touch with what is going on.
UNITAR's study (387/1969) found that only a "handful" of countries
(specifically Iran, India, Thailand, and Kenya) make regular efforts to
locate and inform their nationals of job opportunities at home. The
Committee on Educational Exchange Policy (81/1958) also takes
special note of Iran's efforts in this regard, as does Baldwin (33/1970),
who mentions the successful repatriation programs of both Iran and
Turkey in the areas of health care and higher education. In its section
on India, the Committee on the International Migration of Talent (84/
1970) discusses in some detail India's "scientist pool," noting, however, the economic and implementation problems this program faces.
Another article (199) reports on a Nigerian delegation which toured
American cities during January 1974 to recruit nationals for the
Nigerial oil industry and for social and educational programs.

All the non-empirical works deplore the lack of interest shown by
home countries in maintaining contact with their nationals abroad; the
empirical studies underscore the importance of such social support in
combating talent migration. In her study of Philippine migration to the
United States, Cortes (93/1970) observes that those without jobs waiting
at home exhibit a higher propensity to migrate. (She qualifies this finding, however, with the observation that "government support, when
given during the period of study abroad, substantially attenuates the
influence of all these factors and considerably weakens a person's
propensity to emigrate." Chu's findings are similar (67/1968): students who did not receive job offers from home were less likely to
return, while those receiving job offers in the United States were most
likely to remain. Chu infers from his data that support from the home
culture is more important than from the host. When foreign students
are confronted with a choice between two cultural memberships, they
will look first for support from home. If adequate support is extended,
then they will probably return.

These conclusions find strong support in other literature. Both
Myers (260/1967; 263/1967) and Das (99/1971) associate non-return
with lack of job guarantees. Ritterband's (328/1968) survey of 1,934
Israelis in the United States shows that of those students who had jobs

waiting for them, 74 percent expected to return home, compared with
only 46 percent among those who did not have jobs. Rodriguez' (392/
1974) findings regarding the importance a student's perception of opportunity plays in the decision of whether or not to return leads him to
conclude that governments should create jobs before or after a student
undertakes foreign education.

Glaser (148/1974) found that less than 75 percent in each survey
sample were contacted by employers while abroad, but that those who
were contacted were more likely to return. Similarly, Sheffield and
McGrail's report on the AUCC's Operation Retrieval (346/n.d.) shows
that students quickly lose contact with Canada once they go abroad.
Students said that there was no source of up-to-date information
regarding academic employment in Canada, and their enquiries about
employment were often unanswered.

Summary

Of the six structural conditions associated with the donor country, underdevelopment, systems of higher education, and employment
opportunities appear to bear a particularly strong relationship to talent
migration. This is in part due to the close relationship among these
conditions. Educational systems which educate too many persons, in
fields which are inappropriate to the needs of the country, or which, on
the other hand, do not have facilities for advanced specialized training,
are part of the general disequilibria characteristic of developing countries. Dislocations in the job market are also characteristic, leading
in some countries to severe internal migration, concentrating persons
with professional and technical skills in a few urban centers, and in
other countries to the external migration of these same persons. Talent
migration is stimulated by both the objective condition of the job market, i.e., when there are few opportunities for employment, and by
the potential migrant's perception of the market. The studies suggest
that while the other structural conditions in donor countries—working
conditions, sponsorship, and lack of social support—are significant,
they play a secondary role in migration decisions. Like the others,
they are conditions associated with underdevelopment. As such, they
are usually treated in the literature only as part of a larger inquiry.

Structural Conditions in the Recipient Country

In the previous section, we discussed structural conditions in
the home country which catalyze migration, that is, those elements
which the literature identifies as "push" factors. In this section, we
examine their counterparts, the "pull" factors. In the literature
examined above, the home or donor country was almost exclusively a

developing nation; all the studies discussed here identify developed countries as the host or recipient. The vast majority have focused specifically on the United States. The literature identifies four structural conditions in the developed, recipient countries that stimulate international talent migration: the nature of the professional market; the ability of these nations to fulfill professional needs; the legal aspects of educational exchange and immigration; and the system of sponsorship.

The Professional Market

Eight studies, four empirical and four non-empirical, discuss the nature of the professional market. Adams and Durlam (429/ 1968) observe that talent migration is an index of structural maladjustment in the recipient, as well as the donor, country. The Committee on the International Migration of Talent (84/ 1970) explains this maladjustment as consisting of an oversupply of highly educated individuals in developing countries in relation to demand, and the reverse imbalance, an undersupply in advanced countries.

The view that developed countries are contributing to talent migration by their continuing demands for skilled manpower is supported by case studies of the U. S. professional market. In addition to the general studies of Perkins (307/ 1966), Grubel (156/ 1968), and Van der Kroef (415/ 1970), who found that comparative salary levels and professional opportunities in the United States are significant causal factors, there are two studies which examine the U. S. market in terms of demand for specific skills. Oteiza (290/ 1965) found that migration of Argentinian engineers is strongly influenced by the sustained demand for engineers in the United States. Stevens and Vermeulen (391/ 1972), in their study of foreign-trained physicians, show that much, if not most, of the influx in the last 20 years has been caused by continued U. S. demand for additional hospital house staff.

Fulfillment of Professional Needs

In an earlier section (p. 217), we examined briefly some studies which argue that the home countries' failure to provide adequate working conditions, research facilities, opportunities for advancement, etc., contribute to talent migration. This section will consider the converse: the extent to which the recipient country, principally the United States, attracts migration by offering to fulfill such professional needs. The 16 studies which refer to this issue directly present conflicting evidence as to its significance, particularly regarding salary levels. Several authors believe economic motives are a prime cause of migration to the United States; others believe them to be less dominant.

Eleven studies, nine empirical and two non-empirical, argue that migration to the United States is caused by high salary potentials. In engineering, Oteiza (299/ 1965) finds that unfavorable salary differentials between the United States and Argentina are a major cause of migration. Niland's (289/ 1970) more sophisticated analysis of student non-return from India, Taiwan, Korea, and Japan reveals two aspects of the role played by salary expectations. The first is that salary push-pull forces are a common determinant of all migration decisions: the relationship between salary expected in a certain country and salary required by manpower to enter the labor market in that country provides a qualitative guide to the commitment to migration. In particular, inadequacy of salaries in the home country soon after graduation has an important effect on migration behavior. The second aspect concerns salary levels in the United States specifically. That is, salary levels become an important determinant of mobility patterns as a student's or professional's stay lengthens. In fact, Niland associates a deep commitment to salary with plans for a longer stay. Elsewhere, Niland (288/ 1970) generalizes these findings and states that whereas temporary stay-ons remain to accumulate savings, permanent expatriates are attracted by higher salaries.

These views are corroborated in general by Merriam (242/ 1970) and Ritterband (328/ 1968) in their analyses of scientists and engineers from India and Israel respectively. When Merriam surveyed 206 faculty and senior staff at the Indian Institute of Technology at Kanpur who had returned home from study or work abroad, he found that a desire to earn high salaries was one of four major reasons respondents perceived as causing migration. Similarly, Ritterband states that to argue economic rewards are a determinant of non-return is to argue a truism. Hence, he attempts to locate differential susceptibility to economic factors in certain fields. He finds that among several professions, the greatest difference in repatriation rates was that between engineering and natural science. Most of the differential can be explained in terms of modal economic values of these two groups.

Three dissertations and one non-empirical study examine motives for non-return among foreign students and expatriates, irrespective of their fields. In his survey of 144 foreign students in small private colleges, Palmer (302/ 1968) finds that those motivated by economic considerations tend to remain abroad. Orthman's study (297/ 1971) of 103 persons from the United Kingdom and India employed at the Boeing Company also points to economic reasons as the most listed cause of migration, especially in the case of those from the United Kingdom. Moreover, the results of Dorai's (116/ 1964) empirical analysis of Indian student non-return supports his hypothesis that Indian students remain in the United States for economic reasons. Finally, Henderson (172/ 1964) states that he has observed "important

jobs in Taiwan crying to be filled while former Chinese students, now
fully trained in these fields, were holding down lucrative employment
in American industry." These findings, moreover, support in general
Lefevre's (224/ 1969) and Kao and Lee's (207/ 1973) views that higher
salaries are a major cause of migration.

In this group of studies, only Singh's work (351/ 1970) questions
the absolute strength of salary considerations. When he interviewed
27 Indian graduate students and 17 Indian faculty members at the University of Florida, he found that orientation to home country was a
much stronger predictor of immigration return than was salary. These
studies concur in finding that economic motives and particularly salary
levels are a prime inducement to migration. In the following studies,
the opposite view is presented: that economic considerations are weak
predictors of talent migration.

In Glaser's survey (148/ 1974), foreign-trained professionals
chose income gains less frequently than many other considerations as
controlling their choice of country. The most salient influences in
forming judgments about countries were working conditions, professional needs, quality of colleagues, alienation and discrimination,
politics, and influence of others. Moreover, when respondents were
classified according to possible gains from migration, the differences
had little or no statistical association with plans.

Myers (263/ 1972) reports findings similar to Glaser's, although
they are perhaps not as conclusive. In a case study of non-return
among 476 Peruvian students in the United States, Myers compares
earning streams for returning and non-returning students. Even
though no firm answers were found concerning the dominance of
earnings in decisions to repatriate or remain, Myers' results did not
support the hypothesis that monetary considerations are dominant
considerations when deciding to return home. Use of professional
skills and employment opportunities were more important.

Both Comay (80/ 1969) and Psacharopoulous (318/ 1971) also conclude that high salary levels or potentials in developed countries are
not a cause of migration. In a dissertation analyzing talent migration
from Canada to the United States, Comay finds that salary differentials
are a weak explanatory variable. For his part, Psacharopoulous concludes that variations in emigration bear no relation to per-capita
incomes.

What these four authors suggest is that one must look beyond
purely economic motives to find migration inducements in the host or
recipient country. For Glaser, as for Niland (288/ 1970; 289/ 1970),
Jafari (192/ 1971), Merriam (242/ 1970), and Lefevre (224/ 1969), professional opportunities, career prospects, favorable working conditions,
and research opportunities in developed countries are equally, if not
more important, factors than economic considerations in the decision

to emigrate or return home. To varying degrees, the views of the eight authors discussed above support Baldwin's contentions that the strength of non-salary considerations underlying migration, particularly those related to professional needs, cannot be minimized.

In short, there is ample evidence in the literature to support both sides in this controversy. When viewed more broadly, however, all these studies are focusing on the ability of developed, host countries to meet certain professional requirements of foreign students or foreign-trained professionals, whether economic or non-economic. In so doing, they reveal a significant structural condition in the host country which induces talent migration.

Legal Aspects of Educational Exchange and Immigration

The literature overwhelmingly supports the argument that U. S. immigration laws and visa regulations are a prime inducement to talent migration. Twelve authors discuss the effects of this structural condition on talent outflows from developing to developed countries. All of the studies dealing with U. S. immigration laws concur with UNITAR's (389/ 1971) statement that immigration policies significantly influence migration patterns. Emigration to the United States has increased sharply since the 1965 Immigration Act abolished the previous national-origin quota system which favored persons from Northern and Western European countries. Seventeen thousand (ten percent) of the immigrant places available each year to persons outside the Western Hemisphere are now specifically reserved for professionals. Watanabe's (421/ 1969) non-empirical article on migration from developing to developed regions, Truscott's (378/ 1971) dissertation on professional migration to the United States, and Chang's (66/ 1971) analysis of Chinese students and intellectuals in the United States also point to serious ramifications of these laws. For Chang and Watanabe, U. S. immigration policies are specifically and strongly related to permanent expatriation.

Two empirical studies examine the degree to which the 1965 law reinforces the occupational preferences of the United States by making immigration from developing countries occupation-specific. In his dissertation, Sours (359/ 1971) argues that because this legislation established an occupational quota system, talent migration has been increasingly transformed into a developmental issue. The study by Stevens and Vermeulen for the Department of Health, Education, and Welfare (391/ 1972) traces U. S. policy towards migration of medical talent since World War II, showing that it increasingly emphasizes national rather than international needs. They note, however, the absence of an integrated and recognized American policy regarding the immigration and education of foreign-trained physicians. Similarly,

Van der Kroef (415/ 1970) notes the anomaly of the United States providing various kinds of medical aid to developing countries, while at
the same time "draining" these areas of their trained medical manpower.

Several other studies discuss U. S. visa regulations, another
legal aspect of educational exchange. It is generally agreed that they
are ambiguous and unevenly administered. Furthermore, a correlation can be drawn between migration rates and type of visa held.
Myers (260/ 1967) associates student non-return with self-sponsored
undergraduates who hold an immigrant or student (F) visa, and an
extensive study by Ritterband (330/ 1970) of 1,934 Israeli nationals
in the United States showed that those on exchange visas were more
likely to return than those on student visas. In the Israeli case, different migration rates arise from the process of visa allocation in
Israel. The talented student is often offered employment prior to
completion of graduate studies, frequently including a sojourn abroad.
These applicants are more likely to obtain exchange visas and eventually return home. Hence, Ritterband concludes, the presumed effect
of exchange visas is in actuality a function of the coalescence of the
academic and occupational systems in Israel and visa allocation procedures of the United States.

Several tentative conclusions can be drawn from this body of
research. The consensus of opinion regarding U. S. immigration laws
is that, as presently formulated, they do make it easier for professionals from developing countries to become permanent U. S. residents.
Insofar as the laws are occupation-specific, the results are especially
harmful to these regions. Writers discussing visa regulations agree
that there is a correlation between student visas and non-return. However, as Ritterband points out, this may be due as much to procedures
in the home country as in the host.

Sponsorship

In an earlier discussion (see p. 218), we referred to home-
country sponsorship as an important predictor of return plans or
actual return behavior and cited several studies which show that
students with home-country support are more likely to return. This
section will examine its counterpart: private national sponsorship by
the host government or its institutions and international sponsorship.
It should be noted that in theory, sponsorship from international
sources merits separate treatment as an additional factor in talent
migration. Since, however, the literature does not distinguish between
host-country and international sponsorship of educational exchanges,
they will be treated together here. (In fact, the literature fails to
address the larger question of the role played by international organizations in the entire talent migration process.)

The authors reviewed here suggest that the role played by sponsorship in migration/return decisions encompasses more than simply the source of support. UNITAR (389/1971) questions whether students sponsored by foreign governments or foundations have a return rate comparable to those sponsored by their home governments. In his study for UNITAR on talent migration from developing countries, Henderson (388/1970) states that migration obtains more in private than officially sponsored exchanges. He argues that statistics demonstrate considerable contrast between private intentions and public purposes of foreign education. That is, foreign education seems only in part to have serious concern for development insofar as it appears to be equally or more concerned with different and more private objectives of preparing foreign students for better positions.

This view is echoed by the Committee on Educational Exchange Policy (81/1958) in its argument that educational institutions, foundations, and private organizations which sponsor foreign students do not regard future employment in the home country as a major objective. Finally, Levy (225/1967) cites the "excessively strong influence" of donors or external aid agencies in the selection of scholarship candidates as a major factor impeding a country's formation of a rational policy for international training.

Summary

The literature identifies four structural conditions in the developed, recipient countries that stimulate international talent migration: the nature of the professional market; the ability of these nations to fulfill professional needs of emigres; the legal aspects of educational exchange and immigration; and the system of sponsorship.

Two of these appear to be primary stimuli. Studies which discuss the international market for professionals in general point not only to structural maladjustments in both the donor and recipient countries (that is, both an oversupply and undersupply of highly educated and trained individuals in the respective countries), but also the international mobility of professionals as major factors contributing to talent migration. Case studies of the U. S. professional market support the view that developed countries are contributing to talent migration by their continuing demand for skilled manpower.

A closely related factor is the relative ability of developed countries, principally the United States, to create satisfactory working conditions. Although one may argue whether economic or non-economic motives are paramount, it is clear from the literature that the fulfillment of professional needs is a primary attraction offered by the recipient countries.

The final two conditions seem to be important insofar as they augment the attractive powers of the first two. Given the high level of demand and the satisfactory working conditions in the United States, the added factors of occupation-specific immigration laws and international or host-government sponsorship which does not regard future employment at home as a major objective may tip the balance in favor of migration or non-return.

Circumstantial Variables in the Decision to Migrate

Despite the customary categorization into "push" and "pull" factors, the literature suggests a third category which relates not to objective, structural conditions in the donor or recipient country, but to the subjective circumstances of the individual. They differ from the variables attaching to donor and recipient conditions in that they are associated with the individual's situation or personal circumstances. There are three broad categories of these situational and personal variables—ties to the home country, ties to the recipient country, level or field of study—and a number of miscellaneous variables.

Ties to the Home Country

The authors considered here establish three types of home-country ties which may influence the decision to migrate, to stay on, or to return. They are: family and cultural ties, a feeling of obligation to the home country; and attitudes towards the home country's way of life.

Five empirical studies discuss the importance of family and cultural ties. The findings support Glaser's (148/ 1974) contention that if they are so strong that the student misses his or her family and culture and is lonely abroad, then he or she is far more likely to return. The dissertations of Thames (376/ 1971) and Jafari (192/ 1971) examine factors influencing students' and/ or professionals' plans for returning home. Jafari questioned 300 Palestinian Arabs or Jordanians in the United States: of the 91 percent who were planning to return, the vast majority were doing so in part for personal reasons. In Thames' sample of 100 Korean students in Southern California, the 69 percent planning to return were also motivated in part by a desire to return to family and friends. Singh (351/ 1970) questioned a small sample of Indian students and professionals and found that attachment to Indian culture and family obligations were strong predictors of behavior. Finally, in his interview of 109 returnees to the Republic of China, Wei found that satisfaction with their way of life in the home country was directly related to closeness to parents.

Glaser's study also considers the influence of children on an individual's return plans and behavior. He found that at all stages of sojourn and return and in all surveys, those who desired to have their children educated at home or to work there were more likely to return.

Four empirical studies relate age and ties with the home country to a decision to remain abroad or return. In an examination of Canadian migration to the United States, Comay (80/ 1969) finds that French ethnicity, family formation variables and age deter migration. Cortés (93/ 1970) surveyed Philippine students who had studied in the United States between 1960 and 1965. She found that older individuals migrated much less frequently than younger ones, probably because of greater anchorage at home. This conclusion is supported by Palmer (302/ 1968) in a survey of 144 foreign students who had attended small U. S. colleges. He found that older students, married students whose spouses stayed at home, and those with strong ties with home (such as family, identity, or a desire to serve their country) tended to return. Ritterband's (328/ 1968) study also showed that older persons, in this case Israelis, were more likely to return, especially if they had an Israeli spouse who exerted pressure to return.

Closely related to personal ties is the feeling of obligation to home country. The three studies by Thames, Jafari, and Singh mentioned above and one by Wei (422/ 1970) also find that a desire to serve the home country or a feeling of obligation toward it are strongly influential in and positively related to the decision to return. The same is reported by Merriam (242/ 1970) who questioned 206 faculty and senior staff at the Indian Institute of Technology at Kanpur (IITK) who had studied or worked abroad in a developing country. He found not only that nationalistic feelings were the overwhelming reasons for return, but also that a large majority were drawn back for reasons quite independent of IITK's existence. This latter finding suggested to Merriam that "centers of excellence" need not be created primarily to induce highly trained professionals to return: they will return for other, more compelling reasons. Thus the evidence appears to show that those who have the strongest anchorage in the home country, through family ties or a sense of obligation, are least likely to consider permanent migration.

The third cluster of studies in this section discusses the individual's attitudes toward his or her country's way of life in general and the political characteristics of the national government in particular. Eleven studies discuss such attitudes. The non-empirical works of the Committee on the International Migration of Talent (84/ 1970), Sitler (352/ 1971), and Watanabe (421/ 1969) all contend that political instability, persecution, and other political conditions in the home country can influence the decision to migrate. This view is supported in several empirical studies.

Two authors discuss the formation of critical attitudes before the sojourn. In a study of social-psychological determinants of

non-return, Rodriguez (392/1974) argues that the decision to stay
abroad is in part affected by the home country's political characteristics which determine whether a particular student will receive scholarships, be admitted to a university, or have satisfactory employment
opportunities. Moreover, using path analysis, he finds that the
strongest path to standard-of-living expectations derives from political
instability at home. Carino (60/1970) is more explicit. In her dissertation which analyzes the structural conditions of professional migration
into the United States, she finds that democracy acts as both a motivating factor to migration and one which facilitates emigration to the
recipient country.

The remaining six empirical works discuss the role played by
such attitudes in general, without specifying when they developed or
the reasons for their formation. Palmer (302/1968), Jafari (192/1971),
and Kao (207/1973) all report that dissatisfaction with conditions at
home, including way of life and degree of political freedom, affect the
decision to stay abroad.

Of this group, only one empirical study disagrees with these
findings. In his analysis of expatriation as a function of social support,
Chu (67/1968) does not find a significant relationship between political
stability and anticipated standard of living. His random sample consisted of 106 students from Asia, Latin America, Africa, and the
Middle East.

Ties to the Recipient Country

The literature suggests that ties to the host or recipient country
are of two types: acceptance of its cultural values and satisfaction with
its way of life. Four empirical studies discuss the effects of acceptance
of certain cultural values. Chu (67/1968) examined foreign students'
opinions regarding materialism and the ability to adjust to American
competitiveness. His hypothesis that expatriation would be positively
related to rejection of their own cultural values and acceptance of the
host's was moderately, but consistently, supported by his findings.

Using cross-cultural marriage as one criterion for measuring
acceptance of the host culture, Valipour (413/1967) found that non-
returnees exhibit greater acceptance of that culture by virtue of their
marriage to a host-country national. Myers (263/1972) and Palmer
(302/1968) report similar assimilation effects of cross-cultural
marriage.

Eight studies, seven of which are empirical, discuss satisfaction
with the host country's way of life as a factor in migration behavior.
Elements considered include general adjustment to American life style
and standard of living, and interactions with or attitudes towards
Americans. Shin (348/1972), for example, finds that those Koreans

who are better adjusted to the American way of life will remain. Kao
(207/ 1973) regards satisfaction with American life as a predictor of
migration behavior. Both Merriam (242/ 1970) and Niland (288/ 1970)
find that standards of living in the United States or other developed
countries influence expatriation decisions. Singh (351/ 1970), however,
finds this variable to be a much less important predictor of behavior
than family ties and patriotism.

Finally, four empirical studies speak of interactions with
Americans or attitudes towards Americans. Valipour (413/ 1967) finds
that, in addition to cross-cultural marriage, interactions with Americans are a factor in migration decisions. Those who interact more
frequently with Americans are considered to be better assimilated to
this culture and do not plan to return home. Similarly, Rodriguez
(392/ 1974) observes that such subjective factors as a foreign student's selection of Americans as reference groups are important
factors in the decision to stay or migrate. Only Hekmati (170/ 1970)
and Chu (67/ 1968) report contrary findings. The former finds that
non-returnees do not have more favorable attitudes towards Americans
than do returnees and Chu finds no significant relationship between
potential expatriation and close friendships with Americans.

Thus it appears that acceptance of the host country's cultural
values and satisfaction with the host's way of life will influence migration, but the evidence is conflicting regarding the effects of interactions
with Americans or attitudes towards Americans.

Field and Level of Study

There are 19 studies, 13 empirical and six non-empirical, which
deal with the relationships between migration and the field or level of
study pursued. It is characteristic of these studies that they do not
undertake comparative analyses within broad fields about the level of
study attained and its effect on migration decisions. Rather, level of
study and field of specialization are discussed independently of each
other. The literature does not make clear the extent to which correlations could be established between these two variables.

Ten studies discuss the effect of level of study on migration.
The non-empirical studies of Henderson (388/ 1970) and the Committee
on the International Migration of Talent (84/ 1970) both observe that
mobility of students and professionals rises with level of training. For
Henderson, this raises questions regarding the optimum level of training appropriate to the needs of developing countries.

Moreover, there seems to be agreement among authors regarding
the effects of graduate work in general and doctoral-level work in
particular. In his dissertation regarding Canadian migration to the
United States, Comay (80/ 1969) finds graduate study to be the single

most important variable explaining migration. Myers (263/1972) notes that undergraduates and doctoral students are most likely to remain. Das' research in part supports these views (98/1969; 99/1971). He finds a strong inverse relationship between academic status and likelihood of return. Of his sample of 1,400 foreign students from developing regions, 29 percent of 122 Ph.D. students as compared with 64 percent of 433 who were master's-degree students planned to return. Conversely, 70 percent of all doctoral students planned to remain in the United States but only 36 percent of the master's students. Borhanmanesh (49/1965) reports similar findings.

    Three studies in this group offer somewhat different views. For Cortes (93/1970), the receipt of an American degree at any level of higher education is sufficient to induce migration. Niland (288/1970), in a non-empirical study, states that a positive correlation exists between the quality of institution attended and early return, at least in the case of upper-class students: upper-class students who have attended better institutions are more likely to return early. Finally, Shin (348/1972) concludes that the more strongly the student feels that study abroad will contribute to development of the home country, the greater is that individual's likelihood of return.

    Among the 12 studies which focus on migration within fields of specialization, there seems to be general agreement that medicine, engineering, physical sciences, and humanities are areas of high migration. Myers (263/1972), the Immigration and Naturalization Service (396/1970), Cortes (93/1970), and Henderson (172/1964) discuss these fields in a general manner. In his review of literature, and the IIE census for 1964-65, Myers observes that even though medicine, science, and engineering are the fields in which most migration occurs, non-return differences within broad fields of concentration are not significant.

    Five studies concentrate in whole or in part on the medical professions. Whereas Van der Kroef's study (415/1970) emphasizes medical migration throughout, the Committee on Educational Exchange Policy merely notes migration among medical students and exchange doctors. Henderson and UNITAR (389/1971) examine the losses from the specific countries of Korea, Taiwan, Iran, India, and the Cameroons, Colombia, Lebanon, the Philippines, and Trinidad and Tobago respectively. They both note severe shortages of trained medical personnel in these countries. Henderson further observes that the United States is in the anomalous position of providing aid to the same countries from whom she drains manpower. The most comprehensive study in this area is by Stevens and Vermeulen (391/1972). They present dramatic statistics: one of every five physicians practicing in the United States in 1972 was a foreign medical graduate. The majority of these come from India, the Philippines, and Korea. They argue that this talent outflow is due primarily to the disequilibrium which exists between the output of the American medical educational system and the needs of the health-care delivery system.

Three empirical studies concentrate on engineering migration from different countries. In his dissertation on Israeli repatriation, Ritterband (328/1968) finds the greatest difference in repatriation rates exists between engineers and natural scientists. He explains these differences in terms of modal economic values of these two groups. Oteiza (299/1965) concludes that due to an abundant supply of engineers in Argentina and unfavorable salary differentials between that country and the United States, migration in the engineering profession of Argentina is likely to continue for some time. Finally, Niland's analysis (289/1970) of engineering migration from five Asian countries leads him to conclude that due to the manpower characteristics of the potential emigres, as measured by amount of home-country education, academic status, work experience, and financial support, India suffers a higher per-unit loss than others, especially Japan. Hence, developing countries experience not only a greater incidence of talent migration, but also a greater per-unit loss.

Only three studies consider the fields of education and agriculture. Myers (263/1972) notes low rates of non-return among agricultural students. And whereas the Immigration and Nationalization Service's Annual Indicator for 1969 lists teaching among the leading occupations of immigrants, UNITAR (389/1971) notes that teacher shortages vary between professions and countries. That is, while the Cameroons and Colombia suffer an acute shortage, the Philippines have a surplus.

Finally, two studies refer generally to level of specialization within fields. The Committee on Educational Exchange Policy (81/1958) attributes talent migration to training in a highly specialized field in which positions are not available at home. This finding, which most would accept as true, is disputed by Glaser (148/1974). He states that even though some very specialized and advanced fields have low rates of return, specialization in complex areas is not convincingly related to emigration. Less-specialized fields have even higher rates of non-return. Hence, he concludes that other non-occupational variables, such as working conditions, professional needs, quality of colleagues, alienation, and discrimination are at least as important in determining where a person will live and work.

From this group of 19 studies, one may draw the following conclusions. First, there appears to be a positive correlation between level of study and emigration: specifically, doctoral study is highly associated with non-return. Second, migration is especially high in the fields of medicine, engineering, science, and the humanities for reasons that can be attributed to both home and host countries. Finally, level of specialization within fields has not yet been shown to be closely related to emigration.

Other Circumstantial Variables

Within this final category are miscellaneous variables which have also been found to influence migration behavior: age, socio-economic status, length of sojourn, distance in travel, advice received from significant others, and cultural similarity or historic ties between the donor and recipient countries.

Age

In an earlier discussion (see p. 228), four empirical studies related the variables of age and family ties to the decision to migrate. There are three additional studies, however, which explore the variable of age without relating it specifically to ties with the home country. Myers (263/1972) associates student non-return with arrival in the United States at an early age. Similarly, Shin (348/1972) found that the Korean student who came to this country at a younger age is more likely to plan to remain here than one who comes at a more advanced age. Only the study by Chu (67/1968) finds no significant relationship between potential expatriation and age. Thus, it appears that likelihood of return can be associated with arrival in the host country at an older age, especially when one couples this variable with family ties at home as in the studies of Comay (80/1969), Cortes (93/1970), Palmer (302/1968), and Ritterband (328/1968).

Socio-economic Status

Of seven empirical studies which examine socio-economic status, the majority support the hypothesis that individuals from middle and upper classes tend to return, and, moreover, that they are more satisfied with the home country upon return. Rodriguez (392/1974) attempts to analyze social determinants of non-return among foreign students from developing countries. Using the data gathered by Glaser, Rodriguez concludes that, among other things, a student's status in the country of origin determines the predisposition to migrate, especially if the individual is subject to racial or religious discrimination. Myers (263/1972), Thames (376/1971), Valipour (413/1967), and Hekmati (170/1970) all report that students from a higher socio-economic level intended to return. Explanations for these findings are offered by Niland (288/1970), who suggests that upper-class students are more likely to return because family connections can assure them satisfactory employment, and by Wei (422/1970), who links social status of Chinese returnees to their satisfaction with their country.

Only the study of Cortes (93/1970) does not support what seems to be conventional wisdom. She did not find a greater proportion of students from lower socio-economic levels in the migration group. In fact, the contrary was the case.

Length of Sojourn

Length of sojourn is a variable often thought to influence the decision to remain abroad. Most studies which examine this variable find that the likelihood of return decreases with length of stay abroad. These studies include: Myers (263/1972), Shin (348/1972), and Thames (376/1971). Niland (288/1970), however, qualifies this conclusion by finding that length of sojourn is related to the problem of non-return only for certain countries; he finds a more positive correlation between early return and the quality of institution attended.

Distance in Travel

Three empirical studies question the role of distance in travel, a variable also thought to affect international migration. All conclude that it does little to retard migration to the United States. These studies are by Psacharopoulous (318/1971), who analyzed U. S. and foreign government data and individual research, Comay (80/1969), who analyzed Canadian migration to the United States, and Carino (60/1970), who looked at migration to the United States in the fields of natural science, social science, engineering, and medicine.

Advice of Significant Others

Rodriguez' (392/1974) study examines in some depth the extent to which advice of significant others influences migration. As he points out, "the migration decision is not made in a social vacuum," but is based upon many intertwined circumstances, including the predisposition to migrate, perception of opportunity, and advice received regarding migration. He was able to establish high correlations between advice given by significant others in both the home and recipient countries and non-return intentions. Moreover, he found that advice from certain home-country sources, particularly the spouse, have even higher correlation with non-return intentions. This finding is supported by Ritterband's (328/1968) conclusion that the spouse exerted the most influence in the migration decision. Rodriguez concludes that advice received before arrival in the United States is among the strongest factors affecting the decision to stay abroad or return home.

Cultural Similarity and Historical Ties Between Donor and Recipient

Finally, two studies looked at the variables of cultural similarity and historical ties between the donor and recipient countries. Carino (60/ 1970) could find no relation between cultural similarity and migration, but Watanabe (421/ 1969), considering historical ties, observes that they facilitate migration. Using the examples of Vietnam and certain African countries, he notes their special position as regards immigration into France and explains that historical ties between these nations eliminate some political and cultural barriers to immigration.

Summary

This section has examined the relationships between migration and a number of variables associated with the individual's situation or personal circumstances. Among those which appear to be most strongly related to return are home and family ties, advice from significant others, and a sense of obligation to the home country. Age, class, political orientation, and ethnic background are also important: older students, and those who do not experience poverty or discrimination in the home country are more likely to return. Variables which correlate highly with the decision to emigrate or to remain abroad include acceptance of the host country's cultural values and life style, study at the doctoral level, and specialization in the fields of medicine, engineering, science, and the humanities. In addition, the longer the student stays abroad, the less likely he or she is to return.

Effects of Talent Migration

We have identified 25 studies, 14 empirical and 11 non-empirical, which consider the effects of talent migration on the donor country, the recipient country, or the individual. The majority of these studies, however, treat migration effects as an issue ancillary to the larger question of the structural conditions and circumstantial variables which affect talent migration. Those who address the issue directly are attempting to develop a theoretical framework for measuring such effects. A few authors view this subject from a macro, internationalist perspective, and some from a micro perspective focusing on the individual.

Negative Aspects of Talent Migration

Not surprisingly, the authors who discuss the negative aspects of talent migration consider primarily the potentially harmful effects of this process on the donor country which is, almost exclusively, a developing country. Of the 16 studies in this group, eight refer in some way to the argument that talent migration seriously impedes development effects in such countries. The empirical study of UNITAR (389/ 1971) and the non-empirical works of the Committee on the International Migration of Talent (84/ 1970) and the Committee on Educational Policy (81/ 1958) all make this argument, the latter stating explicitly that "the greatest concern is probably felt by countries having large economic development programs at a stage where trained people are badly needed."

Sitler (352/ 1971) agrees, referring to the emigration of a "critically elite group . . . of professionals who are in demand in all countries." The Committee on the International Migration of Talent discusses the annual migration of an estimated 3,000 to 5,000 persons of the highest ability whose loss can be particularly serious to developing countries. Comay's dissertation (80/ 1969) concerning migration of professional manpower from Canada to the United States further supports these views. He finds no evidence of quality selection in the migratory move to the United States, but this is not true for the return trip: according to his data, the most able are least likely to return.

Several authors disagree with this basic proposition and argue that talent migration does not impede development. Their position is well stated by Johnson (429/ 1968):

> Development is an integrated process of accumulating capital in the broad sense—material, human and intellectual—and of evolving a culture that promotes the efficient use of such capital and of constantly seeking to improve the efficiency of use. It is not likely to be promoted by concentrating attention and economic policy on the accumulation of one type of capital (larger numbers of educated people) on the assumption that all else will follow.

Some empirical evidence is offered by Das (98/ 1969) and Glaser (148/ 1974). Das examines the attitudes of 1,400 Asian, African, and Latin American students towards returning home upon completion of study in the United States. He finds no evidence that development programs have been adversely affected by emigration. Moreover, even though Das does find evidence that developing countries have manpower shortages and are prepared to hire people from other countries, he also finds that representatives of these countries do not complain about non-return. This complaint is instead voiced by American politicians and educators.

Analysis of Glaser's survey data reveals no clear-cut relation between ability and migration plans: as persons are ranked by their grades either at home or abroad, their intentions to return neither increase or decrease. These findings support Kannappan's contention (206/1968) that the assumption that leadership skills of emigres represent an irreplaceable loss is fallacious. He doubts that key ingredients for leadership are to be found among emigres in particular.

Another group of authors discusses talent migration in terms of welfare losses to the donor country. Some believe that the welfare effect of talent migration is more significant than the development effect.

Welfare effects are examined empirically in the dissertations of Dorai (116/1967) and Levy (226/1969). In a cost-benefit analysis of Indian student non-return based on published statistics for 1958-66, Dorai arrives at two conclusions: (1) that social benefits to the United States resulting from Indian student non-return (as measured by the capitalized value of their lifetime savings) far exceed social costs (or savings foregone) to India; and (2) that under certain assumptions, emigration of human capital adversely affects the economic welfare of the home country.

Levy analyzes some of the general welfare impacts on the United Kingdom of the migration of British physicians. He first criticizes the "internationalist" model which has been used to demonstrate that the emigration of scientific and professional personnel is not likely to cause any significant welfare losses in the country of origin. He then develops a theoretical model which shows that under certain assumptions, talent migration will result in a reduction of per-capita income of the non-migrants in the home country. Using this model, he then demonstrates the impact of migration on the allocation of resources to the educational investment and, thus, on human capital formation.

The empirical works of Niland (289/1970) and Devine (114/1971) do not support the findings that the home country suffers economic and social welfare losses through emigration. In The Asian Engineering Brain Drain, Niland argues that talent migration should be perceived as a source of specific economic welfare to both the home country and the individual concerned. He argues that the home country should encourage delayed return rather than immediate return which may represent a greater source of loss or cost.

Devine hypothesizes that the United States, despite its provision of higher ecucation resources for vast numbers of students from developing countries, gains financially from the non-return of a minority of such students. To test this hypothesis, Devine applied the techniques of cost-benefit analysis to data from the academic year 1964-65. He concludes that when high and more realistic rates are used to discount human capital values, the United States is actually a net contributor to the resources of developing countries. Moreover, Devine argues that developing countries' welfare will not suffer it they invest scarce resources wisely, importing educational services in exchange for relatively cheaper, home-produced goods and services.

Two general conclusions can be drawn from this sample of literature. The first is that there appears to be little agreement as to whether migration is harmful to developing countries and, if it is, exactly what its specific effects are. Two types of effects have been studied, the effect on development programs of the loss of the ablest individuals and the welfare effect on the non-migrant population. Within these categories, however, there is no agreement as to whether talent migration does in fact depress development efforts, whether it results in the loss of critical individuals, or whether a country's economic and social welfare suffers as a result.

The second observation is that this area suffers from a lack of both theoretical formulations and empirical research. The basic problem is one of measurement, as pointed out by Henderson (388/1970). If one is trying to assess the impact on development of the outflow of highly skilled professionals, one can only assume that, if they stayed, they would be usefully employed. The failure of a country to achieve a particular growth rate or health target is, for instance, difficult to explain in terms of the contributions which might have been made by those who have migrated. In valuing or assuming a loss to development, the analyst is faced with a non-statistical and unmeasurable problem, and is hard-pressed to produce suitable empirical data.

Positive Aspects of Talent Migration

It is interesting to note that almost as many authors view talent migration in terms of its beneficial aspects as they do its harmful results. There are 13 studies in this group: Adams and Dirlam (429/ 1968), Chang (66/1971), Dorai (116/1967), Groves (155/1967), Kannappan (206/1968), Levy (226/1969), Merriam (242/1970), Orthman (296/1971), Patinkin (429/1968), Psacharopoulous (318/ 1971), Ritterband (327/n.d.), UNITAR (389/1971), and Watanabe (421/1969).

Three authors view valent migration as an aid to development. Concerning India, Orthman concludes that until a better balance is achieved between the output of university graduates and the capability to employ them, talent migration serves a useful purpose in economic development. Similarly, most of the respondents from the Indian Institute of Technology at Kanpur in Merriam's study asserted that migration was an asset to India. Finally, in a non-empirical discussion of talent migration from developing countries, Kannappan assesses the costs and benefits of talent migration to developed and developing countries in terms of four cost categories in the development of human capital: maintenance costs, direct costs of education, indirect costs due to earnings lost, and contributions by developed countries subsidizing the costs of overseas study. In so doing, Kannappan finds it difficult to support the contention that talent migration negates national efforts to augment the domestic stock of human skills and, thereby, development effort.

In addition to these general arguments, several authors cite specific benefits accruing to the donor country through talent migration. First is education and the production of knowledge. The argument is that talent migration facilitates technological transfer, prevents the monopoly of scientific development in one country, and promotes basic research in general and research related to specific development problems of the donor country in particular. Moreover, the studies of Groves and UNITAR argue that migration strengthens business ties between the donor and recipient countries either by influencing investment of foreign capital in projects directly related to development needs or through the formation of partnerships with firms in the home country whereby emigres supply needed information, tools, and products to their partners.

A fourth positive result of migration cited by authors is that of income remittances benefiting both family and the country's balance-of-payments status (UNITAR, Watanabe, Kannappan). A final, intangible benefit Kannappan cites as deriving from talent migration is that of increased understanding of the donor's problems and aspirations among individuals in the recipient country.

Only two empirical studies and one non-empirical study refer specifically to the benefits accruing to the recipient country as a result of talent migration. In his dissertation on Chinese students and intellectuals in the United States, Chang concludes that due to their accomplishments in numerous fields, such individuals have made great professional contributions to American society. Dorai, examining the economic consequences of Indian student non-return, concludes that the social benefits to the United States far exceed the social costs to India. The final benefit deriving from talent migration is cited in reference to Western Europe by Adams and Dirlam. For them, talent migration can help make Western Europe more competitively viable by serving as a force for modernization and stimulating the elimination of a tradition-oriented society.

Two studies, by Levy and Psacharopoulos, concern economic benefits accruing to the individual as a result of migration. Levy, in his dissertation, estimates the rate of return to investment by British physicians in emigrating to the United States and finds it to be very high. Psacharopoulos examines the profitability to the individual of completing a degree in his or her home country and immediately

emigrating to work in a foreign country. He calculates the domestic
rate of return on investment in education for 26 countries and compares
this to the cross-rate of return where the costs are the direct expense
of education, the earnings foregone, and the costs of moving, and
where the benefits consist of the difference between lifetime earnings
at home and abroad. His analysis shows that cross-rates of return
are substantially higher than domestic investments, and that they are
higher than the returns to alternative investments, particularly in developing countries.

Summary

The literature reviewed in this section considered the effects of
talent migration on the donor country, the recipient, and the individual.
Authors discussing the negative or potentially harmful effects of talent
migration do so primarily with reference to the donor country. Among
these authors, however, there is little agreement as to whether migration does in fact have a negative impact on the donor country either
by hindering development efforts, or by affecting the welfare of the
remaining population.

Authors who consider the benefits of talent migration argue that
it serves a useful purpose in development by channeling excess manpower to countries where it can be utilized. Others cite such specific
benefits as education and the production of knowledge, the transfer of
technology, the strengthening of business ties between countries, income remittances, and the like. Those authors who specify the benefits accruing to the recipient country analyze them in terms of social
benefits derived, professional contributions gained, and the ability of
foreign professionals to serve as a modernizing force in a tradition-
oriented society. A final group of studies argues that talent migration
can also bring considerable economic benefit to the individual in terms
of investment returns.

Conclusion

The phenomenon of international talent migration is a complex
and multi-dimensional one. As Rodriguez so accurately states, the
decision to migrate or remain abroad is not predetermined but results
from the interaction of many related factors. Nevertheless, we, like
the authors whose work we have analyzed, have attempted to isolate
groups of factors which influence to varying degrees the decision to
migrate, to stay on, or to return. Admittedly, any categorization into
push and pull factors, structural and circumstantial conditions and the

like is artificial. The literature suggests that some of these factors
are more strongly influential in and positively related to migration intentions or behavior than others. It therefore seems useful to review
what we have termed structural and circumstantial conditions with a
view towards assigning relative weights to their importance in the migration process.

In his article, Watanabe makes a distinction between inducements
to and facilitators of talent migration. Inducements to migration consist of those elements which make migration appear profitable or attractive to the potential migrant. Facilitators ease the decision or the
process by justifying intentions or behavior or by providing a ration-
alization for a decision initially based on certain inducements. Whereas inducements to migration appear as primary elements strongly
related to migration intentions or behavior, facilitators play a secondary and catalytic role. Watanabe's categorization offers a useful
framework in that it permits one to rank and assign relative weights
to the conditions identified in the research findings.

The literature suggests that three of the structural conditions
found in donor countries can legitimately be classified as inducements
to migration: underdevelopment, systems of higher education, and the
state of the job market. Many authors believe that talent migration
is inextricably linked with the disequilibria generally endemic to the
development process. One manifestation of these disequilibria is that
the higher education systems in developing countries create an overflow of talent by their specialized education of more people than the
economy can effectively absorb or by educating too many people in
fields inappropriate to manpower needs. Moreover, the system may
emphasize and inculcate values incompatible with the country's aspirations, leading to the alienation of students from their social and physical environment and cultural milieu.

One consequence of development disequilibria and dysfunctional
university output is that there are more highly trained and skilled individuals in these countries than there are suitable and attractive employment opportunities. It is argued by all authors waiting on this subject that the lack of employment opportunities (or the individual's perception that there are not enough good jobs available), a condition
caused in part by unrealistic manpower planning, is strongly influential
in and positively related to migration intentions or behavior.

It appears that these three structural conditions bear a particularly strong relationship to migration insofar as they make migration
appear attractive and profitable. There are also conditions in donor
countries which appear to facilitate migration. Poor working conditions, principally the lack of research and graduate facilities, and
severe limitations on promotion or advancement, may provide the
final justification for deciding to migrate. Similarly, actual or

perceived lack of social support from the home country, whether in the form of government sponsorship, employment guarantees, or government or employer contacts while abroad, may facilitate migration by weakening the student's or professional ties and/or sense of obligation to the home country.

If we turn our attention to conditions in the recipient country, we find two major inducements to migration. First, the nature of the professional market is such that developed countries have a continuing demand for highly skilled manpower, especially in fields where skills are non-geographic—engineering, medicine, and physical sciences. Case studies of the U. S. professional market demonstrate the attractive powers of this structural condition. Second is the relative ability of developed, recipient countries to satisfy their manpower's professional needs. That working conditions in the developed countries make migration appear both attractive and profitable cannot be too strongly emphasized. Several studies argue that economic motives and particularly salary levels are primary in the decision to migrate. However, other studies (specifically those of Glaser [148] and Myers [262]) present strong evidence that non-economic considerations—opportunities for advancement, quality of colleagues, research facilities and the like—carry more weight than do the purely economic. Whichever view one accepts, it is clear that the recipient country's ability to fulfill various professional needs is a strong inducement to migration.

There are two conditions in the developed, recipient countries which can be identified as facilitators to migration. There is unanimous agreement among authors that United States immigration laws and visa regulations encourage and greatly facilitate the immigration of certain professions to this country. The same is argued for governmental and institutional sponsorship practices which do not view future employment at home as a major objective. Once again, it appears that the migration decision which is induced by the attractive powers of the professional market and the ability of the recipient country to satisfy the migrant's professional needs can also be facilitated, supplemented, or further justified by the legal aspects of exchange and immigration and by sponsorship policies.

The final three inducements to migration are among those factors we have termed personal or situational. There is strong evidence suggesting that the formation of family ties in the recipient country, and acceptance of its cultural values influences and positively relates to the decision to migrate or stay on. This likelihood of non-return or emigration is greater among individuals of lower socio-economic class, particularly if they are subject to racial or religious discrimination at home. Finally, the literature supports the view that the field and/or level of study is strongly related to migration. A positive correlation has been found between level of study and emigration: doctoral students are more likely to emigrate than are undergraduate or master's students. This is also true for the geographically non-specific fields of medicine, engineering, and science.

The remaining personal variables appear to be secondary, or facilitating, elements in the migration decision. That is, the variables of age, length of sojourn, historic ties, and advice received from significant others are factors which further ease the decision to migrate or by which the individual further justifies his or her behavior.

It has been shown that arrival in the United States at an early age and length of sojourn are both positively related to non-return. Historic ties between countries further facilitate migration by eliminating certain cultural and political barriers. Finally, the evidence suggests that advice received from significant others, especially in the home country, has an effect on migration plans and intentions. In any individual case, however, these variables cannot be so neatly isolated. Younger students arrive in the host country with fewer strong family ties at home; a long sojourn further weakens these ties and encourages the acceptance of new cultural values. Similarly, advice from significant individuals and the presence of historic ties between the home and host countries may combine to convince the individual that the decision to migrate, originally prompted by other circumstances, is the correct course of action.

Two conclusions can be drawn from this analysis. The first is that the variables which are causally related to migration can be assigned relative weights according to their apparent influence in the decision to migrate. That is, certain structural conditions in both donor and recipient countries, and certain factors pertaining to the personal situation of the potential migrant can be identified as inducements; they are the most strongly associated with migration. The remaining circumstantial and structural variables play a secondary, albeit important role in migration, and thus can usefully be viewed as facilitators.

The second conclusion concerns the utility of such a distinction for the researcher, analyst, or policy maker, as demonstrated by the major empirical studies of Glaser, Rodriguez, Myers, and Niland. Such a grouping or categorization enables the researcher not only to form possible relationships among disparate elements of the migration process, but also to formulate hypotheses upon which predictions for migration behavior and subsequent proposals for action can be based.

Questions concerning the effect of talent migration on the donor and recipient countries and on the individual are not easily answered. Does migration retard development in donor countries? What are the effects of migration on the social and economic welfare of the remaining population? What effect does the loss of a few highly skilled individuals have on economic growth, research potential, and leadership?

These aspects of talent migration have received less attention, in part because there appears to be an implicit assumption that while talent migration does cause serious problems for developing countries, these problems can be solved only after their causes are identified and understood. A second, and more important, explanation for the relative lack of research on the effects of migration is the lack of analytical and statistical tools for measuring the relationship between migration and social or economic losses. Thus research has focused on why people migrate, particularly to the developed countries, and authors who consider the effects of migration do so within the context of a larger inquiry, treating them as an ancillary part of the migration process. It is clear that the effect of talent migration on both the donor and recipient countries as well as on the individual is one which deserves greater empirical research emphasis and theoretical development.

Recommendations

The remainder of this chapter will present the major recommendations contained in the literature on talent migration. The recommendations for action are much more numerous than recommendations for research. They are principally directed towards donor (developing) countries and recipient (developed) countries, although recommendations are also made for multilateral and international action, as well as for educational institutions and the student and professional abroad.

Recommendations for Developing, Donor Countries

Among the general recommendations for donor countries are that planners and policy makers be aware of emigres' sensitivity to changes in the job market at home, of the closing gap between living standards in developed and developing countries, of the entry of new "classes" into society and business resulting from development, and of the ability of many countries to provide satisfying opportunities in science and engineering.

Other general recommendations include the urgent need for better migration data; the development of new, experimental health-delivery systems to reduce dependence on over-trained physicians; and the institution of some form of compensation scheme whereby either the individual, the employer, or the recipient country reimburse the donor for the cost of publicly financed education.

Development Policies

There are five principal recommendations for development policies. One study urges a review of the relationship between migration and development and a definition of the roles to be played by ministries, research institutes, and universities in development. Four authors recommend that economic development be accelerated through increased capital investment, development of procedures for the administration and organization of human resources, promotion of economic integration, and resistance to political Balkanization. A fourth recommendation urges the establishment of new institutions to evaluate and study the problems facing developing countries. The role of foreign-trained individuals is critical here as they will possess the requisite technical expertise and commitment to national goals. The final recommendation is that skilled manpower be shown that it can fulfill a vital role in promoting development and that a high identification of this group with development be encouraged.

Science and Technology

Two studies make recommendations for policies regarding science and technology. The first is that general science policies be formulated which emphasize and coordinate relevant science and technology, graduate education, measures to improve technological transfer, and study-abroad policies. Science policies should be integrated with regional arrangements for education and employment. The second recommendation urges governments to assume responsibility for promoting the growth of applied science and technology, and for the establishment of productive interfaces between higher education and science and technology.

Higher Education

There are several recommendations made in reference to higher education policies. Five authors urge the restructuring and reorientation of the methodology and philosophy of and investment in higher education and research to suit the needs of developing countries. Similarly, four others recommend that cooperation between nations be extended, particularly through the establishment of centers of excellence. Three recommendations concern the need to increase the production of middle-level skills, to develop innovative work in educational institutions, and to increase funding for experts from developed countries to teach in developing countries.

<u>Study Abroad</u>

There are numerous recommendations for study-abroad policies. As regards selection, three studies recommend that governments identify those high-priority manpower requirements which can only be satisfied by study abroad and sponsor carefully selected students to do so. Another author recommends that foreign students be screened and that preferential treatment be given to those intending to return, although he adds that present screening techniques are inadequate.

As regards sponsorship, four studies recommend that older students, those at a more advanced level or who have already started a career at home, be sponsored for a shorter period of study abroad. Three other authors urge that scholarships be granted to those whose study plans are in accord with their country's needs and whose research activities can be supervised while abroad.

It is also recommended that the number of <u>exchange</u> scholarships be increased (since students with these scholarships are more likely to return), and that loans be tied to a "forgiveness" system. Finally, one author suggests that financial assistance be reduced. He notes, however, that this measure would affect only a small number of government-sponsored students. In the area of pre-departure counseling, two authors recommend that student counseling services be improved in general, and in particular, that counselors urge students to seek a spouse of the same nationality.

The remaining recommendations for education-abroad policies are more general in nature. One author recommends that education abroad be viewed as a development tool. Four others suggest that as many students as possible be educated either at home or in regional centers, and that joint programs be established between universities in developed and developing countries. For those who do study abroad, more attention must be paid to the university environment: it is important to establish programs for graduate students where they will not be overwhelmed by "high-powered" Americans at "high-powered" institutions but will successfully complete their academic programs. Another study recommends that an international meeting be held to discuss the problem of the "private" student and ascertain if and how such students should participate in development. The final recommendation in this section concerns the notion of delayed return. The author suggests that developing countries direct their energies towards averting long-term losses, but without demanding immediate return which may result in greater loss or cost than delayed return.

<u>Inducements to Return</u>

Policy recommendations for encouraging the return of students and professionals is another category which receives considerable attention. Several recommendations are directed towards the idea of offering returnees better opportunities for fulfilling their professional aspirations. For example, six authors urge that effective employment be promoted and eight recommend that salary levels be increased or at least adjusted in favor of desired skills. Working conditions could be enhanced through such measures as special customs exemptions on the importation of research equipment, subsidized return fares, and housing. Four authors also urge that the professional's contribution to development be recognized through the formation of professional organizations, government subsidies for travel to encourage contacts with colleagues abroad, and granting of special status and promotion for work in rural areas.

Two studies recommend improvement in the operations of the labor market; that is, how manpower is recruited, hired, promoted, and retired. It is also recommended that governments review the numbers and kinds of specialists needed to achieve development goals and then support those individuals by developing a sustained, planned commitment to their work and the institutions which employ them.

Two general recommendations for inducing the return of students and professionals are the adaptation of industrialized techniques to local use, and the implementation of policies which recognize the reasons for working abroad. Those who remain abroad after completion of their studies in order to accumulate savings might be attracted home by a policy of preferential interest rates.

Emigration Policy

On this issue, policy recommendations are largely negative: four authors advise governments not to adopt policies which would restrict migration, despite the need to diminish talent outflows. As Rodriguez says, "If countries must balance individual rights with considerations of national welfare, it is hoped that they err on the side of the individual," in accordance with United Nations policies. Two studies, however, do recommend the imposition of an emigration tax and the enforcement of citizenship sanctions against non-returnees.

Retrieval

In the area of retrieval measures, five authors recommend programs which would include visits to the recipient countries by teams composed of representatives from universities, government, and industry, and the establishment of a centralized agency to oversee the program, and publication of employment registers in specific fields. Businesses should also recruit more vigorously in the United States, and one author argues that the home government should commit itself to creating jobs for nationals studying abroad.

Manpower

Implicit in many of the recommendations for developing countries
is the need for coherent manpower planning. Specific development
goals must be identified, and training-abroad programs so coordinated
as to provide the necessary skills and expertise. Five studies recommend that the quantity and quality of education and training be coordinated with realistic manpower policies.

Recommendations for Developed, Recipient Countries

Recommendations in this area are principally directed towards
immigration policies, higher education policies and foreign aid policies of these countries. There are also some general recommendations
for developed countries on the whole and the United States in particular.

General Recommendations

General recommendations for developed countries include the
need for more accurate and comprehensive migration data and the provision of grants to returnees. It is also recommended that governments devise ways to help foreign students return to useful employment
at home. Moreover, two authors argue that developed countries should
try to expand the participation of developing countries in world economic growth through international trade. Finally, it is recommended
that the formal compensation schemes proposed for donor countries
be postponed at the very least and discarded as unworkable at best.
    The literature offers two general recommendations for the
United States. First, the Immigration and Naturalization Service
should provide full statistics on entering foreign nationals and their
visa status, including statistics on how many immigrants are actually
re-entering (former) foreign students. Second, American businesses
should recruit more foreign professionals and technicians for their
overseas operations.

Immigration Policy

Many authors urge reformulation of immigration legislation in
general and re-evaluation of occupational preferences in these laws
in particular. Within this group, four authors also argue for the restriction of immigration through laws, visas, and taxes. An equal
number, however, view the regulation of migration, and especially of
foreign students, as undesirable The third major recommendation in
this group is that developed countries should consult with developing
countries regarding migration policy and establish bilateral agreements

Higher Education

Six authors recommend that the higher education systems in recipient countries must be re-examined in light of manpower demands. Specifically, more nationals must be trained for upper- and middle-level positions in the areas of science, technology, and especially medicine. Three authors recommend that graduate admissions be encouraged, and that selection, admissions, and potential for return be related to the home-country's needs. It is also argued that post-doctoral fellowships in humanities and sciences be increased and conversely, that scholarships and training grants for students from developing countries be decreased. Finally, there are two recommendations that curricula include courses in economic and social development, and that universities and professional associations subsidize materials to be sent abroad.

Foreign Aid

The literature makes several recommendations for changes in the foreign aid policies of recipient countries in light of talent migration. Seven authors recommend that developed countries expand the volume and effectiveness of technical assistance, directing their attention to institutions central to development (such as centers of excellence) which are capable of offering satisfying careers to key nationals or which will aid in the absorption of surplus manpower. Similarly, it is recommended that developed countries use the blocked currencies of developing countries to create international development institutes. In such institutes, and in technical assistance projects, greater use could be made of trained individuals from developing countries. Two authors further recommend that the scope of research grants made to universities and scientific centers of donor countries be increased, and that developed countries finance more in-country training programs.

Recommendations for Multilateral Activity

Three recommendations in this area have also been made in reference to donor and recipient countries: to establish centers of excellence in developing regions, to institute inter-governmental compensation schemes, and to establish bilateral migration agreements between donor and recipient countries.

In addition to these, one author recommends that inter-governmental agreements be negotiated by which authorities of developed countries would be informed of the home country's manpower requirements and could tailor their programs accordingly. Another author argues that educational research and technological institutions be established in donor countries to deal with the large-scale problems of development, education, and science and technology. Finally, it is recommended that in order to reduce professional isolation, developed and developing countries should increase the kind of multinational association exemplified by the Center for Theoretical Physics in Trieste.

Recommendations for International Action

There are four major recommendations in this area. First, it is recommended by two authors that members of international organizations concerned with talent migration provide sufficient funds for the continued study and analysis of this problem and for improvement of data collection on the stock and flow of highly trained and professional manpower. Another author urges the formation of an International Science Foundation, which would sponsor the work of scientists from developing countries on projects of special importance to their home countries.

To increase manpower demands in developing countries, two authors suggest that international agencies use trained individuals from developing countries in technical assistance programs, provide grants to returnees, and sponsor greater numbers of foreign students from developing countries. Finally, it is recommended by one author that in the areas of scientific and technological exchanges, collaboration be arranged between countries in the commercially least valuable aspects of current applied science, such as pollution and road safety.

Recommendations for Educational Institutions

Regarding educational institutions in donor countries, several authors recommend pre-departure counseling programs, improvement in job placement and job-information services, and continued contact with the student abroad, perhaps through cooperation with embassy officials. One author also recommends institutional practices which induce return but do not require substantial resources. As the Indian Institute of Technology at Kanpur has demonstrated, academic freedom, flexible advancement opportunities, firm employment offers made in absentia, and payment of travel expenses home are effective measures inducing the return of professionals abroad.

Recommendations for educational institutions in recipient countries include selection of students whose fields are relevant to the home country's needs and establishment of comprehensive student personnel and guidance services to provide professional counseling during the sojourn. One author also recommends that scholarship policies be reviewed for their adverse consequences. In particular, ethnic minorities should be given special attention to ensure that they are not denied access to educational opportunities.

Recommendations for Students and Professionals Abroad

Only one author focuses his attention directly on the individual. He argues that students and professionals abroad should rethink the obligations and challenges imposed by higher education. Rather than demanding that the home country provide opportunities for "exciting" and advanced technical research, they should appreciate and accept the fact that aiding in a country's development is as challenging as the work they pursue abroad.

Recommendations for Research

In contrast to other chapters, the recommendations for research on talent migration are few and narrowly focused. One author argues that research must be nation-specific, and within that, occupation-specific so that the costs of migration can be assessed and retrieval plans formulated. Other recommendations focus on migration in the field of medicine. It is recommended that WHO study the effects on world health of the migration of physicians and nurses. Specific topics include: (1) analysis of motivations and expectations of migrating physicians, the demographic characteristics of emigres, the role of U. S. government agencies and how foreign physicians learn of training opportunities in the United States; (2) studies of foreign medical graduates in the United States to include their differential location, their perceptions and career expectations, their recruitment by hospitals, their contributions to medicine by specialty, the licensing and characteristics of returning and non-returning individuals; (3) studies of physician manpower in donor countries and in the United States; and (4) studies of Americans in foreign medical schools.

CHART 5.1 - EMPIRICAL STUDIES: MIGRATION OF TALENT

Item No./ Author(s)/ Date	Sponsor- ship	Population Studied/ Geographical Emphasis	Student Specialization/ Long- or Short- Term Stay	Data Collection Methodology/ No. of Respondents	Data Analysis Methodology/ Apparent Disciplinary Emphasis	Key Ideas
429/Adams/ 1968	Non-Gov. Ag. & Gov. Ag.	For. Stud. in US, Ret. Home/ Multi-Nat.	Multi-Disc./LT	Inf. Inter./Ob.	Simp. Anal./ Multi-Disc.	Examines talent migration from four perspectives and recommends social, economic, and political policies for recipient and host.
49/Borhan- manesh/ 1965	Diss., UCLA	For.Stud. in US/Iran	Multi-Disc./LT	Quest./100	Simp. Anal./ Soc.	Examines reasons for coming and factors influencing migration decision.
60/Cariño/ 1970	Diss., Indiana Univ.	Unclear	Med. Sci., Soc. Sci., Phys. Sci./ LT	Unclear	Soph. Anal./ Unclear	Examines certain structural properties of donors which serve as "push" factors and secondary factors which affect choice of destination.
66/Chang/ 1971	Diss., Univ. of Utah	For. Stud. and profes- sionals in US/China (migrants)	Multi-Disc./LT (migrants)	Quest., Int./ 100	Simp. Anal./ Soc.	Shows high level of contribution of Chinese migrants to US life.
67/Chu/ 1968	None	For. Stud. in US/Multi-Nat.	Multi-Disc./LT	Struct. Int./ 106	Soph. Anal./ Soc.	Shows expatriation to be related to amount of social support received from home country.
80/Comay/ 1969	Diss., Princeton Univ.	Unclear/ Canada	Unclear/LT (migrants)	Analysis based on data published	Soph.Anal./ Econ.	Cause of professional emigration from Canada to US must be sought in US.
93/Cortés/ 1970	Stanford Univ.	For. Stud. in US, Ret. Home/ Philippines	Multi-Disc./LT	Quest.	Simp. Anal./ Res. Rev./ Soc., Psych.	Discusses effect of "anchorage" in home country on talent migration.

Item No./ Author(s)/ Date	Sponsor- ship	Population Studied/ Geographical Emphasis	Student Specialization/ Long- or Short- Term Stay	Data Collection Methodology/ No. of Respondents	Data Analysis Methodology/ Apparent Disciplinary Emphasis	Key Ideas
98/Das/ 1969	Diss., Okla. State Univ.	Original study upon which article below is based.				
99/Das/ 1971	None	For. Stud. in US/Asia, Af., L. Amer.	Multi-Disc./LT	Quest./1,400	Soph. Anal./ Soc.	Examines attitudes of foreign students from developing countries towards returning home and effect of attitudes on loss of skills by home country.
114/DeVine/ 1971	Diss., Claremont	Unclear/ Multi-Nat.	Unclear	Analysis based on published data	Soph. Anal./ Econ.	Examines whether US gains financially in student exchange with developing countries as result of student non-return.
116/Dorai/ 1967	Diss., Wayne State Univ.	For. Stud. in US/ India	Multi-Disc./LT	Analysis based on published data	Soph. Anal./ Econ.	Undertakes economic analysis of costs and benefits of foreign education.
148/Glaser/ 1970 (see also Hekmati/ 1963)	UNITAR	For. Stud. in US, Canada, France; For. Stud. ret.to 6 developing countries	Multi-Disc./LT	Quest. admin. by local res. teams	Soph. Anal./ Soc., Psych.	Primarily studies attitudes related to migration and return.
170/Hekmati- Tehrani/1970	Diss., NYU	For. Stud. in US/ Greece, Iran, Turkey, India, Philippines	Multi-Disc./LT	Quest./210	Soph. Anal./ Soc., Psych.	Examines alienation, family ties, and social position as factors related to for. stud. non-return.
171/Hekmati and Glaser/ 1973 (see also Glaser, 1974, above)	UNITAR	A progress report on an extensive study of returned and non-returned students from developing countries who have studied in developed countries. Examines primarily attitudes related to the brain drain.				

Item No./Author(s)/Date	Sponsorship	Population Studied/Geographical Emphasis	Student Specialization/Long- or Short-Term Stay	Data Collection Methodology/No. of Respondents	Data Analysis Methodology/Apparent Disciplinary Emphasis	Key Ideas
388/Henderson/1970	UNITAR	For. Stud. in US and other countries/Multi-Nat.	Multi-Disc./LT	Secondary stat. info. from nat. and int. agencies, Res. Rev.	Analysis of stat. info, res. rev./Econ., Soc.	Primarily an analysis of factors associated with brain drain.
192/Jafari/1971	Diss., Iowa State Univ.	For. Stud. and prof. in US/Palestinian Arabs and Jordanians (migrants)	Multi-Disc./LT (migrants)	Quest./223	Simp. Anal./Soc., Psych.	Examines motivation for remaining in US upon completion of studies.
207/Kao and Lee/1973	None	Prof. in US/China and Taiwan (migrants)	Multi-Disc./LT	Quest./372	Soph. Anal./Soc.	Examines significance of several variables affecting propensity to stay in US.
226/Levy/1969	Diss., Wayne State Univ.	Unclear	Med. Sci.	Unclear	Unclear/Econ.	Criticizes "internationalist" model of talent migration and finds that British system of financing medical education encourages emigration.
242/Merriam/1970	None	Prof. ret. home/India	Phys. Sci., Engr./Multi-Disc.	Quest./206	Simp. Anal./Soc.	Identifies causes motivating individuals to return home after study or work in a developing country.
261/Myers/1967	Diss., Univ. of Chicago	Original study upon which book below is based.				
263/Myers/1972	Carnegie Corp.	For. Stud in US/Multi-Nat. (sub-study on Peruvian stud.)	Multi-Disc./LT	Quest., Int. (of Peruvian stud.), Res. Rev.	Soph. Anal./Econ., Soc.	Theoretical and economic brain drain models proposed, based on available data and evidence.
289/Niland/1970	Nat. Sci. Fdn.	For. Stud. in US/India, Japan, Korea, Taiwan, Thailand	Engr./LT	Quest./447	Soph. Anal./Soc., Psych.	Examines engr. migration to US on micro level and focuses on 5 issues.

Item No./ Author(s)/ Date	Sponsor- ship	Population Studied/ Geographical Emphasis	Student Specialization/ Long- or Short- Term Stay	Data Collection Methodology/ No. of Respondents	Data Analysis Methodology/ Apparent Disciplinary Emphasis	Key Ideas
297/Orth- man/1971	Diss., Univ. of Wash.	Prof. in US/ UK, India (migrants)	Phys. Sci., Med. Sci./Multi-Disc./ LT (migrants)	Quest./103	Res. Rev., Simp. Anal./ Econ.	Econ. reasons seem to be most important cause of migration.
299/Oteiza/ 1965	None	Prof. in US/ Argentina (migrants)	Engr./LT (migrants)	Res. Rev., analysis of census stat.	Simp. Anal./ Unclear	Due to econ. and other development-related factors, emigration of Argentinian engineers to US will continue.
302/ Palmer/ 1968	Diss., Univ. of Mich.	For. Stud. in US and ret. home/ Asia	Multi-Disc./LT	Quest., struct. int./144 for. stud. and 135 for. stud. advisers	Simp. Anal./ Soc.	Examines factors related to return/ non-return and relationships between educational institutions' practices and non-return.
318/Psacharo- poulos/1971	None	Unclear	Unclear	Statistical Analysis based on published data	Simp. Anal./ Econ.	Determines the profit to individual of completing degree at home and then emigrating to US.
328/Ritter- band/1968	Diss., Columbia Univ.	For. Stud. in US/ Israel (migrants)	Multi-Disc./LT (migrants)	Quest., struct. int./1, 934	Soph. Anal./ Soc.	Examines social, psychological, and economic determinants of migration and return.
330/Ritter- band/1970	Office of Education, HEW	Article based on original study above.				
392/ Rodriguez/ 1974 (see also Glaser)	HEW and Bureau of Applied Social Science Research	For. Stud. in US and other coun- tries/Multi-Nat.	Multi-Disc./LT	Based on data gathered in Glaser/UNITAR studies (see Glaser above).		Push-pull factors affecting migration are examined, using a social-psychological model.

Item No./ Author(s)/ Date	Sponsor- ship	Population Studied/ Geographical Emphasis	Student Specialization/ Long- or Short- Term Stay	Data Collection Methodology/ No. of Respondents	Data Analysis Methodology/ Apparent Disciplinary Emphasis	Key Ideas
346/Shef- field and McGrail/ n.d.	AUCC	For. Stud. in US/Canada	Multi-Disc./LT	Grad. students in US visited by Canadian team	Simp. Anal./ Soc.	Canadian students in US lose contact with Canada; would return if jobs were available.
348/Shin/ 1972	Diss., Mich. State Univ.	For. Stud. in US/Korea	Multi-Disc./LT (post-grad.)	Quest./103 of 112 in Michigan	Soph. Anal./ Psych., Soc.	Examines background variables and attitudes as they affect decisions to migrate or return.
351/Singh/ 1970	Univ. of Florida	For. Stud. and Profs. in US/ India	Multi-Disc./LT	Quest., Int./ 27 grad. students and 17 fac.	Soph. Anal./ Soc.	Analyzes attitudes and background which influence decision to migrate.
359/Sours/ 1971	Diss., Univ. of Wash.	Unclear	Unclear	Analysis of published data	Simp. Anal./ Pol. Sci.	Talent migration is viewed as indicator of world interdependence.
391/Stevens and Vermeulen/ 1972	HEW	Prof. in US/ Multi-Nat.	Med./LT	Review of published data	Simp. Anal./ Unclear	Stresses lack of coherent US policy toward immigration and education of foreign-trained physicians and lack of reliable information regarding their roles and expectations.
376/Thames Diss. 1971	Univ. of S. Calif.	For. Stud. in US/Korea	Multi-Disc./LT	Struct. Int./100	Simp. Anal./ Soc.	SES, length of sojourn, familial ties, and nationalistic feelings are seen as factors influencing return.
372/Trus- cott/1971	Diss., Louisiana State Univ.	Unclear	Med. Sci., Engr., Nat. and Phys. Sci.	Unclear	Simp. Anal./ Unclear	US Immigration laws are main factor contributing to migration.
413/Vali- pour/1967	Diss., Columbia Univ.	For. Stud. in US/Iran	Multi-Disc./LT	Unclear	Simp. Anal./ Soc.	Comparison of returning and non-returning students in terms of attachment to home country, acceptance of host culture, and comparative opportunities in each.

Item No./ Author(s)/ Date	Sponsorship	Population Studied/ Geographical Emphasis	Student Specialization/ Long- or Short-Term Stay	Data Collection Methodology/ No. of Respondents	Data Analysis Methodology/ Apparent Disciplinary Emphasis	Key Ideas
389/ UNITAR/ 1971	UNITAR	Unclear/ Cameroons, Colombia, Lebanon, Philippines, Trinidad and Tobago	Med. Sci., Engr., Phys. Sci./ Multi-Disc.	Survey administered by local res. teams	Soph. Anal./ Soc., Econ.	Examines patterns and causes of migration, estimates losses to countries' welfare and recommends policy.
415/Van der Kroef/1970	None	Unclear	Unclear	Res. Rev., statistical analysis of published data	Simp. Anal./ Soc.	Statistical analysis of migration in order to assess severity of problem.
422/Wei/ 1970	None	For. Stud. Ret. Home/China	Multi-Disc.	Quest., Struct. Int./109	Simp. Anal./ Soc., Psych.	Socio-psychological variables play important role in migration decision.

CHART 5.2 – NON-EMPIRICAL STUDIES: MIGRATION OF TALENT

Item No./ Author(s)/ Date	Sponsorship	Geographic Emphasis	Includes Reference to Empirical Research	Key Ideas
30/Asher/ 1970	None	Unclear	None	Recommends actions for developing and developed countries to alleviate talent migration.
33/Baldwin/ 1970	None	E. Asia, S.E.Asia, M. East, L. Amer., India, E. Africa	Some	Talent migration is viewed as "overflow."
58/Calder/ 1967	UNESCO	Unclear	None	Talent migration would decrease if scientific problems of developing countries were more fashionable in developed countries.
64/Cervantes/ 1972	None	M.S. Asia, E. Asia	Some	The brain drain is seen as leveling off in Asia, partly due to increased costs of living in the West, and also because of social and economic changes in Asia.
81/Committee on Educational Exchange Policy/n.d.	Gov. Ag.	Unclear	Some	Discusses reasons foreign students remain in US and suggests actions which US can take to increase likelihood of return.
83/Committee on the Int'l. Migration of Talent/1970		Concluding chapters of book described below.		
84/Committee on the Int'l. Migration of Talent/ 1970	Found., Priv./ Non-Gov. Ag.	E. Asia, S.E. Asia, M.S. Asia, L. Amer., E. Afr., W. Eur., Australia	Much	Regional analyses of talent migration and its impact on modernization.
147/Gish/ 1969	None	Great Britain, W. Indies, India, Pakistan, Africa	None	Great Britain's training of foreign nurses should not be considered as part of educational aid to developing countries.

Item No./ Author(s)/ Date	Sponsorship	Geographic Emphasis	Includes Reference to Empirical Research	Key Ideas
155/Groves/ 1967	None	E. Asia, S. E. Asia, M. S. Asia	None	Discusses contributions made by returnees and non-returnees to Asia.
156/Grubel/ 1968	None	Multi-Nat.	None	Intergovernmental compensation schemes between donor and recipient have greatest merit and least social cost.
172/Henderson/ 1966	None	Multi-Nat.	None	Offers recommendations to US govt. and educational institutions.
396/Immigration and Naturalization Service/ 1969	Gov. Ag.	Multi-Nat.	None	Statistical compilation of professional migration to US in 1969 indicating trends in numbers and characteristics of aliens.
198/Johnson/ 1969 (see also Adams, 429)	Priv. /Non-Gov. Ag.	Unclear	None	Harmful effects of talent migration are usually exaggerated and beneficial aspects overlooked by overly nationalistic approaches.
199/Johnson/ 1972	None	Nigeria	Unclear	Discusses recent actions taken by Nigeria to encourage return of students in US.
203/Jones/ 1966	None	Multi-Nat.	None	Improvement of employment opportunities at home and counseling of foreign students may reverse talent flows.
206/Kannappan/1968	Instl.	Multi-Nat.	Some	Argues that migration does not harm developing countries; recommends action to increase supply and demand for highly-skilled in donor countries.
224/Lefevre/ 1969	None	Unclear	None	Recommends actions for developing and developed countries to reverse talent outflows.
225/Levy/ 1967	None	Unclear	None	Developing countries should create a National Manpower Authority to forecast manpower needs and development programs.
260/Myers/ 1967	None	Multi-Nat.	Some	Examines foreign student non-return, the reasons for it, and the methodological and definitional difficulties involved in examining it.

259

Item No. / Author(s) / Date	Sponsorship	Geographic Emphasis	Includes Reference to Empirical Research	Key Ideas
288/Niland/ 1970	None	Multi-Nat.	Some	Author advocates position between nationalist-internationalist poles, suggestion attention be focused on fulfilling goals of temporary non-returnees.
305/Partha-sarathi/1967	None	India	Some	India's talent migration will not be alleviated until her higher education is restructured and realistic manpower planning is developed.
307/Perkins/ 1966	None	Unclear	None	Root of talent migration lies in US domestic needs: recommends measures for US government and educational institutions.
327/Ritter-band/n. d.	Bureau of Applied Research, Columbia	Unclear	None	Advocates talent migration analysis which takes into account institutional determinants and consequence of foreign study.
352/Sitler/ 1971	Univ.	E. Asia, S. E. Asia, M. S. Asia	None	Talent migration is caused by internal factors in developing countries: recommendations are made in this regard.
387/UNITAR/ 1969	UNITAR	Multi-Nat., Kenya, Thailand	None	Few developing countries are actively stemming talent migration.
421/Watanabe/ 1969	None	Multi-Nat.	Some	Examines magnitude of talent migration, its causes and effects and recommends policies for donor and recipient.

6

**FOREIGN AND
INTERNATIONAL
ORGANIZATIONAL
RESEARCH**

The amount of literature gathered here whose origin is outside the United States is quite small. This is in good part due to the very limited response to our request for materials and publications sent to a considerable number of researchers and institutes abroad. In all, only 35 items were received. More than half represent research by international organizations or persons sponsored by them, leaving only 16 items by scholars in other nations. Some of the material from the international organizations has received attention elsewhere in this review, as have several articles and studies from other countries. This material will be noted here but will not be analyzed extensively.

The foreign literature surveyed here contains 21 empirical items and 14 non-empirical items. Most were published in Western Europe; we received no literature from Africa or Latin America. Among the international organizations, UNESCO was the source of most publications (10). The general subject area receiving the greatest attention was the evaluation or description of specific training programs (14 items). Nine of these concerned the training programs of international organizations. The brain drain is discussed in six items. Other subject areas covered were training needs and facilities, training and economic development, foreign student attitudes, foreign student problems, and degree equivalences. A simple statistical summary of the literature is given in the following tables.

Empirical Studies

Twenty-one items are empirical studies, 13 of them conducted under the auspices of international organizations. Only four of the 21

Table 6.1

Research from Abroad: Type of Study

	International Organizations	From Specific Countries	Total
Empirical	13	8	21
Non-Empirical	6	8	14

Table 6.2

Research from Abroad: Geographic Origin

Western Europe		Asia		Unclear Origin: 2
Great Britain	6	Taiwan	1	
West Germany	2	Oceania		
Norway	2	Australia	1	
The Netherlands	2	The Americas		
France	1	Canada	1	

Table 6.3

Research from Abroad: Problem Areas Studied

Training Programs		Foreign Student		Degree	
International	9	Problems	1	Equivalences	1
Other	5	Foreign Student		National Training	
Brain Drain	6	Attitudes	1	Needs and	
Training and Economic		Statistical	1	Facilities	1
Development	2	Guides	1	Others	2

Table 6.4

Empirical Studies: Auspices

Inter-governmental Organizations	13
University Institutes	3
National Research Foundations	1
None	3
Unclear	1

Table 6.5

Empirical Studies: Geographical Emphasis

Multinational	6
Middle South Asia	6
Africa	5
Western Europe	4
Southeast Asia	3
East Asia	3
Americas	3

Table 6.6

Empirical Studies: Data Collection Method

Questionnaires	11
Structured Interviews	3
Observation and Informal Interviews	3
Research Review	3
Tests	2
Records Analysis	1
Statistical Review	1
Economic Statistical Review	1
Unclear	1

Table 6.7

Empirical Studies: Data Analysis Method

Simple Analysis	14
Sophisticated Analysis	7
Research Review	1
Economic Analysis of Statistics	1

items were published prior to 1967. The data collection method receiving heaviest use was the questionnaire; seven studies employed sophisticated analytical methods. Foreign students and skilled professionals constituted part or all of the research populations of 20 studies.

Thirteen publications were sponsored by international organizations: eight by UNESCO, four by UNITAR, and one by FAO. Two publications, however (on the brain drain), derived from the same research project. All but two of the 13 publications were published after 1970. Questionnaires were employed in ten publications while six used more sophisticated types of data analysis. The two major subject groupings which stand out in this literature are the brain drain (four items) and the evaluation of training programs (five items).

All four publications on the brain drain were sponsored by UNITAR. Glaser (148/1974) and Hekmati and Glaser (171/1973) report on UNITAR's multinational research project on the brain drain. This project, discussed extensively in Chapter 5, surveyed students in the United States, Canada, and France; professionals from developing countries who have studied abroad and are now working in the United States and France; and professionals who have studied in developed countries and have returned to India, Sri Lanka, Korea, Greece, Ghana, Brazil, Colombia, and Argentina. A UNITAR study on the brain drain in five developing countries—the Philippines, Cameroon, Colombia, Lebanon, and Trinidad and Tobago (389/1971)—assesses the loss of investment to the economies of these developing countries resulting from the outflow of trained personnel. This report, and a study by Henderson (388/1970) which examines the emigration of highly skilled manpower from the developing countries by analyzing secondary sources of statistical and descriptive information, are also discussed in Chapter 5.

A group of six items consists of evaluations of training programs by international agencies. Four are studies of UNESCO fellowship programs in India (383a/1971), Iran (383b/1972), Japan (383c/1972), and the Cameroons (383d/ 1973). The program, which began in 1947, offers fellowships and travel grants to mature persons already engaged in careers, for the purpose of improving their academic and personal competence. The Indian fellows responding to the questionnaire criticized the training program for being too short in duration, and for requiring rigid adherence to the program specifications. They also had difficulties with the language of the host countries. The Iranian fellows also cited language difficulties, as well as financial problems, differences in customs and traditions, and lack of proper guidance. Twenty-one percent of them reported employment problems upon return, in that offers of employment were not commensurate with the knowledge and experience they had acquired. In general, however, the Iranian fellows were found to be occupying key positions in educational, scientific, and cultural projects.

The survey of Japanese UNESCO fellows revealed some additional problems: too heavy a concentration of fellows in certain professional specialties, and difficulties with administrative arrangements, such as negotiating for visas. It is interesting to note that the Japanese government has adopted the policy of not making further applications for UNESCO fellowships. Instead, Japan will participate only as a host country. Fellows from the Cameroons reported, again, financial problems and difficulties in finding employment upon return.

Despite the common problems cited, chiefly language, financial difficulties, and employment, the majority of fellows in all four studies agreed that the fellowship had significantly contributed to the development of their professional skill and competence.

The fifth evaluative study is a report on seminars, study tours, training courses, and meetings of working groups of experts sponsored by the United Nations Development Programme (382/ 1968). It suggests that significant improvements in these projects might be obtained by strengthening the purely teaching, as distinct from the substantive, aspects and that a process of continuous evaluation of projects should be initiated. (See Chapter 4, p. 197.)

The last evaluation is a report by Van Ravenswaaij for the Food and Agriculture Organization in which he examines the attitudes and experiences of recipients of FAO fellowships in the field of fisheries, 1965 to 1971 (136/ 1972). Respondents reported problems similar to those found in the UNESCO evaluations discussed above. Language was a problem for 75 percent, with 70 percent reporting that it had directly affected their studies. Forty-seven percent reported difficulties in applying their knowledge and attributed this to deficiencies in the program. Latin Americans had particular problems in applying training while Africans faced more problems in social re-adaptation to the home country. Significantly, one-third of the respondents stated that they were considering settling abroad as soon as an opportunity arose.

As a result of this study, Van Ravenswaaij recommends central coordination of all external training activities, fully supported by continuing research and evaluation. More specifically, he recommends that in selecting experts for participation in training programs, their ability to transmit knowledge and their psychological capacity to function in a different milieu be taken into consideration.

An important report by the UNESCO International Committee of Experts on Training Abroad Policies (385/1971) presents information on the training needs of 47 countries by major priority fields. In Education, a large number of replies listed educational planning and administration as a top priority. Educational research received second priority; teacher training was third; and out-of-school education was fourth. In the Natural Science sector, science policy, planning, and research was listed as a first priority. In the sector of Philosophy, Human Sciences, Social Sciences, and Culture, teacher training was seen as the major need. Training in radio and television was the primary need in the Communication sector. On the location of training, the study indicated that preference is given to training of nationals in their own country whenever suitable training facilities exist. Despite the advantages of training within a given region (fewer problems of cultural adjustment, lesser need for language training, lower living and travel costs), it was reported that respondents are reluctant to use regional training facilities. Some replies, however, suggested the "twinning" of universities and institutes in the developing countries, leading to exchanges of staff and provision of training in the host country directly related to the needs of the sending countries. In a review of the training facilities available in the 47 reporting countries, the fields of special competence included educational planning and administration, educational research, teacher training, training of teachers in the basic sciences, and training of engineers and technicians.

In an article which reports on results of a UNESCO study, Galtung (144/1965) focuses on the impact of study abroad on students from the United Arab Republic, India, and Iran who had returned to their home countries after two or more years of study in the German Federal Republic, the United Kingdom, and the United States. The students reported varying degrees of adjustment to their host countries; the Indian students reported fewer changes than the other two national groups, apparently choosing cultural coexistence rather than conformity to a foreign culture. It was concluded that training in cultural pluralism, cultural distance, image of the home country abroad, and the home country's "rank" in the international system were relevant factors in adjustment and the degree of acceptance of foreign cultures. (See also Chapter 2, p. 63.)

Data from the same study are presented by Eide in Students as Links between Cultures (125/1970), discussed in Chapter 2, p. 68. In a concluding chapter of the same book, Eide explores how student scholars function as culture carriers between their home and host societies. She analyzes four methods by which people of one country tend to learn about another: (1) general cultural knowledge acquired in schools; (2) mass-media communications; (3) images transmitted in the form of goods or things; and (4) direct transfer via nationals from one country to another while pursuing knowledge, recreation, trade, or working as members of international organizations.

The empirical literature from sources other than international organizations consists of eight studies. Four of these are from Great Britain, two from Germany, and one each from France and Taiwan. Three of the studies were published in 1966. The data collection methods varied widely; three studies used a form of research review, two administered tests, and two others used questionnaires and statistical reviews, respectively. Four studies focused on the attitudes of the foreign student.

In a study of 411 foreign students in France, Dupeux (120/1968) found a correspondence between the self-image of a nationality group, constructed from the responses of the students, and the commonly adopted stereotype which defines a particular national character. She suggests that one reason for this conformity is that, in a defensive position in a culture which is not their own, foreign students unburden the problem of their personal existence on others.

A comparative study by Yang (427/1966) examines the motivational and temperamental characteristics of ethnic Chinese from Malaya and Singapore studying in Taiwan. Five personality tests were administered to 500 overseas and 1,000 non-overseas college freshmen and sophomores. In comparison with the Taiwanese students, the Chinese overseas students on the average displayed higher needs for order and endurance and were more emotionally stable, rigid, and sophisticated. No significant differences were found in such areas as the need for achievement, autonomy, aggression, and power.

A 1966 study by Aich explores the social determinants for the political attitudes of African and Asian students in German-speaking countries. Opinions of 709 students were sampled at academic institutions in Germany, Austria, and Switzerland. It was hypothesized that students' attitudes are influenced politically and ideologically during their sojourn, though not always positively. Political orientation is one result of the socializing process and is tied to the individual's personality structure. Results of the survey showed that satisfaction with both academic and social aspects of the sojourn were related to the students' attitudes to the two major powers, the United States and the U.S.S.R. The more dissatisfied students were with their studies, the worse their financial situation, and the greater their dissatisfaction with social contacts and leisure activities, the more negative were their attitudes to the West.

A second German study, by Froehich and Schade (143/ 1966), looks at the problem of readjustment of students from developing countries upon return from their studies in Germany. Informal interviews with 14 returned students indicated that they considered themselves an elite minority which, however, was discriminated against. The behavior structure of the students revealed a compromise between a minimum of adjustment to native culture and a maximum of realization of the cultural norms of an industrialized society.

The remaining four empirical studies are from Great Britain. The Inter-University Council for Higher Education Overseas notes that there is a lack of factual information concerning overseas students in the United Kingdon, not only because of lack of statistical data, but because of data which cannot be compared among educational organizations. The Council, in a rather loose, non-scientific sampling of opinion from university officials in the Commonwealth countries, examined policies and problems of The Overseas Postgraduate (190/ 1972). Statistics are quoted from the Commonwealth Universities Yearbook which show the largest group of students study Social, Administrative, and Business Studies, followed by Biological and Physical Sciences, and Engineering Technology. There is a need, according to this brief study, for British universities to take special interest in the requirements of overseas students and for increased funding for both the students and for research into the relevance and effectiveness of their training.

A study designed to define some of the problems of foreign students in Great Britain is outlined in Exploring Education: Students from Overseas, published by the National Foundation for Educational Research in England and Wales (428/ 1971). It concludes that systematic and effective procedures must be adopted for assessing the academic capabilities of foreign students and assigning them to courses that are suited to their requirements. Criteria for admission that had been found to have predictive value were: grades obtained in previous academic work; English test scores; an assessment of the candidates' financial resources; and an appraisal of the student's capacity to adjust to a new social and cultural environment. The other pressing need noted in this study is for more effective guidance and counseling to be made available during the foreign students' stay in Britain.

An assessment of the training of Pakistanis in Britain under the Colombo Plan is the subject of a report by Symonds (381a/ n.d.). A sample of 129 former trainees and their supervisors was interviewed in 1968. The former trainees were found to be generally enthusiastic about their sojourn in Britain but they felt that stipends were too small, the tours were too short, and there was too little opportunity for practical work experience. Policy recommendations suggested that training should emphasize special courses, with formal degrees to be acquired in Pakistan, and priority in subject matter should be given to public administration. Closer consultation was advised between British representatives and Pakistani departments and institutions, and visits by British professors to Pakistan should be encouraged. It was recommended that training should be closely related to overall manpower needs and that better follow-up techniques should be devised and implemented.

The last empirical study to be considered here is by Wolfson (381b/ 1969) and concerns the training of Ghanaians in Britain. Interviews were conducted with 90 returned students and 35 heads of departments, and an inter-departmental seminar attended by 40 government officials was held as a part of the study. As in the assessment of the Pakistani program, the returned students indicated an enthusiasm for their British experience. While all the trainees returned to their jobs in Ghana, many complained that lack of financial and material resources hindered them from utilizing the skills and knowledge obtained during their sojourn experience. The study concludes that training requirements should be planned as part of a coherent development effort and that Ghanaian authorities should make a determined attempt to identify more clearly their training requirements within each department. Britain is advised to take a more active part in assisting Ghanaian authorities in delineating these requirements and perhaps providing a technical assistance expert to advise on coordination and better utilization of all overseas training offers.

Non-Empirical Studies

Fourteen non-empirical publications originate from sources outside the United States. As with the empirical studies, a division can be made between the publications of international agencies and those from other sources.

Table 6.8

Non-Empirical Studies: Auspices

Intergovernmental Agencies	6
Universities	2
University Associations	2
None	2
Unclear	2

Table 6.9

Non-Empirical Studies: Geographical Emphasis

Multinational	7
Western Europe	5
Americas	2
Oceania	2

Table 6.10

Non-Emprical Studies: Problem Areas Studied

Curriculum	4
Evaluative Reports	3
Brain Drain	2
Degree Equivalences	1
Training and Economic Development	1
International Relations and Exchanges	1
Culture Learning	1
Guides	1

The geographical emphasis of the studies was multinational and Western European. Five studies make some reference to empirical research while the remaining nine make none.

Six of the non-empirical publications issue from international agencies, five of them from UNESCO. In the Final Report of the Working Party on UNESCO Fellowships (426/n.d.), the need for cooperation and coordination, particularly of information among United Nations and administering agencies, is emphasized. On the selection of fellows, it was felt that although UNESCO selection criteria were adequate, many students encountered problems of language ability, inadequate academic preparation, or general adaptability which delayed completion of their programs and led to requests for extensions. It was agreed that more precise estimates of students' expectations and abilities, and length of time required to complete a program were needed. Progress reports by the student and an academic adviser twice a year were also recommended. The issue of the "brain drain" did not appear to be a problem as far as UNESCO fellows were concerned. UNESCO's insistence on obtaining a commitment from fellows to return to their home country after training, and on a commitment from the home countries to employ fellows on return are apparently important factors in the students' return. Suggestions were made as to how the administrative agencies might increase the efficiency and scope of UNESCO's international training. These suggestions included improved methods of reporting and evaluation, provision of up-to-date information on facilities and programs and the coordination of facilities and formulation of coherent policies on foreign students.

Calder, in an article in the UNESCO Handbook of International Exchanges (58/1967), examines the emergence of deliberate and organized international relations and exchanges in the scientific and technological fields since 1945 and notes the following problems: (1) The growing diversity and proliferation of scientific and technical cooperation has created an overlapping of some functions and neglect of others. (2) Fashions and emphases in science are generally set in the highly developed countries and may not be relevant to problems in less-developed countries. If the scientific problems of the less-developed countries were more fashionable in highly developed countries, there might be greater mutual benefit and less brain drain. (3) Advances in technology are often not shared with the less-developed countries. Remedies for this problem could include increasing technological research in universities, and could begin with collaboration between countries in the commercially least invidious aspects of current applied science, e.g., pollution or road safety.

Aside from a short article from FAO concerning its training development and evaluation system (138/1973), the remaining publications of international agencies have been discussed elsewhere in this report. They are a UNESCO report of an international committee of experts on training-abroad policies (386/1972) and an article by Levy recommending National Manpower Authorities to direct international training policies in the context of economic development (225/1963), both reviewed in Chapter 4, and a UNESCO-sponsored description of methods and practices of establishing equivalences between degrees and diplomas from different countries (188/1970), discussed in Chapter 3.

Additional reference should be made to Students as Links between Cultures (125/1970), edited by Eide, the empirical part of which was referred to above. The first section of this book presents articles devoted to different aspects of international educational exchange. Marshall, in "The Strategy of International Exchange," notes factors such as cultural differences, differences in flows of students, differences in educational systems and teaching methods, and economic differences, all of which mitigate against equivalence in exchanges. He points out that the risk of failure in exchange dwindles as the problems become better understood, and emphasizes the need for more comparative research, particularly of students from the same home country who study in different host countries.

Klineberg contributes two articles to the book. In the first, "Psychological Aspects of Student Exchange," he reviews exchange problems from the perspective of psychology. His second article, "Research in the Field of Educational Exchange," is a review of existing literature containing many important suggestions for future research. He finds, for instance, that the effect on the individual of study in the United States has been over-emphasized, and recommends research on (1) the effects of exchange on the host country, (2) the effects of exchange on people in the home country aside from the student (3) the age or level of educational attainment at which a foreign student achieves the most favorable results, and (4) the need for a theoretical framework to guide research on study abroad.

Finally, Breitenbach, in "The Evaluation of Study Abroad," surveys the general development and special problems of research about study abroad. He assesses evaluation as a method of research in the social sciences and offers a definition of the more important functions of study abroad, among them investment in human capital, being part of international aid, furthering scientific and academic learning and cooperation, and facilitating diffusion of cross-cultural patterns. He suggests four main groups of research topics: problems of academic study, problems of informal cultural learning, problems of utilization of knowledge and skills in the home country, and the role of the returnee as an agent of social change or as a culture carrier.

There are eight non-empirical studies from sources other than international agencies. A brief article by Van Ravenswaaij (320/1967) examines the Dutch experience in providing international education for students of developing countries. The Dutch approach, according to the author, tends to limit the brain drain problem. Foreign students are required to have had some years of practical experience in their respective fields and the students' average courses last about one year. Further, courses are offered in English and are specially oriented toward problems of developing countries.

Gish looks at the extent of nursing training for foreign students in Britain and the aid given to such training by the British government (147/1969). A review of the statistics revealed that of 75,500 nurses in training in Britain, 20 percent were from the Commonwealth, five percent from the Irish Republic, and two percent from other countries. Of those from the Commonwealth, one-half were from the West Indies and a fifth were from Africa. The author concluded that it was unlikely that many nursing students would return to their own countries and that those countries should plan accordingly. In addition, it was felt that nursing training for foreign-born women should not (in the main) be considered as part of British educational aid to underdeveloped countries.

Overseas students in Australia and problems of culture learning are the topics of a study by Bochner (47/1972). The problems of the overseas student are put in the context of cultural adaptation and described in terms of the four main roles a sojourner plays in the new environment. As a foreigner, the student needs to achieve rapid understanding of the social rules and customs that regulate interpersonal behavior in the host culture. As a scholar, the foreign student shares the anxieties of all new students. In addition, wrong reasons for choice of department, language difficulties, and cross-cultural differences in academic behavior all pose problems. As a young adult, the foreign student is striving to define his or her own purposes and goals. Contributing to the difficulty of the task may be anxiety about the political situation at home, utilization of skills on return, ambivalence about Western and traditional value systems, and possible conflict between personal goals and the goals of the exchange program. As a representative of a nationality, the student may be sensitive about his or her nation's status in the host country. A suggested alternative method of assisting developing countries would be for the government of Australia to channel more of its educational resources into sending qualified Australian teachers, academics, and technicians to other countries, particularly Asian countries, where they could teach students on their home ground.

The non-empirical literature includes one "guide" or handbook addressed to students from overseas who plan to study in Great Britain (31/1972). The book offers information on courses in various British educational institutions, foreign student entry into life in Britain, expenses involved in British study, and the addresses of the educational institutions.

The remaining items of non-empirical literature have been reviewed elsewhere in this report. Two are brain drain publications concerning the retrieval of Canadian graduate students from abroad, as reported by Sheffield and McGrail (346/n.d.), and measures for dealing with the brain drain from developing countries in general, as outlined by Lefevre (224/1969). Both are discussed in Chapter 5.

Finally, an article by Regueira (323/1966), discussed in Chapter 3, reviews some characteristics of educational courses in economic development.

Conclusion

The empirical and non-empirical literature from sources outside the United States concerning foreign students in countries other than the United States is of considerable variety and varying quality. Again it must be emphasized that this review includes only items received in response to our request and does not pretend to represent all the literature published abroad. What is obviously needed is a systematic bibliographic compilation and evaluation of literature on foreign students published abroad in both English and other major languages.

The material discussed here offers further insight into the subject matter of previous chapters. Evaluations of the UNESCO fellowship program and of two British training programs revealed criticisms very similar to those expressed by AID participants, namely that the sojourn was too short and that more practical experience should be included as part of the program. Respondents also mentioned some problems in the utilization of training, and in two instances difficulty in finding suitable employment after return home. The FAO study raises an important issue that has apparently not been considered in American follow-up studies: the problem of social readaptation to the home society. The empirical work of Galtung addresses this issue, as does the study by Froelich and Schade. In a more theoretical vein, the discussions by Klineberg, Breitenbach, and Eide in Students as Links between Cultures shed light on the question of how study abroad eventually disseminates cultural knowledge and contributes to social change. Further research is needed to identify empirical work which might expand and test these theoretical positions.

Regarding program structure and administration, the studies reviewed here find, as do the U. S. studies, that there are frequent gaps in communication between the student, the program administrator, and the educational institution; that better selection and placement techniques are needed; and that sponsored trainees should form part of an overall manpower development design. One British study also recommended better advising and counseling services for foreign students in British universities.

These studies contain some comments on new approaches to human resource development, discussed more fully in Chapter 4. The Dutch stress short courses conducted in English, thus avoiding the language problems so frequently cited in the evaluation studies. Several authors recommend the development of regional training facilities (Bochner 47, Requeira 323, Wolfson 381b) although one UNESCO study (385) found a reluctance to use such facilities among the 47 countries surveyed. The AID studies discussed in Chapter 2 (e. g. , 14d) also reported lower participant satisfaction when training had been conducted in "third country" sites. The implication is that sponsored students are interested in more than specialized training per se and have other goals in mind when they participate in an overseas training program. This is another area where further research might identify pertinent studies.

7

OVERVIEW, FINDINGS, AND RECOMMENDATIONS

Overview

The preceding chapters, presenting the content, findings, and suggestions contained in studies of foreign students in the United States, indicate that the literature has been

- quantitatively large,
- methodologically uneven,
- conceptually and theoretically unfocused,
- topically wide-ranging but seldom interrelated,
- in results and findings, diverse, sometimes contradictory, and only in some instances significant or original,
- in policy recommendations, scattered, ad hoc, and unconcerned about implementation,
- in research recommendations, broad, seldom mutually related, encompassing a wide spectrum, and within it emphasizing some recurrent themes while ignoring others.

It should be emphasized that the studies surveyed do not represent in any meaningful sense a "unit." Rather, with the few exceptions of studies conducted as a series, the literature surveyed represents a collection of separate items, brought together only by the criterion that most of them were published or issued in the period studied, and because, by topic of inquiry, they fit the frame of this project. This should be borne in mind because, as we refer to the "research surveyed," "the literature," and some of "its" characteristics, trends, or deficiencies, the impression might arise that the extensive body of books, articles, reports, dissertations, etc., may somehow have a unity or cohesion of its own. In fact, the record is vastly heterogeneous. What we have surveyed is an array of studies and other documents, not the result of any overall a priori program, plan, or recommendation for research. This accounts, on one hand, for the variety and richness of the total, and, on the other, the low cumulativeness, comparability, and generalizability of the results.

It should also be noted that the term "research," as generally used, refers to a very wide range of highly disparate endeavors. It includes efforts involving investments of personal thought, with no reference to other views or publications; compilations of data, information, or discussions at meetings; evaluations of other studies; ad hoc marshalings of selected data to justify particular programs or allocations of funds; individual projects using a specific method to generate autonomous findings; comparative studies perusing data generated by other researchers; tests of other inquiries with a view to assessing the (continued) validity of their concepts, methods, or findings; as well as large data-generating inventory undertakings to serve as a basis for policy decisions by organizations or government, or for further research. All of these, and combinations of these, are viewed as "research." Obviously, they differ widely in: (a) form and the clienteles they are meant to serve; (b) their purposes—ad hoc short-term to general long-term; and (c) their methods—from selective compilations or situational statements to disciplined social science inquiry. A review of so diverse an array of materials thus cannot but confront issues of comparability, quality, objectivity, reliability, validity, and sophistication of the various documents, and thus puts a premium on (1) the selectivity, and (2) the judgment of those who would attempt a review. Neither represents a comfortable assignment.

Quantity and Types of Publications

Very substantial effort, intelligence, and concern have gone into the preparation of the some 433 studies surveyed in this report, and of the additional 110 that could only be identified and listed. If we bear in mind that international educational exchange is not now, or yet, a crystallized field of academic study, that it is not fully housed in any one discipline, that it possesses no scholarly journal, that the number of U. S. and world researchers professionally committed to a continuing and systematic interest in international educational exchanges probably does not exceed 50, and that foreign students in the United States constitute only plus or minus 1.5 percent of the total U. S. college and university population, then the extent and variety of attention given to foreign students in the literature must be deemed remarkable.

By function, the items surveyed fall into five major categories.

Informational. Bibliographies; guides; handbooks; directories of personnel, organizations or programs; descriptions of programs or fellowship opportunities; statistical compilations or censuses; newsletters; policy or project releases, etc.

Books and monographs. Descriptions and/or analyses of programs, issues, policies, or functions of educational exchanges; of foreign students as a special component of exchanges; or of a particular aspect of their functioning, impact, or problems.

Reports. Published and/or unpublished resumes of conferences or colloquia; contract evaluations or studies of particular programs, projects, types, or records of research; reports on international organizations, national governmental, foundation, professional organization, or university activities, resources, etc.

Articles or Chapters. Published in scholarly or professional journals or as chapters in compendia. Includes book reviews.

Research Papers, Dissertations. Unpublished analyses or research papers; M.A. theses and Ph.D. dissertations.

Of the above, some 240 were by method and result predominantly empirical, and the remainder predominantly non-empirical, i.e., descriptive, prescriptive, and/or analytical or critical, but not primarily seeking to generate or test original research data. Needless to say, many publications fall into more than a single category by format, method, or content.

Quantity

The period under review, in general, seems to have produced quantitatively more publications than preceding periods. The U. S. Department of State's "Selective Bibliography on Cross-Cultural Education"[1] listed for the longer period of 1946-1964 approximately 150 governmental or government-sponsored and 250 private publications, of which 140 were books, monographs, pamphlets and dissertations, and 110 articles. Since all compilations are selective, and some included "work in progress," no serious comparison with this or with the prior reviews of Cormack, Cussler, and Walton is possible. One aspect, however, merits attention. It is the relative diminution in the number of academic research books which focus on some aspect of the foreign student phenomenon. Between 1955 and 1966, for example, at least 17 books of this nature were published, and they included a number of seminal studies.[2] In comparison, the period since 1967 includes 13 books: by Deutsch (two); Singh; Speakman; Sinauer; Adams; Kidd; Niland; Eide; Melvin; Myers; Kelman and Ezekiel; and Sanders and Ward. Of the above, however, only five research foreign students specifically, and four inquire into the more specialized problem of the migration of talent, including student non-return. The rest are analytical-discursive.

A similar situation obtains in more general books on the international policy implications of educational and cultural relations. The earlier period witnessed the publication of books by Blum, Coombs, and Frankel. Since then, only a revised edition of the book by Blum, edited by Braisted, has dealt with the topic.

While there is no inherent virtue as such in books—they can be significant or not—in the academic research community they tend to exercise a more continuous impact than other types of less permanent and identifiable publications. Judging by the frequency of references to them, and the use of concepts which they introduced, books published between 1955 and 1966 continue to be important for foreign student research. It should be remembered that many of these books were the result of stimulation and support by the Committee on Cross-Cultural Education of the Social Science Research Council. The Committee is no longer in existence and no such program is in operation.

Monographs—intensive treatments of a specific topic—are difficult to compare over time, since they range widely by purpose, content, sponsor, professional field, and type of author. It would seem that their ratio in the total literature may have remained approximately the same as before, that more professional associations or research bureaus are publishing them, and that they do so more regularly.

A particular feature of the foreign student literature is the considerable number of evaluative research reports, mostly sponsored by national governmental units or international organizations. What is particularly valuable is that some of these studies form series which use relatively congruent survey techniques and test mutually complementary populations, thus offering data which, with caution, can be compared. AID's DETRI series (10, 11, 12, 14, 113) are good examples. Other series include those issued by the U. S. Department of State (397, 398, 408), the U. S. Advisory Commission on Educational and Cultural Affairs (309), USIA (409 and others), the U. S. Department of Health, Education, and Welfare (391-396), the Board of Foreign Scholarships (44, 46), UNESCO (383-386), UNITAR (387-389), the Institute of International Education (181-187), NAFSA (264-285), and other agencies, professional associations, university research programs, etc.

Regarding Ph. D. dissertations, a substantial number are devoted to foreign student research topics. We have identified 97, and there are probably more. Of these, not fewer than 40 seem to have been written by Ph.D. candidates who were foreign students themselves.[3] Most dissertations derive from educational, sociological, social psychological, and, in a few cases, professional field backgrounds. Fewer than before are history or foreign-policy oriented, many focus on attitudes and problems of specific student groups, many deal with aspects of non-return and brain drain, others with orientation or problems of administration encountered during the sojourn.

A similar profile obtains with regard to journal articles. Of a total of 112 surveyed, 27 apparently were written by present or former foreign students.[4] This substantial and active research contribution by foreign students is significant in that, often, it involves research that empathetically inquires into special populations, topics, or issues that might not have engaged the attention of the usual American researcher. These scholars have made a special contribution to common knowledge and represent, upon return to their home societies, potential international educational resources which can be drawn upon in the future for collaborative or national home-country research.

Regarding periodicals, the surveyed articles have most frequently appeared—and our selective bibliography may have introduced possibly a major distortion—in the following journals: International Educational and Cultural Exchange (total 38), Sociology and Social Research (total 27), International Development Review (total 6). By field, most articles were published in journals relating to the various facets of education (total 19), followed by those relating to sociology and/or social science (total 15), development (total 13), psychology (total 7), and international relations (total 5). Six articles were published in "international" journals published abroad. It is notable that we have identified few publications relating for foreign students in historical or in cultural anthropology journals.

Method

As noted by Cormack, Cussler, and Walton in their review studies, the dominant methods used in empirical research have been, and continue to be, tabulatory survey techniques which seek to elicit information by means of questionnaires, interviews, or combinations of the two. Many use control groups, and the most technically sophisticated use a variety of statistical correlational techniques to assess validity, reliability, and/or significance of their data. Additional techniques used include multiple regression analysis, Q-sorts, various tests, checklists, searches of records, semantic differentials, etc. The sample populations vary in size, some of them ranging in the thousands and representing almost the entire population studied. Studies of this size, of course, can be undertaken only where substantial funds and/or personnel are available. Such funds can come from interested national governmental agencies, international organizations, and possibly foundations.

In the preponderant number of cases, the interviews and questionnaires were administered in the United States, mostly within the context and locus of one or several universities or colleges. A number of studies used entry or exit questionnaires or interviews. The most massive, sophisticated, and cumulative of the latter type are the DETRI exit interview studies sponsored by AID (113).

There were some 32 comparative studies, most of them the work of doctoral candidates. They compared: different foreign cultures at one university; members of one culture at different institutions; foreign and American students on one campus; multiple-nationality/multiple-country data; foreign students on the same campus at different times; reciprocal groups studying in each country's regions; the effect of two modes of counseling on a single foreign culture; two institutions; two groups at multiple institutions; and/or one culture from two overseas countries studying in a third country of the same culture. What these studies have produced are often individually intriguing findings, but the mere fact that they are comparative does not make them in most instances more useful than single-culture studies criticized in the past. Without common framework, they are not comparable, replicable, or mutually relatable.

The literature surveyed contains very few longitudinal studies focusing on enduring residual effects of the educational experience in the United States within a large population. One doctoral dissertation (374) used file records of foreign students who had attended one university over a 20-year period to construct a predictive model of academic achievement, and a major AID series (14a-f) evaluated persons who had participated in training programs and returned to their home countries over a period of ten years or more. Similarly, the 1963 Gardner Report (309), subsequently published as A Beacon of Hope, reports on an interview study involving almost 2,700 ex-grantees who had studied in the United States between 1949 and 1960. Among international organizations, UNESCO's follow-up study, involving the cooperation of local research resources, is unique (125, 144). Glaser's massive study of the brain drain, sponsored by UNITAR, is exemplary in method and international research cooperation (148).

Broadly speaking, what most of these studies on foreign students produce are aggregate data, elicited and subsequently analyzed around conventional categories of factors. They are probed to yield group and category characteristics, views, and evaluations, contemporary or retrospective. They represent variants on what are now the conventional approaches to social science research. We have found little use of less conventional approaches such as depth studies, autobiography, of Cantril's "self-anchoring" scales, of cultural or international distance scales, of taped life histories as developed by Oscar Lewis, of the use of Morris' "Ways to Live," of "critical path" or "network analysis," or of other known and potentially fruitful techniques.

All too often the approach consists of preparing and mailing out a questionnaire to a selected list or sample of students—on campus, around the country, or abroad—and then analyzing whatever is returned. Pretesting is infrequent. Often, the percentage of response omissions on individual questions, or of questionnaire non-returns is high yet the effect on the findings obtained is not always or fully analyzed.

In all cases, what are received and analyzed are <u>verbal</u> data— verbally elicited and verbally stated. Such data in many instances involve the well-known problems of "courtesy" and "ingratiation," of political calculation, of cultural and linguistic misunderstanding, and, where attitudes are the subject of inquiry, the basic issue of the relation between attitudes, verbally avowed at a particular time to particular researchers in one environment, and their interpretation as bearing on potential overt behavior at another time in another environment. [5] We have found no overt behavior observation studies.

Regarding studies focusing on "sojourn-affected" changes, few of them have been able to elicit pre-arrival or background data, most administer comparison-oriented tests without awareness of the potential effect of various stages in the U-curve, and many incline to an over-interpretation of the degree of sharpness and momentary finality of the response proferred, whether volunteered or offered as a solution to the problem posed by a question. It should be noted that what most studies analyze is their <u>data</u>. Such data do not always or necessarily reflect the greater systemic complexity of those who were asked to supply them.

Finally, it should again be noted that many empirical studies are one-time affairs. The interest in foreign students may be limited to their representing an intriguing, convenient, or assigned research population. Often, the dominant competence to be used and demonstrated is that pertaining to the design, technique, and administration of research. In such cases, foreign students represent only human sites on which to collect data. The lack of substantive knowledge and of protracted pre-inquiry into the complex contexts involved often produces naive questions and superficial, if not artificial, results. Where the focus is method, it is occasionally the method that, in effect, is tested by the foreign student sample, rather than vice versa.

Despite the above critique, which, of course, relates to more than foreign student research, the research literature of recent years has moved the art and science of acquiring knowledge about and from foreign students substantially ahead. Regarding evaluation and follow-up techniques, much has been learned and accomplished in AID, the

State Department, UNESCO, and UNITAR studies above all. The social
psychological studies, relating to attitudes, adjustment, etc., seem
to have reached a plateau where the use of other than the generally
employed techniques may be needed to yield significant new results.
The current stage of social science research could permit cross-
cultural assessments, cross-temporal comparisons, comparisons of
attitude and overt behavior, as well as program-oriented evaluations
of relevance, effectiveness, and impacts of sojourns and education.
The emphasis has been predominantly on the latter (see 365). The need
is for more of the former.

Concepts and Theory

Regarding concepts and theory in foreign student research, they
remain, as Cormack, Cussler, Walton, Klineberg, and Spencer have
noted, underdeveloped. Insofar as concepts are used at all, they are
often those developed in the 1950's and 1960's. The U-curve and two-
way mirror hypotheses were tested in several cultural contexts and
found to apply partially in some, and not in others (38, 65, 88, 101,
340). One study links the two concepts (101). Culture shock was
explored in two studies (358, 428) but only cursorily and without
theoretical intent. The third culture concept was applied to scientists
only, and not explored as theory (324). The conguency theory in attitudes was tested in an Arab student context and found only partially
supported (68).

Only a few researchers have introduced new theoretical formulations or examined those from other disciplines in the context of international education. "Anticipatory adjustment" was proposed as an
hypothesis to explain differences in adjustment between students from
developing and developed countries (38). Kelman's differentiation
between "sentimental" and "instrumental" sources of attachment to
the system was tested and found fruitful in explaining ideological disengagement from both home and host society, while leaving cultural
values least, and "the role of the national" most vulnerable (39). There
was a new interest in "lifestyle orientations" and "national character"
approaches (28, 145, 146). Other studies used human capital models
(80), the theory of congruency in attitude (180), the push-pull model in
interpreting brain drain decisions (60), personality adjustment types
(140), indigenization models (42), etc. On a broader theoretical level,
Eide's "cultural links, carriers, and bridges" approach (124, 125) was
supplemented by M. Kelman's, R. Angell's, and M. Singer's use of
"ties and linkages" as analytical tools.

It is surprising that many theories have, since their original
formulation, elicited almost no research follow-up. No foreign student
research has sought to test E. de Vries' theorem of optimum cultural

tension and discontinuity, [6] Nehnevajsa's "actual <u>versus</u> anticipated events" impact approach to attitudes, [7] or such constructs as "culture themes" (Opler), "multiple loyalties" (Guetzkow), "cognitive dissonance" (Festinger), "self-fulfilling prophecy" (Merton), "subjective culture" (Triandis), "marginal man" theory (Stonequist), "goal shock" (Walton), "cross-pressures" (Lazarsfeld), "coping mechanisms" (Coelho), the "Sapir-Whorf" hypothesis, etc. Research approaches to foreign students' cross-cultural experiences based on such theoretical formulations are at present infrequent. This is also reflected in the unsystematic and halting use that is made of such theory as obtains in cross-cultural communication, emotion, learning, exchange (Homans), perception (Kirkpatrick), patterns of thinking and logic (Pribram; E. Glenn, et al.; M. Cole), etc. In fact, it would seem that the most interesting concepts and theories for future foreign student research are to be found in the general theories of social science which could profitably be applied and adapted to the intercultural experience of students—domestic and foreign.

What then is in the forefront of conceptual attention? In governmental and administrative research, important practical aims are how to formulate and administer criteria for the effectiveness of training programs (365); how to define and conceive of success in education (362); how to define and implement the concept of relevancy regarding education abroad (111), and how to develop measures of management potential that, combined with other exercises, would identify among trainees potentially successful change agents. On the academic side, foreign student research continues to wait for those who may help it to recommence where the 1950's and 1960's largely left off—in efforts to build and develop concepts and theories to give purpose and cohesion to data.

Topics

The topics covered in the literature encompass the whole range of perceived operations, programs, effects, interests, and populations involved in study abroad. They include studies of: histories of particular exchange programs by period, field, or country; specific governmental exchange programs; institutional, professional, or departmental educational or training programs evaluations of the quality, utilization, and effects of orientation programs; international relations implications of foreign student education; administrative procedures, including selection, admission, financing; motivations for coming to the United States for study; particular national, geographic, or gender groups among foreign students; wives and families; particular testing instruments; types and effects of orientation programs; adjustment and coping problems in cross-cultural milieus; attitudes and attitude changes—to self, home country, host country, professional role; counseling and advisory processes and personnel—academic and personal; factors influencing academic performance; contacts, friendships, social life, and residential patterns of foreign students; effects of foreign students on American students, academic programs, universities, communities, and so on; non-return, brain drain, and migration of skilled manpower—by countries, continents, fields, levels of training, psycho-social characteristics, and gain-loss calculations; institution building and technical assistance roles of U. S. institutions; practical training and work experience; the returned student and relations with alumni; and selected concepts and/or theories.

It should be noted that, in contrast to earlier periods, post-1967 studies concentrate on the applied uses of advanced U. S. education, on relevance to careers, on the developmental functions of education abroad, on the determinants and effects of the migration of talent, etc. In the process, attention to the liberal arts functions of education, to growth toward common human values, or to international understanding has very much decreased. Relevance and utility have superseded intellectual broadening and the evolvement of mutual understanding as dominant values. This change in emphasis characterizes much of U. S. higher education, however, and is not unique to foreign student literature.

Student non-return, the migration of talent, and the brain drain claim by far the largest segment of the surveyed literature: six excellent books or monographs and 57 articles, dissertations, or reports. The most recent volume is the multi-national UNITAR study (148), deriving data from students now in the United States, Canada, and France, foreign professionals who now work in the United States and France, and returnees in eight developing countries who had previously studied in developed countries. Four studies seek to assess economic gain and loss (114, 116, 260, 263). A paradigm is developed to classify migrants (263). Preselection is found not to be feasible (288). One study analyzes flows in systems terms and finds the direction of movement indicative of the dominating power (359). While the record of analyses is massive, further research, on specific countries and professions, continues to be needed, not only to serve improved manpower planning and training, but also to permit a more accurate assessment of global, intra-, and inter-regional flows, and their consequences.

Direct concern with attitudes toward the United States, and the direction that such attitudes might take as a result of the sojourn, has substantially decreased since the 1950's and early 1960's. Only one academic (233), one professional (401), and two series of AID studies—and the latter within a much broader program evaluation framework—purposefully sought such information (11, 12). It is

striking that despite the vast changes in the world and the United States
in the last 20 years, the areas of appreciation and criticism of the
United States have remained fairly stable. Americans are consistently
personally liked, certain social practices are condemned (discrimination, poverty, unemployment, the media, etc.), and U. S. foreign
policy is consistently criticized. The studies also point to an unaware-
ness on the part of Americans about the decisive impact on others that
the United States is exercising.

Length of sojourn has remained a confirmed, significant variable
in the social problems area, in academic performance, in decisions to
stay abroad, in satisfaction with training, and in effects on alienation
and marginality (14, 39, 105, 146). One study was wholly devoted to
the interrelationship of time and the personal problems experienced
(105). The length was not found to correlate with the number of problems, but the kinds of problems experienced did change. The U-curve
studies also found that length of time was related to feelings of achievement or dejection, that if affected performance, and that the curve
seemed to be operative in some, but not other, cultural groups. Much
more comparative research in this area is needed. Klineberg asks
whether, if such comparisons were to indicate a generic validity for
the U-curve, this should not be taken into account in deciding on
optimum lengths of studies and sojourns (219). Almost all AID training
evaluation studies found that respondents would have wished for longer
training programs than received (14b, c, d, e, f).

Orientation programs have continued to be studied and analyzed,
whether relating primarily to English competence, cognitive information about the host society, information about college procedures and
programs, or involving intercultural experiences, role playing, simulation, and other experimental techniques (186, 200, 255, 326).
Orientation programs were found to encourage personal contacts and
friendships (157, 230), to reduce anxieties, and to enhance academic
performance on the graduate level (229). There is an ongoing debate
between those favoring structured and cognitive programs (lectures,
questions, etc.) and those viewing orientation in terms of behavioral
and intercultural communication. An evaluation of the experience at
the Washington International Center has led to changes in the latter
direction (10). Two orientation programs, both in South America, are
offered prior to departure (266, 270). It is suggested that they might
be coordinated with NAFSA programs in the United States (276). More
recently, there is emphasis on the need for re-entry/transition
seminars to provide perspectives on problems of personal and professional re-adaptation. A 1975 NAFSA publication, Harriet L. Marsh's
Re-entry/Transition Seminars, recommends organizational and professional measures to develop such seminars, the collection of case
studies, and a search for advice or information abroad. No reference

is made to the essential role that home country personnel could play in such programs.

Judging by the literature, motivations for study seem to vary by type of society, availability of advanced education at home, and the undergraduate or graduate level of students. Students from developing countries indicate that their motivations included the desire to learn English (57), a general interest in the United States (192, 239), the prestige and status of U. S. institutions (49), career considerations (239). On the other hand, reference was also made to restrictions on enrollment in home universities or inability to gain admission due to prior record (192, 329). On the graduate level, superior opportunities for specialization play a significant role (329). There is skepticism about the reliability of data on motivations, since tactical and courtesy considerations often play a role in questionnaire responses.

The area of academic performance, including evaluation and grading practices, has been conceptually, theoretically, and cross-culturally superbly analyzed in Spencer's literature review on the subject (362). He pleads for multicultural selection, education programs, and grading. On the objective level, most studies find foreign students performing approximately as well as American students, a finding consistent with previous surveys (20, 48, 230, 240, 411). Most grade-related studies are of the predictive type, seeking to establish correlations between various factors (English competence tests, age, prior training, etc.) and probable success in studies (56, 131, 152, 235, 369, 374). There is general agreement about the predictive potency of English competence and its relation to grade point averages (292, 369, 379). Grade record files were used frequently as research resources—ad hoc or longitudinally (374).

As mentioned before, attention to culture shock has diminished. Two research studies found it behaviorally confirmed, one noting that in the case of a Nigerian group, job downgrading, isolation, and the sudden experience of cultural differences were component factors (229, 358). The subject is also treated in connection with the U-curve, and in relation to orientation. No single study dealt with the phenomenon as such, nor did any study differentiate its course, depth, and length by personality, or cultural or other variables.

A number of research topics identified in earlier research surveys did not receive appropriate attention in the post-1967 period. The impact of foreign students on the United States has been studied mostly in micro-perspective: impact on American students (222). Four studies focus on black African student interactions, and find them ambivalent and mutually disaggregating (40, 246, 247, 291). In reverse, only one study sought to analyze the long-term impact of returnees on their surroundings (119). Three studies dealt with institution building abroad, one comparing the impacts of British and American university models in Nigeria (33, 87).

Military training was analyzed only in one study relating to Brazilians (259). A major overall assessment, however, is now being readied by Dr. Ernest Lefever of the Brookings Institution.

In most empirical studies, women students are neglected in favor of single males (125, 132, 169, 170, 194, 341, 376). Two studies focused exclusively on women, one on U. S. Government exchange and training programs (406), and one on the female brain drain (R43). Two reports noted the relatively stable percentage—about 23 percent—of women in U. S. Governmental exchange programs over many years (402, 406).

"Successful" grantees were not directly analyzed either in empirical research or in case histories. The academic problems involved in "success," and their cultural referents, however, were discussed by Spencer, who asks whether "success" is to refer to grades, application to work at home, leadership in terms of values rewarded at home, adjustment in the home society, or positive attitudes to the host society (362). After return, too, the question relates to time-points. Success as of "when?" It takes time before real influence can be exercised. Such success can only be studied longitudinally; post-return audits may occur too early. Walton hypothesizes that traditional U. S. graduate education is likely to individualize students too much to return with commitments to work for the benefit of their countries. Only one study, though indirectly, relates to the question (39). It confirms the strengthening of individualistic motivations and the weakening of the self-image as a "national," but also finds the cultural belief system only mildly affected. The hypothesis is significant and needs testing. Only one study refers to academic failures (379).

Findings

The process of isolating research results from the literature surveyed encounters problems related to the highly diverse nature of the material. Some findings are parallel in positions or conclusions, but they may have issued from different types of research or populations studied. In other instances, parallel approaches have yielded divergent findings. Nevertheless, it is possible to list here in somewhat over-categorized manner some of the more recurrent and substantively salient findings.* They will be listed in the sequence of chapters in this report.

---

*The Appendix presents a collation of the original list of working hypotheses with findings in the literature surveyed. It should be consulted in relation to this section.

What Happens to Foreign Students While in the United States

Most students feel that, as a result of the foreign experience, they have to "some extent" changed. The major change is identified as relating to "personal habits" followed by "outlook on life." The U. S. sojourn affects least those attitudes which pertain to basic national, cultural, religious, and symbolic values. It has a greater effect on those that pertain to a student's self-view as a "national," which tends to become infused and amended by individual-centered ideologies.

Traditional cognitive orientation programs at the beginning of the sojourn, while increasing information about the host country, the educational process, and the institution, do not seem to affect beliefs about the host society. There is limited evidence that experimental participatory techniques are more effective than purely cognitive approaches, but the duration of their effects and the role of regular reinforcement have not been adequately explored.

Most students arrive with favorable attitudes toward the United States and their prospective educational and social experience although Europeans tend to be more critical than those from other countries. Many African students arrive with apprehensions about racial discrimination. Some recent studies seem to indicate a diminution in this concern.

Attitudes tend to be modified selectively, not generally, with the easing of anticipated problems in the new environment being a major motivating factor. There is little evidence that these functional modifications persist unchanged after the student has left the environment in which they had proved helpful.

Satisfaction with the educational program and warm relations with individual Americans do not exclude critical evaluations of specific U. S. social practices or of U. S. foreign policies. Critical attitudes are not stable, however. They fluctuate according to the year, events, and the perceived saliency of the latter for the home country. Such negative criticisms may have the function of easing disengagement from the environment in which the student has sojourned.

Attitudes at the end of the sojourn seem to be a composite of attitudes pre-existing at the time of arrival, the pattern of a particular student's personal, social, and academic experience while in the United States, and of the perceived helpfulness of the soujourn in relation to anticipated careers and life goals.

The U-curve hypothesis, apart from placing due emphasis on the significant role of phases and the length of sojourn, cannot be viewed as operating universally. Some studies indicate a reverse U-curve for students from less developed countries.

The "two-way mirror" hypothesis, proposing a relationship between the image perceived to be commonly held by Americans of the student's home society and his or her image of the United States, seems to have found only mild confirmation in the few studies that addressed it.

"Cultural distance," in itself, is not an adequate predictor of need for assistance or of problems in adjustment. Degrees and kinds of exposure, ranging from "cultural co-existence" to "conformity" seem more salient. Persons living abroad without exposing themselves in significant ways to the host society tend to reintegrate into their home society with fewer problems.

Relatively little is known about the effect of foreign students on American students or communities. There is some evidence that exposure tends to be selective, and that contacts frequently occur with Americans who already have an interest in the student's country or in international relationships.

General evaluations of Americans as persons do not seem to have changed from prior periods. They are considered to be hard-working, friendly, informal, solicitous, immature, superficial in friendships, on occasion "superior" in demeanor. They are viewed as poorly informed about foreign countries, with many misconceptions about the mentality, social life, and the level of education and civilization of peoples abroad. They are perceived as unaware of the impact U. S. actions have on other societies. Generally, however, Americans are liked as individuals.

Co-national groups apparently play a major role in easing the informal orientation of new entrants, in offering advice on how to cope with problems, in serving as temporary surrogates for the home society, in nurturing the saliency of home country values and concerns, and in compensating for the social isolation of students who, as individuals or groups, may be experiencing such isolation to varying degrees.

Students with vague career expectations tend to be more satisfied with their U. S. education than those whose objectives are more clearly defined. Among those who successfully complete graduate studies, the level of satisfaction is higher.

Adjustment, participation, interaction, and feelings of personal satisfaction tend to be greater in high-quality small colleges than in large institutions. Personality and national origin are major factors affecting the degree and intimacy of interaction.

Most selection and admissions procedures evaluate applicants by criteria relating to probable academic success. Foreign students, men and women, perform about as well as their American counterparts when success is measured by grade point averages. No studies have analyzed the process of interaction between academic advisers and foreign students. We lack knowledge about whether, to what extent, and in what ways cultural and personal learning needs and problems are taken into account in shaping the course of study and the evaluation

of foreign students. Dual standards are generally rejected but
occasionally practiced.

There seems to be a high correlation between students' proficiency in English as measured by various tests and success in study.
We have inadequate knowledge about the effectiveness of various
approaches in post-arrival language training and their relation to
academic success.

There is major concern about the relevance of U. S. academic
programs in some fields and for some levels and groups of foreign
students. This concern, understandably, is highest in programs
sponsored by governmental or international organizations. There is
continuing debate about appropriate criteria by which to measure
"relevance," as well as the lapse of time after return at which conclusions can reasonably be drawn.

The one study that examined the impact of U. S. campus unrest
found that foreign students had remained largely unaffected.

In addition to length of sojourn, field and level of study appear
to be major determinants in the growth of role attitudes, professional
ideologies, and socio-political orientations. Scientists and engineers
tend to be more confident of using their new competencies than those
in the humanities and the social sciences, although the latter are more
oriented toward social change.

There is little evidence that the presence of foreign students has
exerted any major impact on U. S. academic institutions or programs.
As shown by Deutsch, however, such a presence may lead to extensive
interrelationships with the community and its involvement with academics.

Most post-return studies indicate considerable utilization of the
training received, with variations relating to personal characteristics,
specific organizational milieus, and other factors in the home environment. Technical knowledge seems to find greater application than more
abstract research skills. Desire is consistently expressed for longer
training periods, particularly of the non-degree type, and for practical
experience to be made part of educational programs.

Structure, Administration, and Finance

Few institutions have articulated clear rationales and policies
with regard to international education and the admission, presence,
support, and utilization of foreign students. Those that have such
formulations do not consistently apply them in actual educational or
administrative practice.

Broadly speaking, there is little evidence that U. S. institutions
have attempted to adjust academic programs to the home needs of

foreign students. Practical problems, structured requirements, and the often small number of foreign students in a program militate against major innovations, even where faculty might desire them. The enrollment of a "critical mass" has been recommended, but its implications have not been explored.

Many institutions, particularly those which are smaller and more isolated, do not provide effective specialized support for foreign students. Orientation programs upon arrival and/or prior to departure are often not available in such institutions, or are only perfunctory. Many institutions do not have a specialized foreign student adviser.

Proficiency in the English language, as measured by TOEFL, seems to be a valid predictor of academic success, but linguistic proficiency should not be used rigidly as a criterion for admission if institutions can offer English language training on their campuses.

Foreign student advisers, functionally and administratively, occupy an ambiguous role, often peripheral within overall institutional policies. Expectations on the part of foreign students sometimes exceed the service that is, or can be, rendered. Financial stringencies currently are reducing support for the function and position.

Community services for foreign students, some of which are highly successful, tend to suffer from a lack of coordination, communication with students and/or sponsoring agencies, and regular financing.

There seems to exist a considerable distance between those who deal directly with foreign students—foreign student advisers, counselors, academic advisers, faculty—and those in the administration who determine educational policy. There also seems to be considerable slippage in communication between sponsors, programming agencies, institutional administrators and counselors, and teaching faculties.

There seems to be frequent conflict between the training objectives and expectations of the several units involved in sponsored training: sponsoring governments interested in the enhancement of manpower resources; program administrators interested in the participants' satisfaction with their programs; institutions interested in the allocation of students to their programs; and faculty interested in the development of broader and more individualized competencies than those specified.

Alumni abroad with to maintain contact with their universities for sentimental as well as professional reasons. Universities lack programs or resources, and only in exceptional cases do they cultivate such continuing contacts. Selective personal contact is maintained by some faculty members.

New Approaches to Technical Cooperation in the Preparation
of Human Resources for Development

A considerable number of American universities have in recent
years embarked upon programs, frequently though not exclusively
under U. S. government sponsorship, which have involved them in
technical training and institution building in developing countries. The
impact of such programs on the participating U. S. universities seems
to have been only peripheral, particularly regarding curricula, the
broad involvement of faculty, the teaching materials used in classes,
or special programs designed for the needs of foreign students. In
some instances, inter-university consortia have taken on the responsibility for coordinated conduct of international programs. Only rarely
have they been able to develop effective contact with academic programs
on the home campus.

Technical training generally focuses on developing the skills of
a single individual rather than of a team. Team training would increase
the utilization of new skills upon return home, make the transfer of an
individual to other employment less critical for the home-country
organization, and might enhance the effectiveness of the group as
innovators.

U. S. experts and teaching faculty are often insufficiently cross-
culturally experienced to adapt the technologies proferred to the
current needs of developing countries.

There is a need to develop in industrialized societies training
institutions that could offer specialized training for personnel from
developing societies; recruit and utilize appropriately experienced
faculties; cumulatively improve programs, teaching materials, and
techniques; devise instruments for continuing evaluation; and maintain
professional contact with trainees after their return home.

Migration of Talent and Skills

Most students from developing countries plan to return home
eventually. Those who have not returned often engage in temporary
work to gain experience or to accumulate funds with which to return
later.

The level of economic development of the home country in itself
is an inadequate predictor of tendencies not to return. Structural
imbalances in the market for professions bear a stronger relationship
to non-return or emigration.

In many instances, non-return represents in effect an "overflow
of talent," as measured by effective demand, rather than a loss of
utilizable resources. Where such overflow meets an undersupply in
the host country, non-return may be beneficial to both the recipient
and sending countries.

The main home-country factors cited as affecting non-return include lack of development, the nature of the higher education system, employment opportunities, professional working conditions, the system of sponsorship for study abroad, and the degree of social and cultural support extended to the student while abroad. In general, both the objective lack of professional opportunity and its perception by the graduating student seem to be major factors in decisions not to return immediately. These structural conditions in the home society are supplemented and activated by four major counterpart conditions in the host society: opportunities in its professional market, the ability to fulfill professional aspirations, the nature of immigration laws, and the provision of sponsorships. The two sets of structural conditions complement each other.

Older students with families, and those who do not expect discrimination or unemployment at home are more likely to return. On the other hand, those who feel accepted in the host country, have developed satisfactions within its cultural contexts, have received the doctorate, have been abroad for an extended period, and have specialized in medicine, science, engineering, or the humanities are less likely to return.

Harmful effects of the brain drain are almost entirely analyzed in the contexts of home countries. Relatively little attention is paid to potentially harmful effects on the United States as the recipient country. The exceptions are some studies relating to physicians and nurses.

Benefits of the migration of talent are identified as economic (channeling excess manpower to countries where it can be utilized, financial remittances to home societies), intellectual (enhanced opportunities to contribute to knowledge, transfers of technology), and international (strengthening of ties and of mutual information resources between countries, modernizing impacts of expatriates on their home societies).

Only secondary attention has been given to the broader socio-political consequences of migration. Does it retard socio-political, educational, public welfare, research, and leadership developments in home societies? These questions may be as significant as those relating to effective current demand for manpower.

Recommendations

The preceding overview of the literature surveyed and summary of major findings indicates only a modest degree of coherence, largely because most studies issue from a particular field of experience, from a particular orientation, derive from a specific study just completed, or reflect the particular pre-occupation of an author or period. This literature proffers a number of recommendations for further research, for specific action, and for overall policy directions. Those identified in this section represent the thinking of both the many authors reviewed and of the research team.

Research Recommendations

The publications reviewed do not offer copious recommendations for research. While many studies end by calling for "further research" on the topic investigated, few identify other research needs or consider what knowledge is needed in the broader field of international educational exchange. The following are the major research recommendations contained in the literature.

Data. More complete and accurate statistics on the migration of talent and the foreign student brain drain (263); more complete data in UNESCO's world census as well as in IIE's Open Doors, particularly on financial aid (90, 430); migrants' remittances of funds to their home countries to provide a base for calculating compensatory flows to home countries (148).

Operational. Clearer and more consistent definitions of non-return, migration, remigration, brain drain, brain gain (263); sharpening and refining operational outcome criteria and methods by which the actual "effectiveness" of training programs can be assessed. What is it that should be measured? Utilization? Impact of training on development? (365); studies of goal achievements in exchange programs and ways of enhancing their multiplier effect (212); studies of "cultural distance" in foreign students' evaluations of institutions and behaviors. Particularly, study of cultural co-existence as contrasted with adjustment or conformity as styles of coping with the new environment (125).

Comparative. Study of a variety of colleges and universities to learn how particular institutions create climates favorable to the development of international education programs and activities (111, 430); large-scale research on the role and effect of external agents (government, foundations, etc.) on American institutions of higher learning, with particular focus on how they influence the international commitment of such institutions (111); expanded comparative research on American students abroad (311); comparative studies of alienation in students who complete their studies at home and subsequently specialize abroad, and those whose college or university studies were exclusively foreign (Aich, cited in Klineberg in 125); comparative research on students from the same country studying in different countries, or from different countries studying in the same host country (125); comparative study of the consistency of the time span covered by the U-curve in various cultural contexts and in various cultural groups. If consistent, should this affect the length of sojourn? (Klineberg in 125); comparative study of foreign and American students' opinions on a range of public issues with a view to assessing concordances and differences, and the impact of the latter on the former, if any.

Specific topics. The process and problems in giving academic advice to foreign students (175); relationship of biculturality and cognitive flexibility (290); nation and occupation-specific research assessing the costs of migration and formulating retrieval plans (289); motivations and expectations of migrating physicians (391). Effects of the migration of physicians on world health, to be studied by WHO (388, 391); the role of international exchange in creating positive attitudes toward a world community (89, 125); research on the cultural dimensions of the learning process (430); research on the role of training in socio-political change. "Somewhere in the chain of events that is called change, there is something that is attributable to training, and is also influential in some development activity. That training outcome needs to be identified" (365); systematic study of successful grantees, failures, and drop-outs.

Action Recommendations

Much of the literature surveyed contained either specific recommendations for action to be taken by universities, sponsors, governments, etc., or presented findings which implied the desirability of such action. Many of these recommendations were not new; they recur again and again, with subsequent studies reaching similar conclusions about what should be done to improve the academic and social experience of foreign students in the United States or elsewhere. In this section, therefore, we summarize topically what appear to us to be the most important actions to be taken in this field.

Selection and admission criteria. In formulating policy, colleges and universities might consider, in addition to the foreign candidate's academic and linguistic ability and financial resources, such additional factors as manpower needs, future employability of the candidate in the home country, and the availability of comparable training in regional institutions. Universities might also attempt to develop academic aptitude and intelligence tests based on factors which are culturally, academically, and linguistically related to foreign students' backgrounds.

Relevance of academic curricula. All parties to educational exchange—home government, sponsoring agency, educational institution—should specify and coordinate their objectives and conduct periodic evaluations to ensure that objectives are being met. Special attention might focus on seminars and programs that have been particularly innovative or effective, including those which provide a period of work-study or other practical work experience. Universities should explore the feasibility of recruiting and admitting a "critical mass" of students from particular substantive and/or geographic areas so that they may develop special programs for these students.

Orientation and counseling. Agencies and educational institutions should provide continuing professional orientation and counseling for the foreign student throughout the sojourn. Particularly needed is closer cooperation between the student's academic adviser and the foreign student adviser; these two might form the core of a team that would guide the foreign student during the entire sojourn. Universities might, in addition, consider developing inter-cultural communications workshops for faculty, and especially for academic advisers.

English language training. Institutions enrolling large number of foreign students should develop their own appropriate English language training programs; smaller institutions or those with few foreign students should join in the development of cooperative regional centers. Curricula in these programs should include familiarization with the specialized language ("jargon") and concepts of the field to be studied.

Cultural adjustment. Institutions should consider policies to assist the functioning of co-national communities inasmuch as these serve a vital role in facilitating adjustment. Foreign students' adjustment problems as students rather than as foreigners might well receive more attention from academic administrators.

Contributions of the foreign student. Institutions and communities could make better use of the knowledge and experience which the foreign student brings to the United States, as teaching assistant, seminar participant, research partner, guest speaker at local primary and secondary schools, and in community groups.

Rationales. The U. S. government, and state and private educational institutions, should review or develop new rationales for admitting, supporting, and educating foreign students. Once such purposes are articulated, program administrators, university trustees, and faculty should be encouraged to support and implement them.

University cooperation. U. S. universities should seek to develop long-term institutional linkages with institutions abroad. Such links might include: exchanges of faculty and students; joint development of curriculum; collaboration on technical programs; cooperation in research; dual degree programs; etc. Foreign student programs should be viewed as an integral part of the broader international involvement of the university. The various parts of international programs should interact with and complement each other.

New approaches. New approaches to human resource development should include greater emphasis on regional or in-country training, the training of teams in addition to that of individuals, consideration of technologies appropriate to a country's culture and level of economic development, and attention to the need for periodic re-training and visits to centers of professional innovation.

Migration of talent. While preferably no limits should be placed on the free movement of intellectual talent, some countries' economic development depends on the marshaling of highly qualified national manpower resources. Such resources might best be engaged by positive measures that encourage students and professionals to want to return home rather than by restrictive measures that inhibit or penalize migration. Among the positive factors are the need to maintain contact between the home government or potential employers and the student while abroad, improvement in working and research conditions in the home country, provision for continued contact with colleagues abroad, etc.

Alumni relations. Universities should review their objectives, methods, and organization for maintaining regular contacts with their alumni abroad. They should note that the latter's interests include not only sentiment but also professional need. They can be assisted by, as well as assist the university in a variety of ways: as recruiters and interviewers of prospective students; as providers of specialized literature to departmental libraries; as research partners, etc.

Policy Recommendations with Selected Operational Examples

The years ahead will undoubtedly see the continued publication of research relating to international educational exchange and foreign students. Many of the studies will further contribute to available knowledge—operationally, in terms of data, and conceptually. Judging by the record of past years, however, one might query the overall effect that such research may exert. How many of the studies surveyed have been consulted by those whose professional roles should warrant an interest? Have any been taken into account and resulted in action—

administrative, educational, research? We do not know. We have no
record or follow-up studies of implementation. Other than in research
reviews and some articles and books, references to prior literature
are largely absent. University self-studies have not been reviewed
several years later, at least in published form. Doctoral dissertations
are seldom ready by others than the examining committee. Few of
them are published at home or abroad, even though they might address
issues relevant to a program or country. The absence of a specialist
universe of discourse, the lack of communication between operators
and researchers, the lack of a coordinating research institute that
could monitor international educational exchange research, and of a
journal that would publish it, leave a more purposeful and concerted
future growth in the field more to faith than to strong confidence.

Yet, possible strategic steps can be taken by government, foundations, voluntary associations, universities and colleges, and academics
and researchers, individually or cooperatively. Such steps might
expand the utilization of existing data, stimulate greater cooperation
and communication among researchers, enlarge counterpart research
abroad, provide for a coordinative fulcrum and a journal, and improve
communication in cross-cultural advising and teaching.

Research. More research should focus on broader issues, probing
empricially and building conceptually a theoretical framework conducive
to a more coherent growth of knowledge. Five illustrations are
offered.

1. Attitudes and Behavior. Foreign student research abounds
with attitude studies but lacks studies of actual behavior, during and
after the sojourn. Allan W. Wicker's research review finds little evidence of direct influence of attitudes on verbal expressions and overt
actions. What influences and generates behavior is a research problem
of its own in which attitudes are only one, and not necessarily the most
salient, factor to be considered. "Direct study of overt behavior may
be more conducive to yielding reliable knowledge than drawing infer-
ences from diversely ascertained verbal attitude data."[8]

2. Elite Studies. There is a dearth of studies on the role, behavior, impact, and modernization strategies of new, foreign-educated
elites in otherwise traditional societies. In many new states, public
life is centrally influenced, if not dominated, by university-educated
elites, often tightly knit and culturally supercilious. As suggested by
Sawitzki, "it would seem essential for research, best conducted jointly
with national scholars where this is feasible, to secure more extensive
knowledge of both domestic and foreign university graduates as members of the new elites, in order to possibly reform professional education abroad and prepare [graduates] for public responsibilities and the
difficulties they may face. . . . The real problem of the graduates is

not the successful graduation from a university, but the use of the knowledge in a subsequent career."[9] The same applies to other than governmental elites. It would be useful to undertake a series of studies on individual countries, and subsequently comparative integrating analyses.

    3. Country Impact Studies. Very few studies have so far considered the total impacts on a country or region exerted by returned foreign students, whether educated in one foreign country, several countries, or in all "modern" foreign countries. In some countries, the total of foreign students who have returned from study abroad is in the tends of thousands. What effect have such massive foreign education inputs had? Research has not addressed itself to such questions. The literature surveyed includes only three historical retrospects (119, 216, 380).

    4. International Relations Implications of International Exchanges. The literature lists a relatively small and incommensurate number of such studies (25, 39, 58, 142, 212, 295, 350). Yet, one of the animating expectations and justifications of international educational exchange has been that, in some stated but inadequately researched way, it would contribute to more intelligent and cooperative international relationships and to peaceful change. Emerging theory here should be helpful and needs expansion.[10]

    5. Host Culture Studies. Few studies have focused on generalized or specific aspects of the host culture. We have copious data on foreign students' reactions to, or assessments of, dominant U. S. styles, values, and behaviors, but few synthesizing essays or studies that, with cross-cultural intent, analyze the host culture and attempt to present it in operationally meaningful terms.[11] Analyses of this type, as well as empirical, cross-cultural formulations are needed for better planning of orientation programs, courses, and cross-cultural training seminars.

Research Techniques. A veriety of research techniques, not yet fully utilized in the field of educational exchange, could add significantly to the knowledge of the subject. Four examples are offered.

    1. Depth Histories. Utilization of Oscar Lewis' technique of tape-recorded case histories of individuals, families, or comparable groups of foreign students on one or several campuses, and after return.

    2. Cross-Cultural Research Teams. A notable example of this approach is the study conducted by six psychiatrists at the University of Wisconsin, three of whom were of Chinese ancestry, exploring the "real-life version" of Chinese foreign students' existence, experience, and isolation during their U. S. sojourn. The cross-cultural composition of the team and their professional provenance no doubt accounts for the sensitivity and starkness of the findings (68, 218, 247, R57).

3. Research Syntheses. A series of research reviews ordering
and synthesizing, on the basis of major past studies, current knowledge
relating to: specific national or cultural groups among foreign students
in the United States (Indians, Arabs, Chinese, Brazilians, etc.); evaluative data about the germaneness of curricula offered in major fields of
foreign student enrollment (engineering, business administration,
physics, library science, etc.); a particular problem, operation, or
administrative arrangement (practical work assignment, co-national
groups or organizations, academic advising, etc.).

4. Longitudinal Studies. The need continues for more longitudinal
studies on enduring residual effects of study abroad, utilizing objective
and subjective indicators. The Fulbright program in Italy, for example,
is now 25 years old. Data on Italian participants are available, and,
when supplemented by field follow-ups, could yield vital knowledge,
possibly to be collated with other parallel studies.

Research. In order to provide cumulative data for programs, analysis,
and action, foreign student research should: standardize the project
characteristics that are to be reported in completed studies, including
data about the population studied, methods used, the setting, the points
in time when data were collected, research staff characteristics,
funding, permanent location of research materials, etc.; follow up,
broaden, probe for other aspects, test, review, revise, amend, or
challenge data, hypotheses, models, or findings of prior studies or
publications, thus providing for continuity, growth, and coherence;
replicate or re-test prior studies by (a) the same method or instrument
applied to comparable samples to check for continued validity of original findings, (b) the same method used on commensurate but differing
samples to develop comparisons and identify the variables involved,
and (c) other methods applied to the same or a related sample to test
findings of important studies; and update, periodically and systematically, by revision or re-study, (a) specific inquiries offering research
information of continued generic value, (b) general analyses of continuing program or policy interest, (c) literature reviews in specialized
fields of operations or analysis, and (d) bibliographic compilations and
statistical reports.

Regarding standardization of reporting, important not only for
comparability of research but also for computerization and retrieval,
the leadership might be assumed by the Social Science Research
Council, the National Science Foundation, or another appropriate body.
One of these, in cooperation with researchers, could develop a standardized research and reporting form that would accompany grant
applications and research presentations, be published in appropriate
journals and newsletters, and be distributed at professional meetings
and workshops. Such a form might contain a basic core and develop

additions for various fields, the international educational exchange field being one of them.

The follow-up and replication functions, in large part, will need to rely on the initiative of academics and researchers themselves, except where a research group or program would recommend that a particular document, or group of studies, may merit replication. An example of a study warranting replication is J. R. Crist, S. W. Cook, J. Havel, and C. Selltiz's Attitudes and Social Relations of Foreign Students in the United States, published in 1963 by the University of Minnesota Press.

Up-dating might best be the responsibility of either the original sponsor, or of professional or service organizations. Many of them do so regularly with regard to their own publications. Less often does this occur with studies undertaken by an individual author. Obviously, only in a very few instances will the original author be available to undertake such re-study or updating. If, however, some studies, by substance and approach, should be deemed to be of continued value, government or professional voluntary organizations (IIE, NAFSA, or others) might seek appropriate support to make up-dating, re-study, and publication—optimally as a series—possible. In all cases, the original arrangements, procedures, and data should be juxtaposed with those more current, to permit comparisons and the identification of trends.

Studies that could be considered for up-dating include, for example, Edward C. Cieslak's The Foreign Student in an American College: A Survey and Evaluation of Administrative Problems and Practices, Wayne State University Press, 1955; Homer D. Higbee's The Status of Foreign Student Advising in U. S. Universities and Colleges, Michigan State University, 1961; M. J. Flack's International Educational and Cultural Relations and Their Treatment in International Affairs Textbooks, 1945-70, Report to the U. S. Advisory Commission on Educational and Cultural Affairs, Department of State, 1971.

Contributions. Government, international organizations, and academic institutions could contribute to a more concerted growth of research on international educational exchange by considering the feasibility of some of the following.

1. Government. (a) The regular up-dating, publication, and dissemination of the Guide to International Education Resources. This 1972 publication reported on research projects funded by the Office of Education 1956-1971; subsequent issues might be expanded to cover major data resources beyond OE-funded efforts. (b) Computerization of the extensive record of research on international educational exchange accumulated during 30 years of government research, including findings of major academic studies. This would permit cross-topical,

cross-country, cross-population, and cross-temporal analyses.
(c) Publication, in association with other appropriate organizations, of
regular listings of research in progress in international educational
exchange. This would facilitate research contacts, advice, exchange of
literature, and possible coordination of efforts. (d) Sponsorship, as
suggested by Cormack in 1962, of periodic working conferences of
research specialists in the field of international educational exchange,
to identify on a continuing basis areas of achievement, need, and opportunity, and to articulate research recommendations. (e) Sponsorship,
possibly jointly with UNESCO or UNITAR, of special training programs
for selected foreign academic and governmental researchers and administrators in the field of international educational exchange, to enhance
resources for counterpart research and program cooperation. (f) Cooperation with academic institutions in identifying ways to improve the
academic experience of foreign students on campus. This might lead to
legislative recommendations for innovative programs involving travel
of faculty and foreign students, special academic offerings, and new
strategies for the preparation of human resources for sending countries.

2. Internacional Organizations. (a) Encouragement, systematic
support for, and dissemination of national and international cooperative
research in an expanding number of countries. UNESCO might consider
the establishment of an International Research Council or Fund to support multi-national research on educational exchange. (b) Sponsorship
of annual international conferences of research specialists in educational exchange, relating to and cooperating with the conferences proposed in Recommendation 19 above. (c) Encouragement of contracts
with universities for the development of specially designed training
programs for groups of sponsored fellows under technical cooperation
projects. Such programs would involve academic training, participant
observation and travel, and practical work experience.

3. U. S. Universities and Colleges. (a) Establishment of a
Research Institute on International Educational and Cultural Exchange
to engage in cumulative research, serve as a center for international
documentation, sponsor or host visiting researchers and workshops,
maintain liaison with counterpart institutions in the United States and
abroad, assist in the training of specialized research personnel and
administrators, and publish an internationally-oriented research
quarterly. (b) Encouragement of faculty members active in foreign
student programs to enter into direct communication (through travel
and correspondence) with sponsoring institutions and governments
abroad so as to learn more about the particular needs of foreign students. This would encourage the development of academic programs
tailored to meet more fully the needs of foreign students and contribute to greater relevancy of programs for U. S. students who desire
an international perspective in their studies. (c) Involvement of

qualified foreign alumni in international research projects to maintain and benefit from the research competencies acquired during study, and strengthen the mutual development of international research resources. (d) Introduction of department or inter-departmental courses and research seminars in international educational exchange in appropriate schools or programs (Education, Public and International Affairs, etc.), and encouragement of foreign students to participate in them. (e) Development of annual programs that would offer cross-cultural orientation and familiarization with foreign student research to faculty members advising or teaching students from abroad. (f) Consideration of re-entry/transition seminars prior to departure for the home country, or upon arrival there. A cooperative approach utilizing both home and U. S. personnel could serve as an opportune device for continuously evaluating the relevance of educational programs and for gathering information on the changing needs of the home societies.

NOTES

1. External Research Paper, April 1965.

2. For example, those by Useem; Cieslak; Schwantes; Lippitt and Watson; Lambert and Dressler; Scott; Beals and Humphrey; Bennet, Passin and Knight; Coelho; Garraty and Adams; Morris; Davidsen and Sewell; Higbee; DuBois; Weidner; Crist, Cook, Havel, and Selltiz; Morse and Freeman, and others.

3. For example, nos. 32, 36, 49, 60, 65, 66, 75, 98, 116, 119, 126, 157, 158, 167, 170, 180, 192, 194, 215, 221, 230, 236, 240, 291, 292, 293, 294, 298, 306, 324, 343, 344, 348, 358, 412, 413, 414, 416, and 424.

4. For example, nos. 15, 24, 34, 64, 67, 68, 93, 145 (2), 159, 171, 195, 204 (2), 206, 207, 214, 247, 299, 305, 318, 319, 320, 323, 419, 421, and 427.

5. "One of the few instances in which an attitude is unlikely to be translated into an opinion or an act in any social context is when it is elicited in a rigorously controlled interview situation by highly trained interviewers employing a technically high-quality instrument." Irwin Deutscher in S. Z. Nagi and R. G. Corwin, The Social Contexts of Research (New York: Wiley-Interscience, 1972).

6. E. de Vries, Study and Research Concerning International Relations and Exchanges in the Fields of Education, Science and Culture, UNESCO/IES/22/2. 145, October 31, 1961.

7. J. Nehnevajsa, Comparative Impact on Attitudes of Actual Versus Anticipated Events, University of Pittsburgh, January 1965.

8. A. W. Wicker, "Attitudes Versus Actions: The Relationship of Verbal and Overt Behavioral Responses to Attitude Objects," Journal of Social Issues, 25 (1969): 41-78. But see also the research-derived proposition of Crespi that "favorable attitudes [toward a country] are highly correlated with favorable actions . . . [and] while favorable attitudes are not in every case either necessary or sufficient for favorable actions, in most instances they are a major determinant." Leo Crespi, "The Meaning and Measurement of Program Effectiveness in USIA," a Discussion Paper, December 1973, p. 6.

9. H. H. Sawitzki, "University Graduates as an Elite Group in a Developing Society, Shown on the Example of Afghanistan," (in German), in Afghanische Hefte, 5, 1972.

10. See K. Kaiser, "Transnational Politics: Toward a Theory of Multinational Politics," International Organization, 25 (Autumn 1971): 790-817. Also the final chapter of 212.

11. See, for example, Edward Stewart's American Cultural Patterns: A Cross-Cultural Perspective (Pittsburgh, Pa.: Regional Council on International Education, 1971).

On the following pages we list the working hypotheses which were developed at the inception of the project as a guide to the abstracting and coding procedures. They were meant to express assumptions about foreign students, what happens to them in the United States and after they return home, their effect on the United States, etc. The list was by no means regarded as comprehensive, nor were all hypotheses assumed to be correct. On the chart we have indicated whether the literature reviewed in this report generally supports or rejects each of them. No attempt was made to tabulate exact numbers of studies, in large part because few studies asked questions in precisely the way our hyptheses were expressed. Our attempt in the following is to give a general impression of the weight of direct and indirect evidence vis-a-vis each hypothesis. In addition, comments on the hypotheses which were sent to us by Philip C. Coombs, Margaret Cormack, Johan Galtung, Philip I. Sperling, and Barbara J. Walton are noted and discussed, particularly where they disagree with, or amplify, our findings.

The list has been slightly modified for presentation here: some statements have been reworded, others combined, and a section pertaining to foreign research has been eliminated since we did not receive enough material to make judgments regarding it.

HYPOTHESIS	COMMENT

1. Quantitative

A. The statistics on foreign student and participant training flows into the United States are inadequate: there are overlaps in reporting by different organizations and no one source of information summarizes data on all visitors to the United States which would be useful to universities and others involved in handling foreign students.

Strongly supported. See discussion in Chapter 5.

B. The United States' share, percentagewise, of total fellows sponsored under multilateral organizations is

No evidence from our studies. Sperling believes this to be true.

305

HYPOTHESIS   COMMENT

decreasing, perhaps because of the high cost of study in the United States as compared to other countries.

C. In absolute numbers, the number of foreign students in this country is increasing.	Supported.
D. The proportion of graduate students as compared to undergraduate students from abroad is increasing.	Supported.
E. Available statistics have not been probed for indications of countries or areas of the world that have, over time and presently, had disproportionately few students studying in the United States.	Supported; we found no studies which presented such statistics.
F. Very few studies and publications take pre-1967 data and replicate or update the research with a view to re-testing and keeping the data valid, if warranted.	Supported; we found no such studies.
G. There are probably no data indicating, by overall frequency and magnitude, awards of the various types of sponsors that give fellowships to foreign citizens for study in the United States.	Partially rejected; see, for example, the data published by the Bureau of Educational and Cultural Affairs, discussed in Chapters 3 and 4.

2. Reasons for Coming to the United States

A. Many non-sponsored students come to this country with no clear career aspirations in mind. They are seeking guidance when they come to the United States. Their study in this country affects their career aspirations.	Supported. Walton points out that such indecision is typical of students of college age.
B. There is a significant relationship between the concreteness of career aspirations specified by the	No data, except in case of sponsored students on leave from a post at home, in

HYPOTHESIS	COMMENT
foreign students upon arrival and the actual careers that they enter or re-enter after their return home.	which case, supported. See Chapter 2.
C. A considerable percentage of sponsored students already have some gainful employment and career commitment, and therefore have predetermined career aspirations.	Supported. See Chapters 2 and 5.
D. There are significant differences among the career aspirations of foreign students, depending on the countries from which they come.	No data. Sperling suggests that this is not true.
E. There are significant differences among the career aspirations of graduate and undergraduate foreign students.	No data.
F. The career aspirations of a considerable percentage of foreign students tend to differ from the careers of their fathers.	No data.
G. Large numbers of students, both sponsored and non-sponsored, select study in the United States because of a favorable prior attitude toward economic development conditions in the United States, and/or a positive image of training and educational facilities in this country, and/or the prestige in their own country of a degree obtained at a U. S. university.	Strongly supported. See Chapter 2.

3. What Happens to Foreign Students while in the United States

A. There has been little consideration given to the best academic and social conditions in the United States conducive to preparing students for successful readjustment upon return home.	Supported, although some studies do consider it and, according to Sperling, AID gives it special attention.

HYPOTHESIS	COMMENT
B. There has been much research on attitudes and adjustment problems of foreign students.	Supported. See Chapter 2.
C. There are no studies indicating which of three attitudes—the student's attitude toward his role as (a) a person, (b) a professional, or (c) a citizen, is most affected by his studies in the United States.	Few studies considered these aspects of attitude change, but see Chapter 2. Cormack suggests an additional hypothesis that attitude change may be related to the level of morale in the United States and its international status at the time of the sojourn.
D. There is a typical progression of attitude change closely connected, among other things, with the length of stay in the United States.	An equal number of studies supported and rejected this hypothesis. In addition, several modifications to the U-curve hypothesis were proposed. See Chapter 2.
E. Sizeable numbers of students are somewhat disillusioned after having been here for a period of time and tend to modify their idealistic attitudes downward to more realistic attitudes concerning the United States.	Moderately supported. See Chapter 2.
F. Smaller, though perhaps not insignificant, numbers of students develop antagonistic and negative attitudes toward the American political, economic, and social models during their stay.	Supported.
G. There are probably few studies looking at content relevancy of the curricula available and offered to the foreign student in a variety of universities and colleges.	Supported; only three studies directly addressed this topic, though others looked at student perceptions of relevancy. See Chapter 2.

HYPOTHESIS	COMMENT
H. The goals of graduate study, as seen by most universities, may not be entirely consistent with the goals of training as seen by sponsoring agencies, especially when fellowships are related to technical assistance projects. In essence, most universities see graduate study as preparation for research and teaching in a U. S. institution whereas many sponsored fellowships may be for the purpose of preparing planners, managers, and administrators in educational and governmental institutions.	Strongly supported. In addition, many studies point to divergence in goals between the student and the sponsoring agency.
I. Nationality is a more important factor in interaction with American students than is opportunity for contact.	Supported. Sperling and others note that English-language facility is also important.
J. Little research has been done on the quality and timing of orientation programs for foreign students.	Rejected. See studies and recommendations in Chapters 2 and 3.
K. There has been little consideration given to the idea that cultural "ghettos" fulfill psychological needs of students.	Rejected. See Chapter 2.
L. Few academic departments and professional schools have specialized programs which attempt to develop their curricula or adapt them to the special needs of students from foreign countries.	Supported, although Sperling notes that AID has contracted with many universities for tailor-made courses, and this may be true of other sponsoring agencies.
M. Once in the United States, foreign students probably receive inadequate information on fellowship resources available to them from sources outside their U. S. institution.	No data.
N. Although there are a number of State Department, IIE, government agency,	Supported.

HYPOTHESIS   COMMENT

and non-governmental organization programs to organize and facilitate short-
term tours in the United States of high-
level personnel, these efforts are generally
uncoordinated.

    O. U. S. universities are not well   Weakly supported; little
organized to host short-term foreign visi-   data available.
tors and to provide suitable learning
experiences for them in their areas of
interest.

    P. There has been little research   Supported; only five studies
done on female foreign students or   of women were found.
trainees.

    Q. Many multilateral and foreign-   No data.
government sponsored fellows miss in U. S.
libraries an adequate representation of:
(a) non-English research materials, or of
(b) materials concerning their own country
or region.

    R. Academic performance of for-   Strongly supported. A large
eign students is equal to that of American   number of studies also con-
students.   sider the relationship of
                                              predictive tests to academic
                                              achievement, and the prob-
                                              lems of credential evalua-
                                              tion. See Chapters 2 and 3.

    S. Few studies consider the effect   Supported; only four such
of the college or university environment   studies were found.
on the foreign student: its size, location,
level (two-year, four-year, graduate),
values, degree of competitiveness, quality,
etc.

4. What Happens to the Student After Return Home

    A. Upon return home, attitudes   No data. Sperling feels
toward the political, economic, and social   that this is not true for
structure of the United States depend in   AID participants.
part on the student's success in finding

HYPOTHESIS   COMMENT

satisfying employment which uses U. S.
training. In cases where satisfying
employment is not found, there may be
a tendency to blame this on the training
program and indirectly on the United
States in general.

B. Many students upon return home find that the degree of specialization and level of responsibility that they have been trained to expect in employment is above that offered in job opportunities.

Supported, although some studies do not find this to be true. Even sponsored students, however, who may have a job waiting, occasionally report over-training. See Chapters 2 and 6.

C. Foreign students have played an important role in stimulating technological and social change on return home.

Supported. Sperling notes, however, that the evidence is rather journalistic and one-sided.

D. An unknown percentage of returnees feel that their training in the United States was less than relevant to their professional needs.

Supported. See Chapter 2.

E. More second- and professional-degree holders find posts related to their training than first-degree holders.

Supported; little data available.

F. There are great variations by country and region in the difficulties encountered by returning graduates in finding suitable employment.

Supported; little data available.

G. Many returned students, especially from highly developed countries, and to some degree from developing countries, find that their U. S. training has made little difference in making their skills more marketable and sought after.

Equally supported and rejected; little data available.

H. Few sponsoring agencies or educational institutions maintain regular,

Strongly supported. See Chapters 2 and 4. Sperling

HYPOTHESIS	COMMENT

sustained contact with students after return home; such contacts as exist are generally informal, based on student-professor friendship.

disagrees regarding AID follow-up.

I.   Foreign education leads to the desire to accept political and social responsibility at home.

Equally supported and rejected.

J.   Foreign-educated students have a better chance of employment in tight employment situations.

Equally supported and rejected; little data available.

K.   Social contacts and family position are important factors determining when and how a foreign student will use his or her training at home.

Supported.

L.   Introduction of new ideas by returnee is facilitated when (a) a returnee is flexible and (b) when colleagues are receptive or have also been trained abroad.

Supported, especially part (b).

5. Effects of Foreign Students on the United States

A.   Little attention is paid in universities, communities, and governments with regard to the effects that foreign students have on U. S. institutions, opinion, and knowledge.

Supported; only three studies directly addressed this topic.

B.   In universities and colleges where there have been significant numbers of foreign students, and where there have been opportunities for interaction through activities outside the academic classwork, U. S. students have developed insights concerning other foreign countries that they probably would not have developed had the foreign students not been on campus.

Supported.

C.   At the same time, large numbers of U. S. students are unaffected by

Strongly supported.

HYPOTHESIS   COMMENT

the presence of foreign students on their
campuses for the simple reason that they
have little contact with them.

D.   Those U. S. students who are
affected by the presence of foreign students on campus tend to develop a more
cosmopolitan viewpoint toward international affairs.

Supported, although as
Cormack suggests, it may
be the more world-minded
students who seek out the
foreign students on campus.

E.   There is probably more opportunity for U. S. students to get to know
foreign students at the graduate level, because of the smaller numbers of students
in such programs, the larger number of
seminars, and the possibility to get to
know foreign students more intimately
under such circumstances.

Moderately rejected; little
data available. Cormack
notes that at some under-
graduate colleges, inter-
action is much greater
than at large graduate
institutions.

F.   Many faculty members consider dealing with foreign students a
special chore and problem. This is likely
to result from language difficulties on the
part of the foreign student, and from the
professor's lack of understanding of the
different economic, social, and cultural
contexts from which the foreign student
comes.

Supported.

G.   Only in relatively few cases
have U. S. faculty members changed their
teaching or benefited in major ways from
the presence of foreign students on campus.
This may be because many U. S. faculty
assume that the foreign student is here to
learn and do not make any attempts to learn,
in turn, from the experience of the foreign
student.

Supported.

H.   In many U. S. colleges and universities with large numbers of foreign
students, there exist university-community
programs to involve foreign students in
community activities.

Supported.

HYPOTHESIS   COMMENT

I.   Notwithstanding these activi-   Supported.
ties, a relatively small percentage of
foreign students participate extensively in
such activities. Similarly, only a small
percentage of people in the community are
involved in activities designed to stimulate
interaction between the foreign students and
the community.

J.   On the whole, universities and   Strongly supported.
colleges are organized in traditional aca-
demic fashion, with little change being
introduced as the structure, number, or
fields of interest of foreign students change.

K.   There may be some evidence to   No data.
show that the presence of large numbers of
foreign students on U. S. campuses may have
encouraged social science departments and
the social professions to include more of an
international emphasis in their academic
programs.

L.   There is probably no evidence in   Supported; only one study
the physical and technological sciences and   cited examples of change.
in the medical professions to show that aca-
demic programs have changed to include
subject matter related to the interests of
international students.

M.   There are probably few studies   Supported.
which analyze the effects of foreign students' public writing (letters to newspapers, articles about their country)
while in this country.

N.   There are probably no, or very   Supported.
few, studies of publications about the
United States or U. S. education, written
and published by ex-foreign students in their
countries after their return from the United
States.

O.   Special short-term training   Supported by one study.
ventures (for middle- or high-level

HYPOTHESIS   COMMENT

personnel) in universities and colleges
tend to be handled as separate undertakings
and remain largely isolated from the rest
of the university's programs and life. Thus
they have little impact and exhibit no continuous feedback into academic programs.

6. Structure, Administration, and Finance of Foreign Student Programs

A. Services, other than academic, provided foreign students in the United States are probably inadequate on the average since they depend largely upon the initiatives of individual universities and communities.

Supported by our studies but disputed by Walton and Sperling, and by Cormack who notes that there is considerable variation among universities.

B. Mechanisms for informing both non-sponsored students and sponsored fellows of opportunities in the United States before they decide where they want to go (pre-sojourn) are inadequate in most countries. In essence, the system of making available information on study opportunities in the United States through binational centers, USIA offices, and the like, is probably inadequate.

Strongly supported. Sperling disagrees regarding informational materials provided by AID.

C. Universities abroad vary in their efficiency in informing their students of opportunities to study in the United States.

Supported. Several studies recommend improvements such as the CETC network. See Chapter 3.

D. There is little source of finance for universities and academic departments for development of specialized programs suited to the needs of foreign students.

Supported.

E. There are few organized efforts on university campuses to work with faculty in developing the skills and understandings necessary to work effectively with foreign students.

Supported, although many NAFSA publications seek to fill this gap.

HYPOTHESIS	COMMENT

F.   Programming and placement agencies in New York and Washington tend to deal in macro terms and are not equipped to compare advantages and disadvantages of similar departments of various universities in providing specialized training for the special needs of sponsored fellows. Neither are they up-to-date on new programs and new specialists in major universities and thus do not program short-term foreign specialists to visit them.

Comment: Weakly supported; little data available.

G.   Patterns of organizing for the reception of foreign students on campuses vary widely, but most colleges and universities have at least a part-time foreign student adviser or counselor.

Comment: Supported.

H.   The duties and services of the foreign student adviser, where one exists, are vaguely defined.

Comment: Supported. Many publications, especially from NAFSA, seek to define and professionalize the position but it remains ill-defined from the institutional point of view. See Chapter 3.

I.   The foreign student adviser, in most cases, has little administrative authority or influence on such vital matters as housing, institutional fellowship aid, employment of wives, English-language remedial courses, etc.

Comment: Supported. Many recommendations address this problem. See Chapter 3.

J.   Relatively few foreign student advisers are professionally trained for their positions.

Comment: Supported.

K.   In most U. S. communities and universities, there is little provision for social contacts and experience on the part of multilateral and foreign-government sponsored fellows who, in many instances, as senior persons, have special needs not

Comment: Rejected, at least for AID programs.

HYPOTHESIS   COMMENT

covered by the routine resources of foreign student advisers.

L.   Financial aid from the aca-   Strongly supported. See
demic institution for foreign student   Chapter 3.
scholarships, and for support services
(foreign student advising and counseling,
international clubs) has declined in recent
years.

M.   At the national level, there   Supported.
would seem to be less than adequate coordination among national organizations and
associations offering fellowships for foreign
students. Moreover, there is a lack of coordination and cooperation between the sponsoring agency and the academic institution,
on the one hand, and between the student and
the agency on the other.

N.   Private universities tend to   No data.
offer a greater proportion of fellowships
for foreign students than state universities.

O.   Private universities have more   No data.
purposeful recruitment programs for foreign students than state universities.

P.   Few institutions have a clear   Supported. NAFSA offers
policy regarding the integration of foreign suggestions for useful ad-
students into the campus community.   ministrative devices. See
                                          Chapter 3.

Q.   There is a lack of information   Supported; we found no
on how internationally active foundations studies presenting such
go about selecting and administering   information.
fellows whom they fund.

R.   The needs of sponsored fel-   No data. Walton suggests
lows are becoming increasingly more   that the needs of students
specialized and new forms of dealing   from developing countries
with these specialized technical and   are becoming more inter-
academic needs have yet to be developed   disciplinary and problem-
by universities.   oriented.

HYPOTHESIS   COMMENT

S.   Few institutions have articulated a rationale for the presence of foreign students which would serve as a basis for policy making in such areas as selection, admission, curriculum planning, and non-academic services.

Strongly supported. See Chapter 3.

7. Talent Migration and Brain Drain

A.   The root of the brain drain problem lies in the home country (its attitude towards its nationals abroad as well as economic and social factors).

Strongly supported. See Chapter 5.

B.   Only a relatively small percentage of students sponsored by the U. S. Government, their own government, or by international organizations do not return to their own country.

Strongly supported. See Chapter 5.

C.   The great majority of foreign students who do not return to their own country are self-sponsored students.

Strongly supported. See Chapter 5.

D.   Many former foreign students in the United States who have not returned would return if appropriate employment were available.

Strongly supported, but many studies stress the catalytic effect of other factors, e.g., family and home country ties, in the decision to migrate. See Chapter 5.

E.   In absolute numbers, the greater number of foreign professionals trained in this country who came here or return here are in professions where posts do not exist in the quantities necessary in their own countries to absorb all of the trained nationals in that field.

Strongly supported. See Chapter 5.

F.   In some countries, there is a noticeable leveling off in the migration of trained personnel.

Supported.

HYPOTHESIS	COMMENT
G. Innovation is needed in U. S.- foreign government relationships in studying this problem and to come up with new solutions, such as foreign government effort to place students trained in the United States in appropriate professional positions.	Supported. Many studies make recommendations in this regard. See Chapter 5.
H. Most embassies, and their educational and cultural attaches, do little to keep their nationals studying in the United States informed of employment opportunities and needs in their own countries.	Strongly supported, but with certain notable exceptions. See Chapter 5.
I. Some universities and departments encourage outstanding foreign students, particularly doctoral students, to remain at their institution by offering them teaching or research positions.	Supported.
J. The administration of U. S. immigration laws and the laws themselves are ambiguous and thus facilitate stays in the United States.	Strongly supported. See Chapter 5.
K. Data on brain drain of students and professionals are unreliable due to inadequate statistics and record-keeping and difficulty of identifying student non-returnees.	Strongly supported. See Chapter 5.
L. Students from lower-middle and lower classes as well as minority group members are more likely to stay in the United States.	Strongly supported. See Chapter 5.
M. Brain drain severely hampers development efforts in the less-developed countries.	Equally supported and rejected. See Chapter 5.

HYPOTHESIS   COMMENT

8. Alternate Modes and Models of Preparing Human Resources for Development

A.   There are examples of appar-   Supported. See Chapter 4.
ently successful and much less costly pro-
grams whereby U. S. universities send
teams of professors to offer in-country
training abroad instead of bringing large
numbers of students to the United States.

B.   Most U. S. universities do not   Supported.
have the resources to develop special programs of study for foreign students and with
some subsidy would be interested in developing innovative programs.

C.   A few programs exist whereby   Supported. See Chapter 4.
faculty and students are exchanged in both
directions between U. S. and foreign institutions. There is little concrete research
on the effects of such programs on the
institutions so linked.

D.   More global studies are needed   Supported.
on the total effectiveness of our various
university efforts to train foreign nationals
for effective roles when they return, studies
which would lay the groundwork for innovative proposals for the future.

Commentary

In addition to the comments on specific hypotheses noted above, the letters we received from persons active in international education or research raised some significant points which deserve further mention, not least because they relate to broader issues and principles.

Johan Galtung, of the Peace Research Institute in Oslo, challenges the basic motivations and even the benefits of study as offered in the United States. He attributes to the United States—the government and educational institutions—an interest to tie the emerging elites of the developing countries to essentially liberal-capitalist conceptions of society, conceptions which he does not believe accord with their needs.

Moreover, he asserts that much of U. S. higher education is oriented to the use of massive technologies at a time when, nationally and internationally, serious questions are being raised about both the proficiency and social costs of such an approach. Galtung believes that the education received abroad may thus in fact be "dysfunctional." It should be noted that only one study in the literature surveyed related to the first question. The second question is subsumed in discussions of "relevancy."

Philip C. Coombs, of the International Council for Educational Development, deplores the non-utilization of advanced educated alumni abroad as partners in university or internationally conducted research involving their fields or regions. Not only does such neglect fail to engage significant research resources, deprive alumni of the prestige that attends participation in international research programs, even in some instances make such projects less acceptable, but it also fails to maintain nurturing links with the former institutions and the research skills acquired during study. Additionally, Coombs draws attention to the selectivity, other than for persons who prepare to be academics or high-level analysts, of training in the most advanced, refined, and sophisticated research and computer methodologies and techniques, often at the expense of providing experience and competence in concrete applied techniques of field research.

Barbara J. Walton raises the question whether graduate study at traditional American institutions within the individualized U. S. cultural context may not negatively affect the motivation of foreign students to use their training for the benefit of their community at home. It may, instead, strengthen their desire for professional and personal self-advancement. The massive research on the migration of talent, insofar as it is based on verbal data, has only indirectly touched on the question and has not specifically sought or secured a concrete answer.[1]

Margaret T. Cormack wonders to what extent U. S. higher education is really seriously interested in research on foreign students with a view to "improving American education" as against using such terms to legitimize requests for funds. She notes that inadequate attention has been devoted to foreign students' "search for identity," an old phenomenon that, however, holds new meaning for persons from traditional and changing cultures. She reiterates her 1962 observation that it is intrinsically illogical for Americans to want foreign students to become well adjusted to our culture and then expect them to return happily home when their studies are completed. She draws attention to the limitations of post-return evaluations which, while valuable, are diagnostically inadequate since it may take many years for foreign-trained individuals to achieve positions of authority in the home country. While in junior positions, their impact can be increased if top administrators and decision makers in their institutions are also exposed to international education through short-term sojourns abroad.

Finally, as we too have mentioned, Cormack draws attention to the implications of the potential difference between those foreign students who had experienced or are experiencing the United States in its period of declining morale and international status, and those who had studied here during our ascendant and more "positive" periods. The research surveyed by us has not dealt with this cross-temporal dimension; the one opinion study of 1971 relating to events on U. S. campuses proffers only a benign reassurance.[2] It is essential to generate more recent data.

NOTES

1. See also Becker (39/1971).
2. See No. 401.

ANNOTATED BIBLIOGRAPHY

The annotated bibliography contains complete citations and brief summaries of all studies mentioned in the report. It is arranged alphabetically by author, except that publications by major agencies and private organizations are listed under the name of the agency; where author or editor of such a publication is given, a cross-reference has been included. Works by the same author(s) are given chronologically. Where agencies have published a series of reports, these will be found grouped together.

In the process of collecting materials for this report, the following bibliographic publications were used: Sociological Abstracts, ERIC Abstracts, Social Science and Humanities Index, International Political Science Abstracts, International Bibliography of Political Science, Canadian Education Index, British Humanities Index, Reader's Guide to Periodical Literature, Dissertation Abstracts International (Xerox University Microfilms), and Public Affairs Information Index. The annotations derive from original abstracts prepared by the research team or, in some cases, from printed abstracts appearing in one of these publications. They are intended to convey the scope of the author's work, its research method, and major findings in the case of empirical studies.

1. Ackerman, William C. "Private Support Activities in International Education." Exchange 6, no. 2 (Fall 1970): 1-13.
This article describes the important role played by multinational corporations (Chrysler, Esso, GE, 3M, etc.) in supporting international educational and cultural exchange, chiefly through grants to foreign students for graduate study in the United States.

2. African-American Institute. African Students at U. S. Universities. By Jane W. Jacqz. New York, 1967.
This is a report of a Conference on the Admission and Guidance of African Students held at Howard University, March 17-18, 1967, organized by the African-American Institute with the assistance of AACRAO, CEEB, IIE, and NAFSA. It was attended by 190 invitees representing admissions officers, foreign student advisers, and independent African governments.

According to surveys cited in the report, there were, in 1965-66, an estimated 6,880 students from 47 countries and territories of Africa

enrolled in American colleges and universities; they perform well at
U. S. institutions and are generally satisfied with the academic side of
American life. A significant minority, however, have social and financial problems resulting in dissatisfaction and alienation, and would not
choose to come to the U. S. to study if the decision were to be made
again.

A major issue for debate at the Conference was whether or not
U. S. colleges and universities should be responsive to African manpower needs in admitting and guiding African students. The three
principal speakers, Frederick S. Arkhurst, Ambassador from Ghana
to the U. N., Senator Walter Mondale, and Homer D. Babbidge, Jr.,
believed they should, and that they should assume particular responsibility for encouraging students to return to Africa.

To better respond to African manpower needs, various suggestions were made: improved manpower planning by African governments; stricter control over issuance of passports and expanded use of
bonding; greater emphasis on graduate programs with students receiving undergraduate training in their home countries; more effective
academic counseling in U. S. institutions; provision of information on
African manpower plans and employment opportunities; visits by
recruiting teams to U. S. campuses.

In the discussion of useful resources and practices in the admission of African students, it was recommended that there should be
greater information on U. S. education in USIS libraries, especially
regarding the costs of U. S. study, and that use be made of Educational
Systems of Africa and various standardized tests (PSAT, SAT, TOEFL)
for evaluation of applicants' credentials and academic aptitude.

3. _____. Refugee Students from Southern Africa. By Jane W. Jacqz.
New York, 1967.

This is a report of a workshop held in New York, April 18-19, 1967,
attended by 58 persons representing international agencies, African
governments and liberation movements, European and U. S. governmental and private agencies, and U. S. colleges and universities.

Discussion at the workshop focused on factors affecting training
and utilization of the large number of southern African refugees now
studying in the U. S. The primary goal of training must be to prepare
for participation in the struggle for freedom; secondary objectives are
to prepare students for service among refugee groups or in their country of asylum. Achievement of these goals implied, for many speakers:
(1) restriction of scholarships to students associated with a liberation
movement, (2) emphasis, where possible, on training in Africa,
(3) concentration on science, technology, and medicine at sub-profes-
sional levels, supplemented by practical training and work experience,

and (4) special efforts on U. S. campuses to develop a sense of
"African-ness" through contact with liberation movements. Returned
students should be at the disposal of their parties, but new employment
opportunities must be developed in international organizations, African
organizations, and country of asylum, possibly through a central job
placement mechanism. The "travel document" problem, and the difficulties of border states, deserve special attention.

4. _____. "A Current Assessment of the Southern African Student
   Program." By Damon S. Kletzien. New York, February 1972.
SASP was initiated in 1961 by the Department of State as part of the
Fulbright-Hays Educational Exchange Program in an urgent effort to
provide educational training to African students primarily from those
countries expecting independence and majority rule in the near future.
By January 1972, 465 students had participated in the program, most
completing academic degrees. The hope that this training could be
utilized in Africa has become increasingly unlikely; the continuation of
minority white rule in many countries makes return impossible.
Furthermore, independent African countries hesitate to admit refugees
who may pose a threat to their internal or international security and
for whom, given their small employment infrastructure, suitable jobs
are not available.
    Their ambiguous legal status is a major obstacle for these
students: they lack travel documents which would enable them to enter
friendly African nations, and they encounter extreme difficulty in
obtaining clear documentation of their eligibility for U. S. employment.
    Given the changed circumstances, the emphasis of SASP has
changed from an on-going scholarship program to one of administrative assistance to refugees. Recent efforts include collection and distribution of employment information, liaison with other U. S. and
international organizations concerned with southern African refugees,
development of contacts with African employers, and implementation
of the Transitional Training Program to prepare SASP participants for
jobs offered in Africa.

5. _____. The African Graduate Fellowship Program Annual Report.
   By B. Rotach and J. Haas. New York, 1972.
The AFGRAD program is administered through its secretariat in New
York and AAI representatives in Africa. After selection, candidates
receive orientation in New York and are closely monitored during their
sojourn. Employment assistance is given as grantees approach the
end of their studies.
    In its nine years of activity, AFGRAD has granted awards to
693 African nationals from 31 countries; as of June 30, 1972, 272
AFGRAD Fellows and African Graduate Study Awards (AGSA)

grantees were studying or training in the United States. The overall repatriation rate is 88.6 percent.

Four major changes have occurred since the inception of the program: (1) a growing demand for doctorates has led to an increase in Ph.D. students; (2) the high rate of non-return among medical students forced AFGRAD to reduce its emphasis on medical studies; (3) the development since 1967 of AGSA to aid employed applicants who do not meet AFGRAD standards; and (4) provision has been made for financial aid to grantees wishing to conduct doctoral dissertation research in Africa. In the Appendices, all grantees are listed by name, country of origin, institution, and field of study.

6. _____. The African Scholarship Program of American Universities: Annual Report for the Period July 1, 1972, to June 30, 1973. New York, n.d.

Since 1961 ASPAU has awarded 1,594 scholarships for undergraduate study at American institutions. Major fields of study have been engineering, 32.8 percent; natural and applied sciences, 18.0 percent; liberal arts and social sciences, 14.6 percent; business, public administration, and applied social science, 12.4 percent. The proportion of liberal arts grantees has dropped consistently, reflecting the developing manpower priorities of African nations. Level of participation by country has varied, as has the rate of repatriation. The latter continues to increase: as of June 30, 1973, 55.10 percent of participants had returned and 34 grantees remained in the program, expecting to complete their studies by June 1975. A significant number of students graduating 1973-74 are pursuing graduate education in the United States, with the support of the U.S. academic community and their home governments.

Two recommendations are made: (1) the African Transfer Student Award (ATSA) program, under which students may transfer to U.S. institutions for specialized or advanced training not available in their home countries, should be reinstated; (2) AID should consider using the ASPAU placement mechanism as a service to African governments wishing to sponsor students in U.S. institutions.

7. Agency for International Development. Operations of the Participant Training Program of the Agency for International Development. By Harley O. Preston. Washington, D.C., 1966.

This paper describes the Participant Training Program of AID and the specific standard procedures at each phase: pre-departure, training procedures, selection, pre-departure briefings, processing, training in the United States, orientation in the United States, and exit interviews. Some basic difficulties and problems encountered in using the procedures are noted.

8. _____. "Leadership Training and Summer Enrichment Program:
   The Lisle Fellowship, Inc." By Forrest Clements. Washington,
   D. C., 24 November 1967.
To determine the suitability of the Lisle program for regular AID
participants, nine non-sponsored foreign students joined the six-week
experiment in the summer of 1967. Teams of students worked for
various community agencies for four days, then discussed their experiences in uninhibited seminar sessions held at the Lisle Center. A
final evaluation revealed that although the students were satisfied with
the Lisle experience, no significant change in the group as a whole
occurred.

9a. Agency for International Development—National Association for
    Foreign Student Affairs. Report of the AID-NAFSA Workshop for
    Foreign Student Advisers. Samuel E. Belk, III, and Eugene
    Chamberlain, Co-Chairmen. Washington, D. C., 1970.
Workshop participants met in Washington, 17-18 November 1969, to
exchange information and improve channels of communication between
AID/OIT and university foreign student advisers. Among their suggestions were: (1) that foreign student advisers request information from
AID International Training Specialists; (2) that AID work through the
foreign student adviser entirely, even in original negotiations for
admission; and (3) that AID send copies of all correspondence concerning participants to the foreign student adviser.

9b. _____. Report of the Second AID-NAFSA Workshop, March 8-10,
    1971. Samuel E. Belk, III, and Furman A. Bridgers, Co-
    Chairmen. Washington, D. C., n.d.
Attending this workshop were staff of OIT, NAFSA representatives
including 12 persons from the Community Section (COMSEC), and
others from government agencies and non-government institutions.
Its purposes were to broaden the contacts between AID's Participant
Training Program and NAFSA representatives on campus and in the
community, and to encourage universities to recognize more fully the
needs of AID-sponsored students.
      Presentations included an overview of the Participant Training
Program, an account of the activities of COMSEC, the role of the
Development Training Officer in overseas AID Missions, and a description of OIT which acts as intermediary between the Mission and the
U. S. training institution.
      Working groups presented reports and recommendations on
orientation; counseling; community relations; relationships among
campus, AID, and participating agencies; and evaluation and follow-up.
Recommendations were made on implementing closer communication
between AID and NAFSA.

9c. _____. Human Resources Development: The Foreign Student on
Campus. Report of a Workshop held at the University of Maryland,
28 February-1 March 1972. Ed. by August E. Benson. Washington, D. C., n.d.

The third AID-NAFSA Workshop focused on the task of developing a
set of uniform standards for assisting participants in achieving educational goals as formulated by the student, the home government, and
AID. Dr. J. A. Kieffer of AID, speaking on "Human Resources Development and the AID Program," pointed to the decline of U. S. funding
and stressed the need for developing countries to identify their own
training requirements and evolve their own institutional capabilities.
Dr. F. H. Harbison, Princeton University, concurred and, in his
talk "Human Resources as the Wealth of Nations," said that in the
1970's the overwhelming problem for developing countries will be the
underutilization of manpower. Dr. A. O. Londono of OAS spoke on
"Foreign Student Development: A View from Abroad," urging that the
student's study program be relevant to the home country and, if possible, geared to national development goals.

Workshop groups reported on: (1) "Establishing a Philosophical
Basis for the Development of Human Resource Models and Programs";
(2) "Developing a Program of Relevant Education through Cooperative
Efforts between Campus and Sponsor"; (3) "Developing a Program of
Relevant Community and Social Experiences through Cooperative
Efforts between Campus and Community"; and (4) "Developing a Com-
prehensive Personal and Professional Follow-Up Program with Foreign
Alumni." (See also No. 283.)

10. Agency for International Development, Office of International
Training. Orientation of AID Trainees at the Washington Inter-
national Center. By Paul Kimmel, DETRI. Washington, D. C.,
July 1969.

In 1968, DETRI began a three-year evaluation of the WIC orientation
program for AID participants. This interim report is based on data
gathered between 17 June and 4 October, 1968; the research methodology utilized questionnaires completed by trainees before and after
the week-long orientation program, participants' evaluation of each
of eight lecture-discussions, and systematic observation and ratings
by DETRI observers.

Overall reactions of the trainees to the WIC program were favorable; those who made several friends were especially likely to be
satisfied. Participants showed a gain of ten percent in correct answers
to factual questions about the United States in the before-and-after
questionnaire, but beliefs about the United States changed very little.
A positive relation was found between change in information and change
in beliefs: trainees who had misinformation about American family life,

unemployment, and literacy tended to have a more negative image of those aspects of the United States corresponding to this misinformation than did trainees who had correct information.

Factors which other studies have found to produce changes in information and beliefs among American students did not produce similar changes for the AID trainees. Student-centered lectures, repetition of lecture materials, the number of questions and amount of discussion after the lectures, and the specific mentioning of information to be learned all correlated weakly and unsystematically with both information and belief change.

Several suggestions are made for improving the program: (1) make more use of trainees' information and experiences; (2) place new emphasis on trainees' social accommodation including re-evaluation of the evening program; (3) augment the clarity of the lecture presentations; and (4) review lecture content.

An independent evaluation by Ernest W. Lefever suggests improvements in quality and presentation of the lectures. In a second evaluation, by Edward C. Stewart, a reformulation of the program according to principles of cross-cultural communication is proposed which would facilitate integration between the objectives of instruction and accommodation, establish more unity of themes and concepts, invite more participation from the visitors, and endow the visitor with a more active role.

11a. _____. Participant Assessment of AID Training Programs. First Annual Report. By Paul Kimmel, William Lybrand, and William Ockey, DETRI. Washington, D. C., August 1969.
This report summarizes the experiences of 2,420 participants in AID's Office of International Training Programs and analyzes information gathered through DETRI exit interviews. (See No. 113 for a description of these procedures.)

Five factors were found to relate to the technical and socio-personal satisfactions of all participants: (1) participants who reported irrelevance or duplication of training program content were less satisfied; (2) participants who felt more involved and who believed that their supervisors were more involved in program planning were more satisfied; (3) participants who made American friends, lived with Americans, participated in social, cultural, and recreational activities, and utilized support services provided by AID were more satisfied with the technical and socio-personal aspects of their sojourns; (4) participants who felt they were in some way discriminated against by Americans were less satisfied with the social-personal aspects of their sojourns as were (5) participants who reported difficulties with living arrangements.

Recommendations designed to improve the program in accordance with these findings are presented. A few basic statistics on the training programs show that: 88 percent of the trainees were males; over half were under 35; 59.8 percent had the equivalent of a U. S. college education; and over 25 percent had training programs lasting three months or more.

11b. _____ . Participant Assessment of AID Training Programs.
Second Annual Report. By Paul Kimmel, William Lybrand, and William Ockey, DETRI. Washington, D. C., July 1970.
This second report presents a new finding, that participants who reported difficulties in communicating with their Program Development Officer or Program Officer and who were dissatisfied with that communication were also likely to be dissatisfied with their overall experience. It re-emphasizes the contribution of American friendships to overall participant satisfaction.

Several findings were not replicated from the First Annual Report difficulty with English language, participation in Pre-University Workshops, and difficulties with money allowances were not related to participant satisfactions and dissatisfactions. Differences in participant backgrounds could possibly have been sufficient for these changes. There were proportionately more participants from the Far East and fewer from Africa. The participants in this report are also younger, more likely to be married, and have more years of education than those from the previous year.

11c. _____ . Participant Assessment of AID Training Programs.
Status Report 3. By Paul Kimmel and William Ockey, DETRI.
Washington, D. C., April 1971.
This report contains data on 2,835 Academic and Special Participants and 129 Observation Training Teams interviewed from July 1969 through February 1971. Positive changes noted in Fiscal 1971 included higher ratings by participants of their satisfaction with communication with the government official responsible for their training. They also found daily living allowances more often "adequate." An important negative change was that Academic and Special Program Participants more often were rated by DETRI interviewers as seeing AID as "poor."

The proportion of Academic and Special Participants from Near East-South Asia increased while that of participants from Latin America declined.

11d. _____ . Participant Assessment of AID Training Programs.
Status Report 5. By Paul Kimmel and William Ockey, DETRI.
Washington, D. C., September 1972.
The DETRI exit interviews with AID participants were discontinued in April 1972. This final report contains information from 5,501 Academic and Special Participants interviewed from July 1968 through March

1971. One change noted in the descriptive characteristics of the population was that a larger proportion of those interviewed in Fiscal 1971 were in the fields of transportation or public administration, while more of the participants interviewed in Fiscal 1972 were studying agriculture or education.

Satisfaction with the total experience, with the technical training, and with feeling welcome and accepted in the United States remained high. The downward trend in the DETRI interviewers' ratings of participants' feelings about U. S. society, the American people, and their personal and social experiences, seen in previous reports, had leveled off in Fiscal 1972.

12a. _____. Participant Assessment of Factors Related to the Bureau of the Census. Profile Report. By Paul Kimmel and William Ockey, DETRI. Washington, D. C., April 1971.
From July 1967 through December 1970, 172 participants in Academic and Special training programs programmed by the Bureau of the Census received DETRI exit interviews. Between 58 percent and 62 percent of the respondents rated satisfaction with the total sojourn experience at one of the top two scale positions; between 63 percent and 69 percent rated their feelings of welcome and acceptance in the United States at one of the top two positions. There was the beginning of a possible negative trend in participants' feelings about the United States as a society and about the American people but neither was statistically significant. Between 15 percent and 18 percent of the respondents were rated by the DETRI interviewers as seeing the Bureau of the Census as "excellent."

The report, as do others in this series, gives statistics as to participants' country of origin, type and length of training program, age, sex, etc., and discusses participant reactions to administrative arrangements, planning of training programs, and personal and social activities.

12b. _____. Participant Assessment of Factors Related to the Department of Agriculture. Profile Report. By Paul Kimmel and William Ockey, DETRI. Washington, D. C., April 1971.
Of USDA participants interviewed by DETRI (916 in Academic and Special Training programs, July 1967–December 1970, and 228 in Observation Training Team programs, September 1967–December 1970), between 69 percent and 75 percent rated satisfaction with their total experience at one of the top two scale positions. Satisfaction with total technical training was rated in one of the top two positions by 66 percent to 73 percent of participants in Academic and 50 percent to 56 percent of those in Special training programs. An upward trend is seen in feelings of welcome and acceptance in the United States, but

a declining trend in feelings about the United States as a society. Between 61 percent and 73 percent of the participants were rated by the interviewer as seeing USDA as "excellent" or "good."

12c. _____. Participant Assessment of Factors Related to the Department of Labor. Profile Report. By Paul Kimmel and William Ockey, DETRI. Washington, D. C., April 1971.

This report is based on 293 interviews, September 1968–December 1970. Department of Labor participants gave somewhat lower ratings of satisfaction with their total experience than the combined ratings of observation team participants programmed by other agencies, but gave somewhat higher ratings of satisfaction with their technical training program. Nearly 50 percent gave high ratings of satisfaction to their personal and social activities in the United States.

12d. _____. Participant Assessment of Factors Related to the Federal Aviation Administration. Profile Report. By Paul Kimmel and William Ockey, DETRI. Washington, D. C., April 1971.

From July 1967 through December 1970, 213 participants in special training programs of the Federal Aviation Administration received DETRI exit interviews. Between 78 percent and 84 percent rated satisfaction with their total experience as AID participants at one of the top two scale positions. Similar ratings were given by 76 percent to 84 percent regarding their feelings of welcome and acceptance in the United States, and by 63 percent to 73 percent regarding satisfaction with their total technical training program. Between 68 percent and 80 percent were rated by the interviewers as seeing the FAA as "excellent" or "good."

12e. _____. Participant Assessment of Factors Related to the Internal Revenue Service. Profile Report. By Paul Kimmel and William Ockey, DETRI. Washington, D. C., April 1971.

Analysis of 183 persons interviewed between September 1968 and December 1970 showed that about 17 percent of IRS participants were "extremely satisfied" with their total AID experience, about the same level of satisfaction shown by members of all other observation training teams. IRS participants gave higher than average ratings regarding satisfaction with their technical training programs. About 69 percent of the IRS participants rated satisfaction with their personal and social activities in the United States at one of the top two scale positions.

12f. _____. Participant Assessment of Factors Related to the Office of Education. Profile Report. By Paul Kimmel and William Ockey, DETRI. Washington, D. C., April 1971.

Exit interviews were conducted with 320 participants in Academic and Special Training programs (July 1967 to December 1970) and 161

participants in Observation Training Team programs (September 1968
to December 1970). Between 66 percent and 78 percent of these OOE
respondents rated satisfaction with their total AID experience at one
of the top two positions; this rating was given by 55 percent to 72 percent regarding feelings of welcome and acceptance in the United States.
A significant trend is noted in the interviewers' ratings of participants'
feelings about the United States as a society: in Fiscal 1969 and Fiscal
1970, over 60 percent were rated as becoming more positive toward the
United States, but in the first half of 1971 only 38 percent were so rated.

12g. _____ . Participant Assessment of Factors Related to the Office
of International Training. Profile Report. By Paul Kimmel and
William Ockey, DETRI. Washington, D. C., April 1971.
From July 1967 through December 1970, 2,439 participants in Academic and Special training programs who were programmed solely by
the Office of International Training (AID) received DETRI exit interviews. From September 1968 through December 1970, 72 participants
in Observation Training Team programs for OIT were interviewed.
Among important overall reactions were the following. Between 65 percent and 71 percent of the participants rated satisfaction with their total
AID experience at one of the top two scale positions. About 60 percent
of the Academic participants rated satisfaction with the total technical
training they received at one of the top two rating positions. A downward trend was apparent in the participants' feelings about the United
States as a society.
     Participant reactions toward administrative arrangements,
planning of training programs and personal and social activities were
also discussed.

12h. _____ . Participant Assessment of Factors Related to the Public
Health Service. Profile Report. By Paul Kimmel and William
Ockey, DETRI. Washington, D. C., April 1971.
Three hundred and fifty-eight PHS participants were interviewed from
July 1967 through December 1970. Top ratings were given by between
75 percent and 83 percent regarding overall satisfaction and by between
61 percent and 75 percent regarding feelings of welcome and acceptance
in the United States. Interviewers' ratings of participants' feelings
about the American people were generally stable over time; there was
a trend toward more positive evaluations of the PHS.

13. _____ . Counseling Handbook. Washington, D. C., June 1973.
The OIT counseling staff, whose philosophy, functions, and services
are described in this handbook, offer a chain of supporting guidance
to foreign trainee participants. Major categories of problems encountered include transcultural adjustment problems, basic personality

problems, and problems growing out of the mechanisms of the training program itself.

14a. Agency for International Development, Participant Training Branch. An Evaluation Study: The Indian Participant Training Program, 1951-1960. New Delhi: USAID, American Embassy, 1966.

In 1959, AID requested missions in 40 countries to conduct an evaluation of their returned participants. The objectives of the survey were to ascertain whether participants utilized and transmitted training, whether training was of appropriate level and quality, and to assess non-technical aspects of the program and its administration. The Indian results are based on responses of 1,449 participants trained from 1951-1960.

Less than half reported considerable use of training; many held better jobs than before training but did not think training was responsible. Participants agreed unanimously on factors which influence utilization: availability of material resources, attitudes of colleagues and superiors, and level of progress and organization in India. Recommendations of both participants and their superiors were that training should be longer, that participants need more advance information and opportunity to consult in program planning, and that program content should be more practical, specialized, and relevant.

Regarding non-technical aspects of training, responses show that 75 percent were satisfied with the orientation program in the United States and that participants enjoyed community hospitality and activities. Their one criticism concerned insufficient free time for personal interests.

14b. Agency for International Development, Participant Training Program. Far East: An Evaluation Study. Washington, D. C., 1966.

This study is based on selected data from a survey of 2,567 returned AID participants in Taiwan, the Philippines, Korea, Thailand, and Vietnam collected in 1961 and 1962. The participants were older and more educated than those from other regions. Most were administrative officials or professionals working for their governments at the time of selection. Agriculture was a major training field, followed by education, and industry and mining.

During their sojourn most participants attended orientation sessions and were entertained in private homes. In evaluating their programs, they were somewhat less satisfied than were those from other regions. They were least satisfied with the length of the programs and the number of things they were required to do and see. Utilization of training was examined and found to vary according to training area.

14c. _____ . Latin America: An Evaluation Study. Washington, D. C.,
      1966.
This report presents a synopsis of the nature and long-term effects of
AID Participant Training Programs for eleven Latin American countries:
Brazil, Bolivia, Chile, Peru, Ecuador, Costa Rica, Nicaragua,
Jamaica, British Honduras, British Guiana, and Surinam. Interviews
were held with 3,480 participants (total population 7,051) from 1942 to
approximately 1961. Participants were primarily mature male government officials, in either professional or managerial positions. The
Latin American programs held in the United States or its territories
were shorter than others, lasting a median of 5.5 months. The largest
training field was agriculture, followed by health and sanitation.
      The participants were found to be generally satisfied with their
pre-departure orientation, but they were least satisfied with information about the content of their programs.
      Overall reactions to the training programs showed that Latin
American participants expressed greater satisfaction with their training
programs than did those from other regions. They were least satisfied
with the length of their programs and the variety of their training
experiences.
      In the post-training period, seven out of ten participants returned
to their previous jobs. Sixty-three percent rated their work supervisors as either very or somewhat helpful in using their training.

14d. _____ . North Africa: An Evaluation Study. Washington, D. C.,
      1966.
This survey, based on extensive interviews with 1,122 AID participants
from Tunisia, Libya, Ethiopia, Morocco, and Sudan between 1960 and
1963, was designed to evaluate the effectiveness of training which took
place from 1951 to 1961.
      These participants were much younger and less well-educated
than those from other regions. Most were government officials, one-
third of them from lower-status levels. The participants were slightly
less satisfied with their programs than were those from other regions;
they were least satisfied with program length and with the variety of
training activities. Almost one-half of the programs were conducted
outside the United States. These, especially in Lebanon, were rated
as much less effective.
      Utilization of training programs varied considerably among
training fields. Participants trained in transport and communications,
and industry and mining were high utilizers, while those trained in
health and education were low. Utilization also varied considerably
with the type of training. Those who took on-the-job training tended
to be higher utilizers.

14e. _____. Near East and South Asia: An Evaluation Study. Washington, D. C., 1966.

This report summarizes the findings of surveys of 5,019 AID trainees from India, Turkey, Pakistan, Iran, Greece, Jordan, Israel, Egypt, completed in 1961. The trainees were primarily married men in their thirties and forties, holding university degrees and employed in the areas of agriculture, education, or government administration.

Compared to participants from other regions, these trainees were better educated and more experienced, but had fewer prior contacts with the U. S. Overseas Mission. Two-thirds were very satisfied with their pre-departure orientation. They were least satisfied with information supplied about the content of their programs.

During their period abroad, the participants experienced fewer language difficulties than did participants from other regions.

Evaluations of the programs showed that about half of the participants were very satisfied with their programs and a somewhat larger proportion rated it as "one of the most important things" they had ever done. The trainees were most satisfied with the level of training and least satisfied with the program's length.

Training fields were related to subsequent use of training. Trainees in community development and in health and sanitation were the highest utilizers, followed by those in transport and communications, agriculture and natural resources, and education. Utilization of training did not vary greatly with the type of training program.

14f. _____. Ghana-United States: Participant Training Evaluation Survey, 1957-1967. Accra: Liberty Press, 1968.

This report summarizes the findings of an evaluation survey of 143 (of approximately 300) Ghanians who participated in the AID program from 1957 to 1967. Most programs dealt with agriculture and involved several types of training. Observation tours accounted for the largest proportion of training followed, in rank order, by university programs, on-the-job training, and non-university special groups.

Among the findings of the survey were: (1) Although most judged the programs satisfactory, one-half of both the supervisors and the participants found the sojourn too short, and two-fifths found the funds provided by AID inadequate. (2) The aspect of the program most frequently mentioned as most useful was on-the-job training. (3) Most of the participants (88 percent) reported using their training in their current work, and almost all of them (94 percent) stated that they had, in some measure, transmitted their knowledge or skill to others.

15. Aich, Prodosh. "Soziale Determinanten der Politischen Einstellung der Afrikanischen und Asiatischen Studenten in Deutschsprachigen Landern" (Social Determinants for the Political

Attitudes of African and Asian Students in German-Speaking
Countries). <u>Kolner Z. Soziol, Soz-Psychol</u>. 18 (1966): 482-515.
It is hypothesized that Africans and Asians studying in Western countries are influenced politically and ideologically during their sojourns,
though not always positively. Since political orientation results from
socialization, and is tied to the individual's personality structure,
Western influence can only effect slow changes in the attitudes of
foreign students.

A systematic survey sampled opinions and attitudes of 709 African
and Asian students at eight institutions in Germany, Vienna, and Zurich
who had been living in German-speaking areas for at least ten months.
Satisfaction with studies, housing, social contacts, leisure activities,
and financing was related to political attitudes: the greater the dissatisfaction, the more negative the attitudes toward the West.

16.   Allaway, William H., ed. <u>International Educational Exchange in
       the United States: A National Profile</u>. University of California,
       Education Abroad Program, 13 January 1971.
Allaway uses material from <u>Bridges to Understanding</u> (335), the
<u>University of California Self-Study</u> (410), and <u>Open Doors</u> (185) to dis-
cuss the problems, effects, and implications resulting from the varied
international commitments of U. S. educational institutions. (1) The
influx of foreign students, totaling 134,959 in 1969-70 has resulted in
many organizational adjustments on the campus, specifically in the
areas of selection and admission, English-language requirements and
training, financing, orientation, advising, curriculum. (2) The reverse
flow, of students, teachers, and research workers to foreign countries,
creates a different set of problems: the goals and administration of
study-abroad programs, the place of foreign study or research in the
academic curriculum, the proper conduct of the scholar abroad.
(3) American education has become increasingly internationalized,
largely through the development of language studies, area studies,
comparative studies, and problem-oriented studies. (4) U. S. universities are further involved in international exchange through technical
assistance programs, many of them university-to-university relationships which offer materials, faculty assistance, and training of foreign
students, and through special training courses for overseas visitors or
for Americans planning to work or study abroad. (5) Some structural
changes have occurred on campus in response to the universities' international commitments. Most institutions have created special offices
to handle international programs; the consortia approach, where several institutions combine to support a program of mutual interest, has
become increasingly popular.

In recent years, U. S. institutions have been experiencing
changes which affect the setting in which international programs

operate. It is expected that there will be increased diversity and more specialization; internal structural changes may occur; new patterns of financing will emerge; and broader representation in university governance will be effected.

17. Allen, Donald E., and Arafat, Ibtihaj S. "Procreative Family Attitudes of American and Foreign Students." International Journal of Comparative Sociology 12 (June 1971): 134-39.

It is hypothesized that foreign students, strongly influenced by the host society, fully accept American standards regarding family relations and fertility. Data was obtained from self-administered questionnaires from 100 American and 99 foreign students chosen at random at Oklahoma State University. Attitudes toward the procreative family were compared by social class, religion and nationality; nationality was the most discriminant variable. Of 13 chi-square tests, only two tended to support the hypothesis, leading the authors to conclude that similar education has had very limited consensual effect on the family attitudes of foreign students.

18. Allen, Walter P. "International Student Achievement: English Test Scores Related to First Semester Grades." University of Houston, January 1965.

A comparison of scores on the Michigan Test of English Language Proficiency and first semester grades for 90 foreign students at the University of Houston indicates that there is a slight correlation between the two which is especially marked when only English grades are considered but still holds for grades in other subjects. This correlation is greater with the higher English test scores than with the lower scores.

Althen, Gary L. See No. 274.

19. American Association of Colleges for Teacher Education. Administrative Internships in Teacher Education and Higher Education. Annual Report for 1972-73. Washington, D. C., 1973.

In 1964, as a result of the mutual concern of AID and the American Association of Colleges for Teacher Education, a special type of on-the-job training was designed and implemented for educational leaders in the developing nations. An internship program enabled foreign educators to have a supervised work experience under the tutelage of an American administrator. Since its inception, 131 educators from 34 Asian, African, and Latin American countries have participated.

This report gives participant statistics for 1972-73 and the results of a pilot evaluation study. It is recommended that a follow-up study is needed of the 131 former interns to arrive at some valid conclusions about the overall success of the program.

20. American Association of Collegiate Registrars and Admissions Officers. Report of AACRAO-AID Conference "University-Government Cooperation in Programs for Students from Abroad: An Assessment Based on an AACRAO-AID Study." Washington, D. C., n.d.

This report summarizes the content and outcomes of a national invitational conference, December 8-9, 1970, devoted to presentation and discussion of the AACRAO-AID Study of AID participants (See No. 418). Lee Wilcox, Vice-Chairman of the Study Committee, noted that, contrary to accepted folklore in the admissions community, participants are well-qualified and perform well academically. The study did reveal, however, certain deficiencies, such as incomplete credentials and poor English facility, and discrepancies in the perceptions of participants and in certain AID procedures.

In work groups, the conferees reached general agreement with the findings of the study and presented their suggestions on selection processes in the Missions, placement processes in Washington, admission and academic placement on U. S. campuses, and performance and experience on U. S. campuses.

21. _____. A Bibliography of Reference Materials for Evaluating Foreign Student Credentials. Ed. by Robert Hefling. Athens, Ohio, 1971.

The Academic Advisory Staff (AAS) of AID-OIT analyzes and interprets the academic credentials of AID participants from cooperating countries in terms of the educational system of the United States. To carry out its service, the AAS has developed a library of reference materials for use by credential analysts, educators, and AID staff members. This document lists the references contained in the library, grouped in terms of their content and usefulness on either a worldwide basis or by regions of the world.

22. American Association of Community and Junior Colleges. Foreign Students in Community and Junior Colleges. By Lornie Kerr. Washington, D. C., 1973.

Enrollment of foreign students in a two-year community or junior college offers advantages to both student and institution: the student may be attracted by specialized two-year training, low fees, close association among students, faculty, and community; the institution will be enhancing the image of the United States and enriching its international education programs. This booklet offers detailed advice on admissions procedures, advising and counseling of foreign students, academic and non-academic orientation programs, housing, community volunteer programs, and on-campus programs.

23. American Library Association. Pre-Conference Institute. Papers and Speeches. Detroit, Michigan, 26-27 June 1970.
The four papers in this volume of institute proceedings present: (1) a retrospective, subjective look at foreign-trained librarians employed in North American libraries and foreign students in North American library education programs; (2) statistical analyses of current policies and practices relating to the employment of foreign-trained librarians in North American library education programs; and (3) a review of the current state of library education in selected countries of Latin America and the Caribbean, Europe, Asia, Africa, Australia, and New Zealand.

24. Amir, Shimeon. "Training for Development: The Israeli Experience." Focus: Technical Cooperation 1973, no. 4, pp. 14-16. In International Development Review, 15, no. 4.
The Department of Foreign Training of Israel's Ministry of Agriculture sponsors short training courses of one to six months in which, between 1960 and 1972, some 4,500 persons from 80 countries have participated. Israel, as a still-developing country, offers advantages over established, developed countries, in that students can hear at first hand of progress, experimentation, and transformation, returning home not only with new techniques but inspired by the example of Israel's achievements. The importance of follow-up has been recognized in the formation of Shalom clubs, organizations in each country of the alumni of Israeli training institutions.

25. Angell, Robert C. Peace on the March: Transnational Participation. New York: Van Nostrand Reinhold Company, 1969.
In Chapter 3, "Study, Teaching and Research Abroad," Angell considers whether study abroad encourages the belief that nations can and should learn to accommodate to one another. In examining research in this area, he concludes that whereas most evidence is positive, there is enough that is negative to suggest that systematic differences exist. All other things being equal, transnational participation between representatives of equally developed nations is most likely to foster accommodation. In general, educational exchange fosters accommodative attitudes principally because the positive experiences of students and scholars will be transmitted to members of elites in their own countries and thus affect the climate in which policies are made.

26. Antler, Lawrence. "Correlates of Home and Host Country Acquaintanceship Among Foreign Medical Residents in the

United States." The Journal of Social Psychology 80 (1970):
49-57.
The purpose of this study, partially supported by the Social and Rehabilitation Service of HEW, was to assess the relationship between
adjustment to the host country and (1) contacts among foreign students
from the same country and (2) contacts among foreign students and
host-country representatives. Subjects of the study were 170 foreign
medical residents selected at random from lists of residents in
university-affiliated teaching hospitals. Europeans comprised 31 percent, Latin Americans 23 percent, 24 percent were from the Far East,
and 21 percent from the Near and Middle East. A background information questionnaire plus 19 other instruments were either developed or
adapted for the study. A standard personality inventory, the Gordon
Personal Profile, was also administered to each subject.

The results showed that the subjects' amount of interaction with
home countrymen was of greater significance than was the amount of
interaction with host-country representatives for adjustment, motivation, and attitude.

27.   Arapoff, Nancy. "Discover and Transform: A Method of Teaching
       Writing to Foreign Students." Paper presented at the Third
       Annual TESOL Convention, 5-8 March 1969.
Reading is an important prelude to writing: invariably those persons
who have done the most reading are the best writers. The "discover
and transform" method of learning writing has the students first read
and compare two written models similar in content but different in
form. Aided by a set of questions, the two models are analyzed in order
to understand what grammatical and semantic rules operate to transform
the first model into the second. The "transform" part of the method
has the student apply his competence on a written model.

28.   Arkoff, Abe; Thaver, Falak; and Elkind, Leonard. "Mental
       Health and Counseling Ideas of Asian and American Students."
       Journal of Counseling Psychology 13 (Summer 1966): 219-223.
This paper, which stems from earlier research (Thaver, Arkoff, and
Elkind, 1964), examines the ideas of mental health held by students of
several Asian countries, compares these ideas with those of a similar
American student group and a group of American psychologists, and
explores the consequences of such ideas for counseling and psycho-
therapy. Subjects were 24 Americans, 19 Chinese, 19 Filipinos, 21
Japanese, and 15 Thais, all of the University of Hawaii's East-West
Center, and 20 professional counselors and clinical psychologists.
Each subject completed a 60-item questionnaire, devised by Nunnally.
Relatively more than American students and psychologists, Asians
were neutral or acquiescent toward the questionnaire items, expressed

belief that mental health could be enhanced through exercising will-power and avoiding unpleasant thoughts, and viewed counseling as a directive, paternalistic, and authoritarian process.

29. Arnold, Ruth, and Adams, Harold. "Rationale for International Students I." Presentations in a panel discussion at an AACRAO Conference. College and University 45 (Summer 1970): 530-44.
This report makes a case for the continuation and expansion of inter-national exchange programs. The authors emphasize the need for each institution to analyze its goals and to adjust its policies accordingly. Exchange programs are seen as a means for American universities to pursue their own primary goals—the advancement and transmission of knowledge—while contributing to a primary goal of U. S. foreign policy—the creation and maintenance of free nations around the world. Institutional obligations to foreign students are also discussed. (See also No. 333.)

30. Asher, Robert E. "Brain Drain to Brain Gain." AIFLD Review 2, no. 3 (1970): 45-54.

The brain drain is a multi-dimensional problem requiring action on the part of both developing and developed countries. On the outflow side, the remedies involve measures making it more attractive for talented personnel in less-developed countries to remain at home and, rela-tively speaking, less attractive for them to emigrate. On the inflow side, they involve making it easier for the less-developed country to import professionals of other nationalities and to re-attract its own emigrees. Advanced countries can de-emphasize scholarships and training grants abroad for nationals of less-developed countries, finance more training in those countries, and facilitate the release of highly skilled nationals of their own for temporary duty in less-developed countries.

31. Association of Commonwealth Universities. Higher Education in the United Kingdom. A Handbook for Students from Overseas and Their Advisers. London, 1972.
This book has as its purpose to meet the demand from potential students from many countries for information about opportunities for study in Britain. It offers information on the courses offered in the 35 univer-sities and 29 polytechnics in Great Britain and Northern Ireland, the entrance requirements into such courses, and expenses that will be involved in studying in Britain. In addition, information is presented regarding foreign student entry into British student life and the addresses of the various higher education institutions.

Awe, Ruth. See No. 184.

32.   Bae, Chong-Keun. "The Effect of Traditionalism on Social
       Adjustment and Brain Drain: A Study of Korean Students at the
       University of Wisconsin." Madison, Wis.: University of
       Wisconsin, n.d.
To discover the effects of traditional Korean values on social adjustment and rate of brain drain, a sample of Korean students at the University of Wisconsin, Madison, and a matched comparison group in
Seoul were studied by means of a questionnaire and an interview.
Results showed that the nature of Korean traditionalism is essentially
stable; any change that occurs follows a U-shaped curve so that the
student returns home as traditional as when he left. Traditionalism is
a crucial barrier to satisfactory adjustment of Korean students to
American society. However, it does not decisively influence a student's
decision to remain in the United States or to return to Korea.

33.   Baldwin, George B. "Brain Drain or Overflow?" Foreign Affairs
       48 (January 1970): 358-72.
In examining the problem of talent migration from developing regions of
East and Southeast Asia, India, the Middle East, East Africa, and Latin
America, Baldwin concludes that brain drain is in actuality an overflow
of talent caused by the inability of these economies to absorb high-level
manpower. He bases his conclusion on two findings: that migration of
more realistically and usefully considered from the perspective of
society's "effective demand" than "human needs" for such talent, and
that migration has not depressed economic development of these countries. In analyzing how developing countries can more effectively compete for return of their professionals, he recommends that: (1) migration controls be avoided; (2) counseling services be improved for
foreign students before and after arrival in host country; (3) more
effective "recapture" mechanisms be established for institutions and
countries interested in repatriation; (4) U. S. medical output be greatly
increased; (5) new, experimental health delivery systems be developed
to reduce dependence on over-trained physicians; and (6) the United
States increase its aid for development of foreign institutions capable
of offering satisfying careers to key nationals.

34.   Barrientos, Ivan, and Schufletowski, Frank W. "The Question-
       able Foreign Student." School and Society 96 (April 1968): 243-45.
For academic and political reasons, U. S. institutions should assist
high-calibre foreign students (1) by enforcing a more selective admissions policy, (2) by eliminating excessive academic permissiveness
which encourages double standards, and (3) by creating competently
staffed foreign student offices.

35.   Barry, Jean, S. J. "The Thai Students in the United States: A
       Study in Attitude Change." Ed.D. dissertation, Columbia
       University, 1966.
This study was undertaken to explore the impact of living and studying
in the United States upon Thai students in the areas of religion, occupational values, views on education, and attitudes on courtship and
family life. A structured questionnaire was sent to the 1,214 students
listed by the Royal Thai Embassy in Washington for the academic year
1964–65. Returns represented 85 percent of the population presumed
to have been reached by mail.

Respondents were grouped in five categories according to length
of stay, and a comparison was made between the attitude patterns of
each group. Attitude differences were related to length of sojourn, sex,
age, and source of financial support. Least subject to change were
religious beliefs and values; in education, change was in the direction
of a greater valuation of knowledge and open-mindedness. Students
also wished for greater freedom in relationships between the sexes.

36.   Basu, Arun Chandra. "A Study of Graduate Agricultural Students
       from India at Selected Land-Grant Colleges and Universities in
       the United States." Ph.D. dissertation, University of Missouri,
       1966.
Data for this study were obtained through mailed schedules from 314
respondents at 17 institutions. They represented 85.1 percent of the
relevant population. Personal interviews were held with 55 of the
students.

Satisfaction with graduate curricula was expressed by nearly 90
percent of the subjects, particularly at the doctoral level. Over 80 percent perceived their training to be both helpful and useful in their chosen
professions in India, but most felt a need for additional experience
before returning home. Major non-academic problems mentioned were
homesickness and difficulty in securing foreign-exchange permits prior
to departure.

It is recommended that (1) prospective students obtain adequate
information about graduate programs and requirements; (2) more
emphasis be placed on basic sciences at Indian agricultural institutions;
and (3) Land Grant institutions offer courses geared to the needs of
developing countries and include applied research experience.

37.   Becker, Tamar. "Perceptions and Attitudinal Changes among
       Foreign Students on the UCLA Campus." Ph.D. dissertation,
       University of California, Los Angeles, 1966.
For a published report of this research, see No. 38.

38. _____. "Patterns of Attitudinal Changes Among Foreign Students."
American Journal of Sociology 73 (January 1968): 431-42.
The U-curve hypothesis has achieved the status of undisputed fact
despite research findings which are only tentative and lack statistical
significance. It may be a valid characteristic of European students but
not apply to students from developing countries.

A study of 27 Indians, 25 Israelis, and 25 Europeans at UCLA,
using an open-ended interview schedule and a short two-part Semantic
Differential test, examined the hypotheses that attitudes of students
from developed countries would display a U-curve but that attitudes of
students from under-developed or semi-developed countries would be
characterized by hostility to the United States and idealization of home
country in the initial and final phases of the sojourn, and a relative
detachment from home country and a less stereotyped view of the United
States during the middle phase. When subjects were grouped on the
basis of the difference in percentage of sojourn completed, the findings
supported these hypotheses.

The "anticipatory adjustment" hypothesis is proposed to explain
the differences in adjustment of students from developed and developing
countries. It denotes a process of selective adoption of attitudes on the
basis of their utility in easing the individual's adjustment to anticipated
imminent and drastic changes in his environment. In the course of this
adjustment process, the individual tends to focus on and exaggerate that
which, from his point of view, is objectionable in the environment he is
about to leave, thus making the involuntary departure more palatable.

39. _____. "Cultural Patterns and Nationalistic Commitment Among
Foreign Students in the United States." Sociology and Social
Research 55 (July 1971): 467-81.
Among modes of attachment to the national state, commitment to
national cultural values is least vulnerable to erosion during prolonged
sojourn abroad. Commitment to the "role of the national," on the other
hand, is highly vulnerable and tends to give way to an individual-
centered ideology. In support of these hypotheses, a modified random
sample of 187 students of seven nationality groups was interviewed at
UCLA in the fall of 1967 using an open-ended schedule. In the spring
of 1968, 55 percent were re-interviewed. Median length of sojourn
prior to the first interview was 19.9 months.

40. _____. "Black Africans and Black Americans on an American
Campus: The African View." Sociology and Social Research 57
(January 1973): 168-81.
The article explores the manifestations and causes of strained relations
between black Africans and black Americans on the UCLA campus. As
part of a broader cross-cultural study, 57 black African students were

interviewed (33 participated in a follow-up interview). The results of the study show that higher status and tangible benefits accorded Africans in preference to black Americans, socio-cultural differences between the groups, and perceived rejection by American blacks strengthen the Africans' tendency to emphasize their separate identity and minimize contact with black Americans.

Belk, Samuel E. See No. 9a-b.

41.　　Benne, Max Erwin. "The Influence of Foreign Visitors on the Interest of Certain Adult Members of a Hosting Community in Participating in Internationally Oriented Activities." Ed. D. dissertation, Michigan State University, 1967.

Prior to the arrival of a group of foreign students in the Chesaning, Michigan, area for the 1966 Memorial Day weekend, 175 adult residents completed a questionnaire that included the Sampson World-Mindedness Scale and the International Activities Scale. After the visit, 97 completed a second copy of the IAS.

It was found that the interest of some adults in participating in internationally oriented activities increased, while the interest of others decreased, as a result of the foreign student visitation. The post-visit scores were significantly higher for the adults who hosted a foreign student or talked with one for an hour or more than were those of the adults who only saw the students or read about them in the newspaper.

Benson, August E. See No. 9c, 283.

42.　　Bjur, Wesley Eugene. "Technical Assistance and Institution Building: A University Experience in Brazil." Ph. D. dissertation, Claremont Graduate School and University Center, 1967.

In this study, the institution-building model developed by the Inter-University Research Program in Institution Building is used to analyze the experience of the UN, and later the University of Southern California, in assisting schools of public administration in Brazil 1951-65. A modified "indigenization" model is presented which suggests that the process of institutionalization progresses in sequence through charismatic, professionalization, and legitimization stages on its way to fruition as an established societal institution. These phases are traced in the development of the Brazilian institutions which are studied.

43.　　Bloom, Joyce Neimark Mauser. "Students from Other Lands in the Two-Year College." Ph. D. dissertation, Columbia University, 1970.

This study, based on data obtained in 1964 and verified in 1969, indicates the need to analyze and design the existing foreign student programs in two-year colleges to meet the real needs of this student group. Each college must define its international goals and investigate what is now being done to achieve them. Redesign of all basic procedures including qualified counseling, proper pretesting, a realistic appraisal of the financial need of the students, and work possibilities must follow.

44a. Board of Foreign Scholarships. Reviewing the Commitment: Seventh Annual Report. Washington, D. C., October 1969.
This is the seventh annual report to the U. S. Congress from the Board of Foreign Scholarships, covering academic exchanges between the United States and other countries during the 23rd year of the educational and cultural exchange program from 1 September 1968 through 30 August 1969. It presents statistics summarizing grants made under the various exchange programs authorized since 1959. The Board expresses particular concern over the cutback in both private and federal funding for educational exchange.

44b. _____. Report on Exchanges: Tenth Annual Report. Washington, D. C.: U. S. Government Printing Office, 1973.
During the year beginning 1 August 1971, the Board of Foreign Scholarships marked the 25th anniversary of the educational exchange program by initiating a series of distinguished lectureships, the "Lincoln Lecturers," and by publishing an informal history of exchanges under the Fulbright-Hays Act. A major feature of 1971-72 was the reorganization of the Board and the introduction of a new system of subcommittees to provide more effective liaison with cooperating agencies, to increase contact with small and minority campuses, and to plan participation in the American Bicentennial Celebration. Members of the Board participated in a number of overseas meetings and workshops, discussing program objectives with binational commissions, U. S. diplomatic missions, foreign government officials and educators.

Appendices to this report present statistics on various exchange programs, 1971-72.

45. _____. "Educational Exchange in the Seventies." Exchange 7, no. 2 (Fall 1971): 1-8.
In this policy statement, issued on the 25th anniversary of the first International Education Act, the Board stresses the great value and importance of international exchanges. Noting the greatly changed context in which these exchanges occur, the Board recommends that: (1) participants should be engaged primarily in university-level activities, but should include an increasing number of persons from non-academic professions; (2) exchange activities should concentrate on a few subjects or problems at a time; (3) most grants should continue to

be made to individuals, but experimentation with grants to teams and
institutions is now in order; (4) commissions should expand their support to non-sponsored students, scholars, and educational groups, and
the Department should encourage this by sanctioning appropriate budget
increases.

46.   _____. A Quarter Century: The American Adventure in Academic
       Exchange. Washington, D. C., December 1971.
This report represents an informal history of 25 years of the Fulbright-
Hays Program, and recommends that, in the future: (1) bi-national
commissions should concentrate on three or four broadly conceived
programs and projects; (2) exchanges should be confined to persons in
higher education or professions; (3) funds should be granted to "team
activities" or for the development of "institution-to-institution" programs; and (4) policy should be directed at increasing support from
private sectors and cost sharing by foreign governments.

47.   Bochner, Stephen. "Overseas Students in Australia: Problems in
       Culture Learning." Working Papers of the East-West Culture
       Learning Institute No. 16. Honolulu: East-West Center,
       February 1972.
The problems of the overseas student are put into the context of cultural
adaptation and described in terms of the four main roles a sojourner
plays in a new environment: as a foreigner, a scholar, a young adult,
and as a representative of a nationality. An alternative method of
assisting developing countries would be for the government to channel
more of its educational resources into sending qualified Australian
teachers, academics, and technicians to Asian countries where they
could teach and train young Asian students on their home ground.

48.   Bohn, Ralph Carl. "An Evaluation of the Educational Program
       for Students from Foreign Countries: Emphasis upon Orientation
       Procedures, Individual Problems, and Psychological Variables."
       Ed.D. dissertation, Wayne State University, 1957.
This study was designed as a pilot investigation into the effectiveness
of the foreign student program directed by the Technical Training Section of the Office of Education and financed by the "Point Four" Program.
     In 1955, 36 students of industrial and general educational admin-
istration from Asia, Africa, and South America completed a battery of
tests and questionnaires. While scoring low on language ability, their
grades were equal to or better than those of American students. They
held favorable attitudes to the United States, but one-third indicated
that the educational program had failed to fulfill either their own personal objectives or the original objectives established for study in the
United States. The major causes of this failure were misunderstanding

between the sending country, the Office of Education, and the student; misinterpretation of curriculum offerings; and lack of adequate facilities for learning highly specialized activities.

49. Borhanmanesh, Mohamad. "A Study of Iranian Students in Southern California." Ed. D. dissertation, University of California, Los Angeles, 1965.
An open-ended interview, covering socio-economic, educational and religious background, American experiences, and effects of these experiences on attitudes to the United States and to home country, was conducted with 100 Iranian students attending 13 universities and colleges in Southern California. Most students came because of the prestige of American universities, although availability of part-time jobs was also important. Factors related to non-return were lower class or religious minority background, enrollment in M.A. or Ph.D. programs, marriage to an American, belief in better employment opportunities in the United States.

Brademas, John. See No. 123, 187, 203, 239, 307.

50. Brettell, J. Allan, and Gildseth, Bruce. "Foreign Students at Kansas State University: A Profile." Evaluation and Research Report No. 3. Manhattan, Kans.: Kansas State University, Office of the Dean of Students, 1968.
This report is a profile of the 409 foreign students and the 44 permanent residents enrolled for the Fall Semester 1968 giving age, sex, marital status, nationality, major field, source of financial support.

51. _____. "Foreign Student Programming at Kansas State University: An Inventory." Evaluation and Research Report No. 5. Manhattan, Kans.: Kansas State University, Office of the Dean of Students, March 1969.
This short report presents a brief overview of international student programs at Kansas State University including those of religious organizations, international organizations, and community volunteers.

52. Breuder, Robert L. A Statewide Study: Identified Problems of International Students Enrolled in Public Community/Junior Colleges in Florida. Tallahassee, Fla.: Florida State University, Department of Higher Education, May 1972.
Problems of international students enrolled in public junior colleges in Florida and Florida State University were identified by the Michigan International Student Problem Inventory (which presents 11 problem areas of student personnel services, such as admissions, counseling, health services, and student activities). Three subgroups in the

university and colleges (male/female, on campus less than 12 months/
on campus more than 12 months, and English first preference/English
not first preference) and two types of junior colleges (rural/urban,
enrollment of fewer than 50 international students/50 or more) were
compared. Findings concerning international students at junior colleges
included: (1) most problems are perceived in the areas of financial aid,
English language, placement, and admissions; (2) sex and length of
sojourn caused no significant differences in problems perceived. It was
also found that problems perceived by international students in the
junior colleges were not significantly different from those perceived by
undergraduate international students enrolled at Florida State University. Other findings, as well as recommendations for meeting the needs
of international students, are also presented.

53.   Brickman, William W. Foreign Students in American Elementary
       and Secondary Schools. Philadelphia: International House, Ogontz
       Plan Committee, 1967.
The Ogontz Plan, founded in Philadelphia in 1961, has a dual purpose:
"to promote international understanding by sharing educational experiences" and "to teach the sameness of people while explaining the different values that are the product of varied environments." To achieve
these goals, selected foreign students make scheduled visits to elementary and secondary schools; five students from as many countries
work together, each appearing at the school three half-days per semester, and are paid at substitute teacher rates.
       The author's evaluation of the Plan is based on: (1) discussions
with university, school, and community persons across the country,
and (2) content analysis of 63 questionnaires completed by the University
of Pennsylvania students who had participated in the Plan.
       He concludes that there is widespread approval of the goals of
the Plan, and considerable interest in expanding its activities to other
areas of the country. He recommends that the Plan seek private and
Federal funding, promote greater exchange of ideas on international
education, initiate a study of the extent of change in pupils' attitudes
resulting from participation in the Plan, expand its staff, and improve
the student selection process.

54.   _____. "International Exchange in Higher Education: Europe and
       the United States, 1700-1900." Notre Dame Journal of Education
       3 (Spring 1972): 10-21.
Since its inception, American higher education has had a strong international component consisting of, on the one hand, the foreign training
of American scholars, from the Puritan fathers to the German-trained
scientists of the 1920's and, on the other, the steady influx of European
scholars uprooted by recurrent national crises. Thus U. S. academic

institutions, while developing an indigenous way, have traditionally maintained an international character.

Bridgers, Furman A. See No. 9b, 266, 276.

55.   Burgess, Thomas C., and Marks, Marguerite M. "English Aural Comprehension Test Scores as a Predictor of Academic Success among Foreign Students." Educational and Psychological Measurement 28 (Winter 1968): 1229-30.

The Lado Test of Aural Comprehension (LTAC) is used by many colleges to determine which foreign students have sufficient command of the English language to do well in classes given in English. To determine the predictive validity of the LTAC, test scores, grades in a variable credit course of English for foreign students (Eng GPA), and cumulative grade point averages were obtained on the first-year performance of 89 students who attended Portland State College at some time during the years 1964-1967. It was found that the predictive validity coefficient for general grade point average was not significant, while the coefficient for grades in English for foreign students was significant but low.

56.   Burke, Jack Dale. "The Predictive Validity of English Language Screening Instruments for Foreign Students Entering the University of Southern California." Ph.D. dissertation, University of Southern California, 1968.

For a total sample of 178 foreign students attending USC, as well as four specific subsamples of different levels of judged competency in English, this correlational study was concerned with ascertaining the predictive validity of a battery of six ability and achievement tests given at the beginning of each semester over a period of three years to screen foreign students.

The most noteworthy conclusions were that: (1) the California Reading Test, Speech Interview, and the Larry Ward English Examination for Foreign Students were the three most valid measures of predicting academic achievement; (2) grade point average could be more accurately predicted than academic standing; (3) a composite of predictive variables achieved a greater degree of validity with a criterion than did a single predictor.

57.   Byers, Philip. "Asian Invasion of American Campuses—Why?" Exchange 6, no. 4 (Spring 1971): 58-70.

The number of Asian students studying in the United States has almost tripled since 1961. Byers believes this influx will continue as long as (1) the United States remains a business and industrial leader, (2) English remains the lingua franca of the world, (3) the quality and availability of U. S. higher education is maintained, (4) our economy can absorb all the professional people available and (5) the political situation in Asia remains unsettled.

_____. See No. 279.

58. Calder, Nigel. "International Relations and Exchanges in Scientific and Technical Fields." In UNESCO Handbook of International Exchanges, pp. 29-37. Paris: UNESCO, 1967.
This article concerns the emergence of deliberate and organized international relations and exchanges in the scientific and technological fields since 1945. After discussing the motives for this development, Calder suggests three major problems: (1) The growing diversity and proliferation of scientific and technical cooperation has created an overlapping of some functions and neglect of others. (2) Fashions in science are generally set in the highly developed countries and may not be relevant to problems in less developed countries. (3) Advances in technology are often not shared with developing countries.

59. Canter, Jacob. "American Higher Education for Students of the Developing World." Speech delivered at the University of Minnesota Conference, 13 April 1967.
Raising the question of whether education for American students is relevant to the facts of today's world if it does not include study of the problems, characteristics, and history of the developing countries, the quthor advocates the internationalization of U. S. education, making it valid for both American and foreign students. While there will always be a demand for "area studies," the broader goal should be the inclusion of study of other parts of the world, of other cultures, into the regular curricula. Greater use should be made of foreign students and scholars in the classroom, presenting views on problems of American society as well as on those of their own countries. Technical and scientific curricula could also benefit by inclusion of experience gained in developing countries.

Extra-curricular education for all foreign students should include seminars of specialists from a particular geographic region, a continuing seminar on the liberal tradition in Western thought, and regular analysis and discussion of current events in the United States.

60. Carino, Ledivina Vidallon. "Structural Conditions and Professional Migration: A Study of the Movement of Scientists, Engineers, and Medical Personnel into the United States, 1965-1967." Ph.D. dissertation, Indiana University, 1970.
The central hypothesis of this study was that certain structural properties of sending countries served as push factors for migration. Two

factor-sets were identified: the first set was called "primary" because
the factors were expected to provide the initial push; the secondary
group included factors which affected the choice of destination. Specifically, it was posited that American professional immigration would
be high only where both factor-sets were strong. Regression analysis
was used to determine the individual effect of each variable. The findings tended to support the central hypothesis in both its general and
specific forms.

The nature of the scientific community, a primary factor, affected
the migration negatively, as predicted. The role of development could
be described only among low democracies, where its effect was positive.

Democracy was found to have a dual influence. As an index of the
freedom to migrate, it was a "generalized facility," easing migration
towards any receiving country. It also acted as a motivating factor,
particularly as its low level placed limits on the growth of the professional community and increased its deterrent effect on the outward
movement of highly trained persons.

The influence of instability was found to be curvilinear, with the
medium level being most conducive to migration. Distance was found
to be a strong negative influence, and economic relation as a weak
positive one. The other secondary factors, cultural similarity and
political relationship, had little effect.

Several strategies for further analysis are suggested.

61.   Carnovsky, Leon. The Foreign Student in the American Library
       School. Final Report. Chicago, Ill.: University of Chicago,
       Graduate Library School, 30 November 1971.
The experience, observations, and reactions of foreign students to
American library education are reported in this study. A questionnaire
was sent to each foreign student who graduated from an accredited
American library school between 1965 and 1969. Though most of the
respondents expressed general satisfaction, there were numerous
criticisms, many of them echoing those of American graduates. Suggestions and recommendations are included.

62.   Carpenter, Edward L. "Roles of the Foreign Student Adviser."
       Exchange 4, no. 4 (Spring 1969): 38-43.
Carpenter describes the foreign student adviser's various roles. He
finds that lack of articulated institutional policy regarding the entire
question of foreign students on campus is a major impediment to definition of the adviser's role vis-a-vis students and the community.

63.   Carter, William D. Study Abroad and Educational Development.
       Fundamentals of Educational Planning 19. Paris: UNESCO,
       International Institute for Educational Planning, 1973.

This monograph reviews the study-abroad problem in order to acquaint educational administrators, particularly in developing countries, with recent thinking on more efficient planning techniques within the total educational and development framework. Two major problems have characterized study-abroad programs over the last 20 years: the brain drain, caused principally by the inability of developing countries to provide satisfactory employment for highly trained manpower, and the extreme dispersion in planning and administration of foreign study programs.

Stressing the need for a more integrated approach to training, the author discusses seven interrelated tasks which might serve as a framework of new policies, as proposed by the United Nations Development Programme. They are: (1) to promote greater recognition of the centrality of training in development programs; (2) to improve knowledge of training activities which could improve coordination and suggest new approaches in the field of training; (3) to improve awareness of ways whereby needs and priorities could be identified more effectively; (4) to improve the planning of training programs in general and the training component of specific projects; (5) to improve the capacity of outside experts and "trainers of trainers;" (6) to improve the training of local experts or "counterparts" on projects; (7) to improve the quality of administration of international training at national, regional, and inter-regional levels.

To implement these tasks, an administrative unit in each country is proposed which would correlate information and research, define the criteria needed in negotiating with foreign scholarship donors, define standards of candidate selection, and supervise orientation, placement and follow-up of grantees.

64.   Cervantes, Nestor. "When Brain Drainers Drain Back." The
          Asian Student, 18 March 1972, p. 5.
Although there are signs that the brain drain from Asia is moderating, planners and administrators should give close attention to three factors: economic growth and social change in Asia; narrowing of the income gap between Asian countries and the West; and Asia's growing employment opportunities in science and technology. Brain-drain profiles are given for Taiwan, Philippines, India, and Japan.

Chamberlain, Eugene. See No. 9a.

65.   Chang, Hwa-bao. "A Study of Some Attitudes of Chinese Students
          in the United States." Ph.D. dissertation, University of Texas
          at Austin, 1972.
This study was intended primarily to be an explanatory survey in which several hypotheses concerning some attitudes of Chinese students

toward the United States were formulated and tested. Attitudes were positively associated with the degree of contact with Americans, and perception of the international relations between the United States and home country; but negatively associated with degree of authoritarianism. A U-curve hypothesis concerning attitude changes through time was partially supported by the present findings. The national-status rating differential was found to be somewhat related to the students' attitudes, but the degree of frustration, sex differences, field of study differences, and religious affiliation were found not to be related to the attitudes of Chinese students toward the United States. Identification with the immigrant role and the expectations associated with that role determined, to a certain extent, attitudes toward the United States.

66.   Chang, Shu Yuan Hsieh. "The Views and Contributions of Chinese Students and Intellectuals in the United States." Ph.D. dissertation, University of Utah, 1971.
The data for this study came from interviews with over 100 Chinese in the United States and Taiwan, and from 500 questionnaires completed by Chinese students and intellectuals in the United States. The study concludes that Chinese intellectuals have migrated to the United States in increasing numbers each year. They have enjoyed more chances for academic advancement and more freedom and security to pursue educational activities and to participate socially in community life than they had at home, despite some trouble with the language, financial difficulties, discrimination, and prejudice. They have made tremendous professional contributions to American society, but the majority have expressed their desire to do the same for their home country.

67.   Chu, Goodwin C. "Student Expatriation: A Function of Relative Social Support." Sociology and Social Research 52 (January 1968): 174-84.
Chu examines the problem of student expatriation in a survey of 106 male graduate students from Asia, Latin America, the Middle East, and Africa; data was collected in a structured interview using both open-ended and multiple-choice questions. The potential expatriates were found more likely to be those who had rejected their own cultural values and accepted American cultural values. Expatriation was negatively related to social support from the home culture and positively related to social support from the host, indicating that social support from home culture plays a predominant role in determining whether a student will become an expatriate.

68.   Chu, Hung-ming; Yeh, Eng-Kung; Klein, M. H.; Alexander, A. A.; and Miller, M. H. "A Study of Chinese Students' Adjustment in the U. S. A." Acta Psychologica Taiwanica 13 (March 1971): 206-18.

The cross-cultural adjustment of 67 Chinese students and faculty at the
University of Hawaii was studied by administering a questionnaire
adapted from Yet et al., 1969. Results were compared with the two
groups studied by Yet et al. in Taiwan: 132 Chinese students about to
leave for study in the United States and 108 who were remaining in
Taiwan for graduate study. The questionnaire included a Mental Health
Questionnaire (MHQ), sections on motives and problems regarding study
in the United States, an adjective checklist for describing Chinese character and American character, and an attitude questionnaire evaluating
opinions and feelings about the life of a student in a different cultural
setting.

The students' concept of the character of Chinese and Americans,
their main reasons for coming to the United States, and their expected
difficulties showed a very consistent pattern in the three groups. Students in Hawaii, however, displayed greater symptoms of mental stress
suggesting that "adjustment to the new foreign environment was a strong
stress to the students." Moreover, "the significant negative correlation
between the scores of American character and the MHQ and the significantly higher scores of the MHQ among the students with high Chinese
Character and low American Character can be considered as a valid
variable to predict the future cross-cultural adjustment of Chinese
students at the time of their departure from Taiwan."

69.   Clark, Violet Esther Wuerfel. "Ghanaian Students in the United
        States." Ph.D. dissertation, University of Michigan, 1963.
Academic achievement and academic satisfaction among Ghanaian students were studied. Questionnaires were returned by 144 students (190
were mailed) and by the institution they attended. Academically successful students tended to be government-sponsored, were in the last
two phases of cultural adjustment, and attended accredited universities.
Significantly more students were satisfied who were 30 years or older,
married, held U.S. grants, or were self-sponsored, were in the
United States less than two years and expected to remain less than
three years.

70.   Clarke, Helen, and Ozawa, Martha. The Foreign Student in the
        United States. Madison, Wis.: University of Wisconsin, School
        of Social Work, 1970.
The first section of this book contains general information on international education. It reports, in part, on a study by Chester Ruedisili,
1963, "Foreign Students at the University of Wisconsin," in which
students and faculty responded to a questionnaire regarding numerous
phases of foreign student life on campus.

The second section, an account of Ozawa's experiences as a
graduate student at Wisconsin, offers a glimpse of foreign student
life—a valuable supplement to the technical data.

Clements, Forrest. See No. 8.

71.   Coan, Clark. "A Survey of the Housing of Foreign Students at
       the University of Kansas." Lawrence, Kans.: University of
       Kansas, Office of the Dean of Foreign Students, August 1966.
A questionnaire was administered to 529 foreign students (187
responded) on non-immigrant visas. Off-campus housing was found to
be inferior in quality; many students were unhappy with their roommates, which may reflect the University's on-campus policy of not
permitting foreign students to live with co-nationals. It is recommended that more attractive housing be found for graduate students.

72.   _____. "Foreign Student Housing Study." International Student
       Studies Series No. 22. Lawrence, Kans.: University of Kansas,
       Office of the Dean of Foreign Students, April 1969.
Housing arrangements for foreign students at the University of Kansas
were studied by means of a questionnaire completed by 302 students,
and a statistical break-down of data available to the Office of the Dean
of Foreign Students. It was found that the majority of foreign students
reside off-campus, in accommodations that did not offer both room and
board. Such students spend an average of $15 per week on food and
$56.61 per month on rent. Queried about International Houses, 53.5
percent had heard of them and 30 percent of the single students said
they would like to live in one. Preferences were for coeducational
housing, international food, and U. S. roommates.

73.   _____. "A Dean's Profile." International Student Studies Series
       No. 23. Lawrence, Kans.: University of Kansas, Office of the
       Dean of Foreign Students, 1969.
During the spring term 1969, the Dean of Foreign Students and his
assistant kept a log of their daily activities. Analysis of this log revealed that most of the officials' time was devoted to immigration
advising, counseling, and foreign student activities; least time was
spent on community relations, group meetings, and emergency
situations.

Coelho, George V. See No. 393.

74.   Coelho, Victor Anthony. "Students from India in the United States:
       An Exploratory Study of Some Cultural and Religious Attitudes."
       Ph.D. dissertation, Loyola University of Chicago, 1972.
Coelho uses a case study method to examine cultural and religious
attitudes of Indian students in the United States. Fifty-six students
from the Chicago area, representing India's major religions, participated in open-ended interviews and completed questionnaires. It was

found that increased length of exposure to the technological civilization of the United States produced evidence of less constancy in the students' religious observances. They indicated a desire for greater individual freedom and autonomy in social relationships between the sexes. More women than men believed they had been broadened culturally and were better prepared for their life associations.

75.   Coelho-Oudegeest, Maria de Lourdes Ivonne. "Cross-Cultural Counseling: A Study of Some Variables in the Counseling of Foreign Students." Ph. D. dissertation, University of Wisconsin, 1971.

Foreign student counseling by American university counselors can be regarded as a special instance of cross-cultural communication, thus requiring the examination of culture-bound communication variables associated with the process of counseling. Independent variables selected for this study were language skills and culture-bound attitudes of the foreign student, and a personality variable of the American counselor—openmindedness. The counseling relationship was selected as the dependent variable.

Two hypotheses, that a positive relationship exists between (1) the degree of counselor openmindedness scores and ratings of counselor empathy and warmth, and (2) between client vocabulary and cultural closeness scores and ratings of counselor genuineness and client depth of exploration, were tested in an experimental interview situation with 11 counselors and 24 foreign students. The data was treated statistically by means of analyses of variance and correlation studies. The results did not support the first hypothesis and supported partially the second.

76.   Cohen, Robert Douglas. "The Functions of a Co-National Group of Foreign Students in New York City." Ph. D. dissertation, 1971.

The purpose of this case study was to describe and analyze the functions of a compatriot or co-national group of foreign students in an urban setting. The population chosen for the study were 35 Kenyan students and former students resident in New York City in the summer of 1970. A structured interview was held with each of the respondents; several respondents were interviewed several times for corroboration of the data gathered.

Residence patterns in New York City showed an avoidance of dormitory and host-national residential situations; the Kenyans lived initially with one another, yet eventually fulfilled mutual expectations that one would "find a place of one's own." Data gathered regarding extend of contact among Kenyans revealed much greater contact among Kenyans than between Kenyans and Americans. Two major functions of the co-national group were discovered: the friendship function, which fostered accessibility among co-nationals for helpful interaction regarding personal problems; and the instrumental function, which allowed co-nationals to expect, seek, and secure help from one another in finding residence, getting into a college, and finding employment. The co-national group did not function to further direct contact with the home country; it served only as a local and temporary surrogate for the home culture and society.

It is suggested that the co-national group should be recognized and utilized by the foreign student adviser as a powerful and helpful resource for the welfare of foreign students.

77. Colacicco, Mary Grace. "A Comparison of Item Responses on the MMPI by Selected American and Foreign Students." Ph. D. dissertation, Purduc University, 1970.

Two groups of male foreign students, Indians (53) and Latin Americans (58), were matched to two groups of male American students on age, school, and classification. All 222 subjects were administered a Personal Information Form and the Minnesota Multiphasic Personality Inventory. The data showed the Latin American group to be more prone to illness, more sensitive to others, and more prone to depression than the American student group. The Latin American students also manifested a tendency to behave in unusual or socially inappropriate ways as measured by comparisons on the MMPI.

The Indians and the matched group of Americans were graduate students. Indian students' responses suggested that they are more sensitive to their environment, more illness-prone, more depressed, and more withdrawn from social contacts than their American student peers. The Indians also appear more compulsive and seem to behave in a more unusual manner than American students.

When comparing the two groups of foreign students, a few differences were found. However, most of the differences were not consistently directional in a manner which allows clear interpretation.

78. College Entrance Examination Board. Financial Planning for Study in the United States: A Guide for Students from Other Countries. By Martena Sasnett. New York, 1967.

This booklet is for students who are considering leaving their home countries to enter a college or university in the United States. Its purpose is to provide these students with information about costs of study, what responsibilities they will be expected to assume in meeting these costs, what help may be available from other sources, and how they should plan for the financial aspect of their visit.

79. _____. University, Government, and the Foreign Graduate Student. A Summary of the Colloquium on the Foreign Graduate

Student held at Wingspread, Racine, Wisconsin, 30-31 March
1967. New York, 1969.
This colloquium, attended primarily by graduate deans, focused on
broad questions relating to foreign student graduate programs. Noting
that foreign graduate students sponsored as part of an institution-to-
institution arrangement have the best possibility of being matched to an
appropriate U. S. institution, and that growth in international programs
poses questions regarding the institutional role and functions of the university in the design of its programs and treatment of foreign students,
the participants recommended (1) that institutions aim at a "critical
mass" of five to ten percent foreign students in graduate programs;
(2) that special efforts be made to orient prospective students to the
U. S. educational system; (3) that a double standard for admission and
qualification for degrees has no justification in universities; and (4) that
to maintain the recommended proportion of foreign students, additional
scholarship funds must be sought.

The report contains three papers presented at the colloquium.
The first, "The Foreign Graduate Student: Old Assumptions, New
Questions," by George P. Springer, stresses the academic objectives
of the university, suggesting that foreign student procedures be accom-
modated to those for domestic graduate students, and recommends a
computerized two-way information system making available detailed
information on U. S. graduate programs and on qualifications of prospective students. Daly C. Lavergne, in "University and Government:
Two Views of the Foreign Graduate Student," discusses the mutual
goals of government and institution in assuming the responsibility for
international education and notes the need for greater concern for the
needs and goals of the individual trainee. "An Appraisal of the Behavior
of Universities in International Education," by Albert G. Sims, urges
financial aid which will strengthen universities as educational institutions without involving them in policy formation which is more properly
the role of government. (See also No. 431.)

Colligan, Francis J. See No. 82.

80.   Comay, Peter Yochanan. "International Migration of Profes-
      . sional Manpower: The Canadian Case." Ph. D. dissertation,
      Princeton University, 1969.
The human capital model is shown to be directly applicable to a study
of labor responsiveness to pecuniary and non-pecuniary incentives. A
model is developed to explain Canada-U. S. migration of professionals;
the model is then applied to survey data on the migration of Canadians.
Study in the U. S. is shown to be the most important single explanatory
variable; those who reach the doctorate level are most likely to migrate
and least likely to return. Employee mobility and geographic mobility

are strongly interconnected. French ethnicity, birth outside the United States, family formation variables, and age retard migration, while distance of travel plays a very minor role. No evidence is found of quality selection in the migratory move to the United States. This is not true for the return trip, where the most able are least likely to return. Salary differentials and employment opportunities are statistically significant though weak in their influence.

The costs and benefits of Canadian emigration to the United States are also assessed. Net benefits are estimated for study abroad, taking account of probabilities of migration and return, the relative costs of education in the two countries, and discounted lifetime earnings. Some suggestions are made for action by the Canadian government.

81.   Committee on Educational Interchange Policy. The Foreign Student: Exchangee or Immigrant? New York, May 1958.
The records of four agencies sponsoring foreign-student exchange for 30 years were studied: the Belgian American Educational Foundation, the Commonwealth Fund, IIE, and the Rockefeller Foundation. Of 10,598 former foreign grantees of all nationalities, nine percent are now resident in the United States. Students remain or return to the United States for various reasons: friendship, better professional opportunities, difficulties in personal readjustment at home, changes in political outlook of the home government. Immigration does, however, provide benefits to the United States through cross-fertilization of ideas and better international understanding.

To increase the likelihood of return, administrators should select students who seek training in fields relevant to their country's needs, and who have psychological roots in their homeland. U. S. administrators can encourage students to retain contact with home and, through embassy contacts, terminal orientation and skillful counseling, urge students to consider all factors before making a decision to immigrate. While foreign governments can offer better inducements, students may resent such regulation.

82.   Committee on the Foreign Student in American Colleges and Universities. The College, the University, and the Foreign Student. By Francis J. Colligan, et al. New York, 1963.
The international commitments of American colleges and universities are permanent and increasing. Foreign student programs now in operation should be viewed as part of the total international commitment of each institution and should be coordinated and interrelated with all other aspects of that commitment.

Colleges and universities must provide leadership in assessing program objectives, and in cooperating with government and private agencies in achieving them. Current programs can be improved through greater dissemination of information on U. S. institutions, more flexible admission standards, English language training centers, continuing orientation programs, professional academic advising and personal counseling, and greater budgetary support for foreign student services.

83.   The Committee on the International Migration of Talent. Modernization and the Migration of Talent. New York: Education and World Affairs, 1970.

See No. 84. This pamphlet presents conclusions and recommendations which appear in the final chapters of the book.

84.   _____, Charles V. Kidd, Chairman. The International Migration of High-Level Manpower: Its Impact on the Development Process. New York: Praeger, 1970.

This volume contains regional studies of migration and its impact on modernization, prepared by different authors under the aegis of Education and World Affairs. The regional studies cover East and Southeast Asia, South Asia, the Middle East, Middle Africa, Latin America, Europe, and Australia.

Migration is presently fostered by two circumstances: oversupply of highly educated persons in developing countries, in relation to demand, and the reverse imbalance, namely undersupply in advanced countries. But migration cannot be explained solely through economic supply and demand analysis. Some people migrate not because there are no jobs at home, but because they see no professional future, because they believe they can work more productively elsewhere, because they are not in sympathy with the aims and methods of their governments, or because they do not have professional associates to stimulate them. As a result, it is estimated that worldwide migration from less to more developed countries averages 300,000 persons per year, some 15 percent of whom have professional or technical training. An even smaller group, some 3,000 to 5,000, are persons of the highest ability whose loss can be particularly serious to the home country.

Patterns of movement are varied and complex. The major losers, Indian, Iran, Turkey, Pakistan, the Philippines, Taiwan, Korea, Greece, Colombia, and Argentina, are countries which have expanded educational facilities faster than is warranted by the existence of satisfying career opportunities.

The process of modernization—economic and social development—requires the adoption of technologies and strategies based on indigenous talent. Consideration of manpower required for rural development, e.g., a prime essential for the sustained growth of many countries, reveals both the tremendous gap between the output of many university systems and national needs and the capacity of a technologically oriented segment of the economy to absorb people. Such programs depend on the presence of top-level people possessing professional and political skills and a quality of personal dedication. It is thus of concern that mobility tends to rise with levels of training. Significantly, factors such as opportunities to be creative, a chance to use one's professional training effectively, to work with respected associates, feelings of usefulness and esteem, are as important or more important than higher salaries in affecting migration of exceptional people.

85.   Coombs, Philip H. "International Educational Exchange: A Work for Many Hands." Higher Education 18 (September 1961): 3-6, 18-19.

On the 15th anniversary of the signing of the Fulbright Act, Coombs, a former Assistant Secretary of State for Educational and Cultural Affairs, assesses the accomplishments and failures of the international educational exchange program. Statistics show that the Fulbright and Smith-Mundt programs have reached a cumulative total of about 82,000 grantees; yet the U. S. Government sponsors only ten percent of the foreign students in America. Important advances have recently been made by the government in assuming greater responsibility for non-sponsored students and in achieving better coordination of private and federal efforts.

The increasing numbers of foreigners who will be arriving in the 1960's requires improvements in the structure and administration of our exchange programs. Areas of particular concern are: better pre-departure and academic placement; tailoring of academic programs to special needs of foreign students; increased community contacts; creation of an admissions and guidance office in each major contributing country to serve as a clearinghouse for information on academic and federal programs; increased follow-up on returnees.

86.   _____. The Fourth Dimension of Foreign Policy. New York: Harper and Row, 1964.

It is Coombs' thesis that educational and cultural activities comprise a fourth dimension of foreign policy that can bolster political, economic, and military elements, adding flexibility, breadth, and depth. To fulfill its proper role, educational policies must be shaped by a clear set of objectives, better planning, and more vigorous and imaginative administration, and must have greater political and financial support.

87.   Copeland, W. A. "Universities Cooperate to Stem the 'Brain Drain.'" Development Digest 7 (April 1969): 58-61.

This article, excerpted from "The Pahlavi-Pennsylvania Contract," International Development Review 10, September 1968, pp. 21-23, describes the creation of an American-style university in Iran, Pahlavi University, a joint program with the University of Pennsylvania. The program has achieved notable success in attracting Iranian graduates with American training back to their country.

88.   Cormack, Margaret L. "International Development through Educational Exchange." Review of Educational Research 38, no. 3 (June 1968): 293-302.

In this article, Cormack reviews studies of foreign students in the United States published during the 1950's and early 1960's. The behavioral research which identified the attitudinal U-curve is cited as are other significant studies illuminating the problems of adjustment among various national groups. Various methodologies are discussed and suggestions made for new research aims and approaches.

89.   _____. "International Educational Exchange: Visas to What?" Exchange 5, no. 2 (Fall 1969): 46-63.

This article examines the question of international educational exchange from several different perspectives. Summarizing the history of exchange, 1945-1969, Cormack traces the evolution of American thought on the subject and discusses the motivation of those who study or teach abroad. She recommends a course of future research and assesses the implications and functions of international educational exchange as part of the world community.

90.   _____. Review of Statistics of Students Abroad, 1962-1968. Comparative Education Review 17 (June 1973): 276-78.

Cormack is highly critical of the UNESCO statistics, largely because they are so limited in scope. Although its findings are valuable in showing a few basic trends, UNESCO should now begin to ask "why" questions: Why is there a shift toward the arts? Why do students leave their own countries for higher education? Why do they go to specific countries? And why do they pursue specific fields? The study is also criticized for its over-broad geographical categories (Eastern Europe and the USSR) and its similarly broad categorizations of subject matter fields. It is concluded that UNESCO would be of great service to international education if it provided qualitative analyses that illuminate educational reality.

91.   _____. "American Students in India: Ambassadors or Cultural Polluters?" International Studies Quarterly 17 (September 1973): 337-57.

In this article, Cormack evaluates the four-year-old Callison-in-Bangalore Program through which American students spend their sophomore year at the Indian university. While the general aim of "broadening one's horizons" has been achieved by the program, more specific aims must be formulated which consider the negative experiences of some students and avoid a callous exploitation of the Indian hosts. The major purpose must be intercultural education, based on "a clear intercultural aim, appropriate selection and orientation in relation to this aim, a continuous intercultural seminar in the field, and an integration of the intercultural experience in the ensuing college curriculum."

_____. See No. 398.

92.   Correa, Joseph M. "Intercultural Interaction and the World-
      mindedness of College Students." Ph.D. dissertation, University
      of Washington, 1970.
The hypothesis tested was that American students who have more intercultural interaction with foreigners, i.e., friendship with foreign students, travel and/or study abroad, or foreign-born parents, will exhibit a high sense of world-mindedness. Data were collected on a random sample of 24 undergraduate students at the University of Washington in 1969. Analysis indicated that the students were significantly more worldminded than the general population of the United States but none of the three intercultural factors hypothesized was found to be significant.

93.   Cortes, Josefina R. Factors Associated with the Migration of
      High-Level Persons from the Philippines to the U. S. A.
      Stanford, Calif.: Stanford International Development Education
      Center, 1970.
A sample of Philippine students who had studied in the United States from 1960 to 1965 was surveyed by questionnaire in 1968. From the questionnaire data, the study compares those students who migrated to those who did not in terms of their "anchorage" in the home country, their relative valuation of opportunities in their home country and country of destination, and their motivational orientation. The results show that the propensity to migrate is higher among persons who are weakly anchored in the Philippines, who perceive little opportunity for themselves in that country, who are young and single, who have no job to return to, who are in fields such as physical sciences and engineering, and who have succeeded in getting a degree from a U. S. institution. Government support, when given during the period of study abroad, substantially attenuates the influence of all these factors and considerably weakens a person's propensity to emigrate. The study suggests more Philippine government attention to attitudes of prospective overseas fellows and a concern for improving the "pull" of the Philippines in attracting both sponsored and non-sponsored fellows to return.

Cotner, Thomas E. See No. 394.

94.   Cowan, Susie. English Proficiency and Bicultural Attitudes of
       Japanese Students. Tokyo: The Taishukan Publishing Company,
       1968. Also available in the journal Eigo Kyoiku (The English
       Teachers' Magazine) 17, 1968.
Continuing a research project begun by B. Spolsky and F. Migliazza
in the English as a Foreign Language Program at Indiana University
which was designed to show that foreign students whose overall integrative motivation is high (+IM) have achieved a higher standard of
English proficiency than those whose integrative motivation is low
(-IM), this report seeks to relate the English proficiency and bicultural
attitudes of Japanese students who have all studied English for about
the same length of time in Japan. Data were also obtained from a taped
interview and two questionnaires, the first listing 30 adjectives which
are traits in a person's value system, the second listing reasons for
coming to America.

Figures based on the results show: (1) students with a high total
English score tend to have a +IM sign; (2) length of stay in America is
not a significant factor in determining whether a student has a + or -
sign; (3) there is no positive relationship between reasons for coming
to America and English ability; and (4) most of the students considered
learning English "rather important." The final conclusion is that
Japanese students with high IM—who tend to become somewhat "Americanized"—tend to become better speakers of English.

95.   Craig, W. Bradford. A Report on the African Scholarship Pro-
       gram of American Universities, 1960-70. N.p., n.d.
The ASPAU program originated in 1959-60 as a cooperative venture by
American universities, Nigerian educators, U. S. foundations, and
AAI, in which 24 Nigerian students were enrolled in 24 American colleges. In 1961, AAI contracted with ICA (AID) to become the administering agency for an expanded program providing scholarship support
to 1,594 students from Sub-Saharan Africa, 1961-70.

Selection and placement procedures were outstanding features of
the ASPAU program. Candidates were tested and evaluated by binational committees in each country, using standardized forms which
facilitated final selection by U. S. admissions officers. Various orientation programs were devised, the most successful being a ten-day
stay at Putney, Vermont, headquarters of the Experiment in International Living. As a result of these procedures, plus adequate funding
and continued support and guidance from ASPAU's Cambridge office,
91 percent of the students completed their degree courses; only 136
withdrew prior to completion. As a program to provide trained manpower, ASPAU might be considered only moderately successful,

since only 711 of the 1,338 graduates (53.14 percent) have returned to Africa.

Major problems encountered in the administration of the program were (1) conflict between the training goals of AID and the educative goals of the participating institutions; and (2) rising costs of U. S. education and changes in funding priorities of both educational institutions and U. S. agencies.

96.   Cussler, Margaret T. Review of Selected Studies Affecting International Educational and Cultural Affairs. College Park, Md.: University of Maryland, 1962.

This study analyzes the assumptions and conclusions, the strengths and weaknesses, of major private- and government-sponsored research into cross-cultural education. Future lines of research are suggested; appendices include a survey of relevant doctoral dissertations 1953-61, a bibliography of studies reviewed, and an annotated reading list.

The governmental evaluator has been primarily concerned with proving the effectiveness of programs with survey research focusing on returnees several years after their U. S. sojourn. Aside from the problem of effectiveness of attitude questionnaires in "polite" cultural areas is the lack of adequate funding for extensive overseas research. Nevertheless, the studies under review offer a variety of rich data on background of grantees, value of orientation programs, changes in adjustment by length of stay, status sensitivity, alienation, dissemination of information by returnees.

Review of research leads to the following suggestions for future policy. (1) International education should be based on the spirit of free enquiry rather than on concern for the image of America. (2) Education of former colonials should stress the acquisition of skills with which to develop their own institutions in their own way. (3) Selective adoption of Western technology may be preferable to total Westernization.

97.   Darian, Steven G. "A History of the Teaching of English as a Foreign Language in American Colleges and Universities, 1880-1965." Ph.D. dissertation, New York University, 1968.

The growth of English-language teaching in the United States for foreigners was stimulated by the influx of non-English speaking immigrants beginning in 1890; a heightened awareness, brought about by World War I, of the need to assimilate them; the flight of educated people from Europe prior to World War II; the increasing need of emerging countries to develop trained personnel; and the spread of English as an international language. Early teaching methods used materials built around a semantic topic rather than a specific grammar pattern.

Contrary to popular opinion, the aural-oral method is used less often than writing in the teaching of grammar, at least at the intermediate and advanced levels today.

98.   Das, Man Singh. "Effect of Foreign Students' Attitudes toward Returning to the Country of Origin on the National Loss of Professional Skills." Ph.D. dissertation, Oklahoma State University, 1969.

Data from this study were obtained by questionnaire from 1,400 male foreign students enrolled for the fall semester of the 1968-69 academic year at 20 American colleges and universities. All were on F-1 (student) visas but had secured full-time jobs as a part of their practical training. The random sample was drawn from 31 less-developed and developing countries of Asia, Africa, and Latin America.

Major findings were: Foreign students who have studied in the United States for two years or more and are over 25 years of age are less likely to return to their homes. Students from the less-developed nations are more likely to return than are those from the developed countries. Privately supported students whose families are at home are less likely to remain in the United States than are those whose families accompanied them. Students whose countries provide good employment opportunities are less likely to remain, as are students in agriculture and engineering. Most foreign students do not plan to return home immediately upon completion of their studies; they wish to obtain practical training first.

It is stressed that this is a study of attitudes rather than of behavior.

99.   _____. "The 'Brain Drain' Controversy in a Comparative Perspective." Social Science 46 (January 1971): 16-25.

Summarizing the research reported in No. 98, Das observes that in some cases, migration is eufunctional to host and home countries as well as to individuals. This positive aspect should be more appropriately termed "brain gain" or "brain exchange." Brain drain occurs when migration becomes dysfunctional in that it retards the development of the home country.

100.   Davis, F. James. "Cultural Perspectives of Middle Eastern Students in America." The Middle East Journal 14 (Summer 1960): 250-64.

This study used questionnaires to elicit views of American life from Middle Eastern students at the Universities of Minnesota and Michigan. The general hypotheses tested were: (1) Middle Eastern students experience some surprise upon contact with American life; (2) Middle Eastern students have favorable views of some aspects of American life and unfavorable views of others; (3) Middle Eastern students in America experience problems of cultural conflict; (4) there are differences in cultural perspective among Middle Eastern students in America according to sex, marital status, native country, field of study, and length of time spent in the United States. Results confirmed the general hypotheses.

101. _____. "The Two-Way Mirror and the U-Curve: America as seen by Turkish Students Returned Home." Sociology and Social Research 56 (October 1971): 29-43.
The two-way mirror and the U-curve of favorability to America are patterns previously reported for foreign students in the United States. This study, based on questionnaires and interviews of returnees in Turkey, sought to determine whether these patterns persist over time. It was also hypothesized that favorability would be related to the student's perception of goal-achievement during the sojourn.
Both the two-way mirror and the U-curve of favorability by length of stay were found: those who returned home during the third (or for some attitudes the second) year tended to be less favorable towards America, while those who returned either very soon or after several years tended to be very favorable. Regarding the second hypothesis, some of the findings were supportive, some ambiguous, and some contradictory. There was enough support to warrant further thought and research in terms of goal-achievement and deprivation.

102. _____. "Problems of Development in Turkey as Seen by Turks Returned Home from Study in American Universities." Sociology and Social Research 57 (July 1973): 429-42.
Questionnaire data from 222 returnees to Turkey (one-half of whom were also interviewed) who studied in American universities from 1957 to 1968 indicated a range of developmental problems centering on Turkey's major social problems. Respondents are characterized as "advanced moderns." Dissatisfied with the slowness of change, they were confident of contributing to national development and envisioned a variety of alternative paths for achieving it. The United States was one of the most listed "guideline countries."

103. Davis, James L. Work Experience as a Component of Educational Exchange: A Study of Exchange Visitor Program P-III-4320. New York: Council on International Educational Exchange, 1973.
The purposes of this study are two-fold: (1) to describe the nature of the cross-cultural work experience and examine the extent to which this experience involves the visiting student in the life of this society; (2) to assess the impact of such involvement upon the student in terms

of his understanding of, and attitudes toward, the United States. Out of the 2,888 British and 2,700 Irish students participating in the summer of 1972, eight of each nationality were randomly selected as respondents. Results are based on two questionnaires and two personal interviews.

The working student participates in American life through his job, his place of residence, through contacts with fellow workers, and through efforts of American friends and relatives, but the depth of involvement ranges from the spectator level to full involvement; most are in between. Participation is facilitated by an effective orientation program and by having a pre-arranged job, but most important are personal efforts by friends and relatives. Attitudes toward the summer job fell into three categories: frustration, satisfaction, and fulfillment.

The first few weeks of the sojourn are crucial. By mid-summer, those who will show personal growth and evidence of positive change tend to be substantially involved in at least one aspect of American life. They develop more positive attitudes toward America, while uninvolved students are likely to reinforce or create their own critical attitudes. Both positive and negative attitudes persist at least six months after return home.

104. Davis, James M. "Foreign Students in the Two-Year College." Exchange 7, no. 2 (Fall 1971): 25-32.

This article examines those aspects of two-year community colleges which relate to foreign students and makes specific recommendations regarding admissions, orientation, housing, advising, etc., by which the college may ensure a successful sojourn.

105. Day, Jerry Richard. "A Study of the Differential Effects of Length of Time in the United States on Foreign Graduate and Undergraduate Students with Regard to the Number, Severity, and Category Groupings of Problems He Experiences." Ph.D. dissertation, Oklahoma State University, 1968.

This study sought to determine if graduate and undergraduate foreign students' personal problems significantly increase, decrease, or fluctuate over a length of time in the United States. One hundred and ninety-nine graduate and undergraduate students at Oklahoma State University completed the Michigan International Student Problem Inventory. Respondents were divided into three time groups consisting of students here from one to ten months, 11 to 21 months, and 22 months or more.

Results showed that foreign students at Oklahoma do not experience a greater number of problems as their stay in the United States lengthens, but that specific kinds of problems they experience may change.

106. DeAntoni, Edward. "Foreign Student Career Counseling: A
      Personal View." Exchange 7, no. 3 (Winter 1972): 91-102.
DeAntoni, Assistant Director of the Career Center at Cornell, discusses the problems encountered by the counselor assisting foreign
students in job hunting. In his experience, satisfactory placement
depends on the counselor's knowledge of the student's cultural patterns
of socialization and life-style. Attempts by the Center to provide
liaison between student and home country indicate that countries are
often unwilling to cooperate in attracting nationals home.

107. Deluga, Marvin Raymond. "An Analysis of the Selection Proced-
      ures of Foreign Students at the Undergraduate Level in the United
      States." Ph.D. dissertation, University of Idaho, 1970.
Through a questionnaire sent to 1,231 U. S. educational institutions
(returned by 631), it is concluded that, although IIE, AACRAO, and
EWA materials are widely disseminated, admissions officers and
foreign student advisers generally do not have the specialized training
necessary for evaluation of foreign credentials.
      The diversity of institutions of higher learning makes it impos-
sible to develop a clear-cut controllable series of programs across the
United States, but a majority of admissions officers desire the establishment of a central clearinghouse for the evaluation of credentials or
the reinforcement of existing agencies which would perform the same
function.

108. DeMarco, James Arthur. "The United States National Commis-
      sion for UNESCO: The Higher Education Role." Ph.D. disser-
      tation, Catholic University of America, 1967.
For this discussion of the organization and operation of the United
States National Commission, relevant to its Higher Education role,
100 prominent citizens who compose the Commission and the national
organizations whom they represent provided data by means of questionnaire and interview as did other key persons in higher education and
government.

109. Deutsch, Steven E. International Aspects of Higher Education
      and Exchange: A Community Study. Cleveland, Ohio: Western
      Reserve University, August 1965.
A comprehensive community study was conducted of the foreign students and the international aspects of five colleges and universities in
the Cleveland area. During a two-year period, questionnaires were
administered to samples of foreign students, host families, and American students and faculties. Respondents totaled 1,018. At the same
time, interviews were conducted with educational administrators, labor
and business leaders, staff members of the Council on World Affairs,

and others involved in international exchange programs. Questions probed included: (1) perception of international student programs, (2) social interaction between foreign students and Americans, and (3) evaluation of services and programs in the host community. Among the conclusions were that foreign students interact to a considerable extent with American families, that most felt committed to return to their native countries, and that considerable interest in international education and exchange is emerging in all quarters.

110. _____. "The Impact of Cross-Cultural Relations on Campus."
    Sociology and Social Research 53 (January 1969): 137-46.
This study addresses the questions of student interest and participation in international programs, the relationship between attitudes and participation, the nature of cross-cultural relations involving American students on the campus, and the relationship between educational experiences and career patterns. A carefully selected, stratified, random sample of 376 students from three colleges and universities was surveyed by questionnaire.

    Results show that American students are quite internationally oriented and supportive of international educational exchange programs. There is a complex of relationships which form a configuration in which this attitude is nurtured, and in which cross-cultural relations with foreign students play an important part.

111. _____. International Education and Exchange: A Sociological
    Analysis. Cleveland, Ohio: Case Western Reserve University
    Press, 1970.
In this book, Deutsch reports more fully on the research described in No. 109. Findings are summarized in terms of the various players in the international educational exchange system.

    Foreign students, primarily male graduate students from the less-developed nations of the world, studying engineering and natural and physical sciences were academically satisfied although many felt that much of the theoretical knowledge with which they were presented was inapplicable to practical problems they would face in their home countries. Language was seen as a problem though apparently not a severe one. Most planned to return home after completing their studies.

    American students were interested in and supportive of international education. Those more socially integrated into campus life were more likely to interact with foreign students. Cross-cultural interaction appears to be a product of the individual's international orientation but also seemed to lead to greater world-mindedness.

    Faculty members were generally enthusiastic about international education but were not very knowledgeable about programs or services provided for foreign students.

The survey of college and university administrators showed that
educational institutions generally lacked articulated policies for international education. Administrators were aware of developments in
international education in other colleges and universities but advisory
reports on aspects of international education were seldom read by top
administrators or had little impact on program development and
implementation.

Community hosts to foreign students were found to be active,
well-educated persons who were well above average in income and
occupational prestige. They viewed international education programs
as service-oriented and were less cognizant of their own personal
rewards than they were of the benefits to the foreign students.

It was concluded that there was a considerable interest in international education in all quarters but apparently more interest in student exchanges than faculty exchanges, and more interest in internationalizing the curriculum than in implementing technical assistance
programs. American students and faculty members believe courses in
foreign languages, comparative cultures and institutions, and in non-
Western studies should be further emphasized in the curriculum.

Several research and policy recommendations were made.
Deutsch notes that the most obvious message in most reports on international education is that coordination and planning are of basic importance, particularly on the part of institutions of higher education. It is
recommended that research be carried out in a variety of college and
university settings with the purpose of understanding the history of
international educational interest and in obtaining insights into how a
school develops a climate favorable to the development of such interest.
Large-scale research is also recommended to assess the effect of
external agents of change upon American institutions of higher education and to better ascertain the role of the various organizations,
agencies, and foundations in influencing the international commitment
of colleges and universities.

112.   Development Education and Training Research Institute, The
       American University. Training Institution Profile Report:
       Special Participants at the University of Missouri. Washington,
       D. C., June 1972.
Between July 1967 and February 1972, 37 AID participants who had
special training programs at the University of Missouri took part in
DETRI exit interviews in Washington, D. C. Based on these interviews,
this report presents an overview and statistical analysis of the participants' evaluation of the Missouri program. Most participants, studying in six-month agriculture, health, or education programs were
satisfied with their training, finding the observational and on-the-job
aspects the most relevant.

In only one respect did the Missouri participants differ significantly from participants at all other institutions: proportionately more
indicated that they either disagreed with or were unclear about the
selection of the University as one of their training sites in the United
States.

113. _____. Final Report: International Training Assessment Program.
     By Paul Kimmel, William C. Ockey, and Herman J. Sander.
     Washington, D. C., October 1972.
This report describes three projects of the Development Education and
Training Research Institute (DETRI) under contract to AID-OIT.

(1) Between November 1966 and March 1972, DETRI conducted
exit interviews in Washington, D. C., with 10,825 AID participants
from about 75 different countries, to obtain reliable information on
what participants felt and thought about their United States experiences
before returning home. Interview instruments consisted of a standardized, structured questionnaire, an unstructured but focused oral interview for individual trainees, and for Observation Training Team
participants, a standardized structured oral interview in a group
session. Three major analyses were made of the data to determine
which events and reactions were most strongly related to participants'
satisfactions with their total training and social-personal experiences
and overall evaluations.

(2) In a related project, DETRI reviewed and evaluated possible
means of assessing participants' understanding of and attitudes to
Title IX emphases on "democratic processes and institutions" as they
experience them in the United States, and degree of motivation to
carry out these principles in the home country. The study concluded
that (1) no instrument is currently available for a pre-departure
assessment of AID participants' understanding of popular participation,
(2) an instrument could be developed but it would measure attitudes
rather than behavior, and (3) a general set of items for all participants
would probably not be feasible. Instead it was suggested that measures
of management potential in which assessees engage in individual and
group exercises under the observation of experts in training and evaluation could be adapted by AID to measure participants' skills as change
agents.

(3) Between 1 July 1967 and 31 December 1970, DETRI conducted
a survey of the orientation of AID trainees at the Washington International Center (WIC). Most found the orientation useful and the atmosphere congenial. DETRI recommendations for improving the orientation
included making more use of trainees' information and experiences,
placing a new emphasis on the trainee's social accommodation, and
improving the clarity of the lecture presentations. (See No. 10)

114. DeVine, Bruce Frederic. "The U. S. Student Exchange Program: Reverse Foreign Aid?" Ph.D. dissertation, Claremont Graduate School and University Center, 1971.

This study attempts to test the hypothesis that the United States, despite its provision of higher education resources for vast numbers of students from developing countries, gains financially on student exchange with these countries as a result primarily of the non-return of a minority of such students.

Utilizing cost-benefit analysis and human-capital theory applied to data for 1964-65, DeVine offers the following conclusions. (1) When low (a priori) rates are used to discount human capital values, the United States is a net beneficiary on the exchange transaction. At higher, and probably more realistic rates, the United States is a net contributor of resources to the developing world. (2) Effects of the dollar balance on participant welfare depend on the particular standards set by each when the exchange was entered. In particular, less-developed country welfare will not suffer if the goal was to invest scarce social resources wisely, importing educational services in exchange for relatively cheaper, home-produced goods and services. Student non-return then becomes merely another factor affecting terms of trade between the United States and the developing bloc. (3) Comparison of net balance figures with assistance given by the United States in other forms indicates a range from -1.5 to +4.6 percent of the latter, depending both on the discount rate used to compute student values and on the definition of foreign aid.

115. Donahue, Francis. "The International Student: His Six Roles." Clearinghouse 45 (September 1970): 51-55.

Donahue describes the foreign student's six roles and proposes ways in which the university can foster their fulfillment. The student is discussed as a student, as a person of culture, as a future professional, as a political individual, as a representative of a foreign culture, and as an individual seeking to make friends and enjoy the intercultural experience.

116. Dorai, Gopalakrishnan Chidambaram. "Economics of the International Flow of Students: A Cost-Benefit Analysis." Ph.D. dissertation, Wayne State University, 1967.

In this dissertation, an economic analysis of costs and benefits of foreign education has been undertaken. The theoretical work draws upon models of migration as well as the "human capital" approach to education and training.

The empirical work was designed to test the hypothesis that the non-return of Indian students educated in the United States was motivated by economic considerations. Calculations of various benefit/cost ratios showed that whereas it would be worthwhile for a self-financed Indian student to undertake undergraduate education in the United States and return to India immediately for employment when future Indian incomes are discounted at a five-percent interest rate, it would not pay to do so if we use a ten-percent rate.

The social benefits to the United States resulting from non-return of Indian students during the period 1958-66, measured by the capitalized value of their lifetime savings, far exceed the associated social costs (or savings foregone) by India.

117.   Doseck, Fred P., and Wenger, Roy E. "The Foreign Experiences of Kent State University Faculty Members." Kent, Ohio: Kent State University, 1967.

A study of the foreign experiences of 654 faculty members at Kent State University was undertaken to determine if the university was "keeping pace in contributing to programs of an international nature." Findings from the questionnaire survey relate to the extent of time spent outside the United States, the number and location of countries visited, languages known, and purposes of the trips.

118.   Doty, Theodore E. "Washington State University in West Pakistan, 1954-1969: An Evaluation of Technical Assistance to Higher Education for Agricultural and Economic Development." Ph.D. dissertation, Washington State University, 1971.

The study found that the West Pakistan Project had been relatively successful in meeting its objectives in the field but there was only minimal impact on the donor institution (Washington State University). The essentially qualitative nature of the evaluation prompts the author to underline the advisability of programming evaluation of a project by means of prespecified performance indicators.

119.   Dow, Tsung I. "The Impact of Chinese Students Returned from America with Emphasis on the Chinese Revolution, 1911-1949." Florida Atlantic University, n.d.

Official Chinese policy to educate young men and women in the West began in 1872, the great majority coming to the United States. Yet they played a smaller role in the Chinese revolutions than students returning from Japan and the U.S.S.R. Today, U.S.-educated Chinese are virtually excluded from the decision-making process. This situation results from the scientific and technical orientation of U.S. training, the cultural gap between China and the West, the expatriation and alienation resulting from America's high standard of living.

Although they did not transform China in the image of America, American-trained students have achieved certain significant objectives: (1) Western science and technology have been transferred to China, thus lessening China's inferiority complex vis-a-vis the West; (2) the American mass education system has replaced the ancient Chinese examination system; (3) American-trained scientists and engineers continue to form the nucleus of China's technological elite.

120. Dupeux, Genevieve. "Etudiants etrangers au Travail" (Foreign Students at Work). Revue de Psychologie des Peuples 23 (September 1968): 276-87.
This study was based on personal experience of teaching foreign students, and an inquiry with these same students (N = 411). Identities were established for the students according to groups. Belonging to a nationality group appeared to constitute a separate element for the students. A correspondence was found between the self-image of the group, constructed from the responses of the students, and the commonly adopted stereotype which defines a particular national character. One of the reasons for this surprising conformity is perhaps that, in a defensive position in a culture which is not their own, foreign students unburden the problem of their personal experience on others.

121. Eberhard, Wolfram. "Problems of Students Returning to Asia." Exchange 5, no. 4 (Spring 1970): 41-50.
Eberhard recommends two policies which would mitigate the problems which confront foreign students upon returning home. The first is a guarantee that students who return to assume a research or teaching position may make a return visit to the United States after two or three years in order to keep up with progress in their fields. The second is that the host institution establish a common study program whereby former teachers, colleagues, and foreign students exchange visits every two or more years.

122. Eddy, John. "Factors and Guidelines in Foreign Student Guidance." Journal of College Student Personnel 13 (May 1972): 252-54.
Eddy offers 12 guidelines to institutions regarding the admission and advising of foreign students.

123. Education and World Affairs Study Committee on Foreign Student Affairs. "The Foreign Student: Whom Shall We Welcome?" In International Education: Past, Present, Problems and Prospects. Selected readings to supplement H.R. 14643 prepared for the House Committee on Education and Labor by the Task Force on International Education, John Brademas, Chairman, pp. 335-47. Washington, D. C.: U. S. Government Printing Office, 1966.
Foreign student policies followed at present by many U. S. colleges and universities are ambiguous and conflicting; in particular, selection

and admissions policies need to be formulated which are congruent with
the purposes of the institution.

Admissions decisions are hampered by the lack of reliable information on prospective students, and of adequate means for evaluating
foreign credentials. Additional considerations are the degree to which
admissions policies should be tied to the manpower priorities of developing countries, the relevance of specialized graduate training, and
the danger of permanently alienating these students from their native
culture.

Cooperative planning by educational institutions has resulted in
such programs as ASPAU; efforts must also be made to reduce confusion and conflict in the activities of government and private agencies
responsible for foreign students. Especially urgent is that all concerned
agencies and institutions accept greater responsibility for the large
number of unsponsored students.

124.   Eide, Ingrid. "Students as Bridges between Cultures." Kultura
       17 (1972): 95-110.
Eide explores the relationship between student and society, suggesting
that by the act of studying, the student becomes a bridge between his
or her own culture and those separated by time, space, and social
class. Statistics from UNESCO give a global view of student exchange.

125.   _____, ed. Students as Links between Cultures. Oslo: Univer-
       sitetforlaget, 1970.
The first section of this book presents several articles dealing with
international educational exchange. In "The Strategy of International
Exchange," Thomas Marshall discusses factors such as cultural differences, differences in the flows of students, differences in educational systems and teaching methods, and economic differences, all of
which militate against equivalence in exchanges. Moreover, parties in
an exchange frequently have different motives or goals. He concludes
that the risk of failure in exchange dwindles as the problems are
understood: the need for comparative research is emphasized, particularly of students from the same country who go to different host
countries.

Otto Klineberg contributes two articles to the book. The first,
"Psychological Aspects of Student Exchange," reviews, from a psychological perspective, problems of selection, preparation, the academic
experience, relations with people in the host country, readjustment
upon return home, mental health, and the role of foreign students as
"culture carriers." In his second article, Klineberg examines
"Research in the Field of Educational Exchange." It is suggested that
exchange goals have not always been formulated with sufficient clarity
to give the social scientist guidance as to the direction research should

follow. Friendship patterns, academic failure, adjustment, discrimination and status shock, effect of exchange on host and home countries
are all areas requiring further research.

The final article is "The Evaluation of Study Abroad" by Diether
Breitenbach. It deals first in general terms with evaluation as a method
of research in the social sciences, and then attempts to define the most
important functions of study abroad. A review of research on study
abroad is included, concentrating on studies carried out in the 1950's
and early 1960's.

In the second section of the book, Ingrid Eide summarizes the
results of UNESCO studies on "The Role as Culture Carriers of Eastern
Students who Received their University Education in Western Countries."
Data was collected by interview in 1963 from male students who had
studied in the Federal Republic of Germany, the U. K., and the United
States and had returned to work in their home countries: United Arab
Republic, Iran, and India. Eide speculates on factors that may be of
importance in understanding if and how different cultures are moving
toward more homogeneity. It is concluded that, regardless of the host
country, differences between the three groups of students were maintained. Neither background variables nor social factors could explain
away the characteristic differences between the three groups. (See
No. 144 for another report of this research.)

In a concluding chapter, Eide explores, by means of data from
the empirical studies, four ways in which student scholars function as
fulture carriers between home and host countries: (1) general cultural
knowledge acquired in schools; (2) mass media of communication;
(3) images transmitted in the form of goods or things; (4) direct transfer during contact regarding recreation, trade, or through international
organizations. Observing that the problems of foreign students are
common to all students, she suggests that future research include
control groups of local students in order to see if the findings are
related to the specific status of the foreign student.

126. Ellakany, Farouk Abdelhamid Ahmed. "Prediction of Academic
      Achievement of Foreign Students at Iowa State University,
      1969-70." Ph.D. dissertation, Iowa State University, 1970.
This dissertation investigates the nature of the relationship between
the foreign students' academic achievement at Iowa State University
and the factors of sex, age, language, field of study, marital status,
year of study, and source of support. The 454 foreign students at Iowa
State University in 1969-70 were investigated through interviews and
data from University records. Regression analysis was computed for
prediction. The main effects which were found to be significant were:
sex, age, and source of support (at the undergraduate level only).
Native language and marital status were found to be significant at both
levels.

127. Elliott, Alan J. A. "The Evaluation of International Education:
      An Administrative Approach." Social Science Information 4
      (December 1965): 61-78.
The problems of evaluating foreign study experience have been the
subject of an increasing quantity of literature in recent years but the
author believes an insufficient place has been accorded to the role of
"fellowship administrator" in evaluating the programs for which he is
responsible. "Administrative evaluation" is found to be predominantly
concerned with the accurate recording of concrete fact whereas "social
science" evaluation is defined as a selective process, largely of a
statistical nature, facilitating in-depth examination of specific problems.
The role of evaluation in administrative procedures needs further examination and development. Evaluation is seen, however, as prompting
planners and administrators into being more conscious of the needs for
clear goal statements.

128. _____. "Foreign Students in Perspective." Social Science Infor-
      mation 6 (December 1967): 189-201.
In the rapidly growing body of literature on foreign students, the
approach is sometimes humanitarian in its character, but sometimes
educational and sometimes political. This article attempts to distinguish between these different types of interest and to facilitate and
encourage a broad approach to the problem in general. The phenomenon
of study is first examined from a statistical viewpoint, but here there
are found to be serious limitations on the information that the available
figures can convey. A distinction is then drawn between the different
kinds of sponsorship that a foreign student may enjoy. Regardless of
sponsorship, host and home countries will eventually have to consider
the policies to be adopted concerning foreign students. An examination
is therefore made of some of the factors which should be taken into
account in both the present and the future development of such policies.

129. Elliott, Frederick George. "Foreign Student Programs in
      Selected Public California Junior Colleges: An Analysis of Ad-
      ministrative Policies and Practices." Ph.D. dissertation,
      University of California, Los Angeles, 1967.
Case studies of foreign student programs at several California public
junior colleges lead Elliott to identify five major areas of concern:
(1) establishing a philosophical basis for supporting a foreign student
program, (2) organizing exchange programs, (3) developing admissions
policies and practices in selecting foreign student applicants, (4) providing an adequate instructional program, and (5) maintaining effective
student personnel services. The examination of administrative policies
and practices became the basis for some 20 recommendations concerning the role of the junior college and the effective discharge of that role
in respect to handling foreign students.

130. _____. "The Dilemma of Foreign Student Admissions." Junior
      College Journal 40 (October 1969): 17-20.
American junior colleges are likely to play an increasingly important
role in foreign student exchange programs. The Committee on International Education of the California Junior College Association conducted an in-depth study of seven California junior colleges; this paper
reports on their admissions policies. It recommends that foreign student enrollment be limited to two percent, denying admission to applicants holding visitor visas but accepting genuine students with advanced
standing from foreign universities. Applicants should provide proof of
financial responsibility, health and accident insurance, and be required
to take a diagnostic language test such as TOEFL.

131. Elting, Robert Arthur. "The Prediction of Freshman Year Aca-
      demic Performance of Foreign Students from Pre-Admission
      Data." Ph.D. dissertation, New York University, 1970.
The findings of the study, conducted among 695 freshmen at the University of Miami, Coral Gables, Florida, 1964-69, indicate that prediction of academic performance is possible in the freshman year for
foreign students. A relationship of a combination of independent variables of pre-admission data and the criterion variable (grade point
average) was found to have a very high and significant coefficient of
correlation for the total sample and for various groups and subgroups
as well. Of the eight pre-admission variables, two (class-rank score
and Cooperative English Tests—Level of Comprehension score), in
combination, effectively predicted expected grade point averages.

132. Erickson, Douglas Eugene. "Differential Personality, Academic,
      and Biographical Characteristics of International Graduate Stu-
      dents at the University of North Dakota." Ed.D. dissertation,
      University of North Dakota, 1970.
Forty-three male graduate students (17 Chinese, 11 Indian-Pakistani,
9 Middle Eastern, 6 "other") completed the Mooney Problem Check
List, the Allport-Vernon-Lindsey Study of Values, and a specially
designed questionnaire. Statistical analysis led to the following conclusions: (1) the Chinese were academically superior to the other
groups whereas the Middle Eastern students achieved the poorest
academic results; (2) the "other" group revealed a significantly
greater number of social-psychological problems; (3) the Indian-
Pakistani students were most likely to identify themselves in terms
of avocational interests; (4) the Chinese showed lower economic values;
(5) the Middle Eastern students were least likely to participate in a
foster family program; (6) the similarities among the four groups far
outweighed the differences.

133. Farmer, Richard, and Renforth, William. "Foreign Students in Indiana: Our Intangible Exports." Indiana Business Review, May/June 1971, pp. 12-16.

It is proposed that expenditures by foreign students can be regarded as "exports" with respect to the Indiana State economy. Foreign students contribute an estimated $17.6 million to the state. Of this, 12 percent or $2 million is provided by the federal government through AID scholarships, etc. The final "export" sales figure makes this industry the 14th largest exporter in Indiana.

134. Farrar, Ronald Douglas. "The Non-Visa Foreign Student at Los Angeles City College: A Study of the Relation of Various Administrative and Academic Factors to the Immigrant Student." Ph.D. dissertation, University of California, Los Angeles, 1968.

Compared to the 103 visa students in residence at Los Angeles City College in September 1964, there were 2,046 immigrant students. Almost no research has been reported on the immigrant student or on his academic behavior in the public junior college. Although visa students may receive what amount to special considerations by institutions, immigrant students are subject to the same regulations concerning admission, academic standards and probation as are the native students. They must compete academically with the native students despite possible problems of language and acculturation.

For this study, 268 immigrant students were matched with native students by SCAT score pattern and other criteria, and the records of both groups were compared. It was found that the SCAT had negligible value for predicting academic aptitude of the foreign students; that the foreign students were superior to the native students in grade point average, that present probation and disqualification practices in most junior colleges are not only unfair to the immigrant student but may even operate actively against his profiting fully from higher education.

The dissertation recommends further research on immigrant students.

135. Feinberg, Lillian G. "A Study of Some Selection and Admission Criteria for Foreign Students of Journalism in United States Colleges and Universities." M.S. thesis, Iowa State University of Science and Technology, 1967.

Foreign students are applying in increasing numbers to the hundreds of U. S. institutions offering journalism education. To ascertain prevailing admissions and graduation criteria, 22 mid-Western and Western accredited and non-accredited journalism schools and departments, and members of both NAFSA and the Association for Education in Journalism participated in a questionnaire and interview survey during the summer of 1965. Analysis of results shows that most institutions require complete academic records, recommendations, health certificate, financial statement, and a statement of purpose prior to admission. While the school or department makes the final admission decision, credit evaluation is generally made in cooperation with the graduate admissions officer and/or the foreign student adviser.

A variety of approaches have been developed in journalism schools to accommodate the foreign student who lacks knowledge of American language and culture required for graduation at the same level as native students. Some practice a double standard; the University of Missouri School of Journalism admits only foreign students personnally recommended by alumni; the University of Wisconsin Department of Agricultural Journalism has bilingual staff members, permitting foreign students to write in their native languages; other institutions offer non-degree programs, split-degree programs permitting the student to complete the degree in the home country, and professional seminars.

Fish, Cynthia. See No. 264d.

136. Food and Agriculture Organization. Fellowship Evaluation: Main Findings of a Pilot Study of Individual Fellowships Awarded by FAO in the Field of Fisheries during the Period 1965-71. By Boem van Ravenswaij. Rome, 1972.
Little is known about the efficiency, effectiveness or significance to developing countries of FAO's Fellowship Programme because no systematic evaluation has taken place thus far. This pilot study demonstrates the need for establishing a built-in evaluation system as a tool for more effective planning, programming, implementation, and follow-up. It further draws attention of practitioners and policymakers to several problems which require immediate attention.

137. Food and Agriculture Organization, External Training Coordination and Evaluation Unit. "Evaluation of Group Training Organized by FAO." Rome, August 1973.
In early 1972 the External Training Coordination and Evaluation Unit carried out a survey of education techniques in 27 group training activities organized by FAO during 1971 which revealed that only nine had attempted to evaluate their effectiveness. The Unit subsequently developed a built-in evaluation system to cover all of FAO's training activities.

138. ____. "A Summary Paper on the Training Development and Evaluation System in FAO." Rome, November 1973.
The External Training Coordination and Evaluation Unit has conducted a variety of evaluative researches on FAO training activities and has

developed an extensive battery of research tools. The objective has been to design a standardized yet flexible system offering policymakers and practitioners responsible for development training a management tool to assist them in improving and changing their training-development approaches according to the changing needs of the societies to be served by it. Evaluation thus becomes an integrated part of each training cycle.

Research tools include evaluation by trainees, staff members and employers, and performance tests measuring changes in performance as a result of training.

139.   _____. "Some Questions on Training and Evaluation." By Boem
       van Ravenswaij. Rome, 1973. (Mimeo.)
This paper offers an operational definition of "training for development" and asks: Are FAO training activities subject to review? Is such review feasible? Are there elements of the FAO training program which could be eliminated or invigorated?

140.   Ford, Charles Christopher. "A Case Study of the Adaptational
       Patterns of Asian Graduate Students in Education at Michigan
       State University." Ph.D. dissertation, Michigan State Univer-
       sity, 1969.
The purpose of the study was to investigate how graduate students from other nations react to U. S. academic environments. Fifteen graduate students from the Middle East, South Asia, and Southeast Asia at Michigan State University's College of Education during the academic year 1969 were interviewed intensively over a two-month period. A typology of three adaptational styles was developed: negative-anxious— openly dissatisfied with educational experiences and highly critical of faculty and university; negative-accommodating—generally dissatisfied but accepting conditions as inevitable; positive—generally satisfied because training was useful and relevant.

The major determinants of the adaptational styles were the stu-dents' perception of the relevance of what they were learning, whether or not they had a job waiting at home, and their interaction patterns with members of the faculty and other graduate students.

On the basis of these results, four hypotheses were suggested for further research: (1) If the student has a job waiting, he or she is more likely to view as low the relevance of the educational experience and to adapt in a negative way. (2) If the student does not have a job waiting, he or she is more apt to view as moderate or high the rele-vance of learning and to adapt in a mixed or positive way. (3) The greater the opportunity for interaction with faculty and students, the less the tendency to react in a negative-anxious way. (4) The greater the opportunity for participation, as through assistantships, the less the tendency to react in a negative-anxious way.

A detailed recommendation for an interdisciplinary seminar focused on the problems of education in developing countries is made.

141. Frank, William Wiley. "An Exploratory Study of Attitudes and Perceptions Toward Change among AID Technical Assistance Program Participants." Ph.D. dissertation, Michigan State University, 1965.

The major purpose of this study was to enumerate and describe the differences between training-program participants in terms of reported ability to introduce change upon return to their home countries. The investigation was based on a questionnaire administered to eight groups of participants (N = 317) representing 52 countries, attending communication seminars prior to return home.

A general description of those participants who hold high expectations of their ability to introduce change would be as follows. These participants felt that their training programs were relevant. They did not perceive physical factors as obstacles. They held favorable views concerning past change. They felt their supervisors would agree with their particular viewpoints regarding change.

142. Frankel, Charles. The Neglected Aspect of Foreign Affairs. Washington, D. C.: The Brookings Institution, 1966.

Believing that educational and cultural relations constitute the neglected aspect of U. S. foreign policy, Frankel, a former Assistant Secretary of State for Educational and Cultural Affairs, reviews the administrative, political, and social settings in which U. S. Cultural Affairs Officers (CAO) operate, and analyzes the theory behind such relations. He argues that, if U. S. policy is to be more precise, exchange goals must be reformulated as: lacing together of educational systems; improvement of the context of communication; disciplining and extending of international intellectual discourse; international educational development; and furthering of educational and cultural relations as ends in themselves. Such a reformulation suggests that regional differences, particularly those between developing and developed countries, call for significant variations in U. S. policies.

To achieve these goals, Frankel recommends the upgrading of educational and cultural relations, administrative reforms, and the creation of more cooperative and binding relationships between government and private educational and cultural agencies. Improvement in the position of the CAO, reallocation of responsibilities, and reorganization of educational and cultural affairs are some practical implications.

Frey, James F. See No. 395.

143. Froehlich, Dieter, and Schade, Burkhard. "Zur Frage der Ruckenanpassung von Studenten Aus Entwicklungslandern." (On the Problem of Readjustment of Students from Developing Countries). Kolner Z. Soziol, Soz-Psychol. 18 (1966): 271-99.

Research on the problems of the readjustment of students from underdeveloped countries who have studied in industrialized nations has over-emphasized the negative aspects. A review of the existing literature leads the authors to hypothesize that their sojourn experiences motivate such students socially and professionally to return home. Fourteen returnees who had studied in Germany were interviewed as to their experiences in the West, their motives for return, and their present situation.

Results indicate a complex relationship of the returnee to his society and some strong role conflicts in his position. The returned students constitute an elite minority which is discriminated against. Their behavior structure shows a compromise between a minimum of adjustment to native culture and a maximum of realization of the cultural norms of an industrialized society.

144. Galtung, I. E. "The Impact of Study Abroad: A Three-by-Three Nation Study of Cross-Cultural Contact." Journal of Peace Research 3 (1965): 258-75.

This article reports on a UNESCO-sponsored study of students from the UAR, India, and Iran who had returned to their home countries after two years or more of study in the West. In interviews, they reported varying degrees of adjustment to their host countries. In general the Indians reported fewer changes than the other two groups, apparently choosing cultural coexistence rather than conformity to a foreign culture. This finding cannot be explained satisfactorily by differences between the samples, or by the Indian students' greater possibility of contact with fellow nationals. It is suggested that such factors as training in cultural pluralism, ideologies that regulate degrees of acculturation, cultural distance, the image of the home country abroad, and its rank in the international system are relevant for the students in their adjustments and degrees of acceptance of the foreign culture. (See No. 125 for another discussion of this survey.)

145. Gandhi, Rajnikant S. "Conflict and Cohesion in an Indian Student Community." Human Organization 29 (Summer 1970): 95-102.

This study examines the formation of a subcommunity among Indian students at the University of Minnesota. A self-administered questionnaire was completed by 134 of the 147 Indian students registered for the fall semester 1965. Statistics were supplemented by participant observation and interviews. Gandhi found that residential concentration and common eating arrangements, together with Hinduism, caste, super-region affiliation, and isolation lead to the suppression of regional and linguistic differences and promote the formation of a close-knit community. Identification with a common culture and patterns of mutual trust cause greater interaction within the group than with Americans. The situation is one of unity in diversity and cohesion in conflict.

146. _____. "Some Contrasts in the Foreign Student Life-Styles."
International Journal of Contemporary Sociology 9 (January 1972): 34-43.
Data from the survey described in No. 145 were used to test the hypothesis that contrasting patterns of life styles were due to differences in orientations—the "old style" students would be oriented inwardly toward traditional Indian culture while the "new style" students would be oriented outwardly toward the Western world. Systematic differences in life-styles were found: there were contrasts in students' orientations to Indian as well as host culture, and these contrasts extended to their economic, political, social, and cultural life in America. Length of stay was positively related to life-style differences but regional, religious, and caste factors were not.

Gardner, John A. See No. 390 a-b.

147. Gish, Oscar. "A Note on Aid for Nursing Training in Britain."
Journal of Development Studies 5 (April 1969): 220-22.
Surveying nurses' training in Britain, Fish found that, of the 20 percent who came from Commonwealth countries, 50 percent were from the West Indies, 20 percent from Africa, two percent from India-Pakistan. Almost 50 percent of the foreign-born trainees had been recruited in their home countries. A further study of non-return among foreign-born women trained as midwives leads him to conclude that: (1) It is unlikely that many of the nursing students will return to their own countries, and (2) nursing training for foreign-born women should not (in the main) be considered as part of British educational aid to underdeveloped countries.

148. Glaser, William A. Brain Drain and Study Abroad. New York: Columbia University, Bureau of Applied Social Research, 1974.
Mounting concern over the brain drain prompted the United Nations, in 1968, to initiate research which would clarify the problem, assess its effects, and propose remedies. This monograph reports on results obtained from surveys of students in the U.S., Canada, and France; of professionals from developing countries who have studied abroad and are now working in the U. S. and France; and of professionals who have studied in developed countries and have returned to India, Sri

Lanka, Korea, Greece, Ghana, Brazil, Colombia, and Argentina. Surveys are continuing in other developed and developing countries; this is to be considered a progress report.

The general patterns which emerge are (1) that most students from developing countries plan to return home eventually, although proportions vary widely among countries; (2) that many non-returnees are working temporarily to gain experience after graduation and plan to return, usually after two years; (3) that returnees rarely expect to emigrate permanently in the future; and (4) that many long-term immigrants will return home after retirement, and favor careers at home for their children. It thus appears that migration is not a permanent condition and that changing circumstances at home can cause more changes of plan than is generally assumed.

Significant variations in data from different countries are explored. Whereas level of economic development of the home country has only a limited relationship to brain drain, structural imbalances in the market for professionals have strong relationships. Countries differ in the ability of their nationals to adjust to foreign societies; developed countries vary in their degree of receptivity to immigrants.

Concerning motivation, it was found that the attractions of curricula and facilities in developed countries are the most common reasons for study abroad. Ties with home, eg., family, sponsorship, a guaranteed job, are associated with high return; income differences among countries do not determine brain drain as strongly as is generally believed.

Probably the greatest anxiety about brain drain is the loss of the ablest persons, who can make the greatest contribution to domestic growth. Survey results, however, show no clear-cut relation between ability and migration plans: as persons are ranked by their grades either at home or abroad, their plans to return neither increase nor decrease. A potential benefit of migration is the remittance of money by professionals employed abroad, but more evidence is needed before judging whether the home country is compensated for the costs of the emigrant's upbringing and education.

149.   Gollin, Albert E.   The Transfer and Use of Development Skills: An Evaluation Study of U.S. Technical Training Programs for Participants from Underdeveloped Areas. Washington, D. C.: Bureau of Social Science Research, Inc., 1966.

In 1959 ICA (later AID) initiated a worldwide survey of former participants to evaluate the effectiveness of its training programs, focusing on the administrative characteristics of the programs and their occupational outcomes. Specifically, the study sought to ascertain whether participants were utilizing their training effectively and what factors

contribute to or hinder utilization, whether the technical training was
of the appropriate level and quality, and whether administrative practices and procedures were adequate and effective. The data on which
this report is based were obtained from interviews with 9,688 former
participants in 23 countries, excluding all European and most sub-
Saharan African countries. Interviews were also conducted with
current work supervisors of the participants and with U.S. technicians
familiar with them. Major findings are as follows:

(1) Prelude — Participants approved of the selection process and
criteria; the main shortcoming of trainees, indicative of lax selection
practice, was poor English-language facility. Pre-departure orientation regarding social and cultural patterns in the host country was
generally satisfactory but substantial numbers of trainees complained
about the lack of information on precisely where they would be going
and what they would be studying. Moreover, only two in five helped
to plan their own program to any extent, and three in five reported
no pre-departure contact with the AID Mission in their country. The
advance preparation of trainees thus appears to be a weak program
area.

(2) Sojourn — Seventy-nine percent of respondents were satisfied
with the level of their training program; programs regarded as inappropriate were more often thought to have been too simple (14 percent)
than too advanced (6 percent). This preference for longer programs
is related to the desire to obtain a degree: only about one-fourth of
all university-trained participants do so but the majority of all who
were asked saw distinct career advantages resulting from acquiring
a degree.

To analyze the correlates of satisfaction with the technical
aspects of the program, an index was constructed which summarized
the number of satisfied judgments each trainee made. It was found
that: (1) judgments were far less favorable among technicians and
lower-level trainees than among managers and professionals, while
the top status groups were by far the most often satisfied; (2) the
more comprehensive their orientation, or the more involved they
were in program planning, the more favorable were the participants'
judgments; (3) degree recipients viewed training more favorably than
non-degree trainees; and (4) certain third-country training sites were
associated with a low-level of satisfaction.

As a final measure of overall satisfaction with the training experience, it was found that 96 percent of the participants completed their
programs.

(3) Aftermath — Almost all participants had been employed continuously since their training program, the greatest number (77 percent) returning to the same job and 14 percent to a different but

expected job. It is significant, however, that well over 50 percent
thought they would have had about the same job they held at the time
of the interview if they had never gone on a training program. Age
at time of selection was the primary factor: the older participants
were much more likely to have found training to have made no difference while those under 30 saw training as having aided them in their
careers.

Follow-up with returned trainees appears to be weak. Just over
two-fifths of the participants had had no contacts with USAID since
their return.

(4) Utilization — The ultimate test of a program's value is its
transferability to a participant's work on development projects. A
large majority had made effective use of training in their occupation;
only 12 percent denied making any use of it at all. Almost all said
they had conveyed aspects of their training to others, a "multiplier
effect" that was corroborated by their supervisors. Certain program
or environmental factors were associated with high utilization of training:

a. the more "professionalized" the field of training, e. g.,
   health, education, agriculture, the greater the utilization;
b. programs in the United States or in the Far East tend to be
   associated with better subsequent utilization than those in
   other third countries;
c. programs of longer duration tend to be associated with better
   occupational use than are briefer programs, especially the
   observation tour;
d. utilization was increased when supervisors played an active
   role;
e. the more active role the participant played in program
   planning, the greater the utilization;
f. the more satisfied the trainee is in overall evaluation of the
   program, the greater the utilization;
g. programs which are perceived as contributing to a career
   enhancement are associated with better utilization;
h. evaluations of non-technical aspects of training seem to be
   unrelated to subsequent utilization;
i. the closer the relationship between returned participants and
   USAID, the greater the utilization.

150. _____. "Foreign Study and Modernization: The Transfer of
   Technology through Education." International Social Science
   Journal 19 (1967): 359-77.
This is a brief summary of the research described in No. 149.

151. _____. "Human Skills and National Development: The Processes
     and Social Consequences of a Technical Training Program of
     U. S. Foreign Aid to Underdeveloped Countries." Ph.D. disser-
     tation, Columbia University, 1967.
See No. 149.

152. Grady, William Ellis. "Selected Variables Related to Academic
     Achievement of American and Canadian Male Freshmen at the
     University of North Dakota." Ph.D. dissertation, University
     of North Dakota, 1969.
From tests administered to 31 American and 31 Canadian freshmen
during 1968-69, it is concluded that the American College Test and
high-school grade point average provided the best prediction of college
achievement for the American freshmen. These variables were found
to be related to college achievement but the specific variables differed
somewhat for the two samples of students.

153. Grafton, Clive L. "Foreign Student Patterns in American Com-
     munity Colleges." Junior College Journal 40 (March 1970): 32-3.
Grafton summarizes the results of a NAFSA survey of the foreign
student population of American community colleges. To accommodate
increased enrollment of foreign students, he recommedns that the
colleges expand existing programs of assistance, language training,
and counseling.

154. Grant, Stephen. "Uses of Foreign Students." Amherst, Mass.:
     University of Massachusetts, 1970.
This paper presents ideas on how foreign students at U. S. colleges
and universities may be incorporated into a secondary-school curriculum in nearby school districts. Reference is made to the "Ogontz
Plan" of Philadelphia where city-wide resources are organized for
arranging school visitations by foreign students.

155. Groves, Marion H. "Contributions to Development by Asians
     Who Have Studies Abroad." Exchange (Summer 1967): 13-19.
Asians who study abroad contribute to the development of their home
contries whether or not they return. Returnees contribute through
(1) their ability to solve problems based on knowledge acquired abroad;
(2) their contacts with individuals and literature which provide continuing access to research and development; (3) their determination to
pursue career objectives and apply professional skills to problems of
their countries and (4) their experiences with participation in cooperative enterprises.

Non-returnees contribute by (1) engaging in research relevant
to their countries' needs; (2) by influencing investment of foreign
capital in projects directly related to Asia's development needs; and
(3) by forming partnerships with firms or persons at home whereby
non-returnees supply needed information, tools, and products.

156. Grubel, Herbert G. "The Reduction of the Brain Drain: Problems
        and Policies." Minerva 6 (Summer 1968): 541-58.
Rational policies dealing with the problem of the brain drain must be
based on a clear understanding of the benefits expected and the costs
entailed. Research has not produced reliable estimates of the number
of persons involved or meaningful empirical measures of the welfare
losses of the population in the losing countries. Nevertheless, it is
legitimate to consider the economic and social costs of policies aimed
at reduction of the folow.
        Policies which attempt to narrow income and opportunity gaps
are desirable but require a long period for them to become effective.
Policies designed to make migration more difficult, through laws,
visas, or taxes, appear to be politically unrealistic; they are also
likely to result in inefficiencies and to involve high costs in administration and loss of personal freedom. The proposal for the institution of
inter-governmental compensation schemes for the repayment of educational subsidies invested in the emigrants by the losing country
appears to have the greatest merits and least social cost.

157. Guglielmo, Hector. "Rights and Obligations of Foreign Students
        in an American University." Ph.D. dissertation, University of
        Arizona, 1967.
The purpose of the study was to discover what factors in foreign students' background and experience have a positive or negative relationship to their knowledge of civil regulations regarding immigration,
automobile operator's responsibilities, income tax and social security,
housing, employment, and purchasing and installment buying. The
sample consisted of 146 foreign students at the University of Arizona.
        Major results were as follows. A definite positive relationship
was noted between length of time in the United States and scores on the
questionnaire. There seemed to be little relationship between number
of visits per month with an American family and scores on the questionnaire until the number of visits reached five or more. The amount
of orientation had little bearing on scores. Students that lived with
their families, in most cases immigrants, scored higher than those
living with co-nationals. Participants with employment experience
scored higher.

It is recommended that universities provide specialized orientation in the six areas considered, that they encourage interpersonal contacts, and provide adequate counseling facilities.

Haas, J. See No. 5.

158. Hagey, Abdulla Rashid. "Academic and Social Adjustment of Middle Eastern Students Attending Oregon Colleges and Universities." Ph.D. dissertation, University of Oregon, 1968.
A questionnaire was administered to 272 students from nine Middle Eastern countries in Oregon. Findings are presented regarding: (1) the extent to which academic and/or social adjustment are related to selected factors in the student's past and immediate environment; (2) the extent to which the sample of Middle Eastern students is actually homogeneous in those background areas though to be pertinent to academic and/or social adjustment; and (3) the extent to which the nature of the school setting relates to the kinds of services utilized by the students.

159. Halasz, Sari C. "University of California, Los Angeles Study II: Graduate Students from Indonesia, Korea, Pakistan and Thailand: Fall 1959 through Spring 1967." College and University 45 (Fall 1969): 44-54.
This study presents detailed information on the academic performance of 34 Indonesian, 100 Korean, 21 Pakistani, and 22 Thai students at UCLA as it relates to previous scholarship, post-baccalaureate study, English proficiency, and financial support. (Results of Study I were published in the Fall 1967 issue of the same journal.)

160. Halberstam, Jacob, and Dasco, Michael. "Foreign and United States Residents in University Affiliated Teaching Hospitals: An Investigation of United States Graduate Medical Education.: Paper presented at a meeting of the Committee on Medical Education at the New York Academy of Medicine, 18 March 1965. (Mimeo.)
For this study, sponsored by the Vocational Rehabilitation Administration, HEW, 170 foreign-born and trained and 120 U. S.-born and trained residents were randomly selected and subjected to extensive testing and interviewing. A major finding was that, although the vast majority of both groups expressed basic satisfaction with their academic experiences, their supervisors reported a larger proportion of dissatisfied and poorly performing residents in the foreign group than in the U. S. group. Modification of residency programs for foreign physicians is regarded as urgent.

161. Halberstam, Jacob; Rusk, Howard; and Taylor, Eugene. "For-
    eign Surgical Residents in University-Affiliated Hospitals."
    Annals of Surgery 171 (April 1970): 485-500.
Fifty foreign and 50 U.S. residents in surgery participated in this
study. Each was interviewed by a trained field worker and completed
an extensive battery of tests. The most salient findings show that (1)
foreign surgical residents are remarkably similar to their U. S.
counterparts; (2) they are considered to be competent physicians who
render high-quality care to their patients; (3) they are more readily
accepted as physicians in the United States and find it easier to adjust
to life and medical practice in this country than do foreign medical
residents in other specialities.

    The study suggests that about 40 percent of the foreign residents
intend to become U. S. citizens. The authors believe there is a relationship between brain drain and the relevance of U. S. training for
the foreign surgeon's future at home. They are, however, opposed to
a three-year limit on training as a solution to this problem.

Hall, George. See No 266.

162. Harari, Maurice. "Priorities for Research and Action in the
    Graduate Foreign Student Field." Exchange 6, no. 2 (Fall 1970):
    60-67.
Consultation and collaboration between U. S. educational institutions
and overseas institutions regarding, in particular, selection and training of graduate foreign students is suggested. Policies of U. S. government agencies and foundations will be more sound if based on a coherent
U. S. university rationale which is supported by current and reliable
information concerning education trends overseas and collaboration
with colleagues abroad in identifying development priorities and issues.

163. _____. Global Dimensions in U. S. Education: The University.
    New York: New York Friends Group, 1972.
"International education" is an inclusive term encompassing (1) international content of curricula, (2) international movement of scholars
and students concerned with training and research, and (3) arrangements engaging U. S. institutions in technical assistance and educational cooperation with foreign countries.

    International studies programs on U. S. campuses are currently
threatened by declining financial support, by fragmented administrative infrastructures, and by challenges to the relevance and substantive
value of their goals. While progress has been made in internationalizing U. S. education, too many students graduate without having had
courses with international content. Harari suggests a number of new

approaches based on closer collaboration in training and research
between international studies (area studies) and professional schools,
governmental, private, and international organizations.

With regard to foreign students, Harari urges that universities
assess carefully their goals and procedures in admission, selection,
and training. Departments need to concern themselves with the substantive adequacy of their curricula. There is also a need to promote
a sustained dialog between the public and private sectors with regard
to foreign students in the United States. National policies need review,
and the understanding of state legislatures needs to be cultivated.

Greater interaction is needed between policy-oriented agencies
and operational agencies concerned with relating the educational resources of the United States to the needs of developing nations. U.S.
programs supporting recruitment of faculty for service overseas need
careful review, more flexible funding, more reciprocity, and more
planning and continuity.

The challenge to the U. S. international studies community is
that it has to become cohesive and it has to internationalize itself.
The problems call for a recasting of the predominantly domestic or
bilateral frame of reference into a genuinely multinational approach.

164. Hayden, Rose. "MUCIA - The Consortium Approach to Inter-
         national Cooperation." Exchange 9, no. 1 (Summer 1973): 57-66.
Established in 1964, Midwest Universities Consortium for International
Activities (MUCIA) is a consortium of five universities whose main
objectives are three-fold: to build and sustain academic linkages with
overseas universities and research institutions; to provide more
effective technical cooperation; and to strengthen the international
dimensions of members' campuses through faculty and student participation in international development work. With support of governmental and international agencies and foundations, MUCIA sponsors
programs which include overseas research, institution building,
technical cooperation, study teams, salary guarantees, and exploratory travel.

165. Heath, G. Louis. "The Lodestar International Student Experi-
         ment." School and Society 97 (October 1969): 372-74.
The Lodestar International Student Center was established in 1963 as
a non-profit, non-sectarian educational and recreation center in
northern California. Offering eight one-week sesssions each summer,
accommodating 16 students and one discussion leader, its purpose is
to provide a unique experience in cultural exchange apart from the
educational setting among the many nationalities represented at
northern California universities and colleges.

166.   _____. "Foreign Student Attitudes at International House,
       Berkeley." Exchange 5, no. 3 (Winter 1970): 66-70.
Extended interviews were conducted with 110 graduate and undergraduate foreign students at Berkeley's International House. It was found
that students were favorably impressed by democratic features of
American life but disturbed by discrimination and ephemeral social
relations. Europeans had a less favorable view of the United States
than did non-Europeans and were less apt to be satisfied with the
nature of university training received. Favorable attitudes were found
to correlate with satisfaction toward the sojourn, academic programs,
and frequency of travel.

Heft, David. See No. 295.

167.   Hegazy, Mohammed Ezzat. "Cross-Cultural Experience and
       Social Change: The Case of Foreign Study." Ph.D. dissertation,
       University of Minnesota, 1968.
The study explores the utility of a sociological analysis of cross-cultural educational contact. The major hypothesis, that systematic differences appear between the American experiences of foreign students
of different socio-cultural backgrounds, was tested using a questionnaire sent to 230 British and Egyptian students at five U. S. universities, 1967-68 (148 replies).
       The major findings of the study were: (1) the British students'
knowledge of and feelings about the host country before they came
were less stereotyped than those of the Egyptians; (2) the students in
both national groups reported different feelings about different aspects
of the culture, rather than an overall feeling about the entire system;
(3) the British students associated more with Americans than did the
Egyptian students; (4) the Egyptian students, more often than the British, developed a temporary community within the larger community;
(5) most respondents reported that they had changed during their American stay, but the patterns of change undergone varied with national
origin; and (6) the aspects of personality organization related to core
values, such as religious values, sexual morals, etc., were found to
be more resistant to change than other aspects, such as dress taste,
food and drinking habits, training in the field of speicalization, etc.
Except for two hypotheses about pre-contact knowledge of the host
culture and the difficulties encountered during the foreign stay, the
working hypotheses were verified.

168.   Heil, Donald, and Aleamoni, Lawrence. "Assesment of the
       Proficiency in the Use and Understanding of English by Foreign
       Students as Measured by the Test of English as a Foreign Lan-

guage." Urbana, Ill.: University of Illinois, Office of Instructional Resources, Measurement and Research Division, March 1974.

The objectives of the study were to determine the predictive validity of the Test of English as a Foreign Language (TOEFL) for the academic success of foreign students using first- and second-semester graduate grade point average as the criterion; to determine the predictive validity of the English Placement Examination (EPE) developed at the University of Illinois; to assess the concurrent validity of the TOEFL and the EPE; to assess the predictive validity of the TOEFL scores and the EPE scores using grade in a remedial English course as the criterion; and finally to estimate the magnitude of the change in the TOEFL scores after the subjects have lived in an English-speaking country and taken a remedial English course for one semester.

It is concluded that the predictive validities of the TOEFL appear to be similar to the predictive validities for native American students using admissions test scores as reported by Bowers (1965). TOEFL "appears to be no better or worse than those admission tests used to predict success for native American students." This conclusion was arrived at using a sample of 148 foreign students at the University of Illinois and examinig their TOEFL scores and correlations with first- and second-semester grade point averages.

The description of this research is preceeded by a comprehensive review of the literature on the prediction of academic success of foreign students.

169. Heise, Jan Otis. "The Relationship of Foreign Student's Educational and Vocational Values to Background Variables and Perceived Institutiona Press." Ph.D. dissertation, Stanford University, 1971.

The aims of this study are threefold: to explore the possibility that college influence on student vocational and educational values is circumscribed by pre-graduate school attributes of students; to determine to what extent the college environment influences these values in accordance with Thistlethwait's need-press theory; and to show that the direction of the students' developing values can be predicted if enough information about the student's situation is known.

A questionnaire was sent to 3,000 male foreign graduate students at eight universities. Analysis of the 51 percent of the questionnaires that were returned shows that all foreign students, regardless of any cultural or educational background characteristics, have a similar profile of vocational or educational values; certain pre-school characteristics are, however, influential in varying the degree to which each of the values is espoused, namely geographic area of origin,

choice of academic major, religious background, academic level, and
job prospects.

The faculty and student "press" items were not highly correlated
with the criterion measures of students' vocational and educational
values, with one exception: the educational value of becoming more
acquainted with theories and abstract ideas, or learning research
techniques is more highly correlated with various "press" scales
than any other value.

It is therefore concluded that knowledge of a student's background
will be most helpful in predicting what his values will be since they
appear to be well-established prior to enrollment and change little
during the course of study.

170. Hekmati-Tehrani, Mehri. "Alienation, Family Ties, and Social
      Position as Factors Related to the Non-Return of Foreign Students."
      Ph.D. dissertation, New York University, 1970.
A random sample of 210 students from a base population of 521 male
students from Greece, India, Iran, the Philippines, and Turkey,
enrolled at Columbia and New York Universities during the spring
semester of 1969, served as subjects of the study. One hundred and
ten planned to remain in the United States; 100 to return to their home.

The main findings of the study were that: (1) the non-returning
group experiences a significantly higher degree of normlessness and
powerlessness than the returning group, but the latter come from significantly higher social positions and have stronger family ties; and
(2) the non-returning group does not experience significantly greater
anomie nor does it have more favorable attitudes toward Americans
than the returning group.

171. Hekmati, Mehri, and Glaser, William A. "The Brain Drain and
      UNITAR's Multinational Research Project on the Subject." Social
      Science Information 12 (April 1973): 123-38.
This multinational research project is impressive in scope, and although
not completed as yet, promises much valuable information on the brain
drain and a number of related subject areas. Three standardized
questionnaires are used in obtaining information from a population of
students and migrating professionals from developed and developing
countries.

The study, administered through a network of research centers,
is designed to investigate economic, political, and socio-psychological
explanations of the brain drain. The findings will form the basis for
policy recommendations to both developed and developing nations.

172. Henderson, Gregory. "Foreign Students: Exchange or Immigra-
      tion?" International Development Review 6 (1964): 19-21.

Although firm facts on student non-return are difficult to obtain, it is well known that the United States is draining skilled manpower from countries such as Taiwan, Korea, Iran, India, where it is urgently needed. Particularly affected are the fields of science and medicine. The situation is anomalous in that the United States is providing aid to these same countries.

If the United States is to accept its responsibility to train but not drain, measures should be taken to tighten the administration of visa regulations, to raise admissions standards and concentrate on graduate-level training, and to devise ways of encouraging students to return to useful careers in their home countries.

_____. See No. 388.

173. Henry, David D. "The Latin American Scholarship Program of
        American Universities." Exchange 7, no. 3 (Winter 1972): 30-55.
The Latin American Scholarship Program of American Universities (LASPAU) is a cooperative undertaking of more than 300 North American and Latin American institutions of higher learning which offers Latin American students an opportunity to obtain the academic training required for careers as university teachers in their home countries.

This is a report on the program's operations for the academic years 1969-70 and 1970-71. It details the progress made toward the fulfillment of the program's intermediate goals and suggests the even greater rewards that lie ahead if both partners will exploit the imaginative innovations that various participants in the program have introduced in the last two years.

174. Hickey, Gerald F. "Foreign Student Admissions Procedures in
        Kansas and Nebraska Junior Colleges." Hutchinson, Kansas:
        Hutchinson Community Junior College, March 1967. (Mimeo.)
Four public junior colleges in Nebraska and five private and 15 public junior colleges in Kansas were sent questionnaires regarding admissions procedures in 1966. Three Nebraska colleges, but only two private and nine public colleges in Kansas returned the questionnaire. Finding that the colleges had no standardized admissions procedures and no full-time foreign student advisers, Hickey recommends that standardized admissions procedures be developed, that "drop-in" students be discouraged, that overseas interview services be used, and that college representatives obtain membership in NAFSA.

175. Higbee, Homer. The Status of Foreign Student Advising in
        United States Universities and Colleges. East Lansing, Mich.:
        Michigan State University, 1961.
This important, early research report resulted from a year-long

NAFSA-sponsored inquiry in which some 1,365 institutions participated. Questionnaires to Foreign Student Advisers and a selected sampling of foreign students were augmented by 220 interviews with university officials.

In general, the survey found that the greater the institution's involvement in international education, the greater the clarity of the Foreign Student Adviser's role. In a majority of institutions, however, this office is not given high-level academic or administrative priority.

Among the recommendations of the study were: (1) top institutional officials should be continuously apprised of the demand for an international dimension in education; (2) U. S. institutions should view foreign students and contributing to a mutually beneficial exchange of knowledge; (3) there is an urgent need for English-language centers in the United States; (4) information about U. S. education must be made more readily available to prospective foreign students before they leave their home countries; (5) more attention should be accorded academic advice as an area of need among foreign students; (6) financial aid for foreign students needs penetrating appraisal; (7) the foreign student adviser must be an integral part of an international activity team in each institution.

176. Hill, Jarvis Harley. "An Analysis of a Group of Indonesian, Thai, Pakistani, and Indian Student Perceptions of Their Problems While Enrolled at Indiana University." Ed.D. dissertation, Indiana University, 1966.

Of a total population of 150, 78 students completed a personal-data questionnaire and a checklist covering academic, financial, housing, religious, personal, and social problems. All groups experienced substantial difficulties with academic, personal, and financial problems. Of these, the academic problems were greatest and they were largely related to lack of language proficiency; the women experienced substantially greater difficulties than the men. According to nationality, the Thai students experienced substantially more difficulties with academic problems involving language than did other groups; Thai and Indian students had greater difficulty in getting acquainted with American academic methods than did the Indonesian and Pakistani students.

177. Hodgkin, Mary C. "Political and Cultural Influences in the Formation of Voluntary Associations in an Ephemeral Ethnic Minority." International Journal of Comparative Sociology 8 (September 1967): 165-81.

Hodgkin studied voluntary associations among some 1,999 students from Malaysia and Singapore in Australia. At the superficial level, Asian student associations are similar to those of Western society. There are, however, a number of influences which operate to produce

considerable differences in the actual working of such groups. The
size of the group, outside influences, and political pressures emanating
from the areas from which the students come are contributing factors,
but the main causes of lack of cohesion stem from cultural attitudes to
leadership, to the benefits which accrue from organizational participation, to the status of differing academic qualifications, and to the
educational antecedents of the students. Four major groups of factors
determine the difference between these associations and those of
Western society: (1) the ephemeral nature of the sojourn overseas;
(2) ethnic and cultural diversity; (3) confusion and ambivalence concerning aims and objectives; and (4) the size of the group. Thus the
lack of congruent norms and expectations provides an inadequate base
for integration both within the student group itself and in association
with the host society.

178. Holland, Kenneth. "Statistics and Comments on Exchange with
     the United States." International Social Science Bulletin 8, no. 4
     (1956): 628-37.
The Institute of International Education, in addition to its role as an
administering agency and an information clearinghouse, has become a
source of statistics and publications on exchangees. Four of these are
described: The Central Index of Educational Exchangees, a roster of
Americans who have gone abroad and foreigners who have come to the
United States for educational purposes since 1920; Cultural Attitudes
and International Understanding by Hilda Taba, 1954, which analyzes
the experiences of 45 American students on a European summer-study
tour; Orientation of Foreign Students: Signposts for the Cultural Maze,
a policy statement by the Committee on Educational Interchange Policy,
1956; and The Goals of Student Exchange, by the Committee on Educational Interchange Policy, 1955, which analyzes the conflict between
the goals of sponsoring agencies and those of participants.

179. Hull, William Franklin. "The Influence of a Random Sample of
     International Students upon American Students in a Sensitivity
     Group Experience." Ph.D. dissertation, Pennsylvania State
     University, 1970.
To ascertain whether close interpersonal social contact with foreign
students affects world-mindedness in American students, 41 American
undergraduates at Pennsylvania State University completed a questionnaire before and after participating with foreign students in a weekend
Human Relations Laboratory.
    It was found that the American students demonstrated significant
change toward world-mindedness immediately following the termination
of the Laboratory and that this change remained significant five weeks
later. There was, however, slight indication that the influence of the

international students on the American undergraduate students was
fading by the fifth-week measure.

180.   Ibrahim, Saad Eddin Mohamed. "Political Attitudes of an
          Emerging Elite: A Case Study of the Arab Students in the United
          States." Ph.D. dissertation, University of Washington, 1968.
According to the congruency theory of attitude organization, the
organizing principle of ideology formation, maintenance, and change is
"consistency" among relevant attitudes, and also between attitudes on
the one hand and the individual's value system on the other.
      Data on nationalism, democracy, socialism, and global alignment
was obtained from a ten-percent random sample of Arab students in
the United States (over 400 replies). The empirical findings substanti-
ated most of the theorems derived from general congruency propositions.
The four attitudes were significantly interrelated and were found to be
tied up with the student's social background and to the variety of the
individual's roles and positions in different structures both in the
temporary milieu (the United States) and in the society of origin. The
differential incidence of ethnocentrism and acculturation resulting from
the students' sojourn abroad accounted for a substantial part of attitudinal variance. When the data on single attitudes were reconstructed,
however, using the concept of ideal types, the congruency theory
received only a partial support.

181.   Institute of International Education. The Two-Year College in
          the United States: A Guide for Foreign Students. New York, 1967.
For the foreign student who plans to enroll in a junior college in the
United States, this booklet presents information about junior colleges:
(1) their general nature, location, support, control, and programs;
(2) instructional methods, teachers, calendars, attendance requirements and credits; (3) degrees; (4) student life; (5) admissions
requirements; (6) costs; (7) financial assistance; (8) visa requirements;
(9) procedures on arrival in the United States and at the college; and
(10) a list of accredited junior colleges.

182.   _____. Exporting Technical Education: A Survey and Case Study
          of Foreign Professionals with U. S. Graduate Degrees. By Charles
          Susskind and Lynn Schell. New York, 1968.
A study of two aspects of the problem of foreign students in the United
States was carried out during 1966-67 as part of the Professional
Schools Program initially administered by the Institute of International
Studies on the Berkeley campus of the University of California. The
first part is a statistical evaluation of the performance of foreign stu-
dents who received University of California graduate engineering degrees
during the years 1954-65. The second is a critical survey of previous

studies of returnees by AID and individual researchers, focusing on goals, brain drain, and measures of effectiveness. A summary of recommendations made in these studies, and an annotated bibliography, are included.

The results of the first part are based almost entirely on responses to a questionnaire which was returned by 52 percent of the 676 recipients of advanced degrees over the years under study. Salient results of the survey are: (1) nearly one-third of those who received master's degrees and nearly two-thirds of the doctorates were U. S. residents at the time of the survey; (2) the respondents' comments were overwhelmingly complimentary to their U. S. professional education, with negative comments (mainly about faculty-student relationship and research quality) quite rare; and (3) among returnees, high use of technical knowledge was reported by over half of the master's and by most of the doctorates, and high use of acquired research skills was reported by about one-third of the master's and over two-thirds of the doctorates (and even more by doctorates from developed countries).

183. _____. Closing the Worldwide Learning Gap. How Can Free Enterprise Help? Proceedings of a conference in San Francisco, 29-31 October 1969.
The aim of this conference, attended by leaders in education, business and government, and others interested in international education, was to consider how business and government could cooperate to close the worldwide learning gap. Specific goals, sound organization, operational flexibility, and assured funding were seen to be the four elements essential to any program of cooperative assistance to education in developing nations.

Goals should be defined by competent nationals aware of the capacity of a foundation to achieve them, and should enjoy the support and approval of the private sector, local government, local educators, and others.

An educational foundation was proposed which would have the specific function of developing and administering cooperative efforts between government and business in developing nations. The Instituto Peruano Fomento Educativo in Lima, Peru, was identified as a useful model.

184. _____. International Educational Exchange. A Bibliography. By Richard E. Spencer and Ruth Awe. New York, 1970.
Data sources include library reference works, Ph. D. dissertations, U. S. government agencies, foundations, and universities. Entries cover Exchange of Students, Teachers, and Specialists (admissions,

orientation, adjustment, achievement, returnees, brain drain, immigration policies, etc.), Educational Curriculum, General Works on International Educational and Cultural Exchange, Cross-Cultural and Psychological Studies, and Bibliographies.

185a. _____. Open Doors 1972: Report on International Exchange. New York, 1973.

185b. _____. Open Doors 1973: Report on International Exchange. New York, 1973.
This annual publication is the most frequently quoted source of statistics on foreign students. It seeks to provide a yearly census of the total number of foreign students enrolled in U. S. colleges and universities, their country of origin, field and level of study. Americans studying abroad are also described. The data are as complete as voluntary institutional cooperation permits; because of the narrow definition of "foreign student," those enrolled in secondary schools, trade schools, private English-language schools, etc., are omitted.
        The 1972 edition reports a decline in students from the Far East, Latin America, Europe, and North America, and an increase in those from Africa, Oceania, and the Near and Middle East. The largest increase was in students from Africa. India was for the first time the leader in total number of students; Canada, previously the leader, was second, followed by Hong Kong, the Republic of China, Cuba, and Iran. California led the states with the most foreign students, followed by New York, Florida, Michigan, and Illinois. Miami-Dade Junior College reported the largest number of foreign students of any institution with 5, 871. The proportions of students in various fields of study remained stable from the previous year: engineering 23 percent; humanities 17 percent; physical and life sciences 15 percent; and social sciences 12 percent. Fifty-one percent of the students were undergraduates and 42 percent graduate students.
        In 1973, the total number of foreign students was up four percent over 1971-72, the increase coming primarily from the Far East, the Near and Middle East, and Africa. California again reported the largest number of foreign students, the University of California alone reporting 6, 279. The proportions of students in the major fields continued to show stability, as did the percentage of undergraduates and graduates.

186. _____. English Language and Orientation Programs in the United States. New York, 1973.
This booklet, the result of a questionnaire survey by IIE in 1972, lists and briefly describes 121 offerings of English Language Programs, separate orientation programs with English-language training, and special-opportunity programs at 108 institutions. The booklet also

includes 313 offerings of English-language courses at 312 institutions and degree and certificate programs in Teaching English as a Foreign Language at 54 institutions. Information in the listing includes names and addresses of the institutions, level of instruction of the English courses and programs, costs and length of time of courses and programs.

187. Institute of International Education, Committee on Educational Interchange Policy. "College and University Programs of Academic Exchange." In International Education: Past, Present, Problems and Prospects. Selected readings to supplement H. R. 14643 prepared for the House Committee on Education and Labor by the Task Force on International Education, John Brademas, Chairman, pp. 327-30. Washington, D. C.: U. S. Government Printing Office, 1966.

Three major issues faced by institutions admitting foreign students are: (1) To what extent should curricula be adjusted to meet the needs of students from developing countries? (2) Should foreign students be expected to perform at the same level academically as American students? (3) How much assistance should the university give foreign students with their social and personal adjustment?

188. International Association of Universities. Methods of Establishing Equivalences between Degrees and Diplomas. Paris: UNESCO, 1970.

The methods of establishing equivalences between degrees and diplomas are examined for six countries: Czechoslovakia, France, the Federal Republic of Germany, the USSR, the United Kingdom, the United States. Three major approaches are discussed. The multilateral approach lends itself to groups of countries with related university and general cultural equivalences. The bilateral approach has the advantage of making the process of evaluation easier and of minimizing the risk of errors of judgment. The unilateral approach takes two forms: (1) competent authorities decide each individual case on its merits; (2) the recognition of equivalences is standardized to the extent that lists are drawn up of foreign qualifications deemed acceptable.

189a. International Research and Exchanges Board. Annual Report 1971-72. New York, n.d.

As a result of international political developments, some progress was made toward easing and expanding the exchange of scholars with the Soviet Union, but persistent problems remain, chiefly the pattern of Soviet rejection of Americans working in "sensitive" areas. In Eastern Europe, scholarly exchange has expanded rapidly in recent years, posing problems of an informational and financial nature. Following a meeting in October 1971, IREX agreed to conduct and maintain an inventory of exchange and cooperative opportunities with these countries. The new program of preparatory fellowships, designed to attract promising doctoral candidates into the Soviet and East European field, has proved so successful that additional funds have been obtained for 1973-74.

189b. _____. Annual Report 1972-73. New York, n.d.
During 1972-73, IREX concluded renewed exchange agreements with Bulgaria, Czechoslovakia, Poland, Romania, Yugoslavia, the Soviet Union, and held discussions with Hungary and the German Democratic Republic. Major conferences were organized with Hungary and Romania. While there were some outstanding exchange successes, the report stresses that "it is essential for the academic public to understand that detente has not solved any fundamental problems of scholarly contact with the Soviet Union." IREX funding is currently assured, but efforts must now be made to seek additional sources of support.

190. Inter-University Council for Higher Education Overseas, J. B.
      Butterworth, Chairman. The Overseas Post-graduate. London,
      1972.
Statistics are incomplete but it is estimated that there were 9, 932 foreign students in U. K. universities, 1969-70. The largest group was in social, administrative, and business studies, followed by biological and physical science, and engineering and technology. According to a casual sampling of opinion, there is a need for British universities to take a greater interest in the special requirements of overseas students, particularly the relevance of training, and to provide greater financial support. Steps should also be taken to foster the growth of post-graduate research schools in overseas universities.

191. Irvine, Jack B., Jr. "An Evaluation of Foreign Student Advising
      at Sacramento State College." Sacramento State College, Office
      of the Foreign Student Adviser, May 1968. (Mimeo.)
To determine how students' expectations about advising contrasted with their actual experiences, questionnaires were administered to 208 foreign students (106 returns). Seventy-five percent of the sample checked the overall ratings of "excellent" to "adequate" regarding their advising arrangements. Only ten percent felt that they could communicate neither with their academic adviser nor their foreign student adviser. In general, the level of expectation was higher than warranted by experience. It was recommended that advisers improve techniques of communication and that students' expectations be lowered.

Jacqz, Jane. See No. 2, 3.

192. Jafari, Lafi Ibrahim. "Migration of Palestinian Arab and
     Jordanian Students and Professionals to the United States." Ph.D.
     dissertation, Iowa State University, 1971.
It was the purpose of this study to determine why Palestinian Arabs and
native Jordanians migrate to the United States to study, and what
motivates them to remain in the United States or return home after
completing their studies. A descriptive questionnaire was sent to 300
students and professionals of Palestinian Arab or Jordanian birth who
were living in the United States. Of the 223 respondents, 45 percent
were definitely planning to remain in the United States and 38 percent
were definitely planning to return home. Major reasons for coming to
the United States were admission restrictions to universities at home,
better educational facilities, and to gain higher status and prestige.
Major reasons for non-return were political instability at home, better
career opportunities, better work or research facilities. Ninety-one
percent of those who were planning to return, or were unsure, were
returning because they owed it to Jordan, wanted to live at home,
wanted to return to their families, or wanted to raise their children as
Arabs.

     Jameson, Sanford. See No. 264b.

193. Jameson, Sanford C., and Malcolm, Donald J. "TOEFL—The
     Developing Years." Exchange 8, no. 3 (Winter 1972-73): 57-63.
TOEFL—Test of English as a Foreign Language—measures ability in
listening and reading comprehension, grammar, vocabulary, and
writing. Directed by CEEB and ETS, it has, since its development in
1963, been used extensively by U. S. colleges and universities as a
criterion for acceptance and placement of foreign applicants, and by
government agencies and international businesses and foundations.

194. Jammaz, Abdelrahman I. Abrahim. "Saudi Students in the
     United States: A Study of their Adjustment Problems." Ph.D.
     dissertation, Michigan State University, 1972.
Analysis of a questionnaire sent to 400 male Saudi students in the
United States during 1971-72 (345 replies) yielded the following results.
A high degree of association was found between adjustment and youth,
previous employment at home, attendance at small colleges, majors
in science and engineering, being unmarried.

195. Jarrahi-Zadeh, Ali, and Eichman, William J. "The Impact of
     Socio-Cultural Factors on Middle Eastern Students in the U.S."
     Exchange 5, no. 3 (Winter 1970): 82-94.

Fifty Middle Eastern students at the University of North Carolina, primarily Indian and Arab, and 80 percent male, responded to a questionnaire regarding causes of emotional disturbance. Results were compared to previous studies of American students using the same instrument. While both groups identified academic problems as of major significance, the Middle Eastern students' primary problems related to social adaptation. It is recommended that social integration be fostered by international dormitories, and by the support of student and community groups.

Jenkins, Hugh. See No. 271.

196. Johnson, Dixon C. "Asian Alumni Look Back on Their American Experiences." Exchange 6, no. 1 (Summer 1970): 77-81.
Johnson interviewed 38 Asian alumni of the University of Oregon. Obligation to family was the reason most alumni cited for returning home; only rarely was responsibility to country and national development mentioned. They were satisfied as to the relevance and quality of U. S. education, found Americans to be friendly, and felt that failure of foreign students to make American friends was often due to unresponsiveness on the part of the former.

197. _____. "Problems of Foreign Students." Exchange 7, no. 2 (Fall 1971): 61-68.
Johnson uses data obtained by questionnaire from 214 students at the University of Tennessee. English proficiency and financial affairs were regarded as problems by 60 percent and 55 percent of foreign students respectively, a smaller proportion than expected. American students reported more problems with food than did foreign students, but detachment from family was a greater problem for the foreigners. In every case, American students expected foreign students to have more problems than the latter themselves reported.

198. Johnson, Harry G. "Economic Aspects of Brain Drain." Development Digest 7, (April 1969): 45-54.
In this article (condensed from "An Internationalist Model," in The Brain Drain, ed. Walter Adams, 1968), Johnson suggests that the harmful effects of the brain drain are usually exaggerated, and the benefits of migration ignored, by overly nationalistic approaches. In economic terms, the migration of the educated produces world gains, while losses to particular countries could be covered by compensation arrangements. "Brain drain policy in the countries affected should aim at adjusting the use of educated people to the new prevailing situation of increased relative scarcity by recogniz-ing the higher value of such people in contemporary circumstances,

paying them accordingly, and seeking at the same time to economize
on their use."

199. Johnson, Thomas A. "Nigeria Tries to Lure Graduates Home."
     The New York Times, 17 February 1974, p. 1.
In an effort to persuade Nigerian students and graduates to return
home, an official Nigerian delegation toured several American
cities to inform them of Nigeria's need for skilled personnel in its
burgeoning oil-based economy as well as in a variety of major
social and educational programs.

200. Johnston, Archie B. "FILI, A Pioneer with Potential."
     Tallahassee, Fla.: Tallahassee Junior College, Office of
     Institutional Research, May 1969.
The Florida Inter-American Learning Institute (FILI), which began
at Tallahassee in March 1968, was designed as a half-way house
where foreign students could increase their ability to communicate
in English. Students enroll for one or two 11-week periods during
which they receive instruction in reading, writing, speaking, and
understanding English. When students have reached an established
level of proficiency, they are permitted to attend regular courses
as unofficial auditors. Three additional phases of the program that
have not yet been implemented will provide: Spanish instruction for
American students planning to study in Latin America; English
instruction for international entrepreneurs who wish to do business
with American firms; and Spanish instruction for American business-
men who wish to expand their enterprises.

201a. Joint United States Public Affairs Office. Research Report:
      Survey of Vietnamese Who Studied or Received Training in the
      U. S. — Part I: Cultural and Media Habits. Saigon: JUSPAO
      Planning Office, 23 July 1967.

201b. _____. Research Report: Survey of Vietnamese Who Studied or
      Received Training in the U. S. — Part II: Reaction Profile.
      Saigon: JUSPAO Planning Office, 15 July 1967.
For these studies, 446 U. S.-trained Vietnamese professionals were
surveyed through questionnaires and interviews during 1966-67. Results of Part I show that while American books, magazines, and
newspapers are significant sources of information, foreign radio
broadcasts outrank all other sources on world affairs. Credibility of
the BBC outweighs the VOA by five to one.
        Part II underscores the importance of U. S. education for pro-
fessional and social advancement. Two specific attitudes are reported:

respondents believe people should be more active in democracy and the military is too influential in Vietnam.

202. Jones, Theodore Alan. "The Value to Foreign Student Alumni of Their Education in the United States of America." Ph.D. dissertation, University of Northern Colorado, 1971.
Through the use of a specially designed questionnaire, the effect of U. S. education was described in the areas of the foreign student alumni's vocational lives, attitudes toward the world, personal lives, contribution to their communities or nations, and continued use of English. The population was limited to those who received B.A. or graduate degrees from the University of Northern Colorado or the University of Denver, 1958-70, and who returned to their home countries.

In general, respondents were satisfied with their educations in the United States, were able to move to higher positions, and were contributing to the welfare of their communities or countries. The value of their education was, however, felt to be a total experience and not merely the result of the knowledge and skills learned.

203. Jones, Thomas F. "Should the Foreign Engineering Student Return to His Native Land to Practice His Profession?" In International Education: Past, Present, Problems and Prospects. Selected readings to supplement H. R. 14643 prepared for the House Committee on Education and Labor by the Task Force on International Education, John Brademas, Chairman, pp. 364-66. Washington, D. C.: U. S. Government Printing Office, 1966.
There are cogent arguments on both sides of the brain-drain issue. On the one hand, the foreign engineering student has obligations to his native country which provided his basic education and has need of his specialized skills. On the other hand, by remaining in the United States he is assured of all the opportunity and responsibility he is able to accept. The United States too has invested in his education to the Ph.D. level, and, moreover, has an interest in maintaining its predominance in engineering research and development.

Measures which might reverse the flow are: (1) "urging, counseling and guiding the foreign student to seek a mate of similar nationality;" and (2) "foster the development of opportunities in the homeland equal to those here."

204. Kang, Tai S. "Name Change and Acculturation: Chinese Studies on an American Campus." Pacific Sociological Review 14 (October 1971): 403-12.

The social-psychological implications of identity change symbolized through name change were studied through a stratified random sample of 170 Chinese students at the University of Minnesota. Three hypotheses were tested relating name change to: (1) fuller socialization in the host society; (2) more flexible and varied economic adjustment; and (3) greater access to the lines of influence and power in the host community. Data supported all three hypotheses. Those students who had changed their names displayed significantly more out-group oriented attitudes and behaviors than those who did not change their names. Data suggest that change of name represents a significant shift of social identity.

205. _____. "A Foreign Student Group as an Ethnic Community." International Review of Modern Sociology 2 (March 1972): 72-82.
The hypothesis of this study is that Chinese students, set apart in U. S. society by their physical characteristics, language, and culture, form a highly in-group oriented ethnic enclave which provides an array of institutionalized solutions to the common problems which face aliens in a host community. Results of a survey of 118 randomly selected Chinese students at the University of Minnesota in 1967 supported the hypothesis.

206. Kannappan, Subbiah. "The Brain Drain and Developing Countries." International Labor Review 98 (July 1968): 1-26.
In this study, sponsored by Michigan State University, Kannappan maintains that developing countries will be worse off as a result of migration only if (1) it can be shown that exchange of human skills is on the whole detrimental to them and (2) reduction in the stock of human skills leaves their populace worse off. Investigation of the problem supports neither contention. Recommendations are made whereby developing countries can increase their supply of and demand for trained professionals.

207. Kao, Charles H. C., and Lee, Jae Won. "An Empirical Analysis of China's Brain Drain into the United States." Economic Development and Cultural Change 21 (April 1973): 500-13.
Questionnaires completed by a random sample of 372 Chinese scholars, persons from mainland China or Taiwan holding doctoral degrees and living in the United States, were analyzed to determine the significance of a number of variables affecting their propensity to stay in the United States. Satisfaction with income and the American way of life, length of residence in the United States, degree of

fair competition in Taiwan, political freedom in the United States, and lack of family ties in Taiwan were the six key determinants, in that order of importance, to Chinese scholars' high propensity to stay in the United States. Since no single factor is sufficient to explain the drain, no single policy will reverse the flow. The improvement of domestic non-economic conditions will raise the rate of return and improvement of economic conditions will accelerate it.

208. Kaplan, Robert B. "The Foreign Student and His English
      Language Training." Address delivered at a meeting of the
      Southern California Chapter of the ELS Language Center, Los
      Angeles, California, 1 November 1968.
See No. 209.

209. _____. "English Language Proficiency and the Foreign Student."
      Exchange (Winter 1968): 43-47.
English-language proficiency should not be made a college entrance requirement for foreign students. An institution should not, however, admit students with inadequate comprehension unless it is prepared to support an English-language training program, individually or in cooperation with similar institutions.

210. _____. "NAFSA in the Mod Mod World." Exchange 6, no. 2
      (Fall 1970): 68-75.
NAFSA must encourage educational institutions and government to adjust to the presence of foreign students by making every effort to insure the relevance of U. S. education to global problems, by combating the growing reaction against international education, and by helping to keep down the costs of education.

      _____. See No. 267.

211. Kelly, William. "Horticultural Training of Graduate Students
      from Developing Countries." Paper presented at the 17th
      International Horticultural Congress, College Park, Maryland,
      15-20 August 1966.
Kelly discusses in general terms some of the problems of U. S. horticultural training, chiefly that students from developing countries are trained in basic, rather than applied, horticulture.

212. Kelman, Herbert C., ed. International Behavior. New York:
      Holt, Rinehart, and Winston, 1965.
In his concluding chapter, "Social-Psychological Approaches to the Study of International Relations: The Question of Relevance," Kelman

considers whether international cooperation through educational exchange affects conditions for peace, and therefore whether research in this area has potential political relevance. He finds that international cooperation (1) produces increased openness among key individuals in attitudes to other nations; (2) reduces levels of tension; (3) increases world-mindedness and commitment to internationalist ideology; (4) develops a network of relations cutting across national boundaries. He therefore recommends that applied research be conducted to evaluate goal-achievement of exchange programs and to gain insight into ways of enhancing their effectiveness.

213.   Kent, James. "Foreign Students: An Economic Approach."
       Post-Secondary Education in New York State 1, no. 3 (July/
       August 1973): 1.
Adopting the proposition of Farmer and Renforth (see No. 133), Kent calculates that the 17,294 foreign students in New York State in 1971 contribute $11,601,270 to the State's economy, placing the foreign student "trade" in 18th place among New York State's exporters.

       Kerr, Lornie. See No. 22.

214.   Keshav, Dev Sharma. "Indian Students in the United States."
       Exchange 4, no. 4 (Spring 1969): 43-59.
Under the auspices of the Comparative Education Center of the University of Chicago, the author conducted a comprehensive study of 1,416 Indian students enrolled during 1965-66 at 322 major institutions in the United States. Major findings include: (1) predominant reasons for coming were to gain advanced training, and general interest in the United States; (2) the majority of students did not do extremely well in their studies in India, suggesting that the best students are handicapped by financial inadequacies and faulty information about the United States; (3) Indian students are most satisfied with "general academic standards" and least satisfied with "advisory system;" (4) brain drain is a situational phenomenon and can be cured by situational means alone. Policy recommendations are made for American colleges and universities as well as for the U. S. government.

215.   Kim, Hyung Tae. "Relationships Between Personal Character-
       istics of Korean Students in Pennsylvania and their Attitudes
       Toward the Christian Churches in America." Ph.D. disserta-
       tion, University of Pittsburgh, 1966.
Data were gathered from 137 Korean students (90 percent of the total population) attending the institutions of higher learning in

Pennsylvania, using two attitude scales and a personal information checklist. Analysis supported the hypotheses that there are significant relationships between the students' background characteristics and their attitudes toward the Christian Churches in America and toward selected moral and spiritual values. There was also a significant relationship between their attitudes toward the Churches and their attitudes toward the moral and spiritual values. The students tended to have a traditionally conservative outlook on morality yet seemed to be increasingly progressive in their attitudes toward a socially oriented individualism.

Kimmel, Paul. See No. 10, 11a-d, 12a-h, 113.

216. King, Kenneth J. "African Students in Negro American Colleges: Notes on the Good African." Phylon 31, no. 1 (Spring 1970): 16-30.
King shows that despite its reputation as a "safe" institution, providing segregated, non-political, "industrial" education for Negroes, Tuskeegee Institute in the 1920's exposed its students to the ideas of the American Negro radical intelligentsia. As feared by colonial administrators coping with African desires for U. S. education, Tuskeegee could often be a stimulus to black separatism, an incentive to aggressive business enterprise, and an inspiration for independent, non-sectarian African schools.

217. Kirstein, Laurette. "Community Services for Foreign Students in Metropolitan Areas." Exchange 6, no. 3 (Winter 1971): 55-61.
Community services for foreign students in many metropolitan areas suffer from lack of coordination, communication with students and/ or sponsoring agencies, and regular financing. Practically all programs include home hospitality and tours, programs for wives, seminars, speakers' bureaus, orientation dinners, English conversation programs, and housing assistance. More sponsored than non-sponsored students are served by these programs.

218. Klein, Marjorie H.; Alexander, A. A.; and Tseng, Kwo-Hwa. "The Foreign Student Adaptation Program: Social Experiences of Asian Students." Exchange 6, no. 3 (Winter 1971): 77-90.
As part of a larger project designed to probe the experience of cross-cultural education and adaptation within a multivariate and multidisciplinary framework, the authors present their findings concerning social experiences of Asian students at the University of Wisconsin. The social and interpersonal aspects of the sojourn are satisfactory; nevertheless, many students remain isolated from

American life. It is recommended that the human, rather than the foreign, aspect of the experience be stressed when considering the meaning of intercultural education and adaptation.

Kletzien, Damon S. See No. 4.

219. Klineberg, O. International Exchanges in Education, Science, and Culture: Suggestions for Research. Publications of the International Social Science Council. Paris: Mouton and Company, 1966.

The massive investment in international education creates an imperative challenge to increase the effectiveness of programs at all levels. Existing social science research has usually been conducted in the framework of programs developed within one nation for its own purposes. While extrapolation from one set of circumstances to another is sometimes justified, one objective of future research must be to summarize what has been done and examine the universality of the hypotheses and conclusions presented. The goals of international exchanges have yet to be clearly defined, and a theoretical framework for research formulated. This survey of social science research suggests that efforts be directed to the following areas.

1. In the field of international exchanges involving contact between persons, many publications in the United States deal with the effects on the foreign students of study at a U. S. institution, both in terms of change in attitude toward the host and of individual personality change. Some of the resulting hypotheses need further investigation, particularly in their application to experiences in other countries.

2. Other types of personal contacts are also deserving of research: those resulting from technical cooperation; tourism; sports; immigration; etc.

3. An area suffering from a relative lack of research is the possible contribution to international friendship of materials which can be sent from one country to another without personal intermediaries. Who are the targets of informational programs? What types of information are most effective in promoting positive attitudes? Research should focus on mass media, textbooks, literature, and the arts.

4. Additional suggestions for research include the effect on the individual of governmental policies regulating educational exchange; the role of language skills in success or failure of programs; problems of policy relating to selection and treatment of grantees.

220. Klinger, M. Robert. "Foreign Student Adviser: A Necessary
     Profession." Exchange (Summer 1967): 21-27.
The foreign student adviser is a specialist whose duties—admissions
recommendations, legal and personal counseling, alumni contacts,
etc.—are essential to both institution and student.

Kovach, Joseph W. See No. 283.

221. Kumbaraci, Turkan. "Translated Reading Tests as Culture-
     Fair Measures for Foreign Students." New York: Columbia
     University, n.d.
A comparison of an English-language reading comprehension test
with its Turkish translation and re-translation was conducted. The
instruments consisted of two parallel forms of a reading test of
college entrance level which were translated into Turkish, and then
re-translated into English. The sample consisted of 896 Turkish
high-school seniors and college students and 1,324 American high-
school seniors and college students. Several suggestions were discussed for the perfection of the instruments used for screening
foreign students and for cross-cultural item statistics.

222. Kwochka, Vera Faith. "A Survey of United States Students
     Regarding the Effects of their Residence in the International
     House of New York." Ed.D. dissertation, Columbia Univer-
     sity, 1970.
The goals established by the International House of New York are
(1) to help each student achieve educational and personal goals, and
(2) to give American students an opportunity to broaden their horizons through friendship with people from diverse backgrounds and
cultures. To discover whether these goals are being achieved, a
questionnaire was designed and mailed to natural-born citizens of
the United States who resided in the House for at least two con-
secutive academic terms during the period September 1951 to June
1961. Approximately 1,200 individuals met these requirements;
slightly more than 650 returned completed questionnaires.
     According to the survey, International House is meeting to
some extent the goals established for American residents. A large
minority, however, felt their residence had no effect on their educational progress; many of these respondents did not believe the
House should or could help its residents in this regard. The longer
the length of residence, the more close friendships respondents
established with non-Americans and non-Westerners. Respondents
reported making friends and learning to understand and respect
individuals of other nationalities, ethnic backgrounds, religions,
and races.

Recommendations for more effective aid include increased efforts to achieve a better balance between the numbers of foreign and American residents with regard to their fields of study and educational objectives, to strengthen professional interest groups, and to program more seminars.

223. Landers, Thomas J. "The Erosion of the American Commitment to International Educational Change." Cosmos (Association of International Education, Japan) 2 (1973): 23-27.
Recent trends and events indicate that the American "international era" might possibly be coming to an end, and that a period of domestic introspection, even isolationism, may be setting in. This poses acute problems for the future of international educational exchange. Recommendations are made for reversal of the trend toward declining support for foreign students: (1) reassessment of national goals and renewal of financial commitment to the underlying rationale of international educational exchange; (2) foreign students must be provided equal opportunities for employment, scholarships, and fellowships, this burden to be shifted from the financially troubled local institution to the federal government; (3) overseas counselors should be supplied with more complete information about low-tuition colleges in low cost-of-living areas. [The word "change" in the title of the article is perhaps a misprint and shoud read "exchange."]

224. Lefevre, Th. "How to Deal with the Brain Drain from Developing Countries." Paper presented at the Rehovot Conference on Science and Education in Developing States, 18-26 August 1969.
One contributing factor to the ever-widening gap between rich and poor nations is the concentration of scientific and technical manpower in the developed countries which enables them to achieve an increasing rate of economic growth. In order to reverse this brain drain, underdeveloped countries must devote greater resources to scientific training and research in the context of planned economic growth. Industrialized countries should supply aid which is adapted to conditions in developing countries, and find national solutions to their own manpower problems.

225. Levy, Mordechai M. "International Training Policy in the Context of Economic Development." In UNESCO Handbook of International Exchanges, pp. 17-25. Paris: UNESCO, 1967.
Developing countries, which urgently need to expand the industrial skills and professional knowledge of their populations, should direct their attention to the problem created by unsupervised flow of

students to foreign institutions. Levy recommends that, in each
developing country, a National Manpower Authority be established,
responsible for forecasting the nation's manpower needs and formulating programs for manpower development. A National Scholarship
Board would conduct competitions for state scholarships, selecting
the candidate most likely to fulfill the task for which he is to be
trained. A vocational Guidance Service would direct students to
appropriate foreign institutions, provide educational officers
attached to foreign embassies to maintain continual supervision over
the students, and ensure their return through "bonding" arrangements, frequent home leaves, and contacts with potential employers
in the home country.

226. Levy, Samuel. "Some Aspects of the International Migration
     of Human Capital: The Case of British Physicians." Ph.D.
     dissertation, Wayne State University, 1969.
This dissertation applies the concept of human capital and the
theoretical framework which has been constructed upon it to an
analysis of some aspects of manpower migration. Its major objectives are, first, to analyze some of the general welfare impacts
which migration can be expected to have on the country of emigration and, secondly, an analysis of the effects which emigration of
the highly educated will have on the public provision of higher education on the one hand, and on the private demand for it on the
other. The empirical portion centers on the emigration of British
physicians in an attempt to explore the interrelationships between
the public supply of medical training, the private demand for it, and
the effect which physicians' emigration has had on them.
     The findings suggest that the British system of financing
medical (higher) education actually tends to encourage the emigration of graduates. In addition, the rate of return to investment by
British physicians in emigrating to the United States was estimated
and found to be very high.

227. Lewis, A. B. "Training Foreign Graduate Students in Agri-
     cultural Economics." Journal of Farm Economics 49 (August
     1967): 684-704.
Training in agricultural economics for graduate students from traditional countries poses special problems for American teachers,
chiefly because of the very different habits of thought and social
philosophies of such students. These "non-Greek" habits and
philosophies typify the leadership of traditional countries and hinder
agricultural development in various ways, often leading to the
adoption of unwise national agricultural policies. To transform
traditional scholars into scientists who can and will analyze the

policies and programs of their own country objectively and con-
structively, teachers in each area of specialization in agricultural
economics should put more stress on practical measurement, the
derivation of principles and their application, and should draw upon
examples from many parts of the world. The same kind of teaching
is essential for American graduate students if they are to understand and cope with world agricultural economic problems.

228. Lockett, Betty Alla. "A Study of the Effectiveness of Foreign
    Student Advisers at American Colleges and Universities as
    Reported by Foreign Students Sponsored by the United States
    Agency for International Development." Ph.D. dissertation,
    American University, 1970.

From data collected from 795 foreign students at the American
University Development Education and Training Research Institute
(DETRI) as a part of the AID Exit Interview Project, it was concluded that: (1) foreign student advisers at American colleges and
universities are effective in their role as they are perceived by
the large majority of the foreign students interviewed; (2) the geographic origins of the foreign students did not determine whether or
not they talked with their foreign student adviser; and (3) a major
determinant of the usefulness of foreign student advisers as they
are perceived by foreign students seems to be their availability to
the foreign students. (See No. 113 for a description of this project.)

229. Longest, James W. Evaluating Orientation for Foreign Students.
    Ithaca, N.Y.: State University of New York, College of Agri-
    culture at Cornell, April 1969.

This report is based on research to evaluate an eight-week summer
orientation program for foreign graduate students. It was found that
foreign students do experience a period of adjustment that varies
from one to two semesters. The results indicate that following
orientation the students had: lower transcultural anxiety scores;
significantly higher knowledge of the United States and its universities' requirements; significantly higher English-language test
scores; and lower transcultural anxiety and higher grades than a
control group of students in the first semester of study in the
United States. This study also supported findings of other studies
indicating the positive relationship between English-language scores
and grades achieved, as well as the positive correlation between
prior transcultural experience and higher grades. Suggestions for
future orientation programs and a bibliography are included.

230. Lozada, Rhodelia Corazon Buenaventura. "Foreign Students at
    Purdue University: A Study of Selected Personal and Academic

Characteristics in Relation to Current Experiences and Future Expectations." Ph.D. dissertation, Purdue University, 1970. A 52-item questionnaire was administered to all 809 foreign students attending the spring semester 1969 at Purdue University. Responding to the questionnaire were 476 students representing 58.83 percent of the foreign student population. These students were found to be achieving grades equivalent to those of the average American student. A majority were well-equipped academically for their studies. Upon arrival they experienced language difficulties but these were reported with significantly less frequency after one year.

The chief dissatisfactions were with informal aspects of college life. In general, the students, regardless of academic status, nationality or age, gave the impression that they were satisfied with their study in the United States. About one-fourth, however, felt dissociated from the mainstream of American life and general dissatisfaction was expressed with the strength and nature of the friendships formed with Americans.

A very clear implication is that future foreign students might be helped in their social adjustments if they could be given the opportunity to participate in an orientation program conducted in the United States which focused upon the informal aspects of American life.

Lybrand, William. See No. 11a-b.

231. Major, Randolph T., Jr. "A Review of the Literature on International Exchange." Putney, Vt.: The Experiment in International Living, August 1965.

The research on international education and cross-cultural contact reviewed here is divided into three related categories: (1) Studies of the individual, his or her psychological characteristics and pre-departure environment. These have identified ethnocentrism (Adorno), xenophilia (Perlmutter), motivation (Pool), age, and other cultural and nationality factors as influential elements determining the degree and type of interaction between traveller and host. (2) Studies of the sojourn—length, location, activity, adjustment process, personal relationships. (3) Changes in the individual as a result of travel. Change has been measured in terms of information, opinion, attitudes, images, behavior patterns, personality. Some attitude studies (Leonard, Pool) suggest that travel tends to shift attitudes toward a conservative or national viewpoint rather than towards greater liberalism. While some studies indicate a trend towards positive views of both home and host countries (e.g., Coelho), others posit the development of a "third culture" (Useem) or a multi-cultural personality (Cormack).

All facets of international education research require further theoretical and conceptual development, in particular, the effect of foreign students on the host culture, and secondary effects such as influence on the traveller's family and friends, or the effects of cultural isolation.

232. Maniago, Jo Anne Barker. "The First Peace Corps: The Work of the American Teachers in the Philippines, 1900-1910." Ph.D. dissertation, Boston University, Graduate School, 1971.

This study documents historically the work of the American teachers in the Philippines between 1900 and 1910 and speculates on their success. While producing neither economic stability nor democratic government, the pioneer teachers did provide to the Filipino masses the tools for initiating a Filipino version of democracy.

233. Markham, James W. International Images and Mass Communication Behavior. Iowa City: University of Iowa, School of Journalism, 1967.

A five-year study of foreign students at the University of Iowa 1959-64 examined pre-sojourn images and attitudes about the United States, the nature and extent of manifest change after a period of stay in this country, and the relationships between attitudes and exposure to mass media. Three hundred and forty students were interviewed and tested; there were follow-up interviews with 189 respondents.

Students coming to America were expected to have largely favorable images of the United States, and the analysis of their preconceptions supported this expectation. Comparison of pre-arrival images with later images showed the predominant direction of image change to be negative. Europeans tended to judge America and Americans in more negative terms than did students from other areas. In general, Asians tended to see us in the most favorable light; Africans and Latin Americans were only slightly less favorable.

The students' image change of their homelands was slight during the American stay. Change in homeland images, when it appeared, moved in a positive direction. The mass media were the major sources of images and continued to be important during the sojourn though use of the media dropped slightly.

Comparison in the longitudinal analysis of the earlier and later groups indicated that foreign students of the later period were better qualified scholastically and more extensively informed about America than were those interviewed during the 1959-62 period.

234. Marsh, Harriet Louise. "Foreign Student Advisers in Commu-
    nity Colleges: A Study of the Role and Function in Community
    Colleges of the State of Washington." Ph.D. dissertation,
    Columbia University, 1972.

Through questionnaires and personal interviews, foreign student
advisers in Washington State community colleges described backgrounds, preparation, and various aspects of their positions in the
colleges. Recommendations based on the findings reported in this
study include: (1) designation of counselors as community college
foreign student advisers; (2) special assistance to advisers in
written materials, workshops, consultations, and in-service training, all available through NAFSA; (3) special summer courses on
foreign student matters; (4) formation of institutional policy covering
admission of foreign students, assigned time and job description for
advisers; (5) greater use of community and agency resources; and
(6) inter-institutional cooperative arrangements for evaluation of
admission credentials and possibly orientation and teaching of
English as a second language.

235. Martin, Gale Maclane. "A Model for the Cultural and Statisti-
    cal Analysis of Academic Achievement of Foreign Graduate
    Students at the University of North Carolina at Chapel Hill."
    Ph.D. dissertation, University of North Carolina, Chapel Hill,
    1971.

The empirical portion of this study concerned utilization of TOEFL
as a predictor of academic achievement. Seventy-two foreign male
graduates during their first year of study at the University of North
Carlina at Chapel Hill and having a record of satisfactory marks on
the TOEFL prior to admission were matched with 72 non-tested,
randomly selected peers as to geographic origin and field of study.
Grade point averages were computed for first- and second-semesters'
study for the total population (144).

     In examining the more significant findings of the study, it
appeared that students passing the TOEFL prior to admission
achieved higher grade point averages in both semesters of the
first year of graduate study than their non-tested counterparts.
This held true for all geographic areas concerned. In comparing
each of the five sub-tests of TOEFL with the academic achievement
of the tested group, it was found that none of the sub-tests was
significantly predictive of academic success in either semester of
study.

236. Maslog, Crispin Chio. "Filipino and Indian Students' Images:
    Of Themselves, of Each Other, and of the United States."
    Ph.D. dissertation, University of Minnesota, 1967.

This research explores national stereotypes as revealed by 47 Philippine and 52 Indian students.

237. Mastroianni, George Anthony. "A Study of Attitudes Toward the United States Held by Former Participants in a United States' Educational Exchange Project in Radio and Television." Ph.D. dissertation, Syracuse University, 1971.
Seventy-eight participants in programs sponsored by the Bureau of Educational and Cultural Affairs of the Department of State and 76 non-participants completed a questionnaire. The major conclusion drawn from the findings was that attendance in this exchange program permitted the grantee group to give more discriminating and more definite responses toward attitude statements regarding the Usited States. The grantees were consistently less neutral in their responses.

Matthewson, Douglas E. See No. 272.

238. "Measuring the Impact of Academic Exchange." Far Horizons 10 (Spring 1974): 5-7.
Since 1970, the International Committee for the Study of Educational Exchange has conducted a seven-country survey to investigate international university exchange of students and faculty. Principal topics of the study were the nature and extent of the exchanges, changes in individuals over time, relevant administrative arrangements, and problems encountered. In August 1973, two further studies were approved: (1) "An Investigation of the Consequences of International Educational Exchange" will analyze long-range effects of foreign study on participants; (2) "Mental Health in International Educational Exchanges: A Study of Coping Behavior in a Cultural Environment" will attempt to determine the conditions under which the individual's foreign experience contributes to growth and mental health, and the conditions which are associated with failure and breakdown.

239. Melby, John F. "The Foreign Student in America." In International Education: Past, Present, Problems and Prospects. Selected readings to supplement H. R. 14643 prepared for the House Committee on Education and Labor by the Task Force on International Education, John Brademas, Chairman, pp. 319-26. Washington, D. C.: U. S. Government Printing Office, 1966.
Foreign students come to the United States for three reasons: to get training that will enhance their professional status at home; to get training that will be of direct benefit to their countries; and to learn about the United States. While most are satisfied with their sojourn, many encounter problems such as relevance of their education to

employment opportunities at home, an area in which both foreign governments and the United States might take a greater interest; injustices in American democracy which, as many returnees plan an active political role, may affect international relations; and difficulties in establishing relationships with American students and families despite university-community hospitality programs. Since foreign students, by their mere presence, become a factor in U. S. foreign policy Americans must remember that their experiences and treatment in America will have an important bearing on their attitudes and actions and eventually on the policies of their countries and on our own security and welfare.

240.   Melendez-Craig, Mario. "A Study of the Academic Achievement and Related Problems among Latin American Students Enrolled in the Major Utah Universities." Ph.D. dissertation, Brigham Young University, 1970.

This study presents an account of the academic achievement of Latin American students in the major Utah universities and of related problems as measured by the Michigan International Student Problem Inventory.

The findings indicate that Latin Americans are achieving acceptably; many are outstanding scholars. There is no significant difference between academic achievement and marital status or sex among the group. While there is no significant difference in grade point average among the three schools, upper-division and graduate students achieve better than lower-division students. English proficiency is highly correlated with academic achievement.

Most Latin Americans felt that financial problems are greatest, followed by academic problems, and least important are problems related to religious activities and attitudes.

241.   Meredith, Gerald M. "Why They Came to the East-West Center: A Comparison of Asian Pacific and American Grantees." Washington, D. C.: American Educational Theatre Association, February 1968.

The goals of this study were to (1) identify major reasons for attending the East-West Center, (2) clarify the self-reported motivational structure behind educational-vocational decisions, and (3) examine the relationship of these factors to areas of satisfaction and dissatisfaction with the program.

Dole's Reasons for Going to College Inventory was modified and administered to 216 Asian-Pacific and 106 American grantees, yielding pattern differences between the groups in the areas of reasons, values, interests, influences, and needs related to educational-vocational choice

242. Merriam, Marshal F. "Reversing the Brain Drain: A Case Study from India." International Development Review 12, no. 3 (1970): 16-22.
Data from a questionnaire completed by 206 faculty and senior staff at the Indian Institute of Technology at Kanpur (IITK) revealed that return from study or work in developed countries was motivated by nationalism and was independent of IITK's existence, suggesting that "centers of excellence" do not necessarily induce return. The Institute has, however, policies which attempt to attract professionals without requiring substantial resources and might be implemented elsewhere in India: academic freedom, flexible advancement opportunities, firm job offers made to candidates in absentia, and payment of travel expenses home.

243. Michie, Allan A. "How to Run Programs." College and University Business 43 (November 1967): 56-58.
Observing that there has been a phenomenal growth in international education activities and that the majority of international programs are conducted by a minority of institutions, Michie examines the growth of coordinating administrative structures in educational institutions. Two different approaches to the development of such coordinating offices for international programs are seen. One, typified by such major institutions as Michigan State University and the State University of New York, is the institution-wide approach, by which administration, preferably with faculty participation, works to an overall plan for extending the international dimension throughout the institution. The second approach, exemplified by Stanford and Indiana Universities, is the slower, selective method of identifying and encouraging individuals, disciplines, schools, and colleges within the institution where the international dimension has already become rooted. Between these two approaches, a number of other institutional mechanisms have developed; some further examples are given.

244. _____. Higher Education and World Affairs. New York: Education and World Affairs, 1968.
The target population of this review of higher education and world affairs consists of those institutions just entering the international field. The review therefore includes a survey of the diverse activities which make up international education, an exploration of some common institutional problems, and an indication of the resources which are available to institutions about international education. A fairly extensive bibliography of international education, compiled by Sandra K. Meagher, follows the text.

245. _____, ed. Diversity and Interdependence through International Education. New York: Education and World Affairs, 1967.

This volume presents the major statements and discussions of a symposium marking the twentieth anniversary of the International Educational Exchange (Fulbright) Program held at Columbia University in 1966. After introductory remarks by Senator Fulbright and John Hope Franklin, the principal papers were: "The Responsibility of the Intellectual," by Herman Wells; "The Role of Government," by Charles Frankel; "The Role of the Academic Community," by Oscar Handlin; "What Place for the Arts?" by Howard Taubman; "What Role for Science?" by Caryl P. Haskins; and "Education in the Development Process," by Frederick Harbison.

Conclusions are summarized by Frank B. Freidel in the form of questions: How can the quality of the Fulbright Program be maintained? How can we avoid playing numbers games by supplying live bodies who are not really the people wanted in other countries? Who from other countries could most profit by being in the United States?

246. Miller, Jake Charles. "African Students and the Racial Attitudes and Practices of Americans." Ph.D. dissertation, University of North Carolina, Chapel Hill, 1967.

This study examines the racial image African students hold of Americans. Participants were 130 African graduate students of seven universities.

Results indicated that a majority of the participants came to this country with unfavorable attitudes toward race relations and as a result of their stay here, those attitudes became more unfavorable. Similar majorities believed that the treatment and status of the American Negro were less than favorable and that Americans tended to be too complacent in regard to the apartheid policy of South Africa and white minority rule in general.

A major conclusion of the study was that while a majority of the participants rate race relations high in the overall development of their image of the United States, they also give consideration to other aspects of American life.

247. Miller, Milton H.; Yeh, Eng-Kung; Alexander, A. A.; Klein, Marjorie H.; Tseng, Kwo-Hwa; Workneh, Fikre; and Chu, Hung-Ming. "The Cross-Cultural Student: Lessons in Human Nature." Bulletin of the Menninger Clinic 35 (March 1971): 128-31.

One aspect of a five-year study of students involved in cross-cultural situations conducted by the authors on a Ford Foundation grant investigated the ability of students to achieve "warm friendship and understanding" with people of an alien culture. Their findings, based on questionnaires and interviews with East Asian students at the University of Wisconsin and American students in East Asia, revealed that:

(1) international students' warm intimate contacts are almost exclusively limited to their co-national group; (2) their relations with host-country nationals rarely go beyond superficial pleasantries; (3) they are rather discouraged about any prospects for deep cross-cultural friendships.

248. Miller, Paul A. "The Government-Academic Relationship in International Educational Developments." Bulletin on International Education 5 (14 April 1967): 1-5.
If a mutual and natural interaction is to occur among educators and their institutions in the world community, Miller suggests that it must be practiced and advanced at home. Cooperation between public and private activity and between academic and non-academic interests as well as between government and non-government, would seem to be a necessary condition of public interest.
　　This article is based on general remarks made at the conclusion of an American Council of Education seminar.

249. Miller, Richard Eugene. "A Study of Significant Elements in the On-the-Job Behavior of College and University Foreign Student Advisers." Ph.D. dissertation, Michigan State University, 1968.
This study identifies some 200 significant common functions which are performed by most Foreign Student Advisers, and develops generalizations regarding which functions are performed most effectively. Advisers perceive themselves as working more effectively (1) with people rather than in areas concerning ideas, programs, and organizational structures; (2) with non-university persons and agencies rather than with university personnel; and (3) as they gain more experience in the field. They perceive themselves as working least effectively in academic advising of foreign students.

250. Mishler, Anita L. "Personal Contact in International Exchanges." In International Behavior, ed. by Herbert C. Kelman, pp. 550-60. New York: Holt, Rinehart, and Winston, 1965.
Mishler's review of research leads to the conclusions that: (1) experience of national status deprivation will reduce the possibility of positive experiences by limiting the nature of personal contacts; (2) cultural differences may lead to fruitful cross-cultural relationships when personalities are predisposed to respond favorably to different rather than perceived similarities; (3) the quality of an individual's relationship with home country can be an important factor in sojourn experience; (4) foreign students who come for socio-cultural rather than occupational reasons are more likely to have contacts with host nationals.

251. Mississippi State University, International Cooperative Education
     Program. "Status Report and Development Plans for an Inter-
     national Program in Cooperative Education." January 1967.
Two types of cooperative education programs are proposed: (1) the
U. S. branch of an international firm could provide scholarship support, and the student would be employed by the firm in the home country after graduation; (2) U. S. firms could employ students during
their sojourn.

252. Montgomery, Warner Miller. "The Purpose and Problems of
     AID Educational Assistance to Thailand." Ph.D. disseration,
     University of Michigan, n.d.
This study analyzes the relationship between AID university contract
goals and the problems encountered in the project activities through
an examination of the project operations and the adviser's participation
in them. Five projects in Thailand are described.
     Problem areas included conflict with the AID Mission office over
interpretation of the contract goals, communication between the university team and the Thai institution, and among the American agencies
and institutions working in Thailand, Thai cultural attitudes, frustration with Thai bureaucracy. With few exceptions the goals and activities
were never adjusted to meet the problems. The evidence gathered
and presented in this study strongly suggests that the goals of educational assistance to Thailand have been related more to the anticipated
problems of assistance than to the problems experienced by advisers
in project activities.

253. Moore, Forrest G. "International Education in the Seventies:
     Revolution or Turmoil on the Campus?" Exchange 6, no. 1
     (Summer 1970): 34-46.
Moore proposes changes in immigration regulations, admissions procedures, foreign student offices, curriculum, and university administration in order to reduce unrest and disenchantment among students.

254. Moore, Forrest G., and Forman, Robert E. The University and
     Its Foreign Alumni: Maintaining Overseas Contact. Minneapolis,
     Minn.: University of Minnesota Press, 1964.
The central purpose of this study was to ascertain what foreign alumni
though should be the extent, aim, and method of continued contact with
their U. S. university. Fifty-two alumni of the University of Minnesota in 15 countries, primarily Asian, were interviewed, and questionnaires were completed by 145. In addition, the views of faculty
advisers of foreign students at Minnesota, and of foreign students
advisers and alumni executives from other universities were sought.

It was found that overseas alumni are eager for follow-up and regard it as serving their own needs and those of American faculty members, of the university, and of America. Educational institutions as represented by faculty members, alumni executives, and foreign student advisers believe that continuing relations are well worth emphasizing, but that follow-up programs compete for money and time with many other institutional responsibilities.

Major operational obstacles to improved follow-up are financing, mechanics, and coordination. While the primary responsibility must rest with the educational institution, government agencies and national organizations could assist in funding and in keeping address files current.

255. Moran, Robert; Mestenhauser, Josef; and Pedersen, Paul. "Dress Rehearsal for a Cross-Cultural Experience." Exchange, 10 (Summer 1974): 23-25.
Role playing and simulation exercises are used in a new kind of orientation program being tried at the University of Minnesota for foreign students. The program consists of a 20-hour simulation exercise over one weekend. Simulated problem solving with role playing was found to give participants feedback on the appropriateness of their solutions in this cultural context. Forty-three persons participated in the weekend program: 18 newly arrived foreign students, nine foreign students who had been in the United States at least one year, nine U.S. students, and seven persons from the community. Evaluation of the exercise, using a 20-item questionnaire and the Michigan International Student Problem Inventory, found the orientation to be successful.

256. Moravcsik, Michael J. "The Physics of Interviewing Project." Exchange 8, no. 1 (Summer 1972): 16-22.
To improve the selection of foreign graduate physics students, a team of physics professors from four U.S. universities conducted interviews with 145 prospective students in South Asia. On the basis of subsequent limited data, a "virtually perfect" correlation was found between the interviewer's evaluations and the actual performance of the student in graduate school. It is recommended that similar interviewing trips be organized to a given geographic area every two years.

257. _____. "Foreign Students in the Natural Sciences: A Growing Challenge." Exchange 9, no. 1 (Summer 1973): 45-56.
Reviewing the difficulties encountered by students from developing countries who are preparing for scientific careers at home, Moravesik proposes improvements in pre-sojourn information and interviewing, deferment of fee payment, relevant curriculum planning, and better alumni contacts.

258. Mowlana, Hamid, and McLaughlin, Gerald. "Some Variables
     Interacting with Media Exposure Among Foreign Students."
     Sociology and Social Research 53 (July 1969): 511-22.
From data obtained by questionnaire from foreign students at a southern
state university, it was found that for the entire group, radio and TV
were primary information sources, then U. S. publications, foreign
publications, and personal sources. The self-reported use of information sources for forming an attitude about the United States showed
a highly significant pattern but was not a function of the classification
variables: foreign student's home country, field of study, tenure in
the United States and the place of residence.

259. Mozden, Stanley W. "Military Assistance Training Program:
     A Military Instrument of Foreign Policy." M.A. thesis, Uni-
     versity of Pittsburgh, 1973.
Mozden examines the objective structure and operation of MATP and
assesses its role in Brazilian military training. MATP's impact
should not be underestimated; it is involved in more than one-half of
the world's nations, and it has more participants than all other U. S.
Government programs. It contributes to the capabilities of many
military institutions by assisting in development of personnel and
technical skills. MATP's goals, however, are ill-defined and while
most trainees acquire new skills and knowledge, ther is no evidence
that they are more sympathetic to the United States as a result.

260. Myers, Robert G. "'Brain Drains' and 'Brain Gains.'" Inter-
     national Development Review 9, no. 4 (1967): 4-9.
This article appraises research on the brain drain and points to gaps
in present knowledge of the subject. (1) Attempts to measure the
quantity and rate of brain drain face problems of poor statistics and
ambiguous definitions, and tend to deal only with gross migration
and outward migration, ignoring the flow of migration. (2) There has
been little work exploring country correlates of high-level manpower
flows cross-nationally. (3) Motivations of migrants are complex;
attention should be focused on the home country "push" factors which
are most subject to modification, and on the relationship between a
period of work experience following formal study and the propensity to
immigrate. (4) Losses and gains associated with migration must be
determined from both national and individual viewpoints using monetary and non-monetary theoretical tools.

261. _____. "Study Abroad and the Migration of Human Resources."
     Ph.D. dissertation, University of Chicago, 1967.
Emphasis in this study is on improving concepts and theory in the area
of the non-return of foreign students after study in the United States.

It includes a case study of Peruvian students. Main variables include age, sex, field of study, socio-economic status, sponsorship, type of visa, time spent in the United States and expected earnings. See No. 263.

262. _____. "Some Thoughts on Foreign Student Non-Return."
      Exchange 4, no. 2 (Fall 1968): 45-48.
Summarizing his views on non-return, Myers argues that it should be regarded not as a dichotomy but as a continuum between immediate return and permanent residence. There is no strong relationship between intended non-return and field of study, nor does non-return relate systematically to country development indicators. Although brain drain statistics are weak, non-return is apparently most frequent among young, self-sponsored students, particularly those from low status or marginal groups.

263. _____. Education and Emigration. New York: David McKay, 1972.
Theory, original research, and a comprehensive review of the existing literature on the migration of human resources are employed in this excellent, well-documented study of the brain drain problem. In an overview, it is noted that high-level migrants tend to move more frequently, for longer distances, and over greater periods of their lives; students abroad are a special type of high-level migrant. A paradigm is presented that can be used to classify migrants according to locus of education (home or abroad) and locus of employment (home or abroad). The paradigm incorporates and emphasizes remigration, particularly remigration of individuals educated outside their home area. A qualitative as well as quantitative dimension to migration is included in the paradigm.

   A number of observations are made on the migration of talent, based on case studies and other literature which indicate that the non-return of foreign students and immigration of trained talent vary considerably by country origin and by destination. Medicine, science, and engineering seem to be the fields in which most migration occurs, but among students the differences by broad field are not significant. Foreign student non-return is often associated with holding an immigrant or student (F) visa, with self-sponsorship, with either undergraduate or Ph.D. study, with lack of guaranteed employment at home following study, with arrival in the United States at an early age, with low socio-economic or minority status in the home country, and with marriage to a host-country national. An analysis of foreign student non-return using the IIE foreign student census for 1964-65 confirmed most of these observations, but no one simple set of associations can be established.

Cross-national comparisons of relative losses through non-return were defined in several ways: (1) relative to the total number of foreign students in the United States; (2) relative to the total manpower supply in training at home and abroad; and (3) relative to the effective demand for high-level manpower in the home country determined from the relationship between enrollment per 100,000 population and per-capita income. No consistent relationships emerged between non-return and such indicators such as per-capita income, political elitism and educational development. Certain countries repeatedly appear at the top of the non-return rankings. Nevertheless, Myers warns not to overrate the significance of the cross-national comparisons. The firmest conclusion to be drawn from the analysis is that viewing non-return and associated losses only in terms of the so-called rate of non-return is not sufficient.

The problem of identifying economic gains and losses through foreign student non-return is skirted in the analyses of IIE statistics but a number of methods and applications of human capital concepts to migration are discussed. The rather sophisticated application of human-capital principles fails because the problems of delineating populations have not been solved. Nevertheless, these applications are seen to hold much promise as a means of conceptualizing and analyzing empirically both individual and social investment choices.

A case study of non-return among Peruvian students in the United States using a human-capital model is described. Earnings streams for returning and non-returning Peruvian students were compared but no firm answers were found concerning the dominance of earnings in decisions to remigrate or remain. Generally, however, the results did not support the hypothesis that monetary considerations are dominant considerations when deciding to return home.

Emphasizing the definitional and statistical problems which hamper the analysis, Myers discusses the policy implications of the empirical findings. Formal compensation schemes to losing countries should be postponed and probably discarded as unworkable. Instead, legal restrictions are proposed on student migration, and a policy of restricting emigration to the United States. Restrictions imposed by the sending nations are seen as generally ineffective. Relating selection, admission and return to country needs could be most helpful. Other policy implications discussed include the use of loan funds for foreign students tied to a graduated "forgiveness" system (such as used in the NDEA loans in the United States), reducing foreign student opportunities in the United States, and increasing opportunities in the home country. Improving statistics on student migration is particularly emphasized in order to give a more accurate picture of the migration problem.

264a. National Association for Foreign Student Affairs. The Evaluation of Asian Educational Credentials: A Workshop Report.
Ed. by Lee Wilcox. New York, 1966.
This is one of a series of workshops; each report presents historical
and educational background material on the countries considered, to
enable admissions officers to evaluate correctly the degrees and credentials offered by applicants from those countries. This information
is also of value to those interested in international exchange and comparative education.
At this workshop, held at the East-West Center, University of
Hawaii, 29 November to 10 December 1965, the countries discussed
were India, Japan, the Philippines, and Taiwan.

264b. _____ . The Admission and Placement of Students from the Paci-
fic-Asia Area. Ed. by Sanford Jameson. Washington, D.C., n.d.
This workshop, co-sponsored by AACRAO and hosted by the East-West
Center, University of Hawaii, 1-13 December 1969, discussed Austra-
lia, New Zealand, Ceylon, India, Hong Kong, Malaysia, Pakistan,
Singapore, Okinawa, and the Pacific Islands.

264c. _____ . The Admission and Academic Placement of Students from
Selected Countries of Latin America: A Workshop Report. Ed. by
Joel B. Slocum. Washington, D. C., n.d.
Argentina, Chile, Ecuador, and Peru were considered at this workshop,
co-sponsored by AACRAO, which met at the University of Puerto Rico
in December 1970.

264d. _____ . The Admission and Academic Placement of Students from
the Caribbean: A Workshop Report. Ed. by Cynthia Fish. San
Juan, Puerto Rico: The North-South Center, n.d.
Held in Santo Domingo, Dominican Republic, 4-16 December 1972,
this workshop reports on Cuba, the Dominican Republic, the French
West Indies, Haiti, Puerto Rico, and the U. S. Virgin Islands. It was
co-sponsored by AACRAO.

264e. _____ . The Admission and Academic Placement of Students from
Nordic Countries: A Workshop Report. Ed. by Cliff Sjogren.
Washington, D. C., 1974.
This workshop studied Norway, Sweden, Denmark, Finland, and Iceland.
It was co-sponsored by AACRAO.

265a. _____ . Guidelines: Selection and Admission of Foreign Students.
Washington, D. C., Winter 1966.
The greatest single strength of an admissions program is a carefully
developed institutional policy on the admission of foreign students which
has the wholehearted support of the top level of the administration.

Whether the institution is large or small, the objective must be to admit
foreign students who have the academic financial, and linguistic abilities
to complete their educational objectives successfully and who will benefit
from what the institution has to offer. This booklet presents a detailed
model of the procedure for admitting foreign students from the first request for information to the final admissions decision.

265b. _____. Guidelines: Academic and Personal Advising. Washington,
        D. C., April 1966.
This guideline deals with the day-to-day advising of foreign students.
The adviser sees that institutional resources are being wisely used
according to the special needs and problems of foreign students. The
sources of support, lines of communication and assistance, methods
of informing new foreign students about the institution and the foreign
student services, and a comparison of two activities, advising and
counseling, are discussed.

265c. _____. Guidelines: American-Foreign Student Relationships.
        Washington, D. C., January 1967.
One underlying assumption of any institution in enrolling foreign students is that contact between U. S. and foreign students is beneficial.
Although the development of relationships among students is essentially
a process, programming which creates and implements opportunities
for association should be undertaken by the institution. Under the
guidance of the foreign student adviser, the goals should be considered
and the campus situation as it relates to American-foreign student
relationships assessed.
        Some suggested steps are: combined or overlapping orientation
for American and foreign students; encouraging existing campus groups
to develop an international dimension; identification and utilization of
individuals on campus and in the community with an interest in international programming; provision of a foreign student dimension in
housing, student union, cafeterias, and classrooms.

265d. _____. Guidelines: Housing of Foreign Students. Washington,
        D. C., March 1967.
This guideline is addressed to the foreign student adviser as the coor-
dinator of services to foreign students. It outlines the kinds of housing
information which should be made available to foreign students, and
discusses the responsibilities of the foreign student adviser in this area.

265e. _____. Guidelines: Responsibilities and Standards in Work with
        Foreign Students. Washington, D. C., n.d.
The primary concern of NAFSA and its members is that each individual
involved in educational exchange have the best possible educational and

personal experience while studying abroad. This can be achieved only
if every person who deals with such students is guided by the highest
standards of professional and ethical conduct.

In an attempt to define these standards, the NAFSA Committee
on Professional Development and the NAFSA Board of Directors prepared and approved this statement, 21 October 1970. Responsibilities
and standards of conduct are listed for institutions and for individuals
working professionally with foreign students, including foreign student
advisers, foreign student admissions officers, teachers of English as
a second language, community program workers, advisers to U. S.
students planning to study abroad.

265f._____. Guidelines: English Language Proficiency. Washington,
    D. C., 1971.
English proficiency continues to be an important problem for both
foreign student and host institution. Among the suggestions in this
pamphlet are that a test such as TOEFL be used to measure English
proficiency; that colleges and universities consider regional English-
language centers to provide low-cost language instruction; that English as a Second Language programs should, where possible, constitute a separate entity, offering introductory courses in disciplines
with a high proportion of foreign students.

265g._____. Guidelines: U. S.-Foreign Student Relationships. Wash-
    ington, D. C., 1972.
This booklet, aimed chiefly at foreign student advisers, offers some
very general strategies for encouraging U. S.-foreign student relationships. Basic principles for planning and executing orientation
programs are discussed. A campus team approach is recommended:
students, faculty, and others should be enlisted in a campaign to help
foreign students adjust to American community and campus life.

266.   _____. Report on Predeparture Orientation in Latin America.
    By Furman A. Bridgers and George Hall. Washington, D. C.,
    n. d.
Recommendations for increasing predeparture orientation prompted
NAFSA to undertake a survey of facilities in three Latin American
countries, Mexico, Colombia, and Chile. Interviews were arranged
with government and private agencies and organizations, and representatives from business and academic institutions.

It was found that U. S. Government-sponsored students recieved
predeparture orientation that may be generally adequate, particularly
since further orientation is usually provided in the United States.
Students sponsored by foundations, private agencies, or foreign governments may or may not receive adequate predeparture orientation

depending on the degree of concern for the grantee's needs and the resources available. Non-sponsored students are generally not included in any of the present programs. Moreover, informational materials available, mostly USIS publications, are inadequate and out-of-date.

It is therefore recommended that NAFSA make known the need for developing adequate pre-departure orientation for non-sponsored students and for reviewing and revising informational materials. It is suggested that the Committee on Latin American Students create a Council on In-Country Orientation and plan, in cooperation with local organizations and individuals, pilot projects of predeparture orientation in the three countries.

267. _____. "Towards a Model for International Educational Exchange: A Large University System." By Robert B. Kaplan. Washington, D. C., n.d. (Mimeo.)

Kaplan presents recommendations developed for the Florida State University system. They include: (1) establish a centralized clearinghouse to process admissions, and a system-wide institute for the teaching of English as a second language; (2) create a uniformly defined position entitled Foreign Student Adviser and utilize faculty as academic advisers; (3) make available substantial tuition waivers and a low-cost loan fund for foreign students; (4) develop comparative courses in those units having foreign students in order to maximize use of "informant knowledge;" (5) develop courses which help reorient the student to conditions in the home country; (6) encourage faculty to seek inter-institution and institution-governmental relationships across national boundaries to develop joint curricula, joint degree programs, and joint research projects.

268. _____. The Foreign Student Adviser and His Institution in International Student Exchange. By Ivan Putman, Jr. Washington, D. C., 1965.

Putman briefly reviews the history of international education in the United States, and of NAFSA, founded in 1948. Turning to the responsibilities which educational institutions assume when they admit foreign students, he discusses specialized services; in particular, the institution should have a foreign student adviser. This officer must be able to cope with problems demanding both educational and ethical judgments: the student who wishes to remain for advanced study despite the home country's need for intermediate skills; the student who wishes to immigrate; the community groups who seek to exploit or proselytize the foreign student; the students whose cultural habits conflict with those of the Americans among whom they live. Criteria for selection of this officer should include maturity, interest in and respect for all peoples of the world, ability to command the respect of the academic community. The foreign student office must have adequate clerical and budgetary support, staff continuity, and the wholehearted support fo the administration.

269. _____. Educational and Cultural Exchange with Asian Countries.
     Report of the 18th Annual NAFSA Conference, Chicago, 3-7 May
     1966. Ed. by George B. Stebbins. Washington, D. C., May 1967.
During the plenary sessions of the conference, speakers addressed the
issues of developing cooperative educational relations between nations,
for which a basic theoretical framework for understanding other cultures is essential. Three topics presented in detail were: (1) the changes
resulting from the 1965 amendment of the Immigration and Nationality
Act, (2) the problems of developing countries, in particular those
related to finance and manpower, (3) the role of the intellectual in
developing Asian nations where politics determines his usefulness and
employability. Summaries of workshop discussions are included, covering a broad range of topics relating to Asian educational exchange.

270. _____. Latin American Students in United States Colleges and
     Universities. By Gordon Ruscoe. Washington, D. C., 1968.
Approximately 1,000 Latin American students were studied by questionnaire to provide information about their background, current attitudes, and future aspirations. The majority of the students were found
to be fairly well satisfied with studies and life in the United States,
were reasonably informed about academic life, relatively unencumbered
by academic difficulties, and moderately confident about future educational and occupational success.
     The first recommendation of the study is that greater stress be
placed on in-country orientation programs. A second related recommendation is that such orientation place greater stress on preparing
Latin American students for the informal aspects of college life in the
United States. Thirdly, it is recommended that financial assistance
be awarded stringently on the basis of need to ensure that the increasingly large group of poorer Latin American students will benefit.

271. _____. "Various Proposals for the Improvement of Educational
     Programs Provided for Latin American Students in the USA."
     By Hugh Jenkins. A report prepared for the Sterling Forest
     Conference, 22-23 August 1968. (Mimeo.)
The recommendations of Gordon Ruscoe (See No. 270) are translated
into specific program proposals covering the following areas: Orientation — a pilot orientation course in American higher education, its
institutions, and contemporary developments on campus; admissions
and financial assistance — a meeting of NAFSA admissions representatives with financial officers to discuss the financial needs of Latin
American students; English language proficiency —examination of

standards, and ways to meet the needs of students, including funding
of TESOL programs; relations with the North American community —
workshops involving community and students in programs of mutual
interest.

272. _____. A National Survey of International Students and Programs
     in Community Junior Colleges in the United States. By Douglas
     E. Matthewson. Washington, D. C., 1968.
A questionnaire on topics pertinent to foreign students brought 410
usable replies from 850 junior colleges. The topics were: (1) general;
(2) admission and housing; (3) financial; (4) enrollment; (5) English
proficiency; (6) student activities and community services; and (7)
institutional philosophy. Replies on the topics (in order) showed:
(1) 67 percent have foreign students, but few have a special program,
office, or staff for them; (2) 24 percent required a separate admission
procedure, 19 percent gave an English test, 56 percent provided or
helped with housing; (3) some required financial statements, some
provided financial aid, few took part in exchange programs, about half
located part-time work; (4) few had admissions quotas, 23 percent
felt the technical programs important, 18 percent gave an orientation
course; (5) 23 percent gave special English courses, others felt a
need for them, about half noted that most foreign students already
spoke English; (6) 18 percent had special organizations for the foreign
students, 14 percent had community groups to help them, 43 percent
felt community groups ought to help them, 63 percent said they participated in student activities, most provided special services of some
sort, but only five percent reported foreign or international houses
in the community; (7) most colleges were willing to accept a few
foreign students, many noted the demand for their foreign technical
graduates, 65 percent felt that foreign students were a campus asset,
17 percent planned to extend their program, and many wanted more
information. Various correlations of the data are shown in tables.

273. _____. The Student in the International Scene. Abstracts of
     papers presented at the International Education Year Conference,
     Kansas City, Missouri, 1 May 1970.
Approximately 65 abstracts are presented, covering such topics as
admissions priorities, English-language training, campus environment,
evaluation of community programs, new directions for NAFSA, intercultural workshops, opportunities for student employment, and the
brain drain.

274. _____. Human Relations Training and Foreign Students. By
     Gary L. Althen. United States-Foreign Student Relationships
     Committee Monograph Series No. 1. Washington, D. C., July 1970.

Althen describes two basic types of human relations training currently
in use on American campuses, sensitivity training (T-group, encounter group) and the intercultural communications workshop. The first
type, having personal change as its goal, is essentially culture-bound,
requiring of its participants the American traits of individuality, egalitarianism, frankness, and a belief in the value of change. The workshop, on the other hand, provides a structured setting in which
participants can increase their mutual awareness of the role their
cultural backgrounds play in influencing their values, behavior, and
perceptions. This type of program, when conducted by a skilled
trainer, can be of greater assistance in promoting understanding
between foreign and American students.

275. _____ . Innovations and New Programs of Special Interest in
    Foreign Student Education: A Catalogue. Ed. by Barbara
    Ostrander. Washington, D. C., 1970.
This booklet describes a large number of new programs at U. S.
colleges and universities. A move toward greater foreign student
participation in campus decisions which affect them is a notable tendency among the programs listed. Important new directions in programming include: (1) foreign students as resource persons for local
high schools, (2) in-country and pre-departure orientation programs;
(3) group counseling; (4) intercultural communications and human-
relations training; (5) U. S. business-foreign student programs; and
(6) community action and service.

276. _____ . Report on In-Country Orientation in the Dominican Repub-
    lic and Venezuela. By Furman A. Bridgers. Washington, D. C.,
    1970.
As chairman of the Council on In-Country Orientation of NAFSA,
Bridgers visited the Dominican Republic and Venezuela in 1970 to
evaluate orientation programs. He reports that the greatest promise
for expanding orientation servies in the Dominican Republic lies in
the developing activity of the Fundacion de Credito Educativo, and
that better communication is needed between that organization and
NAFSA.
    In Venezuela, the orientation program of the North American
Association was considered to be highly effective and is recommended
as a model for use in other countries when a one-day program is feasible. However, it is noted that EDUCREDITO, a private agency created
in 1965 to encourage, finance and orient students qualified to pursue
higher education in Venezuela and abroad, has its own special philosophy of education and may want to develop its own kind of orientation.
    Other recommendations to NAFSA include the need to take imme-
diate steps to increase communication with the public and private

agencies in Latin America that provide in-country and pre-departure
orientation, and the need to explore the serious problems of Latin
American students when they return home in securing recognition of
credits and diplomas earned in the United States.

277. _____. Improving the Latin American Business Student's Exper-
     ience in the U. S. University. Washington, D. C., 1971.
A panel of six specialists considered ways to implement change and
improve the educational experience for the Latin American student
within existing U. S. university structures and resource limitations.
They define institutional goals and student motivation, and suggest
modification in the curriculum to make it more meaningful to the
student's home environment.

278. _____. Improving the Latin American Engineering Student's
     Experience in the U. S. University. By Kenneth A. Rogers.
     Washington, D. C., 1971.
The necessity of finding solutions to the special problems of Latin
American students led the NAFSA Committee on Latin American students to convene a panel of engineering educators in Houston, 12-14
March 1970.
     Regarding the prospective student, the participants identified
three aspects of the information gap which often result in a poor
match between student and U. S. institution: lack of information on
programs offered by U. S. institutions, lack of reliable information
on career opportunities in the home country, inability to evaluate
students' educational credentials. Once enrolled, the Latin American
student frequently finds his training irrelevant to his professional
needs at home. Greater flexibility in undergraduate electives and
work experience after graduation are recommended. For the returning
graduate, improved recruitment techniques and follow-up activities
through professional and alumni associations are recommended.

279. _____. The German-American Conference on Educational Ex-
     change. By Philip P. Byers. Washington, D. C., 1972.
The report of this conference, sponsored by NACRAO, NAFSA, and
the German Academic Exchange Service, presents an extensive description of the history and structure of German education at all levels,
an outline of the equivalences between degrees awarded in the Federal
Republic of Germany and the United States, glossary of German ada-
demic terms, and numerous curriculum outlines for many educational
areas and levels—information designed to be useful to those interested
in German-American exchange, to comparative educators, and especially to Americans responsible for admission and advising of German
students.

280. _____. A Survey of Facilities for Latin American Students in U. S. Colleges and Universities. Washington, D. C., April 1973.

This report, prepared by the Committee on Latin American Students, presents raw data gathered by questionnaire from 481 U. S. colleges and universities regarding students from Latin America. For each institution, the following information is given: enrollment of Latin American students as of June 1971; TOEFL requirement and minimum score; presence or absence of special English-language programs, academic options, financial aid, social organizations; and the name of the campus contact person.

281. _____. Report of the NAFSA Task Force on Intercultural Communications Workshops. Washington, D. C., Summer 1973.

Meeting in the fall of 1972, the Task Force reviewed research and materials relating to intercultural communications workshops, a phenomenon which began in Pittsburgh in 1966 and has since spread to a number of colleges and universities. Discussions at the conference and data from a survey conducted in the spring of 1972 (see No. 285) led the Task Force to conclude that the workshop experience, when designed and conducted responsibly, is conducive: (1) to effective intercultural communication; (2) to realization of the participants' goals; and (3) to the effective functioning of persons working with foreign students.

The Task Force recommends that NAFSA undertake research which will lead to a statement of the fundamental philosophy of the workshop and criteria for evaluation. It is also recommended that NAFSA provide training in workshop leadership and coordinate the program nationally.

282. _____. Manual for Program for Foreign Wives. Washington, D. C., 1973.

Suggestions are offered for community programs to assist foreign wives.

283. _____. Guide for the Education of Foreign Students: Human Resources Development. Ed. by August Benson and Joseph W. Kovach, Washington, D. C., 1974.

In the form of a comprehensive checklist covering 10 stages of the educational-exchange experience, this guide outlines the ideal experience for both sponsored and non-sponsored foreign students in American academic institutions and communities. It presents, in condensed form, material developed at the third AID/NAFSA Workshop. (See No. 9c.)

284. NAFSA, Field Service Program. An Inquiry into Departmental
     Policies and Practices in Relation to the Graduate Education
     of Foreign Students. Washington, D. C., 1972.
This report is the product of an investigation conducted by a NAFSA
Task Force on Crucial Issues. During the winter of 1971, 12 universities with foreign student enrollment of over 400 were interviewed as
to departmental policies and procedures regarding foreign graduate
students. Findings are presented as to institutional and departmental
policy, admissions, financial aid, English competency and foreign
student services and programs. The report also contains recommendations for future policy and action in each of these issue areas as well
as general recommendations for future research.

285. NAFSA Task Force on Intercultural Communications Workshops,
     Clifford Clark, Chairman. Intercultural Small Group Experiences
     in United States: A Survey Report. Regional Council for Inter-
     national Education, Intercultural Communications Network.
     Univeristy of Pittsburgh, Pa., n. d.
The Intercultural Small Group Experience (ISGE) has been used extensively on college campuses since 1966. Major findings of a survey
conducted by the Task Force were that: (1) the primary goal of the
ISGE is to encourage an understanding of cultural factors as they influence interpersonal communication; (2) that the leadership of an
ISGE is important to its content and effectiveness; (3) that the majority
of ISGEs had been sponsored by the participants, government agencies,
or by international student offices and that one-third had been initiated
by the leaders; (4) that most are conducted at locations removed from
others and last three days; and (5) that half of the respondents used no
evaluation methods. (See No. 281 for a final report of the Task Force.)

286. National Association of College Deans, Registrars, and Admis-
     sions Officers-National Association for Foreign Student Affairs.
     What's Happening with U. S.-Foreign Student Relations at Pre-
     dominantly Black Colleges? Washington, D. C., NAFSA, Spring
     1973.
As one of three cooperative projects initiated by NACDRAO and NAFSA,
a study of U. S.-foreign student relations at predominantly black colleges was undertaken. Questionnaires were completed by 301 foreign
students and 188 American students studying at 42 institutions.
     The major problem revealed by the survey is not unique to black
campuses: the need for in-depth communication and increased understanding and knowledge of other cultures. Major findings include:
(1) a slight majority of foreign students desired to attend white schools,
believing them to have better academic standards and facilities, but

the vast majority of U. S. students preferred a predominantly black institution; (2) the majority of foreign students believed they should not become involved in American socio-political activities or in campus protest movements, whereas most U. S. students believed such involvement would contribute to the foreign student's understanding of the American system; (3) both U. S. and foreign students felt that any hostility between the two groups was caused by prejudice, misconceptions, and lack of understanding, specifically attitudes of superiority on both sides.

The questionnaire, and tables summarizing responses, appear as appendices.

287. National Liaison Committee on Foreign Student Admissions, Richard Dremuk, Chairman. "Report on Feasibility for Foreign Credential Evaluation Service." College and University 44 (Summer 1969): 414-18.

To determine whether a non-governmental foreign credential evaluation service (FCES) could be established which would serve both academic institutions and governmental and private agencies and, if so, whether it could become self-supporting, information was collected from a representative sample of foreign student admissions officers and agency representatives. There was a strong consensus that a FCES is needed, that it could be operated under non-governmental auspices, that it ought to provide more types of information than are currently being provided by the Office of Education, and that the academic institutions and agencies which would use such an expanded service would be willing to pay for it if the quality of the service were good.

288. Niland, John R. "Foreign Manpower Trained in the United States: Policy Implications of Non-Return." Paper presented at the 23rd Annual Meeting of the Industrial Relations Research Association, 28-29 December 1970.

This paper identifies and evaluates policy alternatives relating to the problem of student non-return (SNR). Manipulation of student in-flow could be initiated by the home country in several ways. (1) Reduction of financial assistance. This would, however, affect only the small percentage that is government-sponsored. (2) Increasing the number of students coming to the United States, assuming that the proportion of non-returnees will remain constant. This is impractical in that the proportion of foreign students at U. S. universities has remained stable over the past decade. (3) Pre-selection of students likely to return. Research has not shown this to be feasible.

Control of outflow could be exercised by the United States through its visa regulations. Home-country alternatives include citizenship sanctions against non-returnees, and attempts to reduce the unattractiveness of home labor-market conditions.

A policy solution should avoid the extreme positions of both internationalists and nationalists. While country-specific policy formulations are preferable, attention might be concentrated on the goals of the temporary non-returnee, such as accumulation of capital, and encouraging rapid realization of these goals.

289. _____. The Asian Engineering Brain Drain: A Study of International Relocation into the United States from India, China, Korea, Thailand, and Japan. Lexington, Mass.: D. C. Heath and Company 1970.
This study examines the phenomenon of talent migration at the micro level, focusing on student non-return and drain of high-level engineering manpower to the United States from India, Taiwan, Korea, Thailand, and Japan. It examines five major issues: magnitude of drain, particularly in a net sense; manpower character of those who might be involved in drain; nature of international mobility patterns; reasons governing international relocation decision; and polity implications of brain drain.

A 12-page questionnaire was sent to 1,200 graduate engineering students from the five countries at 165 U. S. universities during the winter of 1968. Four hundred and forty-seven (49 percent) of the 919 students who received the questionnaire responded; they represented 121 universities.

Niland argues that brain drain has been badly defined, poorly measured, and generally misinterpreted in much of the literature. Insofar as its internal character varies markedly from one country to another, each developing country should be treated as a unique case; actions to abbreviate or modify drain are best implemented by the home country. Moreover, policy makers should alter their perceptions of talent migration so as to view it as a source of specific economic welfare to both home country and the individual concerned.

290. Niyekawa-Howard, Agnes M. "Biculturality and Cognitive Growth: Theoretical Foundations for Basic and Applied Research." Occasional Papers of the East-West Culture Learning Institute No. 1. Honolulu: East-West Center, July 1970.
Defining the ideal bicultural person as "one who does not disidentify with either of his two cultures but appreciates the good aspects of each, and who has learned something that is not culture-specific, namely a general tolerance and understanding of cultures," this paper discusses the phenomenon of biculturality and prepares a foundation for future research through an extensive review of the literature. One avenue of suggested research is non-culture-specific learning resulting from knowing two or more cultures, referred to as the "generalization

effect." A second avenue is suggested by the observation that while all bicultural individuals have the potential to function with cognitive flexibility and to be creative in their thinking, many are inhibited by personality factors and restrictive environments. A study of how bicultural individuals could make the best of their biculturality, and of the relationships between biculturality and cognitive flexibility would be of value to all those directly dealing with international exchange programs as well as to those who are interested in creativity.

Norton, Sherry Mueller. See No. 403.

Ockey, William. See No. 11a-d, 12a-h, 113.

291. Odenyo, Amos Otieno. "Africans and Afro-Americans on Campus: A Study of Some of the Relationships Between Two Minority Sub-Communities." Ph.D. dissertation, University of Minnesota, 1970.
A number of hypotheses are advanced to explain the ambivalence between Africans and Afro-Americans in U. S. universities. The African, for example, fears to be identified with an underprivileged American minority yet envies the American's material possessions. The hypotheses were tested among student groups in Minnesota, using a self-administered questionnaire and participant observation. The findings largely confirmed the hypotheses advanced.

O'Grady, Lorraine. See No. 406.

292. Ohuche, Romanus Ogbonna. "Scholastic Factors Pertaining to the Academic Achievement of Nigerian Students in the United States." Ph.D. dissertation, Iowa State University, 1967.
A random sample of the 1,426 undergraduates and 456 graduate students from Nigeria listed by IIE was contacted in 1966-67. Questionnaire responses were checked by sending a shorter questionnaire to the faculty advisers of the students in the sample. The following conclusions were drawn from the study: (1) previous educational experience could not be used to predict satisfactorily the academic achievement of undergraduates as measured by their cumulative grade point average; (2) undergraduates who completed the equivalent of the higher school certificate examination performed better than those who did not; (3) there was no difference in achievement between scholarship and non-scholarship undergraduates; and (4) no significant differences were discovered between graduate students who received a B.A. in the United States and those who received it elsewhere.

293. Ojiaku, Mazi Okoro. "The Impact of the American Academic
      Tradition on the Development of Higher Education in Eastern
      Nigeria." Ph.D. dissertation, University of California,
      Berkeley, 1968.
This study compares the failure of Ibadan University College, modeled
on the English "red brick" institutions, to the success of the University of Nigeria which, under the leadership of Dr. Nnamdi Azikiwe and
the cooperation of the Michigan State University, adopted the American
Land-Grant philosophy.

294. Olayinka, Moses Siyanbola. "Effectiveness of Two Modes of
      Counseling in Assisting African Students to Adjust to the General
      University Environment." Ph.D. dissertation, University of
      California, Los Angeles, 1970.
Two counseling modes, the Guided Inquiry Mode (cognitive) and the
Advisory Mode (didactic) were tested, using 16 African students from
a total population of 110, and a control group. The results indicated
that counselees in the experimental group reported fewer problems of
adjustment than control group subjects. Counselees perceived white
counselors as more effective and more genuine than black counselors.

295. Organization of American States. "The Training of Foreign
      Students—Its Impact on Tensions Among Nations." by David
      Heft. Unpublished paper, March 1963.
The objective of this paper is to help determine whether and how the
training of foreign students in the United States may contribute to the
reduction of tensions which threaten world peace. Education and
training abroad facilitate advancement in developing countries and
international understanding. Effects of the training of foreign students
are considered under the following headings: (1) effect on foreign
students of training in the United States; (2) effect of training of foreign
students on United States; (3) effect of training of foreign students on
the economic and social development of their countries; and (4) effect
of foreign students on the relations between the United States and other
countries. References in the paper are principally to Latin American
students. Generally, increasing and improving international training
programs will benefit the relations between the United States and other
countries.

296. Orr, James Darby, Jr. "The Foreign Scholar Returned Home:
      A Review of Selected Research." Ph.D. dissertation, Columbia
      University, 1971.
This review of completed follow-up research on foreign students who
studied in American colleges or universities found that most exchangees
considered themselves changed by the exchange experience, having

become more flexible, more insightful, and more sensitive to others.
Many had difficulties in readjustment, particularly younger students,
those most alienated from their own culture, those from countries
distrustful of the United States, those from more rigid societies, and
those uninfluential in the home culture.

Approximately 75 percent of the returnees were able to use their
American training at least partially, and 80 percent claimed to have
conveyed their knowledge and skills to others in the job situation. The
degree of returnee utilization of American training was dependent on
the job setting and the status and authority of the returnee.

The major implications of the data include a need for more pre-
departure planning, closer ties by home governments to the exchange
process, more relevant studies in American institutions, and more
sponsor and home government post-sojourn support of exchangees.

297. Orthman, William George. "Implications of the Brain Drain:
      Verdict of Educated Immigrants in the Puget Sound Area."
      D.B.A. dissertation, University of Washington, 1971.
A literature review and a questionnaire completed by 103 degree-
holding expatriates working in the Puget Sound area in 1969 validated
the following hypotheses: (1) that most brain drain migrants who come
to the United States do so for economic reasons; (2) that economic
reasons are more important to those from the United Kingdom than
those from India; (3) that most of the scientists and engineers from
the United Kingdom have attained professional degrees from British
universities before coming to the United States, whereas their
counterparts from India come as students and obtain jobs in the United
States after graduation; and (4) the United Kingdom has the resources
to alleviate the brain drain, whereas the brain drain from India is a
function of disproportionate capital-labor ratio in respect to certain
categories of highly educated labor.

298. Osman, Osama Abdul-Rahman. "The Transferability of Non-
      Indigenous Administrative Techniques as an Approach to Improve
      Administration in a Developing Country: The Experience of
      American Technical Assistance in Public Administration to
      Iran." Ph.D. dissertation, American University, 1970.
The study focuses on the U.S. technical assistance program in public
administration in Iran, and in particular, the effort to establish program budget and position classification in an attempt to explore the
feasibility of transferring administrative techniques from a more
developed country to a less-developed one. The effort to establish
program budget was successful insofar as the structure of the Iranian
budget is now based on program classification. The concept of position
classification met greater resistance due to the fact that Iranian

culture emphasizes personal status and rank, and such emphases may run counter to the principles of position classification.

Technical assistance can be viewed as a vehicle for transferring knowledge, skills, techniques, and systems. It should not take place, however, without consideration of the social and cultural setting of the recipient country.

Ostrander, Barbara. See No. 275.

299.   Oteiza, Enrique. "Emigration of Engineers from Argentina: A Case of Latin American 'Brain Drain.'" International Labor Review 92 (December 1965): 445-61.

Data from the Argentine Census Bureau show that the percentage of total Argentine immigrants to the United States who fall within the categories "professional workers and technicians," "senior executive," and "skilled workers" is extremely high, approximately 35 percent. Among the graduate professionals in Argentina, physicians and engineers are most numerous and members of both professions emigrate in considerable numbers to the United States. An analysis is made of the employment situation, and supply and demand of engineers in Argentina and the United States. It is concluded that because of unfavorable salary differentials, a sustained demand for engineers in the United States, an ample supply of engineers in Argentina, and other factors, emigration of engineers will continue for some time. The level of demand for engineers in Argentina will depend to a large extent on the momentum of its economic development in the future.

300.   The Overseas Selection of Foreign Students. New York: Education and World Affairs, April 1966.

A worldwide network of counseling, evaluating, and testing centers is needed if U. S. colleges and universities are to cope effectively with the expanding number of applications from students in foreign countries. The basic purposes of the centers would be to provide, in the home country, those services which would assist American institutions in the selection of qualified foreign students, and enable foreign students, both sponsored and unsponsored, to obtain accurate information on U. S. universities, thus facilitating their choice of program

Some private and federal agencies are now providing such services. A coordinated approach is suggested for expanding these facilities: as a pilot project, a center should be established in India under the general supervision of the bi-national commission.

301.   Owen, Wyn F., and Colwell, James L. "Orientation for Foreign Students: The Lesson of the Summer Economics Institute." Exchange (Winter 1968): 48-54.

This article discusses the goals, structure, administration, and accomplishments of the Economics Institute, an orientation program established nine years ago by the American Economic Association and Ford Foundation for foreign graduate students, primarily from developing countries, in economics. It offers summer sessions of intensive instruction in economic theory, mathematics, and/or English tailored to fit foreign students' specific needs. Similar programs have been developed in law (at Princeton) and engineering (at Purdue).

302. Palmer, Roy Virgil. "The Problem of Talent Migration and the Role of the Small Private College in Foreign Student Education." Ph.D. dissertation, University of Michigan, 1968.

This study attempted to determine the extent of migration among foreign students at small private colleges associated with the Churches of Christ. Interviews and a questionnaire were used to assemble the data. Respondents were 144 foreign students and deans and foreign student advisers at four selected colleges.

Findings confirmed those of previous studies. Older students, married students, or those who left wives at home tended to return, as did those with strong identity with the homeland. Those who were selected by government or other agencies, or who received financial help, also tended to return. Factors related to employment seem most decisive. Students with high expectations of satisfactory employment in the homeland tended to return, while those who anticipated threat from unstable political conditions or unfavorable economic conditions tended to remain abroad.

303. Paraskevopoulos, John, and Dremuk, Richard. "Factors Relating to Application Statistics and Enrollment Yield for Foreign Students." University of Illinois, September 1968.

The Office of the University Dean of Admissions and Records of the University of Illinois prepared a study which examined application statistics and enrollment yield to determine the reduction ratio of applicants to registrants and to delineate some of the parameters of this reduction ratio. These statistics were compiled for the years 1966-67 from approximately 5,800 applications for admission from foreign students. The reduction ratio of filed applications to completed applications to admitted applicants to registered students was 58:38:13:11.

The reduction ratio for foreign students was considerably greater than for domestic students. Significant variables were sex and marital status, curriculum, country of origin, level of education, date of application, and age. The low yield of freshmen suggested that freshmen should be discouraged from applying. Foreign students transferring from other colleges in the United States provided a greater enrollment yield, suggesting that better dissemination of information about institutions and their programs is needed. To improve the yield of foreign students and reduce the cost, time, and expertise required for evaluating and processing applications, two methods are suggested: (1) screening students in their home country through realistic counseling; and (2) pooling foreign applications and distributing them among colleges and universities participating in the pool.

304. _____. "Grading Patterns for Foreign Students." Exchange 4, no. 3 (Winter 1969): 55-60.
This article described the results of a faculty study—565 questionnaires completed—at the University of Illinois concerning course requirements and grading standards for foreign students. For foreign students in physical and biological sciences, practically no differential standards were found. In the social and behavioral sciences, where the need for communication skills is greater, a larger proportion (but still a minority) of faculty tended to be sympathetic to language difficulties and to use differential grading standards.

305. Parthasarathi, Ashok. "India's 'Brain Drain' and International Norms." Exchange (Summer 1967): 4-13.
Brain drain from India will not diminish until (1) the methodology and philosophy of her higher education system are re-oriented; (2) a sensible manpower policy is developed which will encourage both the advanced training of individuals and their subsequent absorption by the economy; and (3) Indian students and specialists abroad rethink their obligations and challenges.

306. Pavri, Dina Mehervanji. "A Study of the Scholastic Achievement and Related Problems of Foreign Graduate Students at the University of Virginia from 1957 to 1961." Ph.D. dissertation, University of Virginia, 1963.
This fact-finding study is based on data from University records and from the returns of a questionnaire mailed to foreign students who were in the United States during the period of study. Some of the findings that emerged from the analysis were as follows: (1) there was no significant difference in the scholastic performance of men and women; (2) older students and married students had fewer difficulties; (3) students with scholarships were more successful than those who were self-supporting; (4) 88 percent felt satisfied with the education received at the University, 55 percent were above average scholastically, and 55 percent were successful in getting a degree; (5) the basic problems that affected academic achievement concerned the curriculum, insufficient knowledge of English, lack of money,

lack of sufficient study time, absence of social life, homesickness, and discrimination; (6) only 15 percent had attended any kind of orientation program; none at the University of Virginia.

307. Perkins, James A. "Foreign Aid and the Brain Drain." In International Education: Past, Present, Problems and Prospects. Selected readings to supplement H. R. 14643 prepared for the House Committee on Education and Labor by the Task Force on International Education, John Brademas, Chairman, pp. 354-61. Washington, D. C.: U. S. Government Printing Office, 1966.

The evolution of man from a primitive, tribal condition to integration in a complex, advanced society is a process which may require several generations and results, at first, in the production of only a few talented individuals. U. S. policy of aid and educational exchange programs is influential in this process but it is in conflict with our own voracious domestic appetite for trained manpower which then siphon off the very people who are needed in the developing countries.

Accurate facts and figures on the drain of foreign talent are needed. Moreover, U. S. government agencies and educational institutions must concentrate on a variety of measures designed to encourage return to the home country.

308. _____. International Programs of U. S. Colleges and Universities: Priorities for the Seventies. Occasional Paper No. 1. New York: International Council for Educational Development, July 1971.

International programs in U. S. universities, which expanded enormously after World War II, face problems in the 1970's as both government and private foundations shift their support priorities toward urgent domestic issues. At the same time, however, the private sector is becoming increasingly internationalized, and domestic issues—racial equality, urban development, environmental protection, maintenance of peace—have international components yet to be identified.

To meet these challenges, institutions must restructure the goals and content of their international programs in the light of a new definition of national interest. Specifically, language and area studies centers will have to tie their goals more closely to new domestic and foreign policy directions; study-abroad programs need careful re-evaluation; foreign students in the United States must be elected with greater care and with regard to the needs of developing countries; two-way exchange of visiting scholars should be upgraded and widened to include more institutions; universities should consider, as an approach to funding from international agencies, a procedure in which the contracting agent is an individual rather than the university itself; international programs should become an integral part of the university's basic curriculum.

309. Peterson, R. D. "Some Reflections on Conducting a Foreign Student Training Course." The Journal of Developing Areas 2 (January 1968): 167-86.

This report describes the objectives, organization and problems of Technical Course No. 6 ("The Economics of Agricultural Production and Resource Use") offered by the University of Nebraska's Department of Agricultural Economics under the auspices of AID and USDA. In this graduate-level seminar, presented to six different groups from developing nations in Africa, Asia, Europe, and South America from 1961 through 1966, students were placed in a practical workshop where they could observe the operation of the economic institutions which support modern agriculture. The course focused on methods of conducting and reporting research results, basic principles of agricultural production and resource use, and factors in the institutional framework of a system of commercial agriculture.

310. Pfnister, Allan O. "Expectation and Realization from an American Perspective: A Survey of the Strengths and Weaknesses of Overseas Study Programs with Implications for Accreditation." University of Denver, n.d. (Mimeo.)

This brief review article, oriented toward Americans studying abroad, summarizes (1) research on purposes of overseas study, (2) research on outcomes, such as attitude change and adjustment problems, and (3) recent actions of the U. S. regional accrediting agencies.

311. _____. "Impact of Study Abroad on the American College Undergraduate." Paper presented at the meeting of the National Association for Foreign Student Affairs, Atlanta, Georgia, 4 May 1972. (Mimeo.)

The intent of this review is to show that most research on educational exchange concerns foreign students in the United States and that research is needed in a number of areas relating to American students abroad. A considerable portion of the paper is devoted to an evaluative review of a Study/Service Program operated by Goshen College, Goshen, Indiana.

312. Pierce, Frank Nicholson. "Foreign Student Views and Attitudes Toward Advertising in the United States." Ph.D. dissertation, University of Illinois, 1969.

This study investigates the attitudes of more than 600 foreign students selected from 36 colleges and universities. The sample was statistically projectable by global area to the entire foreign student population in the country at the time of the questionnaire (April 1968). The responses are compared with the opinions of 190 domestic college students who also participated in the survey.

Overall, the saliency of advertising as an institution was found to be low among students in the areas of reported interest, amount of attention paid, and amount of talk about it. Saliency rose sharply in the number of complaints voiced about advertising, then receded somewhat in the perceived need for immediate attention and change in the institution. The most significant finding indicates that the stage of economic development of the students' home countries is a powerful predictor of the amount of favorability the students will show toward American advertising.

Pierson, Constance L. See No. 406.

313. Plaister, Ted. "Reading Instruction for College Level Foreign Students." Paper presented at the TESOL Convention, San Antonio, Texas, September 1968.

This paper describes English Language Institute reading courses offered to non-native speakers of English enrolled at the University of Hawaii. The courses stress: (1) elimination of poor reading habits, (2) training in reading by structures, (3) timed reading exercises, (4) practice in reading different kinds of material in class, (5) lectures on important cultural concepts, (6) practice in taking tests under timed conditions, and (7) vocabulary development using programmed texts.

314. Pool, Ithiel de Sola. "Effects of Cross-National Contact on National and International Images." In International Behavior, ed. by Herbert C. Kelman, pp. 106-28. New York: Holt, Rinehart, and Winston, 1965.

This article deals with the effects of travel on images of the foreigner and of self held by traveler and host. In general, a traveler's images of the host will depend on initial psychological adjustment, retrospective view of experience, and the extent of cultural differences encountered. Travelers distort the host image to fit their own needs and simultaneously acquire a strengthened sense of identity. The net impact of cross-cultural contact on the host is to increase the complexity and differentiation of images of traveler and foreign country.

315. Porter, John Wilson. "The Development of an Inventory to Determine the Problems of Foreign Students." Ph.D. dissertation, Michigan State University, 1962.

This investigation was conducted on the campus of Michigan State University. Subjects included 108 foreign students and 50 U.S. students. Each was given the Michigan International Student Problem Inventory and 46 of the foreign students and 47 of the U.S. students were also given the Mooney Problem Check List—College Form. This procedure was followed to establish the concurrent validity of the MISP Inventory.

The concurrent validity of the MISP inventory was established. Seventy-six percent of the students felt it provided a complete picture of the problems currently troubling them. It was also found that the inventory could satisfactorily differentiate between the problems of U. S. and foreign students. As this was the first administering of the MISP Inventory, the conclusions of this study must be considered tentative.

316. Pratt, Dallas. "The Relation of Culture-Goals to the Mental Health of Students Abroad." International Social Science Bulletin 8, no. 4 (1956): 597-604.

Culture-goals are the traditional culture-specific ways of approaching the ultimate human satisfactions. They are communicated to the young by parents, teachers, and other culture-transmitters. Since culture-goals and institutions, particularly the family, are interrelated, any distortion in the configuration of these institutions may interfere with the individuals' achievement of the ultimate satisfactions necessary for mental health. Culture-goals can be threatened also by confrontation with powerful and attractive alien values.

The culture-goals of several cultures are examined, with particular emphasis on conflicts causing mental health problems. In the Chinese culture, the problem is with the deterioration of "filial piety." In the Jewish culture, especially in Eastern Europe, the view that education for females is undesirable is now being challenged. In the Iberian culture, problems of mental health often revolve around the disequilibrium in the status of the sexes: males fear for their masculinity; women resent their subjugated roles. Northern European cultures, Danes and Swedes, struggle with the goal characteristics of choosing a vocation appropriate to the status of their families and social class.

The emotional conflicts described in the article, it is noted, have little or nothing to do with educational travel, or with the impact of an alien culture. Inability to adjust to American values and the "American way of life" is more likely to be the neurosis of an American student than that of a Japanese student; the latter, if neurotic, is probably having trouble with Japanese values. The emotional problems described, however, would seem to be of great importance to persons dealing with international exchange.

Preston, Harley O. See No. 7.

317. Prince, Raymond. "Mental Health Workers Should be Trained at
      Home: Some Implications of Transcultural Psychiatric Research."
      Paper presented at the American Psychological Association
      Conference, Montreal, August 1973.
The dual effect of Westernization upon health in developing countries—
the improvement of physical health and the deterioration of mental
health—raises a number of important problems regarding the training
of psychiatrists from developing countries in Western nations. A basic
problem is difference in world view: the Western world view is unusual
in its emphasis on personal independence and self-reliance, posing
numerous problems for the more interdependently oriented trainee.
Other problem areas are authoritarianism versus democracy, emanci-
pation of women, and secular versus religious orientations.

      Prince makes the following suggestions: (1) routine training of
psychiatrists and other mental health workers should be carried out
at home; (2) in special circumstances, where Western approaches are
felt to be of interest, a carefully selected flexible psychiatrist could
spend a brief period in a Western country to study the desired techniques, and work out adaptations for the home country; (3) where it is
unavoidable that training be obtained in the West, "adaptation groups"
should be set up for the foreign trainees where various transcultural
problems could be examined.

318. Psacharopoulos, George. "On Some Positive Aspects of the
      Economics of the Brain Drain." Minerva 9 (April 1971): 231-42.
One rarely examined aspect of the brain drain is the profitability to the
individual of completing a degree in his home country and immediately
emigrating to work in a foreign country. The author calculates the
domestic rate of return on investment in education for 26 countries,
and compares this to the cross-rate of return where the costs are the
direct expense of education, the earnings foregone, and the cost of
moving, and the benefits consist of the difference over the entire life
span between what the graduate would earn abroad and what he would
be earning as a secondary school graduate if he remained at home.
Analysis shows that cross-rates of return are substantially higher
than domestic rates of return, and that they are higher than the returns
to alternative investments, particularly in less-developed countries.

      Analysis of other variables thought to influence international
migration shows that variation of the emigration variable bears no
relation to differences in per-capita income and distance from the
United States. Variation in domestic and cross-rates of return, however, explained about 68 percent of the variation in the propensity of
professionals to emigrate to the United States.

      Putman, Ivan, Jr. See No. 268.

319. Raman, N. Pattabhi. "Training of National Staff in Technical Cooperation Projects." Focus: Technical Cooperation 1973, no. 4, pp. 17-19, 23. In International Development Review 15, no. 4.
Common criticisms of technical assistance projects concern delays in the appointment of counterpart project personnel, in aligning national and international inputs of personnel, and in the nomination of qualified candidates for training abroad. Raman finds that evaluation studies show more important problems: (1) the narrowness of approach to counterpart training; (2) deficits in the scope and substance of training; and (3) shortcomings in the planning and execution of fellowships. UNDP-financed fellowships are criticized along these lines.

A recommendation is made for the development of staff capability in the collective sense rather than the preparation of a single individual. Team training would reduce the dependence of projects on individuals serving as single counterparts to experts and provide necessary staff support services.

320. Ravenswaay, C. A. "International Students and Technical Assistance." Higher Education and Research in the Netherlands 11 (January 1967): 38-45.
The Netherlands has designed special post-graduate education courses for use in technical assistance projects with developing countries. These short courses in specially created institutions minimize the dangers of international education: brain drain, irrelevance of training, alienation.

Ravenswij, Boem van. See No. 136, 139.

321. Rayner, Ruth A., and Jones, Bonnie L. "Foreign Nurses: Dedicated Exchange Visitors." Exchange 9, no. 1 (Summer 1973): 36-44.
This article described the Exchange Visitor Program for Foreign Nurses at Columbia-Presbyterian Medical Center in New York. A one-year training program, its main objective is to familiarize nurses with American health services through a program of coordinated educational contact and supervised clinical practice.

322. Regional Council for International Education. The Shape of Change in International Business and Higher Education's Response. Report of a conference in Cleveland, Ohio, 29 June 1973. Pittsburgh, Pa., n.d.
The conference had two principal objectives: to identify the circumstances and forces changing the atmosphere in which multinational corporations must function, and to recommend changes in course content and curricular emphasis through which universities might

better prepare graduates to function effectively in the international
business community of tomorrow. Topics discussed included the need
for practical language training, methods to combat foreign student
alienation, problems of maintenance training of foreign nationals,
changes in professional school curricula to offer more social science
content and flexibility.

323. Regueira, Alberto. "Cursos de formacao em desenvolvimento
      economico: Alguns aspectos caracteristicos" (Educational
      Courses in Economic Development: Some Characteristic Aspects).
      Analise Social 4 (1966): 315-19.
An international review of educational courses in economic and social
development reveals two tendencies: (a) to integrate students from
underdeveloped countries into the regular programs of foreign universities, or (b) to send them to specially created institutions. In solution (a), students often do not obtain knowledge relevant to their
countries' needs; in (b) selection techniques are weak so that not
always the ablest students are chosen for training. Particularly
necessary for these students are: contact with new techniques of
development; an opportunity to tie them in with planning experiences
and elaborate economic policies; and discussions of the multiple
problems which affect backward communities, with use of practical
examples.

324. Restivo, Sal Philip. "Visiting Foreign Scientists at American
      Universities: A Study of the Third Culture of Science." Ph.D.
      dissertation, Michigan State University, 1971.
The significance of scientific activities as a link among societies in
an increasingly interdependent world has been noted but not studied in
depth. The present study focuses on visiting foreign scientists at
American universities as one segment of the international system of
scientific activities. It is organized around three basic themes:
(1) conditions of work, (2) science as ideology, and (3) the modern (as
opposed to traditional, or post-modern) orientation of visiting foreign
scientists.
        Data were collected from a non-random sample of 222 visiting
foreign scientists at seven midwestern universities. Eighty-two
interviews were supplemented with 140 usable returns on a mailed
questionnaire.

325. Riesman, David. "Politica y sociedad en los Estados Unidos:
      Un intercambio con estudiantes brasilenos" (Politics and Society
      in the United States: An Exchange with Brazilian Students).
      Boletin Uruguayo do Sociologia 7 (December 1968): 68-84.
This is a translation of the transcript of a discussion conducted by
the author together with E. Borinski with a group of exchange students

from Brazil at Harvard University. Questions raised concerned social development and changes in the contemporary United States.

326. Rising, Muriel Nixon, and Copp, Barbara M. "Adjustment
       Experiences of Non-Immigrant Foreign Students at the University
       of Rochester, 1967-68." Rochester, N.Y.: University of
       Rochester, 1968.
This pilot inquiry and study was designed to explore some of the adjustment experiences of the foreign students on the University of Rochester
campus to provide information useful in orientation programming, foreign student advising, and counseling. Questions were sent to 45
students and returned by 20 who had matriculated between 1960 and
1967; 22 students who matriculated between 1963 and 1967 were interviewed.
       Respondents' views on four broad areas of adjustment are sum-
marized: (1) adjustment to academic life—problems with English
language, with academic work, and personal relationships; (2) adjustment to U. S. culture—politics, people, religion, social life; (3) adjustment to living at the University of Rochester—accommodations,
difficulties with food, shopping, use of facilities; (4) adjustment within
and across cultures—perceptions of Americans' attitudes to other
countries, conflicts with other foreign students.
       It is suggested that students not be admitted without passing a
good English-language test, that they be given more practical advice
on the mechanics of living, that both U. S. and foreign students be
encouraged to understand cultural differences.

327. Ritterband, Paul. "Toward an Assessment of the Costs and
       Benefits of Study Abroad." Reprint No. A-459. New York:
       Columbia University, Bureau of Applied Social Research, n.d.
The focus of this article is on the human-capital loss incurred by a
country sending a student to study abroad. Ritterband disagrees with
the marginal analysis approach to the brain drain problem because it
ignores the social benefits of education, and does not consider time
perspective when assessing the costs of non-return. The cases of
Japan and India are used for the purpose of clarification and explanation

328. _____. "Out of Zion: The Non-Returning Israeli Student." Ph.D.
       dissertation, Columbia University, 1968.
This study was concerned with understanding the flow of Israeli
students to and from the United States. The major source of information was a mail questionnaire administered to the Israeli student and
alumni population in the United States in the spring and summer of
1966. One thousand, nine hundred and thirty-four persons responded,
a response rate of 67 percent. Documentary and informant interview
materials were collected to aid the analysis.

The major findings of the study can be summarized in two propositions: (1) many of the same factors which explain the motives for coming to the United States, relating primarily to the small size of the Israeli higher education system, also explain and predict the likelihood of returning to Israel; (2) the likelihood of a student's returning to Israel is overwhelmingly determined prior to arrival in the United States. National commitment of the respondent's parents, social class of origin, participation in certain of the youth movements, and rural-urban differentials were all found to be independently significant in generating a predisposition to return to Israel.

329. _____. "The Determinants of Motives of Israeli Students Studying in the United States." Sociology of Education 42 (Fall 1969): 330-49.
Using data described in No. 328, Ritterband analyzes the motivation of Israeli students in the United States. The filter mechanisms in the Israeli educational and social systems are traced to explain the finding that undergraduates tend to be students who either have been tracked out of the college-preparatory system in Israel or have performed poorly, while graduate students tend to come because of the superior educational opportunities offered here in their areas of specialization.

330. _____. "Law, Policy, and Behavior: Educational Exchange Policy and Student Migration." American Journal of Sociology 76 (July 1970): 71-82.
This paper examines the effects of legislation, administrative rules, and policy edicts upon Israelis involved in the educational exchange programs of the United States using data described in No. 328 which revealed that those on exchange visas were more likely to return home than those on student visas. These different migration rates, confirmed by the State Department, arise from the process of allocation of visas in Israel. The talented student is often offered a job prior to completion of graduate education, which frequently includes a sojourn abroad; those having such jobs are more likely to obtain exchange visas and return home. Hence the presumed effect of the exchange visa is actually a function of the coalescence of the academic and occupational systems in Israel and visa-allocation procedures in the United States. It is further argued that State Department policy directives regarding repatriation are ineffective.

331. Rives, Janet McMillan. "The International Market for Higher Education: An Economic Analysis with Special Reference to the United States." Ph.D. dissertation, Duke University, 1971.
The aim of the study is to develop and analyze theoretically and empirically the international market for higher education. The relationship

between the market for higher education and international flows of human capital is stressed, with particular emphasis on trade in U. S. education and on movements of human capital into the United States.

Rodriguez, Orlando. See No. 392.

Rogers, Kenneth A. See No. 278.

332. Ronkin, R. R. "Modifying the Ph. D. Program for Foreign Students." Science 163 (January 1969): 20.
The difficulties encountered by foreign pre-doctoral students in science upon return home would be lessened if U. S. Ph. D. programs included: (1) instruction in learning how to identify research areas which have local relevance and can be pursued with available resources; (2) acquisition of sufficient skill in laboratory maintenance and the correct use of hand tools so that the student can train technicians in these skills; (3) training in the rudiments of science administration including program development, budgeting, procurement, and staffing.

Rotach, B. See No. 5.

Ruscoe, Gordon. See No. 270.

333. Ryer, G. Stephen, recorder. "Rationale for International Students II." Presentations in a panel discussion at an AACRAO Conference. College and University 45 (Summer 1970): 405-14.
This panel discussed, in general terms, the integration and approach of campus and community programs for foreign students. (See also No. 29.)

Sander, Herman J. See No. 113.

334. Sanders, Irwin T., ed. The Professional Education of Students from Other Lands. New York: Council on Social Work Education, 1963.
This book is based on discussions of an interprofessional conference held in 1961 concerning the training of foreign students in social work, education, health sciences, and agriculture. It explores a number of problem areas and contains many recommendations regarding selection, placement, curriculum planning, and follow-up evaluations. Above all, this conference demonstrates the value of interdisciplinary approaches to development of training programs.

335. Sanders, Irwin T., and Ward, Jennifer C. <u>Bridges to Under-</u>
     <u>standing: International Programs of American Colleges and</u>
     <u>Universities</u>. New York: McGraw-Hill, 1970.
This study, sponsored by the Carnegie Commission on Higher Education
and EWA, describes and evaluates, in considerable detail, international
programs and commitments of American educational institutions. Data
were compiled through questionnaires sent to over 1,300 accredited
institutions (replies codified to form the EWA Data Bank), a literature
review, and interviews at over 40 colleges and universities.

In Part 1, the authors discuss with specific examples, the new
approaches developed by institutions to broaden the student's horizons:
language and area studies, comparative and topical studies, study and
work abroad, and the campus environment. Part 2 turns to the university's involvement with the broader international community, including
programs in local high schools, training programs for foreign visitors
and Americans going abroad (e.g., the Peace Corps), exchange programs and technical assistance. The third and final section discusses
the institutional setting—the organizational structure, staffing, and
funding of international programs—and developments on the national
scene which affect such programs.

The authors believe that special international programs and an
enhanced international aspect in all areas of study are central to the
purposes of higher education for the world of today and tomorrow.
Finding that international studies are still largely underdeveloped on
most campuses, and that even present levels of activity are in jeopardy,
they conclude with a list of recommendations addressed to the major
participants in international education: trustees, administrators,
faculty, students, foundations, legislators, government officials, and
citizens.

Sasnett, Martena. See No. 78.

336. Schmidt, S. C., and Scott, John. "Advanced Training for For-
     eign Students: The Regional Approach." <u>Journal of Developing</u>
     <u>Areas</u> 6 (October 1971): 39-50.
Agricultural training in developed countries for students from developing countries has several disadvantages: (1) the inappropriateness of
training for the needs of host countries; (2) long and costly training
periods; (3) paternal attitudes of training institutions; (4) dissertation
research topics often based on the host country's problems; and
(5) the brain drain. Establishment of regionally based research and
training programs in developing countries would allow for more productive orientation of research and education than is now possible in fragmented, short-term programs supported by various foundations and

AID. It would also provide a better chance that students return to their own countries as productive citizens.

337. Schuler, Edgar A. "On the Training of Graduate Students from Other Countries." Rural Sociology 34 (March 1969): 97-98.
Schuler comments on a paper by William W. Reeder, "The Transferability of North American Rural Sociological Training to Other Societies and Other Cultures," presented in Session 7, Training and Work Environment for Sociologists Outside of USA, at the annual meeting of the Rural Sociological Society, Boston, 1968. Reeder suggests far-reaching changes in the orientation and methodology of education in rural sociology. Schuler supports the proposal for graduate training centers in each of the major cultures and asserts that implementation of Reeder's major recommendations will require outstanding ability, creativity, realism, courage, and much persistent hard work.

338. Schulken, Emma Walker. "A History of Foreign Students in American Higher Education from its Colonial Beginnings to the Present: A Synthesis of the Major Forces Influencing Their Presence in American Higher Education." Ph.D. dissertation, Florida State University, 1968.
This study examines, within the context of broad historical perspectives, three major forces which influenced the development of the foreign student movement in American higher education: The Missionary Movement of the 19th Century, the philanthropic foundations active in the first three decades of the 20th Century, and the U. S. Government's role since World War II.

339. Seaquist, Robert Gunder. "A Study to Develop a Planning Base for the Association of Colombian-American Binational Schools." Ph.D. dissertation, University of Alabama, 1968.
This study of the binational schools of Colombia and Haiti (1) considers the history of the American overseas school in its environment in Latin America; (2) compares the schools in the Association of American Binational Schools of Colombia; (3) examines the relationship between the University of Alabama and the Colombian binational schools; and (4) considers the schools in the light of the principles and standards of an accrediting association. In conclusion, some implications and recommendations are suggested.

340. Selby, Henry, and Woods, Clyde. "Foreign Students at a High-Pressure University." Sociology of Education 39 (Spring 1966): 138-54.
Two three-hour semi-structured interviews were given to a group of 18 non-European foreign students to discover the nature and timing of

their adjustment to U. S. university life. Judgments made from the interviews were verified from questionnaire data. Instead of the traditional up-down-up configuration, or U-curve, the students exhibited, in both the interviews and questionnaires, an initial steep decline of morale followed by a gradual recovery over the year. It is concluded that foreign student adjustment could be better understood by considering the impact of the institutions, rather than the impact of the culture at large.

341. Selltiz, Claire; Hopson, Anna L.; and Cook, Stuart. "The Effects of Situational Factors on Personal Interaction between Foreign Students and Americans." Journal of Social Issues 12 (1956): 33-55.

The authors consider the effect on the interpersonal association between American and foreign students of small colleges in small towns, large universities in large cities, and large universities in small towns. It was hypothesized that "foreign students in small colleges in small towns would be most likely to find themselves in contact situations with high interaction potential, and that those in metropolitan universities would be least likely to be in such situations, . . . and that students in situations with higher interaction potential would engage in more frequent and more intimate interaction with Americans. Verification of these predictions would be taken as evidence that interaction is influenced by situational factors and is not dependent upon attitudinal or volitional sets on the part of the foreign students." Three hundred and forty-eight male foreign students attending 35 colleges and universities were interviewed twice, early and late in their U. S. stay so that changes could be measured. The hypotheses are generally supported though it was found that national origin of foreign students is equally important as the interaction potential of the situation in determining interaction with Americans.

342. Shaffer, Robert H., and Dowling, Leo R. "Foreign Students and Their American Student Friends." School and Society 96 (13 April 1968): 245-49.

The socio-cultural interactions and relationships among foreign students and American students on the Indiana University campus were studied to ascertain their impact on the native group and to determine the distinguishing characteristics of friendship patterns and associations between groups. Data were obtained from a background questionnaire, personality and personal preference tests, school records, and personal interviews. It was determined that the friendships under examination were based upon similarities of interests and environmental proximities rather than upon personal or background characteristics, and that initial contacts between the two groups arose from academic and other interests matched in informal and spontaneous meetings. Campus activities and community organizations appeared to contribute little.

343.   Sharma, Sarla. "A Study to Identify and Analyze Adjustment Problems Experienced by Foreign Non-European Graduate Students Enrolled in Selected Universities in the State of North Carolina." Ed.D. dissertation, University of North Carolina at Greensboro, 1971.

To collect data for this study, an inventory was devised covering academic, personal, and social problems. Subjects, selected through stratified, disproportionate, random-sampling procedures, represented the Far East, South Asia, the Middle East, Africa, and Latin America. One hundred and ninety-five completed returns were received; a limited number of respondents were also interviewed.

Statistical analysis showed that, relatively speaking, academic problems were more severe and required a longer time for their resolution than the other two types. Further, there was found to be a strong positive relationship among the three adjustment areas. There is some evidence that student personnel services help in academic adjustment but their usefulness in other areas was not borne out.

Students from South Asia, those who study agriculture, engineering, and physical sciences, and those who are self-supporting, were found to make better academic adjustment than those who came from the Far East or Latin America, those who study social sciences, and those who get money from home, respectively. The variables of length of residence in the United States, age upon entering the United States, varied educational and home backgrounds, and the campus of enrollment were not found to have a bearing on adjustment in the three areas.

344.   Sharon, Amiel T. "Test of English as a Foreign Language as a Moderator of Graduate Record Examination Scores in the Prediction of Foreign Students' Grades in Graduate School." Princeton, N.J.: Educational Testing Service, September 1971.

Scores of foreign students on the Graduate Record Examinations (GRE) Aptitude Tests and the Test of English as a Foreign Language (TOEFL) were combined through multiple and moderated regression to predict grade point average (GPA). It was hypothesized that TOEFL would moderate the relationship between the GRE scores and GPA. According to this hypothesis, students scoring high on TOEFL would be more predictable by GRE than those scoring low. The hypothesis was only partially supported; results suggest that foreign students with low English verbal aptitude can succeed in American graduate schools. The limitations of GPA as a criterion of graduate school success for foreign students is discussed.

345. Shearer, John C. "International Talent Migration and the Foreign
Student." Monthly Labor Review 93 (May 1970): 55-59.
The key to the brain drain problem is the relevance both of the selection
of students and of the U. S. university programs they pursue, in order
to increase the likelihood that training will be appropriate to home-
country needs and that students will find it advantageous to apply their
new knowledge and skills at home.

Two indexes were devised to gauge how the patterns and trends
of U. S. training relate to development needs: a technical index, which
emphasizes improving the quantity and quality of training in the fields
of science, engineering, agriculture, and education; and a structural
index, based on the conclusions of such experts as Raul Prebisch of the
U. N., that technical specialties will not make major contributions to
the general welfare in most Latin American countries until those countries undergo basic structural changes. The structural index gives
greatest weight to the social sciences and humanities.

The indexes showed that among the seven Latin American countries who are major senders of graduate students to the United States,
Venezuela had the highest concentration of students with technical
specialties attending U. S. institutions, and Argentina the highest concentration of students with structural specialties. Generally it was
observed that home governments support the technical specialties to a
greater extent than does the U. S. Government. With respect to the
structural specialties, the situation is almost reversed.

346. Sheffield, Edward F., and McGrail, Mary Margot, eds. "The
Retrieval of Canadian Graduate Students from Abroad." Staffing
the Universities and Colleges of Canada No. 4. Association of
Universities and Colleges of Canada, n. d.
The AUCC in 1965 began Operation Retrieval, a program whereby U. S.
and British universities having a minimum enrollment of 25 Canadian
graduate students were visited by a team representing Canadian educational institutions, and, in some instances, Canadian government agencies. In group and individual sessions it was found that, with few
exceptions, the students wish to return to Canada if suitable positions
were available. They quickly lose touch with developments at home and
have no source of up-to-date information on academic employment.

It is recommended that the Canadian Department of Manpower
should become the central agency for retrieval of Canadian students,
compiling data on Canadians abroad and offering guidance to them on
applying for jobs in Canada. Universities are urged to publish all
staff vacancies and make prompt replies to all enquiries, as should
Canadian industry, which ought to recruit more vigorously on American
campuses.

347. Shepard, Nolan Edgbert. "The Acculturation of Foreign Students
      in Southern Colleges and Universities." Ph. D. dissertation,
      University of Mississippi, 1970.

The study included a representative sample of foreign students from
the 38 universities and colleges in the South in which no less than a
minimum of 25 foreign students were enrolled. A questionnaire concerning the experiences related to the acculturation process was completed by 247 students, 67 percent of the study population.

Most students were pleased with their educational sojourn. A
minority, which ranged as high as 40 percent, were disappointed, feeling unwelcome, lonely, isolated, and friendless. They faced social,
financial, and language difficulties, and often lacked the services of
their institution in confronting the acculturation process.

Recommendations were made regarding the admission and enrollment of foreign students (1) to assure adequate pre-departure information and screening of applicants, (2) to provide better institutional
services, and (3) to make maximum use of the presence of foreign
students to broaden the international dimensions of the American campus.

348. Shin, Kuk Bom. "The Post Graduation Residency Plans of Korean
      Students Attending Selected Universities in Michigan." Ph. D.
      dissertation, Michigan State University, 1972.

Of 132 identified Korean students in seven Michigan colleges and universities, 103 completed mailed questionnaires during the summer of 1971.
Among major conclusions were: (1) Korean students who come to the
United States at a young age, who adjust well to American life, and
whose sojourn is long, are most likely to remain in the United States;
(2) there is no statistical difference between return plans of sponsored
and non-sponsored Korean students, nor are return plans related to
attitudes toward employment conditions back home; and (3) the more
strongly the student feels that U. S. study will contribute to Korea's
development, the greater the likelihood the student will plan to return
home.

349. Sinauer, Ernst M. The Role of Communication in International
      Training and Education: Overcoming Barriers to Understanding
      with the Developing Countries. New York: Frederick A. Praeger,
      1967.

An assessment is made of international training and education in the
United States and other countries; the role of oral, written, visual, and
other modes of communication in meeting educational needs of students
from the developing nations; and financial support for these educational
endeavors. Types of participating agencies and individuals are reviewed with special reference to Israeli programs and course offerings.
Language-training problems, procedures, applications, and objectives

are discussed. Recommendations are made concerning improvements in student classification and curriculum.

350. Singer, Marshall R. Weak States in a World of Powers: The Dynamics of International Relations. New York: The Free Press, 1972.

In his discussion of the impact of international education, pp. 149-67, Singer contends that foreign education and training creates perceptual and identity ties between foreign students and the host nation. International education is thus an instrument of foreign policy; developed countries should educate as many students from developing countries as possible, to reinforce ties between themselves and potential elites. Developing countries, however, should diversify their sources of training and education to prevent excessive ties to a single country.

351. Singh, Kulwant. "Indian Professionals and Students in the United States." Paper prepared for the Annual Meeting of the International Studies Association, Pittsburgh, Pa., 2-4 April 1970.

To identify "push" and "pull" factors that motivate Indian students and professionals to remain in the United States, data was gathered from a stratified sample of 44 respondents at the University of Florida, Gainesville, using a self-administered questionnaire and a structured interview schedule. Results of the study show that there are no significant differences between students and professionals regarding education and social background, motivation for sojourn, professional socialization in the United States, or on the decision to return or stay in America. The dependent variable, remain or return behavior, has some relationship to salary but not to standard of living; hence home-country emphasis on non-economic incentives may prove useful. Orientation toward home country, identified as moral obligation to serve, attachment to Indian culture, and home and family obligations, was a strong predictor of behavior.

352. Sitler, L. Arlene. "The Asian 'Brain Drain'—Factors Contributing toward the Alienation of Returning Graduates and Professional Personnel." Paper presented at the Association for Asian Studies 10th Annual Southeastern Regional Conference, Winthrop College, Rock Hill, South Carolina, 29-30 January 1971.

The brain drain is a problem of increasing concern to developing countries, especially the Asian nations which estimate that over 90 percent of their students in the United States fail to return. Recent research reveals that conditions in the home country are the underlying cause of much talent migration. While international travel and study should not be curtailed, inducements must be found to encourage return. Indigenous or regional graduate education is recommended for developing countries in that it permits education that is better adapted to local conditions and is lower in cost.

Sjogren, Cliff. See No. 264e.

353. Skinner, Maynard Clyde. "The Foreign Student Adviser's Office: Practices, Problems, and Procedures in Selected Colleges and Universities." Ph.D. dissertation, University of Colorado, 1963.
This study discusses: (1) the practices and procedures of the foreign student adviser in American higher education in those institutions having 50 or more foreign students enrolled during the academic year 1960-61; (2) the importance of the foreign student adviser's office in higher education; (3) the apparent trends in duties, status, policies, and philosophy; (4) the concept of the emerging role of the foreign student adviser in higher education in America.

Slocum, Joel B. See No. 264c.

354. Smart, Reginald. "The Goals and Definitions of International Education." International Studies Quarterly 15 (December 1971): 442-63.
Eight basic goals and related definitions of international education are offered: permeation of new ideas; synthesis of value systems and world culture; national development; development of national political power; mutual understanding and cooperation; basic preparation for life in a global context; development of a creative attitude toward diversity; discovery of truth.

355. Smith, Eugene H. "Campus Activism and Foreign Students." Exchange 4, no. 3 (Winter 1969): 39-43.
It is Smith's contention that the university should actively encourage its foreign students to participate "in all forms of lawful political, social and university activism." He stresses that the university must also, through its Foreign Student Adviser, clearly inform foreign students of their rights and obligations vis-a-vis home and host governments, university laws, and regulations of the sponsoring agency.

356. Smith, M. Brewster. "Cross-Cultural Education and Cultural Change." International Social Science Bulletin 8, no. 4 (1956): 585-97.
Cultural impact is one objective of most sponsored programs of educational exchange; it is therefore desirable to understand the conditions and processes by which one culture affects another. Processes discussed include: sojourn learning, both academic and informal; the persistence and transfer of learning; strategic social placement, i.e., the

degree to which the returnee and his new skills and attitudes are accepted by his home culture; and continuing channels of communication with individuals and institutions established during the sojourn.

357. Snipes, Paul David. "Communication Behavior and Personal Adjustment among American and Foreign Students at Indiana University." Ed.D. dissertation, Indiana University, 1969.
One hundred and twelve American and foreign students at both undergraduate and graduate level comprised the research sample. All completed the Sixteen Personality Factor Test (16PF), Forms A and B, published by the Institute for Personality and Ability Testing, Champaign, Illinois, and a Communication Questionnaire.

It was found that foreign graduate students devoted the most time to printed and broadcast media. Undergraduates devoted the most time to social-personal and social-nonpersonal communication activities.

No particular pattern appeared among the correlation coefficients for the 16 PF Factors taken separately and combined and the time devoted to the four communications activities by the groups separately or combined.

358. Sofola, Johnson Adeyemi. "American-Processed Nigerians: A Study of the Adjustment and Attitudes of the Nigerian Students in the United States of America." Ph.D. dissertation, American University, 1967.
The findings in this study confirmed the hypotheses that Nigerian students experience maladjustment due to job downgrading, isolation, and cultural differences bringing about culture shock. The students' positive image of America is influenced negatively by post-arrival experiences but it could not be ascertained that students became more appreciative, or nationalistic, toward Nigeria. Data were obtained through questionnaires and interviews with 265 Nigerian students, principally in Washington, D. C., New York, and Chicago.

359. Sours, Martin Harvey. "The Brain Drain and World Politics." Ph.D. dissertation, University of Washington, 1971.
Sours attempts, through historical analysis and examination of empirical indicators such as U. S. federal budgets and the post-doctoral destinations of Ph.D. recipients, to reconceptualize the brain drain as an indicator of world interdependence. The policy decisions of the great powers exercise a dominant influence as shown by the effects on third-world development of the 1965 U. S. immigration legislation. The brain drain thus can serve as an index of the propensity for systemic dominance of the international system by the United States.

360. Spaulding, Seth. "Needed: New Forms of Technical Cooperation in the Development of Education." Focus: Technical Cooperation 1974, no. 1, pp. 3-7. In International Development Review 16, no. 1.

Spaulding suggests a number of new technical assistance strategies: more funding for large global projects; involvement of more institutions in the technical cooperation process; greater flexibility in the use of funds; better coordination of educational development. Mechanisms to encourage educational innovation are discussed, as is the need for a variety of evaluative activities.

361. Speakman, Cummins E., Jr. International Exchange in Education. New York: Center for Applied Research in Education, 1966.

Speakman examines modern concepts of educational exchange, focusing on the development and content of U. S. programs offered by national and international agencies, both public and private. He identifies a number of problem areas, including selection and admission criteria, manpower shortages in agency staffing, and the need for closer bilateral cooperation in planning major international programs.

362. Spencer, Richard. "The Academic Performance of Foreign Students in American Colleges and Universities: Comments on the Literature 1960-67, with Bibliography." Urbana, Ill.: University of Illinois, Office of Instructional Resources, Measurement and Research Division, 1967.

Research on the academic success of foreign students is found to suffer from restricted and biased sampling, unrepresentativeness, and lack of control over intellectual, linguistic, and cultural factors which might be causal factors in the interpretation of result. Definition of crucial terms, e.g., "foreign student," "success," is lacking; testing practices vary widely. Spencer concludes that research on foreign student problems needs to be improved relative to the definition of terms, application of appropriate statistical models, and selection of adequate samples.

363. _____. "Factors Affecting Successful Performance of Foreign Students: Possible Future Research. A Working Paper." Urbana, Ill.: University of Illinois, Office of Instructional Resources, Measurement and Research Division, 1967.

Factors discussed are grouped into criterion variables, background factors, and situational factors. Spencer then proposes a methodology by which to obtain, evaluate, and organize information on the performance criteria, potential selection criteria, and interpersonal processes of foreign student education.

364. _____. "The Relationship Between Examination Systems and
Cultural Change." Urbana, Ill.: University of Illinois, Office of
Instructional Resources, Measurement and Research Division,
1967.
Spencer argues that the development of instruments to test or identify
those variables which exist among foreign students or other cultures
may not necessarily be equated over the various cultures and linguistic
systems represented. The measurement field is now faced with the
selection and measurement of two types of populations: (1) non-English-
speaking foreigners wanting to study in the United States; and (2) the
social, educational, and professional selection and promotion of individuals in a society other than our own.
    The objectives of foreign students may differ from those of Amer-
icans. The real test of success or failure is not the grade point average
but whether the student succeeds in using his education for the benefit
of his own country.

_____. See No. 184.

365. Sperling, Philip. "Evaluating Training Programs: The AID
Experience." Focus: Technical Cooperation 1973, no. 4, pp. 9-
13. In International Development Review, 15, no. 4.
This report outlines the multi-perspective assessment which AID uses
with its participants: evaluation of the participants, faculty perceptions,
exit interviews, entry questionnaires, and post-sojourn interviews.
Future research must be based on a built-in evaluation system and a
clear definition of the ultimate criterion for determining the success
of training programs.

366. Springer, George P. "The Foreign Graduate Student." University
of New Mexico, n.d.
Springer offers a definition of "foreign graduate student" and discusses
the problems of administering and organizing foreign student programs,
arguing that although some special arrangements are necessary, it may
be best to accommodate foreign student procedures to those used for
domestic graduate students. He recommends a computerized two-way
information system to benefit all participating institutions and domestic
as well as foreign applicants.

Stebbins, George B. See No. 269.

Stevens, Rosemary. See No. 391.

367. Stewart, Edward C. "Cultural Sensitivities in Counseling." Paper
presented at the Division 9 Symposium, "Cross-Cultural Counseling," American Psychological Association, Montreal, August 1973.

When counselor and client come from different societies, the counseling situation can be treated as an event in intercultural communication. The relationship should be marked by empathy, a response at the latent level of communication, based on the assumption of cultural differences, rather than by sympathy, a response based primarily on presumed similarities. In the counseling situation, empathy protects the privacy of the client and relieves both counselor and client from making moral judgments. Topics which have proved useful in developing empathy are lexical markings of adjectives in English, negativism in American society, and negativism in methods of learning.

368. Stone, Benjamin. "Gaps in Graduate Training of Students from Abroad." Science, 6 June 1969, p. 1118.
Stone recommends supplementary training for science students from foreign countries in the identification of research problems, maintenance skills, and basic administrative techniques. There is also a need for more broadly trained and creative scientific personnel.

369. Sugimoto, Roy Atsuro. "The Relationship of Selected Predictive Variables to Foreign Student Achievement at the University of California, Los Angeles." Ph.D. dissertation, University of Southern California, 1966.
University records for 1,375 foreign students with F-1 or J-1 visas at UCLA during 1964-65 were analyzed with the following results: (1) Among the most significant pre-admission predictors of the academic success of foreign student are graduate standing, age, and type of visa held. (2) Least predictive values can be attached to such standard pre-admission items as scores on the English examination, admission status, and the date of entry into the United States. (3) Defined in terms of "university action taken," first-semester grade point average is the best index of the student's eventual academic success.
It is recommended that improved selection criteria be devised for the screening of foreign students, especially those from countries of the Far East, and that the final decision regarding admission or rejection be based upon a consensus of the admissions officer, the foreign student counselor, and the academic adviser.

370. Susskind, Charles, and Schell, Lynn. "Berkeley-Golden Gate for Foreign Engineers: A Study of Foreign Students who Received Graduate Engineering Degrees at Berkeley, 1954-1965." University of California Institute of International Studies, March 1967.
See No. 182. This is a preliminary report of research results.

371. Sutnick, Alton I.; Reichard, J. F.; and Angelides, A. P. "Orientation of Foreign Medical Graduates." Exchange 6, no. 4 (Spring 1971): 91-99.

The authors describe orientation programs organized by the Philadelphia County Medical Society and various community organizations for foreign doctors and nurses serving in local hospitals. A survey by the Association for Hospital Medical Education suggests that orientation programs treat the following major difficulties confronting foreign medical graduates: unfamiliarity with English vernacular; confusion over unfamiliar medical techniques and procedures; unfamiliarity with American methods of practicing medicine; and the structure of hospital organization.

372. Swan, Lee Melvin. "Perceptions Regarding American Graduate Education of Filipino Agricultural and Home Economics Students at Selected Universities in the United States, Their Major Professors, and Their Home Country Authorities." Ph.D. dissertation, University of Wisconsin, 1969.

This study was the first phase of a longitudinal project evaluating the effectiveness of American graduate education for Filipino students. In this segment, 113 Filipino agricultural and home-economics graduate students, and their major professors (68), were interviewed at the ten American Land-Grant Universities having the largest enrollment of such students. In addition, 76 individuals named by the students as a potential employer, supervisor, or colleague upon return (a home-country authority) were interviewed in the Philippines. The evidence suggested that consensus on perceptions of objectives, policies, and procedures in graduate education among the Filipino student, his major professor, and his home-country authority was an important variable associated with satisfaction and performance in the graduate experience. Analysis of study data also revealed that the student's divisional major, his years of work experience, and his years of stay in the United States sojourn, were associated with his perceptions and priorities in the graduate experience.

Symonds, Richard. See No. 381a.

373. Tanner, Shirley. "An Investigation of Friendship Patterns of Foreign Students." Occasional Paper No. 1. University of Michigan, International Center, 1968.

This study analyzes the friendship patterns, obtained through a questionnaire, of 63 randomly selected, non-immigrant, non-Canadian, single male graduate students at the University of Michigan.

The findings were as follows: (1) the theories of friendship allowing for disillusionment, adjustment, satisfaction and general vacillation (Lysgaard and Sweell, 1954-55; Lambert and Bressler, 1956) were supported; (2) there was no relation between meeting places of the students' American friends and their countries of origin nor between discrimination and American friends; (3) students without problems in friendship and customs were more likely to have American friends; (4) students from "Westernized" countries had the greatest number of American friends while other groups had more friendships among their co-nationals; (5) students from Europe and English-speaking countries found American friendships to be most similar to their own nationality friendships; (6) students with the most previous contact with Americans did not stay with co-nationals, whereas those with fewer contacts did; (7) students who lacked adequate knowledge of English were more likely not to have American friends.

374. Telleen, Judy G. Johnson. "A Predictive Model of the Cumulative Academic Achievement of Graduate Students from India: Based upon Data Collected on 54 Variables in a Longitudinal Study of 300 Indian Graduate Students Who Attended the University of Michigan during the 20-Year Period September 1947 to August 1968." Ph.D. dissertation, University of Michigan, 1970.

This study examines and summarizes the academic and background characteristics of 300 Indian graduate students. Of the 54 variables included in the study, 15 were found to be significantly related to academic achievement. By use of the significance of chi-square values, eight variables were selected for use in a predictive model: age, Indian degree classification, matriculation exam grade, name of first Indian degree, name of Indian school, name of most advanced Indian degree, presence of scholarship, source of financial support. The model was found to accurately predict the cumulative letter grade of Indian students who were not a part of the original 300 students in the study.

375. The Tenth Mohonk Consultation with International Students. A Proposal for Pre-Departure Seminars. Mohonk Lake, New Paltz, N. Y.: The Mohonk Trust, 1973.

Thirteen students from 12 countries who are studying in American colleges and universities met to prepare a proposal for Pre-Departure Seminars for foreign students. These seminars were seen as essential for several reasons: (1) U. S. education does not adequately prepare the foreign student to use the skills he has learned; (2) prolonged exposure to a new culture poses a threat to the student's ability to communicate upon his return; and (3) students have lost touch with home societies during their absence.

Several arrangements for pre-departure seminars were proposed. One method would be to hold a single long meeting where students could exchange views. Another arrangement would be a series of three or four separate meetings involving in-depth discussions. A third method could be the incorporation of a pre-departure seminar into a school curriculum as a credit or non-credit course for foreign students.

The members of the Consultation proposed to serve as a task force to assist other groups in the implementation of pre-departure seminars.

376. Thames, John Alsop. "Korean Students in Southern California: Factors Influencing their Plans Toward Returning Home." Ph. D. dissertation, University of Southern California, 1971.

A sample was selected of 100 Korean students attending seven colleges and universities in Southern California. The students were interviewed utilizing a survey which included questions about the general background of the students, their plans concerning returning home, and their attitudes toward certain factors influencing their plans. In analyzing the data, ten factors were cross-tabulated with the degree of certainty of the students to return home and the cross-tabulations were subjected to chi-square analysis.

In general the students least likely to return home were those from lower socio-economic backgrounds, students who had not finished their undergraduate education in Korea, males who had not completed their military obligation to Korea, those supported partially or totally by working in the United States, those majoring in engineering or natural sciences, those who had already spent more than two years in the United States, those who planned to or had already obtained permanent residence in the United States, and female students.

The recommendations included improved job placement, information services, and programs of pre-departure counseling by the colleges and universities.

377. Thompson, Carol B. "International Programs: Communication or Obfuscation?" Exchange 7, no. 2 (Fall 1971): 75-80.

Results of an informal survey of "Big 10" universities, 1970-71, showed diminished participation in International Clubs and planned programs for foreign students.

378. Truscott, Michael Hugh. "The Brain Drain of Scientists, Engineers, and Physicians from the Developing Countries to the United States." Ph. D. dissertation, Louisiana State University and Agricultural and Mechanical College, 1971.

This study examines some of the more important "push" and "pull" forces which are commonly cited as contributing to the brain drain. A basic conclusion is that the immigration laws of the United States are the main contributing factor to the drain from other countries. A second conclusion is that the brain drain is more a symptom of the state of underdevelopment than a cause of underdevelopment. It is symptomatic of the disequilibrium that exists between the typical pattern of expansion of higher education in developing countries and their limited capacity to absorb an expanding number of graduates. The possibility of a reverse drain for the United States presents itself in the very near future.

379. Uehara, Soichi. "A Study of Academic Achievement of F-1 Classed Aliens and Other Non-immigrant Temporary Students at Kapiolani Community College." Honolulu, Hawaii: Kapiolani Community College, May 1969.

This research investigated the difference in academic performance between foreign students who enter the country with a student visa and are thereby required to take the U. S. Consulate English test, and those who originally enter with some other type of visa (no test required). The study included data on the 48 foreign students who have attended or are attending Kapiolani Community College from September 1964 to the present. The percentage of academic failures for the two groups of students was 16.7 percent and 35.0 percent, respectively. Findings included: the degree of English proficiency was closely related to academic success; the majority of temporary visitors had their visa status changed to that of student; and the three measures of English proficiency used by the college yielded similar results. It was recommended that, if the college maintains an open door for foreign students, it must provide a sophisticated remedial English program; if a relatively closed door is to be maintained, then a better measuring device is needed to select those who will attend.

380. Ukai, Nobushige. "Pragmatism Goes West." Saturday Review, 18 February 1967, pp. 88, 91.

Long-range consequences of academic interchange between America and Japan can be classified as tangible, such as new directions in Japanese education, and intangible, for instance, a deepened understanding of American empiricism. Confrontation with Western scholarship has helped to alert Japanese (1) to the necessity for devising social procedures consistent with the concept of the individual as an independent and responsible decision maker in the democratic scheme, and (2) to be more sensitive in the realm of selecting means to achieve a social goal.

381a. United Kingdom Ministry of Overseas Development. Report on the Results of Training of Pakistanis in Britain under the Colombo Plan. By Richard Symonds. Communications Series No. 34. University of Sussex, Institute of Development Studies, n.d.

To assess the results of U. K. training programs for Pakistanis under the Colombo Plan, former trainees (129) and their supervisors were interviewed during 1968. The sample was representative of the fields in which awards had been the most numerous in the last four years and of the principal geographical units from which the trainees had come. Analysis of the program, and interviewees' estimates of its value are given for each training sector: public administration, industry, atomic energy, medicine, etc.

The author recommends that in general, assistance should be in the form of post-doctoral training or special courses, encouraging Pakistani institutions to take the responsibility for graduate degrees. Placement, candidate selection, etc., could be improved by closer consultation in Pakistan between British representatives and the departments or institutions using British aid. Training results could be significantly reinforced if contacts with the training institution were maintained and if trainees were offered subscriptions to professional journals in their fields.

381b. _____. Training Ghanaians in Britain. By Margaret S. Wolfson. Communications Series No. 35. University of Sussex, Institute of Development Studies, October 1969.

In the decade since independence, 400 Ghanaians have obtained training in the U. K. as part of the Special Commonwealth African Assistance Plan (SCAAP). The purpose of this study is to determine, first, whether the orientation and scope of the training has been best suited to Ghana's evolving training needs, and second, whether the officers sent for training have been able to put their additional experience to best use. Informal personal interviews were conducted with 90 returned students and 35 heads of departments, and an inter-departmental seminar attended by over 40 government officials was held.

The purpose of the program has been to provide increased knowledge and experience for middle- and senior-level civil servants through short-term courses and work attachments in the U. K. Its relevance is attested by the lack of drain, and by continuity of employment.

Failure to achieve maximum effectiveness can be attributed to four factors: lack of selectivity with respect both to choice of applicant and choice of training program; lack of effective administrative coordination and planning for manpower requirements in Ghana; inadequate financial and material resources with which to implement improvements desired by returnees; and failure of returnees to participate in conferences or seminars which would diffuse among colleagues the results of their U. K. sojourn.

Although returnees are enthusiastic about their visit to the U. K., it is suggested that consideration be given to development of training facilities in Africa. It is further recommended that the U. K. take a more active part in assisting Ghanaian authorities to formulate training requirements, and appoint a technical assistance expert. The Ghanaian authorities are advised that training requirements should be planned as part of a coherent development effort.

382. United Nations Development Programme. <u>Report on an Evaluation</u>
      <u>of Seminars, Study Tours, Training Courses and Meetings of</u>
      <u>Working Groups of Experts.</u> New York, December 1968.
During the 1967-68 biennium, 213 regional and inter-regional seminars,
study tours, training courses, and meetings of working groups of experts were financed by the Technical Assistance component of the UNDP
As a result of questions raised in recent years about the effectiveness
of these projects, the Administrator undertook an evaluation study based
on a structured sample of 113 projects. Data was obtained from reports
from the participating agencies, questionnaires, comments from Governments and UNDP Resident Representatives, and observations from
the study consultant.

      The study recommends that the coordinating authorities and
UNDP Resident Representatives be more involved in selection of participants, ensuring that the project is clearly relevant to the specific
development needs, opportunities, and resources of the country and
that ample time is allowed for advance preparation. Wider systematic
follow-up ought to be encouraged for better retrieval of experience to
guide future projects. In addition, a process of continuous evaluation
of projects should be initiated.

383a. UNESCO. "Evaluation of UNESCO Fellowship Programme (1964-
      1969). India." Paris, 20 October 1971.
The UNESCO Training Abroad Programme has, since 1947, offered
fellowships and travel grants to mature persons already engaged in
careers, to improve their academic and professional competence.

      This report presents information gathered by questionnaire from
248 Indian fellows who participated from 1964 to 1969. One hundred
and forty-five respondents were working at the same posts as they held
at the time of the award while 95 had been promoted to higher positions
in the same field or had left the occupation for which the fellowship had
been awarded. The consensus of opinion was that the training had
developed their professional skill and competence although, in some
cases, the use of advanced knowledge or skills was limited by lack of
facilities or opportunities.

      Major criticisms of the program included the shortness of the
training period, problems with the extension of awards and rigid
adherence to the program, and lack of knowledge of the language of the
host country. (See also No. 426.)

383b. _____ . "Evaluation Study of UNESCO Fellowships: Iran." Paris,
      1972.
One hundred Iranian fellows, from a total population of 162, replied to
the questionnaire. In general, the fellows were occupying key positions
in educational, scientific, and cultural projects. About 80 percent

declared that their studies and experiences through the fellowship had been of great value in their assignments. Their main problems included difficulty with the foreign language, financial problems, differences in customs and traditions, and lack of proper guidance.

On return to Iran, 21 percent of the scholars had difficulty finding jobs commensurate with the knowledge and experience they had gained. These fellows expressed some regret at accepting the scholarship and going abroad.

383c. _____. "Evaluation Study of UNESCO Fellowships: Japan." Paris, 1972.
The first Japanese UNESCO fellowship was granted in 1951. By the end of 1968 the number of Japanese fellows abroad had reached over 100. One-third replied to a survey questionnaire; they felt the experience was very valuable professionally. Problems included: (1) too brief a sojourn; (2) financial arrangements; (3) too heavy a concentration of fellowships in some fields; (4) difficulties over administrative arrangements.

The Japanese government has now decided to participate as a host country rather than a beneficiary country.

383d. _____. "Evaluation du Programme des Bourses de l'UNESCO en Republique Unie du Cameroun." Paris, 1973.
In 1954 the first UNESCO fellowship was awarded to a scholar from Cameroon. Since that time, 136 Cameroonians have participated. Approximately 60 fellows completed the survey questionnaire. In general, the fellows were pleased with their training; some social impact of the program was positive. Financial problems and some problems with finding employment upon return were noted by the fellows surveyed.

384. _____. "Statistics of Students Abroad, 1962-1968: Where They Go, Where They Come From, What They Study." Paris, 1971.
This volume, an analysis of international trends in student exchange programs, is presented in two parts. Part 1 contains the actual analysis supplemented by an annex of tables which summarize world and regional trends. Part 2 contains country tables for 151 countries and territories in which students abroad are presented according to their country of study and their field of study. This is the first comprehensive study on this subject published by UNESCO; it serves as a reference source for those interested in international exchanges and, more specifically, as documentation for national authorities concerned with manpower planning.

385. UNESCO International Committee of Experts on Training Abroad Policies. "Information on Training Needs and Study Facilities." Paris, 18 October 1971. (Mimeo.)

This brief report is based on replies to questionnaires by 47 countries during 1971. Part 1 identifies priorities in training for the following sectors: Education; Natural Science; Philosophy, Human Sciences, Social Sciences, and Culture; and Communications. On the location of training, replies indicate that preference should be given to training nationals in their own countries whenever suitable facilities exist. Training abroad should be reserved for post-graduate studies and research. The importance of assessing manpower resources is emphasized and it is recognized that establishing fact-finding machinery is of top priority.

Part 2 concerns available training facilities. Main fields of special competence include: Educational Planning and Administration, Educational Research, Teacher Training, Training of Teachers in the Basic Sciences, and Training of Engineers and Technicians.

UNESCO collaboration is deemed helpful in (1) the assessment of manpower needs and resources, (2) improvement of local structures to achieve full use of international assistance, (3) guidance in developing national training policies towards increased equality of education in local and regional institutions and more effective use of educational resources.

386. _____. "Report of a Conference held in Paris, 25-29 October 1971." Paris, 1972.
This report advises UNESCO's Director-General on policies concerning training abroad. It contains general recommendations regarding objectives and strategies of training, and more specific recommendations pertaining to operational aspects of training from selection to follow-up.

387. United Nations Institute for Training and Research. "Policies Affecting the Outflow of Trained Personnel." Development Digest 7 (April 1969): 55-57.
A survey of measures taken by developing countries relating to control of students studying abroad, and to their recruitment for employment at home, indicates that few countries are actively stemming the brain drain. Only a handful of countries (e.g., Iran, India, Thailand, Kenya) make regular efforts to recruit their own students in the United States for home employment. United States visa regulations for exchange visitors are found to be having some effect in combating the brain drain problems. (This article is excerpted from "Outflow of Trained Personnel from Developing Countries," a report submitted by the Secretary-General of the United Nations to the 23rd Session of the General Assembly, 1968.)

388. _____. The Emigration of Highly Skilled Manpower from the Developing Countries. By Gregory Henderson. New York, 1970.

Henderson examines various aspects of talent migration: components of migration, statistics of professional migration, migration by countries, and occupation and migration of middle-level personnel. He also discusses the impact of indigenous and foreign education, economic and social factors motivating outflow, advantages and disadvantages of migration, and certain measures currently underway to alleviate talent outflow. The concluding section contains recommendations for developing and developed countries and for international strategies.

389. _____ . The Brain Drain from Five Developing Countries. UNITAR Research Reports No. 5. New York, 1971.
Five developing countries—Cameroon, Colombia, Lebanon, the Philippines, Trinidad and Tobago—were selected by UNITAR for intensive research into the problem of outflow of trained personnel from developing to developed countries. The research was conducted in each country by a resident national who then met with UNITAR representatives to discuss the studies and their policy implications. The report contains the studies from the five countries, a synthesis of them, policy recommendations, and statistical tables.

Certain features were common to all five countries regarding patterns and causes of migration. The rates of emigration were highest among medical personnel, teachers, science graduates, and engineers, whose destinations were primarily countries offering higher living standards. Among the causes of emigration, economic factors predominated; most developing countries are unable to generate sufficient employment to absorb all trained professionals.

Student emigration appears to be highest among those who pursue undergraduate education abroad although a contractual arrangement between student and home government increases the rate of return.

Among its recommendations for practical action, the report stresses the need for adequate data on migration, the reform of educational systems to make them more closely relevant to the manpower needs of the country, long-range manpower planning, and professional organizations and government travel subsidies to encourage high-level personnel to maintain contacts with colleagues abroad. Developed countries are urged to increase their output of highly trained manpower and continue the technical assistance which will enable developing countries to better absorb their own surplus professionals.

390a. _____ . U. S. Advisory Commission on International Educational and Cultural Affairs. A Special Study on the Effectiveness of the Past Educational and Cultural Exchange Programs of the U. S. Department of State. By John A. Gardner. Washington, D. C., 1963.

This report was subsequently published as A Beacon of Hope. See No. 390b.

390b. _____ . A Beacon of Hope: The Exchange-of-Persons Program.
By John A. Gardner. Washington, D. C.: U. S. Government
Printing Office, 1963.

The U. S. Advisory Commission on International Educational and Cultural Affairs was asked by Congress to appraise the effectiveness of U. S. exchange programs, with special reference to foreign students, leaders, teachers, and others who have come to the United States on State Department grants. An extensive survey was undertaken, which included interviews with 2,696 former grantees from 20 countries, non-grantee leaders and professionals in the same countries, Embassy officials, State Department officers, NAFSA members, and private individuals involved in educational change.

Analysis of these interviews led the Commission to conclude that the exchange program is effective; while it does not bring about a uniformly favorable point of view on all aspects of the American scene, it is particularly successful in promoting mutual understanding and in helping to dispel many misconceptions and ugly stereotypes about American people held by foreign visitors.

In its recommendations, the Commission focused on two areas. First, regarding the grantee, it is recommended that some preference be given to candidates who represent the "have-nots" of their country rather than the upper-income elite, and that they be persons who are sufficiently vigorous and restless to help promote desirable social and economic change. Field-selection centers might be set up to assist potential students in choosing academic institutions and to provide the institutions with information on foreign educational systems and standards. To raise the calibre of Americans who apply for overseas grants, stipends should be substantially increased.

The second area of recommendations is the administration of the exchange program. Studies should be conducted on the role of the Cultural Affairs Officer, and of the problems created by the program's reliance on foreign currencies. Since the character of the exchange program must be determined by the needs of individual countries, country-by-country planning is deemed essential; enthusiasm for work with developing nations should not, however, result in neglect of European programs.

390c. _____ . A Sequel to A Beacon of Hope: The Exchange-of-Persons
Program. Washington, D. C.: U. S. Government Printing Office,
1964.

In its second annual report, the Commission discusses its various activities and notes some modest progress toward implementing the recommendations in A Beacon of Hope, particularly in the coordination of international educational and cultural activities.

In addition to A Beacon of Hope, the Commission has produced two other reports. The first, on the cultural presentations program, recommended that the Department of State resume responsibility for direct management of the program, revitalize the Advisory Commission on the Arts, establish a policy of long-range planning, and increase the public recognition of participants. The second report concerned the functions, program, and operations of the Center for Cultural and Technical Interchange Between East and West (East-West Center). Recommendations included establishment of a National Review Board, maintenance of existing relationships to the University of Hawaii, and development of a plan for orderly growth and expansion.

391. U. S. Department of Health, Education, and Welfare. Foreign Trained Physicians and American Medicine. By Rosemary Stevens and Joan Vermeulen. Washington, D. C., 1972.
The purpose of this study was to bring together available materials on the location, activity, and function of the more than 63,000 foreign-trained physicians in the United States; to review the political, economic, and organizational factors which have led to the current manpower situation; and to analyze these data in terms of physician manpower policies and research. At present, one of every six physicians practicing in the United States is a graduate of a medical school outside the United States and Canada.

Two recurring themes are stressed: (1) the lack of integrated and recognized policy toward the immigration and education of foreign-trained physicians; (2) the lack of reliable information about the basic characteristics, expectations, and roles of foreign-trained physicians in the United States, and more generally, about physician manpower roles in the American health system.

A discussion of major areas requiring additional research includes studies of immigration and emigration, studies of foreign medical graduates in the United States, studies of physician manpower in donor countries, studies of Americans in foreign schools, and studies of manpower in the United States.

392. _____. Social Determinants of Non-Return: Foreign Students from Developing Countries in the United States. By Orlando Rodriguez. Washington, D. C., June 1974.
Rodriguez uses data gathered by Glaser (see No. 148) to develop a social-psychological model of migration incorporating such factors as the

effects of objective social situations and reference-group influences. He finds that students' motivations and advice received before arriving in the United States are the strongest factors affecting their decisions whether to return or stay abroad. The process of non-return is, however, not predetermined from the beginning. Contingencies may arise in the United States which reverse the effect of prior factors. The choice of the students' reference groups in the United States is found to be due more to situational factors than to students' predisposition and advice at home.

A central question in the study concerns the inter-connections between perceptions of opportunity, as indicated by the standard of living expectations, and prior factors in the process of study abroad which lead to non-return. The students' perceptions are found to be due to rational assessment of objective situations; subjective factors, such as the students' selection of Americans as reference groups, have no effects on perceptions.

The conclusions of the study are brought to bear on a number of policy recommendations: (1) Since students on exchange scholarships are much more likely than other students to return, countries interested in increasing the rate of return could increase the number of exchange scholarships. (2) It is assumed that the tendency of minority groups to migrate is due more to the socio-cultural environment than to job opportunities. Therefore no country should formally or informally discriminate against any of its minorities. (3) The most important return problem envisioned by the respondents is sheer lack of job openings. Therefore countries with a brain drain problem should increase the number of jobs for professionals. (4) Since it was found that there is a higher propensity among students holding college and university scholarships to stay abroad, colleges are advised to review their scholarship policies more carefully for possible adverse consequences. (5) Policies restricting migration should be resisted, despite the need to limit the brain drain. If countries must balance the individual's rights with considerations of national welfare, it is hoped that they err on the side of the individual.

393. U. S. Department of Health, Education, and Welfare, National Institutes of Mental Health. "An Investigation of the Consequences of International Educational Exchanges." By George V. Coelho. October 1973.

Following upon the successful university self-studies conducted under the auspices of an International Committee for the Study of Educational Exchange, Coelho proposes two further projects to investigate the impact of international university exchange. Project 1, "Long-Term Consequences of Exchange," would utilize available records, questionnaires, and interviews to study the effects, after some five years, of a foreign sojourn on teachers, research workers, and students. Project 2, "Mental Health in International Educational Exchange: A Study of Coping Behavior in a Cultural Environment," would study the behavior of foreign students who are participating in a formal program of educational exchange for a sojourn of at least one academic year. Coping behavior is defined as the behavior utilized to establish emotional security within a culture distinct from one's own. The results of the coping mechanisms employed would be considered the dependent variables, and the study would be directed toward the discovery of the independent variables in the experience of the foreign students which contribute to psychological success or failure.

394. U. S. Department of Health, Education, and Welfare, Office of Education. "A Summary of the Exchange and Training Programs, Office of Education, U. S. Department of Health, Education, and Welfare, 1939-1967." By Thomas E. Cotner. Washington, D. C., n. d.

Cotner outlines the history and scope of training programs and student and teacher exchange programs administered by the Office of Education, including the International Teacher Development Program and the Leader and Specialist Program. Total number of participants in all programs is 29,531.

395. _____. Report on a Study to Determine the Feasibility of Establishing a Central Foreign Credential Evaluation Service under Non-Governmental Auspices. By James F. Frey. Washington, D. C., February 1969.

The study was conducted to determine whether a non-governmental Foreign Credential Evaluation Service (FCES) should be established and, if so, what services it would provide, what the demand for these services would be, and what financial resources it would require. A survey of admissions officers at 223 educational institutions and representatives of 38 agencies (federal government, private, and state teacher certification and nursing licensing boards) revealed that there is a continuing need for a central agency to evaluate credentials of foreign students and professionals. No consensus was reached on the organizational structure of a new FCES but outside funds would be needed for its first five years, after which it would be entirely self-supporting. The report contains recommendations on staffing, budget, fees, and billing arrangements, and 56 illustrative tables.

396. U. S. Department of Justice, Immigration and Naturalization Service. Annual Indicator of Immigration to the United States of Aliens in Professional and Related Occupations, Fiscal Year 1969. Washington, D. C., June 1970.

This publication, introduced in FY 1967, provides an annual statistical compilation for analysis of trends in immigration to the United States of persons in professional and related groups. Data in this edition show that 11.3 percent of 1969's immigrants fell into the professional and related occupations category, chiefly engineers, teachers, nurses, accountants and auditors, and physicians and surgeons. This represented a 17.1 percent decrease over the previous year; overall immigration declined 21 percent.

397. U. S. Department of State. Fact Sheet on the International Educational Exchange Program: 1946-1966. Washington, D. C., April 1966.

A description of the principal features of this Department of State program includes a summary of the legislation which initiated it, a statement of purpose, and its financial organization. Its history and philosophy are set forth, accompanied by pertinent quotes. Statistical information and a selective bibliography are included.

398. U. S. Department of State, Bureau of Educational and Cultural Affairs. "An Evaluation of Research on Educational Exchange." By Margaret L. Cormack. Brooklyn College, August 1962.

This project was undertaken, in partial implementation of the 1961 Fulbright-Hays Act, to evaluate existing research concerning the problems of educational and cultural exchange. In her analysis, Cormack stresses that the role of research is not the justification of purposes, programs, or their funds, but rather an inquiry into what happens to people under various circumstances within clear value positions. Research must look beneath and beyond programs to personal and social dynamics so that programs can be based on a more intelligent understanding of the processes involved. She then attempts to lay a theoretical foundation for more significant social science research on cross-cultural learning.

In outlining research needs, she recommends that the Bureau act as liaison in the coordination of research by action organizations, academic associations, foundations, and college and university personnel. It should undertake a project to standardize methodology and promote several master research plans to include investigations of variables affecting cross-cultural learning.

399. _____. Summaries of Evaluation Studies of the Educational and Cultural Exchange Program. Washington, D. C., June 1967.

Forty evaluation studies 1951-65 are summarized in this report. Many evaluative criteria are used, but major concern is with attitude change as a result of the exchange program, professional and social consequences of the experience, and general assessments of the problems encountered by the exchangees.

400a. _____ . "Educational and Cultural Exchange-of-Persons and Related Activities under the Auspices of the United States Government and Private Agencies for Argentina." Washington, D. C., December 1968.

These brief reports consist of charts which list government, private, and international agencies involved in exchange with the country under consideration during the previous fiscal year. The number of persons exchanged, their field of study, and financing are also given. Extensive footnotes to the charts provide program details. No claim is made that the data are definitive.

The following were included in this study:

400b. Bolivia, December 1968.
400c. Brazil, December 1968.
400d. Chile, January 1969.
400e. Colombia, January 1969.
400f. Costa Rica, January 1969.
400g. Dominican Republic, 1969.
400h. Ethiopia, June 1968.
400i. Japan, August 1967.
400j. Kenya, August 1968.
400k. Liberia, August 1968.
400l. Mexico, February 1969.
400m.Peru, January 1969.
400n. Tunisia, August 1969.
400o. Venezuela, January 1969.

401. _____ . A Preliminary Study on Foreign Students in America: The Effects of Today's Campus Environment on Their Attitudes Toward America. By Daniel Yankelovich, Inc. Washington, D. C., March 1971.

The purpose of this study was to examine the impact of campus unrest on foreign students. Thirty-five non-European students and 15 faculty members from ten universities participated in in-depth interviews. It was found that foreign students were largely unaffected by student demonstrations, counterculture life style, or the rhetoric of the student left, and two-fifths preferred to associate with other foreign students. They are satisfied with the education they are receiving although they realize that overtraining and Americanization may make readjustment to home country difficult. They disapprove of American foreign policy, especially toward underdeveloped countries, and are dissatisfied with the domestic policy which hinders their finding employment to supplement their meager funds.

402. _____. International Exchange: Leaders for Tomorrow. A Review
      of U. S. Programs for Foreign Students. Washington, D. C.,
      September 1971.

Programs described in this booklet, the 1970 annual report of the State
Department's Bureau of Educational and Cultural Affairs, are indicative
of some of the services and opportunities for foreign students studying
in the United States. Counseling services available to the foreign students and orientation procedures for incoming students are reviewed.
A summary of exchanges and expenditures includes tables on: (1) exchanges with each country, 1949-70, (2) fields of specialization by
category of grantee, (3) distribution of grantees in the United States,
(4) countries which share costs of exchange, (5) total participants in
the program, (6) women grantees as compared to total exchanges,
(7) source of funds, fiscal years 1969 and 1970, (8) total funds obligated, fiscal years 1965-70, and (9) expenditures by country, fiscal
year 1970. Special sections include reference to leaders abroad who
have studied in the United States, 1970 State Department-sponsored
programs for foreign students and young leaders, and a profile of the
Exchange Program 1970.

403. _____. The Asian and Pacific Student Leader Project: An Evalu-
      ation. By Sherry Mueller Norton. Washington, D. C., 27
      December 1972.

One hundred twenty-two past participants in the Asian and Pacific
Student Leader Project, which between 1963 and 1971 sponsored 70-day
multinational group tours in the United States for 221 university student
leaders, were interviewed in their home countries. Their achievements
show that the goals of the project are being realized: a significant number continued in their roles as student leaders after their tour, and
many have begun careers, or intend to, in politics, government
service, business, or international trade. Although critical of some
organizational aspects of the program, participants most frequently
cited increased social and political awareness of the United States and
their home country, and improved understanding of themselves and
their capabilities as the major advantages of the program.

404. _____. "Report on Meeting Re Crucial Issues." Washington,
      D. C., June 1973.

Twenty-six educators met to discuss the current state of foreign student education in the United States. They find the outlook gloomy:
underprivileged groups now have priority access to undergraduate
education; financial support for foreign students has been sharply
reduced; and job opportunities are very limited.

   A number of policy recommendations were suggested to make
the most efficient use of available resources, such as insuring that

students complete their programs, the use of Third Country Programs, development of limited programs (only Master's students, only students with Master's degrees, training for specific objectives; the AID approach); more flexible approaches at the University level to insure education relevant to the student's needs as well as the needs of his country, and better orientation programs to the host-country environment and re-orientation programs to the home country. In addition, a greater effort is needed to involve more educational leaders and the general public in foreign student education.

405. _____ . International Educational and Cultural Exchange.
      Washington, D. C., 1974.
This booklet provides a brief overview of international and cultural exchange and describes a variety of programs such as those between the United States and the U.S.S.R., Eastern Europe, The People's Republic of China, and the Middle Eastern nations. Recent thrusts in exchange are noted including the funding of special U. S.-African projects for black college faculty and secondary-school teachers, the development of institution-based exchange programs, and the growing participation of other nations, in particular, exchanges between Japan and the Federal Republic of Germany. An extensive quantitative section of the booklet describes international exchange by country, the fields of specialization and distribution in the United States of grantees from 1952 to 1972. Sources of funds and total funds obligated for 1971-72, and expenditure by country, under mutual educational and cultural exchange agreements are also shown in tabular form.

406. U. S. Department of State, Bureau of Intelligence and Research, External Research Staff. "U. S. Government Exchange and Training Programs for Women." By Constance L. Pierson and Lorraine O'Grady. Washington, D. C." U. S. Government Printing Office, 1964.
This study describes the activities of U. S. Government agencies involved in training and exchange programs with special attention to programs in which women have participated substantially or exclusively, and presents estensive numerical and geographic data on the participation of women in all programs.

    In Department of State programs, the proportion of women has remained almost constant at 23 percent since 1955; there has, however, been a strong shift of emphasis away from Western Europe to other free-world areas which now account for two-thirds of the total program. In the AID program, the proportion of women has doubled in three years, reaching 12 percent in 1963 although the total number of participants has declined, and here too, there has been a shift in geographic emphasis, with a greater proportion of women coming from Latin

America and Africa. This increase reflects in part the greater educational opportunities for women in Latin America, and in part the characteristics of the programs. Women are clustered in programs for students and teachers (Department of State) and in the fields of health, education, and community development (AID); when these programs are expanded, the proportion of women rises.

Special training or exchange programs for women have been arranged by the Department of State's Bureau of Educational and Cultural Affairs and the Office of Community Advisory Services; AID's Rural Development Training Branch, Education and Health Training Branch, and Public Administration Training Branch; the Peace Corps; the Department of Agriculture; the Department of Labor's Women's Bureau. Although women participate in their programs, USIA, HEW, NSF, and the Armed Forces have not had programs specifically for women.

407.   U. S. Department of State, Office of External Research. Foreign Student Exchange in Perspective. By Barbara J. Walton. Washington, D. C., December 1967.

In this excellent review of research on foreign students in the United States, Walton touches on the major issues confronting educators and researchers, and cites significant studies from many disciplines. During the 1950's, major concerns of program sponsors and researchers were the attitudes and opinions of foreign students about the United States, the development of youth leadership, and the uses of acquired skills and knowledge. Evaluating these studies, Walton concludes that sponsors of foreign student programs should seek intelligent understanding of the United States rather than endorsement or approval. Leadership, whether political, social, or professional, depends upon the development of social responsibility through the educative process and should be of concern to all educators. Educational exchange programs are probably on firmest grounds when they concentrate on professional and technical leadership and on the transfer of skills. While U. S. education can provide such training, use of training by returned students depends on a variety of factors related to the economic, social, and political situation in the home country.

The question of student non-return, or brain drain, has been a hotly debated issue since the early 1960's. Problems of definition and of unreliable data have hampered research but a number of "push" and "pull" factors have been identified. The root of the problem, it is generally agreed, lies in the home country; some countries are initiating repatriation programs, and revisions in U. S. university admissions and hiring policies have also been suggested.

Research in the area of cross-cultural adjustment has yielded many interesting results: identification of foreign student problems;

the U-curve and its subsequent modification into a W-curve; the concept
of culture shock. While the argument continues over whether foreign
student adjustment is different from that experienced by American students, professional services have been developed to ease the foreign
student's transition to U. S. academic life—foreign student advisers,
orientation programs, language training, etc.—and much research has
investigated the relationship between adjustment and academic success.

An area that has received relatively little attention is the impact
of foreign students on American students, the American academic
institution, and on American life in general. Here, as for the other
topics discussed, Walton makes cogent suggestions for further research.

408a. U. S. Department of State, Soviet and Eastern European
        Exchanges Staff. Exchanges with the Soviet Union and Eastern
        Europe, 1968. Washington, D. C., 1968.
This report describes U. S. exchanges with the U. S. S. R., Poland,
Czechoslovakia, Hungary, Romania, and Bulgaria during 1968, including officially negotiated exchanges (such as exhibits, performing arts,
scientists, scholars, artists, etc.) and privately sponsored visits.

408b. _____. Exchanges with the Soviet Union and Eastern Europe, 1970.
        Washington, D. C., 1970.
This report discusses U. S. exchanges with the U. S. S. R., Poland,
Czechoslovakia, Hungary, Romania, and Bulgaria during 1970. It includes officially negotiated exchanges (such as exhibits, performing
arts, scientists, scholars, artists, etc.) as well as privately sponsored
visits.

409. United States Information Agency, Office of Research and Assess-
        ment. Changes in Attitudes and Impressions Concerning the
        United States by Selected Groups of Short-Term African Grantees.
        Washington, D. C., 1971.
One hundred and fifty-four randomly selected grantees completed pre-
tour questionnaires; 119 also completed post-tour questionnaires. Sixty
participated in group discussions. The main findings are: (1) Grantees'
generally favorable opinion of the United States was not changed by
their tour experience. (2) Race relations concerned grantees most and
the visit did not alter this greatly; they found Americans more sympathetic to this issue than anticipated. (3) Personal qualities of Americans, as well as Americans' respect for law, the quality of U. S. education, and racial progress favorably impressed grantees. (4) Grantees
formed more negative impressions regarding Americans' ignorance of
international affairs, weak family ties, participation in domestic politics, and pollution in urban areas. (5) Visits appears to contribute to
formation of less stereotyped and more sophisticated attitudes towards

American life. (6) Many came to learn about American people and culture while also seeking professional skills. Many felt their goals were at least partially achieved.

410. University of California. Self-Study of International Educational Exchange. July 1970.
In June 1969, committees on each of the University of California's nine campuses undertook to study the campus' role in international studies. Statistics were compiled pertaining to foreign students and foreign scholars at the University of California, and U. S. faculty and students abroad. The campuses unanimously asserted a continuing commitment to educational exchange and recommend ways in which current programs and policies at the University of California could be improved.

Responses to the nine studies, including some questionnaire surveys, show that foreign students are attracted to UC primarily by the reputation of its faculty and programs. Most foreign students and scholars find their experience at UC satisfactory and, in turn, make significant contributions to the University in terms of teaching and research.

UC has two major programs which facilitate study abroad by American students and faculty. The Education Abroad Program offers a structured program for the student at a foreign university. While some doubts are expressed as to its academic value, there has been relatively little negative student reaction, and instructors report significant increases in the maturity of returned students. The UC-University of Chile program (the Convenio) has, since 1965, provided a coordinated and mutually beneficial exchange program for students and faculty of both institutions.

411. University of South Carolina, Office of Admissions and Registration. "Academic Performance of Foreign Undergraduate Students: Cumulative Grade Point Ratio as of Fall Semester, 1966." May 1967.
This brief report finds that, almost without exception, students from English-speaking countries or from countries with a close U. S. relationship (Cuba, Puerto Rico, Panama) have no problem in maintaining a 2.0 grade point average.

The foreign undergraduates had a mean grade point average of 2.133 at the end of the fall semester of 1966, suggesting that foreign student admission requirements at the University of South Carolina are adequate.

412. Ursua, Aurora Ricardo. "The Relationship Between Adeptness in the English Language and Social Adjustment of Foreign Graduate Students." Ph.D. dissertation, Catholic University of America, 1969.

The Michigan Test of English Language Proficiency and the Michigan International Student Problem Inventory were administered to 201 foreign students who were grouped according to national origin, world area, sex, age, type of student, language spoken in the home, number of languages spoken in the home, and length of stay in the United States. Results showed low but significant correlations between English language and social adjustment. They suggest the need for improved advising and counseling services at the University.

413. Valipour, Iraj. "A Comparison of Returning and Non-Returning Iranian Students in the United States." Ph.D. dissertation, Columbia University, 1967.
This study found that, on the basis of respondents' perceptions, returning students came from higher socio-economic backgrounds, had a more satisfactory family life, had closer ties with their families and friends, were relatively moderate in their criticism of the political and economic conditions in the home country, and maintained better contact with it while abroad.

The non-returning respondents, on the other hand, were better assimilated by the criteria of the frequency of personal interactions and cross-cultural marriages in the host country.

Recommendations were made for setting up a comprehensive student personnel and guidance program. The philosophy underlying the recommendations was to give educational-vocational guidance to the students with the purpose of helping them to get into the areas of study for which there are pressing demands in Iran.

414. Van de Guchte, Marten. "The Effect of Aural and Visual Cues on the Rating of the Speech of Foreign Students." Ph.D. dissertation, Michigan State University, 1969.
An experiment was designed in which 24 panels of 12 students each rated aural, visual, and aural-visual presentations by 32 foreign students representing Dutch, Japanese, Spanish, and Turkish language groups. Among the conclusions were: (1) foreign students from different language groups can be differentiated on the basis of degree of foreign accent and/or foreign appearance; (2) in the attempt to determine the degree of foreign accent perceptible to an American English-speaking listener, the score achieved by the foreigner on the Fries and Lado Test of Aural Comprehension seemingly provides an accurate predictor; (3) in the rating of foreign students from a given language group, certain aural and visual cues appear to be predominant in affecting judgments of their speech.

415. Van der Kroef, Justus. "The U. S. and the World's Brain Drain." International Journal of Comparative Sociology 11 (September 1970): 221-39.

This article brings together statistics on the brain drain from a number of sources, in order to assess the severity of the problem. Despite questionable data, the problem is shown to be a serious one, particularly in scientific and medical fields. Three causal factors are adduced: (1) the effect of the U. S. immigration law of 1965; (2) low remuneration and restricted professional opportunities for skilled personnel in developing countries; (3) persistent imbalance between training output and manpower requirements in developing countries.

To lessen brain drain, American business could recruit more foreign nationals for its overseas operations. "Draining" nations are advised to re-examine their educational priorities; "gaining" nations should exercise greater care in selection of foreign students for training.

Vermeulen, Joan. See No. 391.

416. Vorapipatana, Kowit. "A Study of the Thai Graduates' Training Program in the Field of Education from the United States." Ph. D. dissertation, University of Utah, 1967.

This study measures the effectiveness of training provided through AID using an attitude survey of 170 graduates and 51 of their immediate supervisors (76 percent and 82 percent response, respectively). Personal interviews were conducted with 25 of the graduates and 15 of their supervisors.

The study indicated that the training program has had a positive effect on the graduates in both personal and professional aspects. The majority were working in the areas in which they were trained and were able to put into practice most of their ideas based on what they learned in the United States.

It is recommended that the program be continued with some modification: (1) practical experiences in the graduates' fields of study should be provided as part of the training program; (2) the training institutions in the United States should be more flexible in designing the required courses for future graduates; (3) an up-to-date record of statistics of manpower classification should be maintained and made available in the Ministry of Education.

417. Vroman, Clyde; Wilcox, Lee; and Tschan, Robert. "Research on AID-Sponsored Students." College and University 45, no. 9 (Summer 1970): 717-23.

This article summarizes the research described in No. 418.

418. _____. The AACRAO-AID Participant Selection and Placement Study. A Report to the Agency for International Development, Office of International Training, March 1971.

This report, prepared by the AACRAO-AID Study Committee, has two broad purposes: (1) to assess the effectiveness of the selection and placement of AID-sponsored, academic participants in U. S. universities and colleges, and (2) to suggest how the total process can be improved.

A sample of AID participants was drawn by selecting the first non-contract participants to arrive in the United States from summer 1967-68, totaling 1,004 persons, three-fourths of whom came from Africa or the Far East. Each completed a questionnaire, two English Language tests, and a Scholastic Aptitude Test. This data was supplemented with biographical details, a review of the relevant PIO/P and academic credentials by an AACRAO credential analyst, a questionnaire completed by an AACRAO representative on campus, academic transcripts, and, for graduate students, an evaluation by a faculty member. Major findings, supported by quantitative data, are as follows:

1. Description. Participants differ significantly from the total foreign student population on geographic and field of study comparisons. They tend to be more mature, more established professionally, and likely to work in the public sector.

2. Academic Qualifications. Participants are generally well-qualified. About half were rated as having previous academic work of a quality above the average, and 80 percent were regarded as capable of doing satisfactory work in an American college or university of average academic competition.

3. Placement. The field of study expected by participants agreed with their prescribed majors 65 percent of the time, and credential analysts and campus representatives agreed on degree objectives for 72.8 percent. Two-thirds or more of the participants' dossiers were complete.

4. English Language. Between one-third and one-half of the participants lacked sufficient English to begin a full academic program on arrival. About one-half of the cases were handled in accordance with formal AID guidelines.

5. Academic Performance. Performance compares very favorably with that of most American students and is superior to that of other foreign students. More than 85 percent met their training objective.

6. Prediction of Academic Success. The SAT-Math was a good predictor of undergraduate performance; verbal scores on U. S. aptitude tests (SAT or GRE) were of little value. English proficiency tests had only marginal value in predicting grades.

419. Wakita, Kayoko. "Asian Studies Survey—Spring 1970." Los Angeles: Los Angeles City College, October 1971.

A questionnaire sent to 1,700 Asian students enrolled in the 1970 spring trimester at Los Angeles City College elicited 659 (38 percent) responses, mostly from persons of Japanese or Chinese ancestry who were categorized as foreign-born, native-born, and from Hawaii. A distinct language barrier between the foreign-born and native-born was evident, the latter being considered inferior because of their inability to speak the ancestral tongue. Native-born, long identified as a minority, reacted strongly to questions on discrimination. Hawaiian-born, experiencing prejudice from both groups, tended to congregate together, considering the native-born unfriendly and the foreign-born too shy.

420. Walton, Barbara J. "Research on Foreign Graduate Students." Exchange 6, no. 3 (Winter 1971): 17-29.
This article, an up-date of Walton's 1967 survey of foreign student research (see No. 407) concentrates on research regarding foreign graduate students. Categories reviewed are: campus and nationality studies, academic performance, U. S. Government studies, brain drain research, business administration, engineering, medicine, economics, social work and education, foreign students as professionals, and research in progress. In her recommendations she again suggests that foreign student research be conducted within the context of American education inasmuch as one cannot discern which problems are unique to foreign students until one knows more about student problems in general. A second area of suggested research concerns the foreign student in relation to social and technological change.

_____. See No. 407.

421. Watanabe, S. "The Brain Drain from Developing to Developed Countries." International Labor Review 99 (April 1969): 401-33.
This article examines the magnitude of brain drain as revealed in government immigration statistics—its causes, effects, and ameliorative measures. Except in a few developing countries, migration of substantial numbers of highly trained professionals will adversely affect both welfare and development. Counter measures must be considered by home and host countries; one solution is to accelerate development and provide better employment opportunities in developing countries.

422. Wei, Yung. "Socio-Psychological Variables and Inter-Nation Intellectual Migration: Findings from Interviewing Returnees in the Republic of China." Paper presented at the Annual Convention of the International Studies Association, Pittsburgh, Pa., 2-4 April 1970.
Although "brain drain" is a frequently discussed topic, lack of accepted measures and scarcity of data on "international intellectual migration"—

a more appropriate conceptualization—has made it difficult to determine the extent or effects of talent outflow. Among the macro-analytic approaches to the problem are (1) the moral-patriotic, often adopted by political leaders who view the outflow as detrimental to the national interest; (2) the legalistic, arguing for greater migration controls; and (3) the economic, which seeks to determine international and national effects.

Believing that "brain drain" is composed of individuals making decisions on personal rather than on purely economic grounds, the author adopts a micro-analytic approach. A three-stage model of international intellectual migration is developed: a predisposition stage leading to the decision to migrate, a conflict stage during which the individual typically becomes disillusioned in the foreign society, and the resolution stage in which a decision is made as to country of residence.

A case study was conducted in Taiwan, where outflow has been severe. A questionnaire was mailed to all students who returned from the United States after 1961, and one in three of those returning 1957-61. One hundred and nine valid answers were received; selected respondents were also interviewed. Major findings are: (1) socio-psychological variables (e.g., expectations of family and friends) played an important role in both the decision to study abroad and to return; and (2) satisfaction with the home country is more closely related to social status, importance of service to society, closeness to parents, than to income level.

423. "Why They Went Home: Asian Alumni of the University of Oregon." Research sponsored by the East-West Center, Honolulu, Hawaii, n.d.

During the summer of 1968 the author interviewed 36 University of Oregon (UO) Asian alumni in their home countries regarding brain drain, training they received at UO, student personnel service, relationships between U. S. and Asian students, and establishment of contacts with UO alumni.

The most frequent reason for returning home was family obligations with the exception of Thai students who felt a responsibility to their country. All felt their education was relevant to Asian situations, and most viewed it as superior to that in their home countries. They reported that, as alumni, they were making contacts with prospective students and returning graduates.

Wilcox, Lee. See No. 264a.

424. Win, U Kyaw. "A Study of the Difficulties Indian and Japanese Students Encountered in Six Problem Areas at the University of

Southern California, 1969-70." Ph.D. dissertation, University of Southern California, 1971.

Ninety-eight (73 percent) of the Indian students and 47 (56 percent) of the Japanese students at the University completed a checklist appraising difficulties met with in six areas: academic, financial, housing, religious, personal, and social.

The chi-square values obtained for each of the 50 items on the checklist revealed differences between the two nationality groups. Japanese students encountered more difficulties than Indian students in registration, understanding lectures and textbooks, reciting in class, preparing oral and appropriate courses. Both Indian and Japanese obviously needed the help of an adviser in all six problem areas but generally showed unwillingness to seek it from foreign student advisers except in legal and financial matters.

Greater efforts should be made to provide orientation programs with regularly scheduled follow-up sessions to insure that foreign students learn how to use the library, write essay examinations, take objective tests and prepare research papers.

425. Witman, Jeanne. "COSERV's First Decade in One Community in Pittsburgh, Pennslyvania." Exchange 7, no. 4 (Spring 1972): 16-24.

This article discusses the administration, structure, and financing of the Pittsburgh Council for International Visitors (PCIV), a community volunteer organization designed to welcome international visitors to Pittsburgh.

Wolfson, Margaret S. See No. 381b.

426. Working Party on UNESCO Fellowships. Final Report. Occasional Paper No. 8, Canadian Commission for UNESCO, n.d.

The Working Party, meeting in Vancouver, 29-31 May 1972, brought together personnel from agencies in North America and Oceania responsible for administering UNESCO Fellowships to discuss the training abroad programs and related administrative problems.

It was agreed that more exchange and coordination of information was needed among UN agencies and administering agencies. In addition, UNESCO needs more accurate information on existing host-country training facilities in both academic and practical fields.

Concerning selection of fellows, it was felt that although UNESCO selection criteria were adequate, many students encounter problems which delay completion of the program and lead to requests for extension. It was agreed that more precise estimates of students' expectations and abilities, and of length of time required to complete a program, were needed. Brain Drain, however, does not appear to be a problem.

The report concludes with suggestions as to how administrative agencies might increase the efficiency and scope of UNESCO's international training. (See also No. 383a-d).

427. Yang, Kuo-shu. "A Comparative Study on Motivational and Temperamental Characteristics of Malaya and Singapore Overseas Chinese Students in Taiwan." Bulletin of the Institute of Ethnology Academia Sinica 22 (Autumn 1966): 139-68.
Five standardized tests were administered in Taipei, 1964, to 500 overseas and 1,000 non-overseas freshmen and sophomores. Some of the findings are: (1) In comparison with the non-overseas students, the overseas on the average displayed higher needs for order and endurance and lower needs for intraception and dominance. No significant overseas-non-overseas differences were found on the need for achievement, deference, exhibition, autonomy, affiliation, succorance, abasement, nurturance, agression, and power. (2) In comparison with the non-overseas student, the overseas on the average tended to be more emotionally stable, rigid, "thick-skinned," and radical, and less generally active, reflective, timid, and sophisticated.

428. Yates, Alfred, ed. Exploring Education: Students from Overseas. London: National Foundation for Educational Research in England and Wales, 1971.
Students entering college for the first time are often confronted with serious adjustment problems; such problems are multiplied in the case of the foreign student. On the basis of a study of foreign students in Great Britain, it is clear that there is a need for systematic and effective procedures whereby the academic capabilities of foreign applicants may be assessed so that they can be assigned to courses that are suited to their requirements. Criteria for admission that have been found to have predictive value are: grades obtained in previous academic work; English test scores; an assessment of the candidate's financial resources; and an appraisal of the student's capacity to adjust to a new social and cultural environment. The other most pressing need for foreign students is the need for more effective guidance and counseling to be made available after their arrival in Britain and throughout their stay.

Addenda

429. Adams, Walter, ed. The Brain Drain. New York: Macmillan Company, 1968.

This collection of papers, presented at an international conference held at Lausanne, Switzerland, 1967, examines the phenomenon of international talent from four different perspectives. The first section discusses early migration, modern migration, and migration's multi-lateral aspects. In the second section an analytical framework for talent migration is constructed. Internationalist and nationalist models are presented as well as models illustrating the national importance of human capital and examinig migration in terms of push-pull differentials. The third section relates study abroad to emigration and examines possible causes of, and solutions to, foreign students' failure to contribute to the development of their home countries. The final section contains case studies of talent migration from France, Greece, the European Economic Community, Africa, India, and an article giving a "less alarmist view" of brain drain from developing countries.

In summarizing the participants' conclusions, it is recommended that policy makers identify and quantify factors which contribute to the attraction of developed countries of dissatisfaction with developing countries, such as salary differentials, professional opportunities, lack of receptivity to change in the home country, relevance of foreign training, lack of realistic manpower policies, technology gap, political balkanization, discrimination on non-economic grounds, and monopolistic restrictions in advanced countries.

430. College Entrance Examination Board. The Foreign Graduate
      Student: Priorities for Research and Action: A Summary of
      a Colloquium held at Wingspread, Racine, Wisconsin, 16-17
      June 1970. New York: 1971.
Participants at this Colloquium, sponsored by the National Liaison Committee on Foreign Student Admissions, noted that graduate student exchanges in 1970 are taking place in conditions quite different from those obtaining in 1960. In the United States, although applications from foreign students continue to rise, costs of education are soaring and universities are increasingly sensitive to the demands of minority/poverty American students. Abroad, foreign countries are experiencing problems of educational glut, brain drain, and the inability to provide educational and research facilities which would attract nationals home. These changed conditions require the development of new national and institutional rationales for offering graduate education to foreign students and the rethinking of policies and practices.

Presentations at the Colloquium were by Homer Higbee, Francis Sutton, George H. Huganir, Jr., and John Richardson, Jr. Among the recommendations made by the participants were: (1) There is need for a long-range national policy on international exchange of graduate students to which individual institutions and graduate schools can relate their own policies. (2) Each university should develop an explicit rationale for the admission of foreign students. (3) In developing policies for the admission and training of foreign graduate students, efforts should be made to consult with appropriate people overseas concerning national manpower objectives. (4) There is a need for a more complete annual census of foreign students, going beyond the data reported in Open Doors and including the financial aid received. (5) Fellowship-support programs sponsored by various government agencies should be maintained. (For an earlier Colloquium, see No. 79.)

431. Practical Concepts, Inc. "Evaluation of ASPAU, AFGRAD, and INTERAF: Impact of Regional Scholarship Programs on Manpower Needs in Africa." Washington, D. C.: 1973.
This evaluation was designed to develop a factual basis for further AID efforts in assisting African countries to meet their needs for trained manpower. Among its major conclusions are that: (1) the problem of coordinating training goals with the educational goals of U. S. institutions has not been fully resolved; (2) work-study programs and on-the-job experience are of considerable value and, in many instances, non-degree programs may be preferable to degree programs; (3) degrees sought by participants were often in areas not relevant to African development priorities; (4) about 20 percent of those who returned held "high leverage" positions; and (5) the intermediary programming organizations played an important and critical role in the success of the programs. Research needs are also identified.

432. United Nations Institute for Training and Research. The Search for New Methods of Technical Cooperation. By Harold Caustin. New York: 1974.
This pamphlet reports on a weekend seminar in 1972 attended by representatives of all types of technical cooperation programs. It was convened to discuss obstacles impeding a more coherent pattern in the management of technical cooperation, bilateral or multi-lateral; to consider alternative methods, practices, and channels which might ease the flow of development aid and heighten its effectiveness, and, at the same time, to foresee to the extent possible how best to seize the opportunities arising from the greatly expanded dimensions of aid which the application of scientific and technological knowledge now offers for the accelerated advancement of less-industrialized countries.

Six broad areas were identified in which existing practices might be improved: (1) contacts could be expanded between international organizations and particular departments within a national administration and might also include such intermediaries as non-governmental organizations, research institutes, volunteers, and the business community; (2) the responsibility of the governments themselves should be enhanced particularly in the bilateral field; (3) the role of the "expert" and the national "counterpart" needs further examination and definition; (4) the procedures of international organizations should be more flexible and better coordinated; (5) more research is needed to provide information on the choice of techniques and the selection of the appropriate technological aid for a given country; and (6) a new conceptual approach, such as regarding scientific and technical knowledge as an "international resource," is required to understand better the variety and scope of the problems raised by the introduction of development aid in any society.

433. Weintraub, Leon. MUCIA Foreign Alumni. Madison, Wis.: University of Wisconsin, Office of International Studies and Programs, September 1971.

Information was sought regarding institutional contact with foreign alumni of the five universities comprising the Midwest Universities Consortium on International Activities (MUCIA). In general, maintenance of relationships with foreign alumni was found to be minimal at the departmental or college level. Personal and informal contacts were maintained but could not be inventoried. Alumni Association records were often inaccurate and out-of-date. It is suggested that much could be done to improve and regularize relationships between MUCIA, its foreign alumni, and foreign institutions.

R1. Adwere-Boamah, Joseph. "Intellect and Commitment: A Potential for Educational Change in the New Nations." Interna-tional Journal of Comparative Sociology 13 (June 1972): 99-112.

R2. African-American Institute. Annual Report, 1972. New York, 1972.

R3. Agency for International Development. Worldwide Evaluation of Participant Training. By Forrest Clements. Washington, D. C., March 1966.

R4. _____. University Resources for International Development. By Chester M. Alter. Washington, D. C., 1968.

R5. _____. A Survey of AID Educational Cooperation with Developing Countries. Washington, D. C., June 1970.

R6. _____. Participant Assessment of AID International Training: Exit Interview Questionnaire Contents and Instructions. Wash-ington, D. C.: The American University, Development Education and Training Institute, June 1971.

R7. Catalogue of Selected AID Publications. Washington, D. C., 1974.

R8. _____. Training for Development in Partnership with the Private Sector. Washington, D. C., 1972.

R9. _____. Participant Handbook. Washington, D. C., July 1973.

R10. Altbach, Philip G. and Uphoff, Norman T. The Student Inter-nationals. Metuchen, N. J.: Scarecrow Press, 1973.

R11. Althen, Gary. "Arab Students Outside the Classroom: An Inquiry into Social Life Adjustments in Pittsburgh and Recommendations for Further Research and Improvement of Orientation Programs." Master's thesis, University of Pittsburgh, 1966.

R12. Aronson, J., et al. "Basic Techniques of Foreign Student Research." College and University 47 (Summer 1972): 379-86.

R13. "Augmentation de 3,000 Etudiants Etrangers aux Universites Canadiennes en Deux Ans." University Affairs 10 (September 1968): 20.

R14. Barry, Jean. Thai Students in the U.S.: A Study in Attitude Change. Cornell Thailand Projects, Series 11, No. 66. Ithaca, N.Y.: Cornell University, Department of Asian Studies, 1967.

R15. Board of Foreign Scholarships. "Educational Exhange in the Seventies: A Statement." International Educational and Cultural Exchange (Fall 1961): 1-8.

R16. _____. International Educational Exchange: The Opening Decades, 1946-1966. Washington, D.C., 1966.

R17. Braisted, Paul J., ed. Cultural Affairs and Foreign Relations. Washington, D.C.: Columbia Books, 1968.

R18. Bristol, Jane F., and Dugan, Robert. A Pilot Study of Participant Training in the United States: Executive Report. Washington, D.C.: Institute for International Services, June 1963.

R19. The British Council. The British Council in Britain: The Origins and Work of Home Division. London: 1966/67.

R20. _____. Annual Report, 1972-1973. London, 1973.

R21. _____. Overseas Students in Britain: Statistics, 1971-1972. London, July 1973.

R22. Chemers, Martin. "Cross-Cultural Training as a Means for Improving International Favorableness." Human Relations 22, no. 6 (December 1969): 531-546.

R23. Chorafas, I. N. The Knowledge Revolution: An Analysis of the International Brain Market. New York: McGraw-Hill, 1968.

R24. Cohen, Peter. The Gospel According to the Harvard Business School. Garden City, N.Y.: Doubleday, 1973.

R25. Commission Federale des Bourses pour Etudiants Etrangers. Report of the Commission. Berne, Switzerland: Department de Politique Federal, April 1970.

R26. Commission on International Education. The Role of Higher Education in Governmental Planning for International Education. Washington, D.C.: American Council on Education, April 1963.

R27. Committee on Foreign Affairs, House of Representatives. African Students and Study Programs in the United States: Report and Hearings of the Sub-Committee on Africa. Washington, D.C.: U.S. Government Printing Office, 1965.

R28. Committee on Culture and Intellectual Exchange. Report of the White House Conference on International Cooperation. Washington, D.C., 1965.

R29. Deutsch, S. E. "Impact of Cross-Cultural Relations on the Campus." School and Social Research 53 (January 1969): 137-146.

R30. Dugan, Robert; Bristol, Jane; and Miller, Hope. A Pilot Study of Participant Training in the United States: Technical Report. Washington, D.C.: Institute for International Services, June 1963.

R31. Education and World Affairs. The Overseas Selection of Foreign Students. New York, 1966.

R32. _____. A Crisis of Dollars: The Funding Threat to International Affairs in U.S. Higher Education. New York, 1968.

R33. Flack, Michael J. International Educational and Cultural Relations and Their Presentation in International Affairs Textbooks, 1945-1971. Prepared for the U.S. Advisory Commission on Educational and Cultural Affairs, Department of State, 1971.

R34. Food and Agricultural Organization. Fellowship Evaluation: Main Findings of a Pilot Study of Individual Fellowships Awarded by FAO in the Field of Fisheries during the Period 1965-1971. Rome, 1972.

R35. Ford Foundation. "The Foundation and the Less Developed Countries: The Decade of the Seventies." Staff Working Paper, April 1972.

R36. Fox, Melvin J. International Educational Exchange. New York: Ford Foundation, 1966.

R37. Garrity, John A.; Klemperer, Lily von; and Taylor, Cyril J. H. The New Guide to Study Abroad. New York: Harper and Row, 1974.

R38. George Washington University. The Implications for Arms Control and Disarmament of the United States Exchange Program with the Soviet Union and Eastern Europe. Washington, D.C.: U.S. Arms Control and Disarmament Agency, 1967.

R39. Glaser, William, and Habers, G. Christopher. The Migration and Return of Professionals. New York: Bureau of Applied Social Research, Columbia University, 1973.

R40. Gorney, Sondra K. "Annual Educational Exchange Statistics." School and Society 95 (April 1967): 234-236.

R41. "Graduate Student Followships for Africans." School and Society 98 (October 1970): 338.

R42. Guyer, David. "International Student and Faculty Exchange, 1967-1968." School and Society 97 (January 1969): 31, 34.

R43. Habers, G. Christopher. "The Universal Minority: A Study of the Female Brain Drain of Students From Developing Countries in Three Developed Countries." Master's Thesis, Columbia University, 1972.

R44. Hart, Thomas; Mauch, James; Way, James; and Chaparro, Jose. "Final Report on Contract AID-529-255-T/Venezuela Program of Graduate-Level, In-Service Training for Faculty and Others at UDO" and "An Interim Report on the Continuation of a Cooperative Program between Universidad de Oriente, Cumana, Venezuela, and University of Pittsburgh, Pittsburgh, Pennsylvania." Pittsburgh, Pa.: University of Pittsburgh, 1973.

R45. Herder, Robert W.; Harr, John B.; Sheppard, William B.; and Fioro, Lois R. A Review of AID Training. Report submitted to the Administrator, AID, January 1969.

R46. Hodgkin, M. C. Australian Training and Asian Living. University of Western Australia Press, 1966.

R47. Institute of International Education. Handbook on U.S. Study for Foreign Nationals. New York; 1973.

R48. International Council for the International Christian Youth Exchange. "The Old and the New in ICYE: Program Priorities for the '70's." Geneva: January 20, 1972.

R49. "International Development Education." Review of Educational Research 38, June 1968.

R50. International Labour Office. Technical Cooperation Activities of the ILO 1950-1972: Statistical Tables. Geneva, 1973.

R51. "International Migration of Intellectual Talent: The American Academic Community and the Brain Drain." Bulletin on International Education 4 (November 1966): 1-8.

R52. International Telecommunications Union. "ITU Technical Assistance Activities (Fellowship Component)." n.d.

R53. Johnson, Harry. "The Economics of the Brain Drain: The Canadian Case." Minerva 3 (Spring 1966): 299-311.

R54. Kao, Charles H. C. Brain Drain: A Case Study of China. Taipei: Mei Ya, 1971.

R55. Kelman, Herbert C. "The Role of the Individual in International Relations: Some Conceptual and Methodological Considerations." Journal of International Affairs 24 (1970): 1-17.

R56. Kelman, Herbert C., and Ezekiel, Raphael S. Cross-National Encounters: The Personal Impact of an Exchange Program for Broadcasters. San Francisco: Jossey-Bass, 1970.

R57. Klein, M. H.; Alexander, K.-H. Tseng; Miller, M. H.; Yeh, E.-K.; and Chu, H.-M. "Far Eastern Students at a Big University." Bulletin of the Atomic Scientists 27, no. 1 (January 1971): 10-19.

R58. Klemperer, Lily von. International Education: A Directory of Resource Materials on Comparative Education and Study in Another Country. Garrett Park, Md.: Garrett Park Press, 1974.

R59. Klineberg, Otto, and Ben Brika, Jeanne. Etudiants du Tiers-Monde en Europe. The Hague: Mouton, 1972.

R60. Library of Congress, Congressional Research Service, Foreign Affairs Division. Brain Drain: A Study of the Persistent Issue of International Scientific Mobility. Prepared for the Subcommittee on National Security Policy and Scientific Development of the Committee on Foreign Affairs, U. S. House of Representatives. Washington, D. C.: U. S. Government Printing Office, 1974.

R61. Limbird, Martin. "Iowa's State Univeristy in Ghana: Summary of the Current Involvements of Iowa State University Alumni in Ghana." Ames, Iowa: Iowa State University, 1973.

R62. Little, Arthur D., Inc. Management Education Program for Administrators of Agro-Industrial and Industrial Development: A Syllabus, October 1972-July 1973. Cambridge, Mass., 1973.

R63. Livingstone, A. S. The International Student. Manchester: Manchester University Press, 1964.

R64. Lugert, Alfred; Graf, Diemut Gundula; Kirsteuer, Rolf; Kirsten, Christian; and Angermann, Erhard. Die Fremde Elite: Massenkommunikation und Stereotype Auslandischer Studenten. Vienna: Osterreichische Forchungsstiftung fur Entwicklungschlife, 1969.

R65. Margolis, Harold, and Bloch, Lucille. Foreign Medical Graduates in the United States. Cambridge, Mass.: Harvard University Press, 1969.

R66. Marks, Gregory. "Yank at Oxford." Twentieth Century 179 (May 1971): 37-38.

R67. Melvin, Kenneth. Education in World Affairs. Lexington, Mass.: D. C. Heath, 1970.

R68. Merritt, Richard C., ed. Communication in International Politics. Urbana, Ill.: University of Illinois Press, 1972.

R69. Myers, Robert G. "International Education, Emigration, and National Policy," Comparative Education Review 17 (February 1973): 71-90.

R70. Moll, Richard. "Aid Me in the Education Sphere." Saturday Review 50 (18 February 1967): 85-87, 100.

R71. Mowlana, Hamid, and McLaughlin, Gerald W. "Some Variables Interacting with Media Exposure Among Foreign Students." Sociology and Social Research 53 (July 1969): 511-522.

R72. National Association of Foreign Student Advisers. The Cultural Dimensions of International Education: A Report on the Fifteenth Annual Conference of the National Association of Foreign Student Advisers. Pasadena, Calif. 1963.

R73. National Association for Foreign Student Affairs. NAFSA and the Student Abroad. By Hugh Jenkins. Washington, D.C., 1973.

R74. National Association for Foreign Student Affairs and the American Association of Collegiate Registrars and Admissions Officers. A Guide to the Admission of Foreign Students. Washington, D.C.: n.d.

R75. Operational Policy Research, Inc. Foreign Students in the United States: A National Survey, A Report to the U.S. Advisory Commission on International Educational and Cultural Affairs. Washington, D.C., 1964-65.

R76. Overseas Liaison Committee. 1973 Annual Report. Washington, D.C.: American Council on Education, 1974.

R77. Palmer, Stephen E. Toward Improved U.S. Immigration and International Education Programs (Preliminary Draft). Cambridge, Mass.: Harvard University, Center for International Affairs, 1974.

R78. Putman, Ivan, Jr. "The Foreign Student Adviser and His Institution in International Student Exchange." Part I of Handbook for Foreign Student Advisers. New York: NAFSA, 1965.

R79. Revenswaaij, C. A. van. The ISS Alumni Report. The Hague: Institute of Social Studies, 1965.

R80. Salisbury, E. R. First Aid for the Foreign Student Adviser. Detroit, Mich.: University of Detroit Press, 1972.

R81. Schlagintweit, Reinhard. "Foreign Cultural Policy and Foreign Policy." Aussenpolitik (English edition) 25, no. 3 (1974): 255-271.

R82. Schumacher, Henry A. "Utilization of United States Graduate Agricultural Programs by Peruvian and American Students." Ph.D. dissertation, University of Pittsburgh, 1972.

R83. Shibli, Khalid. "Brain Drain: Myth, Magic, or Reality." Paper prepared for the Commission for Planning in the Eastern Region, March 1974.

R84. Slemenson, Marta, et al. Emigracion de Cientificos Argentinos: Organizacion de un Exodo a America Latina - Historia y Consecuencias de una Crisis Politica-universitaria. Buenos Aires: Instituto Torcuato di Tella, Proyecto de Investigacion Inter-Centro, 1970.

R85. Stevenson, A. Russell. Graduate Study in the United States: An Introduction for the Prospective A/D/C Fellow. New York: Agricultural Development Council, 1968.

R86. Sutton, F.X.; Ward, F. Champion; and Perkins, J. A. Internationalizing Higher Education: A United States Approach. New York: International Council for Educational Development, 1974.

R87. Swedish International Development Authority. "Information on SIDA's Policy with Respect to SIDA Fellowships and UN Fellowships." Stockholm, February 1972.

R88. Swedish International Development Authority and Mount Carmel International Training Centre for Community Services. "MCTC/SIDA Follow-up Survey on Participants Trained in Courses at the Mount Carmel International Training Centre, Haifa, Israel, and on Projects in Handicraft and Home Industries in Ethiopia, Tanzania, Lesotho, Botswana, and Swaziland." Stockholm: SIDA, 1973.

R89. Sweet, Charles; Vickelwait, Donald R.; Stevenson, Richard S.; and Harris, Pamela. The Senior Fulbright Program and its Domestic Impact. A Study prepared for the Bureau of Educational and Cultural Affairs, Department of State. Washington, D.C.: Development Associates, 1973.

R90. Tajfel, Henri, and Dawson, J. L., eds. Disappointed Guests, London: Oxford University Press, 1965.

R91. Than, R. J. "De-Americanization of Emile." Journal of College Placement 33 (February 1973): 84-87.

R92.   Thomson, Harold. "International Interchange." Education and
        Culture (Strasbourg: Council of Europe) No. 23 (Autumn/
        Winter 1973): 18-25.

R93.   Tysse, Agnes N., comp. International Education: The Amer-
        ican Experience, A Bibliography. Metuchen, N. J.: Scarecrow
        Press, 1974.

R94.   United Nations. Policies and Procedures Governing the Admin-
        istration of United Nations Fellowships. New York, 1965.

R95.   _____. A Survey of UN Fellows from El Salvador. New York,
        n. d.

R96.   United Nations Development Programme. Evaluation of the
        United Nations Training Programmes for the Period January
        1967 to December 1972; UNDP (TA) Programme. New York,
        October 1973.

R97.   UNESCO. Report of the Working Party of Representatives of
        the Various Agencies in Europe Which are Responsible for the
        Administration of UNESCO Fellowships. Paris, 1970.

R98.   _____. "Training Abroad: A Study of UNESCO Fellowships and
        Travel Grants 1948-1968." Paris, January 1971.

R99.   _____. Guide to UNESCO Fellowships. Paris, 1972.

R100.   U.S. Department of Health, Education, and Welfare, Office of
        Education. International/Intercultural Education Reports,
        Washington, D. C., April 1973.

R101.   U.S. Department of State. Educational Exchange Grants.
        Washington, D. C.: International Educational Exchange Service,
        Bureau of Public Affairs, 1959.

R102.   _____. Higher Education and the World: Proceedings of the
        National Foreign Policy Conference for Leaders in Higher
        Education. Ed. by Frank Klassen and Raymond Schultz.
        Washington, D. C., 1972.

R103.   U.S. Department of State, Bureau of Educational and Cultural
        Affairs. International Exchange: 1967. Washington, D. C., 1967.

R104.   ____. International Exchange: People's Diplomacy in Action. Washington, D.C., 1972.

R105.   ____. International Educational and Cultural Exchange: A Human Contribution to the Structure of Peace. Washington, D.C., March 1974.

R106.   U.S. Department of State, Council on International Educational and Cultural Affairs. Some Facts and Figures on the Migration of Talent and Skills. Washington, D.C., 1967.

R107.   Wei, Yun. "The Problem of Brain Drain and the Role of Western-Trained Intellectuals in the Developing Nations: The Case of Taiwan, Republic of China." Paper presented at the Annual Convention of the International Studies Association, Dallas, Texas, 14-18 March 1972.

R108.   Winegard, W. C. "We Must Plan Faculty Exchange with Lesser-Developed Countries." University Affairs 9 (February 1968): 15.

R109.   Wood, Richard. U.S. Universities: Their Role in AID-Financed Technical Assistance Overseas. New York: Education and World Affairs, 1968.

R110.   Young, Francis A. "Educational Exchanges and the National Interest." ACLS Newsletter 20, no. 2 (1969): 1-18.

Numbers refer to items listed in the Annotated Bibliography. Those in the Annotated Bibliography preceded by R will be found in Additional References.

The number of each item in the Annotated Bibliography is followed by the pages in the book on which that item is mentioned. Some items, although not directly discussed in the book, were nevertheless included in the Bibliography; their numbers have been omitted from this list.

ABOUT THE AUTHORS

SETH SPAULDING is Professor of Education and Economic and Social Development in the School of Education and the Graduate School of Public and International Affairs, University of Pittsburgh. He has served as Director of the Department of School and Higher Education, and of the Department of Higher Education and the Training of Educational Personnel, UNESCO. Previously he was Senior Advisor in the Ford Foundation's Overseas Development Program in Rangoon, Burma. Dr. Spaulding received his Ph.D. from Ohio State University.

MICHAEL J. FLACK is Professor of International and Intercultural Affairs, Graduate School of Public and International Affairs, University of Pittsburgh. He has taught at Tufts University, Vassar College, and the University of Oregon, and has been Visiting Professor at the Institute of Social Studies, The Hague, and the Institute of International Politics and Economy, Belgrade. Dr. Flack earned his M.A.L.D. and Ph.D. at the Fletcher School of Law and Diplomacy.

SEAN TATE is Research and Development Associate with World Education, Inc., New York. He holds a B.A. and M.A. in political science from the University of New Hampshire, and is completing doctoral requirements in the International and Development Education Program at the University of Pittsburgh.

PENELOPE MAHON is a doctoral student and Graduate Assistant in International Affairs at the Graduate School of Public and International Affairs, University of Pittsburgh. She received a B.A. from Bryn Mawr College, where she majored in political science.

CATHERINE MARSHALL is Assistant Editor at the University of Pittsburgh Press. A graduate of Vassar College and the University of London, she has been a teacher, a co-author of articles in cross-cultural anthropology, and has directed an air pollution research project.

MINORITY REPRESENTATION IN HIGHER EDUCATION
IN THE UNITED STATES

> Frank Brown and
> Madelon D. Stent

IMMIGRANT PROFESSIONALS IN THE UNITED STATES

> Bradley W. Parlin

COMPARATIVE HIGHER EDUCATION ABROAD:
Bibliography and Analysis

> Philip G. Altbach

EDUCATIONAL COOPERATION BETWEEN DEVELOPED
AND DEVELOPING COUNTRIES: Policies, Problems,
and Innovations

> H. M. Phillips

HIGHER EDUCATION IN DEVELOPING NATIONS: A
Selected Bibliography, 1969-74

> Philip G. Altbach
> and David H. Kelly